THE COURT OF THE LAST TSAR

ALSO BY GREG KING

The Fate of the Romanovs

The Last Empress: The Life and Times of
Alexandra Feodorovna, Tsarina of Russia

The Duchess of Windsor: The Uncommon Life of Wallis Simpson

The Man Who Killed Rasputin: Prince Felix Youssoupov and the
Murder That Helped Bring Down the Russian Empire

THE COURT OF THE LAST TSAR

*Pomp, Power, and Pageantry in
the Reign of Nicholas II*

Greg King

WILEY

John Wiley & Sons, Inc.

Copyright © 2006 by Greg King. All rights reserved

Published by John Wiley & Sons, Inc., Hoboken, New Jersey
Published simultaneously in Canada

Text illustrations courtesy of: Pp. 14, 15, 34, 35, 50, 53, 55, 60, 73, 79, 80 (both), 82, 83, 84, 87, 98, 106, 135, 138, 146, 161, 178, 211, 212, 243, 254, 272, 274, 278, 280, 283, 292, 316, 318, 326, 443, 449, 463, 472, 474, author's collection; p. 19, Daniel Briere; pp. 33, 37, 39, 40, 49, 57, 143, 174, 181, 198, 200, 214, 256, 260, 275, 289, 312, 314, 320, 329, 335, 361, 364, 372, 377, 378, 382, 391, 393, 415, 416 (both), 417 (both), 421, 422, 425, 442, 464, Antonio Perez Caballero; p. 128, Penny Wilson.

Insert illustrations courtesy of: Plates 1, 2, 3, 4, 5, 7, 13, 17, 24, 25, 39, author's collection; plates 6, 8, 11, 12, 15, 18, 27, 35, Daniel Briere; plates 9, 10, 14, 16, 19, 20, 21, 22, 23, 26, 28, 29, 30, 31, 32, 33, 34, 36, 37, 38, 40, 41, 42, 43, 44, Antonio Perez Caballero.

Design and composition by Navta Associates, Inc.

For general information about our other products and services, please contact our Customer Care Department within the United States at (800) 762 2974, outside the United States at (317) 572-3993 or fax (317) 572-4002.

Wiley also publishes its books in a variety of electronic formats. Some content that appears in print may not be available in electronic books. For more information about Wiley products, visit our web site at www.wiley.com.

Library of Congress Cataloging-in-Publication Data:

King, Greg, date.
  The court of the last tsar : pomp, power, and pageantry in the reign of Nicholas II / Greg King.
     p. cm.
  Includes bibliographical references and index.
  ISBN-13 978-0-471-72763-7 (cloth: alk. paper)
  ISBN-10 0-471-72763-6 (cloth: alk. paper)
  1. Russia—Civilization—20th century. 2. Russia—Social life and customs—20th century.
3. Russia—Court and courtiers. 4. Nicholas II, Emperor of Russia, 1868–1918—Family.
5. Romanov, House of. I. Title.
  DK247.K56 2006
  947.08'3'08621—dc22

                                                                2005017409

Printed in the United States of America

10 9 8 7 6 5 4 3 2 1

For Susanne,
a literary malachite column

CONTENTS

AUTHOR'S NOTE

In this book, readers will encounter a variety of titles: "emperor," "empress," "tsar," and "tsaritsa." Until 1721, all Romanov rulers were called tsar, which was commonly believed to have derived from the Latin word *caesar* but was actually adapted from the Greek translation of the Byzantine title *basileus*, signifying a Christian emperor. Peter the Great, enamored of all things Western, officially adopted the title *gosudar imperator*, or sovereign emperor; until the end of the empire, this was the correct form of address. Despite this, the emperor was often referred to as tsar, and his wife, bearing the title *imperatritsa*, or empress, was commonly called tsaritsa in Russian; tsarina, familiar to some readers, never existed in Russian. In official documents, Nicholas II was called emperor, although, as a Slavophile, he preferred the older title of tsar; conversely, his wife, Alexandra, preferred the Western title of empress. In this book, I have used emperor and empress, leaving tsar and tsaritsa in place only for direct quotations.

Peter the Great also altered the title of the heir to the throne from tsarevich, meaning "son of the tsar," to tsesarevich, a higher distinction derived from Byzantine models. Nicholas I refined the title to *gosudar naslednik*, to include his status as sovereign heir. Without altering original sources and quotations, I have attempted to use the correct form of tsesarevich.

Paul I established a number of rules governing the imperial family, which also spelled out the distinctions in their titles. A male was a *velikii knyaz*, translated by the imperial court, which used French as its official language, as grand duke; a female was a *velikaya knyazhna*, or grand duchess. Married females were marked with a subtle difference, *velikaya knyaginia*, although there was no change to their designation as grand duchesses. In 1886, Alexander III restricted the use of grand duke and grand duchess to the children and the grandsons of an emperor; lesser members of the imperial family were thereafter titled a prince or a princess of the imperial blood. In recent years, people unfamiliar with the nuances of the Russian language—and attempting to relate these styles to more familiar European models—have resorted to tortured literal translations of these titles, resulting in uncomfortable appellations such as grand prince or great princess and ignoring Paul I's declaration of grand duke and grand duchess. I have used the latter titles, employed by the imperial court itself, as correct.

Titles used by the imperial court present their own unique difficulties. Court offices followed Peter the Great's Table of Ranks, or *Chin*, a system he introduced that established sixteen categories of officials, arranged according to their hierarchy. Although French was the official language of the court, its officials largely bore titles originally drawn from German models but transliterated into their own, peculiar Russian form: *ober-tseremoniimeister* (grand master of ceremonies), *kamer-junker* (gentleman of the chamber), and *fligel-adjutant* (aide-de-camp). An additional corruption stems from the fact that in the Russian language, there is no letter "h." Titles copied from German models, such as *Hof-Marschall* (master of the court) and *Hof-Meisterina* (mistress of the court) therefore become, in Russian, *gof-marschal* and *gof-meisterina*. This led to a mixture of German and English, such as *freilina* (maid of honor). As such, they stand as curiosities, and often their English translations are awkward. I have given English translations as the Russian versions of these titles appear in the text, though I have moved freely between these three languages throughout, in an effort to not only maintain the flavor of Nicholas II's court but also ease the task for readers. A complete listing of official court titles and offices can be found in appendix C.

A Russian has two names: a Christian name and a patronymic derived from his or her father. The masculine form takes the father's first name and adds "vich" to the ending, indicating "son of." Thus the last emperor was Nicholas Alexandrovich, the son of Alexander. For daughters, "ovna" is added to the end of the father's name: Marie Pavlovna, the daughter of Paul, for example. During the reign of Nicholas II, the imperial family included some sixty individuals, who often shared Christian names. To distinguish between them, I have therefore frequently used patronymics in the text, with the hope that this will make the complex relationships in the imperial family easier for readers to follow, with one exception: Grand Duchess Marie Pavlovna, the wife of Grand Duke Vladimir Alexandrovich, is referenced using her husband's title, to avoid confusion with another Grand Duchess Marie Pavlovna, the daughter of Vladimir's brother Paul.

In transliterating Russian names, I have followed the Library of Congress method, with some exceptions. Christian names—and those names familiar to English-speaking readers—have been rendered in English: thus, we have "Nicholas" for "Nikolai," "Alexandra" for "Aleksandra," "Marie" rather than "Mariya," and "Tchaikovsky" in place of the unfamiliar "Chaikovsky."

Until spring 1918, Russia used the Julian calendar rather than the Gregorian one that is used in the West. As a result, dates in the nineteenth century were twelve days behind those in the West; in the twentieth century, the Julian calendar was thirteen days behind the Gregorian calendar. As this book focuses on the period from 1894 to 1914, I have elected to render dates according to the Julian calendar then in use in Russia; where important for the reader's understanding, or when events took place in Europe, I have given dates according to both calendars or to the Gregorian calendar. When discussing issues of finance, I have used a calculation based on a 1905 valuation of the ruble; modern equivalents are roughly ten times the 1905 figures and are noted in the text where important.

INTRODUCTION

"The Russian imperial court," Prince Christopher of Greece recalled, "was the most magnificent in Europe. There was something still barbaric in its splendor." It was, he said, "a world of fairy tales, a land of centuries-old traditions, a civilization still deeply rooted in the past." He marveled at the "medieval, sudden contrasts of vast riches and desperate poverty," noting the ermine and sable lap rugs in carriages drawn by horses adorned with gold and silver harnesses as they sped past "an unrest that crept silently in the dark like a furtive beast."[1] So overwhelming was this opulence that even a proudly republican French ambassador was moved to remark on the "pageantry, luxury of setting, and that inimitable exhibition of pomp and power in which the Russian Court has no rival."[2]

Nearly a hundred years after their brutal execution, the dramatic, passionate tale of Nicholas and Alexandra continues to fascinate. Hidden behind this most haunting of royal love stories, however, was a world of extraordinary luxury. This three-times great-grandson of Catherine the Great and the granddaughter of Queen Victoria resided within a string of glittering palaces, wore brilliant uniforms and fashionable gowns, took holidays in seaside palazzos and in secluded country estates, traveled on private trains and elegant yachts envied by the monarchs of Europe, and lived surrounded by a retinue of thousands.

This was the world of the Russian imperial court: a cloistered, insular universe of privilege and power. A potent underlying mythology drove its participants to enact the pageantry of medieval, Orthodox Russia—infused with the sensibilities of Versailles—against a backdrop of fading Edwardian splendor. This spectacle of archaic ceremonies was carefully orchestrated as a lavish stage upon which Nicholas II played out his tumultuous reign. Despite the immense body of literature devoted to the last of the Romanovs, the court of Nicholas and Alexandra is largely cloaked in mystery.

As the nineteenth century slipped into the twentieth, the Russian imperial court—alone of Europe's monarchies—remained a bastion of Byzantine ritual and elaborate ceremony. National tradition and religious symbolism shrouded its public spectacles, which were enacted against a backdrop of sumptuous palaces and watched principally by members of a ruling class whose world was cushioned from reality by a carefully conceived mythology. The underlying message ran deep. "It's very high up to God," went one favorite peasant proverb; "it's a very long way to the Tsar!"[3] Uneducated and denied access to this world, the Russian peasant still understood the enormous gulf that separated him from those who controlled his destinies in the golden city of St. Petersburg. The proverb recognized the futility of hope, while reinforcing the otherworldliness of the two dominant forces within the empire: the spiritual authority of God, in the guise of the Russian Orthodox Church, and the temporal authority of the autocratic sovereign, chosen—according to belief—by the Lord Himself and endowed with divine rights.

This was not true for all previous rulers. The Romanovs who sat upon the imperial throne at the dawn of the twentieth century had come to their position by accident and through democratic election. In the fifteenth century, Ivan the Terrible became the first Russian sovereign to wrap himself in the mantle of religious privilege. His grandmother, Zöé Paleologue, had been a niece of the last Byzantine emperor, Konstantin, who died fighting the Turks in a futile defense of Constantinople in 1453. When Zöé came to Russia, she brought with her the traditions of the Byzantine court, and Ivan's father had adopted the Byzantine double-headed eagle as his own symbol. When Constantinople fell, the faithful declared Moscow to be the true seat of Orthodoxy. Ivan the Terrible embraced this heritage; at his coronation, he himself placed the Cap of Monomakh atop his head, a crown that had belonged to the twelfth-century ruler who had unified Russian territory before the Mongol and the Tartar invasions. It was a symbolic gesture, signifying Russia's claim to empire. And Ivan solidified this proposition by proclaiming himself not grand prince, as all other rulers had done, but as the first tsar, a title loosely based on the Latin *caesar* but also derived from the Byzantine rank *basileus*, or Christian emperor.[4]

Ivan was the last true sovereign of the great Rurik Dynasty that had ruled Russia since 862; he was followed by a number of feeble puppets controlled by a council of *boyars*, or nobles, who imposed their own representatives as regents. The death of Boris Godunov in 1605 opened the Russian throne to a succession of pretenders, years known as the Time of Troubles. Then, in January 1613, an assembly of nobles, the Zemsky Sobor, voted to offer the throne to a sixteen-year-old boy, Michael Romanov, the grandnephew of Ivan the Terrible's wife, Anastasia, and set off for the Volga River village where Michael lived with his mother.

It was a race against time, for a group of Poles had set out to kill young Romanov. After losing their way, they ordered a village elder, Ivan Susanin, to take them to the boy. Susanin dispatched his son-in-law to warn Michael before leading the Poles into a deep forest, where he was killed for his efforts. The representatives of the Zemsky Sobor found Michael at the Ipatiev Monastery in Kostroma, and the terrified young man eventually accepted the throne as the first Romanov tsar. Russia was saved, and the story of Ivan Susanin became one of the greatest of all Russian legends, commemorated in Michael Glinka's patriotic opera *A Life for the Tsar.*

The new Romanov Dynasty was a product of its times and a mirror of the Russian Orthodox Church: insular, medieval, and suspicious of Western influences. It was Michael's grandson, Peter the Great, who rebelled against this isolation, conquering territories, constructing new cities, and driving his subjects toward an alien European ideal. His great capital of St. Petersburg, founded as Russia's "window to the West," signified his determination to break with the cloistered world of the Moscow court. For the first time, the Byzantine traditions of Muscovite rule were infused with European symbolism. Until the end of the dynasty in 1917, these two conflicting ideals waged war with one another in an imperial court that copied Western motifs, yet set them against a backdrop firmly rooted in a religious, medieval past.

Throughout the eighteenth century, first in the reign of Peter's daughter Empress Elizabeth, then in that of her eventual successor Catherine the Great, the Russian court made concerted efforts to sever itself from unpleasant reminders of its Muscovite roots. In St. Petersburg, palaces copied first Italian baroque, then French neoclassical models, and their rooms overflowed with delicate furniture from London and Paris. The sovereign and the aristocracy spoke

French; drowned their sorrows in wines imported from Italy, France, and Germany; and entertained themselves at performances of Italian operas and French comedies. Such liberal borrowing from foreign models indelibly framed the Russian court in artificial terms, highlighting its distinct position and reinforcing its power through rituals that only separated it from the emperor's subjects.

The struggle against Napoleon finally showed up the hollow underpinnings that held the imperial court in magnificent isolation. Fighting to defend Russia, the empire's soldiers marched into Paris in 1814, only to find themselves the subject of scornful gossip. Officers moved through the city's salons, followed by barely disguised laughter at their coarse manners and European pretensions. In the years that followed, the Russian court again turned inward. It maintained its familiar European uniforms, titles, ceremonies, and manners but coupled them with a strong nationalistic flavor.

Nicholas I came to the Russian throne in the midst of the Decembrist Uprising, a rebellion organized by leading aristocrats and members of the Imperial Guards Corps. Although loyal troops suppressed the revolt, it was an unpleasant manifestation of the dangers of Western thought. European ideas and aspirations, grafted clumsily onto the Russian ruling class, had led only to discontent; the emperor therefore adapted European models to suit the promotion of the autocracy as a Russian institution. The imperial court wrapped itself in costumes designed after traditional native models; worshipped in new cathedrals built according to old Slavic architecture; read the works of new Russian authors like Lermontov and Pushkin; and listened to the music of Glinka, Borodin, and Mussorgsky.

Nicholas I ruled his court with an increasing eye to self-promotion. After the scandalous reigns of his grandmother Catherine the Great, with her string of lovers, and his father Paul I—openly believed to have been insane—Nicholas I sought to invest the autocracy with representations of moral clarity. In so doing, the emperor unwittingly revealed his private life and that of his family, submitting it not only for observation but for critical comment as well. As the lines between public and private behavior became blurred, the autocracy itself fell victim to this cult of personality, and increasingly the strength of the institution was judged according to the personality of the emperor. This fusion deprived the imperial court and the autocracy of much of the mystery that itself functioned as justification for the isolated privilege in which the Romanovs lived.[5]

Under Nicholas I, this new moral emphasis heightened the prestige of the imperial family and court, but during the reign of his son, Alexander II, the first cracks appeared. Alexander II cast himself in the mold of reformer and launched a series of extensive measures designed to improve the lives of his subjects, including the liberation of the serfs in 1861. Then, in 1866, Alexander II took a lover, Princess Catherine Dolgorukaya, a seventeen-year-old student from St. Petersburg's Smolny Institute for Noble Young Ladies. He made no secret of his affair and, indeed, flaunted it and its bastard offspring before not only his wife and family but the whole of the imperial court as well. Society matrons, accustomed to the dignified court of Nicholas I, expressed shock while reveling in gossip about the emperor's private life, while others looked upon the affair as a license to indulge their own passions without fear of imperial censure.[6]

A literal conflagration finally ended this charade. On Sunday, March 1, 1881, Alexander II was driving through the snowy streets of St. Petersburg with his ordinary Cossack bodyguard when anarchists threw two bombs at his carriage. Within minutes, members of the imperial family and court—scattered across the capital—rushed to the Winter Palace; there was never any thought, such was the state of things in Russia at the time, but that the sound of the distant explosions had signaled an attempt on the life of the emperor. They found Alexander II on a camp bed in his study, one leg missing, the other a shattered pulp. "His face was deadly pale," recalled his grandson, the future Nicholas II. "There were small wounds all over it. His eyes were closed. My father led me up to his bed. 'Papa,' he said, raising his voice, 'your sunshine is here.' I saw the flicker of an eyelid. Grandfather's blue eyes opened and he tried to smile."[7] It was a terrible, agonizing scene, forever seared into the memories of those who looked on in horror as the emperor bled to death before their eyes. "From that moment on," wrote Countess Marie Kleinmichel, "the Reaction began."[8]

Under Alexander III, the Russian court gradually disintegrated. He refused to reside in the Winter Palace, much to the chagrin of his wife; instead, he selected the country estate at Gatchina, some forty miles south of the capital, which could be more easily defended. It became, in the words of one writer, "the citadel of autocracy."[9] This seclusion set an ultimately fatal pattern that would be repeated under his son Nicholas II. Alexander, who hated society and balls, reduced imperial entertainments at the Winter Palace, giving rise to a second, rival court, led by his brother and his sister-in-law, Grand Duke Vladimir and his wife, Marie Pavlovna, as society looked elsewhere for its pleasures and approval.

Alexander III was an immense man: at six feet four inches, he literally towered over both his family and his empire. A Slavophile at heart, he became the first Russian sovereign since the eighteenth century to sport a beard. His grandfather had first invoked the nationalist spirit for the imperial court as a reaction against the corrupting influence of the West on his empire; Alexander III took this a step further. Nationalism now became the predominant theme in the autocracy itself. "Orthodoxy, Nationality, Autocracy!" went the favored formula; coupled with the oft-repeated slogan "Russia for the Russians!" it defined an imperial ideal that was quickly stamped on every aspect of the court.[10] The uniforms of all military regiments were redesigned to eliminate Peter the Great's Prussian models; new laws established the primacy of the Orthodox Church to the persecution of other religious faiths; and the Pan-Slavist movement reached its zenith, with a proliferation of Russian music, art, and architecture that took its inspiration from medieval models.

Against this backdrop, Nicholas II acceded to the throne in 1894. He presided over an imperial court that embraced some fifteen thousand individuals; in reality, fewer than a thousand people held posts that entailed actual service. Even so, the court was a fluid entity, expanding and contracting with each new ceremony or presentation, with access carefully regulated according to birth and position. In its most impressive and elaborate displays, such as coronations, weddings, and funerals, the court included not only the emperor and his immediate family but also all of his relatives; those who held ranks within the apparatus of the court itself; members of the aristocracy; Orthodox clergy, who enacted its services; government officials, whose power—as it was understood in Russia—stemmed solely from the autocrat himself; and even members of the elite Imperial Guards regiments, who provided scenic spectacle in their array of brilliant uniforms as they marched in processions.

"You can't possibly hope to describe the imperial court," an elderly Russian émigré told me a decade ago, on reading an early draft of this book. "You had to have lived within it to understand it." Such considerations have perhaps led to the lack of evaluation of this vanished world, which plays so deeply into the story of Nicholas and Alexandra, and which—through the popular dissemination of their tale, as well as those of Rasputin and Anastasia—has come to be known to millions, albeit in vague terms. And yet, with the exception of the important study by Professor Richard Wortman, the significant wealth of material on the imperial court has been all but ignored.

The Court of the Last Tsar is a humble attempt to correct that lack of information. This limits itself to the form and function of the imperial court from 1894 to 1914, from the accession of Nicholas II to the outbreak of the First World War, which marked the end of this gilded life. From sketching the lives of the principal players on the imperial stage to placing them within the frame of their palaces and describing their wealth, clothing, jewelry, yachts, country estates, and court ceremonies over which they held sway, I have tried to add color and depth to the familiar portrait of Nicholas and Alexandra. I have examined the memoirs, diaries, letters, and official accounts that offer diverse glimpses of this vanished world, but this present work can serve only as a general introduction to the characters, ceremonies, possessions, and power of the last imperial family of Russia. A complete study would require numerous volumes, but I hope that I have evoked a vivid picture of the pomp, power, and pageantry of the lost world over which Nicholas II presided.

PROLOGUE
St. Petersburg

ON THE EDGE OF THE CLEAR BLUE WATERS of the Gulf of Finland, swept by chill sea breezes and frozen in its long, desolate winter, the city slumbered. It had been the vision of one legendary man, Peter the Great, and had been nurtured and embellished through the years by his crowned successors. Gifted and brilliant artists and craftsmen—painters, architects, builders, carpenters, sculptors, and gardeners—had lent their collective genius to its creation. It was a strangely artificial place, neither European—despite the work of its numerous Italian, French, German, English, and Swiss architects—nor entirely Russian.

Under Soviet rule, the ravages of war and decades of neglect lay across its pastel palaces, whose once vibrant facades were ignored by the endless queues of beleaguered babushkas waiting in chill winds throughout the long days. Silent political posters of Lenin and Marx gazed out across the city's greatest avenue; the noisy trams, smart carriages, and shining new motorcars that had previously thronged its pavement in the days before the Revolution had been replaced by crowded buses and lonely taxis rumbling along its dingy edge. St. Petersburg, the former capital of imperial Russia, had all but disappeared beneath the Soviet grime that shrouded Leningrad.

Here and there, at the ends of the city's canals or mirrored in the frozen sheet of the Neva River, stood lonely sentinels of the vanished empire: a brightly colored onion dome crowning an abandoned church that bristled with arches; a golden spire atop a lemon-yellow building, echoed by the burnished glow of a thin needle, topped with a guardian angel that spread its gilded wings over the city and rose above a grim stone bastion; a monument carved with the face of the city's founder; and a forgotten mansion, plaster crumbling, its garden choked with weeds behind a rusted iron fence. The heart of the city, both in the glory that was St. Petersburg and in its schizophrenic life as Leningrad, was a vast square, dominated by an immense building festooned with pilasters and scrolled pediments and fringed with a balustrade adorned with urns and classical statuary.

Within, the enormous halls, embellished with columns of marble, malachite, and lapis lazuli, once rang with the music of Tchaikovsky, Glinka, and Chopin, as men in crisp uniforms and ladies in brocaded gowns swirled across its elaborate inlaid floors. As the famed Winter Palace, it witnessed the opulent pageantry of the Russian court, windows ablaze with light against the pervasive winter nights while privileged guests danced and dined at the invitation of the Emperor of All the Russias. Now, its rooms echoed with the sounds of tourists, heels clicking and cameras whirling as they marveled at the wonders gathered here in its life as the Hermitage. Dour attendants sat silently in gilded chairs, watching as the occasional foreigner followed groups of red-kerchiefed schoolchildren, sailors on leave, elderly couples, and art students seeking inspiration as they strolled from masterpiece to masterpiece collected by Catherine the Great and her successors or confiscated from the private palaces of the country's vanished aristocracy.

Ringing the city, a necklace of former imperial estates evoked the fragile world of the Russian court, with manicured gardens, glittering enfilades of richly decorated rooms, and ornate pavilions erected at the caprice of a succession of Romanovs. The estates had been occupied by Hitler's soldiers during the Second World War. Their neoclassical and baroque facades were left scorched and pocked with shells, the exquisite rooms within victim to devastating sheets of flame. Soviet architects, craftsmen, and artists struggled for decades to resurrect their former glories. Other palaces and pavilions lay abandoned, their parks clotted with weeds, as wind whistled through rooms invaded by snow and rain, the shattered walls and collapsed colonnades illuminated in the pale northern light. Their forgotten rubble, concealed by the encroaching wilderness of time, and the magnificent city they fringed whispered of an epoch submerged in history, a vanished world of brilliance and mirth. These broad, carefully planned avenues, large parade grounds, tranquil canals, and ornate palaces served as the mise-en-scène for the glittering world of Emperor Nicholas II, the court of the last tsar.

. . .

On May 16, 1703, Peter I, the tsar of Russia, stood on the bank of the broad Neva River, gazing at the thick forests and the cluster of islands that ringed the mouth of the Gulf of Finland. As a group of courtiers looked on, the tsar took a bayonet and cut a cross in the mud, declaring that here, in this desolate spot, he would build a fortified port: a "window on the West," as the poet Alexander Pushkin later described it in his epic poem *The Bronze Horseman*.[1] The idea of raising a citadel in this wasteland was madness, but no one dared question Peter's resolve. Conditions were considered impossible: the land had only recently been won back in battle after centuries of Swedish occupation, and early laborers were often forced to fight off constant invading forces. The northern latitude posed its own difficulties: incessant snows fell throughout the long winters, while the spring thaw drove the Neva over its banks, flooding the land and creating a breeding ground for the cholera, typhoid, and malaria that ravaged many of the laborers.

Peter forbade all masonry construction elsewhere in Russia, and ships arriving at his new port had to carry stones for foundations and walls. Thousands of tons of earth were shoveled to fill the marshes, fields were crossed with deep trenches, and entire forests were felled for their wood. Seven years passed, and work went on day and night, winter and summer. Prisoners, captured in the Great Northern War with Sweden, were forced to chop trees, plow fields, chip stones, and carry bricks, clad in little more than rags. Thousands died; their names were forgotten, their bodies buried in mass graves or left to rot beneath the palaces they built.

Gradually, a city rose from the archipelago of dank marshes and deep forests, christened with the Dutch name of Sankt Pieter Burkh. Within a decade, Peter had installed his court in this savage wilderness: all government offices, along with bureaucrats and their families, were forced to move here, as were unwilling aristocrats. No one was certain the land would remain in Russian hands, and the inhospitable atmosphere—with its roaming packs of wolves and dangerous epidemics—did little to endear the settlers to their new home, but no one dared refuse. By the time of Peter the Great's death in 1725, St. Petersburg—as it had become when spoken by the Russian tongue—had displaced Moscow as the empire's capital.

St. Petersburg was built upon water, earning its epithet of "Venice of the North." At its center, the swift, steel-gray waters of the Neva River cleaved the city in half. The river was the heart of St. Petersburg, riveting in its attention, a silent witness to momentous events that played out along its banks. One visitor recalled the Neva "dancing in perpetual movement, brilliant with the play of innumerable lights, furrowed by the ceaseless movement of ships, barks, tugs, and barges, and itself broad as a gulf, rushing impetuously towards the Gulf of Finland."[2] The Neva wrapped itself around the city's innumerable islands, themselves crossed by the winding ribbons of the Moika, the Catherine, and the Fontanka Canals. Bridges of wood, stone, and iron, adorned with turrets, statuary, and gilded griffins and christened with such evocative names as the Potseluev Most (Bridge of Kisses) and the Pevchesky Most (Bridge of Song), linked parks and palaces to parade grounds. Hundreds of ships lay at anchor along the granite quays, their tall masts swaying gently in the rhythm of the tides. By the beginning of the twentieth century, St. Petersburg had come to embody Peter's wish: it was a great seaport and a center for Russian trade with the rest of Europe.

The new city was a deliberate contrast to Moscow. The former capital was circled with narrow streets, crowded with wooden buildings, and dominated by a forest of spires, brightly painted cupolas, and gilded onion domes topped with burnished Orthodox crosses. Moscow was vertical, medieval, and ringed with intrigue, superstition, and fear of the outside world. Peter's new city was horizontal, wide and flat, echoing the three-quarter-mile breadth of the Neva, the encircling forests of birch, and the long northern sky. It was a visible rejection of ancient Muscovy, and citizens in St. Petersburg regarded Muscovites as backward, their city "fat and indolent."[3]

St. Petersburg became a theatrical stage, upon which Peter forced his compliant courtiers to enact a bizarre pantomime of half-learned European manners, while costumed in uniforms and gowns carefully copied from those he had seen in Holland, Germany, and England. In this artificial world, the formerly powerful nobles found themselves at the mercy of the determined tsar. He dictated every aspect of their lives in his new city: how they should dress; what materials they must use in building their new houses; what foods to serve at a proper, European-style dinner; how to dance according to European standards; and even how to wear their hair, according to the latest Western models. For two centuries, St. Petersburg struggled to come to terms with these aspirations, which drove it away from the soul of the empire and beckoningly toward Europe. It sought acceptance from the West in its baroque, rococo, and neoclassical palaces and refined manner, yet hovered uneasily around the traditions that infused its inhabitants. By the beginning of the twentieth century, it was a city that enchanted, yet, having abandoned so much of its native culture, seemed empty, lifeless, a pale if grand imitation of the very thing it tried so hard to achieve. Nevertheless, it remained thoroughly Russian in temperament. "No mistake could have been made as to the ultimate nationality of the city," recalled Grand Duke Alexander Mikhailovich, "that ordered its champagne by the magnum, never by the quart."[4]

The capital was a cosmopolitan mixture of cultures and nationalities. As the largest city in the multiethnic empire, its streets were peopled with Russians, Ukrainians, Germans, Balts, Finns, Poles, Swedes, Latvians, Lithuanians, Georgians, Turks, Jews, and Mongols. They mingled with thousands of international visitors to the capital: British diplomats, American attachés, Italian tourists, and French academics, all making their uncertain ways from the train stations and the docks through the noisy streets. From the sea, these visitors approached the city across the silvery length of the Gulf of Finland. "The huge city rises gradually into sight," recalled one early tourist, "its many golden domes and spires glittering in the sun like gigantic sparks in the distance."[5]

Once travelers were ashore, their impressions grew more vivid. "In St. Petersburg," wrote one visitor, "everything that pertains to the Imperial power is built upon a massive scale. The streets are broad and give magnificent prospects. The squares are extended with a lavish hand, regardless of site values. The Palaces are enormous. Churches, domed like the heavens and pillared like the firmament, blaze with Byzantine splendor. The colossal monuments are frequently carved from a single stone. The river is embanked with titanic blocks of hewn granite."[6]

Despite the European trappings in which the city wrapped itself, visitors were immediately struck by St. Petersburg's exotic qualities. Meriel Buchanan, the daughter of the British ambassador, vividly recalled her first impressions of "a church with blue domes painted with golden stars; a huge red palace; carriages and coachmen with bright velvet caps; policemen in long black, fur-trimmed overcoats; a big yellow building with a pale green roof; a golden spire that shone against the sky; and a huge bridge spanning an immensely broad river."[7] The wife of an American diplomat wrote, "I felt a million miles away. The enormous padded coachman on the Ambassador's sleigh, and the footman in the outlandish garb of the ancient Russian chasseur, with his hunting dagger dangling from his belt, proudly sported, both of them, the American colors in their cockades. But it only enhanced their strangeness. The domes and towers of the churches, overlaid with gold leaf or blue enamel, flashed out above the snow-mantled city. Unfamiliar Cyrillic letters were over the dingy little shops. . . . The young secretary from the Embassy who had come to the station smiled at my enthusiasm, and tucked the fur robe closer in. It was bordered with sable, the richest, softest, most costly fur in the world, and never in extreme caprice of fancy had I imagined sable carriage robes. But I recalled that I had been told I should find life in St. Petersburg with a background of magnificence seen in no other place in Europe."[8] This kaleidoscope of buildings, people, animals, and scenery was overwhelming. "The whirlwind of human activity and the noise of a great capital give one a sort of dazed feeling," recalled the nineteenth-century French author Théophile Gautier. "The traveler passes, as in a dream, by unknown objects, wishing to see everything and seeing nothing."[9]

Inevitably, all of these visitors were drawn to Nevsky Prospekt, the city's rival to Berlin's Unter den Linden or the Champs-Elysées in Paris. "Nothing could be finer than Nevsky Prospekt," wrote Nicholas Gogol, "at least not in St. Petersburg; it is the be-all and end-all. It positively gleams and sparkles—the jewel of our capital."[10] A French architect, Alexander Le Blonde, had laid out the Prospekt, slicing through three and a half miles of forests to create a wide avenue from the edge of the Neva to the Alexander Nevsky Monastery. At all times of the day and night, the Nevsky pulsed with life. Strollers, wrapped in heavy furs in winter and carrying parasols in summer, wandered arm in arm on afternoon promenades; officials and civil servants rushed from one meeting to the next, their uniforms heavy with gold braid; and ranks of soldiers and sailors marched from one post to the next. The great Prospekt witnessed them all: grand dukes and prostitutes, lovers and murderers, poets and artists, side by side among starving workers and their crying children. They dodged speeding trams, bells and horns blaring in a great cacophony of sound. In winter, sleds and brightly painted troikas raced passengers to ballet performances and midnight suppers, while in summer, coaches and landaus jostled for room. "Nowhere else can there be seen so

Nevsky Prospekt, 1900, looking toward
the Admiralty Spire

С.-Петербургъ.   Невскій проспектъ. Аничкинъ Дворецъ.
St. Pétersbourg.   Perspective de Nevsky. Palais Anitchkin.

Anichkov Palace, 1900, seen from Nevsky Prospekt

cosmopolitan a crowd as that which throngs its pavements," wrote one visitor. "Every nationality and almost every costume of Europe and Asia is represented. Ladies in exquisite Parisian toilettes, and elegants who might have stepped from Bond Street or Hyde Park; officers in smart uniforms, and fierce-looking Cossacks and Circassians; peasant women with kerchiefs on their heads, and mujiks in their red shirts; priests with long hair falling over their shoulders and strange frocks and broad-brimmed hats—all combine to make the Nevsky such a sight as will long remain in the memory of the visitor."[11]

In early morning, the Nevsky presented a docile face. Against the pale light, merchants shambled to their shops, the silence of dawn broken by the rattle of wheels over the uneven cobbles. Gradually, the avenue was overtaken by merchants, officials, and, as Gogol recorded, a contingent of foreign nannies and governesses, "pale English misses and rosy-cheeked Slav maidens," walking "in stately fashion behind their lightsome, fidgety girls, commanding them to hold their heads high and backs straight."[12]

By afternoon, the crowd had changed, as fashionable elements thronged Nevsky Prospekt for their usual promenade. "All that meets the eye on the Nevsky Prospekt," wrote Gogol, "is replete with decorum: on every side you will see men in long frock coats with their hands in their pockets, ladies in pink, white, and pale blue satin redingotes and bonnets."[13] Théophile Gautier noted "officers of the Guard, in gray mantles with a mark on their shoulder to indicate their rank. Their breasts are nearly always starred with decorations and they wear caps on their heads. Next come the officials in long overcoats pleated at the back and drawn in by a belt. Instead of a hat they wear a dark cap with a cockade. Young men, who are neither officers nor officials, wear coats trimmed with fur whose price fills the stranger with astonishment."[14] At four, the elegant strollers disappeared, replaced by lonely clerks and tired merchants making their way to dingy apartments, fighting for space along the sidewalks with a contingent of men armed with ladders who moved from one post to another, lighting the gas street lamps that dotted the avenue.

At all hours of the day and night, the Nevsky pulsed with traffic. "A perpetual stream of carriages pours down it at full speed," wrote Théophile Gautier, "and to cross the Prospekt is an operation not less perilous than to cut across the Boulevard in Paris."[15] People driving these vehicles never failed to amaze Western visitors. "On his head," noted Gautier, "is a low hat with a bulging crown and a brim turned up at the sides and sloping down over the forehead and neck. He wears a long blue or green blouse closed under the left arm by hooks or silver buttons and pleated around the hips and fastened at the waist by a Circassian belt embroidered with gold, his muscular throat encircled by a cravat, his long beard falling over his breast, his arms held out straight, a rein in each hand, and it must be acknowledged that he presents a magnificent triumphal appearance, that he is indeed the coachman of his equipage. The bigger he is the higher his wages; entering into your service thin he demands increase of wages as he increases in flesh."[16]

Nevsky Prospekt served as a grand introduction to the capital's eclectic mixture of baroque and rococo churches and palaces, washed in pale yellows, ice blues, Venetian reds, and sea greens. Successive Romanovs imposed their own tastes on the city. Peter the Great's daughter Empress Elizabeth sponsored the great Italian Bartolomeo Rastrelli, who applied his theatrical sense to St. Petersburg's countless buildings. Later, Catherine the Great commissioned proponents of neoclassicism, including Charles Cameron, Giacomo Quarenghi, and Antonio Rinaldi. Her grandson, Alexander I, continued the tradition, transforming St. Petersburg—with the assistance of Carlo Rossi, whose Empire style succeeded in unifying the great avenues and enormous buildings—into a single, cohesive, artistic expression of the autocracy. "Each," wrote W. Bruce Lincoln, "was an Imperial monument, conceived and executed on an immense scale, and the massive three dimensional renderings of pagan deities and Russian national heroes that their builders set against backdrops of soaring columns and massive façades left no doubt that Russia's Emperors identified their triumphs with the glories of ancient Rome."[17] At the beginning of the twentieth century, obelisks, triumphal arches, grand avenues, and columned buildings lent the capital a severe, harmonious beauty unlike anything to be seen in Moscow.

The Alexander Nevsky Monastery marked the southern end of the Prospekt. Founded by Peter the Great in 1710 to commemorate the thirteenth-century victory of Alexander Nevsky over the Teutonic knights, it later became one of four *lavra* in the Russian empire, the most important rank a monastery could hold. The complex included the Theological Academy of the Russian Orthodox Church and several cemeteries where the city's famous were buried. Dostoevsky was interred there, along with Tchaikovsky, Rimsky-Korsakov, Borodin, Glinka, Mussorgsky, and Lomonosov.

The most fashionable stretch of Nevsky Prospekt began where the avenue crossed the Fontanka Canal. Here, on each corner of the Anichkov Bridge, a rearing bronze horse held by a groom towered over the placid water, the work of sculptor Peter von Klodt. Although a man of immense talent, von Klodt frequently clashed with his greatest patron, Nicholas I. The emperor freely offered suggestions that were little short of demands and angered von Klodt by presenting several of the sculptor's first casts for the bridge to his brother-in-law the king of Prussia. So enraged was von Klodt at this unwelcome imperial intervention that he was alleged to have depicted the emperor's features in the swollen groin vein of one of his bolting Anichkov horses.[18]

Just off the avenue stood Alexandrinskaya Square, dominated by Carlo Rossi's Alexandrinsky Theater, a yellow and white structure whose tall portico of Corinthian columns was crowned by a statue of Apollo and four prancing horses.[19] The back of the building formed the end of Rossi's famous Teatralnaya Ulitsa (Theater Street), an avenue of magnificent proportions housing the Russian Imperial Ballet School, whose strict regime produced Nijinsky, Pavlova, Karsavina, and other brilliant dancers.[20]

Down the Nevsky, and opening off the opposite side of the avenue, a boulevard led to Mikhailovsky Square, rimmed with a complex of neoclassical buildings designed by Rossi in the first half of the nineteenth century. The Mikhailovsky Theater on the northern side of the square offered French comedies, operas, and ballets; it stood adjacent to the Hall of Nobles, whose lemon-yellow facade ornamented with white pilasters concealed an immense ballroom decorated with Corinthian columns and hung with enormous crystal chandeliers. But the centerpiece of the square was Rossi's Mikhailovsky Palace, designed in 1819 for Alexander I's younger brother Michael Pavlovich. The palace facade, stretching 350 feet along the eastern side of the square, was a symphony of white Corinthian columns, projecting pediments, Venetian windows, and richly carved classical friezes set against pale yellow walls.[21] In 1895, Nicholas II purchased the palace and created within its walls the Alexander III Museum of Russian Art.[22]

Farther down the Nevsky stood Rastrelli's Stroganov Palace, adorned with baroque window frames, banded columns, and scrolled pediments perched high above the Moika Canal. A dozen churches dotted the avenue, an ecumenical mixture reflecting the capital's diverse population. Within a mile of each other stood the Dutch Reformed Church, St. Catherine's Catholic Church, the Lutheran Church of St. Peter and St. Paul, and an Armenian church. At one end of the Catherine Canal rose the Church on the Spilt Blood, a pseudo-medieval pile of towers, tent roofs, and onion domes, erected on the spot where Emperor Alexander II had been assassinated by a Nihilist's bomb in 1881. At the distant end of the canal stood the beautiful St. Nicholas Cathedral, designed by Rastrelli's pupil Savva Chevakinsky, its blue and white baroque facade crowned with five golden onion domes. The most important church on the avenue was Kazan Cathedral. With its tall dome and colonnaded wings, it was as much an immense secular monument to the Russian victory over Napoleon as it was a religious structure.

Fashionable shops lined Nevsky Prospekt. The largest was the Gostiny Dvor, or Merchant's Row, a classical arcaded bazaar designed by Jean Baptiste Vallin de la Mothe where merchants from all corners of Russia sold their diverse wares.[23] Within its stalls, shoppers found "rare old pictures, silver, coins, and drinking vessels . . . beautiful lace, made by the peasants . . . linen from Kostroma, Orenburg shawls of lovely design, lacquer work, and fine gold and silver enamels" from the provinces. "Occasionally," recalled one visitor, "a shock-headed Cossack from the Don, having spent all his rubles in cards and vodka, would sell his family treasures—drinking cups dating from the days of Catherine, old French snuffboxes jeweled with pearls and diamonds, captured from officers and generals of the Grand Armee, or similar items of tempting value."[24]

Nearby stood Elisieev Brothers, an immense food emporium with a gilded hall, encased behind an art nouveau facade that attracted much attention when

The Church on the Spilt Blood, erected on the spot along the Catherine Canal where
Alexander II was assassinated in 1881

it was built in 1903. Druces imported British goods that, at the beginning of the
twentieth century, were in vogue among smart society: its regular stock included
English soaps, scents, bright chintzes, Scottish woolens, Irish crystal and linen, as
well as furniture from Maples Department Store in London. Brocards dealt
exclusively in French perfumes, soaps, and colognes. There were stores for all

manner of housewares, the most popular being Gambs Brothers, whose Louis XVI–revival pieces filled the palaces of both the imperial family and the aristocracy. Half a dozen bookstores and newsagents, including Watkins and the famous Belizard's, displayed the latest books, newspapers, and magazines, not only in Russian but also in English, German, Spanish, Hebrew, Italian, Polish, and French, the official language of the imperial court. Filipov's Bakery, and Wolf and Beranger's, provided delicate and imaginative confections to satisfy the most demanding tastes of the aristocracy, while, farther down the avenue, the showrooms of jewelers such as Hahn, Bolin, Bulgari, Tillander, Fabergé, and, later on, Cartier, offered more precious bibelots for discerning buyers.

These shops catered to all nationalities and classes. Signs in windows proudly proclaimed, "English spoken," "*Ici on parle Français*," and "*Man spricht Deutsch.*" For those unable to decipher foreign tongues or even the elaborate Cyrillic lettering in gold, many signs simply illustrated the wares to be found within. "Golden bunches of grapes, carved or painted, indicate the wine merchant," wrote Théophile Gautier. "Further on hams, sausage, tongues, boxes of caviar, point out a shop for edibles. Boots, slippers, rubber shoes, most realistically painted, say to the feet that cannot read, 'Enter and you will be shod.' Gloves crossed over each other speak a language intelligible to all."[25]

A host of hotels—of varying character and quality—stretched across St. Petersburg, offering visitors a brief respite from the bustle of the city. "Most of the really Russian hotels," recalled one English visitor, "are furnished with great magnificence, but are often dirty and dusty beyond belief."[26] The Hôtel de Russie, at a corner of Mikhailovsky Square, offered comfortable rooms favored by French travelers; the Hôtel de France, on Bolshaya Morskaya Street, was the province of Russian officers and English journalists, who regarded its oak-paneled bar as their private club.[27] For most of Nicholas II's reign, the most fashionable accommodation could be found at the Hôtel d'Europe, situated in an unprepossessing building at a corner of Nevsky Prospekt. The architect Feodor Livdal extensively remodeled the hotel in the art nouveau style after the turn of the century; in 1910, he added a magnificent restaurant, crowned with a stained glass skylight, at the top of the hotel.[28] For all its stylish splendor, however, one guest complained that it was "not particularly cheap or comfortable."[29] In 1912, its place as the preeminent hotel in the imperial capital was lost to another Livdal structure, the Astoria, built onto the existing Angleterre Hôtel on the eastern side of St. Isaac's Square.

At the northern end of the avenue lay the Admiralty, housing the Ministry of the Navy. Peter built his first shipyard here in 1704; by the beginning of the nineteenth century, the old wooden buildings and storehouses had fallen into disrepair, and Alexander I commissioned Andrei Zakharov to design a new structure that stretched a quarter mile along the Neva embankment. A tall tower, pierced by an arch surrounded by allegorical statuary and sculpture depicting tridents, anchors, globes, and nymphs, dominated the center of the facade; above the columned tower, a slender golden spire surmounted with a gold-leafed weathervane in the form of a ship rose toward the sky. From the long, narrow garden behind the Admiralty, St. Petersburg's three main arteries led into the distance: Nevsky Prospekt, Gorokhovaya Street, and Voznesensky Prospekt.[30]

The Admiralty.
See plate 1.

Across the Neva, surrounded by a deep canal and guarded by thick walls, a pale, slender spire of gold marked the city's oldest structure, a fortress named after St. Peter and St. Paul. Although built as a defensive measure against invasion by the Swedes, the fortress never saw military action; its walls shook only from the noise of cannon salutes and the firing of the noonday gun. Six triangular bastions, of brick faced with granite and named after Peter's favorite courtiers, abruptly thrust their sixty-foot-thick walls out from the center of the fortress, their tops lined with cannons.[31]

The fortress
cathedral.
See plate 2.

In the center of the fortress's cobbled square stood the Cathedral of St. Peter and St. Paul, designed by an Italian, Domenico Tressini, and dominated by a stepped bell tower topped with a spire rising some four hundred feet into the northern sky.[32] Like St. Petersburg itself, the cathedral represented Peter's fierce determination to break with the confines and traditions of the Moscow court. Inside, twelve scagliola columns, topped with gilded Corinthian capitals, divided the cathedral into three wide naves. Rather than the traditional frescoes, the walls were decorated with pink, gray, green, and white scagliola, lending a cool, colorful splendor to the interior. Beneath the high dome, a wooden iconostasis, or altar screen, elaborately carved and decorated with tassels, fringed curtains, and bells, separated the nave from the sanctuary.[33] Here, below tombs of white marble embellished with golden Orthodox crosses, lay Peter the Great and his crowned successors; the only exceptions were the tombs of Alexander II and his wife, Empress Marie Alexandrovna, his of green Altai jasper, hers of blood-red rhodonite.[34] At the end of the nineteenth century, the fortress confined the country's most dangerous political prisoners; ironically, from the windows of their cells in the Trubetskoy Bastion, they could look across the river to the heart of the empire, the Romanovs' Winter Palace.

Cathedral
interior.
See plate 3.

Palace Square.
See plate 4.

The Winter Palace stretched a quarter mile along the Neva embankment, its heavy baroque facade cloaked in a coat of Venetian red and adorned with banded columns, statuary, and tall windows that danced against the mirror of the dark river. On the opposite side of the immense building lay Palace Square, pierced in the middle by the Alexander Column commemorating Russia's victory over Napoleon in 1812 and rising 150 feet into the sky. It took workers two years to shape the 700-ton monolithic polished-granite column and another year to bring it from the quarry in Finland to St. Petersburg, where the French architect August Ricard de Montferrand supervised its erection, mixing the mortar in the base with vodka, according to legend, to keep it from freezing. Two thousand veterans of the conflict with Napoleon raised the column in less than an hour, using an intricate system of ropes and pulleys, but once the column, topped with an angel holding a cross, was in place, nothing was done to secure it to its base. It was held in position simply by its own weight.[35]

In the reign of Alexander I, the square was transformed into a suitably regal frame for the Winter Palace. In 1819, the emperor commissioned Carlo Rossi to design an enormous building to house the General Staff and Ministries of Foreign Affairs and Finance. The resulting structure, the longest building erected in Europe at that time, enclosed the southern end of the square in semicircular arms, pierced in the middle by two successive triumphal arches leading to Bolshaya Morskaya Street and Nevsky Prospekt.[36] Atop the final arch, a massive bronze sculpture depicted a Roman chariot pulled by six prancing horses, a clear and symbolic reminder of the Romanovs' imperial aspirations. The sculpture was so large and so precariously balanced atop the arch that everyone feared it would collapse. Unperturbed, Rossi himself ascended the scaffolding at the moment of dedication, declaring that if the sculpture fell, he would tumble with it.[37]

From the Winter Palace, a bridge spanned the Neva and led to the Strelka on the tip of Vasilevskiy Island. Here, beginning in 1805, the French architect Thomas de Thomon erected a stock exchange, modeled on the Temple of Paestum and ringed with two rows of forty-four Doric columns. This bourse ranked among the most important financial centers in Europe. At the edge of the Neva, where granite quays curved down to the water, de Thomon built two distinctive brick rostral columns; on public holidays, flames roared into the night sky from the gas lamps atop the columns.[38]

The western quay of Vasilevskiy Island housed many of St. Petersburg's academic buildings. Here stood Peter the Great's Kuntskammer, its five-storeyed polygonal tower set between wings of blue adorned with white pilasters and cornices. Peter had envisioned it as Russia's first scientific museum and paid handsomely for the hundreds of specimens that filled its halls. But his tastes leaned toward the bizarre: an entire gallery was filled with two-headed fetuses, skeletons with extra arms, the remains of dwarfs and giants, two-headed animals, an enormous severed penis, and, in Peter's day, several unfortunate live exhibits, including a man with only two fingers and a very unwilling hermaphrodite, who eventually managed to escape. To encourage visitors, Peter offered all who came to view his exhibition a free glass of vodka, often a necessary inducement to steady nerves and calm stomachs.[39] Farther down the quay were the Twelve Colleges of St. Petersburg University, the Imperial Academy of Sciences, and the Imperial Academy of Fine Arts, its granite quay graced with two Egyptian sphinxes, discovered during an excavation at Thebes and presented to Nicholas I.[40]

The English Embankment stretched along the opposite side of the Neva, framing the vast expanse of the great river. It was named after Quarenghi's English Church, a simple neoclassical structure with mahogany reredos and stained-glass windows. The first stretch of the embankment was lined with the Senate and Holy Synod Buildings, their pale yellow facades ornamented with stark white Corinthian columns and cornices and linked together by an arch. The Senate, created by Peter the Great in 1711, gave its mandatory assent to imperial proclamations and helped rule the country, while the Synod controlled the Orthodox Church. At the center of the quay, Senate Square was home to the city's most famous sculpture, Etienne Falconet's statue of Peter the Great. Commissioned by Catherine the Great, the giant equestrian memorial—called *The Bronze Horseman* by Pushkin—showed Peter astride a rearing mount, its base engraved with the simple inscription: *Petro Primo, Catherina Secunda.*

St. Isaac's
Cathedral.
See plate 5.

Facing Senate Square and dominating the city's skyline with its great gilded dome was St. Isaac's Cathedral, the most impressive of all the capital's churches. The cathedral enclosed one side of a square ringed with architectural masterpieces; at its center stood a huge equestrian statue of Nicholas I atop a pedestal of granite, porphyry, and various types of colored marble.[41] At the far end of the square, beyond the immensely wide Blue Bridge spanning the Moika Canal, was the Mariinsky Palace, built for the favorite daughter of Nicholas I and used, at the beginning of the twentieth century, as the seat of the Imperial Council. To the west was Giacomo Quarenghi's Horse Guards Manege, a riding school hidden behind a facade adorned with columns. Originally, the pedestals

Peter the Great,
Senate Square.
See plate 6.

on either side of the portico held Italian marble sculptures representing the sons of Zeus; the Holy Synod, however, objected to enormous statues of naked men so close to the cathedral, and these were duly removed.[42]

From the Manege stretched Konnogvardeisky Boulevard, the scene of frequent exercises by the Horse Guards Regiment, whose barracks lay behind the riding school. The boulevard ended at Ascension Square, dominated by Andrei Stackenschneider's immense, Italianate Nikolaievsky Palace, built in 1851 for Grand Duke Nicholas Nikolaievich, the brother of Alexander II. A profligate, adulterous man whose enormous debts and unofficial second family bankrupted his estate, the grand duke was abandoned by his wife, Alexandra, who after twenty-six years of marriage became a nun. He himself went slowly mad, said to be suffering from syphilis, and spent his last tormented years locked away under guard. After his death, his sons were forced to sell the palace to the state to pay his debts. Under Nicholas II, it became a school for girls, named after the emperor's sister Grand Duchess Xenia Alexandrovna.[43]

Between mansions and canals stretched squares, gardens, and parks, their shaded walks offering a cool retreat from the brief but fierce summer heat. A mile down the Neva Embankment from the Winter Palace, past the imposing marble palaces of the Romanov grand dukes lining Millionnaya Street, stood the thirty-acre Champs de Mars, the great imperial parade ground, known derisively as "the Petersburg Sahara" owing to its blinding swirls of dust in summer.[44] Along its western edge lay the massive Pavlovsky Guards Regiment Barracks, its long lemon-yellow facade adorned with classical porticos, pediments, and rows of white Corinthian columns. A string of impressive buildings enclosed the northern side of the Champs de Mars, including the Marble Palace, home to Grand Duke Konstantin Konstantinovich; the Betskoy House, built in the 1780s by Jean Baptiste Vallin de la Mothe; and the Saltykov Mansion, which housed both the British Embassy and the princes of Oldenburg in Nicholas II's reign.[45]

Rising like a menacing sentinel at the southern end of the Champs de Mars was the grim Mikhailovsky Castle, built by Emperor Paul at the end of the eighteenth century. One night, Paul declared, the Archangel Michael had appeared in a dream and instructed him to build a church on the spot where he had been born. Convinced that such a building would offer a sanctuary from the intrigues of the Russian court, the emperor ordered Rastrelli's old summer palace, the place of his birth, razed and in 1796 commissioned Vassili Bazhenov to design a great fortress that would incorporate the ordained church. A year later, Vincenzo Brenna took over the commission and finished the Mikhailovsky Castle. In his haste to move in, Paul ripped pediments, cornices, and moldings from his mother's palaces, to speed the decoration of the interior. When he took up residence, the plaster on the walls had not even dried, and the tapestries and fabrics covering the furniture soon rotted.[46]

Paul lived in his hulking fortress for only forty nights. On the evening of March 11, 1801, conspirators crept into the fortified structure and bludgeoned and strangled him to death. After that, no Romanov wished to live within the castle's tainted walls, and it was given to the Training Academy of the Military Institute of Engineers.[47]

East of the Champs de Mars stretched Peter the Great's Summer Garden, laid out by Le Blonde in imitation of the patterned gardens that Peter had so admired in England, France, and Holland. Le Blonde created a paradise crossed with long avenues, shaded with clipped linden and maple trees, and adorned with parterres in golden box, geometrical flowerbeds, and allegorical statuary. Peter imported apple trees from Sweden, cedars from northern Russia, and a variety of exotic tulip bulbs from Holland that exploded with color at the beginning of spring, all enclosed by a decorative wrought-iron railing set with gilded grilles, designed by Yuri Velten.[48] The Summer Garden was a favorite spot among both St. Petersburg's aristocracy and its demimonde, with "dogs and lower ranks"— in the words of one general—being strictly forbidden.[49]

The harsh weather of the North dominated the life of the city. Autumn came early, wrapping St. Petersburg in its soft, golden glow. "The sun made great splashes of light on the bright yellow trees and the golden leaves littering the avenues," noted a September visitor to the Summer Garden.[50] By October, the city was submerged in a perpetual fog, the swirling mists and gray rains cloaking the golden spires and baroque facades of the palaces and cathedrals. "Winter could be sensed, waiting to strike," recalled one lady.[51]

November brought the first real signs of the approaching deluge, as the city was "wreathed in dark clouds and swept by chilling winds."[52] Light fell from the sky by three o'clock in the afternoon, wrapping the city in a veil of darkness. Snow was relentless, blanketing the capital until it disappeared beneath the white powder. Through the next six months, the gas streetlamps along Nevsky Prospekt glowed round the clock, casting pale halos of soft light on the bundled masses who carefully made their way across drifts of snow. The canals and the Neva froze, great sheets of blue ice so thick that tram tracks could be laid over the surface of the river. "The sky is clear and blue, though of an entirely different shade from the azure of the south," noted Théophile Gautier. "This is steel blue, or ice blue, of a charming tint never yet produced by any brush. The dazzling, cold light, the frozen sun, brings a blush to the cheeks of some little pink cloudlets. The snow, sparkling like diamonds, as brilliant as marble, has grown doubly white under the hardening touch of the frost. The trees, covered with icy crystals, seem turned into silver flowers, fit for the garden of the fairies."[53]

By Easter, the snow had begun to melt, turning the streets to slush as the city waited for the Neva to thaw, a sure sign that spring was on its way. Grand Duchess Marie Pavlovna recalled, "Dull, cracking noises rose from the depths of the ice, rifts appeared here and there, disclosing black water. Soon, the river was furrowed by gaps that kept widening. Immense pieces of ice broke away with a crash and whirled downstream, obstructing the current. They smashed against one another, with a dry sound, turned, and climbed one upon another. The river swelled, the turbulent water, muddy and yellowish, swept its burden at full speed towards the sea."[54] And one German visitor noted, "The houses seem to recover a firm footing on the ground, the lively green of the painted roofs, and the azure star-spangled cupolas of the churches, with their gilt spires, throw off their monotonous icy covering; the eye revels again in the long, un-tasted enjoyment of color, and the river, divested of its wintry garment, flows again in unrobed majesty, and gaily mirrors the palaces ranged along its banks."[55]

Spring in St. Petersburg was brief; by June, the lush greenery of the trees lining the avenues and embankments had burst forth, and birds filled the sky with their songs as gentle breezes off the gulf carried wafts of warm salt air over the city. The famous White Nights came in the middle of June. Summer sunsets over the Neva were fiery spectacles of crimson, purple, and gold, streaking the sky with an overwhelming, burning intensity made even more magnificent by the reflections of palace windows shimmering on the surface of the sapphire water. At midnight, the expansive sky was strewn with a diffused glow of luminous blues, pinks, azures, and fragile mother-of-pearls. A low, gauze-like mist hung over the Neva, filtering soft light across the golden spires and silent canals. The still, glassy surface of the water mirrored the monochromatic pastels of the sky above; from the tip of Vasilevskiy Island, the long, columned facade of the Winter Palace seemed to hover as if by magic, floating against this surreal backdrop. Even at two o'clock in the morning, St. Petersburg glowed with a strange, iridescent light, silhouetting the spires and domes of the churches against the pale sky.

"People took advantage of the light to walk at ten or eleven o'clock at night in the outskirts of the city, in the lovely part of the Neva," recalled Prince Nicholas de Basily. "One could watch the sun sink beneath the horizon and reappear almost immediately and the diaphanous light enhanced the beauty of gardens intersected by arms of the river. Carriages rolled by one after another, and friends greeted friends. Pretty women drew admiring glances."[56]

Summers in St. Petersburg could be miserable. In August, a quiet settled over the city as it simmered in a blaze of heat. The air was still, heavy, humid, and without the slightest hint of a breeze. The only sound was the rhythmic lapping of water against the granite quays lining the canals. Meriel Buchanan, the daughter of the British ambassador, wrote that it was "like plunging into a furnace; the walls of the houses seemed to radiate heat, the sun blazed through a copper-colored haze, the river was like molten lead with an oily reflection on its absolute stillness. The little white passenger steamers passing to and fro hardly made a ripple on the smooth surface; even the fussy black tugs dragging the heavy painted barges seemed oppressed by the weight of the air and the acrid scent of burning wood."[57]

Midnight in
St. Petersburg.
See plate 7.

Members of the aristocracy and the upper classes fled their mansions and flats for the bucolic relief of the Islands. Here, at the mouth of the Gulf of Finland where the Neva emptied its waters into the Baltic Sea, an archipelago of dozens of small islands formed a marshy delta. They were peaceful, near to the city center, yet isolated by stretches of water and thick groves of birch and pine trees. Many government ministers and members of the diplomatic corps went to stay there during the summer, renting dachas and secluded villas lost at the ends of sandy roads. "Shutters were opened up in summer homes," wrote Helene Izvolsky, "and nightingales trilled until dawn; lovers picked jasmine blossoms and lilies of the valley, or rode around the lakes in small boats between patches of water lilies. There was also something unreal or dreamlike about this atmosphere, which hardly harmonized with the tensions and unrest of the city."[58]

Afternoons were filled with polo matches, picnics, games of lawn tennis, boating on the canals, and rides through the forests. Meriel Buchanan recalled "the voices of children in the next door garden, the sound of bells from the little yellow church with the bright green domes on the other side of the river, the whistle of passing steamers, the voices of men in brightly-colored shirts who rowed the little green boats across the river, sometimes the sound of a concertina from one of the barges, a voice singing an endless folk song, long drawn out, sad with the hopeless sadness of the Russian race. . . . Here and there, through the trees, one would catch a glimpse of silver waters, from the little villas scattered along the road, would come the sound of a gramophone, the echoes of laughing voices, the clatter of teacups. . . . A crowd of little rowing boats dotted the quiet water, a yacht with a scarlet sail painted with a black skull tacked slowly across the river, coming in from the wide shining Gulf that stretched away into a soft purple haze of heat."[59]

The end of the unbearably humid summer brought the return of thousands of families from peaceful holidays in the country as the onset of autumn marked the beginning of a new school year. In 1900, there were more than a hundred secondary schools in St. Petersburg, a dozen of which were regarded more or less as the exclusive domain of the aristocracy. Of these, the most important and prestigious were the Corps des Pages and the Alexander Lyceum for boys, and the Catherine and the Smolny Institute for girls.

Alexander I had founded the Alexander Lyceum, Russia's most exclusive place of education, to ensure an education for his younger brothers. In time, members of the aristocracy were admitted, destined for the diplomatic corps, civil service, and the legal professions. One of its most famous graduates had been Alexander Pushkin. Pupils, selected on a basis of family background and academic achievements, were enrolled between the ages of ten and twelve. Clad in white trousers and waist-length blue cotton tunics, they mastered subjects ranging from history and the sciences to military maneuvers over the course of their six-year terms.

The daughters of the aristocracy had several choices, including the Catherine Institute Boarding School for Young Ladies of Noble Birth, housed in an impressive neoclassical building along the Fontanka Canal. It was the Smolny Institute, however—a rambling complex along the banks of the Neva, dominated by Rastrelli's baroque ice-blue and white Cathedral of the Resurrection—that was St. Petersburg's most prestigious girls' school.

Cathedral of the Resurrection. See plate 8.

Originally, the site held a tar yard, used to service the ships of Peter the Great's fledgling navy. By the middle of the eighteenth century, the tar yards had been abandoned, and in 1744, Empress Elizabeth founded a convent here.[60] When Catherine the Great came to the throne, she established the Smolny Institute in its buildings. To house its growing body of students, she commissioned Giacomo Quarenghi to build a severely classical structure whose long facade was dominated by a central portico of eight white Ionic columns. At the beginning of the twentieth century, the institute was open to daughters of the nobility, who entered at the age of six and left its halls at eighteen. Each morning, assembling for breakfast in the main hall, the young girls curtsied to a large canvas of Nicholas II's mother, Dowager Empress Marie Feodorovna, the school's patron. During their twelve years in the school, pupils, clad in plain white cotton and muslin dresses covered with aprons and finely starched shoulder capes, learned all that was required for life as gentlewomen: music, drama, drawing, dancing, painting, embroidery, and languages, as well as riding, croquet, archery, and lawn tennis. In keeping with the cosmopolitan nature of the capital, students at the empire's premier school for young ladies spoke German on Mondays, Wednesdays, and Fridays; French on Tuesdays, Thursdays, and Saturdays; and English between classes. Russian was used only on Sundays.[61]

By the beginning of the twentieth century, St. Petersburg was restless, a place of unsettled aspirations, immense wealth, and power alongside grinding poverty and despair. This magnificent city, with its architectural masterpieces, appeared like a mirage, some distant echo of the vanished imperial world of Rome or the legendary Atlantis, its privileged inhabitants sitting atop a smoldering volcano of discontent whose flames licked at the railings of their palaces. It was marked with a curious flavor, distinct from other cities in the empire, a place inhabited by the ghosts of Tchaikovsky, Dostoevsky, and Pushkin and flowering with the genius of Diaghilev, Stravinsky, Nabokov, and Kandinsky. Over this collection of beauty and opulence ruled Nicholas II, emperor and autocrat, the eighteenth sovereign to sit on the Russian throne and destined to be the last.

Part One

PERSONAGES

1

THE LAST TSAR

ON OCTOBER 20, 1894, AT HALF-PAST TWO in the afternoon, Alexander III of Russia died of nephritis at his Livadia Palace in the Crimea. The once powerful emperor lay in agony, his massive frame wasted. His last hours were passed with his family until, with a dying breath, he uttered a short prayer and kissed his wife. Alexander was only forty-nine. Although he had been unwell for months, his premature death came as a shock, both to his family and to his empire.

"Sandro, what am I going to do?" the new emperor, Nicholas II, tearfully asked his cousin and brother-in-law, Grand Duke Alexander Mikhailovich. "What is going to happen to me, to you . . . to all of Russia? I am not prepared to be a Tsar. I never wanted to become one. I know nothing of the business of ruling. I have no idea of even how to talk to the ministers."[1]

The twenty-six-year-old man who stood weeping on his cousin's shoulder in the dim light of an October sunset was the eighteenth sovereign of the Romanov Dynasty to accede to the Russian throne. By blood and marriage, he was related to the royal houses of Great Britain, Spain,

Nicholas II, painted by Liphart, 1900

Sweden, Germany, Denmark, Romania, and Greece. The wealthiest man in the world, he possessed an empire that stretched across one-sixth of the land surface of the globe and encompassed 140 million subjects. As an autocrat, Nicholas II was responsible to no one. Imbued with a deep belief that his was a role ordained by God, he relied only on his own conscience for guidance as his empire entered the turbulent waters of the twentieth century.

Yet it is hard to imagine a man more incapable of this onerous burden than Nicholas II. Shy, thoughtful, and exceptionally polite, Nicholas came to the throne obsessed with the idea that he was ill prepared to rule and was pursued by fate. Even the date of his birth—May 6, 1868, the Feast of St. Job in the Orthodox liturgical calendar—played into this self-fulfilling prophecy. Like Job, Nicholas felt himself tested and tried at every turn, a victim of divinely mandated misfortune. With a tragic sense of fatalism, Nicholas would ascribe every catastrophe that befell his empire to "God's will."

Nicholas was the eldest of six children born to Alexander and his wife, Marie Feodorovna. A second son, Alexander, lived less than a year; a brother, George Alexandrovich, followed in 1871; a sister, Xenia Alexandrovna, in 1875; another brother, Michael Alexandrovich, in 1878; and a second sister, Olga Alexandrovna, in 1882. Alexander III had dominated his family in much the same way he did his empire: his word was law, his decisions uncontestable. Capable of great warmth and indulgence, he was, at the same time, "ruthless even with his children," recalled an official at court, "and loathed everything that savored of weakness."[2] He despised his eldest son's gentle character, once loudly complaining, "You are a little girlie!"[3] Nicholas feared the unpredictable behavior that followed his father's drunken carousals; when Alexander became violent, his wife gathered their children and escaped to an apartment in St. Petersburg's Tauride Palace.[4]

The future Nicholas II with his two brothers, George and Michael, and eldest sister, Xenia, 1886

Marie Feodorovna provided a warm refuge, but her protection took the form of an oppressive cocoon that stifled maturity, and Nicholas remained innocent

PLATE 1. The Admiralty

PLATE 2. The Cathedral
of the Fortress of
St. Peter and St. Paul

PLATE 3. Interior of the Cathedral of the Fortress of St. Peter and St. Paul

PLATE 4. Palace Square

PLATE 5. The dome of St. Isaac's Cathedral at sunset

PLATE 6. *The Bronze Horseman*—Falconet's statue
of Peter the Great in Senate Square

PLATE 7.
Midnight in St. Petersburg
during its famous
White Nights

PLATE 8.
Rastrelli's Cathedral of
the Resurrection at the
Smolny Institute

PLATE 9. Empress Alexandra, painted by Mueller-Norden, 1896

PLATE 10. Marie Feodorovna, painted by Flameng

PLATE 11. St. Isaac's Cathedral

PLATE 12. The interior of St. Isaac's Cathedral

and childish. The cloistered world of the imperial palaces, with their fawning servants and gold-braided courtiers, did little to encourage independent thought. Instead, Nicholas was subject only to emotion, relying on instinct and on passion in making important decisions. From his sixth birthday on, a string of teachers, military instructors, generals, and government officials tutored Nicholas in history, Russian literature, the classics, geography, arithmetic, science, languages, and religion, yet it was an education conceived along idiosyncratic lines. On his father's orders, instructors were not allowed to question him, nor were his studies graded, leaving Nicholas's mistakes and opinions unchallenged.[5] The role of his mother was equally damaging. Fearing the loss of her dominance, Marie Feodorovna personally selected men of limited capabilities, arranging lessons so that Nicholas never saw the same tutors for more than two successive days to avoid any lasting influences.[6]

The future Emperor Alexander III and his fiancée, Marie Feodorovna, 1866

Nicholas had an excellent memory. He spoke Russian, French, German, Danish, and English, the latter with a perfect accent; his Russian, as Prince Andrei Lobanov-Rostovsky noted, was even tinged with "a slightly English accent."[7] In May 1890, he jubilantly recorded in his diary: "Today I finished forever my education!"[8] Short, with blue eyes and a chestnut beard and mustache, Nicholas made his first forays into official life, though the results were far from encouraging. One Russian referred to him derisively as "just a little, fair officer. He comes up to my shoulders."[9] The wife of an American diplomat noted, "The men of the Imperial Family are such large, tall, fine-looking men that the Russians will find it difficult to connect the idea of majesty with one who is so small."[10] He lacked, recalled one courtier, "the inspiring presence of his father; nor did he convey his mother's vibrant charm."[11] At official receptions, his boredom gave offense. Yet his father, himself poorly trained, did nothing to prepare Nicholas for his eventual role. When Nicholas was twenty-three, Alexander III dismissed his son as "nothing but a boy, whose judgments are utterly childish."[12]

Like any other young aristocrat, Nicholas joined the Imperial Army, immersing himself in the carefully regulated world of the Russian military. He had a liaison with the prima ballerina Mathilde Kschessinska, but his true passion lay elsewhere. He first met Princess Alix of Hesse *und Bei Rhein* in 1884 at the wedding of her sister Elizabeth, known as Ella, to his uncle, Grand Duke Serge Alexandrovich. After a week together, the sixteen-year-old tsesarevich was utterly convinced of his love for the shy and solemn golden-haired girl, but it was to be five years before they met again. Alix spent that winter of 1889 with Ella and Serge, and Nicholas lavished her with attentions, much to the consternation of his mother, who, recalled one aristocratic lady, "made no attempt to disguise her displeasure at her son's infatuation."[13] St. Petersburg society thought her ill humored and unsmiling, but Nicholas was determined. "My dream is to one day marry Alix H.," he confided to his diary.[14]

Empress
Alexandra, 1896.
See plate 9.

The politically unimportant German state of Hesse, stretched along the banks of the Rhine and centered round the medieval city of Darmstadt, had long provided brides to the Romanov Dynasty. Only six when her mother, Queen Victoria's second daughter, Princess Alice, died, Alix had been raised according to the dictates of her powerful grandmother. Under her direction, Alix developed into a shy but serious young woman with a stubborn will and belief in the superiority of her own morality and intelligence. Her cousin Princess Marie Louise later complained that "from her earliest childhood, there was that strange, impregnable obstinacy that nothing could overcome."[15] She never developed the social skills necessary to her rank, giving the impression of boredom, of disinterest, and of distinct unease. The most powerful influences in her life were her mother, her grandmother, and her sisters. Her father was easily dictated to, and her brother Ernie was equally submissive. These models of feminine power, weak men, and domination characterized her youth and later marriage.

Alix was confirmed into the Lutheran Church at sixteen, and her devotion to her faith became for Nicholas an almost insurmountable obstacle. "I can never change my religion," she wrote to his sister Xenia Alexandrovna.[16] This was welcome news to Nicholas's mother, who "remained in a negative state of mind" over her son's obsession, according to one official; she even "forbade" him to meet Alix during her 1890 visit to Russia.[17] Nicholas was persistent, and circumstance conspired in his favor when, two years after her father's death, he traveled to Germany to attend the wedding of Alix's brother Grand Duke Ernst Ludwig IV to his cousin Princess Victoria Melita of Edinburgh, known as Ducky within the family. Conspiring with him were Alix's brother and her sister Elizabeth, his aunt

Grand Duchess Marie Pavlovna—known in the family as Miechen—and his and Alix's mutual cousin, Kaiser Wilhelm II. Nicholas's efforts weakened her resolve, and changing personal circumstances ultimately led her to accept his proposal.

Six months later, Alexander III's death brought Nicholas to the throne. Alix, who had come to the Crimea to receive the dying emperor's blessing for the betrothal, converted to Russian Orthodoxy, embracing her new faith with a fervor bordering on exaltation and taking the new name of Alexandra Feodorovna. A week after Alexander III's funeral, the couple wed, beginning a marriage that was one of history's greatest love stories. For twenty-four years, husband and wife remained true to each other. "Even after many years of marriage," remembered Prince Christopher of Greece, "they were like young lovers."[18]

Few Russians took to the empress, nor did members of her husband's own family, particularly his difficult mother, who regarded her with jealousy and treated her with barely disguised contempt. In contrast to her husband, Alexandra at least looked the role. "A real Empress she is," declared one diplomat, "tall, golden haired, and a pink and white face."[19] "Much of her beauty comes from exquisite coloring," recalled one woman, "and there is about her a subtle charm impossible to picture and difficult to describe." The woman was particularly struck by her expression: "a singularly wistful and sweet sadness that never went quite away even when she smiled."[20]

Alexandra flung herself into her new role, filled with enthusiastic ideas that were often met with scorn. Increasingly, noted one aristocrat, she suffered "from the misinterpretation of everything she said and did, and even her thought, her unspoken word, was a source of eternal suspicion and persecution."[21] As she fell under Orthodoxy's spell, Alexandra grew even more serious. "There had always been something strained about her," recalled her cousin Queen Marie of Romania. "She had no warm feeling for any of us and this was of course strongly felt in her attitude, which was

Grand Duchesses Olga and Tatiana Nikolaievna, 1913

never welcoming. Some of this was no doubt owing to shyness, but the way she closed her narrow lips after the first rather forced greeting gave you the feeling that this was all she was ready to concede and that she was finished with you."[22]

The Russian court, with its scandals, gossip, and flaunted love affairs, shocked Alexandra. "Most Russian girls," she complained, "seem to have nothing in their heads but thoughts of officers."[23] Inevitably, Alexandra struck those she encountered as "very distant and unapproachable," as Princess Anatole Bariatinsky recalled.[24] The St. Petersburg ladies who attended her first reception left with distasteful impressions: her shyness was ascribed to haughtiness, her dislike of ceremony to indifference or hatred of Russia. Society mocked her, as did members of the imperial family: Grand Duke Nicholas Mikhailovich made no secret of his feelings, deeming the empress "the Abominable Hessian," "the Hessian Tigress," and, most amusingly, "the woman who wanted to set Christ straight."[25]

Through her influence, Nicholas began a gradual withdrawal from society. Residing for most of the year in the Alexander Palace at Tsarskoye Selo, fifteen miles south of the capital, the imperial family remained hidden from the outside world. Nicholas and Alexandra valued the sanctity of their family and regarded public duties as an encroachment on their private lives. Four daughters came in quick succession: Olga was born in November 1895, followed by Tatiana in 1897, Marie in 1899, and Anastasia in 1901.

Olga most resembled her father, with her light chestnut hair and blue eyes. Her broad face and slightly turned-up nose detracted from her beauty, though, as Gleb Botkin, the son of an imperial physician, recalled, her personality made her "the most attractive" of the girls.[26] She was not only the quietest of the children, but also the most intelligent. The tutor Pierre Gilliard noted that she "possessed a remarkably quick brain. She had good reasoning powers as well as initiative, a very independent manner, and a gift for swift and entertaining repartee."[27] Her serious nature echoed that of her mother. Alexandra imbued all of her children with a sense of purpose, but Olga, as the first, bore the most criticism. She could be willful, "very straight-forward, sometimes too outspoken," as a member of the court recalled.[28] Resenting this treatment and armed, as Anna Vyrubova wrote, with "a strong will" and a "hot temper," Olga occasionally clashed with her mother.[29] Confined to a world where even simple friendships were rare, she sought solace in religion.

With her lean figure and fine features, Tatiana most resembled her mother. Proud and refined, she impressed everyone with her grace and character. "She was a poetical creature," recalled the empress's friend Lili Dehn, "always yearning for the ideal and dreaming of great friendships."[30] In manner, Tatiana was "gentle and reserved," according to Anna Vyrubova, "kindly and sympathetic," looking after her younger sisters and brother with "such a protecting spirit" that they called her "the Governess."[31] Of all the girls, it was Tatiana who most inherited her mother's sense of authority and acceptance of their privileged positions, and Alexandra indulged her second daughter, confiding in her in a way she found impossible with the headstrong Olga. Tatiana tried to emulate her mother's religious piety but was unable to exhibit the same depth of feeling; instead, she assumed the role of caretaker, surrounding her mother with constant attentions.[32] In contrast to her mother, however, Tatiana was the most social of the sisters, and her natural charm and beauty made her immensely popular with her father's subjects.[33]

Marie was the most beautiful of the sisters, with thick, golden hair and deep blue eyes so large that within the family they were known as "Marie's Saucer's."[34] Modest and warm-hearted, she was, recalled one courtier, "kindness and unselfishness personified."[35] She flirted with the young officers surrounding the family, slipping into their dining room to chat about their families. Marie paid little attention to her lessons, preferring walks in the park. Of all the girls, she seemed the most confined by her position. Her dream, she said, was to marry and raise a large family.[36] Like Olga, Marie was headstrong, "energetic and determined to get her own way," recalled Alexander Mossolov.[37] As a third daughter, Marie suffered from the idea that she had been unwanted, and her elder sisters exacerbated the situation, refusing to include her in their activities and, as courtiers recalled, treating her like an outcast and calling her "fat little bow-wow."[38]

The idea that she, too, had been unwanted undoubtedly resulted in the famously roguish behavior of the youngest daughter, Anastasia, deemed "the most amusing" of the four by one courtier.[39] Her small, boyish frame was suited to her wild pursuits: she climbed trees and refused to come down, terrorized her tutors with practical jokes, and made frequent, often barbed, comments at those around her. Her cousin Princess Nina Georgievna

Grand Duchesses Marie and Anastasia Nikolaievna, 1913

remembered her as "nasty, to the point of being evil."[40] Short and somewhat overweight as a girl, Anastasia eventually developed into a beauty, with auburn, shoulder-length hair and, as Tatiana Botkin recalled, "the most extraordinary blue eyes of the Romanovs, of great luminescence."[41] Although the least intellectual of the children, Anastasia was perhaps the brightest of the five. General Count Alexander von Grabbe remembered, "Whenever I talked with her, I always came away impressed by the breadth of her interests. That her mind was keenly alive was immediately apparent."[42] Her aunt Grand Duchess Olga Alexandrovna later said, "Her teachers called it laziness. But I am not so sure. I think books as books never said much to her."[43]

The isolation enforced by their mother was meant to safeguard her daughters from what she considered the temptation, loose morals, and self-indulgence of society. Alexandra did not understand that even as royal children, they needed outside influences. As Anna Vyrubova wrote, "The Empress dreaded for her daughters the companionship of over-sophisticated young women of the

Empress Alexandra with her new son, Tsesarevich Alexei, 1904

aristocracy, whose minds, even in the schoolroom, were fed with the foolish and often vicious gossip of a decadent society. The Empress even discouraged association with cousins and near relatives."[44] Such isolation moved their grandmother to once speak of them as "hostages to their mother's paranoia."[45] Not surprisingly, the grand duchesses remained immature. "I never heard the slightest word suggestive of the modern flirtation," recalled Alexander Mossolov. "Even when the two eldest had grown into real young women, one might hear them talking like little girls of ten or twelve."[46]

The grand duchesses aroused public curiosity, but they were mere ceremonial adornments in their father's world. The primogeniture of the Romanov succession laws demanded a male heir. After four daughters, Nicholas and Alexandra grew frantic, seeking the intervention of a number of dubious holy men in an effort to produce a son. Finally, on Friday, July 30, 1904, Alexandra gave birth to an heir, Tsesarevich Alexei. Within six weeks of his birth, however, the first signs of hemophilia appeared, a discovery that shattered the couple's lives forever. Nicholas submissively accepted his son's illness as "God's will," while Alexandra, her physical and mental health devastated by the knowledge that she had passed on the disease, turned to mystics for comfort. When, in 1905, Gregory Rasputin first appeared, both Nicholas and Alexandra readily accepted him and his mysterious ability to alleviate their son's illness.

Alexei grew up to be a tall, thin young boy, closely resembling his mother. "He had a long, finely chiseled face," recalled Pierre Gilliard, "delicate features, auburn hair with a coppery glint in it, and large blue-gray eyes."[47] The emperor and the empress assigned two sailors, Derevenko and Nagorny, to watch over their son. They watched while he played, warned him when he exerted himself, and carried him when he was unable to walk. Constrained by his illness, Alexei allowed his emotions full range. One of Nicholas II's adjutants later recalled, "Despite his good nature and compassion, he promised to have a stubborn and independent character in the future. From his earliest days he did not like to obey and would only do so, like his father, when he was completely convinced of it himself."[48]

"His mother," recalled the tutor Gibbes, "loving him passionately, could not be firm with him, and through her, he got most of his wishes granted."[49] Wild and uncorrected when young, he often embarrassed family members. After his wife lunched with the imperial family, Grand Duke Konstantin Konstantinovich recorded in his diary: "He wouldn't sit up, ate badly, licked his plate, and teased the others. The Emperor often turned away, perhaps to avoid having to say anything, while the Empress rebuked her elder daughter Olga, who sat next to her brother, for not restraining him. But Olga cannot deal with him."[50] Although eventually Alexei began to grow out of this churlish behavior, neither Nicholas nor Alexandra did much to correct the problem.

But Alexei was also capable of great charm. Alexander Grabbe recalled him as "an extremely handsome boy . . . svelte, elegant, intelligent, and with unusual presence of mind. He possessed, moreover, other winning qualities: a warm, happy disposition and a generous nature which made him eager to be of help and enabled him quickly to establish rapport with others."[51] He had a great sympathy for those who also suffered and could be unusually thoughtful for a boy of his age.

The tsesarevich's hemophilia remained a carefully guarded secret within the imperial family. The public knew only that the heir to the throne was frequently ill, and rumor replaced fact. The reasons for the imperial couple's reliance on Rasputin were never revealed, and the swirl of gossip and sexual innuendo surrounding the peasant attached itself to Nicholas and Alexandra, further undermining public affection for the Romanovs.

Nicholas II did little, if not to win public sympathy, then at least not to alienate it. In the first days of his reign, he found himself overwhelmed with the onerous duties he had assumed. "I don't know anything," he once complained. "The late Emperor did not anticipate his end, and thus did not train me in anything."[52] And, as he admitted to his cousin Grand Duke Konstantin Konstantinovich, Alexander III "had never once mentioned the responsibilities that awaited him." When the dying emperor was asked frankly if he had counseled his heir, Alexander replied, "No. He himself knows everything." Nicholas, however, knew little, complaining that his father "had never given him any instructions and had left him to act as he thought best."[53]

"He was very young when he ascended the Throne," wrote Count Paul von Benckendorff, who knew Nicholas well, "with no experience of life or of affairs, and his character never had a chance to be formed. To the end of his life he lacked balance, nor could he grasp the principles that are necessary for the conduct of so great an Empire, hence his indecision, his limitations, and the fluctuations that lasted throughout his reign."[54] Nicholas maintained a firm reserve with all. "I found him invariably pleasant and gracious," noted Alexander Grabbe, "yet inscrutable. As I was soon to learn even with persons of his immediate Entourage he seldom revealed what he thought or how he felt except in trivial matters, never showed like or dislike, and never made his position known on any subject."[55] By reducing many encounters to trivial conversation, Nicholas surrendered any opportunity to hear informed opinion on the crucial events of the day; the few who ventured into such territory were quickly reminded of the emperor's displeasure.[56]

The early twentieth century presented Nicholas with challenges both to his authority and to the nature of the Russian empire. Social and economic aspirations of an ever-increasing working class had been kept in check during the reign of his father, and the revolutionary movement was forced underground after ruthless suppression. Nicholas's reign saw these forces coalesce into a powerful alliance, but he was unable to understand the problems and form a cohesive response.[57] Instead, believing that God ordained the autocracy as the only just power in Russia, Nicholas resisted efforts that hinted at an infringement on his rights. He perceived the autocracy in spiritual, not political, terms, inheriting, wrote one official, "an unshakable faith in the providential nature of his high office. His mission emanated from God. For his actions he was responsible only to his own conscience and to God."[58]

Nicholas was hostage to the peculiarly Russian idea of *sud'ba*, or fate, a manifestation of predetermined events that controlled every aspect of life. The autocracy, as Nicholas understood it, was a mystical force, ordained by God and therefore not subject to the ministrations of man. He felt no need to question the many disasters of his reign or understand the factors that had caused them; instead, all events were ascribed to fate, a view that absolved Nicholas of all personal responsibility. Believing, as his cousin recalled, that "the mysterious forces emanating during the sacrament of taking the oath on the day of Coronation provided all the practical data required by a ruler," Nicholas relied only on intuition to navigate the tumultuous events of the day.[59] He ruled by resignation, unwilling and unable to question the mystical nature of the autocracy that had been inculcated into him since birth.

As emperor, Nicholas perceived himself as a modern monarch, while clinging desperately to a medieval view of his own prerogatives. "He lived a totally Western life in St. Petersburg in surroundings more English than Russian," writes Anne Odom, "and in his early years he often traveled to Western Europe. Increasingly, however, he sought refuge from the strains of ruling over a modern society by turning to his romantic view of the reign of Tsar Alexei . . . which he considered to have been a peaceful period of harmonious relations between Tsar and people."[60] In his view, the autocracy stood apart from the institutions of the Russian state and the government. Distrusting most officials, he made no effort to work within the system as his predecessors had done. In the world inhabited by Nicholas, he and he alone was the source of all authority and power. He considered, as Richard Wortman notes, the "formal apparatus of administration as alien and anti-monarchical."[61]

"The ministers I knew," recalled Sir Samuel Hoare, "told me that there was no intimacy between the Emperor and his Government. If they saw him, it was in official audiences, in uniform, with portfolios under their arms, and for a fixed and limited time."[62] Nicholas once complained that Prime Minister Peter Stolypin had provided too much leadership, thereby distracting attention from himself. "Do you suppose I liked always reading in the papers," he petulantly asked, "that the President of the Council has done this, or the President of the Council has done that? Don't I count? Am I a nobody?"[63] He viewed the student unrest, strikes, and pleas for reform that ringed the disastrous Russo-Japanese War of 1904–1905 as direct attacks against his divine mandate, and he ruthlessly crushed them. During the Revolution of 1905, some ten thousand Russians were executed by the government, with thousands more in the years that followed.[64] "No Romanov before Nicholas," wrote W. Bruce Lincoln, "had ever put down his subjects on such an enormous scale."[65]

Nicholas's response to the 1905 Revolution underlined his conviction that the autocracy was indissoluble from the Russian empire. With the country collapsing around him, Nicholas was forced to take decisive action to save his throne: on October 17, 1905, he reluctantly signed a manifesto creating the Duma, Russia's first elected legislature. Although he granted civil liberties, freedom of religion, speech, and assembly and enfranchised the majority of his subjects, Nicholas did not view this as an infringement on the autocracy. He recognized that he had transformed the empire into something approaching a democratic monarchy, yet he refused to acknowledge the change to his own power. To Nicholas, the Duma gained its power directly through his benevolence: it was his gift to Russia, subject to his whims and orders as an extension of the autocracy itself. Although he had promised to "keep unchanged the institutions I have granted," both the First and the Second Dumas were closed on Nicholas's orders and their deputies put into the street when they insisted on launching investigations into government-sponsored pogroms.[66]

In 1907, in anticipation of the Third Duma, the emperor illegally altered the voting laws, to narrow the chances of socialists winning seats.[67] In 1913, he again tried, unsuccessfully, to limit the power of the Duma and to revoke it altogether.[68] The October Manifesto had been wrested from an unwilling emperor, and in the years that followed, he turned away from not only his ceremonial duties as sovereign but also from bureaucrats, officials, ministers, the aristocracy, and the court—in short, from educated Russians, the very people he believed had driven a wedge between him and his people. To the end of his life, he firmly believed that the majority of Russians—the simple, uneducated masses far away from the corrupting influences of St. Petersburg or Moscow—remained steadfast in their devotion. Seeking validation, he began to appeal directly to the people, taking great pains—as Alexander Grabbe recalled—to seek out peasants during his walks, to confirm his beliefs.[69] Even so, Nicholas, according to Mossolov, spoke to them "as if they were children," reinforcing his own view of himself as national father.[70]

This appeal to popular sentiment eventually found voice in a burgeoning twentieth-century media. Bowed by discontent and modern expectations, Nicholas cleverly adapted to the changing world and recognized the inherent propaganda value of its mass media. By utilizing modern methods, he strove not only to assert the archaic prerogatives of a vanished autocracy but also to retain control over the only aspect of his life that had not fallen victim to the tide of change: the presentation of himself and his family.[71] It was no accident that in the last decade of his reign, he increasingly turned to public ceremonies and presentations of his idealized family, with innumerable postcards and souvenirs of his beautiful daughters and handsome son issued with imperial approval in an effort to win back the interest and affection of a public alienated from the throne and excluded from the imperial court.

These efforts reached their zenith in 1913, when Nicholas authorized a biography, published to mark the Tercentenary of the Romanov Dynasty. Publication of *The Reign of the Sovereign Emperor Nicholas Alexandrovich* marked a turning point in the history of the Russian monarchy. Never before had a ruler authorized a biography or allowed such intimate glimpses into every aspect of his life. Written by Major-General Andrei Elchaninov, a member of the Imperial Entourage, the book presented Nicholas as he saw himself: he personally read through the manuscript prior to publication, making revisions in his own hand.[72] It emphasized that which Nicholas wished to be known and ignored that which he found troublesome. Although the First World War was still a year distant, it was no accident that in addition to the Russian edition, English and French translations were also published in London and Paris in 1914—the two countries to which Russia had allied herself.

Elchaninov presented Nicholas as a man who stood in direct communication with God; the legal, bureaucratic, and spiritual institutions of the empire were superfluous to Nicholas's autocratic role. The portrait was one of dedication and an almost supernatural ability in every aspect of his life. "He never lays down his work," Elchaninov asserted, "on week days and weekends, resting only during his short period of sleep, offering in small things, as in great, a lofty example of loyalty in the performance of his duty."[73] This is how Nicholas wished to be seen, and the book continued in a hagiographic tone, stating that the emperor had "full and exact knowledge of every subject dealt with" in his daily meetings with officials, a portrait at odds with the experiences of hundreds of those whom he encountered. Such statements, though they reflected Nicholas's view of himself, elevated his abilities to the point of absurdity.[74]

In commissioning the book, Nicholas II crossed a fragile line. Everyone could now read—with the emperor's approval—of his daily life within the palace walls. This, too, presented Nicholas as he saw himself and as he wished to be seen—a model husband and father, completely devoted to his family to the point of abjuring his imperial obligations. "Entertainments at the Palace," Elchaninov wrote, "are comparatively rare. Great balls and processions are presented only when necessary, as a duty of service. A modest, frugal way of life is evident here, too."[75]

Thus, for the first time, dereliction of the ceremonial role of the Russian sovereign was presented as a deliberate virtue.

Elchaninov's book reflected Nicholas's attempts to reassert himself as a focus of national unity after a frequently catastrophic twenty years on the imperial throne. Yet such claims were balanced against the near-isolation in which the emperor and his family lived, leaving his subjects unaware of their real personalities and existence behind the walls of their palaces. As the first years of the twentieth century crept toward the oblivion of 1914, the empire contented itself with the proliferation of souvenir postcards and flickering newsreel images of its ruling dynasty, while the few privileged participants enacted its archaic rituals for an audience about to be swept away in the flood of revolution.

2

THE IMPERIAL FAMILY

NICHOLAS II WAS NOT ONLY SOVEREIGN of Russia, but also head of the House of Romanov, presiding over his extended family. In addition to Nicholas and his family, the principal members of the Imperial House included his mother, Dowager Empress Marie Feodorovna; his two sisters, Grand Duchesses Xenia and Olga Alexandrovna, and their families; and his brothers, Grand Dukes George and Michael Alexandrovich.

Dowager Empress Marie Feodorovna had occupied the Russian throne at her husband's side for thirteen years. Born Princess Marie Sophie Frederika Dagmar in 1847, she was one of the remarkable children of King Christian IX who, before ascending the Danish throne, had been duke of Schleswig-Holstein-Sonderburg-Glucksborg, a German principality; her mother, Queen Louise, was also German, of Hessian ancestry. Despite these Teutonic influences, Christian's children were imbued with a hatred of Germany, a bitter legacy of Denmark's unsuccessful military struggles against Prussia. To the end of her life, Marie Feodorovna loathed everything German, poisoning both her husband and her eldest son and using her considerable influence over them to cement alliances that led to the First World War. "I heard it at the dinner table twenty times every day," Nicholas II once candidly said of his mother's fiery hatred.[1]

Her early life had been simple. Court protocol was largely ignored, and formal education was regarded with suspicion. Perhaps it was this early sense of deprivation that drove the Danish princess. Asked at an early age what she most wanted, Dagmar declared that she wished for "power and influence."[2] In 1863, her sister Alexandra married Albert Edward, the prince of Wales, Queen Victoria's eldest son and heir; a few years later, her brother William accepted an invitation from Athens and became King George I of the Hellenes. Dagmar herself was not particularly beautiful: small, with a slender figure, she charmed with her large, luminous eyes and indulgent smile. Nor was she a gifted conversationalist; her parents, by circumstance and inclination, had forgone the usual governesses and tutors for their children, and none of their daughters were very well educated. Even when she became an elderly widow, there remained something slightly carefree and childlike about Marie Feodorovna. But she was socially adept and knew how to win affection. In 1864, this vivacity led to an engagement with Tsesarevich Nicholas, the eldest son of Alexander II. If it was not a love match, both partners certainly found the other attractive. Within a few months of the announcement, however, the tsesarevich fell ill with cerebrospinal meningitis, and he died in April of 1865.[3]

In the Romanov family, legend had it that with his last breath, the tsesarevich had begged his brother Alexander to take care of Dagmar and joined their hands atop his chest.[4] "It makes a touching story," noted one historian, "but one suspects that it was invented to mask the indecent haste with which Dagmar was expected to switch her affections."[5] Indeed, talk ran high that Dagmar should marry the new heir to the throne, Alexander Alexandrovich. She was amenable to the idea, but Alexander, in love with a lady in his mother's suite, was coerced and threatened by his father before finally asking for Dagmar's hand.[6] Despite his misgivings, Alexander and Dagmar were engaged. She converted to Orthodoxy, taking the name Marie Feodorovna, and in October 1866, the pair was married.

Marie Feodorovna. See plate 10.

From the beginning, Marie Feodorovna took to her role with a frivolous abandon, relishing the power, wealth, and prestige of imperial Russia. "For the first time in her life," writes Coryne Hall, "she could have as many pretty dresses as she wanted, and it was a heady experience for a girl of just nineteen."[7] She used her position to strengthen her own popularity and coerced her husband—who hated such frivolities—to reluctantly join her in lavish balls that entrenched her hold over society. Despite her own narrow intellect and pettiness, she won the respect of St. Petersburg's elite.

Marie Feodorovna was less successful as a mother. One official condemned her as "a foolish, untalented woman," writing that she spent "most of her time on gossip and dresses. She loves dancing until exhausted and considers this more important than the rearing of her children."[8] The youngest children, at least, considered this a blessing. "It was indeed fortunate that her days were so crowded that few of our escapades came to her notice," said her daughter Olga.[9] Coddling and cosseting her sons, and fearful of losing primacy in their affections, she contributed greatly to their marked immaturity. "My sons," she proudly declared, "were not allowed their separate residences until they married. I was advised to grant them each a separate home and their own entourage when they became of age but I would not. They lived with me."[10] So intense was this jealousy that Alexander and Marie Feodorovna even denied their eldest son his annual allowance on reaching his majority, to keep him under their control.[11]

With her daughters, Marie Feodorovna's behavior reflected a reserve bordering on indifference, and neither felt much true affection for their mother. The empress feared any influence that might come between her and the power she wielded over them. When Xenia was ten, it was suggested that the empress appoint a governess to begin proper instruction. But she protested, "We had no governess when we were children!"[12] "Going to her rooms was a duty laid on me by Nana," Olga recalled. "I never felt at my ease. I tried to be on my best behavior. I could never bring myself to speak naturally. She had a horror of anything beyond the frontiers of etiquette and propriety."[13]

Marie Feodorovna, noted her niece Grand Duchess Marie Georgievna, "was not very tall, but she held herself in such a way that she could never have been taken for anything but an Empress. Though not strictly pretty she had wonderful velvety brown eyes, dark hair, and a personal charm."[14] Dressed in expensive and extravagant gowns adorned with lace and fringe, she swathed herself in a sweet perfume so heavy that its scent lingered long after she had gone.[15] Although an inveterate smoker, Marie Feodorovna, recalled her nephew Prince Christopher of Greece, "wanted no one to know it but the family, so if anyone else entered the room she would immediately hide her cigarette behind her back, oblivious of the clouds of smoke arising like incense."[16] Her voice—"extremely musical," as one lady remembered—was "low" and "husky," with "a curious guttural timbre."[17]

Empress Alexandra in Russian court dress; she wears her pearl and diamond tiara by Kurt Hahn, circa 1906.

Marie Feodorovna, circa 1890. She wears
Russian court dress and, around her neck,
the Imperial Riviere Necklace.

Above all, it was her "charming affability" and habit of "saying an endearing word to everyone," as Vladimir Gurko recalled, that cemented her reputation. "At receptions she knew what to talk about with anyone introduced to her. She knew the interests of the people she spoke with and was invariably aware of their station and ancestry. One thus got the impression that the Empress herself was interested in the people she met."[18] Even so, noted her nephew, "she had a tragic aptitude for ignoring facts and believing only what she wanted to believe."[19]

It was this stubborn, proud woman who, after the premature death of her husband, found herself dowager empress. Her son's marriage to Princess Alix became a source of perpetual animosity. Alexandra thought her mother-in-law stubborn and insipid; in turn, Marie Feodorovna resented her daughter-in-law's intelligence and hold over Nicholas II. A thin veil of cordiality disguised a deep-rooted dislike, and there were battles over the crown jewels, which Marie Feodorovna refused to relinquish despite tradition; patronage of the Red Cross; and which empress should come first in the prayers for the imperial family. By Easter of 1895, relations between the two women were so strained that Alexandra refused to pay half the cost of her mother-in-law's Fabergé egg.[20]

By January 1896, mourning for Alexander III had ended and the social season began, bringing a myriad of difficulties for both empresses. According to tradition, a dowager took precedence over a reigning empress, and Marie Feodorovna, still young and vibrant, refused to relinquish her position. "Quite openly," recalled her daughter Olga, "my mother enjoyed being the first lady in the Empire."[21] Marie Feodorovna, remembered Prince Christopher of Greece, "was the one person who could have saved the situation, but she could not bring herself to do it. Although she never acknowledged it, she was bitterly jealous of her son's wife and, half-consciously perhaps, fostered the feelings against her."[22] Another critic was less kind, asserting that the dowager empress "thrust aside her daughter-in-law in a most unceremonious way, and instead of drawing the latter's attention to her mistakes she magnified them."[23]

Comparisons between Alexandra and her vibrant mother-in-law were bold and unfavorable, and the dowager empress did nothing to halt the criticism. Baroness Sophie Buxhoeveden later recalled the atmosphere of the dowager empress's court where, as she wrote, "everything done" by the emperor and his wife "seemed rash, and even a little wrong."[24] Marie Feodorovna deliberately caused scenes to remind Alexandra of her own precedence. Alexandra's brother recalled how the dowager empress "would always arrive at the same time as her son and daughter-in-law, and often kept them waiting. Nicholas II always had to appear with both Empresses, his mother on his right, Alix on the left; on entering the room it was always Alix who, through lack of space, was obliged to step back. Nicky, with his fierce sense of tact, constantly tried to find some sort of *modus vivendi*, but each time he ran up against the iron will of his mother."[25] Such actions, recalled one member of her court, left Marie Feodorovna with "barely disguised delight in causing bitter scenes to upset the Court at Tsarskoye Selo, and especially the Empress."[26]

As time wore on, it was her relationship with her eldest son, however, that became most strained, as she deluged him with unsolicited political advice. One aristocratic critic later declared that Marie Feodorovna openly "dreamed of her own autocracy, the unbounded expansion of herself."[27] According to one diplomat, she encouraged in Nicholas "a lack of decision in every act, that became the tragedy of his entire existence."[28] Nicholas himself usually bore this intrusion in silence, only rarely pointing out to his mother that he, as emperor, had to make his own decisions. The dowager empress, recalled Foreign Minister Serge Sazonov, was "too outspoken and impetuous. The moment she begins to lecture her son, her feelings run away with her and she sometimes says the exact opposite of what she should; she annoys and humiliates him."[29] Soon all St. Petersburg bristled with tales of her influence over the emperor. The British journalist W. T. Stead once boldly raised the issue with her, but she insisted that she wielded no influence. "I have nothing to do with these things! I never meddle in politics."[30] She justified her denial, and her continued involvement, by repeatedly appealing to Nicholas not as an adviser but as a mother. "My heart bleeds to have to write you all these painful things," she declared to her son, "but if I don't tell you the truth, who will?"[31]

In the capital, Marie Feodorovna lived in splendor at Anichkov Palace, perched on a corner of Nevsky Prospekt and the Fontanka Canal. Beyond its columned ballroom and enfilade of reception rooms adorned with colored damask, carved pilasters, and gilded moldings, she occupied a suite filled with Victorian fringe, overstuffed furniture, and potted palms that transformed the palace into a house swollen with the worst excesses of the era.[32] One visitor was surprised to see "quantities of ill-assorted objects," writing: "It is incredible that these people can have lived surrounded by such bric-à-brac, when they could have had the most beautiful things in the world: there were Japanese screens from the bazaars, portraits done from photographs like the ones one sees in concierges' lodges, stuffed monkeys under glass domes, and the most hideous furniture."[33]

Yet here, in these bizarrely decorated rooms, Marie Feodorovna felt at ease. She used her precedence to live far more luxuriously than had any of her predecessors or even her own son and daughter-in-law did. "She traveled with a retinue of two hundred people," writes Coryne Hall. "Servants, bodyguards, maids, ladies-in-waiting all poured from the train as the fascinated crowd stood and stared. . . . There were no tiresome problems about money."[34] No one intervened, and the dowager empress's "right to do as she chose and spend as much as she wished was unchallenged," writes Hall. "She developed a streak of selfishness and a determination to get her own way."[35]

In the first decade of Nicholas II's reign, Marie Feodorovna not only dominated her son and isolated and humiliated his wife, but also presided over a number of increasingly corrupt institutions. Scandals over missing funds from her charities were concealed, and she intervened on behalf of friends who had embezzled millions of rubles that had been intended to help orphanages, hospitals, and famine victims.[36] Not surprisingly, as one official noted, the "lesser nobility, unable and unwilling to earn their living legitimately, gravitate to Marie Feodorovna."[37]

In time, Alexandra exerted her influence and alienated Nicholas from his powerful mother. The gulf widened and affected other members of his family, who were forced to choose up sides and sympathies. Increasingly, relations worsened, and attitudes became more firmly entrenched until the dowager empress felt isolated. With her sisters she purchased a villa near Copenhagen, where she spent more and more time. Her trips abroad, extended to England to stay with her sister Alexandra, increased in frequency, until her presence in Russia was a mere shadow of her former glory on the imperial throne.

Grand Duchess Xenia Alexandrovna, Nicholas II's eldest sister, inherited her mother's dark beauty. According to Prince Felix Yusupov, her future son-in-law, she possessed "a rare, delicate charm," and he asserted, "Everyone who came near her fell a slave to her grace, modesty, and kindness of heart."[38] The grand duchess, noted one contemporary, "is very shy with strangers, which makes her at times appear stiff. She feels completely at ease only in her own intimate set. She has inherited her mother's lovely eyes and beautiful skin, but her manner lacks the latter's assurance."[39]

A woman of limited intellect, Xenia married her father's cousin, Grand Duke Alexander Mikhailovich—known in the family as Sandro—in 1894, just a few months before Alexander III's death. Educated by tutors in the Caucasus, where his father, Grand Duke Michael Nikolaievich, served as viceroy, Alexander Mikhailovich entered the Imperial Navy as a midshipman in the Garde Équipage in 1885. Tall, with a dark mustache and beard, he traveled the world, losing his virginity to an American prostitute in a Hong Kong brothel.[40]

Grand Duchess Xenia, her husband, Grand Duke Alexander Mikhailovich, and their eldest child, Princess Irina, 1895

Marie Feodorovna had opposed the match, as her daughter Olga explained, because she "did not want to lose all control over Xenia. She meant her to stay on as a companion to herself."[41] Xenia's romance with Alexander, when it came, was fast and furious, intense to the point of embarrassment. Nicholas reported to his brother George, "They have become quite impossible, presumably from prolonged yearning and being so used to each other. They spend the whole day kissing, embracing and lying around on the furniture in the most improper manner."[42] A month later George, having spent some time with his sister and her fiancé, was forced to agree: "I was indeed amazed at the gymnastics, sucking, sniffing and similar activities which these two people indulged in all day long. They almost broke the ottoman and behaved in the most improper way; for instance they would lie down on top of each other, even in my presence, in what you might call an attempt to play Papa and Mama."[43]

Together, Xenia and Alexander had seven children: Princess Irina Alexandrovna, who later married Prince Felix Yusupov, the principal assassin of Rasputin; and six sons, the Princes Andrei, Feodor, Nikita, Dimitri, Rostislav, and Vassili Alexandrovich. These imperial cousins were among the few members of the Romanov family whom Empress Alexandra trusted as playmates for her children, and, in the early years of Nicholas II's reign, the two families were exceptionally close.

The grand duke, recalled one lady who knew him well, "was the most human, the most natural, and the kindest of all the members of the Imperial Family."[44] Not particularly intelligent, he was ambitious and believed himself gifted with talents and insight, traits that earned him a reputation for arrogance. He influenced Nicholas II to pursue colonization of the Korean Peninsula, a move that led to the disastrous war with Japan. In the 1905 Revolution, and amid the chaos of naval mutinies, he resigned his official posts, unable to maintain control of the volatile situation. Instead, he devoted his energies to aeronautics, establishing the first Russian School of Aviation in 1909 at the suburban imperial estate of Gatchina. Nor did he prove to be a faithful husband. He formed a liaison with a woman in Biarritz, an affair that became the talk of St. Petersburg.[45] True to her Romanov heritage, Xenia countered by taking her own lover—the husband of Alexander Mikhailovich's paramour—a curious situation that led to indiscreet rumors in the capital.[46]

Grand Duchess Olga Alexandrovna, Nicholas II's youngest sister, was an intelligent young woman who lived in her mother's shadow. Born in 1882, she was among the most popular members of the imperial family, known for her generosity and lack of pretension. In a family renowned for its regal demeanor and impressive appearance, Olga Alexandrovna was something of a disappointment. One official uncharitably described her as "rather plain; her snub-nosed, Mongoloid face is compensated only by extremely beautiful eyes, kind and clever, looking right inside you."[47]

Grand Duchess Marie Pavlovna, however, called her "light and supple," and "remarkably gifted in sports; she was gay, of a child-like and disarming simplicity, and had a generous heart. She loved to surround herself with simple people: peasants in particular fascinated her and she knew how to talk with such people and win their confidence."[48] Another observer called her "a true Russian and the most warm-hearted woman imaginable. She is clever and talented, and her watercolor drawings have often been exhibited or given for sale to charity bazaars. Her unconventionality frequently gets her into trouble with her family. She does not like to be reminded of what is due to her position."[49]

In 1901, Olga was engaged to a distant cousin, Prince Peter of Oldenburg. The couple had absolutely nothing in common: Olga was nineteen, her future husband thirty-three; she loved art, music, and literature, while he detested such pursuits. What Peter liked was gambling, and he lost enormous sums at the gaming tables. Apparently, Olga was the only person in St. Petersburg who did not know of his homosexuality. "His appearance falls well short of satisfactory," wrote one member of the Russian government. "Despite his age, he has lost almost all his hair and generally gives the impression of being feeble, in poor health, and altogether unlikely to engender a large family. Obviously considerations that have little to do with ensuring a successful married life were given first priority and this will surely in time give cause for regret."[50]

Olga was convinced that her mother had arranged the match; she knew nothing of it until Peter proposed. Having lost Xenia to the ambitious Grand Duke Alexander, the dowager empress seemed determined to keep her youngest daughter close at hand. "I was just tricked into it," Olga later complained. Peter proposed during the excitement of a party, and Olga was so taken aback that she could only mumble "Thank you" before the other guests burst in with their congratulations. She spent the rest of the night crying on her brother Michael's shoulder.[51]

The dowager empress, with typical self-denial, concealed her machinations, expressing surprise at the engagement. "I am sure you won't believe what has happened," she wrote to Nicholas. "Olga is engaged to Petya and *both* are very happy. I had to consent, but it was all done so quickly and unexpectedly that I still cannot believe it."[52] Nicholas responded with incredulity: "Though today is not the 1st of April, I cannot believe Olga is actually *engaged* to Petya. They were probably both drunk yesterday, and today don't remember all they said to each other. . . . It all still seems rather queer."[53]

Grand Duchesses Xenia and Olga
Alexandrovna, about 1910

The marriage was a disaster from the beginning. Olga spent her wedding night alone, crying herself to sleep, while her new husband gambled at his favorite club.[54] Thereafter, they lived on friendly but platonic terms. "During the fifteen years the marriage lasted," she later said bluntly, "Prince Oldenburg and I were never husband and wife."[55] While her new husband squandered his wife's dowry of a million rubles at gaming tables, Olga made herself intensely popular with the public by forgoing etiquette, focusing instead on her undoubted talents as a painter.[56]

For the first long year, Olga Alexandrovna suffered in silence. She had a nervous breakdown and lost all of her hair.[57] The grandson of her former English nanny, Elizabeth Franklin, recalled how Olga Alexandra often sought "refuge" with her former nurse, often arriving "pale and distressed, almost as if she had been crying."[58] Then, in 1903, she fell in love with Nicholas Kulikovsky, a handsome officer in the Cuirassier Guards. With her forthright manner, she went straight to her husband, asking for a divorce. Prince Peter refused, but he appointed Kulikovsky as his adjutant, ensuring him a regular place in the Oldenburg household. This ménage à trois continued for many years; finally, however, Olga abandoned her husband, and the marriage was dissolved during the First World War. Just three months before the Revolution, Olga finally wed Kulikovsky, a morganatic union attended only by her mother. Although the dowager empress and her eldest son attempted to dissuade Olga from the scandalous move, neither protested too vehemently, recognizing the years of unhappiness she had suffered.

Nicholas II also had two brothers. The elder, Grand Duke George Alexandrovich, was born in 1871. Shy and intelligent, George was undoubtedly the best educated of the children. At eighteen, he joined the army, eventually becoming colonel in chief of the Life Guards Ataman and the 93rd Irkutsk Regiments. Military training, however, was difficult. George had always been delicate, and in 1891, after months of coughing up blood and fainting, he was diagnosed with tuberculosis. The onset of the illness was rapid, and George was eventually sent to live in the Caucasus, at Abbas Touman, where it was hoped the warm mountain air would improve his condition. At first, his health did improve, and he was able to exercise and even entertain visiting relatives. But behind his doctors' backs, he continued to smoke a half-pack of cigarettes a day, which left him exhausted and coughing blood.[59]

When he rallied, George occasionally journeyed abroad, renting the Villa des Terrasses at Cap d'Ail on the Côte d'Azur. "Resigning himself to the inevitable," recalled a member of the French police, "he strove to enjoy the last few pleasures that life still held for him: the sunlight, the flowers, and the sea; he sought to beguile the anxiety of his suite and of his doctors by assuming a mask of playful good humor and appearance of youthful hope and zest."[60] Inevitably, though, these holidays only exacerbated the grand duke's illness. On "the first news of a slight relapse on the part of the illustrious patient," recalled his French minder, the dowager empress would rush to his side. "More than once, I detected the anguish of the mother stealthily trying to read the secret of her son's hectic eyes, peering at his pale face, watching for his hoarse, hacking cough, as he walked beside her."[61]

As the grand duke's health declined, he returned to the Caucasus, slipping into a mysterious existence. According to rumor, he contracted a morganatic marriage with a Caucasian woman who bore him a child before the union was dissolved. In 1894, he was said to have married a second time, to a Mlle. Orkovskaya, who bore him two sons and a daughter, allegedly given the surname of Romanovsky. Evidence to support either of the unions disappeared after the Revolution.[62]

After he became emperor, Nicholas II rarely saw George. Travel was difficult for the young man, and Nicholas's duties prevented him from visiting the Caucasus. In his last letter to his brother, George wrote, "Life here is pleasant, and I cannot complain of my fate; this autumn I will have been here eight years, and despite myself I have grown used to the life and the place. . . . I am no longer fit for any kind of service. I am no longer able to walk at all, for instance, because of shortness of breath."[63]

One July day in 1899, George left his villa at Abbas Touman and failed to return. Officials discovered his body on the side of the road, the victim of a sudden and catastrophic pulmonary hemorrhage. His funeral was an ordeal for the entire family, and Nicholas II openly wept throughout the service. Grand Duchess Xenia wrote in her diary: "Mama did not sit down once, but stood there quite composed, without crying, but with an expression of profound suffering on her face. When they started to lower the coffin into the tomb, Mama, who had been holding me tightly by the hand, suddenly staggered, collapsed onto me (with eyes wide open, yet seeing nothing) and said loudly, 'Home, let's go home, I can't stand any more!' and then she tore herself away from me! Nicky took hold of her from one side but she kept pushing forward, trying at all costs to get past the tomb to go out, but it wasn't possible just then, as the tomb was open and there was no way past. Sandro was standing there and supported Mama." As soon as the priest pronounced the final blessing, the dowager empress quickly grabbed her son's hat from the top of his coffin and fled the cathedral; Xenia found her collapsed in her carriage, the hat clutched to her breast as she wept uncontrollably.[64]

Grand Duke Michael Alexandrovich, dressed for the 1903 Medieval Ball

Michael Alexandrovich, Nicholas II's youngest brother, was born in 1878. Tall and slim, he was, recalled his stepdaughter, "very sensitive" about his premature hair loss. "He had tried every method and cure, from quack remedies to prolonged and expensive treatments, and always said he would give a fortune to anybody who made his hair grow again."[65] He had grown up utterly unconcerned with politics and was known for his naiveté; his father once remarked that Michael "believed without hesitancy anything and everything anyone told him."[66] His "inborn kind-heartedness, simplicity, and unfailing courtesy," remembered Colonel Boris Nikitine, "charmed all those who came in contact with him."[67] And Dimitri Abrikossow, a Russian diplomat who knew him well, recalled "how little he knew about real life." Abrikossow remembered, "I must say I have never met another man so uncorrupted and noble in nature; it was enough to look into his clear blue eyes to be ashamed of any bad thought or insincere feeling. In many ways he was a grown up child who had been taught only what was good and moral. He did not want to admit that there was wickedness and falsehood in this world and trusted everybody."[68]

In 1898, the grand duke entered the Imperial Army, serving first with the Preobrazhensky and the Horse Guards Artillery Regiments before becoming colonel in chief of Her Majesty's Cuirassier Guard Regiment and commander of the Chevalier Guards.[69] Nicholas II appointed his brother to the Imperial State Council, and Michael, between the death of Grand Duke George Alexandrovich in 1899 and the birth of Tsesarevich Alexei in 1904, became heir presumptive to the Russian throne, a role that required a certain amount of political knowledge, which Michael duly attempted to learn. His grasp of affairs was sufficient to impress one British diplomat, who described him as a "tall, handsome figure of a man with charming manners and an easy-going disposition; he struck me as a prince who might have made an excellent constitutional monarch."[70]

Michael had two obsessions: automobiles and beautiful women. He met his cousin Princess Beatrice of Saxe-Coburg-Gotha in 1902, when she was seventeen, and he twenty-four. At first, his passionate letters convinced Beatrice of his sincere intentions. Orthodox custom, however, forbade marriage between first cousins, and when Michael raised the issue, his mother and his brother both warned that he could never contract such a union. After a year, Michael callously informed Beatrice that he had never had any interest in an alliance with her. Not surprisingly, her family condemned Michael's dishonorable behavior.

Michael's next romance came in 1905, when he fell in love with Alexandrina Kossikovsky, a *kamer-freilina* to his sister Olga. Although Alexandrina was a commoner—and thus, by Romanov family laws, ineligible as a bride for a Romanov grand duke—Michael recklessly pursued the liaison. Nicholas II was horrified. "Three days ago," he wrote his mother, "Misha wrote asking my permission to marry. . . . It is infinitely easier to give one's consent than to refuse it—but in this case I will never do it! God forbid that this sad affair should cause misunderstanding in our family."[71] The dowager empress fully agreed, writing, "We must do everything to save him from himself."[72] The affair came to an abrupt end in 1907, when Michael met the beautiful Nathalia Sheremetievskaya, the daughter of a prominent Moscow lawyer.

Born in 1888, Nathalia Sheremetievskaya was the wife of Captain Vladimir Wulfert, an officer in Grand Duke Michael's Cuirassiers Regiment stationed at Gatchina. Even worse, she had already divorced one husband, Serge Mamontov, with whom she had a daughter. Nathalia was a strikingly handsome woman, yet, as her friends were quick to point out, she was "ambitious" and lived for "flattery."[73] Stronger than the young grand duke, she was determined not to let opportunity pass and wove a web of intrigue that captivated the innocent Michael. As a loyal soldier and a monarchist, Wulfert knew his duty, maintaining a discreet silence over his wife's burgeoning affair.

Soon, Wulfert agreed to a divorce. In 1910, while waiting for the decree, Nathalia gave birth to the grand duke's bastard son, whom the couple named George after Michael's late brother. Wulfert received 200,000 gold rubles ($2,000,000 in 2005 figures) from the Imperial Treasury in exchange for a formal renunciation of Nathalia's son, allowing Michael to claim him as his own. For the next two years, Michael and Nathalia lived quietly; then, in 1912, while on holiday in Bavaria, they slipped across the Alps to Austria and were secretly married in Vienna.[74]

The emperor was stunned at this development, and his mother was beside herself with rage: "I have just got a letter from Misha in which he announces his marriage! It is unbelievable—I can hardly understand what I am writing—it is so appalling in every way that it nearly kills me! I beg only this one thing of you: that it be kept absolutely secret to avoid another scandal! There have been secret marriages in the past which one pretended to know nothing about. I think this is the only way out—otherwise I won't be able to show my face anywhere for the shame and disgrace of it all!"[75]

Michael's marriage, without his brother's consent and to a commoner, was illegal. Nicholas stripped him of his official position as regent for Tsesarevich Alexei and deprived him of his military offices. For several years, the couple lived in

The Vladimirs, 1897. From left to right: Boris, Kirill, Grand Duchess Vladimir,
Grand Duke Vladimir, Andrei, and Elena

exile; only at the beginning of World War I did the emperor relent and allow the
scandalous lovers to return to Russia. Nicholas granted his sister-in-law the courtesy title of Countess Brassova after her husband's country estate; her son was
styled "Serene Highness," and Michael took command of his army regiments.
But neither Nicholas nor his consort would receive the twice-divorced commoner; to his mother, Nicholas described Nathalia as "a cunning, wicked
beast."[76]

Embittered by this reaction, Nathalia soon gained a reputation as a domineering, spiteful schemer. "It was you Romanovs who brought Russia to such a state!"
she once exclaimed during a luncheon with her husband's cousins.[77] She
befriended the most liberal politicians who conspired against Nicholas and
Alexandra, at the same time clinging desperately to the comforts of her husband's

position.[78] Maurice Paleologue recorded that she was working with her gullible husband "to secure him his revenge in another field. Ambitious, clever and utterly unscrupulous, she has been parading very strong liberal opinions for some time. . . . In Court quarters she has already been accused of betraying Tsarism— a fact that pleases her immensely, as it makes her views notorious, and lays the foundations of her popularity. She becomes more independent every day, and says the most audacious things—things which in the mouth of any other would mean twenty years of Siberia!"[79] In despair, the dowager empress once deemed her "a brazen adventuress intent on seeing herself crowned as Empress, and poor Misha too naïve to see it."[80]

But the proud countess's plans to force Nicholas II's abdication and her husband's succession to the throne fell victim to the Revolution. Within four years of their return to Russia, Michael and Nathalia were again separated when the Bolsheviks exiled him to Siberia. Following his execution in 1918, Nathalia escaped to Europe, where she later died in near poverty, all but forgotten by the surviving Romanovs.

3

A RIVAL COURT

JUST DOWN THE EMBANKMENT from the Winter Palace, facing the dark blue waters of the Neva, stood the Florentine-style Vladimir Palace, the home of Nicholas II's most powerful uncle. Here, at the side of his sophisticated wife, Marie Pavlovna, Grand Duke Vladimir presided over a court rivaling that of the emperor in its opulence. Born in 1847, Grand Duke Vladimir Alexandrovich was the third son of Emperor Alexander II. When, on their father's death in 1881, Alexander III became emperor, Vladimir could scarcely contain his resentment. The idea that an accident of birth had kept him from this great destiny preyed on Vladimir: to him, Alexander was a simple, unintelligent brute. Alexander III kept his brother's ambitions in check, but Nicholas II faced an uncle he feared and regarded as his intellectual superior.

Tall and handsome, with "piercing eyes under beetling brows" and a closely trimmed beard, Vladimir, recalled Meriel Buchanan, "made every other man look insignificant."[1] During an 1871 visit to Queen Victoria, he was described as "rather stout for so young a man; he speaks English very fairly and is affable and pleasant in conversation."[2] Consuelo Vanderbilt found him "autocratic and overbearing"; she thought he needed "only to have a knout in his hand to complete the perfect picture of the haughty Russian aristocrat."[3]

As president of the Imperial Academy of Fine Arts, Vladimir supported the latest painter, dancer, or musician. His sponsorship allowed Serge Diaghilev to create his famous Ballet Russes, though the grand duke often interfered, once halting a performance to jump up on stage and lecture the dancers before a startled audience.[4] With his air of haughtiness, Vladimir regarded most of his relatives with disdain. His cousin Grand Duke Alexander recalled his "roughness" and "shouting voice," adding, "He treated the younger Grand Dukes with a maximum of contempt. None of us could have engaged him in conversation unless prepared to discuss subjects of art or the finesses of French cooking."[5]

Jealous and angry over his junior position at court, Vladimir's dissatisfaction took the form of arrogance and self-indulgence. One critic declared that he "was undoubtedly clever, with that cleverness which consists in appropriating other people's ideas, or repeating other people's words as if they were one's own; but at the same time he was in reality very ignorant, ambitious and intriguing. His memory was good, his wit and conversation brilliant, but it was all superficial. . . . Towards women . . . he was nothing but vicious."[6]

In 1874, Vladimir married Marie, the twenty-year-old daughter of Grand Duke Friedrich Franz II of Mecklenburg-Schwerin, a minor German court on the Baltic coast, a match arranged by Alexander II in an effort to curb his wayward son. When told of his impending engagement, Vladimir commented candidly, "Poor girl! What sort of husband shall I make? I am drunk every night and cure the headache of the next morning by getting drunk again!"[7] Known as Miechen within the imperial family, Grand Duchess Marie Pavlovna had been a shy, unsophisticated young woman, but her marriage wrought a stunning transformation. In place of the quiet, provincial girl arose a charming, worldly woman who soon became the toast of St. Petersburg.

In the first years of their marriage, noted one aristocrat, the lives of the Vladimirs were "the eternal source of the gayest stories of the *chronique scandaleuse.*"[8] St. Petersburg gossips whispered of orgies over which the grand duchess was rumored to preside, or they speculated on which guards officer found favor in her bed.[9] One night, the couple, joined by Vladimir's brother Grand Duke Alexei Alexandrovich, threw a midnight supper for a troupe of French actors led by Lucien Guitry at a St. Petersburg restaurant run by the famous Monsieur Cubat. The dinner quickly dissolved into a drunken brawl, as the sounds of china being smashed and furniture being broken filtered from their private room. The manager rang General Gresser, the prefect of the St. Petersburg Police, who rushed to the restaurant to deal with the potential scandal. In the interval, Vladimir had seized Guitry's mistress and, as she struggled against his embrace, repeatedly kissed her. Seeing this, Guitry did the same to Marie Pavlovna, and Vladimir attempted to strangle him as screams filled the establishment. Grand Duke Alexei freed Guitry from his brother, only to throw the actor out of the restaurant and directly at the feet of the newly arrived, startled prefect. When the officer interrupted the drunken party inside, Alexei flung a dish of caviar into his face and blocked the door to the private room. Soon, more police officers arrived, and—amid the uproar of screamed obscenities—forcibly removed the imperial guests. On learning of the incident, Alexander III ordered the Vladimirs into a six-month French exile.[10]

Such behavior did nothing to endear the Vladimirs to Alexander III or his consort. "I know that my mother did not care for the Vladimirs any more than the rest of us did," commented Grand Duchess Olga Alexandrovna.[11] The dowager empress eventually developed such antipathy toward Marie Pavlovna that in private, she often referred to her caustically as "Empress Vladimir."[12]

It was not only Marie Pavlovna's hedonistic manner that fueled Marie Feodorovna's intense dislike: she despised her simply because the grand duchess was German. In public, Marie Feodorovna and Marie Pavlovna made polite conversation, but away from the emperor and the empress, the grand duchess openly criticized her husband's family to anyone who would listen. Occasionally, her complaints were genuine. In 1883, the grand duchess was stricken with the measles just before Alexander III's coronation. Still recovering throughout the ceremonies and plagued with a high temperature, Marie Pavlovna confessed that she was dreading the coronation ceremony itself, when she would have to stand, in a heavy Russian court gown of silver tissue complete with tiara and veil, for six hours in the cramped, hot Assumption Cathedral. She asked Marie Feodorovna if she might have a chair at hand in case her temperature rose or she felt faint. But the empress angrily dismissed her request, saying that she "had to stand all the time, too."[13]

With her dark eyes and abundant brown hair, stylish clothes and exquisite jewels, Marie Pavlovna was a formidable figure. "There is a smartness about her that no one else can attain," wrote Queen Marie of Romania.[14] Like her husband, the grand duchess polarized those she met. Grand Duchess Marie Georgievna wrote that she "had the greatest charm any woman ever possessed. She was always most sweet and kind to me."[15] The British ambassador called her "a *grande dame* in the best sense of that term, but without any pretensions as regards the strict observance of court etiquette."[16] The American heiress Elizabeth Drexel remembered her as "naturally charming and gay, with a flair for saying precisely the right thing at the right time."[17] And Foreign Minister Serge Sazonov added, "*She's* the woman we ought to have had as Empress!"[18]

Grand Duchess Vladimir came to considerable power and influence during the reign of her brother-in-law Alexander III. Following the assassination of Alexander II, the new emperor and his family retired to the safe confines of the suburban palace at Gatchina, leaving Marie Pavlovna to fill the void. The entertainments at her husband's palace on the Neva embankment and at their country palace at Ropsha, near the military camp at Krasnoye Selo, made the Vladimirs famous. The powerful flocked to the weekly drawing rooms given by the grand duchess, and she, in turn, established herself as the ultimate arbiter of taste and fashion in the empire. Her entertainments and costume balls were social triumphs, though inevitably Alexander III despised this profligate style of life. During a fishing exhibition attended by the imperial family, Alexander III noticed some barely clothed peasant women processing a net of half-rotted fish. He turned to his sister-in-law and, in a loud voice, suggested that the scene before them was a fitting model for Marie Pavlovna's next costume ball. "In everything," noted one official, "the attitude between them grows more aggravated with each day."[19]

Marie Pavlovna retaliated in her own manner. In candid letters to Princess Bismarck in Berlin, she mentioned the possibility of influencing a Russo-German alliance. She foolishly left these letters on her desk, where her husband's adjutant Count Paul Shuvalov discovered them. Knowing his duty as a loyal subject, Shuvalov carried them straight to Alexander III. Furious, the emperor summoned his sister-in-law to an uncomfortable audience, warning that she was not to continue her political maneuvers. Alexander advised Vladimir that he should take his wife abroad for a holiday. Marie Pavlovna was beside herself with rage and never spoke to Count Shuvalov again. Even after the adjutant's death, she refused to receive his widow, Countess Betsy Shuvalov.[20]

In 1888, Grand Duke Vladimir and his wife were on holiday in France when they learned of a railway accident near Borki involving Alexander III and his family. On hearing the news, the grand duke neither returned to Russia nor inquired as to his brother's safety. The emperor never forgave his brother, commenting, "Imagine Vladimir's disappointment when he learns we are all alive!"[21] Indeed, Marie Pavlovna was said to have declared, "We shall never have such a chance again."[22]

Relations between the Vladimirs and the throne were no better under Nicholas II. "He's nothing but an immature schoolboy!" the grand duke once exclaimed of his nephew.[23] In the summer of 1895, when the court was in mourning for Alexander III, the grand duke and his wife gave an elaborate party, complete with gypsy bands, at Ropsha. When the dowager empress learned of this, she complained to Nicholas II, "The Vladimirs seem to have forgotten everything already. . . . It is so unseemly and I cannot understand that Uncle V. is unable to restrain her." Without a sense of irony at her own style of life, she added, "With her, pleasure goes before everything."[24]

Vladimir flaunted his power over Nicholas II, who complained that it was "unfair to take advantage of my youth, and position as your nephew. Please remember that I am now head of the family, and have no right to ignore any of their actions that I find wrong or inappropriate."[25] The grand duke ignored him, and his palace witnessed an amazing cross-section of society: artists like Ilya Repin, the famed singer Boris Chaliapin, the pianist Serge Rachmaninov, ministers, and foreign diplomats, all paraded through its halls. Through the clouds of cigarette smoke, guests found the lavish rooms crowded with roulette wheels on baize-covered tables or filled with excited shouts as immense fortunes were wagered at baccarat.[26] Nicholas was too uncertain to stand up to his persuasive uncle. "To avoid quarrels and strain in the family," he once wrote, "I constantly concede, and end up looking like an idiot, without will or character!"[27]

Not surprisingly, few outside their privileged milieu were generous in describing the grand duchess and her circle of friends. "Her own set is not only fast but vulgar," wrote one contemporary, "and unfortunately, the admittance is easy. It is sufficient to have money, to be rich enough to entertain her, to talk slang, to go every year to Paris, and to give her money for all the bazaars she patronizes."[28] Grand Duke Nicholas Mikhailovich condemned her frequent guests as "a pack of international parvenus."[29]

But, as Meriel Buchanan wrote, much of this criticism was simply inspired by the grand duchess's success in her role:

> It was inevitable that anybody with her vivid personality should have enemies in a society like that of St. Petersburg, and it was perhaps natural that aspersions should have been cast upon both her moral and her public character by censorious busybodies, for she was fearless and of too strong a character ever to be ignored or thrust into the

background. Her vigorous mentality could not but deplore the attitude of the young Empress, but though she took a keen interest in both foreign and international politics, she was never guilty of an anti-Russian intrigue, and never anything but dignified, regal, and gracious in public.[30]

The Vladimirs spent enormous sums of money entertaining and on their carefully contrived surroundings. Their palace reflected both the age of historicism in which it had been built and the aspirations and tastes of its owners. Of all the St. Petersburg palaces, it most closely resembled the fashionable mansions of the European nouveau riche and those of the American Gilded Age that rose in New York and Newport. With its mixture of cosmopolitan styles and lavish ornament, it provided an impressive evocation of the splendor of the Russian imperial court, but at the same time it stood as a bold declaration of intent, a visible symbol of the grand duke's determination to dominate St. Petersburg society.[31]

The Vladimirs surrounded themselves with all the sumptuous trappings the grand duke's fortune could provide. Not satisfied with the usual liveries worn by members of the grand ducal courts, Marie Pavlovna ordered more extravagant uniforms for her own household. Footmen in the Vladimir Palace wore scarlet coats, swords, and square caps, and carried maces while on duty. This evocation of a princely Renaissance court, with the allusions to patronage and autocratic power, was deliberate. In much the same way, the Vladimirs ordered a gondola tied at the pier in front of their palace and drove along the city streets in a gilded carriage decorated with Vladimir's coat of arms and accompanied by footmen attired in smart uniforms of scarlet and green.[32]

With an unrivaled passion for jewelry, Marie Pavlovna spent thousands of rubles acquiring a collection of diamonds, pearls, emeralds, and sapphires third only to those owned by the two empresses. When Jacques Cartier opened a shop in St. Petersburg, the grand duchess became his most valued client, ordering necklaces and tiaras of unparalleled magnificence. She was an imposing presence as she received visitors, "the thick fur of a white bearskin at her feet," recalled one guest, "with the ferocious mouth open and the terrible teeth hanging out, her luxuriant, regal figure clothed in the gorgeous blue robes of the native Russian costume, the gown and the head dress ablaze with jewels and the long velvet train carpeting the floor behind her. She stood [as] the personification of Russian feminine beauty, enchanting in its touch of barbaric wildness and its tinge of Oriental voluptuousness."[33]

Inevitably, such sybaritic behavior became the talk of the imperial capital. Vladimir was one of the wealthiest grand dukes. Each year, in addition to the 250,000 gold rubles ($2,500,000 in 2005 currency) he received from the state, the grand duke could count on a further 35,714 gold rubles ($357,140 in 2005 currency).[34] Despite this, it was widely believed that he extorted funds to enrich his private coffers. There were questions surrounding missing donations to build the Church on the Spilt Blood, erected on the site where Vladimir's father, Alexander II, had been assassinated, and gossip during the Russo-Japanese War ascribed armament and supply shortages to the grand duke's greed.[35]

In the first decade of Nicholas II's reign, the grand duchess attempted to befriend the young empress, "eager to guide all her movements," recalled one aristocrat, "and took offense when this failed; afterwards she used her considerable influence in Society to work against her new rival."[36] Although Empress Alexandra and the Dowager Empress Marie Feodorovna had never got on well together, both were united in their disapproval of Marie Pavlovna. Grand Duchess Vladimir knew better than to criticize the popular dowager empress, but she made no secret of her dislike of Alexandra. Once, Alexander Mossolov attended a particularly brilliant reception at the Vladimir Palace and congratulated the grand duchess on an enjoyable evening. "One ought to know one's job," Marie Pavlovna declared haughtily, her tone pregnant with condemnation. "You may pass that on to the Great Court."[37]

The Vladimir children grew up accustomed to privilege and power. Of the four, only Grand Duchess Elena, born in 1882, caused few difficulties. "She had the loveliest eyes imaginable," wrote Prince Felix Yusupov, "and everyone fell under their charm."[38] And Baroness Sophie Buxhoeveden recalled her as "the idol of all the young folk and a great deal of entertainment was given in her honor."[39] As an only daughter, the dark-haired grand duchess was indulged and doted on by her father, who filled her with an appreciation of art and music; yet she was above all else her mother's daughter, domineering and regal. She once declared her priorities were "God first, then the Russian Grand Dukes, then the rest."[40]

Grand Duchess Vladimir initially arranged an engagement with Prince Max of Baden. When he abruptly changed his mind, Elena was publicly humiliated, and her mother, according to Grand Duke Konstantin Konstantinovich, was "desperate to find another husband" for her daughter.[41] After a proposed match with the future King Albert of Belgium fell through, Elena met the dashing Prince Nicholas of Greece. Grand Duchess Vladimir, however, summoned the prince and, as Grand Duke Konstantin Konstantinovich recalled, "told him not to count on Elena, because, as the third son of a King, he was not a suitable match for her." After two years, the ambitious Marie Pavlovna was forced "to change her mind, as her search for other suitors for her daughter has been in vain."[42] Elena married Nicholas at Tsarskoye Selo in 1902; one of their daughters, Marina, later married the duke of Kent, the son of King George V of Great Britain.

The three sons of Grand Duke Vladimir caused considerable scandal during Nicholas II's reign. In view of their parents' dilettantish styles of life, it is not surprising that Grand Dukes Kirill, Boris, and Andrei Vladimirovich inherited a taste for hedonistic pleasures. Their rank and fortunes allowed them to indulge these passions, and none of the three was slow to take advantage.

Boris Vladimirovich was a charming, reckless young man. Born in 1877, he graduated from the Nikolaievsky Cavalry School and entered the imperial guards in 1896, joining the Hussar Life Guards Regiment. Promoted to the rank of major-general *à la suite*, he eventually commanded the Life Guards' Ataman Cossack Regiment, but military duties were an obligation forced on him by virtue of his birth. "Gay or sulky by turns," remembered his cousin Queen Marie of Romania, "he had an attractive, rather husky voice, kind eyes, and a humorous smile which crinkled his forehead into unexpected lines. Not exactly handsome, he had nevertheless great charm, and a slight lisp added a certain quaintness to his speech."[43] One relative called Boris "a very agreeable man, but inclined to drink too much," while another termed him "a badly brought-up, spoilt drunkard."[44]

During the Russo-Japanese War, Boris was attached to the viceroy of the Far East and proved a capable soldier. He was more concerned, however, with pleasure. In one year, Boris spent 25,000 rubles dining in restaurants ($250,000 in 2005 figures) and another 8,000 ($80,000 in 2005 figures) on his motorcars; in comparison, he gave 46 rubles ($460 in 2005 figures) to the Russian Orthodox Church.[45] Visiting America in 1902, he made headlines by drinking champagne from the satin slipper of a dancer and handing out $20 bills as tips to showgirls.[46] The grand duke's debts overwhelmed his annual income from the Imperial Appanages Department; inevitably, when he found himself unable to pay his creditors, his mother dispatched bribes to conceal his indiscretions.[47]

In 1895, he built a large, English-style house, complete with half-timbering and interiors commissioned from the London firm of Maples, at the edge of a lake in the suburban enclave of Tsarskoye Selo, filling it not only with expensive furniture, tapestries, and paintings, but also with an immense collection of wines.[48] Dimitri Abrikossow recalled a luncheon here in the midst of the First World War: "Looking with sadness on his collection of wines, Boris bemoaned the possibility of its loss to the Germans, as if there was no greater tragedy that could befall Russia. None of these people seemed to realize the crisis through which Russia was passing; they could not deprive themselves of the pleasures to which they had been accustomed all their lives."[49] In this artificial world, Boris added to the surreal atmosphere by keeping a pet pig, Auguste, on which he doted. Auguste had free run of Boris's villa, as Prince Christopher of Greece recalled, and "used to trot round after his master like a dog, beg for tidbits from the table."[50]

The grand duke's overwhelming passion, though, was for women. He made no distinction between the unattached, the affianced, and the married and used his military connections to entertain—and then bed—the wives of his fellow regimental officers, aware that the law, as well as court etiquette, protected his indiscretions. Nevertheless, a fair number of men protested, and several challenged Boris to duels. His tastes were never consistent, and he left a trail of scorned women scattered across St. Petersburg. In 1913, he turned his attention to Grand Duchess Olga Nikolaievna, the eldest daughter of Nicholas and Alexandra. Through his mother, he suddenly declared that he wished to marry her, news that reduced the empress to "mortified tears."[51] Alexandra quickly put a stop to further inquiries.

His brother Andrei Vladimirovich was somewhat more discreet. Born in 1879, he was the only one of the children to receive a truly thorough education, attending classes at the Mikhailovsky Artillery School before joining the Horse Guards Artillery Regiment. During his military career, he also attended law classes at the Alexandrovsky Military Juridical Academy, from which he graduated in 1905. While commanding several regiments of the Horse Guards Artillery, the grand duke also served as a member of the Imperial Senate.[52]

A quiet, shy man, the grand duke was tall and thin, with a receding hairline and a small mustache. But he caused an enormous scandal, involving not only himself, but also Nicholas II's former mistress Mathilde Kschessinska and his own cousin Grand Duke Serge Mikhailovich. Mathilde Kschessinska was a dark, petite beauty seven years his senior; in her prime, she had been one of St. Petersburg's most famous ballerinas, winning fame through her sensual charm. Her well-known affair with Nicholas, when he was still tsesarevich, ended abruptly on his engagement in 1894, although the ambitious Mathilde immediately took up with his second cousin, Grand Duke Serge Mikhailovich. Within a few years, however, Mathilde grew bored with Serge and began an affair with his cousin Andrei Vladimirovich. Serge Mikhailovich was so enamored of the ballerina that he raised no objection, and Mathilde openly boasted of her sexual game.[53] When Prince Konstantin Radziwill told her, "You should be proud to have two Grand Dukes at your feet," she replied imperiously, "What's surprising about that? I have two feet."[54]

Matters were further complicated when Mathilde gave birth to a son, Vladimir, in 1902. No one knew with any certainty whether the father was Grand Duke Serge Mikhailovich or Andrei Vladimirovich. The latter recognized the boy as his own, though Vladimir himself later openly expressed doubts.[55] Mathilde took advantage of this situation to enrich herself, building an extravagant art nouveau–style mansion in the imperial capital and appearing in increasingly expensive jewels as gossips clucked their tongues in astonishment. Vladimir Teliakovsky, the director of the imperial theaters, became Kschessinska's most enthusiastic critic. He termed her "morally impudent, cynical and brazen," a woman "living simultaneously with two Grand Dukes, and not only not concealing the fact, but on the contrary, weaving this 'art' as well into her stinking, cynical wreath of human offal and vice."[56]

It was Grand Duke Kirill, however, who caused the greatest of all the scandals among the Vladimirovich sons. Born in 1876, the tall, handsome Kirill was as ambitious as his father and as charming as his mother. He passed the Naval Academic Examination in 1896 and entered the Garde Équipage, serving aboard the cruiser *Nakhimov* as lieutenant-commander. When the Russo-Japanese War erupted in 1904, he was the only member of the imperial family to volunteer for active duty. A year later, he was aboard *Petropavlovsk* when it struck a mine in the Strait of Tsushima. The blast threw Kirill into the water, where he managed to grab hold of some floating debris. Eventually, a nearby member of the convoy rescued the grand duke; 631 of those aboard had perished, and Kirill was one of only 53 survivors. On his return to St. Petersburg, he suffered a nervous breakdown and was temporarily released from his military duties.[57]

Sympathy for Kirill's injuries, however, did not extend to his marriage to Princess Victoria Melita. Known in the family as Ducky, she was one of the daughters of Queen Victoria's son Alfred, duke of Edinburgh and his wife, Marie, daughter of Alexander II. In 1894, Victoria Melita had married Grand Duke Ernst Ludwig IV of Hesse, the brother of Empress Alexandra; it was at their wedding that Nicholas had proposed. Queen Victoria had arranged the marriage between Ernst Ludwig and Victoria Melita, and it proved spectacularly unhappy from the very beginning. The grand duke found his new wife arrogant, domineering, and spiteful, while she took absolutely no interest in his consuming passion for the arts. After she discovered him in bed with a young male servant, the marriage ended in an acrimonious divorce.[58]

Although Kirill Vladimirovich and Victoria Melita were first cousins, they became lovers. Kirill's father complained that his son "had been seduced by a married woman."[59] Kirill wandered round, as Grand Duchess Xenia Alexandrovna recalled, with "a languid expression of persecuted innocence." She herself believed that "the only honorable thing for him to do is to marry her and take the corresponding punishment."[60] Kirill consulted Father Ioann Yanishev, the personal confessor to the imperial family, who told him "that, from the point of view of Canon Law," there was no impediment to the marriage, a curious stance in view of the Church's prohibition on marriage between first cousins.[61] In the end, this is just what Kirill did: in October 1905, he wed Victo-

Victoria Melita, Grand Duchess Kirill ("Ducky"), about 1910

ria Melita at a villa outside Munich. The marriage remained a virtual secret; Kirill left his new wife in Coburg, while he himself returned to Russia to inform the emperor of his fait accompli.

Nicholas II, however, learned of the union before Kirill made it to the palace. The emperor dispatched Baron Vladimir de Freedericksz, the minister of the imperial court, to the Vladimir Palace at Tsarskoye Selo, where he informed the Vladimirs that Kirill was to leave Russia within forty-eight hours, be stripped of all of his military ranks, lose his grand ducal income, and be deprived of his title of Grand Duke of Russia and the style of Imperial Highness.[62] The Vladimirs were outraged. Marie Pavlovna complained, "The blind vindictiveness and rage of the young Empress has, for sheer malice, exceeded everything the wildest imagination could conceive. She stormed and raged like a lunatic, dragging her weak husband along with her until he lent her his power and so made it possible to revenge herself on her ex-sister-in-law."[63]

The following morning, Vladimir burst into his nephew's study, first pleading with, and then threatening, the emperor, if he did not rescind his orders. When

Nicholas refused, Vladimir ripped the medals from his dress tunic, the epaulets from his shoulders, and the aiguillettes from his chest and threw them at his startled nephew, resigning his post as commander in chief of the Russian Army and his rank as personal adjutant-general to the emperor.[64]

Kirill later wrote, "We were dumbfounded by the severity of this decision, as the Emperor had at no time indicated or even vaguely hinted at such drastic steps, but had, quite on the contrary, whenever I had mentioned this matter to him, expressed his sincere hope that things could be straightened out."[65] Within three days of his decision, however, Nicholas relented. "I wonder whether it was wise to punish a man so publicly to such an extent, especially when his family was against it," he wrote to his mother.[66] Nicholas eventually granted official recognition to the marriage in a decree of the Imperial Senate on July 15, 1907, bestowed a grand ducal title on his former sister-in-law, who, having converted to the Russian Church six months earlier, took the name of Grand Duchess Victoria Feodorovna. The emperor also granted their children born before the Revolution, Marie and Kira, membership in the Imperial House, with succession rights. Duly restored to their positions, although not entirely to imperial favor, Kirill and his wife returned to St. Petersburg.

After Grand Duke Vladimir's death in February of 1909, his widow assumed her late husband's position as president of the Imperial Academy of Fine Arts, continuing his generous patronage. During the First World War, Marie Pavlovna became the most vehement of Empress Alexandra's numerous enemies. But the grand duchess's own position evaporated when her nephew abdicated from the throne in March 1917. Marie Pavlovna scarcely managed to escape Russia, dying in Contrexéville as a dispossessed exile three years later, her years of triumph lost in the haze of revolution.

4

THE ROMANOVS

AT THE BEGINNING OF THE TWENTIETH century, the Russian Imperial House encompassed some sixty individuals.[1] The Romanov family was related by blood and marriage to nearly every other ruling house in Europe, which often led to highly incestuous relationships. Grand Duchess Marie Georgievna later wrote, "Both my sister and I married our mother's first cousins. My father's second sister, Empress Marie Feodorovna, was the sister-in-law of Grand Duke Paul, my sister's husband, who was the youngest brother of Emperor Alexander III; therefore, my sister became her own aunt's sister-in-law! My husband's father was my grandfather's brother. I think I became my own aunt!"[2]

Their lives were governed by two distinct sets of regulations issued by Emperor Paul I in 1797. The first, the Pauline Laws, dictated the succession to the imperial throne. From the moments of their births, members of the Romanov Dynasty automatically entered an artificial hierarchy that decreed that all eligible males within the imperial family took precedence over females in line to the throne; women could succeed only when the last legitimate male dynast expired. In this world, the seniority of one's father's position within the Imperial House determined that of any sons and daughters, separating the various grand dukes into senior and junior branches. The second law, and the one that had the most direct impact on members of the dynasty, was Paul I's *Statute of the Imperial*

Family. In conjunction with the *Fundamental Laws of the Russian Empire*, the statute governed nearly every aspect of the Romanovs' lives, from whom they could marry to the annual amounts each received from the Imperial Appanage Department that administered the family fortune.

The Romanovs, commented Dimitri Abrikossow, "had ideas that were centuries old, that they did not know how the rest of Russia lived, and did not want to learn. Fundamentally they felt that Russia existed for the Romanovs, not the Romanovs for Russia."[3] Alexander III held his relatives in check: he once had Grand Duke Nicholas Mikhailovich arrested for appearing in public with his coat unbuttoned and a cigar clenched between his teeth.[4] Less than a decade later, at the Epiphany Ceremony in 1903, a shocked official noted that Grand Dukes Alexei Alexandrovich and Nicholas Nikolaievich had left the religious procession and stood along the Neva, smoking, "a very public violation of their elementary Grand Ducal obligations."[5]

One contemporary critic of the grand dukes observed, "Guided not by considerations of policy, but solely by family interests, their influence in affairs of state is characterized by increasing efforts to exploit the State for their own political welfare."[6] He was not alone in his judgment. "To know the Grand Dukes and Grand Duchesses," commented Infanta Eulalia of Spain, "is to realize that they neither understand the aspirations of the democracy nor sympathize with them, for, reflecting the glory of Autocracy, they are more firmly convinced than any other Royal persons in Europe that a gulf divides them from the rest of mankind."[7]

The emperor had four uncles, the Grand Dukes Vladimir, Alexei, Serge, and Paul. Queen Marie of Romania remembered them as imposing, "like tall trees," who smelled "deliciously of Russian leather, cigarettes and the best sort of scent."[8] But the public face hid a darker reality, as Grand Duke Alexander Mikhailovich later wrote,

> Nicholas II spent the first ten years of his reign sitting behind a massive desk in the Palace and listening with near-awe to the well-rehearsed bellowing of his towering uncles. He dreaded to be left alone with them. . . . They always wanted something. . . . They all had their favorite generals and admirals who were supposed to be promoted ahead of a long waiting list; their ballerinas desirous of organizing a Russian season in Paris; their wonderful preachers anxious to redeem the Emperor's soul; their miraculous physicians soliciting a Court appointment; their clairvoyant peasants with a divine message.[9]

Alexei Alexandrovich was called "the Beau Brummell of the Imperial Family" by his cousin, Grand Duke Alexander Mikhailovich.[10] Born in 1850, he had served in the Russo-Turkish War as head of the Naval Command on the Danube. Alexander III appointed his brother grand admiral of the Russian Fleet, a post he held until the devastating loss of the empire's forces at Tsushima during the Russo-Japanese War in 1905. One courtier described Alexei Alexandrovich as "a *bon vivant*, fond of cards, wine and women," while Serge Witte called him "a very fine and decent man, but he was more interested in his private pleasures than in the affairs of state."[11]

Alexei cared only about his ships and his string of mistresses, whom he lavishly kept in both St. Petersburg and Paris. He once presided over a dinner at which a young French actress was carried to the table on an enormous silver tray, naked and adorned only with rose petals.[12] He had a famous liaison with one of his mother's *freilinas*, Alexandra Zhukovskaya, a woman eight years his senior. In 1870, the pair fled to Italy, where they were believed to have married, an illegal union said to have been annulled.[13] The grand duke was quickly packed off on a three-month tour of America, the first Romanov to visit the United States.[14] Only on his return did he learn that Madame Zhukovskaya had borne him a son, Alexei Alexeievich. This son, raised by his mother but supported by the grand duke's considerable private fortune, was eventually recognized and given the title of Count Belevskii-Zhukovsky by Alexander III.[15]

The grand duke soon fell in love with Zenaide de Beauharnais, the wife of his distant cousin the duke of Leuchtenberg. One evening, the duke returned to his palace to find his bedroom door locked; from within came the unmistakable sounds of his wife in the throes of passion. When the duke demanded admittance, Alexei appeared from within, grabbed him, and threw him down the staircase. Humiliated, the duke spent the night on a sofa but the next morning went straight to Alexander III, demanding revenge. Alexander listened to his complaint, finally commenting that if Leuchtenberg could not control his own wife, he could not expect the emperor to do so. He forbade the duke to institute divorce proceedings, saying that he would not allow public scandal to tarnish his brother's reputation. Thereafter, the duke slept on the sofa in his library, while his wife continued to entertain her lover in her bedroom above.[16] St. Petersburg gossips relished the intrigue; once, noted a scandalized official, Alexei was observed riding in an open carriage, the duchess at his side, "as if a married couple."[17]

Tall and somewhat stout, the grand duke was genuinely popular, the only member of the imperial family to have a brand of cigarette, manufactured by the

St. Petersburg tobacconist A. Petrov, named after him. His nieces and nephews adored him; Prince Nicholas of Greece remembered him as "full of fun," with "an irresistible charm" that won him many admirers.[18] Grand Duke Kirill Vladimirovich recalled his "huge, naval voice" and his "strange garb of his own choosing and invention, which gave him the appearance of a real showman. It was a kind of red-striped flannel suit, a Mephistophelean affair, of which he alone among all men on earth was the proud possessor. He was pleased with it, and liked to be seen about in this fantastic get up."[19]

During the Russo-Japanese War, Alexei lavished money and attention on his current mistress, the ballerina Elizabeth Balleta, who was said to have black-mailed him with compromising letters.[20] When some 2 million rubles ($20,000,000 in 2005 figures) designated for the Red Cross went missing, gossip held that much of it had gone to the shop of Fabergé, to purchase Balleta's magnificent jewels.[21] In December of 1904, eleven months into the war, the grand duke appeared at the Michael Theater in St. Petersburg, Madame Balleta at his side. The audience caught sight of her magnificent diamond and ruby cross and, turning to the grand duke's box, interrupted the national anthem with screams: "The Red Cross! Down with the Red Cross! Give back the money!"[22] "Tongues were soon busy with this affair," noted one visitor to the capital, and Alexei resigned his post rather than expose himself to further disclosures.[23]

Alexei fled to Paris with Elizabeth Balleta in tow. Here, and in Biarritz, Cannes, and Monte Carlo, the couple lived in comfortable exile, popularly believed to be financed by money stolen from several charities.[24] Only occasionally did he return to Russia, preferring to remain with his mistress. Surprisingly, in light of his indiscreet life, Alexei remained Nicholas II's favorite uncle until his death in Paris in 1908.

Grand Duke Serge Alexandrovich, Nicholas II's uncle and also brother-in-law, epitomized the darkest characteristics of earlier Romanovs. Grand Duke Alexander Mikhailovich remembered him as "snobbish and unapproachable," with "boredom and contempt written on his young face."[25] His niece Queen Marie of Romania termed him "the most frightening of all the uncles. . . . His eyes were steely gray, and his pupils could narrow like those of a cat, till they became mere pinpoints, and then there was something almost menacing about him. . . . I must admit that even at his sweetest moments, there was nothing soft nor particularly encouraging about Uncle Serge; there was a tyrant within him, ready at any moment to burst forth; there was something intolerant, unbending about him; instinctively, one felt that his teeth were clenched."[26]

In 1884, he married Princess Elizabeth of Hesse, the elder sister of Empress Alexandra. Known in the family as Ella, she quickly charmed those whom she encountered. "Her eyes, her lips, her smile, her hands, they way she looked at you, the way she talked, the way she moved, all was exquisite beyond words, it almost brought tears to your eyes," recalled Queen Marie of Romania.[27] Although not a particularly solicitous husband, Serge Alexandrovich was a jealous one, and he controlled every aspect of Ella's life, selecting her clothing, appointing her Household and staff, and charging his aides to spy on her. He was horrified when he discovered her with a copy of *Anna Karenina* and immediately forbade her to read it, fearing that she would be exposed to "curious and unnatural thoughts."[28] "She and my uncle never seemed very intimate," said Grand Duchess Marie Pavlovna. "They met for the most part only at meals and by day avoided being alone together."[29] In public, Serge criticized her "in the harshest of language and most brutal of terms," according to Queen Marie, and delighted in humiliatingly referring to her as "My child" before complete strangers.[30]

In 1891, Emperor Alexander III appointed his brother governor-general of Moscow, ushering in a period of harsh repression for Moscow's Jews. "Jews," he once exclaimed, "ought to be crucified!"[31] Indeed, as Alexander III confessed, Serge refused "to go to Moscow until it is cleansed of Jews."[32] In his first year as governor-general, the grand duke expelled some twenty thousand Jews who had been living in the city illegally, sending them to the infamous Pale of Settlement in Western Russia.[33] Those who did remain were often given a distasteful choice: renounce their religion and become Russian Orthodox, or face expulsion; young girls who remained were registered as prostitutes.[34]

After the morganatic marriage and the exile of their father, Grand Duke Paul Alexandrovich, his children by his first wife—Grand Duchess Marie Pavlovna and Grand Duke Dimitri Pavlovich—were taken in by Serge and

Grand Duke Serge Alexandrovich (right), his wife, Elizabeth ("Ella"), with her niece Marie Pavlovna, and Grand Duke Paul Alexandrovich with his son Dimitri Pavlovich, 1892

Grand Duchess Elizabeth
Feodorovna ("Ella") in Russian
court dress, circa 1890

Grand Duchess Elizabeth
Feodorovna in her robes, 1910

Ella. While Serge doted on them, their aunt, recalled Marie Pavlovna, "showed no interest in us or in anything that concerned us, and she saw as little of us as she could."[35]

Rumors of all descriptions surrounded Serge and Ella's married life and what one contemporary referred to as his "unmentionable vices": that she was terribly unhappy; that Serge was homosexual, a sadist in the bedroom who inflicted untold sexual indignities upon his helpless wife; that the grand duke frequented the slums of Moscow in search of prostitutes to satisfy his bizarre desires; and that he was a pedophile, with a taste for the young cadets in the city's military training schools.[36] "His private life was the talk of the town," declared Alexander Mossolov.[37] His homosexuality was a poor secret; Serge Witte said that he was "always surrounded by comparatively young men, who were excessively affectionate toward him."[38] And another author commented, "It was well known that the Grand Duke Serge was one of those unhappy men cursed with the failing of loving only their own sex."[39]

Nor did Serge Alexandrovich confine his activities to those on the fringes of society: there were rumors that his young nephew, Dimitri Pavlovich, had fallen victim to his sexual appetite.[40] In January 1891, Kaiser Wilhelm II reported that the grand duke was in the midst of a bitter fight with an elderly cleric in the Orthodox Church, who "discovered that Serge was buggering his handsome young domestic chaplain. He transferred the latter at once. This so enraged the pious Prince that he contrived to have the old man transferred!"[41]

The grand duchess refused to admit any suffering; her letters to family and friends were filled with warm, glowing reports of her happiness as the grand duke's wife and tales of his loving attentions, assertions in stark contrast to the observations of others. Knowing how despised her husband had become, she cast up a net of self-imposed illusion that shrouded the darker realities from the inquisitive eyes of the public.

An assassin finally brought the grand duke's repressive rule to an end. In February 1905, as Serge left the Kremlin, a bomb ripped his carriage apart. Ella was in the palace when she heard the explosion. Screaming, "It's Serge!" she rushed out to find charred and bloody pieces of flesh scattered over the crimson snow.[42] The grand duke's death freed his wife from their marital prison, but by this time, she had become so mystical that she willingly withdrew from her former life.

Several years after her marriage, Ella had converted to Orthodoxy. Her cousin Kaiser Wilhelm II asserted that she had converted from "an inordinate pursuit of popularity, a desire to improve her position at Court, a great lack of intelligence, and also a want of true religiousness and patriotic feeling." Along with several other relatives, he believed that she had done so to regain favor with Alexander III and his wife, who knew of her continued attempts to facilitate the romance between Tsesarevich Nicholas and her sister Princess Alix.[43] In time, her fervor became an obsession. Orthodoxy not only drew her closer to the undecipherable character of her mystical husband, but also provided her with an emotional communion that her marriage failed to offer. "Uncle Serge regarded with anxiety his wife's increasing absorption in things spiritual, and ended by regarding it as immoderate," recalled Marie Pavlovna.[44]

After Serge's death, Ella divested herself of many of her personal possessions, returning some of her fabled jewelry to the Crown but leaving the majority of her pieces to Dimitri Pavlovich and Marie Pavlovna. Her nephew also gained the extravagant rococo Sergeievsky Palace in St. Petersburg, where she and Serge had lived before moving to Moscow.[45] Much of what remained was sold, including—significantly—her wedding ring, and she used the money to establish a religious community of nursing sisters in Moscow.[46]

Ella insisted that her novitiates assume the title of "Deaconess," and she waged a public battle with the members of the Holy Synod, the Church's ruling body, which declared that such a request was unheard of in Orthodoxy, where clerical ranks were confined to men. She was publicly opposed by Bishop Hermogen of Saratov, one of the Church's leading clerics, who went directly to Nicholas II and complained about his sister-in-law's behavior.[47] In time, however, Ella won. She became the head abbess of the Order of St. Mary and St. Martha, devoting the rest of her life to caring for the sick and the poor. She commissioned the famed religious artist Michael Nesterov to design robes of soft gray baize with white cambric wimples and white wool veils for herself and her sisters; her own robes were executed by the House of Pacquin in Paris.[48] With a last touch of vanity, she also commissioned ceremonial robes for herself, in pearl-colored baize. When she appeared with the imperial family on public occasions, the dowager empress once caustically remarked that she presented herself as "a theatrical martyr, relishing the attention" drawn by her exotic costume.[49]

Grand Duke Paul Alexandrovich, circa 1882

Grand Duke Paul Alexandrovich, born in 1860, entered the Imperial Army, rising to commanding officer of the guards cavalry division and of the guards corps. Nicholas II, who enjoyed a close relationship with his uncle, appointed the grand duke to the Imperial Suite in 1897 as an adjutant-general.[50] In 1889, Paul had married Princess Alexandra of Greece, the daughter of his first cousin Queen Olga of the Hellenes. Two years later, having given birth to a daughter, Marie, in 1890, Alexandra bore the grand duke a son, Grand Duke Dimitri Pavlovich, only to succumb from complications. Her tragic death left Paul lonely, and he soon began a discreet liaison with the divorcée Olga Pistolkors, "a very pretty woman, with radiant brown eyes that have the power of being caressing or full of mirth at will," as one contemporary recalled.[51] The grand duke's mistress was a well-known figure in St. Petersburg society; her former husband had been an adjutant to Grand Duke Vladimir Alexandrovich, and she had befriended many important ladies at court.

The situation changed at the beginning of 1897, however, when Olga Pistolkors gave birth to Paul's bastard son Vladimir. Paul showered his mistress with jewels, including a famous suite of diamonds that had been left to him by his mother, Empress Marie Alexandrovna. Olga made the mistake of wearing them to a ball at the Winter Palace, where the dowager empress recognized them and promptly informed Empress Alexandra, who immediately had Olga Pistolkors escorted from the palace. By the following day everyone knew of Olga Pistolkors's humiliation. Her censure too much to bear, Olga fled to Italy. Alexander Mossolov, on behalf of the emperor, warned that Paul would not be allowed to marry her, but the grand duke's mistress insisted that Nicholas II would not punish him for making legal a situation everyone knew existed.[52]

Paul, who previously had no intention of marrying his mistress, now did just that, while on holiday in Italy in 1902, insisting that he had been forced to do so in order to save her honor. On learning of this, Nicholas II wrote to his mother, "How painful and distressing it all is and how ashamed one feels for the sake of our family before the world! What guarantee is there now that Kirill won't start

Sergeievsky Palace at the corner of Nevsky Prospekt and Fontanka Canal, the St. Petersburg home of Grand Duke Serge Alexandrovich and his wife, Elizabeth, 1900

the same sort of thing tomorrow and Boris or Serge Mikhailovich the day after? And, in the end, I fear, a whole Russian colony of members of the Imperial Family will be established in Paris with their semi-legitimate and illegitimate wives!"[53]

Not only was Olga Pistolkors of unequal rank, but also her status as a divorcée marked her as doubly unacceptable. Nicholas stripped his uncle of his military rank and posts, severed his official salaries, and banished him from Russia. The two children from his first marriage, Marie Pavlovna and Dimitri Pavlovich, were made wards of Grand Duke Serge Alexandrovich, and Paul was forbidden any say in their upbringing. Paul fled to Paris, taking with him two suitcases filled with 3 million gold rubles ($30,000,000 in 2005 figures).[54] In 1904, Luitpold, the prince regent of Bavaria, bestowed upon the former Olga Pistolkors the courtesy title of Countess Hohenfelsen, and Nicholas himself eventually granted his uncle's wife the title of Princess Paley, with the style of Serene Highness. She and Paul spent the next decade in Paris, where she gave birth to two daughters, Irina, born in 1903, and Nathalia, born in 1905.

The grand duke's return to imperial favor was slow and never complete, and it was several years before he was finally allowed to bring his family to Russia.

Even then, relations with the imperial couple remained strained, and Paul and his morganatic wife lived on the fringes of accepted society. *The Almanach de St. Petersbourg*, an annual handbook published under the authority of the imperial court, refused to acknowledge the marriage; the entry for Paul Alexandrovich listed only his deceased wife and their two children, making no mention of his second family.[55]

Empress Alexandra dictated further humiliation: the countess could be presented to members of the Romanov family but not formally through their official suites, as ordinary aristocratic women were—only in private and only by her husband. She was also required, when visiting the imperial palaces, to leave her card rather than being allowed to sign her name in the guest book, as were other ladies of the court.[56] Such deliberate slights left Paul Alexandrovich angry. He later spoke of the "many insults at the hands of my Imperial relatives and their satellites, mostly men and women of social degeneracy," and referred to his uncle the emperor as "one of the principal persecutors of myself and my family," terming him "a political imbecile."[57]

Grand Duchess Marie Pavlovna, the daughter of Paul Alexandrovich, 1908

The two children from Paul's first marriage, Grand Duchess Marie Pavlovna and Grand Duke Dimitri Pavlovich, lived with Serge and Ella after their father's exile. Born in 1890, Marie Pavlovna was often referred to as "the Younger," to distinguish her from her aunt, Grand Duchess Vladimir. She was, remembered Grand Duchess Marie Georgievna, "full of life and very jolly, but inclined to be self-willed and selfish and rather difficult to deal with," while another aristocrat termed her "capricious."[58] Yet one acquaintance described her as "a charming woman, not exactly pretty, but with a clever, interesting face and a figure slender, graceful and straight as a dart . . . possessed of intellect, will, and lofty ideals."[59]

In 1908, she married Prince Wilhelm of Sweden, the second son of King Gustav V, a union secretly arranged by Ella, who appeared to be eager to rid herself of her young charge. She did not even bother to inform her niece of the situation, and Marie Pavlovna learned of her pending nuptials on reading a cable her aunt had accidentally left on a desk.[60] "Her haste to have me married," Marie later recalled, "and the complete absence of any thought as to the sentimental side of such a compact, revolted me."[61] Her father, Grand Duke Paul Alexandrovich, complained of Ella's "complete lack of common sense and humane feelings."[62]

Marie learned Swedish, gave birth to a son, called Lennart, and made herself popular by taking on charitable work, in contrast to her allegedly homosexual husband, who suffered bouts of depression and uncontrolled weeping.[63] By 1913, Marie Pavlovna, finding her life intolerable, reached her breaking point. Telling Wilhelm that she intended to seek a divorce, she fled Sweden, returning to St. Petersburg, where she implored the emperor to grant her an annulment. It took a year to work out the details, but in 1914, the grand duchess finally won her freedom.[64]

Grand Duke Dimitri Pavlovich was only ten when his father was forced into exile. "Tall and slim, pale and delicate looking," recalled his friend Meriel Buchanan, "he lacked the virile magnificence of some of his uncles and cousins, but although he was still a little shy and uncertain of himself, he possessed all the Romanov charm."[65] In 1911, the young grand duke was promoted to the Horse Guards Regiment, and the following year he led Russia's equestrian team at the 1912 Olympic Games in Stockholm, himself coming in seventh in the jumping competition. His true passion, however, was the pursuit of pleasure. He avoided, as Meriel Buchanan recalled, the usual round of expected balls "on the pretext that his military duties were too strenuous to permit him to stay up late every night," although he did so in order to attend "all the smaller, more intimate, and certainly more entertaining, dances given by the young married women." He enjoyed, Meriel declared, being "pursued, made much of, and flattered."[66]

Dimitri was believed to have fallen hopelessly in love with Princess Irina Alexandrovna, the only daughter of Nicholas II's sister Xenia and her husband, Grand Duke Alexander Mikhailovich. This may have been true, although he also harbored an intensely romantic devotion to her eventual husband, the flamboyantly homosexual Prince Felix Yusupov. After Irina and Felix married in 1914, Dimitri Pavlovich, recalled one of his friends, became "helpless and desolate."[67] And Meriel Buchanan remembered that he "became more recklessly dissipated."[68] Certainly, Prince Felix continued his affections, and their relationship, which spawned much rumor, eventually culminated in their combined assassination of Gregory Rasputin in 1916.

The emperor also had a number of relatives from the marriages of his great uncles, the brothers of his grandfather, Alexander II. Grand Duke Konstantin Nikolaievich had been an imposing figure, with a distinguished career in the

Imperial Navy that spanned nearly forty years. In 1848, he had married Princess Alexandra, the youngest daughter of Duke Josef of Saxe-Altenburg.[69] On converting to Orthodoxy, she took the name and the title of Grand Duchess Alexandra Iosifovna; the family called her "Aunt Sanny."[70] She was, recalled Baroness Buxhoeveden, "a commanding old lady with snow white hair, beautifully coiffed. She had kept a great sense of dress and her black, tight fitting princess frocks set off her tall, erect and slim figure."[71]

The grand duchess bore her husband three sons who lived to adulthood, Grand Dukes Nicholas, Konstantin, and Dimitri Konstantinovich, and two daughters, Olga and Vera. Both daughters married outside of Russia: Olga Konstantinovna wed Empress Marie Feodorovna's brother King George I of the Hellenes in 1867, while her sister Vera married Wilhelm Eugen, the duke of Württemberg, in 1874. Grand Duke Konstantin Nikolaievich, however, proved a less-than-faithful husband, referring to Alexandra caustically as his "government-issue" wife.[72] He flaunted an affair with the ballerina Anna Kuznetsova, whose children bore not "the slightest resemblance" to their supposed, legitimate father, and he lived with them, "almost openly" as Alexander III noted in disgust, in the Crimea.[73] When he died in 1892, few mourned his passing.

The eldest Konstantinovich son, the handsome Nicholas, was believed to have suffered from syphilis caught, it was whispered, from the numerous prostitutes who regularly filled his bed. In the fall of 1873, the grand duke met a beautiful young American, Henrietta Blackford; the resulting sexual misadventure shocked the imperial family and ultimately led to Nicholas Konstantinovich's downfall. One night, with the assistance of his adjutant, the grand duke smuggled Blackford into his father's Marble Palace. The trio got drunk, then crept into Grand Duchess Alexandra's room and made love together on her bed. Nicholas presented his mistress with one of his mother's valuable diamond necklaces and tore the jeweled crown from one of her icons, handing the diamonds to his adjutant to pawn.[74] A few days later, Blackford was spotted wearing the stolen necklace at the ballet; arrested, she declared it had been a gift from her lover the grand duke.[75] She was promptly banished from Russia but took her revenge in exile, writing a scandalous account of her adventures, *Le Roman d'une Américaine en Russie*, which appeared the following year in Belgium.[76]

Nicholas Konstantinovich was declared unstable, although few were convinced of the verdict. In exile, he fathered an illegitimate child by a married woman; in 1882, he contracted a morganatic marriage with Nadezhda Dreyer and fathered two sons, Artemy and Alexander, who bore the style of Prince and the surname of Iskander. Dissatisfied, he purchased the sixteen-year-old daughter of a local Cossack, who bore him three children, and in 1900 at the age of fifty, he secretly, and bigamously, married a seventeen-year-old student. Not surprisingly, most of the imperial family ignored his existence.[77]

Konstantin Konstantinovich, the second son, was perhaps the most intelligent and accomplished of all the grand dukes. Born in 1858, he was, recalled Baroness Buxhoeveden, "very good looking, with his mother's regular features and the short fair beard of a Renaissance portrait."[78] Although he had little taste for military life, Konstantin followed the expected course, rising to the rank of infantry general and commander of the Preobrazhensky Life Guards Regiment. Yet the grand duke was more interested in intellectual pursuits. In 1889, he became president of the Imperial Academy of Sciences; he established the Higher Women's Course Academy in St. Petersburg and served as chairman of the Imperial Archaeological Institute.[79]

Grand Duke Konstantin Konstantinovich, about 1884

In 1884, Konstantin wed Princess Elizabeth of Saxe-Altenburg, who took the name Elizabeth Mavrikievna on her marriage. Known as Mavra in the family, she refused to convert from Lutheranism, which caused her husband endless torment. "I argued with her, and she listened to my reasoning that one cannot fully serve a people without being at one with their customs," Konstantin wrote. "She said that God has not thus far moved her to convert, and so she won't. I wanted her to note that this makes me sad, so sad that I don't know what to do with all my grief, except to pray to God. Was there ever such a heavy blow?"[80]

Konstantin Konstantinovich and Elizabeth Mavrikievna had nine children, making theirs the largest single branch within the Romanov family. The first child, Prince Ioann, was born in 1886; Prince Gabriel was born in 1887; Princess Tatiana was born in 1890; Prince Konstantin Konstantinovich was born in 1891; Prince Oleg was born in 1892; Prince Igor was born in 1894; Prince George was born in 1903; Princess Nathalia was born in 1905; and Princess Vera was born in 1906. They enjoyed a peaceful, happy life in the capital's Marble Palace and in their country estates at Pavlovsk and Strelna near St. Petersburg and at Osta-shevo outside Moscow.

But Konstantin was a tortured man, haunted by his own homosexuality. Twenty years after his marriage, the grand duke wrote candidly in his diary of what he termed "familiar characteristics" mentioned by one of his young male lovers, including the fact that the man had "never felt drawn to a woman." Konstantin, as he wrote, "knew these feelings from my own personal experience."[81] He frequently indulged in sexual encounters with young men in bathhouses in the imperial capital and at Krasnoye Selo. Shortly after the birth of his son Oleg, he made an effort to restrain his desires. "I started out on the right path," he wrote. "I began to struggle earnestly with my main vice, and did not sin for seven years, or more correctly, only sinned in my thoughts." By 1900, temptation became too much, and he succumbed once again. After this, he managed to again resist for a year, but during a trip in 1902, he noted, "I sinned a lot." The following year, he wrote, "I have completely gone astray and have lived in a constant state of war with my conscience." It was, he said, a battle against what he called "unclean thoughts and desires." By 1903, he wrote, "They have taken over me again. I keep struggling, telling myself that God has given me the heart, intellect, and strength to fight successfully. The misfortune is that even though I could fight, I don't want to."[82]

If his wife suspected, she never revealed her thoughts to another. On the surface, they lived the happiest of family lives with their children, admired by other members of the Romanov family for their moral rectitude. When Konstantin died in 1915, his wife found that his will stipulated that his diaries could not be read by anyone for ninety-nine years. Discussing this peculiarity with her, Grand Duke Andrei Vladimirovich wrote, "He hadn't let anyone—even her—read them in life, and she used to tease him that he was writing all sorts of complaints and criticisms about her in there."[83] Elizabeth Mavrikievna died without ever learning of her husband's secret life.

The grand duke's most enduring legacy, though, was his contribution to the arts. A poet of some repute, he published his verse under the initials "K. R." for Konstantin Romanov. Peter Tchaikovsky was so impressed by these efforts that he set many of the poems to music. Konstantin translated the works of Byron, Goethe, and Schiller and produced the first Russian version of Shakespeare's *Hamlet*, taking the lead in a performance at the Hermitage Theater in 1900. He also wrote and performed his own plays, including *The King of Judea*, in which he played Joseph of Arimathea before the entire imperial family in 1913.

Dimitri Konstantinovich, born in 1860, grew up an artistic and introspective young man. From his youth, he had a passionate interest in the military and, at eighteen, joined the Mounted Grenadier Regiment, where he eventually rose to the rank of commander in chief.[84] Fair, with light brown hair and blue eyes, he was, remembered Sophie Buxhoeveden, "extraordinarily tall and thin, with legs that seemed endless in his tight cavalry breeches."[85]

Alexander Mikhailovich declared that his cousin was "in love with horse flesh." He kept a large and successful stud farm at Dubrovsky near Poltava, over which he took the greatest care, breeding exquisite Orlov trotters and providing many of the fine thoroughbreds for his regiment and for the imperial cavalry.[86] "I would like you to see my yearlings!" he would call out to visiting relatives, leading them on a tour of his stables.[87] "Between breakfast and dinner," recalled his nephew Prince Gabriel, "we rode horses, and talked about horses."[88]

Alexander Mossolov described him as "full of good sense," remarking that Dimitri Konstantinovich "was the one among all the Grand Dukes who was most deeply imbued with the sense of his duty as a Prince and a cousin of the Emperor."[89] Once, the grand duke dispatched a hefty portion of his annual Civil List income to support a struggling church. When Mossolov learned of this, he warned, "If you make gifts everywhere on this scale, your revenues will not last." But Dimitri replied that the stipend was "not intended to enable us to live as sybarites; this money is put into our hands in order that we may augment the prestige of the Imperial Family."[90]

For all of his equanimity, the grand duke was "a confirmed and enthusiastic woman-hater," recalled his cousin.[91] "Beware of skirts!" he warned his young male relatives at every chance.[92] It was rumored that like his older brother Konstantin Konstantinovich, Dimitri may have been homosexual; it is also possible that he harbored such sweeping views after having witnessed the humiliation inflicted on his mother by his father's affair with Kuznetsova.

His greatest joy came in 1914, when war with Germany finally erupted. For years, he had pored over the Bible, according to his cousin Alexander Mikhailovich, and was utterly convinced that the end of the world was near.[93] "The war with Germany is imminent!" he would cry, predicting disaster.[94] He took the outbreak of hostilities as evidence that his prophecy had been correct. By this time, however, the grand duke was nearly blind. At his mother's funeral in 1911, Dimitri, unable to see clearly, bent forward to kiss an icon in her fingers; he misjudged the distance, missing the coffin and tumbling off the steps with a loud thud. Relatives rushed to his side, but the grand duke appeared unfazed and went on as though nothing had happened.[95] Much to his chagrin, his poor eyesight kept the grand duke from the conflict, and he had to content him-self with a job training the cavalry regiments.

In 1891, Nicholas II's great uncle Grand Duke Nicholas Nikolaievich died. His had been a life of scandal; married in 1856 to a distant cousin who took the name Alexandra Petrovna, the grand duke did not conceal the fact that he found his wife less than appealing. Within four years of his marriage, he had taken a mistress, the famed ballerina Catherine Chislova. In 1868, Chislova gave birth to the first of his five bastard children. His brother Alexander II granted the chil-dren the surname of Nikolaiev but advised the grand duke to move Chislova away from the wagging tongues of court gossips.[96]

By 1881, Alexandra was no longer content to engage in the public charade and moved to Kiev, where she established the Petrovsky Convent of Nursing Sisters and became its mother superior. Refused his requests for a divorce, the grand duke openly expressed the hope that his wife would soon die, thus freeing him to marry his mistress. But it was Chislova who unexpectedly fell ill and died in the Crimea, a twist of fate that drove her lover insane. Suffering from delusions, he molested every woman he met, convinced that they were in love with him. After one ballet performance, the grand duke became so aroused that he went back-stage and tried to seduce everyone he saw. He was finally pulled off a young male dancer who struggled against his kisses and wandering hands. He eventually died under house arrest in the Crimea, where he was attended by an elderly valet, the only member of the household who was safe from his amorous attacks. His hated wife outlived him by more than a decade.[97]

This family scandal deeply affected the grand duke's two legitimate sons, Nicholas and Peter Nikolaievich. Nicholas Nikolaievich Jr.—called Nikolasha in the imperial family—was a career army officer, eventually taking the supreme command of the Russian Army at the beginning of the First World War. Immensely tall, with a lean figure, closely cropped beard, and piercing blue eyes, he evoked the very image of the proud Romanovs. "One could not describe him as being particularly brilliant," recalled Grand Duchess Marie Georgievna, "nor was he very popular while he commanded the Guards, before the War, because he was terribly severe and rather hard."[98] Behind his back, members of the Impe-rial Guard called him "the Evil One" and "old Nick," an unsubtle reference to his Mephistophelean reputation. He delighted, recalled one officer, in "the dress-ing down of his subordinates."[99] Prince Andrei Lobanov-Rostovsky remem-bered, "He inspired us with absolute terror, for it was known that he never minced words if anything went wrong." He recalled a review of young cadets, when the grand duke "had abused them in such language that all the ladies present blushed."[100] Something of this cruelty once appeared during a dinner party when the grand duke, eager to demonstrate that his was the finest sword in the military, called for one of his pet borzois and cleanly sliced through the pathetic animal as his guests looked on in horror.[101]

His brother Peter had less talent and taste for military life. Born in 1864, he served in the Lancer Life Guards Regiment but was forced into long periods of rest from exhaustion and recurring bouts with pneumonia and tuberculosis.[102] In 1889, Peter married Princess Militsa, the second daughter of the future King Nicholas of Montenegro. Militsa was as tall as her husband, with refined, slightly dark features that earned her and her sister Anastasia several court monikers: the kinder appellation referred to them as "the Black Pearls," for both their complexions and their homeland, Montenegro, or Black Mountain.[103] Their enemies twisted this into the far more sinister "Black Peril," expressing the distaste with which they were often regarded.[104]

Militsa's sister Anastasia married the widowed Duke George of Leuchtenberg, a junior member of the Romanov Dynasty. Within a few years, George of Leuchtenberg abandoned his wife and openly lived with his mistress in Biarritz, leaving Anastasia humiliated and alone with his two children, Serge and Elena. As Elizabeth Naryshkin-Kuryakin noted, Empress Alexandra "was very sorry" for Anastasia, looking on her "as a neglected wife." With the empress's prodding, Nicholas finally agreed to grant the unhappy Anastasia a divorce.[105]

In time, the bond deepened, and the two Montenegrin sisters introduced the empress to their own particular brand of mysticism. In the first years of their marriage, Peter and Militsa lived at Znamenka, the immense Nikolaievich palace on the Gulf of Finland adjoining the imperial estate of Peterhof. After her divorce from Duke George of Leuchtenberg, Anastasia also had an apartment here, as did Peter's brother Grand Duke Nicholas Nikolaievich, launching the beginning of a romance that would lead to their eventual marriage in 1907.[106] Nicholas and Alexandra gradually fell under their mystical influence and met a succession of dubious prophets and pilgrims, ending in 1905 with the introduction of Gregory Rasputin.

Finally, there was Grand Duke Michael Nikolaievich, who presided over the Imperial Council, the ruling administrative body of ministers before the creation of the Duma. Born in 1832, he had served as viceroy of the Caucasus. Gossip held that his wife, Olga Feodorovna, a former princess of Baden, was the product of her mother's alleged affair with an American Jewish banker named Haber.

Both Alexander III and Nicholas II referred to her contemptuously as "Auntie Haber," while Empress Alexandra later condemned one of her sons as "a bad man, grandson of a Jew!"[107] To relieve her boredom, or so it was whispered, she took a number of lovers, flaunting them before her resigned husband.[108] Nevertheless, when she died unexpectedly in 1891, her husband mourned her to the end of his life, sleeping with her parasol, her hat, and a pair of her gloves every night.[109]

Grand Duke Michael Nikolaievich's descendants were commonly referred to as the Mikhailovichii within the imperial family; in precedence, they fell below the Vladimirovichii, the Konstantinovichii, and the Nikolaievichii, making them the junior branch in the Imperial House. This status, coupled with their time in the Caucasus and the common belief that Grand Duchess Olga Feodorovna had a Jewish father, led the Romanovs to view them as provincial and uncultured. They were also believed to hold liberal views and were condemned as "dangerous radicals" by most of the Imperial House.[110]

Michael Nikolaievich and Grand Duchess Olga had six children who lived to adulthood. Anastasia, the only daughter, was tall and slim, with "Grecian features and a small head, which she carried haughtily," recalled Baroness Agnes de Stoeckl. "In fact, she seemed the ideal Princess."[111] In 1878, her mother forced her marriage to Grand Duke Friedrich Franz III of Mecklenburg-Schwerin, whose sister had married Grand Duke Vladimir. The pair had three children, including two daughters who themselves made illustrious matches, Alexandrine to the future King Christian X of Denmark and Cecilie to Crown Prince Wilhelm of Germany. Anastasia was unhappy and sought comfort in the arms of a servant; when she learned that she was pregnant, she claimed illness and hid herself until the child was born and spirited away. Her husband, despondent over this development, was rumored to have killed himself on learning the truth.[112]

Of the Mikhailovich sons, Grand Duke Nicholas Mikhailovich, the eldest, was undoubtedly the most talented. Born in 1859, he was, recalled Helene Izvolsky, "a broad shouldered man, with a black beard and dark eyes full of kindliness and intelligence," though with age he grew rotund and lost most of his hair.[113] Called "Bimbo" within the imperial family, the grand duke never married, though he was believed to have fathered several illegitimate children by a number of mistresses.[114] A distinguished historian, the grand duke was also believed to be a dedicated liberal; his fellow Guards officers bestowed upon him the nickname "Philippe Égalité."[115]

His true passion was history, and he produced a number of works: a five-volume collection of Russian portraiture; a multivolume set of annotated diplomatic correspondence between Russia and France; an acclaimed two-volume biography of Emperor Alexander I; and a biography of Alexander's consort, Elizabeth Alexeievna.[116] The latter earned him much scorn. Countess Marie Kleinmichel called the grand duke "a scandal-monger, who ransacked history for the sake of gossip. The eighteenth century was his happy hunting ground, but he did not neglect either the nineteenth or the twentieth century. He felt very happy, for instance, when he discovered that his great aunt Elizabeth Alexeievna, the wife of Alexander I, whom Russia venerated as a saint, had had a lover, and he published with loving care every item of information he could find concerning the young officer."[117]

In the reign of Nicholas II, Nicholas Mikhailovich settled into an increasingly unpleasant and bitter existence. He made no attempt to couch his strongly held beliefs in acceptable language. "I can blurt out insolent things," he admitted. He dismissed Nicholas II as "a man of insufficiently grand stature," while condemning his wife as a "narrow, cold soul."[118] As a result, he often alienated the very people he had hoped to influence.

Grand Duke Michael Mikhailovich, known as "Miche-Miche" in the family, was born in 1861. During a European holiday, he met and fell in love with the beautiful Countess Sophie von Merenberg, the daughter of Prince Nikolaus of Nassau and his morganatic wife Countess Nathalia von Merenberg, and a granddaughter of the famed poet Alexander Pushkin. In February of 1891, they married in San Remo. The marriage was not only morganatic but also illegal under the *Statute of the Imperial Family*. When his mother heard of this, she deemed her son "simply evil."[119] The strain and humiliation proved too much, and Olga Feodorovna suffered a heart attack shortly thereafter.[120]

News of the marriage also shocked Empress Marie Feodorovna, who deemed the grand duke "a swine."[121] As punishment, Alexander III stripped Michael Mikhailovich of his military offices and awards, deprived him of his position as adjutant at the imperial court, and forbade his return to Russia.[122] The grand duke and his new wife, who was given the courtesy title of Countess de Torby by the grand duke of Luxembourg, settled in London, where they lived in splendor in Kenwood House.

Grand Duke George Mikhailovich was born in 1863. Called "Gogi" within the imperial family, he strained to break free of the expectations forced upon him by virtue of his birth. As a young man, he became an adept painter; when he expressed a wish to pursue a career in the arts during a family luncheon, he was met with silence and deprived of dessert for his impudence.[123] An injury to his leg left him with a pronounced limp. For anyone else, it would have prevented military service, but George Mikhailovich was forced by tradition to enter the imperial guards, serving in Her Majesty's Lancer Regiment.[124]

Tall and slim, standing six feet four inches, with brown eyes and a short cavalry mustache, the grand duke lost his hair early. In 1900, he married Princess Marie, the daughter of King George I of the Hellenes. Theirs was scarcely a love match. He proposed to her over a game of billiards. When Marie gave her reluctant assent, he ran round the table to kiss her, but she was quicker and kept him on his feet as he chased her in circles before she finally relented.[125] His bride, who took the name Marie Georgievna, was unhappy. She later admitted that she "never liked living in Russia" and regarded her union as "a marriage of convenience."[126] They had two daughters, Princess Nina, born in 1901, and Princess Xenia, born in 1903.

In time, George Mikhailovich's injured leg forced him from military service. Nicholas II appointed him director of the Alexander III Museum of Russian Art in St. Petersburg, and the grand duke began a lengthy career as an art historian. His particular specialty was numismatics. He composed ten important volumes on the subject, and after the Revolution, portions of his own coin collection—the finest in the Russian empire—eventually found their way to the Smithsonian Institution in Washington, D.C.[127]

Born in 1869, Serge Mikhailovich entered the Horse Guards Artillery Regiment in 1888, rising to the rank of commanding officer in 1903 and inspector-general of the Russian Imperial Artillery two years later.[128] Standing six feet three inches tall, with blond hair and blue eyes, he cut a striking figure, though his sister-in-law Grand Duchess Marie Georgievna termed him "decidedly ugly." She once asked him, rather tactlessly, why he was so ugly, but the grand duke simply smiled and said, "That is my charm."[129]

Although he remained unmarried, the grand duke carried on a scandalous affair with the ballerina Mathilde Kschessinska, who manipulated his affections to further her own ambitions. His infatuation remained intact even amid her permanent liaison with Grand Duke Andrei Vladimirovich and the birth of her son of questionable paternity. Eventually, however, Serge grew tired of her games. After the Revolution, he commented bitterly, "It is only surprising that the old woman didn't somehow manage to get herself enthroned!"[130] Of all the

Mikhailovichii brothers, only Grand Duke Alexander, who had married Nicholas II's sister Xenia, maintained close ties with the emperor and the empress.

After the Revolution, the emperor's youngest sister, Olga, remarked, "It is certainly the last generation that helped to bring about the disintegration of the Empire. . . . All those critical years, the Romanovs, who should have been the staunchest supporters of the Throne, did not live up to their standards of the traditions of the Family. . . . Too many of us Romanovs had . . . gone to live in a world of self-interest where little mattered except the unending gratification of personal desire and ambition. . . . That chain of domestic scandals could not but shock the nation."[131]

These sentiments aptly summed up the decay that hung over the dynasty as it entered the twentieth century, as the fear and respect that had once surrounded the Imperial House slid into public antipathy and alienation. The House of Romanov seemed lost, both in the numerous tragedies of its centuries past and in an impending sense of doom that shrouded the imperial court. Shortly after the last emperor came to the throne, the young writer Dimitri Merezhovsky ominously recorded, "In the House of the Romanovs . . . a mysterious curse descends from generation to generation. Murders and adultery, blood and mud. . . . Peter I kills his son; Alexander I kills his father; Catherine II kills her husband. . . . The block, the rope and poison—these are the true emblems of Russian autocracy. God's unction on the brows of the Tsars has become the brand of Cain."[132]

5

THE RUSSIAN COURT

IN 1895, THE WIFE OF THE AMERICAN ambassador in St. Petersburg wrote to a friend, "I have come to the conclusion that Their Majesties are to people here what the sun is to our world; I do not expect you to understand it; it must be seen and felt."[1] The reverence and respect of the courtiers was real enough: their very lives and existence depended solely upon the continuing presence of the emperor and the empress on the imperial thrones. "Until I became an Adjutant to the Emperor and had served for a while," recalled General Count Alexander Grabbe, "I had only a vague notion of the nature and composition of the Imperial court. I certainly had no idea that there were so many high ranking officials connected with it."[2]

The Russian court was Russian in name and location only. Italian architects had designed its palaces, French was its official language, and its dynasty was almost exclusively German by blood. Many court offices were based on German models, as transliterated by the Russians, and carried titles such as *ober-tseremoniimeister* (grand master of ceremonies), *ober-shtalmeister* (master of the imperial horse), *ober-gofmarschal* (grand marshal of the imperial court), *kamerger* (chamberlain), and *fligel-adjutant* (aide-de-camp).[3]

In 1826, Nicholas I established the Ministry of the Imperial Court, which was charged with administration of court appointments and ceremonial functions. By

Count Vladimir de Freedericksz, the Minister of the Imperial Court, about 1905

the beginning of the twentieth century, the Russian court consisted of 16,500 persons, of whom 15,000 were members of the Household, or servants. Of the remaining number, nearly two-thirds held honorary positions, for which they received no financial compensation. Only the top five hundred officials, members of the Suite and the Entourage, received salaries.[4]

The Ministry of the Imperial Court supervised thousands of officials and members of the Household. So immense were its functions that the ministry itself required a staff of thirteen hundred, their salaries and ceremonial expenses billed to the Russian government at a rate of 12.7 to 17 million rubles each year ($120,700,000–1,700,000,000 in 2005 figures).[5] At its head stood the *ministr imperatorskogo dvora*, or minister of the imperial court, who controlled the imperial budget, handed out salaries and stipends to grand dukes and servants, issued manifestos in the emperor's name, advised him on matters of protocol, and published the *Pridvorny Kalendar*, or "Court Calendar," a list of official engagements undertaken by members of the imperial family.

Nicholas II had two ministers of the imperial court. The first, Count Hilarion Vorontzov-Dashkov, had also served under Alexander III. Born in 1837, Vorontzov-Dashkov entered the Horse Guards Regiment in 1856, rising through the ranks of the Imperial Army to command both the Hussar Life Guards and the imperial cavalry.[6] Count Serge Witte called him "a typical Russian noble of the old school, a man of firm principles, an honorable and worthy official."[7]

Vorontzov-Dashkov's attitude toward the new emperor was almost parental in manner. Though Nicholas did not mind, others, including Empress Alexandra, were offended. After the Khodynka disaster during the coronation in 1896, at which over a thousand people died, Vorontzov-Dashkov found himself pitted against Grand Duke Serge Alexandrovich, who, as governor-general of Moscow, bore ultimate responsibility. The grand duke won the battle, and Vorontzov-Dashkov was publicly humiliated. In submitting his resignation, the count declared that he had planned to retire, remaining through the festivities only because he "felt it my duty to lend my new Master the benefit of my experience" for the occasion. Privately, however, he complained that he "was not used to working with people who could not keep their word."[8]

Vorontzov-Dashkov was replaced by a fifty-nine-year-old Baltic nobleman, Baron Vladimir Borisovich de Freedericksz, "a fine, gallant old gentleman," as one man recalled.[9] Born in 1838, he began his military career in the imperial horse guards. In 1871, he was made *fligel-adjutant*, or aide-de-camp, to Alexander II, and eight years later, having risen to commander of the Horse Guards Artillery Regiment, was appointed major-general à la Suite.[10] His wife, Alexandra, "a tiny, ethereal looking old lady with enormous eyes and white hair," held the ranks of *starshaya dama* and *dame à portrait* in the Imperial Entourage.[11] The couple had two daughters: Eugenia, who married Vladimir Voyekov, the commandant of the Imperial Palaces; and Emma, who served as a *freilina* to both Marie Feodorovna and Alexandra Feodorovna.[12]

Nicholas and Alexandra were devoted to this slightly stooped figure, referring to him as "our old man," a kind of honorary grandfather. When he was unwell, Alexandra knitted little gifts and dispatched notes to his house.[13] Freedericksz, in turn, called the imperial couple *mes enfants*, a gesture of intimacy allowed no one else at court.[14]

Freedericksz held an unbelievable concentration of power. Not only minister of the imperial court, he also served as chief minister of the Emperor's Military Secretariat and of the Imperial Appanages Department, assisted in the latter role by Prince Victor Kochubey. Freedericksz was thus responsible for the finances of the imperial court and the emperor's personal wealth. He served as adjutant-general in the Imperial Suite, was a member of the State Council, and acted as chancellor of the Sovereign and Regal Orders of the Russian Empire.[15] Despite his knowledge and loyalty, Freedericksz was not immune from criticism. One contemporary alleged that he "takes very little active interest in his office," adding, "He is far too kindly and generous, and Court appointments are as plentiful as blackberries in autumn."[16]

Age gradually affected Freedericksz's ability to perform his job efficiently, but the imperial couple were too attached to the minister to replace him. Once, Prince Anatole Bariatinsky arrived to present a military award to Nicholas II. Freedericksz went off to announce him but "on his way from one room to the other, forgot what he was supposed to do, and wandered off, leaving the emperor to wait for the prince in one room and the prince to wait for the emperor in an adjoining room, both bewildered and angered at the delay." On another occasion, Freedericksz, in the midst of a state dinner, strode up to the emperor and, looking at him suspiciously, asked, "Did His Majesty invite you for dinner tonight?"[17] Nevertheless, Freedericksz was handsomely rewarded for his decades of service at the imperial court: in 1913, Nicholas II appointed him a count of the Russian empire.[18]

Count de Freedericksz presided over the Imperial Entourage—those members of the court who had direct access to the imperial family. Directly below him, the *ober-gofmarschal*, or grand marshal, was responsible for all questions of precedence and the routine operation of the court. He supervised the Household and the staff, invoiced groceries for the imperial table, distributed imperial warrants to favored shopkeepers, and coordinated all state visits, both to and by the sovereigns. He was also responsible for domestic arrangements at the court, including the supervision of palaces and entertaining.[19]

Nicholas inherited his first grand marshal of the imperial court, Count Konstantin Pahlen, from his father's Suite. Pahlen organized the first three major ceremonial events of Nicholas II's reign: the funeral of Alexander III, Nicholas's wedding to Princess Alix of Hesse, and the coronation in 1896. Like Vorontzov-Dashkov, Pahlen was incensed by the behavior of Grand Duke Serge Alexandrovich after the Khodynka disaster, and he tendered his resignation in protest.[20]

Prince Alexander Dolgoruky succeeded Pahlen; on his death in 1912, Count Paul von Benckendorff took the post.[21] Born in 1853, Benckendorff came from a family of Baltic courtiers. Educated in Paris, he returned to Russia and entered the elite Corps des Pages. Following his graduation, he joined the Horse Guards Regiment, saw action in the Russo-Turkish War, and rose to the rank of general in the Imperial Cavalry. At the end of the war, he was appointed an adjutant to Alexander II. After the emperor's assassination in 1881, he served Alexander III and Nicholas II, being promoted to the rank of general-adjutant in the Suite.[22]

Tall and broadly built, Benckendorff had a vast knowledge of his post, and his dedication made him a favorite of the imperial couple. The son of the imperial physician Eugene Botkin recalled, "He looked, with his aquiline nose, his gray side whiskers and his monocle, like some ancestral portrait suddenly come to life. He was not only loyal to the Emperor, but had a profound, and almost paternal affection for him. But he was free of every sort of servility, and personally, completely disinterested. Nobody, I believe, ever saw Benckendorff catering to anybody's whims, even those of his Sovereigns, or doing anything for the purpose of making his own position more secure. He was just himself, and people had to like him as he was or not at all. As a matter of fact, not many people did like him, interpreting his aloofness as a sign of conceit and haughtiness, but most people respected him."[23]

Assisting Benckendorff was his son-in-law Prince Vassili Dolgoruky, who, as *gof-marschal*, remained one of Nicholas II's few trusted intimates. Born in 1868, Dolgoruky was the son of Prince Alexander Dolgoruky, who had replaced Pahlen as grand marshal. Called "Valya" by the imperial couple, Vassili Dolgoruky graduated from the Corps des Pages in 1890 and entered the Horse Guards Regiment. Dolgoruky was a great favorite among his fellow courtiers, respected and well liked; Baroness Buxhoeveden recalled his "impassive face, which hid great depth of feeling."[24] Nicholas responded to his loyalty and in 1907 named him a *fligel-adjutant*. Seven years later, he was promoted to major-general à la Suite in 1914, at which time he joined the Imperial Suite as deputy marshal of the court.[25]

A third position, head of the Court Chancellery and director of the Emperor's Secretariat for Petitions, involved a more delicate balance. Until 1900, this was held by General Otto Richter, a Baltic aristocrat who had served as a companion to Alexander III when he was tsesarevich.[26] On his retirement, he was replaced by Lieutenant-General Alexander Mossolov, who came to the court from the Guards Regiments. The head of the Chancellery acted as general secretary to the court, receiving visitors and petitions, members of the imperial family, and government ministers. He was also responsible for court censorship and the enforcement of Russia's press laws when writing about the imperial family, no easy task in the reign of Nicholas II, with the numerous scandals of both his Romanov relations and of Rasputin. In this task, he was, ironically, assisted by Alexander Tanyeev, the sergeant of the Court Chancellery and the father of Anna Vyrubova, one of Rasputin's most ardent supporters.

The last of the four senior posts at court was *ober-tseremoniimeister*, or grand master of ceremonies, first held during Nicholas II's reign by Baron Paul von Korff and then by Count Vassili Hendrikov. Unlike some officials, Hendrikov was known for his jovial manner, which occasionally made him the unwitting butt of practical jokes. Shortly after her marriage to Grand Duke George Mikhailovich, Grand Duchess Marie Georgievna faced her first diplomatic *cercle*. Hendrikov had been dispatched to prepare her, but the grand duchess, accustomed to the formalities, feigned terror, warning the horrified count that she was too shy to endure the ordeal and "very likely to have a nervous breakdown and run away." Though the grand duchess enjoyed his "awful state of anxiety" as the event approached, on the appointed day she collapsed into laughter as Hendrikov looked on in surprise.[27]

In 1911, Count Alexei Ignatiev, who had previously served as one of fourteen masters of ceremony, succeeded Hendrikov. Even in the vastly diminished world of the imperial court under Nicholas II, Ignatiev's duties necessitated a large, capable staff. Prince Peter Kochubey acted as Ignatiev's vice-master of ceremonies; under him were Edvard Volkov, the chief master of ceremonies, and his assistant, Nicholas Rudmann. Nicholas Evreinov, as head of the Ceremonial Department, acted as a liaison between the grand master and the grand marshal.[28]

It was the grand master of ceremonies who actually planned and dictated the intricate balls and receptions, parades, and state occasions that distinguished the Russian court. His office overflowed with heavy leather volumes edged in gilt, detailing processions and precedence, seating charts for state dinners, and clothing regulations for appearance at court. Before important events, the grand master of ceremonies could be found wandering through the palace, measuring distances, marking out positions on the floor in faint chalk, and clambering over tables to adjust immense sprays of exotic, out-of-season flowers.[29]

Other positions in the Entourage included the *ober-gofmeister*, or grand master of the imperial court, a post held first by Prince Serge Gargarin and then by Prince Nicholas Repnin. The grand master coordinated official events with branches of the Ministry of the Court, complex demands supervised by George Alexeiev, who acted as honorary adviser to the grand master. Six assistant masters of the imperial court acted as adjuncts to the grand master, while the assistant of the imperial court, Lieutenant-General Prince Dimitri Golitsyn, worked as liaison between the Emperor's Suite and the office of the *ober-gofmeister*. The Entourage also included Lieutenant-General Artur von Grunwald, who held the post of *ober-shtalmeister*, or master of the imperial horse; the *ober-truchsess*, or palace steward, a position held in the reign of Nicholas II by Prince Odagevski and Alexander Bobrinsky; and the emperor's flag captain, Admiral Konstantin Nilov.[30]

The second group of officials under the minister of the imperial court was the Imperial Suite, divided into two classes. The first class consisted of 150 officers of the Suite, including 64 major-generals à la Suite and admirals of the Suite, and 56 *fligel-adjutants*, who served as aides-de-camp; while the second class encompassed lieutenant-generals and generals, including 73 who served as adjutants-in-ordinary, and 76 with the rank of adjutants-extraordinary, who served as equerries and worked on twenty-four-hour, rotating shifts, accompanying the emperor throughout his day.[31]

The first class of officials also included fifteen diverse offices, including the *ober kamerger*, or grand chamberlain, a post held in Nicholas II's reign by P. N. Kripensky and Count Konstantin Pahlen; the master of the Imperial Hunt; the commander of the Imperial Apartment, Nicholas Evreinov; N. N. Novosselsky, the chief of Court Manufacturers and Imperial Warrants; the *ober-fonschneider*, whose sole duty was to wait on the emperor during his coronation banquet; and the *ober-Shenk*, or grand cup bearer. The second class encompassed 134 positions entailing actual service and 86 honorary posts, including the assistants of the imperial court; the grand esquire trenchant; the *gof-marschals*, or imperial marshals; Vladimir Teliakovsky, the director of the imperial theaters; Prince Serge Trubetskoy, Ivan Vsevolozsky, and Count Dimitri Golitsyn, who successively served as directors of the Imperial Hermitage Museum; Grand Duke George Mikhailovich, the director of the Alexander III Museum of Russian Art; Grand Duchess Marie Pavlovna, the director of the Imperial Academy of Fine Arts; A. A. Bobrinsky, the director of the Archaeological Institution; Vassili Scheglov, the director of His Majesty's Own Library; Alexander D. Sheremetiev, the chief of the Court Orchestra and Choir; Karl Stackelberg, the director of the Imperial Orchestra; and the *tseremoniimeisters*, or 28 lesser masters of ceremony.[32] There were 287 *kamerherren*, or chamberlains; 309 *ober-kamerjunkers*, or chief gentlemen-in-waiting; 3 harbingers; 5 *ober-truchsesses*, or chief stewards; 103 additional stewards; 6 chief *chasseurs*; 20 secondary *chasseurs*; 45 *kamer-fourriers*, equerries-in-waiting; and 40 *kamerjunkers*, or gentlemen-of-the-imperial-bedchamber.[33]

Twenty-two ecclesiastics were posted to the second class of officials.[34] They included the adviser to the imperial court, Proto-Presbyter Father Ioann Yanishev; the personal confessor to the imperial family, Proto-Presbyter Father Petrovich; and the emperor's personal confessor, Proto-Presbyter Father Alexander Vassiliev. Also attached to the Imperial Suite was the ecclesiastical staff at the Feodorovsky Cathedral at Tsarskoye Selo where the imperial family often worshipped, including Proto-Presbyter Father Afanasy Belyaev and Colonel Dimitri Loman, the church warden.[35] Vassiliev was a particular favorite at court, for he had a comforting manner of responding to confessions. Regardless of what the penitent might say, Vassiliev always assured them with a smile. "Don't worry, don't worry," he would say. "The Devil does none of these things. He neither smokes nor drinks nor engages in revelry, and yet he is the Devil."[36]

The second class of officials also included 38 physicians.[37] There were 8 physicians-in-waiting to the imperial family, 4 personal physicians-in-ordinary, two dentists, two honorary surgeons-in-ordinary and two honorary surgeons, and four pediatricians-in-ordinary.[38] All were subject to the rigid, formal etiquette of the imperial court. "I shall never forget," recalled Prince Christopher of Greece, "seeing the American dentist working busily at Olga's mouth with his tail coat carefully pinned back, his sleeves tucked over his wrists, and an imposing row of orders glistening on his breast."[39]

Of these physicians, the most respected was Dr. Eugene Sergeievich Botkin, appointed personal physician-in-ordinary in 1908. Botkin was one of the few members of the Imperial Suite who was conversant in a number of languages. He was proficient in German and often spoke to the empress in her native tongue. Equally adept at English and French, he occasionally acted as her translator when she had to receive Russian delegations by herself.[40] The imperial family relied heavily on Botkin, and he was a favorite among the children. "Your brother is a true friend to me," Nicholas once said to Peter Botkin, "we take everything to heart, and we feel comfortable describing our maladies to him."[41] Habitually attired in an immaculate waistcoat, jacket, trousers, stiff-shirt, and tie, Botkin wore a gold-rimmed pince-nez perched midway down his nose. His one indulgence was scent: the grand duchesses used to tease him by chasing him round the palace, sniffing the air to follow his trail.[42]

The composition of the Imperial Entourage and Suite reflected the privileged position of Russian aristocrats at the beginning of the twentieth century. Fifteen members of the imperial family held court positions, along with 17 princes of the imperial blood; 17 counts; 9 barons; and 111 other nobles.[43] Only the well-born and well-connected could ever hope to attain a position in the Entourage, such was the stratification of Peter the Great's Table of Ranks, first established in 1722. The only exceptions to this rule were the Military Retinue, which included officers still on active duty seconded to the court, and whose salaries were paid by the Imperial Army and Navy, and members of the second class of officials in the Suite. Not surprisingly, the court thrived on gossip and intrigue. Eugene Botkin, exasperated by the poisonous atmosphere, once declared, "You would need to have a mind as perverted as theirs and a disordered soul to defeat all of their unbelievable plots."[44]

The empress maintained her own Suite, numbering well over six hundred. At its head stood Count Peter Apraxine, the *ober-gofmeister*, or master of the empress's court, from 1913 to the Revolution. Apraxine worked closely with

Count Ivan Rostovtsov, the chief of Her Majesty's Chancellery and the private secretary to the empress, who also acted as chief of the Secretariat for the Imperial Children. Count Vassili Hendrikov held the post of general-adjutant to the empress, assisted by Baron Feodor Meyendorff and Admiral Konstantin Pilkin.[45]

Sixty-six of the 240 ladies in the Empress's Suite held the rank of *kaval'er-dama* and the Order of St. Catherine. The most powerful was the *ober-gofmeisterina starshaya dama*, the empress's mistress of the robes, and the senior lady-in-waiting, held for most of Nicholas II's reign by Princess Marie Golitsyn. Appointed by Alexandra's mother-in-law, the princess, noted one critic, was "ambitious, intriguing, and unsparing in her criticisms." She "acted as if it was beneath her to show kindness to those persons with whom she came into contact, and did what she could to accentuate the cold way in which Society was held at a distance by the Empress."[46] The princess freely shared her strong opinions with the young empress, "brusque" advice, as Grand Duchess Olga Alexandrovna remembered, which Alexandra perceived as criticism from the emperor's mother.[47]

Only on Golitsyn's death in 1909 did Alexandra finally offer the position to a lady of her own choice, Princess Elizabeth Naryshkin Kuryakin.[48] Born in 1840, the princess, known as "Zizi," had previously served as *starshaya dama* to Empress Marie Feodorovna. During her tenure at the imperial court, she was made a *kaval'er-dama*, or dame of the Order of St. Catherine, an honor reserved for the most distinguished women in service. While serving as *ober-gofmeisterina* to Alexandra, she directed a number of charitable institutions devoted to the relief of former convicts and exiles.[49] Somewhat short and plump, as Buxhoeveden remembered, she had "strongly marked features" and "shrewd eyes" that took in "everything."[50]

The mistress of the robes acted as an intermediary between the empress and her Suite, supervised and trained the ladies-in-waiting, and delegated their appointments. She attended all official and state functions, personally presented the most important diplomats and guests on such occasions to the empress, and served as the emperor's official hostess in his wife's absence from ordinary luncheons and dinners. On important ceremonial occasions, she immediately followed the empress in procession. She also kept the roster of the Empress's Suite. This included the *starshiye dami*, or ladies-in-waiting of the highest rank; the *dames à portrait*; the *kamer-freilini*, or personal ladies-in-waiting; the *starshiye freilini*, or ordinary ladies-in-waiting; the *kaval'er-dami*, or dames of the Order of St. Catherine; and the *freilini*, or maids of honor.[51]

Anna Vyrubova, in her Russian court
gown as a *freilina* to Empress
Alexandra, about 1907

The *kamer-freilini* worked on a rotating basis, spending two weeks on duty, with four weeks off. They alternated holidays and vacations with other women.[52] On public occasions, at least one attended the empress, holding flowers, handing her speeches, acting as escort, and smoothing over any problems. At these appearances, each wore a *chiffre* with the empress's initials set below a golden crown studded with diamonds, against the blue sash of the Order of St. Andrei. Ladies-in-waiting were well trained: they never intruded, always walked several steps behind the empress, and rarely spoke. At the palace, they routinely dealt with correspondence, answering the numerous requests that came to the empress, and arranged ordinary requests for audiences.[53] Baroness Buxhoeveden remembered being told on her appointment that she "had to avoid anything like conversations on political subjects"; as a result, she said, "I knew nothing of what was said outside the press." Ladies-in-waiting were forbidden to ever be seen on public transport; they were provided with court carriages or motorcars. Nor could a member of the Empress's Suite ever venture into a restaurant, a café, or a nightclub, or attend any dinner or reception without the written consent of the mistress of the robes.[54]

Alexandra had numerous ladies-in-waiting, among them Baroness Sophie Buxhoeveden. Born in 1884, she became a *kamer-freilina* in 1913, at the age of twenty-nine.[55] As one of the youngest women at court, she often accompanied the grand duchesses on their official engagements, taking the place of their frequently ill mother. The girls, especially Olga and Tatiana, looked on her as their confidante, calling her "Isa" and bestowing on her the friendship their mother prevented with girls their own age. Another trusted *kamer-freilina*, Countess Anastasia Hendrikov, was the daughter of Prince Vassili Hendrikov, who served as master of ceremonies under Alexander II and Alexander III. Like Buxhoeveden, she was quite close to the elder grand duchesses, who called her "Nastinka." Buxhoeveden remembered her as "a lovely creature, whose moral personality was in keeping with her looks," and Olga Voronoff recalled that "she was heart and soul devoted to the Empress."[56]

There were a number of *freilini*, maids of honor to Her Majesty.[57] Of these women, undoubtedly the most famous was Anna Vyrubova, who became the empress's most trusted confidante. She was the daughter of Alexander Tanyeev, a secretary of state and a sergeant of the Emperor's Chancellery. Her family had served at court for decades, and her mother was a Tolstoy.[58] In 1903, she was appointed a *freilina* to the empress, who arranged her marriage to Alexander Vyrubov, a young naval officer, in 1907. The marriage quickly failed, as Anna was unwilling to abandon her long hours spent with the imperial family, or even allow her new husband to share her bed. When Vyrubov complained that his wife was neglecting him, she fled to the house of her parents and spread rumors that her husband "had lost his reason in consequence of his excitement at the battle of Tsushima."[59]

Anna successfully played on the empress's feelings of guilt, and soon a court official informed Vyrubov that Alexandra wished him to grant his wife a divorce. The young lieutenant, recalled Princess Naryshkin-Kuryakin, "was very much grieved; in fact, he wept, but gradually began to realize that a happy life with Anna had become impossible." He eventually married again and fathered two children.[60] Anna used the situation to ingratiate herself into the very center of the imperial family. She had "the mind of a child," claimed Pierre Gilliard, "and her unhappy experiences had sharpened her sensibilities without maturing her judgment. Lacking in intellect and discrimination, she was the prey of her impulses."[61]

In time, Anna was condemned for her role as intermediary between the empress and Rasputin, arranging meetings at her little house on the corner of Srednaya and Zerkovnaya Streets in Tsarskoye Selo. Grand Duchess Olga Alexandrovna deemed her "utterly irresponsible, childish to the point of silliness, and much addicted to hysterical outbursts."[62] Countess Nostitz wrote of her "sweet, fresh face" but complained that her full figure and lack of grace made her unattractive to men. "Her only evening gown," she recorded, "was a tomato red plush, in which she looked like an armchair."[63] Those closest to the court willingly believed the worst of her. Gleb Botkin thought she was an exhibitionist, writing that she insisted on taking off all of her clothes just to have her throat examined. He also repeated a bit of salacious gossip concerning Anna's behavior in the Crimea. According to Botkin, her room was opposite the sentry post, and the soldiers "complained officially to their officers of the anguish she caused them by constantly appearing at her window in a state of nudity."[64] It was even hinted among aristocratic St. Petersburg that the empress and Anna were lovers.[65]

Mademoiselle Catherine Schneider served as the empress's lectrice. A niece of the former imperial physician Dr. Hirsch, she was born in 1856 into a Baltic family. Anna Vyrubova called her "a rather difficult person in some ways, taking every advantage of her privileged position, but she was undeniably valuable and was heart and soul in her devotion to the family."[66] Called "Trina" by Alexandra, Mademoiselle Schneider not only read to the empress, but also sought out the newest books of interest from London, Berlin, and Paris. She shared the empress's strict morality, once forbidding the grand duchesses from staging a play that contained the word *stockings*.[67]

Positions in Alexandra's Suite were filled according to rank, either that of the husband or of the father. The lowest, largest rank was that of *freilina*, or maid-of-honor in ordinary attendance, given to highly born, unmarried young women. "This title," recalled Olga Voronoff, "carried with it no duties except those of attendance twice a year if there were official receptions."[68] The rank of maid of honor allowed the young women to wear the empress's *chiffre* on their bodices at court functions. Above them were the *kamer-freilini*. The highest rank in the Suite were the *dames à portrait*, reserved for married women of many years' service, whose position was distinguished by the Empress's Personal Order, a small oval portrait of Alexandra painted on ivory, surrounded by diamonds, and hung upon a blue moiré bow.

Against the entourages and the suites, one group stood apart: the imperial security forces. Guarding the imperial family was the escort, with soldiers drawn from both the guards' regiments and the Cossack *Konvoi* Regiment. Members of the imperial guard were stationed at careful intervals round the railings of the Imperial Park, supplemented by a garrison of some five thousand infantrymen attached to the emperor and empress's residence at Tsarskoye Selo. Each weekend, a different military attaché did duty at court, serving as security liaison between the commander of the palace and the security staff.[69] Sentries on duty within the palace worked twenty-four-hour shifts; each was given an armchair, and, in quiet hours, was allowed to undo the chin-strap on his helmet and take off one of his white gloves.[70]

Security at the imperial court was tight, an ever-present reminder of the uncertainty surrounding the lives of Russia's rulers. More than 250 plainclothes police agents were assigned to the palace commandant.[71] Each soldier, guard, and police agent on duty kept a small notebook, in which comings and goings of all to the palace were recorded. Each time a visitor arrived at the Alexander Palace, a telephone call alerted the commandant. The same degree of security extended to the imperial family. When the empress ordered a carriage for an afternoon drive, the footman to whom the request was conveyed immediately alerted the nearest police agent, who telephoned the palace commandant, who himself rang the Imperial Stables and the office of the Military Secretariat to organize security. From the moment the empress entered her carriage at the doors of the palace until she returned, she journeyed under dozens of watchful eyes. At the rear of her carriage stood Nicholas Pustnikov, Alexandra's *kamer*-Cossack, attired in a dark green coat, a black fur hat, and black boots, and the entire route was lined with security agents.[72]

Plainclothes agents and members of the Emperor's Personal Security Service stood stiffly on street corners, notebooks in hand, ready to jot down the slightest incident, while, behind bushes and trees, dozens more agents lay in hiding, to observe and to protect the empress from any harm. If Alexandra asked the coachman to stop so that she might speak to someone on the way, as soon as her carriage rolled out of sight, a policeman approached the individual, notebook ready, and inquired, "What is your name and for what reason had you conversation with Her Imperial Majesty?"[73] The Romanovs were unable to escape this obtrusive surveillance, and they were constantly shadowed, even during simple strolls in the park. Nicholas despised these men, referring to them contemptuously as "nature lovers" after the obvious manner in which, on sighting a member of the imperial family, they suddenly began to study the surrounding trees or sky.[74]

Responsibility for this security was divided between three separate posts. First there was the commander of the palace and head of the court police, a position held by Generals Trepov, Diedulin, and Hesse; Prince Paul Engalychev; and, from 1913 on, by Major-General Vladimir Voyekov. A tall, prematurely balding man with large ears and a "stiff, pomaded mustache," Voyekov was born in 1868 and, after graduating from the elite Corps des Pages, was promoted first to the Chevalier Guards, rising to the rank of colonel, then to the Hussar Life Guards Regiment, which he commanded from 1907 to 1913.[75] Voyekov married Eugenia de Freedericksz, the daughter of the minister of the court, and worked closely with his father-in-law on official matters.[76] Alexei Ignatiev called him "an intriguer and personally a most uncongenial colleague, but he instilled in us a mighty respect for his business ability. . . . The outstanding characteristic of this disagreeable little man was stinginess, which reached such heights that despite his enormous fortune he would contrive to tailor his service uniform coat himself, re-cutting and re-dying his own clothes."[77]

The commander of the palace controlled His Majesty's Premier Personal Escort. Founded in 1811 by Emperor Alexander I, His Majesty's Premier Personal Escort was commonly known as the Cossack Konvoi Regiment, owing to its composition. In 1890, the Caucasian Squadron was formally dissolved and replaced by the Kuban and the Terek Cossack Regiments, which, in 1906, were established as His Majesty's Premier Personal Escort.[78] They stood out from other members of the imperial guards, being dressed in scarlet Circassian coats or traditional black Caucasian cloaks and *papakhii*, distinctive tall lambskin hats.[79] From 1908 to 1914, the Konvoi regiment was commanded by Prince Yuri Trubetskoy, a former colonel in the Garde à Cheval Regiment.[80] In 1914, Trubetskoy was replaced by General Count Alexander Grabbe. Born in 1864, Grabbe was educated at the Corps des Pages and was one of the young men selected to serve as a dancing and skating partner to the future Empress Alexandra during her visit to St. Petersburg in the winter of 1889.[81]

The Cossack Konvoi Regiment was reinforced by members of His Majesty's Combined Regiment, consisting of four battalions of infantry and cavalry guards totaling some five thousand soldiers. This division had been formed by Alexander III after his father's death, in an effort to ensure the safety of both himself and his family, and was led by the *dezhurnyi* general, or general on constant duty, a post held for most of Nicholas II's reign by Alexei Ressin.[82] These men also did sentry duty and were stationed at interior posts in the imperial palaces. Unlike His Majesty's Premier Personal Escort, those who served in the Combined Regiment were specially recruited from both the officer and the enlisted classes and represented those units of the imperial guard that had a member of the imperial family as honorary colonel in chief.[83]

Finally, Voyekov had under his general charge His Majesty's Railway Regiment, consisting of two battalions with a total of one thousand soldiers. Commanded by General Labl, the Railway Regiment was responsible for imperial journeys within the empire. Before any journey, its members personally inspected the imperial train and traveled the length of the intended route in an effort to prevent any accidents or terrorist attacks. As commander, General Labl always traveled with the imperial party to supervise security.[84]

These imperial regiments supplied visible and ceremonial security at court, but real responsibility for the Romanovs' personal protection fell to His Majesty's Military Secretariat, which controlled two independent divisions. The first of these was the Imperial Police Force, commanded by General Gherardii, with a total of 250 soldiers. The final division was the emperor's personal security force, created in 1906 and commanded by General Alexander Spiridovich, a tall, dashing man with a jaunty little mustache. Spiridovich had general charge of some 300 officers and was responsible for security beyond the imperial palaces. Thus, Spiridovich traveled with the imperial family on every railway journey, every cruise on their yachts, and every foreign visit. Spiridovich was constantly briefed by officials of the Okhrana, the Emperor's secret police, to help him in his task.[85]

Supervising everyone was the chief of the Military Field Chancellery, a post occupied for most of Nicholas II's reign by General Prince Vladimir Orlov. Born in 1868, Orlov was promoted to the Horse Guards Regiment following his graduation from the Corps des Pages in 1889, and he came to know the young Tsesarevich Nicholas during his tenure at Krasnoye Selo. In 1901, Nicholas appointed his friend assistant commander of the Military Field Chancellery; five years later, he named Orlov as its head.[86] Orlov, a man of culture and sophistication, was a personal favorite of the emperor. His immense girth earned him the nickname "Fat Orlov." He was so large that when he sat down, he could not see his own knees.[87] No horse could hold him: at imperial parades and reviews, as the emperor and his suite rode on horseback, Orlov ran alongside, panting desperately for breath.[88] His wife, Princess Olga, who served as one of Alexandra's *starshiye freilini*, was, by contrast, exceptionally tall and thin, remembered by one young lady as "the most elegant woman in Petersburg."[89] When the curious pair appeared together at court balls, wags remarked, "Behold the Prince and the Princess Orlov, in flesh and bone."[90] Orlov eventually fell out of favor, owing to his opposition to Rasputin.[91]

The rewards for these courtiers often came in the form of orders and medals awarded by the emperor as marks of special favor. While the ultimate authority of imperial orders and awards was the emperor himself, the actual power rested with Count Vladimir de Freedericksz, who served as chancellor of the Russian Imperial Orders. He advised on recommendations for various awards and organized the annual order celebrations, marked with religious services and banquets. Gentlemen awarded the various imperial orders were known as kavaliers, or knights, and were obligated, by tradition, not only to attend the annual festivities related to their particular order, but also to participate in certain state occasions. *Kavaliers* were required to participate in the most important state occasions, including coronations, weddings, and funerals, as well as ordinary imperial public processions and the Nicholas Ball, the first and largest imperial ball of each season.[92]

Peter the Great created the first Russian order, of St. Andrei, in 1699. The emperor, as chief of the order, bestowed it on members of the imperial family, foreign heads of state, diplomats, and officials. The Order of St. Alexander Nevsky, initially created as a military award, was later given for both distinguished military and state service. Catherine the Great added the Order of St. George in 1769. The highest level, restricted to twenty-five living individuals at any one time, was awarded for outstanding military bravery. Supplementing the Order of St. George was the Cross of St. George, designed for ordinary soldiers and noncommissioned officers. The Order of St. Vladimir was awarded for military bravery or for thirty-five years of distinguished civil service. There were two Polish orders, added after the 1831 annexation of the former independent kingdom: the Order of the White Eagle marked state or military service, while that of St. Stanislav awarded outstanding accomplishments. For women, there were also marks of imperial favor. The oldest was the Order of St. Catherine, established by Peter the Great in honor of his second wife, Catherine I, and reserved for women of the imperial family and their ladies-in-waiting. The other feminine order was that of St. Anna, introduced by Paul I but originally founded by the emperor's grandfather Karl-Friedrich of Schleswig-Holstein. Although mainly reserved for women, it was also awarded to distinguished men at court.[93]

As the empire moved closer to destruction, these courtiers "slumbered peacefully on the brink of an abyss," in the words of Dr. Eugene Botkin's son Gleb, "lulled by the sweet songs of the be-whiskered sirens who gently hummed *God Save the Tsar*, attended church with great regularity . . . and from time to time asked discreetly when they were going to receive their next grand cordon or advance in rank or raise in salary."[94]

6

BELOW STAIRS
AT THE PALACE

SERVANTS FORMED A PART of the ordinary life of the imperial family. A small army took care of the Romanovs, and the number of servants required at the Russian court was staggering. In the Winter Palace alone, just over a thousand were in constant attendance; when the emperor and empress were in actual residence, up to six thousand might be in service.[1]

The Alexander Palace at Tsarskoye Selo, where the imperial family spent most of the year, was like a well-run ship, and a thousand servants were required to maintain a constant state of perfection.[2] Throughout the day, servants filled the corridors, from the impressively attired *skorokhodi*, or court runners, to liveried footmen and discreet maids. There were hundreds of coachmen, chauffeurs, and stable boys; kennel boys and veterinarians; mechanics and artisans employed in the palace workshop; gardeners and florists; cooks, assistant cooks, pastry chefs, and wine stewards; telephone operators; and, under Nicholas II, several personal photographers and film developers.[3]

Many of those employed by the imperial court had come into service through family connections, as descendants of earlier employees. Most male servants were drawn from the military, thus were considered fit for imperial duty after years of unquestioning allegiance. There was glamour in working at the Russian court, no matter how menial the job, and many servants enjoyed a close proximity to, though not familiarity with, the imperial family. Their wages were minimal, but meals and accommodation, along with liveries and uniforms, were often included. In addition, service jobs at court often meant free education for a servant's children, regular imperial gifts at Easter and Christmas, and a guaranteed pension on retirement. All grand dukes and duchesses maintained their own suites and households. Grand Duke Nicholas Mikhailovich, the wealthiest member of the dynasty next to the emperor, kept some four hundred servants in St. Petersburg alone.[4] Grand Duchess Olga Alexandrovna recalled, "I had a staff of nearly seventy in St. Petersburg, and that was considered quite a modest establishment for the Emperor's sister, and all of them had so many children, and all of them wanted their sons to be trained as doctors and engineers. So you can imagine that the expense was enormous."[5]

Each morning, as dawn broke over the sleepy village of Tsarskoye Selo, rows of windows in the Alexander Palace slowly filled with light, as maids, stewards, footmen, valets, and pages readied for their long days. At eight, one of Nicholas's *kamer-diners*, or valets, gently rapped on the door of the imperial bedroom, waking the emperor. Alexandra rarely rose at this early hour, and Nicholas, in his monogrammed nightshirt and a dressing gown, quietly crept across the corridor to his dressing room. A footman delivered the emperor's morning coffee or tea, and while Nicholas ate a simple breakfast, one of his valets drew his bath.[6]

While the emperor bathed, the *kamer-diner* on duty retrieved the clothing chosen for the day.[7] These men kept the emperor's wardrobe, selecting his clothes according to rules laid down in heavy, gilt-edged volumes that detailed the decorations and orders to be worn with various uniforms and sashes. Nicholas ordinarily wore a uniform. Like his father, he was extremely frugal and wore his trousers and shirts until they had bare patches. Firms in St. Petersburg, including Nordenstrem on the Nevsky Prospekt, tailored his military uniforms. His naval uniforms were usually provided by the firm of Henry, run by Henry Fallenweider from his shop at No. 18 Bolshaya Morskaya; alterations to other uniforms were occasionally undertaken by tailors attached to regiments posted at Tsarskoye Selo. Generally, court purveyors who supplied specific items of clothing or accessories also cleaned or mended them when necessary; thus gloves purchased from the firm of Morrison were also sent to this firm to be cleaned.[8]

When Nicholas finished his bath, he was shaved and his beard was trimmed; twice a month, his hair was cut. Nicholas did not always keep a barber on staff, and these duties were filled by one of his valets or by a man sent from the firm of Maulle G. Clara, Coiffeur et Fournisseur, in St. Petersburg.[9] After dressing, Nicholas went directly to his private study. The emperor's chief *fligel-adjutant*,

P. A. Basilievsky, or one of his assistants, presented him with the morning newspapers, and he settled down to the day's business. Ministers were received on alternate days, papers read through and initialed, and correspondence dealt with. The emperor was unique among European monarchs in that he had no private secretary. "He was so jealous of his prerogatives," wrote Alexander Mossolov, "that he himself sealed the envelopes containing his decisions. He had to be very busy before he would entrust his valet with this relatively trivial task. And the valet had to show the sealed envelope so that his master could satisfy himself that the secrecy of his correspondence had not been violated."[10]

The empress also maintained a Personal Household of private staff and servants. The *gof-meisterina*, or woman in charge of Alexandra's Household, Madame Geringer, attended to the empress's personal or business needs. She was also responsible for the selection of gifts distributed in the empress's name to members of her Household at Christmas, at Easter, and on their name days. Alexandra was particular about the characters of her Personal Household. She kept them separate from other servants, housing them in small rooms on the upper floor. All shared a single bathroom, following an intricate schedule that dictated who had first right to its use and for what duration. Their uniforms were worn over corsets; Alexandra insisted that it was improper to forgo this convention, though the constriction it brought often made daily work difficult and painful as tightly bound girls scrubbed floors and engaged in their round of duties. Alexandra initially asked her maids to wear starched white aprons and caps with their black dresses, but the women found this outfit too uncomfortable, and, after many protests, the empress allowed them to simply wear the dresses, with white ribbons in their hair.[11]

The most senior servant in the Empress's Personal Household, Madeleine Zanotti, held the title of *ober-kamer-jungferi*, or chief of the young ladies of the chamber, a post equivalent to that of first lady's maid. Of Italian and English ancestry, Zanotti had grown up in England and had worked for Alexandra before her marriage.[12] With Alexandra, Zanotti always spoke English. Anna Vyrubova remembered her as "very clever, and as usual with one in her position, inclined to be tyrannical."[13]

Zanotti had overall charge of the empress's wardrobe and jewelry; under her were eight other *kamer-jungferi*. Her chief assistant, Marie Tutelberg, was born in 1863 in the Baltic Provinces. Known as "Tudels," she was a dedicated servant, though Anna Vyrubova recalled that she and Zanotti were "mortal enemies."[14] As she grew older, Tutelberg became forgetful. "Tudels is such a bore!"

Alexandra once complained to Nicholas. "Never remembers anything, asks hundreds of times the same thing."[15] As much as she grumbled, though, Alexandra was devoted to her household, and she never gave any thought to asking Tutelberg to leave her post. Elizabeth Ersberg joined Alexandra's household in 1900 at the age of eighteen. Her father had served as a palace stoker under Alexander III, working at the Anichkov and the Winter Palaces in St. Petersburg and at the country estate of Gatchina. He was among those traveling with the imperial family aboard the imperial train in 1888 when it crashed near Borki, and Nicholas Ersberg succumbed within a year from his injuries. After his death, his daughter Elizabeth became an unofficial ward of Empress Marie Feodorovna, who guaranteed her education and gave her a position as a *komnatnaya devyushka*, the rough equivalent of a parlor maid. At the court of Nicholas II, she rose to the rank of third *kamer-jungferi*.[16]

At nine each morning, the *kamer-jungferi* on duty woke Alexandra, bringing a protein drink blended from cream and egg yolks, before disappearing into the adjoining dressing room, where the empress had left her clothes from the previous evening.[17] These were collected and taken to the laundry or the wardrobe room, and then a bath was drawn for the empress. Alexandra, crippled with shyness, maintained a deliberate distance between herself and her maids. None were allowed to become familiar, and their duties were restricted by the empress's modesty. She never allowed her maids to attend her when she undressed or was in her bath; they only saw her after she had dressed and slipped on a Japanese kimono to have her hair arranged around the pads deemed necessary to achieve the correct shape.[18] The *kamer-jungferi* cared for Alexandra's clothes, which were held in wardrobe rooms on the mezzanine floor and kept fresh with sachets of violet. They worked with a retinue of *kamer-frauen*, young women who served as wardrobe maids and kept books that catalogued every article of clothing in detail.

Alexandra's Personal Household also included three *kamer-diners*, who served mainly in honorary positions, having little responsibility.[19] Her principal *kamer-diner*, Alexei Volkov, had been born in 1859, the son of a peasant family from Tambov Province. At the age of sixteen, he joined the Pavlovsky Life Guards Regiment where he met Grand Duke Paul Alexandrovich, Nicholas II's uncle, who hired him as his batsman. In the aftermath of the grand duke's morganatic marriage in 1902, the emperor gave Volkov a position in his own Household. After a few years, however, he took over as the empress's *ober-kamer-diner*.[20]

Madame Geringer supervised the female servants at the palace. Only unmarried women were hired for such general positions as second and third *komnatniye devyushki*, linen maids, and the *kamer-frauen*. If they married during their employment, they were expected to resign. Older women, hired for more responsible positions, were always accorded the courtesy title of "Madame," whether they were married or not. There were three *komnatniye devyushki* specifically attached to the Empress's Personal Household, all Russian and, unlike the *kamer-jungferi*, all required to wear the regulation black dresses, white aprons, and white caps.[21] They were charged with the daily cleaning and maintenance of the private apartments and the rooms of the imperial children on the floor above.[22]

Perhaps the most notable, owing to her eventual fate alongside the imperial family at the hands of a Bolshevik firing squad, was Anna Demidova. Born in 1878, Demidova was a tall, statuesque woman, with light blond hair and blue eyes. She became friendly with Elizabeth Ersberg, who held the position of third *kamer-jungferi* at the imperial court, in the years surrounding the 1905 Revolution. After some enquiries, the latter was able to secure her friend a position at court as a *komnatnaya devyushka*. The pair became inseparable, and Demidova fell in love with Ersberg's brother Nicholas, an official for the State Railway Inspection Board. At one point, they were engaged, but, for unknown reasons, the proposed marriage dissolved.[23] Later, Demidova became enamored of Charles Sydney Gibbes, the young English tutor to the imperial children; the homosexual Gibbes, however, seemed to take no notice. He once described her as "of a singularly timid and shrinking disposition."[24]

Although Nicholas and Alexandra preferred to remain cloistered in the Alexander Palace at Tsarskoye Selo for most of each year after 1905, they could not abandon all of the requisite duties that accompanied their privileged positions. Visitors to the Alexander Palace were dazzled by the opulent interiors and the varied display of costumes as they were led from hall to hall. "Resplendent in snow white gaiters, the footmen ran before us up the carpeted staircases. We passed through drawing rooms, ante rooms, banqueting rooms, passing from carpets to glittering parquet, then back to carpets. . . . At every door stood lackeys, petrified in pairs in most varied costumes, according to the room to which they were attached: now the traditional black frock coats, now the Polish surcoats, with red shoes and white stockings and gaiters."[25]

Footmen took guests through the labyrinth of passages in the palace, to one of several visitors' suites in the western wing. If a guest had not brought a valet or a lady's maid, palace servants would be assigned to him or her for the duration of the stay. These servants unpacked the luggage and took away whatever needed to be pressed, after they announced the day's schedule. Visitors were briefed on court protocol. No one ever sat or smoked in the imperial presence unless invited to do so; no one spoke to a member of the imperial family without first being addressed; and it was anathema to ever contradict a member of the imperial family. To both Nicholas and Alexandra, etiquette upheld the prestige of the dynasty; lapses, therefore, were always treated as marks of disrespect, not only against their persons, but against the throne as well. This careful etiquette worked both ways. Members of the imperial family were known for their elegant manners and exceptional politeness. Nicholas was an expert at making his guests feel at ease. Within the Romanov family itself, the emperor and the empress were always treated with the deference due their positions. The emperor's own sisters and children invariably curtsied to him, and no one thought it odd for an elderly aunt to sink to the floor before one of the young grand duchesses.

As the morning wore on, waves of maids spread through the palace. Cedar-lined rooms on the mezzanine held the imperial linen collection, presided over by a contingent of *ober-beschliesserin* or upper linen servants. They dispersed freshly laundered sheets, pillowslips, tablecloths, and bath towels to the *komnatniye devyushki* from the thousands of pieces in the imperial collection. Several of the *kamer-frauen* were employed simply to make repairs and embroider these linens with the imperial monogram.[26] As soon as bedrooms were vacant, the *komnatniye devyushki* went to work. All of the beds, remembered Baroness Buxhoeveden, were equipped with "thick cerise satin quilts still bearing large monograms of Catherine II. They were stone hard and slid off the bed all of a sudden whenever one turned."[27] Beds were stripped, linens collected, mattresses turned, fresh sheets tucked in, pillows encased in crisp slips, blankets spread, and eiderdowns folded on the end of the bed.

Used linens, not only from bedrooms but from bathrooms, pantries, larders, the kitchen, and servants' rooms, were bundled by the *beschliesserin* into cloth sacks—each one labeled according to its contents—and placed in large wicker baskets in the laundry room, which was tucked into a basement room in the far corner of the palace. Clothing was also collected and divided: servants' uniforms, along with most of the everyday linens, were sent to the main imperial laundry at Anichkov Palace in St. Petersburg; clothing belonging to the imperial family was normally laundered within the palace itself.[28] Clothing, once returned to the palace, was taken from its tissue paper wrapping, smoothed and ironed, then hung or rewrapped before being taken to its owner. Goffering irons were used on petticoats and frilled dresses, to reset their fine pleats.

Throughout the morning, dressing rooms and bathrooms were cleaned and scrubbed, flower arrangements replaced with bouquets sent from the palace's florist's shop, writing paper stocked, and letters collected for posting. Tables, desks, and chests were dusted, looking glasses polished, floors swept, and curtains and carpets vacuumed and brushed. Drinks trays, with small crystal decanters, were replenished, as were cut-crystal bowls holding sweets or biscuits. "The sweets were varied," remembered Queen Marie of Romania, "and nowhere else in the wide world were they as good. Long-shaped fruit drops wrapped on white paper with little fringed edges of blue, red, or yellow, according to the sweet inside. Flat, cream caramels, too luscious for words, these also wrapped in thick white paper, double fondants of coffee, and also those little paper baskets of fresh strawberry sweets."[29]

While the housemaids were busy with their duties, male servants were also at work. Windows were washed; floors in the state apartments polished; chandeliers cleaned, dusted, and checked for burned-out lightbulbs or candles; and a hundred clocks wound. If any of the priceless paintings, sculptures, tapestries, carpets, ornaments, or pieces of furniture needed attention, they were removed to the palace workshops where skilled artisans carried out the necessary repairs.

Aside from the imperial couple's Personal Households, the only other members of the Household to enjoy intimate contact with the imperial family were the children's attendants: nurses, governesses, tutors, and bodyguards. These men and women held a special position within the court, as they were considered neither members of the Entourage and the Suite nor servants in the Imperial Household. Although Empress Alexandra nursed her children, she had also employed three wet nurses to assist her.[30] Until her death in 1906, the most influential of these attendants was Mrs. Mary Anne Orchard, who, having served as Alexandra's nanny, had come to Russia to assist her former charge.

These nannies were expected to maintain Empress Alexandra's prim Victorian standards; in an effort to avoid the temptation of gossip, they were even forbidden to take Sunday tea at the English Governesses' Club operated by the English Church in St. Petersburg.[31] Still, their dedication to their duties often left much to be desired: one was discovered to be an alcoholic, a situation undoubtedly exacerbated by the fact that according to court tradition she was provided with two bottles of wine and a half bottle of liquor every day. She was eventually dismissed when found in bed with a member of the Cossack escort.[32]

Another, the Irishwoman Miss Marguerite Eager, was obsessed with the Dreyfus case. On one occasion, when bathing the young Grand Duchess Marie, she simply forgot about the child, according to the emperor's sister, Olga

Alexandrovna, "and started discussing the case with a friend. Marie, naked and dripping, scrambled out of the bath and started running up and down the palace corridor. Fortunately I arrived at just that moment, picked her up and carried her back to Miss Eager, who was still talking about Dreyfus."[33] Miss Eager, who had served at the court since 1898, ultimately left the court in 1904, shortly after the birth of Tsesarevich Alexei.[34]

As the girls grew up, it became necessary to direct their educations, and the empress appointed Mlle. Sophie Tiutcheva as their *kamer-freilina* and governess. For many years the empress had no complaints, until Rasputin became a fixture in the lives of the imperial family. Tiutcheva protested his presence within the palace and particularly his visits to her young charges in their bedrooms, when Rasputin would pray before they retired. In 1910, Marie Vishnyakova, who acted as a nurse to the grand duchesses, accompanied Rasputin on a visit to his Siberian village of Pokrovskoye. One night, according to Vishnyakova, Rasputin raped her. On her return to Tsarskoye Selo, she told not only Tiutcheva but also the empress, who dismissed her from service. Outraged, Tiutcheva went to the empress, complaining of the peasant's behavior, but Alexandra refused to listen. In 1912, unable to continue in what had clearly become an unbearable position, Tiutcheva resigned her post.

The tsesarevich had two personal bodyguards or *dyadi*, Andrei Derevenko and Klementy Nagorny, employed to ensure that the boy did not harm himself while playing. Derevenko, the older of the pair, was a tall, rather stout man, with dark eyes and a small mustache. During official ceremonies, Derevenko, clad in dark trousers and a simple sailor's shirt and cap, would carefully shadow the tsesarevich when he was well and would carry him when he was unable to walk. His assistant, Klementy Nagorny, had—like Derevenko himself—been a member of the Garde Équipage and served aboard the imperial yacht *Standart*. Born in 1886 in a small village in the Ukraine, he was a tall, muscular man, with jet-black hair and vibrant eyes.[35]

The imperial tutors enjoyed a more privileged position at court. A number of instructors taught specialized courses: Vladimir Voyekov taught history; Father Alexander Vassiliev instructed them in the Orthodox catechism; M. Sobolev lectured on mathematics; and there were regular lessons in music, drawing, and various languages. Peter Petrov, a member of the empire's hereditary nobility, acted as a tutor in the Russian language and literature. A former army officer, Petrov served as a special adviser to the Military Training Institutes in St. Petersburg.[36] While his prowess as an academic was not outstanding, Petrov managed to win over his young charges with his open, friendly manner, and the imperial children adored him.

Born in 1879 in Switzerland, Pierre Gilliard joined the imperial court in 1905. He had previously worked as a tutor to Duke Serge of Leuchtenberg, the son of Duke George of Leuchtenberg and his then wife, Anastasia of Montenegro.[37] Although undoubtedly devoted to the imperial family, he was, Gleb Botkin recalled, "a very ordinary type of French teacher," and whatever abilities he brought to his position were largely constrained by both the empress's attitudes and the children's disinterest.[38] Gilliard was one of the most senior tutors at court, and inevitably he made enemies, his fellow tutor Charles Sidney Gibbes among them. Gibbes's son George later recalled, "Father thought that he was arrogant, and used his position at Court to gain personal advantage."[39]

In 1908, Alexandra hired Charles Sidney Gibbes to act as an English tutor to her children. Born in 1876 in Yorkshire, Gibbes moved to St. Petersburg, where, as a member of the St. Petersburg Guild of English Teachers, he worked for several years as a tutor to various aristocratic households. A quiet, homosexual young man, Gibbes enjoyed a good rapport with his imperial students, though he frequently clashed with the headstrong Anastasia. In 1913, he began instructing Tsesarevich Alexei, whom he found a much more difficult pupil.[40]

While the tutors were thus engaged in their morning lessons, preparations were under way for luncheon. Alexander Bobrinsky, the *ober-truchsess*, or palace steward, was in charge of the male servants and reported directly to the *ober-gofmarschal*. Directly below him was the *ober-kamer-fourrier*, who supervised the palace kitchens; much to the chagrin of the Russians, every *ober-kamer-fourrier* from the reign of Alexander III on was French.[41]

The *ober-kamer-fourrier* planned the daily menus, consulted with the emperor and the empress on selections for state dinners, and had overall charge of the *suite de cuisine*. Each week, he presented the empress with a leather-bound folio of suggested menus for the next seven days. Alexandra occasionally made alterations or suggestions; when a state dinner was planned, she worked with the *ober-gofmarschal* and the *ober-truchsess*. The *ober-kamer-fourrier* was assisted by the *haus-gofmeister*, a position roughly equivalent to that of butler. Footmen and pages, as well as china, silver, and pantry stewards, all took their orders from the palace steward.[42]

At the Alexander Palace, the domestic Household included 4 assistant *fourriers*, 34 ordinary footmen, 18 footmen-in-training, 54 waiters, and an additional 24 officers attached to domestic service.[43] During balls, state banquets, and receptions, the *ober-truchsess* worked with the *ober-gofmarschal* to coordinate the intricate procedures.

Every morning, as the neoclassical facade of the palace still lay in deep shadow, long streams of carts, trolleys, motorcars, and trucks, all loaded with provisions, arrived at the kitchens, wheels rattling as they swept past the trim sentries to disgorge their supplies. The quantity of food consumed by the court, from the imperial family down to the lowest page, was immense, and on any given day a hundred pounds of beef, a hundred pounds of mutton, and a hundred pounds of fresh fish might be delivered to meet the culinary requirements. Alexander III had made it a rule that where possible, these provisions were to be drawn from the imperial estates, a measure designed to cut the enormous daily expenses of the court. Beef thus often came from special butchers appointed to imperial farms, fish and fowl from the nearby estate at Gatchina. Milk from the imperial dairies and vegetables from extensive kitchen gardens supplemented the day's fare.[44]

The imperial kitchens were situated in a separate building, in the same neoclassical style as the Alexander Palace. At the time they were constructed in 1794–1795, this separation served a dual purpose: it eliminated unwelcome odors and noise from the palace itself and at the same time protected the main structure in the event of a fire.[45] It also meant, however, that all of the food served at the Alexander Palace had to be carried or pushed on trolleys, no matter the weather, some five hundred feet across the garden to the main building. Not only was this inconvenient, but it also meant that most of the food arrived cold. To solve this dilemma, a tunnel was dug between the kitchen and the palace basement; although the food still had to be carried, this passageway at least saved the servants from the temperamental Russian weather. Built round a central courtyard, the imperial kitchen was a warren of rooms given specific designations. Aside from the principal kitchen, there were ice rooms for the preservation of food; pastry rooms; confectionary offices; meat lockers; a room fitted with immense hardstone tubs for live fish; rooms for the storage of caviar; larders; offices; storerooms for food, china, silver, and crystal; and rooms fitted with deep sinks for the cleaning and washing of china.[46]

In overall charge of the imperial kitchens was the *chef de cuisine*, Monsieur Cubat, a Frenchman of refined taste and exquisite training. He had come to St. Petersburg in the reign of Alexander II, opening an establishment that was soon considered the most fashionable restaurant in the capital. After the scandalous incident at Cubat's between Grand Duke Vladimir and the French actor Lucien

Guitry, Cubat had returned to Paris, opening a restaurant on the Champs-Elysées that was said to have been funded with money he received from Alexander III to maintain his silence. Only after Alexander III's death did he return to Russia, where he took the chief position in Nicholas II's kitchens.[47] For his services, Cubat received a salary equivalent to some $45,000 a year, making him the highest-paid member of the domestic household.[48]

Cubat supervised an immense staff that included 2 chief assistant chefs, Lucien Penecte and M. Olivier; 6 assistant chefs; 38 cooks; 20 apprentice cooks; 32 kitchen boys; Monsieur Bosselet, the pastry chef; 2 bakers; 2 confectionary chefs; 20 assistant confectionary chefs; and kitchen and scullery maids.[49] For special occasions at Tsarskoye Selo, additional cooks and assistants were drawn from the staff of the Winter Palace.[50]

Nicholas and Alexandra preferred simple foods. The emperor enjoyed borscht, fresh fish, and slices of suckling pig with horseradish sauce. Alexandra's diet reflected her upbringing. Having grown up in a relatively poor German court, her tastes had never been sophisticated. Even at the court of her grandmother Queen Victoria, the food was simple and often of dubious quality. Her tastes ran to eggs, baked apples, roast beef, and rice puddings; in her later years, she became a vegetarian, although she did not impose her taste on the imperial table. During state banquets, when important guests with more cultivated palates were present, Cubat would stand in the doorway, waiting hopefully for a summons to the imperial table to receive compliments.[51]

Count Benckendorff was in actual charge of the kitchens. He supervised the three daily divisions of meals within the palaces: first was Their Majesty's table, the service dedicated to Nicholas, Alexandra, their family, and important visitors; then came the court marshal's table, which fed the more important courtiers, members of the Entourage and the Suite, and any lesser visitors; and finally, the domestic service, which was divided into two ranks according to the position of each servant. Cubat cooked only for Their Majesty's table; other services were assigned to assistant chefs.[52]

The emperor and the empress often hosted luncheons and dinners. These could range from an informal meal for ten to small banquets for up to a hundred; larger entertainments always took place elsewhere, either at the nearby Catherine Palace, if the imperial family happened to be in residence at Tsarskoye Selo, or in St. Petersburg. For luncheons, up to twenty wine stewards, butlers, and footmen might be required. The *ober-gofmarschal* selected footmen and waiters from the

Imperial Army, chosen for their height and bearing. The most imposing were detailed to be in attendance at the imperial table, with their less illustrious counterparts assigned to particular rooms. Footmen, attired in their intricate liveries, and waiters, clad in black tailcoats, white tie, and gloves, all wore soft-soled shoes to muffle their footsteps. In their position, these men were often privy to intimate dinner conversations and indiscreet talk. "Every time that we were at the Palace," remembered Peter Kropotkin, "we had lunch or dinner there, and the footmen would whisper to us bits of news from the scandalous chronicle of the place, whether we cared for it or not. They knew everything."[53]

Luncheons began with *zakuski*, a Russian form of hors d'oeuvre consisting of caviar, smoked salmon, smoked ham, pickled herring, cheeses, vodka, and wines laid out on a sideboard. After this, the emperor led the guests to the table; on most occasions, Alexandra sat at his right, with guests and members of the Suite arranged according to rank.[54] There were usually three courses served at lunch, "one of eggs or fish," as Mossolov remembered, "and one of white or red meat," followed by fruit and cheese. "When there were no guests, coffee was served at the dining table. The Emperor lit a cigarette, saying that the Empress had given permission. If there were guests, the company rose from the table after dessert." Coffee, as Mossolov remembered, "was then taken standing, the Sovereigns conversing with their Entourage. Smoking was allowed as soon as the Emperor had lit his cigarette."[55]

After lunch had been cleared, the kitchens were again busy, preparing for tea at four o'clock. The pastry chef and the palace confectioner produced a steady stream of sweets and pastries, but most of these were reserved for special occasions or for the tables of the Entourage or the Household. Tea was, by tradition, the same as it had been in the reign of Catherine the Great, down to the rolls, plates of bread, and pastries standing next to the bubbling samovar. Alexandra complained that "other people had much more interesting tea" but found that she was "unable to change a single detail of the routine of the Russian Court."[56] Alexandra always presided, pouring from the samovar and handing round the plates of tiny sandwiches and pastries to the adults and little vanilla-flavored wafers called *biblichen* to the children. During tea, the emperor smoked and read aloud to the family, while the empress and her daughter knitted or did embroidery, and Alexei played with his tin soldiers.[57]

Dinners at the palace were rarely informal affairs; even when Nicholas and Alexandra had no guests, they changed, Nicholas into uniform and Alexandra into a gown and dazzling jewels. As with any occasion at court, no matter how secluded from the eyes of the public, a dinner with the emperor and the empress was a carefully stage-managed affair. The tables were set with priceless collections of imperial china, silver, and crystal. Nicholas II's father, Alexander III, had commissioned the Raphael Dinner Service in 1883 from the Imperial Porcelain Factory in St. Petersburg for the palaces at Tsarskoye Selo. Of six thousand pieces, the service was decorated with grisaille motifs inspired by Raphael's Vatican loggias, with pale pink, blue, and gray classical figures and mythological beasts round the rims and in the center of each plate.[58]

Nicholas II added five new services. The Alexandra Turquoise Service, ordered in 1899 from the Imperial Porcelain Factory, replicated the look of Sèvres porcelain, which featured turquoise-colored, highly glazed plates edged with gilded, rococo-style scallops and decorated with paintings of cherubs. The service contained 1,290 dinner plates alone, with five different center designs.[59] The 1,690-piece Purple Service, commissioned in 1903, was executed in the rococo style, with cartouches encasing woodland scenes executed in soft shades of gray and mauve and cherubs surrounding the gilded rims.[60]

The six-thousand piece Bird Service featured hand-painted scenes of exotic fowl, while the Tsarskoye Selo Service took its inspiration from the country estate's pavilions, palaces, and the park. The largest commission was the Coat of Arms Service, consisting of 47,000 pieces whose plain white plates rimmed with gold and decorated with double-headed eagles repeated the design of Alexander III's Coronation Service.[61]

Places at the tables were set with an array of crystal and silver. The two largest crystal services in use at the turn of the century were the Minister Service, ordered by Emperor Paul from Waterford; and the Prigorod Service, commissioned in 1823 from the Imperial Glass Factory in St. Petersburg.[62] There were a number of silver services in use, including remnants of the famous Orlov Service and Nicholas I's London Service, ordered in 1844 from Garrard in the British capital.[63] The service principally in use, however, was the Governor Silver Service, commissioned by Catherine the Great as a gift for her son and intended exclusively for the Alexander Palace. Inevitably, many pieces of china and silver were damaged or went missing. One silver steward, it was said, deliberately made nicks in hundreds of pieces so that he could sell them to the American Consulate in St. Petersburg.[64]

Guests were escorted to the room where dinner was to be served. Nicholas and Alexandra both preferred to sit at a table prepared in one of the State Apartments, alternating rooms each evening rather than using a permanent dining room. Small dinners were often held in the empress's Corner Salon, where up to thirty guests could be seated at ten round tables.[65] For large gatherings, generally tables were set up in the Semi-Circular Hall; most occasions called for round tables of ten or twelve, covered with immaculate white damask cloths sewn with the imperial monogram. For more important dinners and state occasions, workers erected a U-shaped table. Each place setting, carefully measured with a ruler and laid out with great precision, was marked with an individual parchment in a silver holder that carried not only the menu but also the musical program for the evening. Arrangements of fresh flowers cascaded from Chinese, Sèvres, and Meissen vases and bowls, interspersed with tendrils of ivy and shimmering silver candelabra topped with white silk shades.[66]

Abyssinian Guards, black men who worked in pairs, stood at attention before the closed doors of the private apartments, waiting to admit the imperial couple. The Abyssinian Guards were one of the most famous fixtures at the Russian court. "They were not soldiers," wrote Anna Vyrubova, "and they had no function except to open and close doors, and to signal by a sudden, noiseless entrance into a room that one of Their Imperial Majesties was about to appear."[67]

These men had formed a part of the Russian court since the days of Peter the Great, and his successors continued the tradition. By the middle of the nineteenth century, they were recruited by the Russian Consul in Ethiopia or were presented as human gifts by the Ethiopian emperor. The only requirements were that the men be Christians and that they stand immensely tall, with imposing figures. But not all of these men were from Ethiopia. At least two Americans were in service to Nicholas II.[68] One, named Sam, had come from the Riggs Plantation in Georgia; when once asked about his curious journey to the Russian court, Sam replied simply that he had followed the money.[69]

But the most famous of the men was Jim Hercules. Born to former slaves in the American South in 1867, Hercules took advantage of the freedom after the Civil War and moved to New York City, where he became something of a famous boxer. In the 1880s, he toured Europe, finally settling in London and taking British citizenship. Empress Marie Feodorovna invited him to Russia, where Alexander III offered him a position as an Abyssinian Guard. Each year, Hercules returned to America for several months to visit his family, returning to Russia with homemade jellies as gifts for the imperial children.[70]

Hercules and his compatriots stood out from the other servants not only because of the color of their skin, but also because of their unique attire. They wore coats of black wool embroidered with double-headed eagles in gold thread over short white jackets that shielded waistcoats of crimson velvet, with wide, scarlet wool trousers and pointed boots of Moroccan leather embellished with gold stitching. Atop the head of each guard was a white or a red turban or a red velvet fez adorned with a gilded tassel.[71] "Tall, splendidly built, in their wide trousers and scarlet turbans they stood immobile as though they had been cast in bronze," recalled Prince Christopher of Greece.[72]

Inevitably, their privileged positions at court caused resentment. "They were not supposed to be overly popular with the palace servants," recorded one diplomat's wife, "and one night, when they were costumed in dazzling white and naturally made a sensation, an envious servant who was passing with the fish sauce for supper pretended to slip and then spilt the contents of the dish completely over one of them."[73]

Dinner consisted of five courses, starting with either thick or clear soup, served with cheese on toasted bread or pastries stuffed with meats and cheese. This was followed by a fish course, often sterlet in a rich sauce. The emperor was also exceptionally fond of oysters and had them shipped in by train from Ostend.[74] The third course was often roast game or fowl, followed by a fourth course that might include beef, venison, ham, or lamb, accompanied by a vegetable course. The fifth course was almost always cheese and assorted fruits, including pears sent from Paris and apples, melons, and grapes from the Crimea.[75] The meal ended with a dessert course, including cakes, assorted pastries and tarts, and ice creams and sorbets.[76] During the meal, guests were serenaded by a small orchestra; the selections were largely dictated by Empress Alexandra, who favored Wagner and Brahms.[77]

The *ober-shenk*, or court sommelier, selected the wines and other liquors for every meal. Generally, Madeira accompanied the first course, succeeded by a variety of white and red wines for the courses that followed. Most of these wines were German Rhine or French Bordeaux, although those from the imperial vineyards at Massandra in the Crimea appeared from time to time. Champagne was French, and Nicholas favored that from the Charles Heidsieck Company in Rheims. From an early age, on the advice of the imperial doctors, all of the children drank St. Raphael wine with their meals. At the end of the meal, liqueurs were served, including a variety of flavored brandies and sherry.[78]

"At all the great banquets," recalled Prince Christopher of Greece, "a Court official stood behind the chair of every royal guest to hand the champagne for the toasts. This was a matter of solemn ritual. The wine was first poured out by a footman, then it had to be passed to a page who, in turn, passed it to the hander."

These men were often elderly, and, as Prince Christopher remembered, accidents were frequent. "I can still remember my sister's distress when her favorite pale blue velvet Court dress turned a vivid green in patches after her hander had spilt six glasses of champagne over it."[79]

Following dinner, there might be a light musical performance or scenes acted from a theatrical piece; on Saturday evenings, dinner guests were often asked to join members of the imperial family as they watched a film. These screenings usually took place in the Semi-Circular Hall of the Alexander Palace, where a small hole had been cut into the wall of an adjoining room to accommodate a Pathé projector.[80] Servants erected a large portable screen in the bow, surrounded, as the French ambassador Maurice Paleologue recalled, by "armchairs and a dozen or so smaller chairs." Members of the Entourage and the Suite were often invited to join the guests, while "groups of servants and chambermaids thronged all the doorways" as they looked on.[81]

"The choice of films was a troublesome business," Alexander Mossolov recalled. "The Empress had settled the program, once and for all, as follows: first, as news films, the record taken during the week by the Court photographer Jaguelsky of the firm of Hahn; then an instructional film or a series of attractive views; finally, something amusing for the children."[82] The imperial family enjoyed American comedies and serials, as well as light French romances, although each film had to be carefully screened, to ensure that no offending scenes existed.[83] Responsibility for these decisions often fell to Princess Elizabeth Naryshkin-Kuryakin. "She was a pitiless censor," Mossolov remembered. "Again and again, the brightest spots in a film would be condemned as indecorous, and Jaguelsky's scissors got to work at once on them."[84] Inevitably, though, as Vladimir Voyekov recalled, the princess missed a kiss or a passionate glance, which sent the imperial children into howls of laughter.[85]

If there was no film, members of the imperial family bade their guests goodnight at nine

Jim Hercules, 1891

and retired to their rooms, gathering in the empress's boudoir, where Alexandra and her daughters did their needlework or pasted photographs into leather albums while the emperor read aloud to them. Alexei played checkers or some other game with Anastasia on the carpet. The empress adored music and often would put a record of her favorite operas by Wagner on the gramophone.[86] At eleven, tea was again served, and the children retired to their rooms; Nicholas and Alexandra usually remained up for an hour or two, talking and reading, before finally going to bed.[87]

By midnight, the palace was usually quiet, although its darkened windows shielded a flurry of activity. Tables were dismantled, chairs put away, flowers prepared for delivery to hospitals the next day, floors swept and cleaned, shutters closed, and candles snuffed out. In the sculleries and pantries, dishes, silver, and crystal were carefully cleaned and polished before being passed to stewards, who carefully marked off each piece into books as they were replaced in appropriate chests and cupboards. Invariably, valuable pieces of porcelain were broken, silver went missing, and crystal was shattered, and every damaged or missing item had to be listed as well. Only when the *ober-truchsess* was satisfied were the servants dismissed and the palace wrapped in slumber, to await the start of the new day.

7

THE MILITARY

IN THE YEARS BEFORE WORLD WAR I, the Russian empire maintained a standing army of one and a half million men. Of this number, some forty thousand were officers, drawn from the ranks of the Imperial Guards Corps. Such was their importance that in the social hierarchy of the empire, they ranked directly after the imperial family, holding precedence over members of the imperial court, the State Council, the Committee of Ministers, and other government agency officials.[1]

Officers of guards regiments were drawn from the various military institutions and training schools scattered across the country. The most famous was the Corps des Pages, founded in 1802 by Alexander I. Admission to the school was strict, based on both social background and academic capabilities. Boys destined for the Corps des Pages were often enrolled at birth; only those whose fathers or grandfathers had reached the rank of lieutenant-general, vice-admiral, or privy councilor were admitted, and then only after passing rigorous examinations.

The institution was housed in the former Vorontzov Palace, a large building originally designed for Empress Elizabeth's vice-chancellor and given to the school by Alexander I in 1810. Students were admitted at the age of eleven or twelve and followed a five-year course of general education, with another two years of officer training and specialized military instruction at one of the six military academies.[2] In their final year, the top students served as *kamer-pages* to the imperial court. "This was considered a great honor," recalled Peter Kropotkin, "and moreover, the young men upon whom this honor was bestowed became known at the Court, and had afterward every chance of being nominated adjutants of the Emperor or of one of the Grand Dukes."[3] Their court uniforms were complicated affairs: tight, white doe-skin breeches; highly polished, black Wellington boots; and scarlet and gold tunics with embossed collars. Off duty and in winter, they wore black trousers with thin red piping down the sides and black tunics with gold collars, cuffs, and waistbands; white gloves were obligatory.[4]

The best pupil was made the emperor's very own page. Each grand duke and duchess was assigned one young man, while the dowager empress and Empress Alexandra each had four. At the end of their court service, the young men received gold watches bearing the monogram of the person they had attended.[5] One page, Alexei Ignatiev, recalled his presentation to Empress Alexandra at the Alexander Palace in 1895: "In the middle of a large room bathed in flowers and permeated with the scent of court perfumes stood a tall, well-shaped, and handsome blonde woman, clad in a light gray *crepe-de-chine* dress. It was for me to go up to her first and kiss her outstretched hand; but whether she did not raise her hand in time, or whether in embarrassment I did not bow low enough, the result was that the kiss landed in the air, and I noticed that her face became covered with unsightly blushes, which further confused me. I only just managed to catch a barely audible phrase, spoken in French, to the effect that she was very happy to make our acquaintance."[6]

At the end of their term, the young officer candidates joined the army. "Only the Guards in St. Petersburg were acceptable," recalled Prince Andrei Lobanov-Rostovsky.[7] These regiments, His Majesty's Life Guards, were the most important of all military divisions, their officers known for their good looks, impeccable manners, and loyalty to the throne. By the beginning of the twentieth century, these regiments included the Preobrazhensky, the Semyonovsky, the Izmailovsky, the Finland, and the Litovsky Guards; the Lancers and the Hussars; the Chevalier Guards and the Cuirassiers Gardes; the Horse Guards Artillery; the Grenadier Guards; the Pavlovsky Guards and the Uhlan Guards; the Life Guard Grenadiers; the Garde Équipage, from which all naval officers were drawn; the Guard Sapper Regiment; and the Garde á Cheval. Finally, there was the Konvoi guard, consisting of Cossack regiments that were personally attached to the Household of the imperial family.[8]

Power within these regiments was rigidly defined. Prince Andrei Lobanov-Rostovsky recalled "the very intricate methods of saluting" and the complicated system of formal address. Simple acknowledgment called for a peculiarity of honors: officers to the rank of general were addressed as "High Well-Born"; above them, as "Excellencies," or "Super-Excellencies"; princes and counts were "Shining"; and serene princes were "Becoming Brighter." Discipline, as he wrote, "was extremely severe, and punishment was meted out for the slightest neglect." There was no separation between military and private life. A senior officer, passing down Nevsky Prospekt in a carriage, expected to be saluted by all junior officers, who were only to walk on the left side of the avenue; failure to do so, to be caught unaware, was considered an insult. Officers were forbidden to smoke on the street, enter cafés or restaurants, or appear in civilian dress. So intricate was this layer of rigid etiquette that minor breaches were regarded as deliberate provocations, and duels resulted from perceived insults.[9]

Uniforms followed the dictates of tradition and etiquette, with each regiment assigned unique parade and dress uniforms. The colors of the jackets and tunics changed from regiment to regiment; officers' dolmans, worn loosely over the shoulder, were trimmed with fur and sewn with stitching, galloon, and buttons unique to each unit. Row upon row of shining medals, order insignia, and moiré cordons decorated the chests of elderly generals, with aiguillettes and gold braid denoting rank. Military peaked caps were covered with broadcloth and piping to match the regimental colors, decorated above the brim with order stars or insignia. Hats were plumed with ostrich or eagle feathers, shaped with fur, peaked or brimmed, while helmets were of chased ormolu or silver, decorated with double-headed eagles. Officers' broadswords and sabers, in delicately chased metal scabbards, hung from the waist.

Members of the Chevalier Guards Regiment wore white tunics and breeches, with cuirasses of silver, silver helmets topped with double-headed eagles, and knee-high black leather Hessian boots. For imperial balls, they substituted a crimson waistcoat, adorned with the Star of the Order of St. Andrew, for the uncomfortable breastplate. From the tops of their boots to their tunics stretched elk-skin breeches. Protocol dictated that the breeches, which had to be skin-tight, could not have the slightest crease. To achieve this, the breeches were dampened, smeared with soap, and then pulled on with the assistance of several comrades.[10] The Gardes á Cheval wore nearly identical uniforms, the only difference being their cuirasses, of silver gilt to match their helmets surmounted by a double-headed eagle. On formal occasions, crimson waistcoats adorned with double-headed eagles replaced their cuirassiers. Soldiers in the Cossack regiments inevitably stood out in their long blue broadcloth Circassian coats decorated with gold galloon, gold belts, and bandoliers across their chests; atop their heads, they wore the traditional papakhii of Astrakhan and Persian lamb. On ceremonial occasions, they wore scarlet *kosakhins*, long Circassian coats, over blue breeches and white *beshmet* shirts decorated with gold buttons and gold galloon.[11]

Nicholas I established the Golden Grenadiers as a personal guard for the imperial residences, and he designed their uniforms: a long gray coat, worn over gray trousers; atop their heads were tall golden helmets designed after those worn by the army of Friedrich the Great, with gold chains looped beneath the chin and distinctive golden tassels hanging from the side. On ceremonial occasions, they wore white breeches and exchanged their golden helmets for tall *kalpaks*, the Russian equivalent of the British busby.

Three of the regiments in the imperial guards wore uniforms modeled on foreign dress. The uniform of the Hussar Guards Regiment derived from traditional Hungarian models. Officers wore black trousers trimmed with a single red stripe, white silk beshmets with gold galloon, and crimson jackets ornamented with silver and gold galloon. Over their shoulders, they wore white dolmans, adorned with silver and gold galloon, with sable-edged collars and cuffs. The uniform of the Lancer Guards was copied from Polish dress, with blue trousers, a blue jacket with gold galloon, and scarlet waistcoats ornamented with gold stitching. Atop their heads, they wore the traditional *czapska*, with its jaunty feathered plume. Members of the Pavlovsky Guards wore blue breeches and jackets adorned with gold galloon, with tall brass miter helmets ornamented with double-headed eagles, modeled on the uniforms of the army of Friedrich the Great of Prussia.

Many of the imperial guards regiments had personal attachments with the imperial family. Members of the Cossack Konvoi Regiment and the Garde Équipage were assigned to the imperial family. The Garde Équipage had been formed in 1867, when all of the Russian naval companies were joined together into groups, or *équipages*, of around two thousand men each. They were part of the imperial guards, rather than of the navy, and served on the yachts in the summer, as well as doing winter duty in St. Petersburg as part of the city garrison.

In time, many of the soldiers became friendly with the families they protected. Nicholas II's sister Olga Alexandrovna recalled the special relationship she and her brother Michael had with a regiment assigned to their country palace at Gatchina. "I made friends with as many as I could, and it was fun when Michael and I slipped away into the barracks and listened to the men's songs. My mother strictly forbade such pranks, and so . . . every time we carried it off we felt we had achieved something. The men used to play games with us and toss us in the air. Peasants though they were, they never behaved roughly."[12] Olga's childhood playmates were not officers but common foot soldiers. Protocol would have prevented such free expression by aristocrats, but the regular soldiers, unaware of the niceties of imperial decorum, endeared themselves to the children, though often horrifying their nannies and nurses.

These soldiers provided much-needed amusement for the cloistered imperial family. Olga Alexandrovna recalled coming upon nude soldiers bathing in the lakes and rivers of the palace gardens. Alarmed at the sudden approach of a carriage bearing a member of the ruling family, these men would jump out of the water and make a mad dash, not for their uniforms, but rather for their caps. Nude, but caps in place so that they might properly salute, these soldiers stood solemnly at attention as the Romanovs passed.[13] On other occasions, these men were asked to play the parts of extras in productions of the opera and ballet. Olga remembered a performance of *Aida*: "It was a riot, to see those tall, husky men, standing awkwardly on the stage, wearing helmets and sandals and showing their bare, hairy legs. Despite the frantic signals of the producers, they would stare up at us with broad grins."[14]

Military training was dictated by tradition: all Romanov grand dukes were expected to seek some career in either the army or the navy. Even the women of the imperial family were not exempt from military duties: during the reign of Nicholas II, Empress Alexandra served as honorary colonel in chief of the 5th Alexandriiski Hussar Life Guards Regiment and of the Uhlan Life Guards Regiment. Nicholas and Alexandra's daughters were also given honorary colonelcies on their name days when they turned fourteen: Olga served as colonel in chief of the 3rd Elizavetgradsky Life Guards Hussars Regiment; Tatiana, of the 8th Uhlan Voznesensky Life Guards Lancers Regiment; Marie, of the 9th Kazan Dragoon Life Guards Regiment; and Anastasia, of the 148th Caspian Infantry Guards Regiment. In these roles, the girls often attended regimental dinners and participated in reviews under the approving eye of their father.

Grand Duchesses Olga and Tatiana, August 1912.

Special attention was lavished on the military associations of the tsesarevich, as future emperor. Alexei served as honorary colonel in chief of a number of regiments, including the Life Guards Ataman Cossacks, the Finland Guards Regiment, the 12th Siberian Rifles Regiment, and the 51st Lithuanian Infantry Regiment. He was also enrolled in a new organization, the Poteshnye or Play Regiments, derived from Peter the Great's first military units. Modeled along the lines of the Boy Scouts, but with a military overtone, the Poteshnye Regiments were used to promote the ideas of patriotism and loyalty to the imperial throne among Russian youths.[15]

Nicholas II was expected to lead not only his nation but also his soldiers. At his birth, he had been made honorary colonel in chief of several regiments, and he spent his youth surrounded by these soldiers and their colorful uniforms. When he was ten years old, Nicholas was gazetted as a lieutenant in His Majesty's Preobrazhensky Guards Regiment and was given the first of his many uniforms to wear at official parades and receptions. His grandfather, Alexander II, presented him with his kit, saying that it was now Nicholas's duty to be attentive to all concerns around him in preparation for his eventual role.[16] On holidays and name days, he received delegations of soldiers, each bearing gifts for the little boy and carefully attired in their regimental uniforms.

Nicholas enjoyed military life, but it was not until 1887 that the nineteen-year-old tsesarevich was finally given permission to leave his parents' palace and embark on a career in the imperial guards. In June, Nicholas was gazetted as a second lieutenant in the 1st Company of His Majesty's Preobrazhensky Guards Regiment and moved to the military camp at Krasnoye Selo, fifteen miles southwest of St. Petersburg, where he took up residence in a roomy wooden villa. After rising from a subaltern to division commander, Nicholas spent two seasons in His Majesty's Life Guards Hussar Regiment; here, he obtained the rank of squadron commander. He finally ended his military career with a year as colonel in chief of the Horse Guards Artillery Regiment.

Krasnoye Selo was a world unto itself, a small village based around a great parade ground, fringed by "the lush green of a grove of beech trees." Ornate wooden dachas, home to the camp's officers, lined wide sandy roads, and rows of white tents sloped down to the banks of the Dudergov and the Ligovka Rivers. At the beginning of summer, recalled Alexei Ignatiev, "flowers would fill the air with scent, the paths were strewn with bright yellow sand, and the dusty highway would be watered several times a day, from barrels drawn by one horse carts." During the encampment, he declared, Krasnoye Selo "almost bore the aspect of a luxurious holiday resort."[17] Reviews, parades, receptions, and drills gave way to afternoons swimming in the Ligovka River, while, in the evenings, operas and ballets were given in the camp theater.[18]

Military life appealed greatly to Nicholas. With his passive character, he was always happier taking orders, following a regimented routine with a rigidly defined hierarchy. In the army he faced no question of choice: his senior officers laid out his entire path for him. Thus, he could dedicate himself to those aspects he most enjoyed: uniforms, parades, exercise, and entertainments. His was a dilettantish existence, best exemplified when he had a direct telephone line installed between his villa at Krasnoye Selo and the Mariinsky Theater in the capital, so that he could enjoy the opera without leaving the comfort of his own house. Like most officers, he spent his evenings enjoying the pleasures of youth: dancing, listening to the gypsies, and, inevitably, drinking.

As emperor, Nicholas relished his role as supreme head of the Army, and he returned each summer to Krasnoye Selo for the annual maneuvers. On their first day at the camp, the emperor and all of the grand dukes, on horseback, reviewed the soldiers and the officers drawn up in ranks outside their barracks and villas. The men of the imperial family were followed by a procession of open landaus and victorias carrying Empress Alexandra, the dowager empress, and all of the grand duchesses. At the end of the review, the soldiers all joined together in singing "God Save the Tsar" as the emperor took the salute.

The highlight of the stay was the great review, held on an enormous parade ground beyond the camp. The two empresses led the women of the imperial family in a carriage procession to the Emperor's Mound, an artificial hill at the side of the field crowned with a white canvas tent from which they watched the proceedings. Soon, Nicholas appeared on horseback; attired in the uniform of a different regiment each year, he led the grand dukes and the court officials to the parade ground on horseback.

For the next hour, a stream of men—both officers and regular soldiers—slowly filled the field, forming a sea of thousands of faces. The emperor rode up and down the drawn ranks, receiving the salutes of men before taking up his position for the grand march past. Regimental bands played rousing military marches as Nicholas took the salutes of the men, his hand frozen in place next to the brim of his cap. At the end of the review, the regimental bands massed at the front of the field. A lone drummer recited the Lord's Prayer over the thousands of men, followed by a hymn of blessing. Finally, the bands struck up "God Save the Tsar"; all of the soldiers fell to their knees as they sang, an impressive sight as row after row of thousands of men bowed before their emperor. At the end of the review, the emperor and the empress hosted a luncheon in a tent for the regimental commanders, during which the young men of the Corps des Pages were promoted to the rank of officer.[19]

Military reviews were not confined to Krasnoye Selo. St. Petersburg was a military city. Soldiers and officers rushed through the avenues, and different regiments paraded through the streets to take up their posts. Above all, the sounds of the military men and their bands floated over the capital, as one man recalled, "A regiment marching to church on a Sunday or holiday, a general's funeral, the daily changing of the Guard at the Winter Palace by the Preobrazhensky and Semyonovsky Regiments. Boys flocked to the sounds of the band. It was particular fun when troops returned from the ceremony after a funeral: on such occasions the bands played merry music. Brisk marches were played when the troops went to church, though not, of course, during Lent. Softer sounds came from the spurs of the servicemen's boots. Officers were very particular about the kinds of sounds their spurs made."[20]

In 1901, Nicholas II revived the tradition of reviewing his troops on May Day. A large wooden pavilion, hung with white canvas awnings and decorated with the double-headed eagle, was erected in front of the Oldenburg Palace, with chairs for the women of the imperial family. Grand dukes, astride impressive mounts and decked with rows of gleaming medals, waited in the quadrangle of the Winter Palace for the emperor and the empress. Just before eleven that morning, the emperor, in the uniform of the Preobrazhensky Life Guards Regiment, rode his mount into Palace Square. At his side, an open landau carried Empress Alexandra and the dowager empress, both in white gowns and shaded by lace parasols.[21]

A mounted escort of Chevalier Guards accompanied their procession, as recalled by one witness: "Starting from the Palace, along the embankment to the Summer Garden, there were rows of Horse Guards; the bands were playing *God Save The Tsar* as the Emperor rode

Grand Duchess Olga riding in a regimental parade, 1912

along in a dark uniform with a blue sash beside the Empress's carriage; behind him came the various uniforms of the Adjutants and Generals. The regiments . . . began to cheer, but very much by numbers, giving one very little sense of enthusiasm. Of course, no one was allowed near the Embankment, on foot or otherwise, and the Imperial procession went slowly by the ranks of soldiers moving down an apparently deserted street."[22]

Along the way to the Champs de Mars, the regiments were saluted with salvos fired from the guns of the Fortress of St. Peter and St. Paul across the Neva. They marched along the quays, each preceded by a standard bearer carrying the colors and ribbons of valor awarded to the company. Once at the parade ground, the review began. Stands for the well-born spectators lined the length of the field, "which the high price of the seats," recalled Alexei Ignatiev, "made accessible only to the well-to-do, and which were principally occupied by ladies who desired to show off their spring toilettes and the latest Parisian fashions." Ignatiev continued, "Following the review of the troops, the Emperor halted in front of the Imperial Box, attended only by the trumpeter of his Personal Escort, mounted on a gray horse and wearing a crimson-colored Cossack coat." At a signal, the march past began, led by two squadrons of Cossacks; they were followed by "the battalion of the Pavlovsky Military College, and next, the Mixed Battalion, of which the 1st Company were the Pages, their helmets recalling a long forgotten epoch." A regimental band announced the approach of the imperial guards regiments: "The red uniforms of the Preobrazhensky Regiment gave way to the blue of the Semyonovsky, the white piping of the Izmailovsky, the green of the *Chasseurs*. The regularity of the regimental uniforms was interrupted only by the Pavlovsky Regiment, marching past in cone-shaped head dresses dating from the period of Friedrich of Prussia and carrying their rifles at the slope as a traditional privilege earned in battle. In the artillery that followed the infantry, what caught the eye were the mature bloodstock horses of the finest breed harnessed to the guns, sorted out by color of their hides in a way Russians liked, the leading batteries drawn by chestnuts, the second by bays, the third by blacks."[23] With each advance, noted the illustrated weekly *Niva*, the crowd "erupted into immense 'Hurrahs!'"[24] That afternoon, Nicholas reviewed 27,821 soldiers and promoted more than 1,300 men as officers.[25]

Nicholas preferred quieter occasions, enjoying regimental dinners and celebratory luncheons. On such festive days, long tables laden with silver plate-trays, bowls, cups, vases, candelabra, and the Russian *kovshi*—or drinking ladles—awaited the officers. Trumpeters saluted toasts, and balalaika players strummed their instruments, providing a soulful atmosphere to the proceedings. "Nicholas II," recalled Ignatiev, "would seat himself in the place of the presiding officer and without muttering a word to anyone quietly drink goblet after goblet of champagne, listening till morning in turn now to trumpeters, now to the singers."[26]

The emperor took his rank as commander in chief of the Russian Army with the utmost seriousness. In 1909, when the army redesigned the infantry kit of the common soldier, Nicholas ordered one delivered to Livadia in the Crimea, where he was staying at the time. Early one morning, he put on the uniform of a private of the 16th Rifle Regiment, strapped on the pack and a bedroll, hoisted the rifle onto his shoulder, then silently crept out of the palace, intent on marching twenty-five miles over the mountains to test the comfort of the new design. He told only two people of his plans, Count de Freedericksz and the commander of the palace, making each promise that he would not be followed. With him, he carried the regulation weight of cartridges, as well as a ration of black bread and water.[27]

Apparently, no one recognized him as he marched across the rugged Crimean coast. At the entrance to one estate, the gatekeeper turned him away. "You cannot pass through here!" the man bellowed. "This is private property!" Without a word, Nicholas turned round.[28] Nicholas returned to Livadia at twilight, pulled off the uniform, and began a careful inspection of both the kit and himself. The uniform had been comfortable, he declared, and he did not have any blisters from his adventure.[29] As soon as word of this endeavor reached the Kaiser, Wilhelm II was angry that he had not thought of the idea first.[30] As a souvenir, the emperor filled out an ordinary soldier's service card: "Name: Nicholas Romanov. Rank: Colonel." In the space provided for special notes, the emperor wrote, "No special privileges until I am dead."[31]

8

THE ARISTOCRACY

BEFORE THE REVOLUTION, there were 870 titled families in Russia.[1] Many Russian aristocrats lived lives of unparalleled luxury. They built summer and winter palaces filled with Louis XVI furniture and surrounded by exquisite English gardens, took holidays in Italy and the south of France, spoke English and French but avoided Russian, and entertained on a scale without equal in Europe. The great aristocratic families were inexorably linked with the ascendancy of the Romanovs themselves: Bariatinskys, Dolgorukys, Sheremetievs, Orlovs, Shuvalovs, Golitsyns, Naryshkins, and Vorontzovs all enjoyed unique positions as ancient supporters of the Imperial House.

By the beginning of the twentieth century, most of these families had accumulated vast fortunes, lavishing their wealth on palaces, estates, jewels, and works of art. Not all aristocrats had amassed private fortunes, but riches were still to be had, if not through family inheritance, then through the newer means of high finance and industry. The Benckendorff family, for example, owned an estate that produced half of the world's annual supply of platinum.[2]

The aristocracy was known for its entertainments. One reception, given in the dead of winter, took the theme of some imaginary peasant holiday. A ballroom was decorated to resemble a cottage; live cows wandered through the gilded drawing rooms, adding a touch of authenticity, while servants, who handed drinks from silver trays to the quaintly costumed guests, themselves wore peasant tunics, blouses, skirts, and breeches. "The whole arrangement was charming," recalled one of the guests in this noble charade.[3]

This eccentricity often extended to the aristocrats themselves. One Russian prince bought the highest mountain in the Crimea on a whim and gave it to his wife as a birthday present. Then there was the Bagratian family, of the Georgian Royal House, who claimed direct descent from King David of Israel and thus considered themselves relatives of Jesus Christ. Each year, on the Feast of the Assumption of the Virgin Mary, the elderly Princess Bagratian wore mourning, declaring that it was an occasion for "family" grief.[4]

From the nineteenth century to the end of the Romanov Dynasty, aristocrats played pivotal roles in the empire. Shaping the economic and cultural development of the country, they stood near the apex of society. At the same time, it was from their ranks that the Decembrist Uprising of 1825 was launched. Travel exposed them to Western ideas, holidays in Europe to new cultural and intellectual enlightenment. They assimilated and absorbed these philosophies, at the same time often ignoring their practice in Russia. Over time, the aristocracy developed a stubborn belief in its innate superiority, coupled with a philosophy that, in theory, dictated equality for all. The battle to reconcile these contradictory beliefs waged until the Revolution.

Aristocrats began life endowed with the privileges of birth and position but often crippled by a lack of parental affection. Aristocratic fathers were consumed with their own interests, and many saw their children only at tea or before dinner, when a nanny might bring her young charges—carefully bathed and dressed in smart frocks or sailor suits—to the drawing room to greet their parents. There was little social interaction. Nor were many aristocratic mothers more comforting, devoted as they were to social obligations. Pregnancy was a distasteful ordeal, and few mothers doted on their babies, preferring instead to hand them—and responsibility for their care—off to a retinue of nurses. "Our daily lives were quite separate from theirs," recalled Olga Voronoff. "We were not often allowed out of our quarters, except when we were to kiss our parents good morning or good night, or on those occasions when we were sent for."[5]

While relations between children and servants were warm and loving, they also set the tone for aristocratic life, laying the foundation for the roles into which children would one day accede. Inevitably, inflections of social hierarchy infused these childhood influences, when young charges witnessed their beloved caretakers often capriciously ordered about and made to bend to the whims of their masters; the example thus reinforced the aristocrat's belief in his or her own innate superiority.

Education began at an early age, with sons separated from daughters. For the latter group, there were few expectations: girls needed languages, classes in the arts, and perhaps a few rudimentary lessons in history and literature. Aristocratic girls were viewed not as contributors to society, but instead as social adornments and future wives, roles that did not call for astute intellect or highly developed thought.

Boys were subjected to a more rigorous system, often at the hands of strict and severe military tutors who passed quickly over the niceties of literature and the humanities in favor of more practical pursuits designed to pave the way for military and bureaucratic careers. When they reached the age of ten or twelve, most sons were sent away to boarding schools run along military lines and designed to shape them into subservience. As a result, they rarely saw their families; some educational institutions, such as the famous Corps des Pages in St. Petersburg, even refused their pupils ordinary leave for family holidays.

Members of the Russian aristocracy straddled a precarious knife-edge; brought up to exhibit impeccable manners, they attempted to mold themselves according to idealized European forms. Yet they could never completely conceal their Russian heritage, and a sense of inferiority often infused their lives. It was an echo of the struggle of old versus new, East versus West, Moscow versus St. Petersburg, a collision of expectation concealed by nuance.

On the surface, the charade was barely discernible. Théophile Gautier recalled the Russian aristocratic manner as "polite, caressing, and highly polished. They are conversant with all the details of French literature. They are great readers, and many an author little known in France is widely read in St. Petersburg." The latest Parisian scandals, he noted, were well known in the Russian capital even before they managed to cross the salons of French dowagers. In their imitation of the European ideal, Gautier reported, "the conversation is always in French, especially in the presence of a stranger."[6]

Countess Marie Kleinmichel dressed for the Medieval Ball in 1903

Aristocratic families dominated St. Petersburg society through their positions, wealth, and brilliant entertainments. Without doubt, the most famous hostess of Nicholas II's day was Countess Marie Kleinmichel, an extraordinary woman who possessed a superb education, an immense fortune, and passion for parties. Grand Duchess Olga Alexandrovna remembered her as "a *grande dame* to the tips of her fingers . . . uncannily shrewd and clever. Somehow or other she succeeded in learning the intimate secrets of practically everyone in society. Her house was known as a hotbed of gossip."[7]

Crippled with a debilitating illness, the countess rarely left her splendid house on St. Petersburg's Sergievskaya Street. It was a tribute to her reputation that society clamored for the privilege of calling upon her, eager to join in her legendary receptions. One member of the Russian court recalled, "A woman of brains, highly cultured and very talented, the Countess is extremely fascinating. . . . She seems to electrify the whole company and compel them to enjoy themselves and feel happy. She has a sweet smile or a pleasant word for all. . . . Being well-read, clever in discussions and smart at repartee, the Countess Klenmichel is much appreciated as a conversationalist."[8]

Countess Kleinmichel's chief rival was Countess Elizabeth (Betsy) Shuvalov. Born in 1855, she had married Count Paul Shuvalov, one of the wealthiest members of the aristocracy. Meriel Buchanan remembered her "gaiety and love of life, and buoyant good humor that made it possible for her to overcome the sorrows of her private life. At the same time she was every inch a *grande dame* of the old school, and nobody would have dared take a liberty or behave in an unseemly way in her presence."[9] When Count Shuvalov died at the turn of the century, he left his widow one of the largest private fortunes in all Russia. She spent her widowhood in an immense palace sprawling along the Fontanka Canal. Beyond the heavy Renaissance facade lay an enfilade of drawing rooms hung in crimson, blue, and gold moiré panels framed in dark Circassian walnut pilasters supporting vaulted ceilings.[10]

The countess received at the head of her marble staircase, inevitably dressed in a black satin gown and wearing a magnificent wheat and oak leaf cluster diamond tiara atop her head. One intimate called her "a very independent woman, and her position in society is quite an exceptional one. . . . She is kind hearted and generous."[11] Indeed, the countess was known for her largesse. She lived in splendor, but she also donated large amounts to workhouses and schools. On her own country estates, she established training schools for peasant girls. The latest gowns, coats, and lingerie from Paris were studied and carefully copied by these highly skilled women, and the results, priced for members of the middle and

working classes, were sold in special boutiques and the profits given to the seamstresses on the estates.[12]

In Nicholas II's reign, three American beauties competed for social dominance
in St. Petersburg. Suzanne, Princess Serge Beloselsky-Belozersky, was the daughter of an American army general. Originally from Boston, she was, remembered
one lady, "very popular, a tall, slender brunette whose face was full of charm
if not actual beauty, and who had the additional charm of being not ashamed
of having been born an American."[13] She married Prince Serge Beloselsky-
Belozersky, who had served in the Hussar Life Guards Regiment before being
attached to the Russian embassies in Berlin and Paris.[14] Although the family had
once been immensely wealthy, by the middle of the nineteenth century, the family's fortunes had fallen considerably, forcing its members to sell their baroque St.
Petersburg mansion to the imperial crown in 1884; it became the official residence of Grand Duke Serge Alexandrovich and his wife, Elizabeth.[15] Thereafter,
the family lived in a rococo villa on Krestovsky Island, hidden from the center of
St. Petersburg by the spidery fingers of the Neva and a lush forest of birch,
where, enamored of all things English, they presided over afternoon games of
cricket, croquet, and polo.[16]

Julia, Princess Michael Cantacuzené, was the granddaughter of President
Ulysses S. Grant. Her husband, who also held the title of Count Speransky,
served as an officer in the Chevalier Guards. A third American, Lily Bouton, married Count Gregory Nostitz after her divorce from the German baron Guido von
Nimptsch. The union, one witness recorded, "created a sensation, for Count
Nostitz was looked upon as the beau-ideal of an eligible suitor. For days the feminine tongues of society wagged—mamas of marriageable daughters were aghast
to find this coveted prize escape their grasp, and the marriageable daughters
themselves likewise were not pleased to see their maiden charms outstripped by
those of an unknown American. . . . Society was eager to pick a hole in the pretty
Countess, and mischief-makers tried to ferret out something unfavorable in her
past. But all malignant efforts were in vain; the Countess carried all before her,
disarming everyone by her tact, her charming manner, her never failing amiabil-
ity, and her magnificent receptions."[17]

Of all these families, the wealthiest and most important were the Yusupovs.
They traced their descent from ancient Tartar khans who had murdered, raped,
and pillaged their way to power. They were created princes of Russia and
awarded the title of Yusupov after one of their ancestors, Abdul Mirza, converted
to Orthodoxy, a bold and clever decision that probably saved the family from

Zenaide and Felix Yusupov, dressed for the
Medieval Ball in 1903

obscurity. By the early nineteenth century, the Yusupovs had consolidated their power to such a degree that Prince Nicholas acted as a personal adviser to four Romanov sovereigns—Catherine the Great, Paul I, Alexander I, and Nicholas I.

At the end of the nineteenth century, it was a young woman, Princess Zenaide Yusupov, who stood as sole heir to the family fortune. With her "exquisite, rose-leaf complexion, luxuriant black hair, and cornflower blue eyes," immense fortune, and generous character, Zenaide Yusupov found herself courted by eligible scions from noble families across Europe.[18] But rather than making a grand match, she instead fell in love with the poor and socially unimportant Count Felix Sumarakov-Elston, an officer in the Chevalier Guards. When they married, he received imperial permission to add her family's name to his own and to that of any children born to the union. The couple had two sons, Princes Nicholas and Felix. Both boys adored their mother, but relations with their domineering father were strained and formal. He took no interest in their lives, asked no questions, and Nicholas and Felix, in turn, never confided in their father.

These sons were born into a world of privilege. The family fortune was incalculable: one pre-Revolutionary estimate of their real estate holdings alone placed the figure at $350 million.[19] They had invested wisely through the years, owning racing studs, industrial works, mineral and oil reserves, real estate, and one of the world's greatest private art collections. One of their relatives declared that they were so wealthy that they themselves "didn't really know how much" they were worth.[20] Even the Romanovs considered themselves poor in comparison with their Yusupov subjects.[21]

By the beginning of the twentieth century, the Yusupovs owned an impressive number of palaces and estates. There were an elaborate mansion in St. Petersburg, villas at nearby Tsarskoye Selo and at the Krasnoye Selo Army Camp, a Moscow house that had once been the hunting lodge of Ivan the Terrible, a country estate near the former capital, estates in central Russia, and three different mansions in the Crimea. But the centerpiece of the Yusupovs' world was their palace at No. 94 Moika Canal, a collection of drawing rooms, reception rooms, ballrooms, and art galleries that made it the most elegant of all the private houses in the imperial capital. A Moorish Room with a central fountain had been copied from an apartment in the Alhambra. Zenaide's bedroom, hung with blue damask, contained long rows of cabinets filled with her priceless collection of jewels. Furniture that had belonged to Marie Antoinette and a chandelier of rock crystal owned by Madame de Pompadour evoked the lost splendor of Versailles. Paintings by Rembrandt, Tiepolo, Fragonard, Bouchier, Watteau, and Robert graced the walls, while tables held bowls of uncut diamonds, rubies, emeralds, and sapphires, used as mere decorations.[22] At one end of the palace was a private Louis XV theater, in cream and gold.[23] In these elaborate surroundings, the Yusupovs held court on a scale equaled only by the imperial family. Orchestras and ballet companies were hired for evening entertainments, and a thousand guests might dine on solid gold or silver plates, lulled into a state of enchantment by the perfection of the setting.[24]

A jealous husband killed Prince Nicholas Yusupov in a duel in 1908, leaving his twenty-one-year-old brother Felix as sole heir to the family fortune. Felix was a curious young man, handsome and cultured, eccentric and dissolute. He had gone through a rapid succession of nannies and tutors, frightening them away with his uncontrollable behavior. Desperate, his parents finally sent him to a military school, and he completed his education at Oxford. When he returned to Russia, he was more mature, but his dissipation had grown to encompass opium and alcohol along with sexual pleasures. He was, noted one woman, "tall and slender, and almost too handsome. With his fine features, dark, melancholy eyes, and ivory skin he might almost be called effeminate in appearance. One sees such young men only in very old families where the vigor has begun to run low."[25]

Felix was an unconventional young man, consumed with a taste for pleasure and an enviable ability to flaunt his controversial, hedonistic style of life and still charm those he encountered. His most flamboyant excess was dressing as a woman; wrapped in his mother's clothes, he frequented St. Petersburg's fashionable cafés, flirting with young officers and sipping champagne.[26] His father was horrified when he learned of this, although he himself apparently kept a number of young male lovers in his private household.[27] The son's scandalous love affairs, rumored to include both the beautiful young women and men of St. Petersburg, were the talk of the gossip-hungry capital. It was in keeping with his flamboyant reputation that Felix Yusupov, in 1916, engineered the theatrical murder of Gregory Rasputin, who was shot, bludgeoned, and stabbed in the basement of the palace on the Moika Canal.

Sublime palaces and grand balls characterized the capital's aristocrats, but in the short, intense St. Petersburg summers, they fled their exquisite surroundings for their country estates. These ranged from large wooden dachas surrounded by working farms to extensive, lavish manor houses set in landscaped parks. Country estates were a world unto themselves, evoking both the privilege of their owners' positions and their commonality with the peasants who resided on them. Nowhere were the ties between the aristocracy and the peasant as close as they were on the country estate, and nowhere were their attitudes toward each other, from the aristocratic feelings of patriarchal obligation to the peasant feelings of important servitude, as marked as on these rural holdings. "It is in the country," noted one American visitor, "where one finds them really Russian."[28]

The majority of the great country estates were built in the eighteenth century, at a time when the Russian aristocracy was exposed to Western influences. Traveling abroad, they glimpsed the estates of European aristocrats that captured the way of life these aristocratic Russians were seeking. "The Russian nobility," writes Priscilla Roosevelt, "was the last European elite to express its identity in country living. Russians began building elaborate country houses in the mid-eighteenth century in an attempt to replicate, virtually overnight, a way of life that elsewhere had developed over the centuries."[29]

These estates, large or small, were self-contained worlds. Surrounding the house and the park were stables, barns, and kennels. As hermetic worlds, these estates formed the center of peasant work and life. In popular conception, estates were little more than tyrannical seats run by cruel landowners who exploited the peasants for their own gain. It is true that certain aristocrats ruled their estates on capricious, selfish whims, treating the peasants as personal slaves. Young, attractive girls were often subjected to the amorous advances of their masters. One Russian aristocrat who owned a large estate built six pavilions in his park, each modeled on a different historical style. He kept the pavilions staffed with a virtual harem of peasant girls, each of whom was required to dress in the French, Spanish, Chinese, or classical manner, according to the style of the building to which they were attached. The park itself was filled with empty pedestals; when the master went for a walk, his peasants, stripped naked and painted white, were forced to pose for hours atop the plinths, adopting classical poses. Eventually, during one of these endless tableaux, his Venus and Hercules jumped from their pedestals and clubbed him to death.[30]

For those living in the shadow of the great house, life was far from the carefree, bucolic ideal envisioned and eagerly believed by most Russian aristocrats. Helene

Izvolsky witnessed the church services, the peasant fairs, and the folk dances in dusty squares, "the joyful aspects of rural life. But it had another side, which was dark and grim."[31] She noted "children playing in the mud, their feet bare and stomachs swollen from malnutrition."[32] Even Grand Duchess Marie Pavlovna was unable to reconcile the scenes she saw in the country and wondered why her family—the ruling dynasty—showed such little concern for Russian peasants. In Europe, she noted, farmers "lived in clean houses, behind muslin curtains, and their children were college graduates."[33]

The larger estates employed hundreds of peasants. Special schools were often set up to educate the most gifted, producing talented architects, painters, dancers, and singers. Other peasants were trained to be stable boys, grooms, farm workers, gardeners, and craftsmen. House servants were almost always drawn from the local village, and maids, cooks, pages, footmen, stewards, housekeepers, laundry and scullery maids, pantry boys, and wet nurses all formed an essential part of an estate. Children had peasant nannies and riding instructors, while their parents employed men and women to sew their clothes, shine their shoes, and brush their hair.[34]

Many aristocratic families visited their country estates only in the summer, to escape the humidity of St. Petersburg or Moscow. From the nearest rail station, a string of carriages conveyed the family, its guests, and trunks down dusty roads and through deep forests of birch to the park surrounding the estate. The driveway to the house would be lined with village peasants, who reverently bowed as their masters passed them. The safe arrival of the family was celebrated with a special thanksgiving service in the nearest church, before the aristocrats finally settled in for a long, languid summer.

Baroness Buxhoeveden recalled her grandfather's country house near Kazan as "a vast and impressive gray stone building. From the marble staircase onward—purchased by Grandfather during his travels in Italy in the 1850s and brought, God knows how in those pre-railway days, to Kazan—it was all hideous and opulent. There were a few fine pictures and statues. . . . There was a vast ballroom upholstered in canary colored damask. Beside it was a sitting room with massive furniture in grass green silk with tremendous sofas and couples of unwieldy armchairs connected by small tables. Huge mirrors reflected the polished floors. In the smaller drawing room pale gray damask with white china buttons and a carpet with gigantic pink roses excited my admiration—but only mine—and the dining room was an orgy of carved light oak furniture and walls *en suite*. These sumptuous apartments were on the first floor, off my mother's rooms. Our nurseries were on the top floor and Grandfather lived by himself on the ground floor. Electricity did not yet exist and homely oil lamps were the only illumination on ordinary occasions. . . . Water, however, was laid on with great expense and Grandfather had his own bathroom with hot and cold water downstairs and a bath that was another souvenir of Rome, a huge sarcophagus with carved *bas-relief* figures all round."[35]

Throughout the summer, as the fields surrounding the estate lay thick with golden wheat and the gardens were in full bloom, life on the estate reached a crescendo. "In June," remembered Baroness Buxhoeveden, "the haymaking began and all the village girls and lads gathered in the meadows. Haymaking time was the courting time in the village. . . . The weather was glorious, and the girls decked themselves out in their best to fascinate their swains. There was a lot of giggling and romping about in the sweet smelling hay in the evening when the long day's work was done. Huge stacks were driven home with pretty buxom girls sitting on top of them, good humouredly chaffing and laughing at the lads who were walking wearily alongside."[36]

Peasants celebrated the season with a traditional village fair. "Tradesmen came from all the neighboring towns," recalled one man, "and many thousands of peasants flocked from thirty miles round to our village, which for a couple of days had a most animated aspect. Our fair lasted only a little more than twenty-four hours. On the eve of the fête, the great open space given to the fair was full of life and animation. Long rows of stalls, to be used for the sale of cottons, ribbons, and all sorts of peasant women's attire, were hurriedly built. The restaurant, a substantial stone building, was furnished with tables, chairs, and benches, and its floor was strewn over with bright yellow sand. Three wine shops were erected, and freshly cut brooms, planted on high poles, rose high in the air, to attract the peasants from a distance."[37]

Aristocrats often appeared at these fairs, gazing from the comfort of their carriages or strolling along the dusty village street as they received the bows of the peasants. Even as they looked on, however, the great house bustled with activity, as servants busily packed trunks and loaded carts with precious possessions. The end of the harvest marked the end of these languid summers, and with last looks at the shadowed facades of their great houses, aristocrats fled the country and returned to their busy lives in St. Petersburg, leaving behind estates that stood as the apogee of aristocratic life, visible reminders in stone of privilege destined to vanish forever in the tide of the Revolution.

9

THE RUSSIAN ORTHODOX CHURCH

A Russian cannot be godless. As soon as he
becomes godless, he ceases to be Russian.

—Dostoevsky

THE ORTHODOX CHURCH EVOKED the extremes of Russian life, its exuberant celebrations and quiet, introspective contemplations echoing the diversity of the world beyond its onion-domed cupolas. At once, it was the setting for pomp and pageantry on a scale unrivaled even at the imperial court, and, at the same time, it was a social equalizer, where aristocrat and peasant participated in glorious rituals dating to the beginning of Christendom. They respected the Church, lived in fear of God, kept Orthodoxy's feast and fast days, and reverently bowed and crossed themselves before glowing icons while enveloped in the ancient chants and pungent fragrance of incense.

Like the Russian empire itself, the Orthodox Church remained isolated from the rest of Europe. In 1054, the Orthodox Church, in a conflict over the correct form of worship and the supremacy of the Roman Pope, broke away from the West, and Constantinople became the center of the Orthodox world. Orthodoxy, untouched by the enlightenment of either the Renaissance or the Reformation, turned inward. In 1453, Constantinople fell to the Ottoman Turks, and Moscow proclaimed itself "the Third Rome." The metropolitan was elevated to the position of Patriarch, the spiritual keeper of the Orthodox flock, while the ruler became not only Defender of the True Faith, but also temporal heir to the emperors of Byzantium and the caesars of Rome, endowed with unlimited power and absolute authority.[1]

As Orthodoxy took hold, and its power and influence spread, churches and cathedrals were built for the faithful. Inside, these churches were often decorated with frescoes depicting the lives of saints, the rewards of Heaven, and the punishments of Hell, illuminated in the eerie, flickering light of hundreds of votive candles. Russians considered it disrespectful to sit before God; no matter how long a service, Orthodox celebrants stood. At the front of each church stood an iconostasis that shielded the sanctuary. Each iconostasis contained three doors: the center one, called the "Royal Door," was used only on festive occasions. Only priests of the Church could enter the sanctuary; even the emperor was restricted to entering but once—at his coronation, when, for the only time in his life, he celebrated the liturgy as a priest of Orthodoxy.

The worship in these churches was a rich blend of Western theology and Eastern opulence. Smoking censers filled the churches with the sweet fragrance of perfumed incense, to purify both the structure and the celebrants themselves. No musical instrument was allowed in the church; instead, exquisitely trained choirs sang beautiful chants, their melodic voices resonating in joyous worship. The liturgy itself contained elements of worship dating back to the beginning of Christianity, providing a link between the ancient and the modern, uniting the Orthodox faithful in ritual and reverence throughout the stretches of its influence.

Peter the Great, in his reorganization of the Russian empire, made the Orthodox Church subordinate to the state. He refused to appoint a new Patriarch when the post fell vacant. Instead, in 1721, he created the Holy Synod, a body composed of various bishops and other clergy. The establishment of Orthodoxy as the state religion invested the emperor, as head of state, with even more power and prestige, a position reinforced by Emperor Paul, who claimed for himself and his crowned successors supreme guardianship of the Church.[2]

The Holy Synod consisted of the over-procurator, who headed a panel of three specially selected bishops and nine ordinary priests. The most famous man to hold the post, and the most controversial, was Konstantin Pobedonostsev, the emperor's former political tutor. Pobedonostsev's highly nationalistic Pan-Slav views, accompanied by an intolerance for other faiths, were a contributing factor to the terrible pogroms carried out against Russian Jews during the last years of the empire. Directly beneath the procurator were the metropolitans of the empire's four lavra: St. Petersburg, Kiev, Sergeiev Posad, and Moscow. Below these men stretched a rich collection of archbishops, bishops, deacons, archimandrites or abbots, priests, and monks. The Orthodox clergy formed two groups: the white, or married clergy, from whose ranks were drawn most parish priests; and the black, monastic clergy.

The Orthodox Church stressed that God often endowed simple men with remarkable gifts, able to preach and lead others to salvation without any official religious affiliation. These wandering holy men were called *strannikii.* There were also monks in the Church who lived their lives as spiritual guides to the wealthy and powerful. Such a man, called a *starets*, was thought not only to heal the spirit but also to interpret the will of God to those seeking answers. Archimandrite Theophan, the director of the St. Petersburg Theological Seminary, once declared, "God's men still exist on earth. To this day our Holy Russia abounds in saints. God sends consolation to his people from time to time in the guise of righteous men and they are the mainstays of Holy Russia."[3]

Such beliefs appealed to Nicholas and Alexandra. Having been raised in the Church, Nicholas approached its mysticism with a philosophy rooted in his overwhelming acceptance of the idea of *sud'ba.* As supreme guardian of the Church, he was anointed and consecrated at his coronation and joined the Orthodoxy clergy as a priest of the faith. These sacraments endowed the sovereign with the outward signs of benediction and grace, elevating him from a mere political into a spiritual realm where it was believed God directed his every action and thought. Through such actions, the role of the emperor was perceived as a kind of autocratic priesthood, an inseparable union of Church and State in one man. It was a view shared by both Nicholas and Alexandra, who saw any criticism against the emperor as a direct threat to Orthodoxy and a divinely inspired order.

When Alexandra converted to Orthodoxy, she did so with all of the fervor that burned within her soul. At first, she was instructed by Father Ivan Basarov, who served as priest at the Russian Embassy in Stuttgart; he quickly found her a difficult pupil, eager to question the faith. Exasperated, he abandoned his position to Father Ioann Yanishev, Alexander III's personal confessor. Yanishev, too, found the young Hessian princess a diligent but difficult pupil: he later referred to her religious instruction as "no easy task."[4] Despite the precedent, Alix refused to denounce her former faith, arguing that while she accepted the teachings of the Orthodox Church, there were no heresies within the Christian Church, only "various religions."[5]

For Alexandra, there were no backward glances. Increasingly, she turned to religion for comfort, and as she did so, her views widened considerably to encompass less than Orthodox alternatives. Alexandra had little time to absorb her instructions: received into the Orthodox Church the day after Alexander III's death, she was immediately plunged into the complicated rituals. Her devotion was extraordinary to most at the Russian court. Yet she found in her new faith great strength. "Our Church service and prayers," she explained to her aunt, Princess Louise, "are most beautiful and consoling, and to partake oftener of Holy Communion brings such peace and resignation."[6]

Beyond the great palaces, peasants bowed reverently before icons and knelt in front of chanting priests, but in the St. Petersburg of Nicholas II's reign, an air of cynicism had invaded the aristocracy. Society, bored and complacent, sought new experiences, new theologies; increasingly, aristocrats viewed Orthodoxy as a restraining force, not only on their frequently amoral lives, but also on their societal and cultural aspirations. Orthodox traditions were viewed as superstitious, the sphere of peasants who accepted a universe ordered by unseen forces, where their own lives were submitted to the authority of others. Mysticism and spiritualism were rampant. Thus, it was not uncommon to find wandering holy men in aristocratic salons, peasants cloaked in rags and dirt enthralling jaded audiences with exotic tales of salvation and supernatural visions. Curiosity overcame piety, and séances and sexual adventure, all in the name of religion, became fashionable in the smart salons of the capital.

Nicholas and Alexandra themselves began to delve into this religious quagmire. "Given her dull, egotistical character and narrow world view, given the intoxicating effects of the luxury of the court," wrote Serge Witte of the empress, "it is not odd that she should have completely succumbed to what I call Orthodox paganism."[7] Even those more kindly disposed to the empress freely admitted that she delved into more questionable forms of religion, including spiritualism, the Theosophist movement, and study of obscure medieval religious tracts.

Shortly after the turn of the century, the imperial couple invited a steady stream of wandering holy men into their palaces. One of these was Mitya Kolyaba, endowed, or so it was said, with a gift of prophecy. According to one man, he was "bow-legged, misshapen, almost mute, with a withered arm. He had to be led as his eyesight was very poor; his hearing, too, was deficient, and his speech consisted of a few horrible sounds, uttered in painful gasps. Whenever he was shaken by an epileptic attack and began to shriek his voice changed from an uncanny whisper into the sinister howling of an animal. Finally, it would become an unnerving and fear-inspiring roaring and baying. The repulsive impressions thus created were enhanced by the insane flailings of his deformed arms. Indeed, one had to have extremely strong nerves to endure the presence of this imbecile."[8]

The most famous of the pre-Rasputin holy men, however, was a French citizen named Philippe Nazier-Vachot. Nicholas II first met Nazier-Vachot while on a state visit to France at the turn of the century; both he and Alexandra were so taken with the man's philosophies and apparent gifts of prophecy that they issued an invitation to visit them in Russia. From the time of his arrival in Russia, the emperor's diary makes continual reference to "Our Friend," as the imperial couple called Philippe. They met often, usually at the Palace of Znamenka, which belonged to the emperor's uncle, Grand Duke Nicholas Nikolaievich Jr. It was here that the two Montenegrin sisters, Militsa and Anastasia, actively promoted Nazier-Vachot as Russia's new savior. "At 2:30 we went to Znamenka and sat in the garden until 5 o'clock," Nicholas II wrote on July 13, 1901. "Our Friend was with us. . . . After dinner we again spent the evening all together at Znamenka."[9] And a few days later, Nicholas II noted, "We listened to Our Friend all evening."[10]

On several occasions, Nazier-Vachot predicted that the empress would give birth to a male heir. At first, Nicholas and Alexandra naively clung to this hope. Then, in the spring of 1902, Nazier-Vachot told the empress that she was again pregnant. For the next few months, Alexandra waited in anticipation; her menstrual periods ceased, and she began to gain weight. But it was all an illusion. On 17 August, Dr. Ott, the imperial obstetrician, examined the empress and declared that rather than expecting a child, she was instead only suffering from anemia. It was publicly announced that the empress had miscarried. After this failure, even the imperial couple was overcome with doubts about Nazier-Vachot. Eventually, the Russian police, armed with clear evidence that Nazier-Vachot was a charlatan, expelled him from the country on the emperor's orders. Before he left Russia, however, Nazier-Vachot predicted that God would soon send another "Friend" to comfort and advise the imperial couple. That "Friend" appeared in 1905: Gregory Rasputin.

Contrary to the decades of legend that cloak his life, Rasputin was never a priest or a monk. He was simply a peasant, believed to be possessed, like the strannikii and startsi, of gifts of healing through prayer. In this, he was promoted by two of St. Petersburg's most prominent and influential clergymen at the turn of the century: Archimandrite Theophan, the director of the St. Petersburg

Theological Seminary; and Father Ivan of Kronstadt, who presided at the Cathedral of St. Andrei at the base of Russia's Baltic Fleet, Kronstadt, on Kotlin Island in the Gulf of Finland. Theophan frequented the most fashionable drawing rooms and salons of the capital, often introducing to society the latest wandering holy man or peasant to arrive in the city. With a glowing recommendation from such an illustrious patron, it was easy for a man like Rasputin to attract the attention of the imperial couple.

By the outbreak of the First World War, the Siberian peasant had risen to the pinnacle of his extraordinary power. "One name was on all lips—Rasputin," recalled Countess Nostitz. "One heard it whispered reverently by the Empress's favorite, Vyrubova, sneered at contemptuously by society, spoken with superstitious awe by the lower classes. The dirty, unkempt peasant who, not so many years before, had left his native village to tramp, knapsack on shoulders, staff in hand, pilgrim-wise from monastery to monastery, had become a legendary figure, acquired an importance that was more fictitious than real."[11] This fiction replaced fact, and the imperial family—living far away from the public eye—became inexorably linked to the peasant's foibles and exploits, of which there were many. With Alexei's illness a carefully guarded secret, no one knew why Rasputin's presence was tolerated, and his continued favor was put down to corruption, stupidity, and a whole host of nefarious deeds, including hypnotizing the imperial couple or keeping them drugged. Nicholas was powerless to fight against his wife, who refused to give up her reliance on the peasant. "Better one Rasputin than ten hysterical scenes a day," the emperor once commented in a rare moment of candor.[12] And so, with reluctance, he left Rasputin alone, to cavort his way across the imperial capital, providing ample ammunition for the wagging tongues of society gossips.

If the idea of an intelligent, educated society enraptured with such bizarre spiritual concerns seems more in keeping with medieval Russia, the Orthodox Church itself taught that such things were real, that miracles and saints played a part in contemporary life. Nicholas II eagerly embraced this philosophy and, indeed, contributed to it. In the years before the First World War, the Russian Orthodox Church canonized three saints, Theodosius of Chernigov in 1896, Seraphim of Sarov in 1903, and Iosef of Belgorod in 1911.

Seraphim's canonization, in 1903, came about as a direct result of the emperor's personal intervention. Born in 1759, Seraphim had entered the Sarov Monastery, where he became a monk. For many years, he lived as a hermit in a simple wooden hut outside the monastery walls and soon gained a reputation as a holy man. A number of miracles were ascribed to Seraphim, both before and after his death in 1833, and he had long been considered a candidate for sainthood.

In 1902, it was suggested to Nicholas and Alexandra that if Seraphim were canonized, the empress might conceive a son, and the imperial couple took up the cause. There was an enormous outcry, as Seraphim's body was found in an advanced state of decomposition; the preservation of a candidate's remains was one of the principal tests of saintliness. Bishop Anthony of Tambov Province protested against the canonization, but the emperor silenced him by stripping his rank and sending him to a new post in Siberia. Even the procurator of the Holy Synod, Nicholas's former tutor Konstantin Pobedonostsev, insisted that Seraphim did not meet the Church's established criteria. Empress Alexandra, however, was determined. In July of 1902, she told Pobedonostsev that she wanted Seraphim canonized within six days. When the procurator strenuously objected, Nicholas II himself stepped in, demanding that the canonization take place within a year. Such autocratic interference in purely religious affairs was unheard of. When Pobedonostsev reminded the imperial couple that the Holy Synod was the ultimate arbiter of glorification, Alexandra was furious, saying, "Everything is within the Emperor's power, even to the making of saints!"[13]

On January 24, 1903, under intense imperial pressure, the Church finally declared Seraphim worthy of canonization, stating that the preservation of hair, teeth, and bones was ample evidence of sainthood. This contradicted hundreds of years of accepted Orthodox tradition, and, when the canonization finally took place, the Holy Synod was flooded with hundreds of letters condemning the action.[14] St. Petersburg society, largely indifferent to religious affairs, saw it as yet another example of Empress Alexandra's influence over her husband. Philippe Nazier-Vachot's part in the affair soon became known, and wags in the imperial capital were heard to remark, "It would be difficult to know where Philippe ends and Seraphim begins."[15]

Nearly the entire imperial family attended the canonization that summer. Sarov was not on a rail line; the imperial train pulled to a halt at an isolated railway siding on July 17, and the emperor, the empress, the dowager empress, and members of the imperial family drove across the dusty roads in a string of open barouches. Thousands of peasants had turned out, and the emperor ordered the carriages stopped to greet them. His sister Olga recalled, "And there he was, in a crowd of pilgrims and others milling round him, all struggling to kiss his hands, his sleeve, his shoulders. It was too moving for words. We were traveling with the customary Cossack escort, but there was not a soul for them to watch. Nicky was just *Batushka*—Tsar—Little Father—to all those people."[16]

Half a million pilgrims had gathered at Sarov to join in the canonization.[17] That evening, the bells of the Cathedral of the Assumption rang out, announcing the start of the ceremonies. The emperor and his family drove to the cathedral, where Metropolitan Anthony of St. Petersburg and a crowd of more than sixty priests met them. Some thousand gonfalon bearers joined in the Procession of the Cross as it wound its way to the Church of St. Zosima and St. Savvaty where Seraphim's relics were kept. "The impression was tremendous," Nicholas wrote in his diary, "to see how the people, and especially sick cripples and the unfortunate, regarded the Procession of the Cross."[18] As the Choir of the Holy Synod, brought from St. Petersburg for the occasion, intoned the liturgy, Metropolitan Anthony offered prayers for Seraphim's intercession. At the end of the service, Nicholas II and several of the grand dukes carried Seraphim's coffin on their shoulders to the Assumption Cathedral, placing it in a silver and marble shrine, a gift from the emperor and the empress.[19]

Nicholas and Alexandra also visited Seraphim's small cabin, located in a forest nearly a mile from town. It was a brilliant day, and they deliberately walked the route, keenly observed by thousands of peasants who stood quietly at a respectful distance. After a liturgy at the cabin, the imperial party returned along the same route. The crowd had grown to over a hundred thousand people, but the provincial governor had been ordered not to prevent their assembly. Nicholas elected to take a shorter path back to Sarov, one that took him directly through the crowd, which immediately surrounded him. "I saw the Emperor disappear in the peasant flood," remembered Alexander Mossolov. As he tried to make his way through the gathered crowd, Nicholas shouted, "Let me through, little brothers!" No one paid any attention, and the crowd round the emperor swelled even more. Finally, Mossolov and an adjutant lifted the emperor in their hands, so that all could see him. "There was a veritable thunder of hurrahs!" Mossolov recalled, and the crowd parted to allow the imperial party to pass.[20]

Nicholas returned to St. Petersburg overwhelmed at the canonization. At Sarov, noted S. S. Oldenburg, "he found himself intimately surrounded by untold multitudes who were overcome by emotions the same as his and who affectionately expressed their devotion to him. He met peasants, clergymen, and noblemen. Subconsciously it came to him that the sedition that had plagued him for the past year, and which posed such a threat to his ministers, was an alien, non-Russian, and distinctly urban phenomenon. In contrast the heart of Russia was still healthy and it still beat in unison with the heart of the Emperor."[21]

The emperor viewed the countryside, and even Moscow, as bastions of the Orthodox faith. St. Petersburg bristled with churches, their onion domes and tall spires floating over the pastel colors decorating their baroque facades, designed to transport worshippers beyond their rational existence into the mystical realm. Yet there was little of the traditional spirit within their European-inspired walls, and most churches in the imperial capital impressed only through their sheer size and wealth of decoration. The two greatest churches in the capital—Kazan Cathedral and St. Isaac's Cathedral—were not mere sanctuaries dedicated to God; they were public celebrations of the glories of Orthodoxy, of the Russian empire, and of imperial splendor.

Midway down Nevsky Prospekt, where the broad avenue crossed the Catherine Canal, stood Kazan Cathedral. Paul I had commissioned the building in 1801 from the architect Andrei Voronikhin, and it was completed a mere decade after its inception. In order to conform the structure to the traditional east-west axis, Voronikhin was forced to place the main entrance down a side street, with the door to the north transept facing Nevsky Prospekt itself. To solve this problem, he crowned the north transept with an immense portico and flanked it with twin, curved colonnades, copied from those at St. Peter's in Rome, that fanned outward in a semicircle to create a grand entrance court. At their center, beneath the massive northern portico, tall double doors of cast bronze depicted Lorenzo Ghiberti's famous *Gates of Paradise* portals on the Baptistry in Florence.[22]

Inside the cathedral, double rows of columns, each cut from a single block of pink Finnish granite and topped with gilded Corinthian capitals, supported the vaulted ceiling.[23] Above the mosaic floor, of black, gray, and pink Karelian marble framed in red granite, the dome rose 233 feet, adorned with coffers inset with gilded rosettes.[24] At the front of the cathedral, embedded in the great silver iconostasis, was the *Miracle Working Icon of the Kazan Mother of God*, the protector of the House of Romanov. The icon, reputed to have considerable healing powers, was one of the most venerated of all Orthodox symbols.[25] But the centerpiece of the cathedral was the tomb of Russia's great hero, General Field Marshal Prince Michael Kutuzov, who had turned Napoleon out of the empire in 1812. Surrounding the tomb, and hanging above the columns, were hundreds of captured French standards and regimental banners, as well as keys to the towns that Kutuzov had captured during the conflict.[26] Kazan Cathedral, for all of its glory and imperial trappings, was a cold, almost severe church. The same could not be said of the capital's other great church, the Cathedral of St. Isaac, which stood between the Mariinsky Palace and Senate Square, down the Neva from the Winter Palace.

St. Isaac's Cathedral was the masterpiece of August Ricard de Montferrand, a Frenchman with no formal training in architecture, a fact that resulted in nearly a decade of delays. Not until 1825 was a working set of plans finally produced, and work began in earnest. Thousands of wooden supports were sunk into the marshy ground to form the foundation, and thirty-five years of construction began. Thirty-five years later, it was finished and sanctified, its great gilded dome rising majestically above the imperial capital. The effect was stunning. "Nothing is so beautiful," recorded Théophile Gautier, "as this great temple of gold, bronze, and granite, standing on a carpet of spotless ermine under the blue rays of a winter moon."[27]

The cathedral was built of red granite and more than fourteen varieties of marble. On each facade, Montferrand placed a large portico, modeled on those of the Pantheon in Rome. The porticos on the northern and the southern facades contained sixteen columns of polished red Finnish granite, fifty-four feet high and seven feet thick, each resting on a base of gilded bronze and topped with a gilded bronze Corinthian capital.[28] On the roof, small bell towers with gilded cupolas rose above massive piers, while enormous bronze angels holding torches stood guard at the four corners. All around the roof, Montferrand placed bronze statues of the Apostles and the Evangelists, gilded to catch the sun. Crowning all was the ribbed dome, rising to a gilded cupola nearly 350 feet above the cathedral floor; according to legend, some six thousand workers died of lead poisoning while applying the gilt.[29]

Tall bronze doors cast with elaborate reliefs opened to the cathedral's interior. Massive piers, sheathed in pink, gray, and red marble, rose to the vaulted ceiling. Hundreds of richly composed mosaics adorned the walls, shimmering with 43 different varieties of minerals and precious stones, 900 pounds of gold, and 16 tons of malachite.[30] At the front of the cathedral, the iconostasis rose 200 feet between columns of pink, gray, and red marble and pilasters faced with malachite and lapis lazuli, all decorated with gilt bronze bases and Corinthian capitals.[31] By the time it was completed, the cathedral had cost some 25 million gold rubles ($250,000,000 in 2005 figures).[32] Grand as it was, St. Isaac's remained a surprisingly delicate, sublime building, with a pleasing mixture of color and light that made it one of the world's most inspiring cathedrals.

Kazan Cathedral

It was here, at St. Isaac's Cathedral—the greatest religious structure in the empire—that the most revered and important Orthodox celebrations took place. In the entire liturgical calendar, no feast or celebration was as important or as joyous as Pascha, Easter, and no other church could match its impressive service. Easter celebrations officially began in February, with *Maslenitsa*, or Carnival. All of St. Petersburg was thrown into a frenzied panic, a speeding whirlwind of increasing parties, entertainments and balls, tremendous feasts, and long evenings at the theater, before the beginning of Lent called a halt to the festivities.

Street fairs and circuses were thronged with customers; along the frozen Neva River near the Winter Palace, hundreds of people gathered to watch jugglers, puppet shows, performing animals, and dancing gypsies. "There was an animated fair along the vast esplanade," recalled one St. Petersburg lady, "with booths, shops, puppet shows, music, and folk dancing . . . so much enchantment and magic—a creation of the primitive imagination of the peasant and the sophisti-cated artistry of city people."[33]

The largest fair took place on the Champs de Mars, filled—as one lady recalled—with "jostling, hurrying, laughing, swearing, singing, and sweating crowds of men, women, and children, moving up and down between shod-dily timbered stalls."[34] Small booths, gaily decorated with bunting and flags, sold roasted nuts, gingerbread, and tea and spiced drinks. "Food stalls abounded," recalled Tamara Talbot Rice, "and although the wealthy feasted at home on pancakes filled with caviar and other delicacies, the poor gorged at the fair on hot pancakes dripping with butter. Caged birds and finery could be purchased, cheap jewelry, lace collars, satin ribbons, vividly pat-terned cotton and woolen head scarves, wooden toys intricately carved and gaily painted by village craftsmen and, most exciting of all, small glass tubes filled with pink or mauve-colored liquid—I believe some sort of spirit—in which little black glass imps were imprisoned; called for some inexplicable reason either Carthusian Devils or American Inhabitants, these imps could be made to career up and down their cages merely by warming the tubes in one's hands. The noise was gloriously deafening, the gaiety sublime."[35] At the center of the gatherings, lines of eager adults and children waited to ride the high switchbacks, roller-coasters built upon the icy ground, or to sled down the long, snow-covered slopes of the Russian Mountains, enormous ice mounds rising into the misty sky.[36]

St. Isaac's Cathedral.
See plate 11.

The seven days before the beginning of Lent were known as Butter Week. "It was a week of gluttony," recalled one lady, "of abandonment to sheer delight, a time when we children could be almost as foolish as we felt inclined, and when even the poor shared in the feasting and fun, for the week's dissipation served as a prelude to the Lenten fasts and abnegations that succeeded it."[37] At the end of the week, a masquerade ball took place at the Mariinsky Theater, thronged with thousands of brightly costumed revelers. At the stroke of midnight of *La Folle Journée*, all dancing, eating, laughing, sledding, drinking, and entertaining came to an abrupt end, and the Great Seven Weeks' Lenten Fast began.

Interior of
St. Isaac's Cathedral.
See plate 12.

The Great Fast was the strictest of all Orthodox fasts. Wednesdays and Fri-days were specific fast days, while the general fast encompassed the rest of each week. All meat was excluded from the diet, along with milk, butter, eggs, and sugar. All celebrations ceased, the great theaters and concert halls went dark, and the ballrooms in the palaces lining the Neva embankments were shrouded in dustcovers. Clothing changed as well. For society women, no elaborate velvets, satins, or tulles could be worn, and jewelry was restricted to a string of pearls. Church services were held daily, and all the clergy abandoned their elaborate copes and stoles in favor of black monastic dress. The only relief in this subdued period came on Palm Sunday, when religious parades were held, presents were exchanged, and Easter eggs were waxed, dyed, and colored in festive designs in anticipation of the coming festival.[38]

On Good Friday, every Orthodox Church in the nation was opened to reveal the *Plashanitza*, an effigy depicting Christ in His tomb, standing before the iconostasis. All lights and candles were extinguished, and the Royal Door lay open to the empty sanctuary, stripped of its fittings. Hundreds of hushed worshippers crowded into these churches, praying before the icons and listening to public readings of the appropriate scriptural passages. A heavy sense of anticipation hung over the crowd, as they waited for the great celebration of Easter itself to begin.

Although every church and cathedral in the empire was filled to capacity on Easter Eve, there was no more moving celebration of the festival than the midnight liturgy at St. Isaac's Cathedral. This was considered the official, or state, celebration, attended by all members of the Diplomatic Corps accredited to the imperial court, many of the aristocracy, and occasionally even members of the imperial family themselves. Celebrants arrived at the cathedral having passed through darkened streets, for nearly every lamp and fire had been dimmed or extinguished in anticipation of the festivities. The crowd of fourteen thousand filled the dark cathedral, occupying every available space. Below the dome, before the iconostasis, seats were specially placed for the Diplomatic Corps, who arrived in formal mourning dress: striped trousers or knee breeches, black frock coats, and white tie; and black velvet, satin, and silk gowns for the women. The men wore their decorations—order sashes and medals—while the women sparkled in diamonds hidden behind lace and tulle veils. All round them stood members of the aristocracy, dressed in thick coats of sable, mink, and fox, jostling for space with the ordinary workers and peasants in their Sunday best. The only light in the entire cathedral came from four tall candles burning in front of the iconostasis, their eerie shadows flickering across the expectant crowd. A massed choir, robed in black, chanted ancient and solemn hymns, while the cathedral quickly filled with the sweet smell of burning incense. The Royal Door of the iconostasis stood open, revealing the dim interior of the sanctuary, emptied of its glittering chalices and caskets.

At eleven in the evening, a mass of black-robed priests, led by the metropolitan of St. Petersburg and the ranking bishops of the Church, slowly marched down the main aisle to the front of the cathedral, chanting the Russian Office for the Dead. Just after half-past eleven, the metropolitan, assisted by the bishops, removed the silken Plashanitza that had stood at the front of the cathedral for a week and closed the Royal Door of the iconostasis. Turning to the congregation, the metropolitan announced that the tomb of Christ was empty and ordered an archimandrite to search for the missing Savior. Carrying a gilt lantern, the archimandrite, followed by a handful of bishops or priests, wandered through the cathedral. After reporting that the building was empty, the metropolitan ordered that they search outside, and the group disappeared through the high bronze doors. At three minutes before midnight, they returned, marching slowly to the front of the cathedral.

At the first stroke of midnight, the iconostasis doors opened, revealing the metropolitan, surrounded by his bishops and priests, attired this time in blazing white and silver copes and stoles, embroidered with thousands of tiny diamonds, pearls, rubies, and emeralds, all sparkling in the light. In a moment of pure theater, which not even the imperial court could have better staged, the bells of the city's churches announced the arrival of Easter, joined by the booming of guns from the Fortress of St. Peter and St. Paul. At the same time, the cathedral was suddenly filled with light. Above the heads of the congregation, lining the edges of the cornices and the circumference of the dome, thousands of unlit votive candles had been carefully placed, their wicks linked by a single, oiled thread of gun cotton. At the stroke of midnight, the end was lit, and a flame raced along the thread, from wick to wick, until, as if by magic, the cornices and the dome were illuminated with the flickering flames of the votive candles. Below, members of the congregation also lit their own individual tapers, until the entire cathedral was flooded with the soft, shimmering light.

The metropolitan turned to the congregation and announced, *"Khristos Voskrese!"* ("Christ is risen!"). With one mighty voice, the crowd replied joyously, *"Voistini Voskrese!"* ("Verily, He is risen!") before the choir burst into the Easter liturgy, its rising harmonies floating through the cathedral. Outside, bright spotlights played on the cathedral walls, flames roared into the night sky from the torches held aloft by the bronze angels perched at the corners of the roof, and fireworks exploded over the icy waters of the Neva. For one moment, emperor and prince, peasant and student, were united, as they began the Pascha celebrations and great feasts after weeks of deprivation.[39]

Part Two

PALACES

10

THE WINTER PALACE

IMPERIAL PALACES WERE THE MOST visible symbols of the Russian court. These buildings, with their ornate baroque and classical facades, stood as tangible reminders of the court and the autocratic power it supported. They spoke of the dynasty's glory in their facades adorned with sculpture; echoed fallen empires in their ranged pilasters and elaborate pediments; and, through sheer magnificence, transcended their role as shelters to give witness to theatrical ambition and to the enormous gulf that, in imperial Russia, lay between the governing and the governed.

The Winter Palace was the most important of all imperial residences. Only Versailles could rival its magnificence. "The riches, gems, and treasures of this Palace," wrote one nineteenth-century visitor, "are like the fancied contents of those described in *The Arabian Nights*, and the magnificence of the vases, jars, tables, and consoles of porphyry, jasper, and malachite, is perfectly astounding."[1] Few of the Romanovs were fond of the enormous edifice. "How I hated that Palace!" recalled Grand Duchess Olga Alexandrovna. "Alone of all the family, my mother liked it."[2] Nevertheless, the Winter Palace remained the official residence of the Russian imperial court until the Revolution.

Peter the Great built the first Winter Palace in 1711, on the edge of the forest encircling his fledgling capital. A simple, one-storey structure in the Dutch style, Peter's palace was a warren of low-ceilinged rooms, crowned with a massive hipped roof and a tall golden spire. It took its name from the Winter Canal, a narrow channel that flowed from the Neva to the winding Moika. Just five years after its construction, however, it proved too small, and between 1719 and 1720, the German architect Georg Johann Mattarnovi replaced it with a larger, two-storeyed building adorned with pediments, pilasters, and an elaborate cornice.[3] It was here, in the second Winter Palace, that Peter the Great died in 1725.

Empress Anna, like many of the Romanovs, was obsessed with architecture and built several, increasingly larger, versions of the Winter Palace in an attempt to surround herself with suitably regal trappings. Peter's Winter Palace was razed; in its place, the architect Domenico Tressini erected a three-storeyed building of more than a hundred rooms, ornamented with pilasters and cornices. Anna, however, was not satisfied.[4] One of her courtiers, Count Apraxine, had built a mansion just down the Neva River, and Anna made no secret of her displeasure that an aristocrat should have such a luxurious house. To curry favor, Apraxine presented it to his sovereign, and in 1732 Anna ordered the rising young Italian architect Bartolomeo Rastrelli to remodel the mansion into a new, fourth Winter Palace. Stretching five hundred feet along the Neva, it was the largest structure in St. Petersburg.[5]

Empress Elizabeth was even more enamored of building than her predecessor had been. She wanted a palace to rival Versailles, and Rastrelli began work on the new, fifth Winter Palace in 1755. Thousands of peasants and workers, drafted into service, labored round the clock to give form to Rastrelli's grand vision. Six years later, the enormous building was completed. It stood as mute testament to Rastrelli's brilliance, an immensely long structure of three storeys, ranged round an internal quadrangle, one facade thrown toward the great Nevsky Prospect, another echoed in the mirror of the swift Neva River. The architect's theatrical flair proved equal to Elizabeth's extravagant tastes, combining the baroque and the rococo in a structure of bold assertion and subtle nuance, its undulating facade, adorned with pilasters, caryatids, and statuary, cast in the sunlit summer splendor and dappled winter shadow of the northern capital.

On the evening of December 17, 1837, fire erupted in the palace. Crowds watched in disbelief as orange flames raced from window to window, glass shattering and bursting over the frozen ground to reveal glimpses of burning silk, crashing chandeliers, and collapsing columns within the inferno. Servants and members of the Imperial Army formed a human chain, conveying furniture, paintings, tapestries, and sculptures to safety.[6] When Nicholas I caught sight of a group of soldiers attempting to enter the hellish interior to save a looking glass, he cried, "Your lives are worth much more to me than a mirror, lads! Get out!"[7] After two days, only the charred, smoking walls remained.

It would have been easy to raze the ruins and begin anew, but the Winter Palace was a building rich in history, intimately connected with the Romanovs and their empire, so Nicholas I ordered the building restored to its former grandeur. Work went on round the clock; at night, the ten thousand laborers built fires to keep warm, mixing cement with vodka so it would not freeze in the chill Russian winter. As great a feat as it had been for Rastrelli to raise his structure in six years, Nicholas managed to do better and cut the original construction time by two-thirds. In two years, the sixth Winter Palace, completely restored and more brilliant than ever, had risen from the ashes to once again dominate St. Petersburg.[8]

The Winter Palace was a building of immense drama. The scale of the structure was horizontal; it complemented the breadth of the wide Neva, from which St. Petersburg drew so much of its inspiration. Rastrelli used massed columns, moldings, carved window lintels, and statuary to lend each of the facades a subtly different look. To the north, the palace overlooked the river; to the west, a small private garden, enclosed behind a tall iron fence, stretched along the Neva; to the east stood the buildings of the Hermitage; and to the south, the building enclosed Carlo Rossi's great Palace Square, dramatically framed in the triple arch of the General Staff Building and enclosed along the eastern side by Bryullov's Guards' Corps.

The palace had more than 1,050 rooms and 117 staircases.[9] The Winter Palace was built round a quadrangle; above the lead roof a golden cupola marked the cathedral. The building was so large that a peasant once employed there brought his entire family to live with him, unannounced and unknown to the palace authorities. He even managed to smuggle a cow into the building and up the staircases, to provide fresh milk for his children. They were only discovered when the smell of manure became intolerable.[10]

The palace was a cold, stark building, conceived as a statement of power. The Winter Palace was a stage upon which the ceremonial of the Russian court could be enacted, a majestic backdrop for military reviews and parades. The main halls of the palace, enormous, opulent enfilades, were empty, bereft of furnishings or any sign of humanity. The private apartments, by contrast, were a warren of small rooms, crammed with overstuffed sofas and chairs, and every inch of available space covered with the most ordinary of personal souvenirs. These two faces, public and private, the majestic and the common, provided a revealing window into the lives of the last emperor and his family.

The main entrance to the Winter Palace, a triple arch that echoed Rossi's great triumphal approach on the opposite side of Palace Square, pierced the center of the southern facade. Fifteen-foot-high iron gates, adorned with gilded foliage, garlands, laurels, and double-headed eagles, opened to the quadrangle, ornamented with pleached limes and a splashing fountain. Visitors entered the palace through the Rastrelli Corridor, its vaulted ceiling resting on clusters of banded columns; here, before imperial balls, guests moved between a tropical forest of potted palms and orange trees, casting furtive glances in enormous pier glasses as they made final adjustments to their intricate uniforms and expensive gowns. The Rastrelli Corridor swept through the ground floor until it reached an immense arch, thrown across the passage to dramatically frame the main ascent to the State Apartments, the Jordan Staircase.

The Jordan Staircase took its name from the Ceremony of the Epiphany, held each year on January 6, when the emperor presided over the blessing of the Neva River. A wide flight of steps, their white Carrara marble cloaked beneath crimson runners, rose and divided into twin flights, curving between balustrades adorned with ormolu and alabaster candelabra to meet at the first floor, where gray granite columns stretched to a painted ceiling depicting *Russia in Triumph*. Tall windows pierced the white scagliola walls, washing the gilded putti, swags, and heraldic reliefs in the blinding light of day. At night, with the glow from the candelabra and gilded chandeliers reflected in the rows of mirrors, the staircase glittered in the soft golden light.[11]

From the landing of the Jordan Staircase, immensely tall doors, ornamented with gilded carving, opened to the first of the State Apartments or Parade Halls in the Great Enfilade, the Field Marshal's Hall. Rising two storeys, its white scagliola walls were adorned with stucco military trophies set between pilasters supporting a narrow second-floor gallery. Above the parquet floor hung three massive, hand-carved wooden chandeliers, their gilding a perfect mirror to the glow of their candles. A delicate stucco cornice and the grisaille paintings in the lunettes provided the only decoration.[12] It was a deliberately austere room, a deliberate contrast to the next room in the enfilade, the Small Throne Room.

Here, white and gold Corinthian columns supported a vaulted ceiling decorated with hundreds of shields encased in gilded laurel wreath borders. From the center hung a solid silver chandelier, swirling above a floor of mahogany, rosewood, yew, sandalwood, ebony, and beech, inlaid in intricate geometric patterns. The walls, covered in crimson velvet brocade from Lyon woven with double-headed eagles in silver thread, were hung with two immense paintings depicting Peter the Great during the Northern War against Sweden. A dais, set below an arched apse, held Empress Anna's carved, gilded throne; behind the throne, jasper columns framed an allegorical canvas of Minerva guiding Peter the Great.[13]

The Hall of Armorial Bearings was a room of unrestrained splendor. Twenty-two arched windows overlooked the quadrangle, matched by twenty-two mirrors set within gilded frames on the opposite wall. Sixty-four gilded Corinthian columns and pilasters supported a second floor gallery; above the second tier of windows, arched lunettes filled with carved and gilded cartouches burst up to join a gilded frieze adorned with carved acanthus leaves. Here, all was white and gold: plain scagliola walls were ornamented with gilded heraldic shields of the Russian provinces, echoing the escutcheons that graced the eleven great ormolu chandeliers that filled the hall with a dazzling glow.[14]

Visitors paused in the 1812 Military Gallery, its two-hundred-foot length covered in red velvet brocade and lined with 332 portraits of Russian and allied commanders in the war against Napoleon. Massed columns supported a barrel-vaulted ceiling whose three large skylights flooded the gallery with light. Dominating the gallery was an immense equestrian portrait of Emperor Alexander I by Franz Kruger, set beneath a gilded canopy hung with crimson velvet and crowned with a golden double-headed eagle.[15]

From the Military Gallery, fourteen-foot-high doors opened to the sanctum sanctorum of the Winter Palace, St. George's Hall. Walls of white Carrara marble rose between paired Corinthian columns, supporting a second-floor gallery; two tiers of windows bathed the room in sunshine, producing extraordinary light. Against the white walls and columns, the bases and capitals of the columns were gilded, as were the gallery balusters and surrounds framing delicate stucco relief wall panels. Beams decorated with embossed gilt rocailles divided the ceiling into coffers embellished with golden cartouches, the pattern repeated in the inlaid floor composed of sixteen rare woods, all bathed in the glow from twelve ormolu chandeliers adorned with gilded double-headed eagles. At the eastern end of the hall, beneath a sweep of red velvet brocade sewn with the Romanov coat of arms in silver thread, stood the imperial thrones.[16]

The richly decorated Picket Hall led to the Cathedral of the Savior Not Made with Hands, named after a precious icon. Designed by Rastrelli in the baroque

The Jordan
Staircase in the
Winter Palace.
See plate 13.

style, it rose the full height of the palace. White walls, ornamented with gilded cartouches and statuary and divided by golden Corinthian columns, glowed in the soft, flickering light of hundreds of votive candles. Intricate, wrought-iron railings with delicate ormolu medallions divided the nave from the sanctuary, concealed behind an elaborately carved iconostasis awash with gilded cherubs and angels who danced against the blue sky of heaven painted across the dome.[17]

Beyond, corridors led to the Hermitage at the eastern end of the palace. Like her predecessors, Catherine the Great was enamored of architecture, yet she despised the baroque splendors of Rastrelli's palace. In 1764, she asked the architects Jean Baptiste Vallin de la Mothe and Yuri Velten to erect a three-storeyed building in her favorite neoclassical style. Called the Small Hermitage, its reception rooms and galleries surrounded an inner courtyard on the first floor. Here, above what had once been the palace stables, she built a fantastic Winter Garden, complete with lawns, graveled walks, palm trees, fountains, and free-flying hummingbirds, enclosed by a cast-iron and glass roof.[18]

Before the Small Hermitage was finished, Catherine ordered a second addition, known as the Old Hermitage. Constructed between 1771 and 1787 by the architect Yuri Velten in the neoclassical style, it balanced the Small Hermitage at the opposite end of the Winter Garden.[19] In 1783, the Italian architect Giacomo Quarenghi added long galleries, copied from Raphael's famous loggias in the Vatican, providing an exquisite stage against which the empress and her court could promenade in the long Russian winters.[20] The rooms within were as elaborate as anything in the Winter Palace, with walls of Italian marble; intricate floors of rare, contrasting woods laid in elaborate, geometric designs; columns of malachite, jasper, porphyry, and lapis lazuli, adorned with gilded bases and capitals; and doors inlaid with tortoise shell, mother-of-pearl, and bronze.[21]

St. George's
Hall in the
Winter Palace.
See plate 14.

Nicholas I and Alexander II extensively remodeled the two buildings.[22] The architect Andrei Stackenschneider gutted much of the Small Hermitage to create his extraordinary Pavilion Hall, a perfect jewel of neoclassical, Arabian, and Renaissance design. The room was two storeys high; its walls were faced in white Carrara marble, broken by columns of green Siberian marble framing apses set with classical sculpture. Corinthian columns supported a second-floor gallery, embellished—like the segmented ceiling—with finely wrought gilt medallions. Twenty-eight Bohemian crystal and ormolu chandeliers hung above a mosaic floor copied from the baths of the Roman emperor Titus. It was a stunning room, enlivened by marble and onyx fountains that played to soothing effect.[23]

By the nineteenth century, Nicholas I commissioned the New Hermitage, designed by the German architect Leo von Klenze. Rising at the southeastern end of the Winter Palace, the New Hermitage was ornamented with a portico decorated with ten 16-foot-high *Atlantes*, carved from solid gray granite.[24] A white marble staircase, rising between walls of yellow Siena marble, gave access to more than sixty rooms filled with works of art. Nicholas I opened the new museum to the public so that commoners, with their tickets from the grand marshal of the imperial court in hand, could admire the priceless collection of Romanov art.[25]

Catherine's mania for building was matched only by her passion for collecting. As her reign continued, the Hermitage complex became an architectural necessity as the empress filled its rooms with imported French furniture; Gobelin tapestries; Sèvres, Meissen, and Wedgwood porcelain; sculpture; and objets d'art. The more than two hundred paintings Catherine purchased from a Berlin merchant in 1764, including three Rembrandts, formed the nucleus of the imperial collection.[26] Four years later, she added Rembrandt's *Return of the Prodigal Son*, followed by a hundred more canvases from an official at the Saxon court, including four Rembrandts, five by Rubens, and works by Watteau and Caravaggio.[27] Her most impressive additions came in 1779, when she purchased the collection of Great Britain's Sir Robert Walpole, including twenty works by Van Dyck, nineteen by Rubens, eight by Titian, three by Veronese, two by Velasquez, and canvases by Raphael, Rembrandt, and Poussin.[28]

In the reign of Alexander II, the Hermitage was incorporated as a department of the imperial court, and for the first time official charge of its administration fell to the Ministry of the Imperial Court, a move that marked a sharp downturn in the museum's fortunes.[29] Thereafter, tsarist bureaucrats, rather than skilled curators, were responsible for the collection. Although they occasionally added works of art, neither Alexander II, his son Alexander III, nor his grandson Nicholas II took much interest in the museum's preservation. The last connoisseur to hold the post of director was Prince Serge Trubetskoy; when he resigned in 1899, Nicholas II replaced him with Ivan Vsevolozsky, a former diplomat more concerned with the administration of the imperial theaters. He held the post for a mere ten years, before being replaced by Count Dimitri Golitsyn, who arranged the museum's last major purchase, Leonardo da Vinci's *Madonna of the Rocks*, from Maria Benois in 1914.[30]

At the end of the Hermitage complex, an arched gallery spanned the Winter

Cathedral of the Winter Palace

Canal to Giacomo Quarenghi's Theater, built for Catherine the Great. The empress rejected plans for a conventional theater of tiers and boxes; instead, Quarenghi designed an amphitheater, modeled after Andrea Palladio's Teatro Olimpico in Vicenza, with benches padded in red velvet descending in semicircular steps to the orchestra pit. The walls, faced with light yellow and pink scagliola, were decorated with Corinthian columns set between niches holding classical sculpture. Five hundred guests could be accommodated, and, as Catherine had wished, there was not a single bad view, although the benches themselves were terribly uncomfortable.[31]

Quarenghi also designed the most magnificent set of halls in the Winter Palace. Known as the Neva Enfilade, these three rooms opened on the western side of the Jordan Staircase. From the landing of the Jordan Staircase, guests entered the anteroom, a perfect cube decorated in pastel yellow and white and flooded with light from two tiers of windows overlooking the Neva. Lunettes and the *plafond*, painted in grisaille, offered a stark contrast to the shimmering Romanov Gold Plate, displayed on shelves lining the walls.[32]

Mahogany doors, ornamented with gilded inlays, opened to the Nicholas Hall, the largest room in the Winter Palace. Two tiers of eleven windows, high above the Neva, pierced the northern wall; between them, framing the white scagliola walls, Corinthian columns of Italian marble rose to a segmented ceiling adorned with intricate plaster reliefs picked out in gold. Eleven immense Bohemian crystal and ormolu chandeliers hung above the inlaid wooden floor, where up to five thousand guests could dance to the music of an orchestra hidden in a second-floor gallery.[33]

The Concert Hall was the most extravagant interior in the palace, a dramatic space of white and cream circled with pairs of Corinthian columns. Marble statuary, representing the Muses, rose from a deeply sculpted cornice; lunettes, painted in grisaille, stretched to a ceiling ornamented with stucco reliefs. Between the bands of paired Corinthian columns, sculpture stood in niches hung with white stucco garlands against a grisaille ground. Above the inlaid wooden floor hung five massive Bohemian crystal and ormolu chandeliers, each holding more than five hundred candles.[34]

The Concert Hall marked the end of the Parade Halls and the beginning of the palace's private apartments. Doors opened to the Blackamoor Hall, its name derived from the colorfully costumed court Abyssinians who stood sentinel beneath its vaulted ceiling, restricting entrance to the imperial family's private rooms. Beyond the Concert Hall lay the Malachite Hall, one of the most luxurious rooms in the palace. Designed by Alexander Bryullov in 1838, it was circled with eight malachite pilasters and eight malachite columns, set on gilded bases and topped with ormolu Corinthian capitals. A coved ceiling, covered with elaborate, heavily gilded papier-mâché, rested on a similar frieze, stamped with intricate designs in gold leaf matched by the carved, gilded doors. Between the columns and pilasters, three allegorical murals—*Poetry* flanked by *Day* and

Night—offered relief from the white scagliola walls. The fireplace mantels, decorative urns, vases, clocks, and table tops were also finished with malachite, contrasting with the heavy crimson damask across the windows and upon the furniture. Beneath it all, the floor, laid in elaborate geometric swirls, had been created from nine rare woods.[35] It was a sumptuous and opulent display of the mineral wealth of the Russian empire.

The private apartments of the imperial family, at the western end of the first floor, encompassed just under fifty rooms. Alexander II had been the last sovereign to live here, and his rooms remained as they had been in 1881 when he was assassinated. A visitor left a vivid description of the study where the emperor had died: "The half-smoked cigarette lies upon the ash-tray in a glass tube. The little revolver lies before the mirror. Upon each of the tables and several of the chairs is a loosely folded clean handkerchief, for it was the tsar's wish to have one of these always within reach of his hand. Here are his toilet articles—a plain, small set of bottles and brushes, from a rusty Morocco folding case, evidently bought in England before we invented the modern luxurious dressing-bag. It is modest beyond belief. In three places is his actual shed blood to be seen. As I stood by his bed, my own guide, taking advantage of the old official's back being turned, lifted the coverlet and pointed silently to the broad, rusty stain upon the faded linen."[36]

Into this world of artifice and funereal gloom came Nicholas II and his consort. Shortly after her marriage in 1894, Alexandra asked her sister Grand Duchess Elizabeth Feodorovna to assist in decorating the private apartments here. The grand duchess recommended two well-known St. Petersburg architects, Alexander Krasovskii and Roman Meltzer. Krasovskii, born in 1848, had designed numerous buildings in the capital before his appointment as technical officer of the court authority in 1891, a post that gave him architectural responsibility for the Winter Palace; he had also supervised redecoration of the Sergeievsky Palace for the grand duchess.[37] But it was Meltzer, born twelve years after his colleague, whose influence proved most lasting. A graduate of the Imperial Academy of Fine Arts, Meltzer presided, with his brother, over a family empire. Their father, Feodor Meltzer, had founded one of St. Petersburg's most fashionable furniture stores, displaying and selling pieces he designed and built himself, including commissions for the imperial family. There was a scandal in the reign of Alexander III; suspecting that the firm had attempted to unduly bill the Treasury, he refused to work with it any longer.[38] It was Empress Alexandra who returned imperial commissions to the brothers.

Roman Meltzer was one of the foremost proponents of the fashionable art nouveau style, advocating a mixture of form and function adorned with sensuous curves and exaggerated lines. It was all as Alexandra herself wished. Her brother Grand Duke Ernst Ludwig IV of Hesse transformed his capital of Darmstadt into a shrine to the *Jugendstil*, or art nouveau movement, a style that heavily influenced Alexandra's own tastes. She sought to re-create interiors from her childhood, introducing middle-class taste and comfort into the palace. As a result, in contrast to the grandeur of the Parade Halls, the private apartments offered a deliberate statement of the imperial couple's early desire to withdraw into their own private realm.

Alexandra selected fourteen rooms at the northwestern corner of the palace's first floor; their windows looked out over the Neva to the Fortress of St. Peter and St. Paul on the opposite shore and west to the Admiralty. Krasovskii followed Alexandra's wishes, gutting the existing interiors and transforming the high-ceilinged rooms, with their vaults and neoclassical details, into models of late Victorian taste. Delicate stucco reliefs were knocked from walls, replaced by abundant woodwork that struggled with heavy brocades for primacy.[39] Nicholas Nabokov supervised the decoration, commissioning furniture from the St. Petersburg firm of Nicholas Svirskii. Additional furnishings included Biedermeier pieces in birch and mahogany, and rococo-revival sofas and chairs from the firm of Peter Gambs, with elaborately carved and gilded frames.[40] Gifts from fellow monarchs completed the furnishings of Nicholas II's rooms, including a number of cabinets and tables made by the children of workers on the Sandringham estate of the British royal family in Norfolk and presented to the emperor by his cousin King George V.[41]

Nicholas and Alexandra moved into their new rooms on New Year's Eve, 1895.[42] "We both slept wonderfully in our new home," the emperor wrote in his diary. "The sun lit up my study most pleasantly as I was working in the morning. . . . After luncheon we went to our old rooms and collected the pictures, photographs and last things to take over to the Winter Palace. In the afternoon we sat at home and arranged everything."[43]

Directly off the Malachite Hall, Krasovskii and Meltzer decorated a small dining room in the Louis XV style, its rococo theme echoed in the French-provincial table, chairs, and china cabinets. Stucco rocailles framed Russian tapestries representing *Asia*, *America*, and *Africa*. Above the dining table hung a mirrored, eighteenth-century crystal chandelier concealing a music box; when wound, it slowly revolved above the heads of the diners, sending prisms of shifting light across the white walls to the accompaniment of soft music.[44]

The Malachite Hall in the Winter Palace

The neoclassical Empire Drawing Room, draped in yellow silk and circled by a wainscot carved with gilded rosettes, acanthus leaves, and palm fronds, opened Nicholas and Alexandra's private apartments. For the room, Svirskii designed a suite of Empire-style furniture, painted white and adorned with rosettes and acanthus leaves picked out in gilt. From the painted ceiling, Alexandra hung an Empire-style ormolu chandelier, designed to match the crystal and ormolu candelabra from the Imperial Porcelain Factory.[45]

The adjoining Silver Drawing Room, designed in the Louis XVI style, was a more formal space, where Alexandra received important visitors. The walls were hung with light gray moiré, woven with silver thread; later, they were decorated with a series of Gobelin tapestries, presented to the emperor and the empress in 1914 by President Raymond Poincaré of France.[46] The ceiling, painted with rococo floral garlands, was encased in a sculpted cornice of solid silver rocailles, from which the room took its name.[47] In keeping with the room's function, the empress filled it with a number of exquisite pieces, including an eighteenth-century secretary by the French craftsman Risener and a carved, gilded Schroeder piano, painted by Ernst Liphart with scenes from *Orpheus*.[48]

Alexandra's private drawing room filled the northwestern corner of the suite. Gold silk, woven with a motif of floral wreaths, hung across the arched windows and covered the walls and Svirskii's overstuffed sofas and chairs. Portraits of the empress's parents, family photographs, icons, porcelain, and bronzes added to the incoherence, the repetition of pattern leaving the eye with no place to rest.[49] Neither the eighteenth-century mirrored crystal chandelier, once owned by Catherine the Great's paramour Prince Gregory Potemkin, nor the large mirror, encased in a gilded rococo frame above the white Carrara marble fireplace, relieved the oppressive decor.[50]

Nicholas and Alexandra shared a large bedroom, their double bed hidden behind an arcade of four white Corinthian columns. Honey-colored Karelian birch circled the lower walls and framed upper panels covered with light pink and green floral English cretonne, ominously copied from the rooms of Marie Antoinette at Fontainebleau.[51] Simple cretonne covered the walls of Alexandra's adjoining dressing room; a door at the rear opened to her bathroom, overlooking a small inner courtyard. A hand-painted frieze of wisteria and floral garlands, enclosing Alexandra's initials, adorned the empress's boudoir, hung in silver-and-mauve-striped silk.[52] It was, recalled one visitor, "an exquisitely feminine room and distinctly individual." She noted the call bell, "a curiously beautiful bit of ivory carving, representing elephants in trappings of gold and jewels standing on a piece of jade. One bore a huge diamond on his back, another a great sapphire, and the other a huge star ruby."[53]

Nicholas preferred dark, masculine rooms. Krasovskii used Turkish pine for the walls of his dressing room, tucked behind the bedroom and ornamented with patterned tiles, while birch and lemonwood panels lined his bathroom. Even the seat of his toilet was of cypress. Nicholas was given to one peculiarity: in each of his palaces, he had immense sunken tubs installed, copied from one at his Polish estate of Bielovezh. At the Winter Palace, eight marble steps descended to an iron tank, set in a recess lined with concrete and faced with Dresden tiles, where he could immerse himself in fresh or salt water.[54]

Two narrow rooms, joined by open arches, formed the emperor's private study, designed by Krasovskii in the gothic style. Dark oak, carved with medieval designs, framed glazed walls and twisted in elaborate columns to the deep coffers of the wooden ceiling, hung with a silver chandelier. Arched doors, inset with brass traceries and locks, rose between built-in cozy corners; above, shelves were crammed with family photographs, icons, and a collection of Asian artifacts. Sofas and chairs, upholstered in green leather, clustered round the hooded fireplace, covered in ceramic tiles, and Nicholas's immense desk, guarded by a large jade Buddha set with rubies, a gift from the Buddhists of St. Petersburg when they established their own temple in the capital.[55]

Krasovskii continued the gothic theme in the emperor's library. Two tiers of elaborately carved walnut bookcases circled the room, beneath a mezzanine reached by a small stairway. Krasovskii covered the walls in crimson leather, stamped and gilded in an intricate, medieval-style pattern, offering a rich contrast to the gray tones of the massive Caen stone fireplace. Gothic-revival sofas and chairs, carved with trefoils and heraldic shields, lay across the Oriental carpet; above, from a segmented ceiling of dark walnut adorned with carved rosettes, hung two large, solid silver chandeliers.[56] The bookcases held a small portion of His Majesty's Own Library, a collection of rare volumes that eventually grew to encompass some 34,000 works. The responsibility for this priceless collection fell to Vassili Shcheglov, the director of His Majesty's Own Library. New books were catalogued on receipt; paperback works were sent to the Imperial Bindery and provided with new covers: brown leather for works in Russian, blue for those in French, red for those in English, and green for those in German. Each volume was fitted with an inventory number and adorned with an imperial bookplate representing either the emperor's initials or a double-headed eagle and Nicholas's monogram encased by stylized laurel wreaths.[57]

The emperor's billiard room was decorated in classical style, with dark glazed walls and a floor of rare contrasting woods taken from the palace's old Pompeian Dining Room.[58] His reception room contained an impressive collection of

Alexandra's private drawing room in the Winter Palace

Oriental works of art, collected by Nicholas II during his visit to the Far East, as well as elephant tusks and hunting trophies. The silk-covered walls were hung with two enormous paintings by Becker of Alexander III's coronation.[59] Beyond the reception room, which opened to the Saltykov Staircase, a passage called the Dark Corridor connected the palace's western end. The final room in Nicholas and Alexandra's private apartments was the chapel, set at an angle overlooking the quadrangle and flooded with light from five windows. At its front, an intricate, curved iconostasis of white marble—adorned with columns and set with semiprecious stones—shielded the altar.[60]

The Gothic
Library.
See plate 15.

For the first ten years of his reign, Nicholas and Alexandra lived within the Winter Palace's baroque walls, presiding over St. Petersburg's glittering social season. In these brief months, Rastrelli's exquisite building came to life. The music of orchestras mingled with whispered gossip as aristocrats moved through its cavernous halls scented with out-of-season flowers and exotic incense, windows blazing against the black night like a thousand suns as snow shrouded the statues marching across the roof. Then, the outbreak of the Russo-Japanese War, followed by the uncertainties of the 1905 Revolution, left its windows dark, as the imperial family retreated to the safety of Peterhof and Tsarskoye Selo. Fireplaces grew cold, dust caressed the gilded chandeliers, twilight descended, and the Winter Palace, brooding and empty, sat in silent shadow until the Revolution in 1917.

11

TSARSKOYE SELO

FIFTEEN MILES SOUTHWEST OF St. Petersburg, where a sweep of land rolls gently into a series of low, wooded hills, stands Tsarskoye Selo, the Tsar's Village. Over the centuries, the complex had become the Russian equivalent of Louis XIV's great palace at Versailles. Like Versailles, Tsarskoye Selo had an immense park, filled with palaces, pavilions, formal gardens, and stretches of water, yet they fulfilled vastly different functions. Versailles was a showplace for Louis XIV, a public expression of absolute power, while Tsarskoye Selo was always a private retreat, a place of pleasure for the imperial family.

Tsarskoye Selo, from its inception, was an anachronism. Its palaces rose even as, across Europe, monarchs fell victim to the whims of an increasingly vocal populace. To those privileged few admitted to this world, Tsarskoye Selo was an artificial universe where theatrical rhetoric displaced reality to celebrate the triumphs of the dynasty. There was no ambiguity here: the

The Catherine Palace.
See plate 16.

manicured gardens and shadowed halls bore witness to the unaltered power of the imperial family. Gleb Botkin called it "an enchanted fairyland to which only a small number of people had the right of entry. It became a legendary place. To the loyal monarchists, it was a sort of terrestrial paradise, the abode of the earthly gods. To the revolutionaries, it was a sinister place where blood-thirsty tyrants were hatching their terrible plots against the innocent population."[1]

Catherine I built a small palace here, but her daughter Empress Elizabeth left the greatest legacy at Tsarskoye Selo.[2] As the proud mistress of Bartolomeo Rastrelli's magnificent Winter Palace, Elizabeth found her mother's humble structure unbecoming, and the talented Italian was commissioned to replace it with a more suitable structure.[3] The Catherine Palace, named for Elizabeth's mother, was a rococo structure of some two hundred rooms, in the style of Rastrelli's acclaimed Winter Palace, though surpassing it in beauty.

When Catherine the Great came to the throne, she imposed her own tastes upon the rococo exuberance of Tsarskoye Selo. While she did not pull down Elizabeth's great palace, she did replace many of its interiors with neoclassical rooms designed by her favorite architects, Charles Cameron and Giacomo Quarenghi. Catherine also commissioned Quarenghi to build a neoclassical palace for her favorite grandson, the future Emperor Alexander I, adjacent to her own. The Alexander Palace, in contrast to the Catherine Palace, was a large but comfortable Palladian-inspired house, situated in a quiet corner of the Imperial Park.

In 1837, Tsarskoye Selo became the first town in the Russian empire to be connected to St. Petersburg by a railway line. From the ornate train station, with its steeply pitched roof, a long avenue, lined with the villas and palaces of the aristocracy, ran to the gates of the Imperial Park.[4] Some thirty thousand people lived here, making it the largest of St. Petersburg's suburban towns. Even so, it was still a town perched on the edge of a "barren swamp," an "urbanized wilderness" in the midst of "pristine savagery," as Charles Sydney Gibbes described it in the reign of Nicholas II.[5]

Tall iron railings enclosed the Imperial Park. At thirty-yard intervals stood Cossack guards, forever on duty to protect the imperial family; in addition, mounted Cossack sentinels regularly patrolled the park. A large pair of Egyptian-style gates, designed by the Scottish architect Adam Menelaws, marked the northern boundary of the park; to the south, a set of gothic gates opened onto a driveway leading to the Alexander Palace and the park. But the most magnificent of all the gates were the ones at the main entrance to the Catherine Palace: designed by Rastrelli, they were of gilded wrought iron, elaborate in pattern and detail, stretching twenty feet, with a gilded double-headed eagle surmounted by the imperial crown at the center.[6]

On the other side of these gates and railings spread an Elysian paradise. Groves of birch trees, dark pines and firs, and majestic oaks opened to meadows overgrown with wildflowers, while paths sliced through forest glades decorated with groups of statuary. Follies in the rustic and gothic manners—dairies, farmhouses, mock-ruins, and thatched cottages tucked away in quiet gardens—lay at the end of circling paths.[7] Beyond these woods, an immense landscaped park covered the undulating terrain. "At present I love English gardens to distraction," Catherine the Great wrote to Voltaire. "I love curved lines, soft slopes, ponds and archipelagoes, and I strongly disdain straight lines and double alleys. I hate fountains that torture water in order to make it change its natural course."[8] She commissioned John Bush to transform the park after those of England designed by Lancelot "Capability" Brown and Humphrey Repton. Here Romanticism prevailed, where Arcadian scenes were depicted in the pastoral works of Claude Lorraine and Nicolas Poussin came to life amid the northern wilderness.[9] Rose, lilac, and rhododendron bushes perfumed the spring air, beneath hundred-year-old trees whose branches had been reinforced with iron bars for safety.[10]

Visitors to Tsarskoye Selo entered a world of historicism and artifice formed from the work of Russia's most talented architects. Sloped grass shoulders framed axial walks skirting geometric beds of vibrantly colored flowers, their centers dotted with clusters of gilded lead putti glistening with pluming jets of water. Allées of pleached lime led to bosquets decorated with groupings of classical statuary whose brilliant white marble shone against manicured hedges.[11] Descending into a small valley, they encountered a large artificial lake, fed by streams and cascades crossed by bridges of gothic and Oriental designs. In the middle of the lake rose a marble and granite rostral column crowned with a bronze eagle, commemorating the victory of the Russian Navy over the Turks at Chesme. At one end of the lake stood an exotic pink and white bathhouse designed to resemble a mosque, complete with arabesque traceries on its dome and a tall minaret. Rastrelli's Baroque Grotto, a deep-blue confection adorned with banded columns, stucco garlands, and tritons in brilliant white, echoed its position across the placid stretch of water.[12] Throughout the park, obelisks rose toward the sky, groups of statuary encircled amphitheaters, and mock-ruins, overgrown with ivy and wild roses, provided a suitably Arcadian atmosphere to delight and amuse the imperial family.[13]

At the edge of the formal gardens, Catherine the Great constructed two grand pavilions, the work of Charles Cameron. The Agate Pavilion evoked the opulent world of ancient Rome in a collection of rooms adorned with marble, jasper, agate, lapis lazuli, and malachite.[14] An oval staircase of red agate descended beneath a coffered dome to plunge baths of richly colored Siberian marbles.[15] Adjoining the Agate Pavilion, Catherine built a long, classical Ionic colonnade providing a cool, shadowed refuge from which she could look across a sweeping

The Cameron Gallery.
See plate 17.

vista of lake, pavilions, and gardens below. She filled the colonnade with fifty-three bronze busts of those whom she admired, including Cicero, Voltaire, and, in an unusual tribute, its architect who, in honor for his service, was informed that it would henceforth be called the Cameron Gallery.[16]

The Catherine Palace lay at the center of the Imperial Park. It was Rastrelli's masterpiece, a delightful piece of sensual fantasy, exuberant in its theatricality and imposing in its grand rococo excesses. His Winter Palace was larger, and Peterhof enjoyed a lovelier situation, but the Catherine Palace outshone them in its sublime grandeur and beauty. Prince Christopher of Greece called it "the most beautiful palace in Europe."[17]

It was the longest of all imperial palaces, just under a thousand feet. To relieve the potential monotony of such an enfilade, Rastrelli introduced a number of projecting bays, their columns and pediments breaking the straight lines of the facade and providing a shifting face to soften the effect.[18] Of three storeys, the palace mingled the baroque and the rococo, its deep-blue facade enlivened with white Corinthian columns and gilded bands, caryatids, stucco swags, and nearly a hundred *Atlantes*.[19] The masses of pediments, statuary, and windows created a pleasing repetition of light and shadow, a piece of three-dimensional stagecraft that sparkled in the northern light. At one end stood the cathedral, capped with five brightly gilded onion domes, while in front, two long, curving service wings embraced a courtyard that witnessed regimental parades and reviews.[20]

Empress Elizabeth was the complete antithesis of her frugal father, Peter the Great; what she wanted, and what she got in the Catherine Palace, was a visible representation of the splendor of the Russian court. Thus, Rastrelli was forced to introduce certain elements that, by the middle of the eighteenth century, had already faded into oblivion. The State Apartments, on the principal floor of the Catherine Palace, contained no grand corridor or connecting hallways. The progression through the palace harkened back to the seventeenth-century idea of the royal levee, where the approach toward the private apartments indicated imperial favor. Rastrelli created grand vistas within the palace, providing brief, tantalizing views of the succession of rooms, an architectural masterpiece that came to be called "The Golden Gallery," owing to the heavily gilded door frames.[21]

At the center of the palace, a handsome white marble staircase ascended in twin flights to the principal floor, providing a ceremonial but deliberately restrained introduction to the splendors beyond. The adjoining anteroom rose the full height of the palace and was lit by a tall row of double windows overlooking the park. Rastrelli used gilded cherubs, cartouches, and reliefs to ornament the white walls; on the ceiling above, the brothers Pietro and Francesco Gradichi painted an immense mural, *The Marriage of Bacchus and Ariadne*.[22] From the room's double doors, visitors could peer into the heart of the palace, the Great Gallery.

Rastrelli modeled the Great Gallery on the Hall of Mirrors at Versailles, but it was a French apartment filtered through a Russian lens as viewed by the Italian architect. The Great Gallery spanned the entire width of the palace, rising two storeys to a magnificent trompe l'oeil ceiling depicting *Russia Triumphant*. Two-hundred-sixty feet long, the hall was lit down each side by thirteen rows of double windows; between them, Rastrelli inset floor-to-ceiling mirrors, covering the shorter walls with large pier glasses surrounded with elaborately carved and gilded frames sprouting playful cherubs, garlands, foliage, and rocailles. Above, circling the ceiling, was a fantastic cornice rich with caryatids, garlands, swags, bands of foliage, and crowns, all adorned with twenty pounds of gold leaf. A floor, composed of parquet laid out in a checkerboard surrounding alternating strips of rare woods, centered on alternating inlaid stars, sunbursts, squares, and ovals, creating vibrant and exotic patterns. At night, fifty-six chandeliers and tall candelabra cast their glow across the room, the mirrors lining the walls reflecting a magical, seemingly endless vista of flickering candlelight and burnished gold.[23]

The Great Gallery of the Catherine Palace. See plate 18.

Along the courtyard side of the palace, carved double doors, embellished with gold leaf, opened from the Great Gallery to the Cavalier's Hall, one of four dining rooms in the palace. The simple white walls and the parquet floor stood as a deliberate contrast to the painted ceiling, where Apollo drove his chariot through a blue sky strewn with clouds. Gold leaf spread across delicate boiseries and shone from elaborate lintels framing the doorways. In the midst of this splendor stood a typically Russian touch: a large porcelain faience stove, whose blue Delft tiles rose in a series of arcaded levels marked with tiny columns, niches, and arches.[24] The State Dining Room beyond was more feminine, with sinuous gilding encasing the panels of white silk on the walls. An impressive collection of paintings by I. F. Groothe, depicting swans, peacocks, partridge, and other fowl, echoed the shifting whites, creams, and dove grays of the patterned damask. The Crimson and Green Pilaster Rooms were decorated with columns inset with colored foil pressed beneath glass, a fragile technique that, along with the gilded rocailles and scrollwork, lent to them an unusual elegance.[25]

In the Portrait Room, guests passed between walls hung with silver moiré that provided a stark contrast to the gilded woodwork. Under their feet, the floor was inlaid in an intricate pattern with red and black palm and rosewood, creating an explosion of color. Eyes swept across portraits of previous Romanov sovereigns before resting on the room's centerpiece, a large canvas of Empress Elizabeth. Beyond lay the Picture Hall, whose magnificent floor was a swirl of arabesques inlaid with mahogany, redwood, rosewood, yew, sandalwood, and birch. The walls were covered with 130 canvases from various European schools of the seventeenth and eighteenth centuries, the doors guarded by gilded caryatids supporting lintels carved with golden reliefs of Minerva and cupids, astonishing in their rich detail.[26]

In 1716, King Friedrich Wilhelm of Prussia gave Peter the Great fifty-five panels of light, honey-colored amber in exchange for some Russian soldiers.[27] The panels, composed of fragments of amber painstakingly pieced together between amber moldings, were first placed in Peter's Winter Palace. In 1755, Rastrelli transported them to Tsarskoye Selo, mounting them between gilded frames to panel his new room. To surround them, Rastrelli designed gilded boiseries and adorned the walls with marble, agate, and jasper mosaics, framed by twenty-four mirrored pilasters. In the light of the hundreds of candles set within their gilded sconces, the honey-colored amber glowed and sparkled beneath a cornice of gilded putti. It was the triumph of the palace, a room renowned across Europe for its subtle beauty and lustrous, jewel-like setting.[28]

On state occasions and liturgical feasts, processions walked along a ribbon of crimson carpet, between stark white marble walls, to the anteroom, whose walls were hung with golden silk embroidered with pheasants, peacocks, and swans.[29] They passed through double doors to the cathedral, painted a startling deep blue and embellished with gilded boiseries, cartouches, and cherubs. An iconostasis, its lemonwood frame carved and gilded and flanked by columns inlaid with marble, malachite, and precious gems, sparkled in the light from the five golden domes two storeys above.[30] In this brilliant setting, the last generation of the Romanovs celebrated the weddings of grand dukes and grand duchesses, as well as christenings, including that of Nicholas II's first child, Grand Duchess Olga Nikolaievna.

Cameron designed a suite of private apartments that ranged along the northwestern side of the palace for Catherine's son Tsesarevich Paul and his wife, Marie Feodorovna. These were cool, classical rooms, with walls covered in handpainted Chinese silks and soft pastel colors, white woodwork, and Wedgwoodstyle reliefs and adorned with delicate columns, creating a feminine atmosphere deliberately unsuited to the difficult, militaristic tsesarevich.[31]

Paul loathed his mother, and it was an ordeal whenever duty forced him and his wife to remain under her roof. In the Catherine Palace, it was no accident that

nearly six hundred feet of state apartments and guardrooms separated the bedrooms of the empress and her son. Beyond the Great Gallery and several ante-
rooms, Rastrelli's rococo excesses gave way to the mannered delights of the Age
of Reason. The Fourth Apartment opened with the Arabesque Hall, its name
derived from the subtle Pompeian decoration. Lightly colored arabesques and
traceries covered the pale yellow walls, surrounding oval mirrors and adding an
exotic note amid the Corinthian pilasters. Above, a rich blue frieze, adorned with
oval medallions and sculpted bas-reliefs, rose to a ceiling painted *en grisaille*.[32]
Reason gave way to splendor in the Lyon Salon, its walls hung with light yellow
silk from Lyon set between pilasters and panels of rare lapis lazuli. The floor was
inlaid with twelve contrasting woods, including blackwood, olive, and rosewood, alternating with strips of luminescent mother-of-pearl.[33] Later, the architect Ippolito Monighetti designed an extraordinary suite of furniture for the
room, gilded and decorated with lapis lazuli.[34]

Catherine lived in the Age of Reason, but she also had a taste for the exotic.
From the Lyon Salon, doors opened to the Chinese Hall. Cameron covered the
walls with black and red floral lacquer panels, set against rich green panels decorated with gilded chinoiserie carvings. Above the suite of ebony furniture hung
Chinese-style gas chandeliers, adorned with dragons.[35] Beyond the Chinese Hall
lay the Fifth Apartment, intended for Catherine the Great's personal use.
Cameron designed the dining room to resemble the interior of a Roman villa,
with screens of Corinthian colonnades creating apses beneath the central dome.[36]
Catherine's study was faced with solid silver panels delicately engraved in red
with Pompeian-style designs. Large mirrors, framed with silver and red pilasters,
and mirrored French doors enhanced the magical quality of the light.[37]

The empress's bedroom, executed by Cameron, opened from her study. The
walls, covered with panels of pearl-colored glass, were ornamented with Wedgwood cameos and columns of lilac-colored glass.[38] This same decorative use of
glass was utilized in the boudoir, called the Snuff Box Room, whose walls were
set with panels of translucent white glass adorned with blue enamel engravings
encased in gilded moldings.[39]

The Alexander Park was isolated from the rest of the imperial estate, separated
by a series of canals and languid stretches of water. Bridges, railed with lacy iron-
work, led to roadways twisting through groves of birch and oak skirting the lakes.
Small islands, lush with carpets of green turf and artificial mounds, held pavilions. The children of Nicholas II had a secluded island playhouse; here, too, in a
tiny cemetery, they buried their family pets.[40]

The Scottish architect and landscape designer Adam Menelaws laid out the Alexander Park in the English style, abandoning the carefully contrived allées and parterres favored by Empress Elizabeth.[41] At the center of the park stood the Chinese Village, constructed during the reign of Catherine the Great to house her adjutants. Charles Cameron, Yuri Velten, and Ilya Neelov had all contributed to the complex, which formed the largest collection of chinoiserie in Europe.[42] A private theater, designed in 1777 by Antonio Rinaldi and decorated with menacing-looking dragons perched on gilded eaves, was the scene of elaborate masques held by the empress.[43] Nearby stood the Grand Caprice, a man-made mound of earth and rock pierced in the middle by an arch topped by a Chinese pagoda.[44]

Northwest of the Alexander Palace, hidden across a lake flanked by meadows and screened by trees, stood a piece of pure theater: a neo-medieval Russian-style village, the Feodorovsky Gorodok. It began life in 1895, when the architect Vladimir Maximov built a barracks here for members of the Cossack Konvoi Regiment. He took his inspiration from the Novgorod Kremlin, replicating its thick walls, tall towers, and broad, hipped roofs.[45] Nicholas II, who had always nursed a love of medieval architecture, was delighted at this anachronistic fantasy, and he soon commissioned additional buildings in similar styles. A medieval-style Kremlin, with tent roofs and vaulted arcades, featured intricately decorated stone staircases, painted deep red. The White Palace evoked the medieval Russian architecture of Pskov, Vladimir, Rostov-Veliki, and Novgorod, with decorated stone arches, wings with shadowed arcades, and arched windows flanked by carved and twisted columns. Its eight-sided tower contained a chapel, topped with a tent roof and a golden weather vane in the form of a double-headed eagle. Inside, the dining hall rose two storeys to a vaulted ceiling, decorated with colorful foliage and arabesque designs copied from the rooms of the Terem Palace in the Kremlin.[46]

Fringing the southwestern end of the Gorodok stood the Palace of Battles, originally intended as a court theater. Designed in 1913 by Serge Sidorchyk in a complementary medieval style, it was the last structure built, its progress impeded by the outbreak of the First World War a year later.[47] Just beyond the Gorodok's protecting walls stood the emperor's private railway station, its medieval-style arcades offering a horizontal contrast to its tower and steeply pitched roof.[48]

The Feodorovsky Sobor. See plate 19.

At the heart of the Gorodok was the Feodorovsky Cathedral, named after the Feodorovsky icon of the Mother of God, with which the first Romanov tsar, Michael Feodorovich, had been blessed and consecrated on accepting the throne in the Ipatiev Monastery at Kostroma in 1613. Designed by Vladimir Pokrovsky as the regimental church of the Combined Infantry Regiment and the Cossack Konvoi Regiment, it was modeled on the Annunciation Cathedral inside the Moscow Kremlin, itself styled after old churches in Pskov.[49] On August 20, 1909, Nicholas II laid the cornerstone, and three years later, it was formally consecrated with a liturgy attended by the imperial family. "It has turned out remarkably beautifully," Nicholas wrote, "and is quite in the spirit of the ancient Moscow churches. We liked it enormously."[50]

The west doorway, whose portal was decorated with a colorful mosaic depicting the Feodorovsky Mother of God, opened to the sanctuary, where four massive columns held aloft a vaulted roof pierced by a central dome. The iconostasis rose in four tiers and was decorated with silver, gold, malachite, and precious stones. When members of the imperial family attended services, they used a private entrance at the southeastern corner of the cathedral; another door led to a small spiral staircase that descended to the crypt. Here, Alexandra built a special chapel for private prayer, dedicated to St. Seraphim of Sarov and decorated by the famed artist Victor Vasnestov with medieval-style frescoes.[51]

At the end of the park, across the glistening lakes and past the thick glades of trees, visitors could catch tantalizing glimpses of the distant Alexander Palace, its pale yellow facade rising from the soft green carpet of turf. Catherine had commissioned the palace from Giacomo Quarenghi in 1792 as a gift for her grandson, the future Alexander I. Four years later, the new Alexander Palace was finished, although the exterior brick walls remained without plaster until 1800.[52] This was Quarenghi's masterpiece, a classical structure of clean lines and sublime harmony.

The Alexander Palace stood in stark contrast to the nearby Catherine Palace. Here, all was historicism: classical references to the architecture of ancient Greece and Rome, drawn from interpretations by Andrea Palladio. Built in a U-shape, its three sides surrounded a large courtyard facing north; two smaller wings, ending in tall, arched portes cocheres, also extended from the central block, joined together by an open, two-storey Corinthian colonnade. These columns, along with a cornice and a simple balustrade that ran the perimeter of the roof, were the only external decoration on the building.[53] The Alexander Palace, unlike many of the other imperial residences, relied on the simplicity of its lines and the beauty of its classical form for its adornment.

Nicholas II had first brought Princess Alix of Hesse to the Alexander Palace during her 1889 visit to St. Petersburg to attend a small dance. In 1895, she

The Alexander
Palace's
Semi-Circular
Hall enfilade.
See plate 20.

The Alexander Palace
at Tsarskoye Selo.
See plate 21.

decided to make the palace their first home after she had married Nicholas. She liked the quiet solitude of the park and the comfort of the hundred rooms, which reminded her of country houses in England. The couple moved into the palace on August 31, 1895; after the 1905 Revolution, the Alexander Palace became their permanent home.

At the center of the southern facade, marked by a two-storey bow crowned with a low dome, was the Semi-Circular Hall, linked to the Portrait Hall to the east and the Marble Hall to the west by tall screens of agate scagliola Corinthian columns. Quarenghi employed a subdued color palette in these three rooms, covering their walls with white, cream, and gray scagliola ornamented with accents of yellow Siena marble and circling them with heavily dentilated white cornices.[54]

Immense ormolu chandeliers, designed by Quarenghi and decorated with double-headed eagles, hung from sculptured bas-reliefs set into the vaulted ceilings, and tall Venetian windows flooded the rooms with light. These were deliberately formal rooms, furnished with gilded consoles and Louis XVI–style chairs covered in blue silk and adorned with potted palms and portraits of previous Romanov sovereigns.[55]

The Imperial Anteroom occupied a corner to the southern facade, its two Venetian and two regular windows overlooking the park. Quarenghi faced the walls with white and gray scagliola ornamented with pilasters and inlaid panels, above a floor of black and white marble squares. Despite its austere grandeur, the room more often rang with laughter than with the hushed and respectful tones of ceremony. Here, Nicholas I had placed a wooden slide, known as a Russian Mountain, on which the palace's children often played. At the opposite end of the southern facade, Alexandra had converted the old Crimson Drawing Room, an elaborate neoclassical space with pale green and cream scagliola walls, Venetian windows, and an alcove framed by Corinthian columns, into the palace chapel in 1899.[56] An iconostasis was placed across the western end of the room, while the columned arcade was fitted with a glass screen, behind which the imperial family could worship in private.

Nicholas II and his family had their private apartments in the east wing, extending from the central block and overlooking both the front and the great lakes. When Empress Alexandra decided to make the Alexander Palace her home in Russia, she hired the architect Roman Meltzer to redecorate the private apartments.[57] As a result, many of the rooms in the private apartments were startling in their decor, with swollen sofas and armchairs, tables crowded with souvenirs, and doorways hung with dark portieres, as the neoclassical mingled with the Victorian and the art nouveau in a bewildering, indiscriminate battle for dominance.

Under Nicholas II, the Alexander Palace underwent two intensive renovations, the first in 1896–1898, and the second in 1902–1903.[58] The first renovation, directed by Meltzer, resulted in the private apartments for Nicholas and Alexandra, creating two enfilades separated by a corridor. By 1902, with four young daughters, the emperor and the empress decided they needed more space to house their growing family. Although they had the whole of the palace at their disposal, Nicholas and Alexandra wanted a new suite for their children built directly above their own rooms. A quarter of the eastern wing was occupied by the immense Concert Hall, a two-storeyed room designed by Quarenghi to serve as the palace ballroom, divided down the center by an arcaded gallery and decorated with scagliola walls and Corinthian columns and pilasters. Several architects were called in to advise on the project, attempting to work out various schemes that would preserve the largest and most significant room in this, Quarenghi's architectural masterpiece. But none of the designs or the entreaties that accompanied them could dissuade Nicholas and Alexandra, and at their direction Meltzer demolished the room.[59] In its place, he created two new rooms on the first floor, one for the emperor and one for his wife, while the new second storey allowed for a dozen extra rooms for the imperial children and members of the Imperial Suite.[60]

The imperial family lived a self-contained life within several dozen rooms scattered across the two floors of the palace's eastern wing. From the imperial vestibule at the northern end of the building, with its marble floor and walls covered with glazed cloth, a long corridor divided the wing in half. This was a dark, gloomy space, without any exterior light. In an attempt to lighten the passage, Alexandra hung the walls with a number of lighted paintings, including several by Repin. In time, entire collections of imperial odds and ends—keys to various cities in the empire, gifts of porcelain, and other presents to the emperor and the empress—collected here, dispelling any attempt at coherence. Alexandra's rooms were on the eastern side of the corridor, overlooking the garden and the lakes beyond, while those of the emperor, facing the front courtyard, were to the west.

The imperial children had rooms directly above those of their parents. The tsesarevich's suite included a bedroom furnished with a simple camp bed next to a paneled corner hung with icons. The curious tradition of the camp bed dated from the reign of Nicholas I, who had decreed that none of his children should have anything more elaborate than a simple army bed, in an effort to leave them unaffected by their privileged positions. Next to the tsesarevich's bedroom were his bath and dressing rooms, a small projection room, and a suite of rooms for the tutor Pierre Gilliard and for his *dyadya* Andrei Derevenko.

There was a large playroom on a corner of the second floor, filled with light from seven windows overlooking the park. It was only created in 1903 and used mainly by the tsesarevich and his sisters Marie and Anastasia. A frieze of peacocks against a green background circled the amber-colored walls, contrasting with the yellow and green overstuffed sofas and chairs and the pale green carpet.[61] The room was filled with expensive toys. One visitor observed "great railways, with dolls in the carriages as passengers, with barriers, stations, buildings and signal-boxes, flashing engines and marvelous signaling apparatus, whole battalions of tin soldiers, models of towns with church towers and domes, floating models of ships, perfectly equipped factories with doll workers, and mines in exact imitation of the real thing, with miners ascending and descending. All the toys were mechanically worked, and the little Prince had only to press a button to set the workers in motion, to drive the warships up and down the tank, to set the church bells ringing and the soldiers marching."[62]

West of the central corridor on the second floor were rooms reserved for members of the Household, while, to the east, the children had their apartments. "These rooms," recalled Grand Duchess Marie Pavlovna, "light and spacious, were hung with flowered *cretonne* and furnished throughout with polished lemonwood. The effect was luxurious, yet peaceful and comfortable. Through the windows you could see the Palace gardens and guard houses, and a little beyond, through the grille of a high iron gate, a street corner."[63] There was nothing regal about these surroundings, and the imperial children were raised in rooms dominated by their mother's bourgeois tastes. A small dining room, furnished with a large table and bentwood chairs, opened to the Crimson Drawing Room, where the girls received their few visitors. Their classrooms had floral-covered walls lined with glass-fronted mahogany bookcases and writing tables covered with simple oilcloth. The four girls also shared a large combination dressing-bathroom, divided in half by a curtain hung from a brass rod and circled by a whimsical frieze of hand-painted seagulls.[64] One wall was lined with tall wardrobes; against the other stood one of the only true luxurious items in the entire palace, a solid silver bathtub. Installed during the reign of Nicholas I, it was engraved with the names of all the imperial children who had used it.[65]

Grand Duchesses Olga and Tatiana shared one bedroom, Marie and Anastasia another. These rooms were large and airy, decorated in soft pastel shades of green and pink with white accents, and stenciled, art nouveau–style friezes depicting flowering vines and golden dragonflies. Sofas and chairs were covered in bright English chintzes and pale, striped green silks, with desks, dressers, and dressing tables of lemonwood and maple enameled white.[66] The simple beds, covered with silk eiderdowns sewn with each girl's initials, were hidden behind chintz-covered screens. Dozens of family photographs, watercolors, portraits, and icons covered the walls and the surfaces of desks and dressers, creating an intricate web of faces and scenes.

If the second floor remained the isolated territory of the imperial children, the rooms below were regularly filled with members of the Russian court. Visitors calling on the emperor with official business were conducted by footmen to the Imperial Waiting Room, a large space with dark, oak-paneled walls that had formerly served as a dining room.[67] As they waited, their attention was drawn to the room's dominant feature, an immense Levitan painting, *A Cemetery in the North*, which hung alongside two watercolors depicting Peter the Great's visit to France and a portrait of Empress Alexandra painted by Mueller-Norden in 1896.[68] Above their heads swirled an elaborate art nouveau–style bronze chandelier. Comfortable sofas and chairs, covered in English calf leather, were arranged round the walls, while tables were set with both domestic and foreign newspapers and periodicals.[69] The adjutant on duty greeted visitors here, noting their arrival in the leather-bound appointment books that filled his desk. Standing before the doorway to the emperor's study, an Abyssinian Guard blocked the approach of the unwelcome.

Nicholas's study had two windows and was lined with dark walnut cabinets, bookshelves, and paneling to a height of eight feet; above this, reaching to the cornice, hung patterned red silk. A corner fireplace, faced with tiles, warmed the room, which was filled with a small round table spread with maps, as well as comfortable green leather sofas and chairs, some covered with Persian rugs.[70] A bronze, medieval-style chandelier hung from the ceiling. It was a masculine space, dark and purposeful, but Nicholas dotted the room with sentimental reminders of his life. The tops of the bookshelves held a number of vases and porcelain pieces from the emperor's private collection.[71] Although Nicholas covered the edges of his desk with family photographs in elaborate Fabergé frames and souvenirs, he was very particular about the arrangement of his personal papers. According to Anna Vyrubova, everything "was always precisely in its proper place. The Emperor often said that he wanted to be able to go into his Study in the dark and put his hands at once on any object he knew to be there."[72] Nor was anyone allowed to touch his books, with older titles carefully shelved and new arrivals sorted by the emperor himself.[73] This same rule applied to his family. "I went to your room to see if any papers had come," Alexandra cautiously wrote to her husband, "and found the door locked but the key was there. It looked beastly dreary. I told them to bring any papers sorted there and am going to lay them carefully on the chair next to your writing table. Is that right?"[74]

The emperor's large bathroom, decorated in Moorish style, was split down the middle by an intricate fretwork partition separating the bathing area from the rest of the room. Dark oak panels and a matching ceiling hinted at the masculine taste.[75] His white-tiled bath, designed by Count Nicholas de Rochefort in 1902, was encased in a sunken concrete and lead container, hidden behind the screen and reached by several marble steps. When full, it held nearly 5,000 gallons of water, and two plumbers and a woman whose sole duty was to clean it each day were kept on staff to tend it.[76]

Beyond this lay Nicholas's dressing room, where the emperor displayed a number of rifles from the Tula Arms Factory, antique pistols, and a collection of cigarette cases.[77] Nicholas also kept an exercise bar and other gymnastic equipment here. "I remember finding him swirling around the exercise bar one day when I expected him to be deeply engrossed in his Study," recalled his sister Grand Duchess Olga Alexandrovna. "I need the blood in my head to be able to think," the emperor told her with a smile.[78] Adjoining the dressing room was the emperor's wardrobe room, its walls painted a vivid blue-green. Here, in cabinets of ash lined with cedar, and on the mezzanine floor were the emperor's uniforms, evening clothes, and suits.[79] Wardrobes, adorned with small oil paintings representing various regimental officers, held polished helmets, military caps, and plumed headdresses.[80] Below were drawers lined with rows of white, brown, and black kid gloves; white shirts embroidered with the imperial monogram; starched collars; and crested handkerchiefs and underwear sewn with crowns.

Restored formal study. See plate 22.

Following a small room for the adjutant on duty was the Emperor's Formal Study, with four tall windows overlooking the inner courtyard. Roman Meltzer had designed the formal study in the art nouveau–style between 1903 and 1906, and Alexandra had selected the colors and decor. Nicholas, too diplomatic to protest, disliked the results, preferring his study for his daily work.[81] The upper walls were painted in pale green, covered with a darker stenciled design, while the lower walls of the room were circled with dark mahogany paneling, cabinets, and bookshelves. The long wall opposite the windows was broken by a projection that formed a recessed bay. A dark mahogany staircase twisted up to a mezzanine gallery adorned with polished gray marble columns, their bases and capitals of gilded bronze. These columns sup ported the mahogany ceiling, which was divided into panels by strips of beaten bronze.[82] Bookshelves on the mezzanine contained dozens of albums, covered in dark blue leather and embossed with the imperial monogram in gilt. The albums held thousands of photographs, many of them taken with their Kodak cameras by the imperial family themselves and pasted onto the pages. Nicholas, Anna Vyrubova noted, "was neater about this work of pasting photographic prints than any other member of the household. He could not endure the sight of the least drop of glue on a table."[83]

In the corner of the recess, beneath the gallery, stood a tiled fireplace crowned with stepped mahogany shelves and a built-in art nouveau cozy corner. Next to this, Nicholas had placed an English billiards table and some comfortable sofas and chairs. Large Oriental carpets covered the floor; in the middle of the room stood a round table, covered with a white cloth and surrounded by mahogany Chippendale-style chairs from Vienna, upholstered in fabric ordered from Liberty and Company in London. Hanging over the table was a brass lamp from the Tiffany Company in New York.[84] A massive portrait of Alexander III by Serov dominated the southern wall. In one corner hung a painting by Edouard Detaille, *Review Passing before the Tsesarevich*, which showed the emperor at a review of His Majesty's Life Guards Hussars, of which Nicholas had been a squadron commander while tsesarevich.[85]

Just beyond the imperial vestibule, on the eastern side of the main corridor, was a small elevator, installed in 1899 to link Alexandra's room with those of her children above.[86] At the north end of the imperial corridor, doors opened to a small hallway, leading to the room used during the day by Alexandra's lady's maid. The bathroom beyond was a dark, windowless room hung in chintz, whose porcelain toilet was draped with a loose cretonne cover by the prim Alexandra when not in use. Alexandra's dressing room was hung with paintings, photographs, and souvenirs from her visit to Italy before her marriage.[87] A small fireplace warmed the room when Alexandra dressed. The dressing table, recalled the empress's friend Lili Dehn, was covered with bottles of Verveine toilet water and Atkinson's Rose Blanche, Alexandra's favorite perfume.[88] Just outside this room, a wooden staircase—installed during the 1896 renovation—ascended to a mezzanine floor and then to the children's rooms above.[89] The mezzanine held wardrobe rooms and cedar closets filled with Alexandra's dresses and gowns, tucked beneath an ornamental ceiling painted by Scotti at the beginning of the nineteenth century.[90] There were also rooms with electric irons and steam presses and rooms where seamstresses mended and repaired the imperial family's clothes.[91]

Nicholas and Alexandra's large bedroom had two tall windows looking out over the Great Lake. Alexandra hung the walls with a light floral silk, woven with a pattern of green wreaths tied with pink ribbons and adorned with pink flowers, from the London firm of Charles Hindley & Son.[92] The delicacy of the effect was diminished when she used the same fabric on the upholstery of the cream-colored furniture and for the curtains, leaving the eye no place to rest. A wooden partition of slender white columns sheltered an alcove, draped with the same floral silk that hung on the walls, concealing twin brass beds. Like the other rooms in the Alexander Palace, the imperial bedroom was crowded with Victorian clutter: bronze sculptures, family photographs, potted palms, and hundreds of icons. To the right of the beds was a small enclosed toilet. On the opposite side was a

Alexandra's Mauve Boudoir in the Alexander Palace

private oratory, used by the empress, with a small, carved iconostasis adorned with gilded columns, a folding table set with a prayer book, and a cushion. It was dimly lit by the silver and red glass *lampadka* that perfumed the space with a heavy scent of rose oil.[93]

Alexandra commissioned the Mauve Boudoir that followed from Roman Meltzer in 1896, just after she and Nicholas first moved into the Alexander Palace.[94] Everything here was mauve, Alexandra's favorite color, from the floral silk coverings on the furniture to the flowers in the Chinese bowls and hand-painted irises on the frieze round the ceiling. The walls were hung with a light gray and mauve striped Parisian silk and dotted with hundreds of family photographs and icons.[95] An Annunciation, painted by Nesterov, hung below a portrait of the empress's mother, while Paupion's *Dream of the Mother of God* dominated another wall. "The effect," recalled Grand Duchess Marie Pavlovna, "was frankly ugly, but comfortable and gay."[96] A chaise longue stood in one corner, set against a paneled half-wall. Here, the empress spent endless hours, reading, writing, watching her children at play, and, in later years, reposing when unwell. Screens and potted palms divided the remainder of the space, which was filled with a mixture of overstuffed sofas and chairs built into the cream-colored enameled paneling and delicate neo-rococo pieces in lemonwood, along with a white upright Becker piano.[97] A large writing desk, piled with trays, held a supply of heavy vellum paper stamped with the empress's monogram and crown. The walls were lined with low cabinets and bookshelves of lemonwood, enameled in cream, their doors covered in the same silk that hung on the walls. In the middle of the western wall stood a fireplace lined with dark green tiles. Above the mantel, between the open shelves that rose between columns and arches, was a large mirror, reflecting Alexandra's collection of art nouveau vases. The empress kept the Mauve Boudoir filled with fresh flowers—"the air was fragrant with masses of lilac and lilies of the valley," remembered Lili Dehn.[98]

From the Mauve Boudoir, doors led to the Rosewood Drawing Room. The wainscot, doorframes, and lintels were of highly polished rosewood. Above the wainscot, the walls were hung with yellow moiré from France, reaching to a cornice adorned with a stylized garland frieze.[99] In one corner stood a fireplace, with a mantel and side shelves filled with the empress's favorite photographs, vases, and souvenirs. The room was a virtual shrine to Alexandra's childhood in Darmstadt: visitors could view a screen covered with watercolors of Hessian palaces and castles; a large canvas showing her family's Schloss Romrod; photographs of her father, brother, mother, and sisters; and a copy of Von Angelli's portrait of her mother.[100]

The Maple Drawing Room in the Alexander Palace

Beyond the Rosewood Drawing Room was the Maple Drawing Room, created by Meltzer between 1903 and 1906 in the eastern half of Quarenghi's former Concert Hall and, at a cost of 32,000 rubles, the single most expensive interior undertaken at the palace.[101] The walls of the Maple Drawing Room, painted pale pink, were adorned with delicate bas-reliefs depicting trellises of roses that reached in sensuous tendrils to a hanging cornice equipped with concealed lighting. The coved ceiling, painted pale green, was also decorated with carved plaster roses. A mezzanine gallery spanned the southern end of the room, reached by a wooden staircase. Although the stairs and railings were simple enough, Meltzer decorated the maple pilasters and columns of the bowed balcony with richly carved roses, vines, and garlands.[102] Beneath the balcony stood a fireplace, flanked by walls faced with dark maple paneling and a cozy corner framed by display cases. A large painting entitled *The Entrance of Their Majesties into the Anichkov Palace, 14 November, 1894*, hung on one wall, commemorating the wedding of the emperor and the empress.[103]

The entire room was filled with potted palms and assorted Victorian bric-a-brac, scattered across the pale green carpet and a mixture of Oriental rugs and bearskins. In the northern corner of the room, next to a doorway leading to the Rosewood Drawing Room, was a built-in curved sofa topped with a wooden display ledge that Alexandra covered with family photographs and busts. In the corner above the ledge was a vitrine with a curved glass front; here, Alexandra's Fabergé Easter eggs and other precious objets d'art were kept. One visitor recalled, "The furniture was of light polished wood and bamboo, upholstered in pale green satin with a peculiar flower design. The green lampshades were also decorated with flowers mostly water lilies of a sickly hue. This setting would have suited a play by Ibsen or Strindberg."[104] Beyond this room, wrapped around a corner of the wing, was a balcony lined with wrought-iron railings and covered with an iron roof supported by intricately worked wrought-iron pilasters, manufactured at the St. Petersburg Metal Works and installed in 1898.[105] Oriental rugs covered its stone floor, on which stood wicker chairs and chaise longues; white canvas curtains provided privacy and shielded the balcony from the summer breezes that blew off the lakes.

The last room in the suite, the Corner Salon, marked the entrance to the State Apartments. It was lit on two sides by seven tall windows, each hung with white lace and crimson brocade curtains. The walls were faced in white scagliola, topped with a heavily carved cornice that edged a ceiling hung with a cut crystal, ormolu, and crimson glass chandelier. The Corner Salon was decorated with a rich Savonnerie carpet, neo-rococo revival chairs, and sofas covered in green silk brocade.[106] A Roentgen desk, gilded consoles, and tables held priceless Sèvres and Meissen vases and bowls filled with fresh flowers, family photographs in Fabergé frames, and busts of Alexander I and Paul I. In one corner of the room hung a Gobelin tapestry of Marie Antoinette and her children, a copy of the famous painting by Vigée-Lebrun, which was presented to Empress Alexandra by President Emil Loubet of France during his 1902 visit to St. Petersburg.[107] It was an ominous touch, a poignant and visible reminder of the people's vengeance.

The Alexander Palace said a good deal about the middle-class predispositions, hidden beneath the trappings of imperial splendor, of the last emperor and empress of Russia. The imperial family certainly enjoyed the benefits of a comfortable home, rather than an antique-filled museum. For Nicholas, Alexandra, and their children, the palace became an isolated bastion, a fortress that the empress believed protected them from the immoral influence of the St. Petersburg upper classes she so despised. Ironically, this cloistered existence sheltered them from the gradual collapse of the empire itself until the Revolution forever vanquished their way of life.

12

PETERHOF

TO THE WEST OF ST. PETERSBURG, the countryside rose and fell in a series of low hills, flanked by thick forests of pine, chestnut, oak, and maple, and descending in natural terraces to the Gulf of Finland. Lakes and marshes stretched to the shore, the tranquility broken only by the occasional mewing of a gull or the whistle of a passing launch. The Volkonsky High Road, skirting the crest of the hillside above the Gulf, sliced through "little woods and wet green fields where black and white cows were grazing," recalled one French diplomat, "their color standing out sharply against the green background and the intense blue of the sea."[1] Here, in these serene surroundings, the Romanovs created Peterhof, one of the most magnificent palaces in the Russian empire.

Shortly after founding his new capital, Peter the Great began building a summer palace here. At first, he wanted only a small cabin from which to supervise the construction of the naval base at nearby Kronstadt.[2] Peter liked the location and in 1710 commissioned a small palace, Mon Plaisir, with a park laid out at the edge of the sea. For the next fifteen years, up to thirty thousand workers labored on the estate, carefully creating gardens, fountains, avenues, and pavilions.[3] Eventually, as a concession to the demands of the throne, he commissioned Alexander Le Blonde to erect a larger, three-storeyed palace atop the hill half a mile away.[4] Empress Elizabeth, Peter's daughter, hired Bartolomeo Rastrelli to completely remodel her father's modest building; by the time Rastrelli finished, Peter's palace was unrecognizable.

The Grand Palace
and Cascade.
See plate 23.

Peterhof was the most exquisite formal park in Russia and one of the most impressive water gardens in the world, boasting hundreds of fountains, all intricate and amazing marvels of eighteenth-century technology devised by the hydraulic engineer Vassili Tuvolkov, who dug a series of canals to carry water from the Ropsha Heights, some fifteen miles south, to ornament Peter's garden. The fountains at Peterhof worked on gravity alone; water flowed through a system of pressurized pipes to the Upper Park, before being fed through tunnels beneath the palace to burst forth in the Grand Cascade. The natural slope of the site resulted in fountains of great complexity and height.[5]

From the Volkonsky High Road, the Grand Palace suddenly appeared, set against the lush green of the Upper Park, with its glistening fountains and pristine statuary.[6] It sat at the edge of a natural terrace, its projecting and recessed bays rising three storeys to a double mansard roof. Rastrelli ornamented the yellow facade with baroque details: white quoins, pilasters, and cartouches framing the windows; pavilions, linked to the Grand Palace by enclosed two-storey galleries, extended the length of the building to nearly nine hundred feet.[7] The eastern pavilion, topped with five brightly gilded onion domes, contained the palace church. The one to the west—called the Coat of Arms Pavilion—was decorated with nearly twenty pounds of gold leaf.[8] Atop its central onion-domed cupola perched a golden eagle with three heads, designed so that from any vista it always appeared to be double-headed.

The vestibule, floored in gray and white marble squares, wound its way through the ground floor, its walls and cornices completely unadorned. But any impression of simplicity was soon abandoned on reaching the grand staircase, a perfect symphony in white and gold created by Rastrelli. Wide flights of marble steps ascended to the *piano nobile* amid intricate wrought-iron railings embellished with gold leaf and gilded statuary, beneath walls painted with grisaille cartouches and trophies ornamented with gold. Above stretched a glorious trompe l'oeil ceiling, supported in a gilded frame held aloft by cherubs. Glittering statuary, boiseries, garlands of flowers, carved shell ornaments, and enormous mirrors increased the play of light from the high windows and hundreds of candles.[9] This was Elizabeth's palace, and, from this room on, Peter's simple tastes had been replaced with luxurious splendor.

The Ballroom.
See plate 24.

The State Apartments on the principal floor, glittering with gilt and sunlight, were luminous rooms, distinctly feminine in tone. From the head of the grand staircase, visitors were ushered through the Blue Reception Room to the Ballroom, rising two storeys to a coved, painted ceiling depicting Empress Elizabeth in the guise of Parnassus. Double rows of windows, surrounded by intricately carved and gilded boiseries adorned with ormolu sconces, flooded the room with light.[10] The Chesme Room that followed took its name from twelve large canvases by Jacob Philippe Hackaert, depicting the Russian naval victory over Turkey in the Mediterranean, the Aegean, and the Adriatic Seas in the early 1770s. When Hackaert worked on his commission, the Russian Navy actually had a sixty-gun frigate blown up as it lay at anchor, so that the painter might accurately reflect the horrors of battle.[11]

The Throne Room.
See plate 25.

Beyond lay the Throne Room, the largest of the palace interiors, spanning the entire width of the building, its twenty-eight windows arrayed in two tiers overlooking the Upper and Lower Parks. Yuri Velten had executed the classical decoration for Catherine the Great, leaving only Rastrelli's elaborate, geometric inlaid wooden floor. Classical sculptural stucco reliefs of garlands, oak leaves, laurels, and roses in white were set against the delicate soft blues and grays of the walls. At one end, a dais held a throne of carved and gilded oak covered with red velvet sewn with a double-headed eagle in silver thread.[12] Large mirrors stood between the lower windows, framed by panels adorned with ormolu sconces. A heavily dentilated cornice circled the room, supporting the stuccoed vaults of the tall ceiling. The ceiling was painted with allegorical themes and hung with twelve cut crystal and smoked amethyst glass chandeliers, their pendants shaped as oak leaves, balls, and faceted stars.[13]

The Audience Hall preserved Rastrelli's baroque decoration, its white walls enriched with gilded boiseries and garlands, cartouches, putti, and rocailles enclosing mirrors.[14] Yuri Velten designed the White Banqueting Hall for Catherine the Great, adorning its walls with bas-reliefs of cherubs, garlands, foliage, and fruit designs set within stucco moldings of delicate aquamarine. Two rows of windows overlooked the Grand Cascade and the Gulf of Finland beyond, and five immense, multitiered eighteenth-century amethyst and smoked crystal chandeliers hung from the ceiling.[15]

A startling surprise followed: the West Chinese Lobby, one of two rooms executed by Vallin de la Mothe in the fashionable, eighteenth-century chinoiserie style. It was balanced by the East Chinese Lobby. Both rooms were decorated in almost identical fashion: their walls were faced with black lacquer panels and either inset with Chinese details and paintings, their moldings detailed in gilt, or hung with fine damask hand-painted with flowers and Oriental scenes. The floors were the most intricate in the palace, of garlands, circles, rosettes, and geometric designs, inlaid with more than two thousand pieces of thirteen different kinds of rare woods, including mahogany, amaranth, sandalwood, rosewood, birch, maple, and ebony. Above, dangling on golden chains held in the teeth of angry-looking gilded dragons, hung frosted glass lanterns. On tiny shelves and ledges built into the walls, some of the imperial collection of porcelain was displayed, perfectly at home in these ornate jewel boxes.[16]

The East Chinese Lobby. See plate 26.

At the center of the palace, the Portrait Room spanned the width of the building, with French doors opening to balconies looking out over the Upper and Lower Parks. Also called the Hall of Modes and Graces, its walls were entirely covered with 368 paintings set within gilt frames, the work of artist Pietro Rotari. Above, a frieze of medallions and cartouches depicted representations of *Glory*, *Truth*, *Time*, *Poetry*, *Patriotism*, *Virtue*, and *Wealth*, along with paintings of Neptune, Mars, and Apollo.[17]

The East Chinese Lobby marked the end of the State Apartments; the private apartments that followed were divided into two suites, one for the emperor and one for his consort. The empress's suite, which stretched along the northern side of the palace, opened with the Partridge Room, named for its blue-silk wall coverings patterned with partridges, flowers, and cornstalks.[18] The next room held a low Turkish-style divan, set at an angle against the walls behind a white balustrade and piled with silk cushions and Japanese silk coverings. The exotic theme was further carried out on the wall coverings of hand-painted Chinese silk depicting scenes of rural Chinese life, set between gilded stucco moldings.[19] A series of smaller rooms ended at the Blue Drawing Room, hung with light blue Brocatelle silk surrounded by delicately carved and gilded boiseries and dominated by an immense crystal, ormolu, and cobalt glass chandelier of forty-eight lights, made at the Imperial Porcelain Factory in 1851.[20] A gallery beyond led to the Church of St. Peter and St. Paul, a baroque concoction of white and gold, with elaborate gilded cherubs, rocailles, and moldings, and a massive carved and gilded iconostasis, which occupied the eastern pavilion.

The rooms along the southern enfilade were originally reserved for the emperor; by the reign of Nicholas II, they often housed important visiting heads of state and other dignitaries. Most of Rastrelli's original decoration had been left unaltered, and these rooms were rich examples of his favored baroque and rococo tastes, with intricate carvings, silk-hung walls, inlaid wooden floors, and gilded boiseries. The State Bedroom was hung with hand-painted Chinese silk, set below a cornice decorated with gilded stucco moldings, while the paneling was painted in shades of cream and white. The ceiling was painted with a canvas showing Venus and Adonis, surrounded with a grisaille border of a garland of roses.[21]

At the northern side of the Great Palace, a wide terrace overlooked the Lower Park and the Gulf of Finland beyond. Gilded bronze vases and fountains shot plumes of water into the air and across the Grand Cascade's twin flights of marble steps, their spray glistening against the golden statues lining the hillside. At the foot of the cascade, a wide basin, encircled with gilded tritons, dolphins, naiads, and sirens, offered a shifting, rippling mirror shielded by a sparkling mist.[22] In the middle of the basin, atop an island of rocks, stood a gilded statue of Samson prying apart the jaws of a lion, symbolizing Russia's victory over Sweden on St. Samson's Day in 1709 in the Great Northern War. From the lion's jaws, a single jet, nearly a hundred feet high, thrust itself toward the sky before plummeting back to join the rush of water in the Great Canal as it swept toward the Gulf of Finland.[23]

West of the Grand Canal, at the end of a long allée, stood the Hermitage, a baroque building encircled by a deep moat and reached by a narrow wooden bridge. The entire first floor was given over to a single dining room, lit by nine tall windows and its walls covered with 124 paintings by European artists, separated by thin gilt frames.[24] The Hermitage had a mechanical dining table that could be raised and lowered by winches to serve each new course to the sovereign and his guests. In 1797, the mechanism failed, leaving Emperor Paul stranded until servants could fetch a ladder. The experience left him so outraged that he ordered the mechanism torn out.[25]

The Hermitage was the first structure at the edge of the Marly Garden, one of several complexes in the Lower Park built around pavilions and small palaces. The Marly Garden was the most formal at Peterhof, built in imitation of Le Notre's designs at Versailles. Here, three great, long avenues met: the central Marly Avenue, the northern Malieban, and the southern Birch Walk. To protect the garden from harsh sea breezes, Peter the Great constructed a grass mound, reinforced by a brick retaining wall with curved bays topped by a stone balustrade. On the other side of the wall, a basin was dug, balanced by a semi-circular pond crossed by three bridges. They met at the center of a small island, on which Peter built a small palace called Marly, after the French palace of Marly-le-Roi near Paris. Marly was designed in the simple Dutch style favored by Peter the Great, a two-storeyed building with whitewashed quoins and a lemon yellow facade topped by a mansard roof.[26]

On the slope above the palace stood the Golden Hill Cascade, a marble staircase with gilded copper risers surrounded by a balustrade decorated with Carrara marble statues. Three Carrara marble statues of Neptune, a nymph, and a triton stood guard along the cascade's top wall; beneath them, set into the wall, were three *mascarons* surrounded with cartouches, all in gold leaf. From their mouths, three jets of water shot forth over the marble platform, tumbling down the steps in wide sheets to end in a wide basin at the bottom.[27] The area below the Golden Hill Cascade was known as the Garden of Bacchus and contained several important fountains from Peter's reign. Two were known as the Menager Fountains, each consisting of a single jet of water rising some fifty feet into the sky from the middle of large basins. They received their name from a French device installed within their bases, which forced an enormous burst of water around a central obstruction and up through a narrow shaft, forming a hollow spray.[28] There were also four Triton Cloche Fountains, each formed of a bronze sculpture of a triton holding aloft a large disc with a jet above; the water was forced from the jet and formed a ball, or *cloche*, as it descended down the disc.[29] The nearby Lion Fountain was one of the most elaborate of all the Peterhof waterworks: an open pergola of Ionic columns enclosing a basin, it was surrounded by jets of water from vases and foaming bowls and guarded by lions whose open jaws spat forth white sprays.[30]

From the terrace of the Grand Palace, a broad, sweeping walk descended to the eastern half of the Lower Park. An ornate baroque orangerie nestled against a lush green backdrop. From the hillside, a stream of water poured from the Checkerboard Cascade down a series of black and white steps, fed by jets from the open jaws of brightly painted Chinese dragons.[31] Farther east stood the Pyramid Fountain, set upon a small mound enclosed with a marble balustrade topped with vases and urns. In the middle of the square basin was the fountain itself, composed of 505 individual jets, rising in stepped levels, to form a pyramid with their spray.[32]

Beyond lay the Mon Plaisir Garden, its groves of birch and fir crossed with winding gravel paths and surrounded with small pools. In the woods, Peter installed a number of trick fountains, a favorite eighteenth-century fantasy. Several were made of green metal disguised as fir or oak trees; when the unsuspecting visitor stepped upon a certain stone or sat upon a nearby bench, he was unceremoniously drenched with water from the hollow trunks. Another fountain took the form of a large Chinese umbrella providing shelter for a round bench; when the bench was sat upon, a deluge of water cascaded from the rim of the umbrella, trapping those beneath its canopy.[33]

At the edge of the Gulf of Finland, where the forest of pine, chestnut, oak, and maple opened, Peter created a garden with beds of roses, tulips, and begonias. Its simplicity complemented the nearby Mon Plaisir Palace, a long, single-storeyed structure of red brick, built in 1714 at the edge of the sea.[34] In the interior, however, the frugal Peter made surprising concessions to his high office, with marble floors, colorfully painted ceilings, and elaborate stucco work.[35] For this autocratic man of simple tastes, Mon Plaisir was the perfect retreat from the constraints of the St. Petersburg court. Peter would sail to the small dock at the end of the terrace, bringing an adjutant for company. He rarely spent the night here; when the weather turned on him, he would pace restlessly up and down the long galleries, listening to the raging sea.

Peterhof eventually grew to encompass six large parks, four of which had their own palace complexes. Across the Volkonsky High Road from the Upper Park was the Colonist Park, laid out by Stackenschneider for Nicholas I. Originally, Catherine the Great had given large tracts of this land, once known as "Hunter's Marsh," to German immigrants.[36] A wild stretch of marshes, lakes, islands, and meadows was transformed into an elysian vista of Palladian-inspired temples and monuments. The classical Tsaritsyn Pavilion, constructed in 1844 by Andrei Stackenschneider, was marked by a tower overlooking the lake; within, Nicholas I finished the rooms with Finnish, Italian, and Siberian marbles.[37] In the middle of another lake stood Olga Island, named after Nicholas I's favorite daughter and containing a neoclassical pavilion with a three-storey tower, used for entertaining, as well as an open-air amphitheater where ballet and symphony performances were often given for the emperor and his guests.[38]

The Meadow Park, laid out between 1825 and 1857, stretched farther south. High above the rolling fields near the Babigon Canal, Nicholas I built a Grecian temple christened the Belvedere. From its portico, ringed with Ionic columns, the emperor and his guests could gaze across stretches of water, forest, and meadow to the distant fountains of the Imperial Park and the blue expanse of the Gulf of Finland shimmering in the distance.[39] There was also a small pavilion on the shore of the lake and an elaborate little Russian-style dacha.[40]

In 1779, Catherine the Great selected an area called New Peterhof, southwest of the Great Palace, as the site for a new park, landscaped in the English manner after the works of Humphrey Repton and Lancelot "Capability" Brown. Laid out by James Meader, the English Park featured a serpentine stretch of water, carefully arranged clumps of trees planted to appear as if they had been randomly strewn across the undulating lawns, and classical pavilions.[41]

At the center of the park stood the English Palace, built for Catherine by Giacomo Quarenghi in 1786–1796, its pale walls gleaming in the mirror of the languid lake. The English Palace was Quarenghi's first substantial commission in Russia and his first for the Romanovs, a severe, Palladian-style building of two principal storeys resting upon a raised ground floor. At the center of the main facade, Quarenghi placed a large portico of eight Corinthian columns, reached by a broad flight of stairs, while on the garden side, he created a large, two-storey loggia. In Nicholas II's reign, its fifty ornate rooms were used to house important visitors.[42]

The Cottage Palace.
See plate 27.

The gardens at Mon Plaisir marked the boundary of the Lower Park. To the east, stretching from the shoreline of the Gulf of Finland to the Volkonsky High Road at the crest of the hillside above, lay Alexandria, a natural, English-style landscape park.[43] In 1826, Nicholas I gave the park to his wife, naming the estate Alexandria in her honor.[44] The Alexandria Park, thick with groves of evergreen, birch, and oak trees fringing golden meadows, was laid out by the Scottish architect Adam Menelaws as a pure exercise in the Romantic movement, with rustic streams tumbling over carefully contrived cascades, mock-ruins, and vistas over fields grown wild with flowers to the shimmering waters of the Gulf of Finland. Narrow paths laced through emerald-green grass, shaded by linden and maple trees planted by successive emperors, to arbor-framed walks ending in pavilions and groups of statuary. It was a tranquil spot, isolated and completely free from the hectic life of the imperial court.[45]

In the middle of the park stood the elaborate Chapel of St. Alexander Nevsky, designed by the German architect Karl Friedrich Schinkel and built in the gothic style by Menelaws and his colleague Joseph Charlemagne in 1832. The chapel took the form of a massive two-storey tower, with an arched porch, stained glass windows, and a facade adorned with forty-three statues of various saints. Within, the vibrant sky-blue walls were adorned with white stucco trefoils and tendrils, supporting a dome sprinkled with golden stars.[46]

Through a stretch of woodland lay the Farmhouse Palace, built by Adam Menelaws in 1828–1830 in the Finnish style, with plain stuccoed walls and a steep, hipped iron roof to house the future Alexander II. When the existing building proved too small, Andrei Stackenschneider added two larger wings. The

The Lower Palace at Alexandria, Peterhof

Farmhouse Palace, bristling with lacy gables, balconies, and dormer windows, was a gothic-revival villa, its rooms adorned with intricately carved wooden paneling, arched stained-glass windows, and traceried ceilings and filled with English chintzes and Biedermeier-style furniture of Karelian birch.[47] Nicholas and Alexandra occasionally stayed here in the first years of his reign, and their second daughter, Tatiana, was born at the Farmhouse Palace in 1897.

At the center of the Alexandria Park, high on a bluff overlooking the Gulf, stood the Cottage Palace. In 1826, Nicholas I commissioned Menelaws to design a secluded country house here as a gift to his wife, Alexandra. The Cottage Palace was a piece of pure Victorian whimsy. Its lemon yellow facade bristled with gothic details: arched and leaded stained-glass windows; tall bays set with lancet windows; open porches decorated with lacy cast iron latticework adorned with roses, shamrocks, quatrefoils, and oak clusters; balconies with white railings; and abundant gingerbread fretwork, all set below a steeply pitched roof.[48] The rooms inside the Cottage Palace were small in scale, though richly decorated with stucco traceries, vibrant colors, and Biedermeier furniture. Subsequent emperors used the building on a regular basis, preferring its relatively human scale to that of the Grand Palace. During the reign of Nicholas II, it was Dowager Empress Marie

The Lower Palace at Alexandria, Peterhof, seen from the edge of the Gulf of Finland

Feodorovna who frequently occupied its splendid rooms, along with her unmarried son Michael and her daughter Olga.[49]

The last, and in the reign of Nicholas II, most important of all the buildings in the Alexandria Park was the Lower Palace. Every May, shortly after returning from the Crimea, Nicholas and Alexandra happily abandoned the rigid formality of the Alexander Palace for the fresh sea breezes and intimate atmosphere to be found here. Because it was so small, the palace was rarely filled with the uniformed servants and members of the Suite who usually crowded the imperial family's daily life. Largely left alone, attended by only a handful of officials and staff, Nicholas, Alexandra, and their children could relax in a way precluded by the daily ceremonial of life at Tsarskoye Selo—itself a refuge from the etiquette of the court in St. Petersburg.

The Lower Palace began as a military structure. In 1833, Nicholas I commissioned Joseph Charlemagne to build a four-storey tower near the shoreline; from here, telegraphic signals were regularly conveyed from the naval base at Kronstadt to similar devices installed in the tower of the St. Petersburg City Duma and in a belvedere atop the Winter Palace.[50] By the reign of Alexander III, the tower regularly housed members of Alexander III's family, and in 1882 the emperor commissioned Anthony Tomishko to enlarge the structure. The architect found the building in too great a state of disrepair, however, and soon presented plans for a new villa. The emperor's only request was that the new structure be built in the Italian Renaissance style.[51] In August of 1882, the old signal tower was razed; construction began in 1883 and lasted three years.[52] It was here, in the midst of the ceremonies marking the 1884 wedding of Alix of Hesse's sister Elizabeth to Nicholas's uncle Grand Duke Serge Alexandrovich, that the young tsesarevich brought the twelve-year-old girl who would one day become his wife. "Alix and I," the tsesarevich noted in his diary, "wrote our names on the back window of the little Italian house (we love each other)."[53]

This early sentiment drew Nicholas and Alexandra to Tomishko's villa. Nicholas wrote in his diary: "I came to our lovely Alexandria with a feeling of joy and sadness and entered our house by the sea. It seems so strange to live here with my wife. Although there is not enough space here, the rooms are pretty and the premises are ideal."[54]

As Nicholas noted, the existing building was too small to meet the needs of his family. In 1895, he therefore asked Tomishko to enlarge the villa. Tomishko built a second structure, the new wing, to the east of the existing villa and connected with a passage above an arched porte cochere; corridors dug in the foundation linked the two basements.[55] The members of the imperial family moved into their new enlarged villa in the summer of 1898. "We love this place," Nicholas wrote to Queen Victoria, "and especially our house, which is built quite on the border of the sea."[56]

Tomishko's building was christened the Lower Palace; throughout Nicholas II's reign, it was also called the New Palace, the Lower Dacha, and the Emperor's Own Dacha. These impressive names cloaked the building in a mantle of suggested grandeur; in reality, however, the Lower Palace was not really a palace at all, but rather a moderately sized villa, its two wings filled with a jumble of small rooms and narrow staircases. Poorly planned and executed, it amounted to little more than a dozen major rooms, tacked on haphazardly and shielded in a uniform exterior to disguise the villa's humble beginnings. The Lower Palace was a four-storeyed building, faced in a distinctive polychrome red and yellow brick laid in decorative horizontal bands and dominated by a tall Italianate tower. Loggias, columns, pilasters, and window surrounds of gray Putilov stone added contrast and visual interest, and projecting rounded bays emphasized the picturesque nature of the exterior. The entire structure was topped with steeply pitched roofs resting on heavily bracketed eaves, the varying heights pierced with small dormer windows and crowned with elaborate chimneys faced in yellow and red terra-cotta.[57]

The interior, decorated by Roman Meltzer, was a virtual temple to art nouveau. At the head of a staircase, double doors opened to the drawing room, its walls hung with an English paper of subtle mauve and white stripes adorned by clusters of pink roses below the cornice; trailing vines, set at regular intervals and dotted with roses, lent a strong vertical element to the room. Sofas and chairs, their white enameled woodwork carved with roses contrasting with the floral cretonne upholstery, stood across a pistachio-colored carpet woven with a herringbone pattern of trellised roses. In one corner, atop a raised platform, stood a built-in sofa topped with mirrored panels, its shelf lined with Alexandra's collection of art nouveau porcelain from St. Petersburg, Copenhagen, and Darmstadt. Small tables, covered with fringed brocades, displayed family photographs and marble busts of the imperial children, lit by elaborate art nouveau bronze lamps in the form of water lily stems and flowers topped with rose-tinted glass shades.[58]

The dining room used the vibrant colors and sinuous curves characteristic of the period, with blue walls paneled in white-enameled wainscoting topped by a shelf filled with porcelain. A recessed, white-enameled buffet, edged with mirrors

The dining room in the Lower Palace

and tiered shelves, contained a dumbwaiter connecting to the kitchen below. In the center of the room, above the rectangular table surrounded by white-enameled chairs upholstered in light and dark blue leather, hung four pierced bronze lamps. Cream-colored curtains, sewn with dark blue poppies and green leaves, hung across the windows, while the floor was covered with a deep carpet of blue-green, woven with dark blue medallions.[59]

The windows of the glassed-in winter garden looked out over the lawns and the shoreline. Alexandra's friend Lili Dehn called it "a lovely tropical place, full of flowers and palms. It was exactly like a Garden of Dreams, at least I thought so until I saw the prosaically comfortable garden chairs and noticed some toys and a child's dolls' house."[60] Alexandra often spent her afternoons here, surrounded by free-flying hummingbirds and the bowers of sweet-smelling, exotic flowers.

The emperor's reception room, recalled visiting journalist W. T. Stead, "was painted in a creamy white, with a painted ceiling like Hampton Court. There was a picture . . . I think of the Emperor at autumn maneuvers, a pastel portrait of the Empress, a portrait in color of the Emperor, and several pretty landscapes and seascapes. There was also a piano in the same cream color. A table with a large lamp occupied the center of the room. Before the windows, which had blinds down, were high vases with white flowers."[61] In contrast, Nicholas's study was lined with carved panels of dark walnut topped with open shelves displaying porcelain and bronzes; above this hung blue silk. The emperor used a large desk for receiving official reports; his work desk stood to one side, between windows hung with brocade sewn with medallions in gold thread. Against the walls stood cabinets and bookcases and several built-in sofas, upholstered, as were the matching square-backed chairs, with black Moroccan leather that was decorated with stamped gilt designs and studs.[62]

The empress's reception room returned to the art nouveau theme, hung in cretonne depicting bunches of cornflowers woven with green and gold bands. The lower walls were circled with a wainscot of Karelian birch, which was also used in the mantelpiece, door lintels, and window frames, while the floor was covered with a velvet carpet woven with light gray flowers and rocaille scrolls. The Meltzers also designed the suite of Karelian birch furniture, ornamented with ormolu mounts and upholstered in the same floral cretonne that hung upon the walls.[63]

Nicholas and Alexandra's bedroom on the second floor was hung with white cretonne patterned with blue cornflowers above a low mahogany wainscot. A painted frieze and a molded cornice circled the plasterwork ceiling. The carpet, of mauve velvet, was woven with light gray wreath medallions. A screen hung with the same cretonne as on the walls hid the double bed. Beyond were dressing rooms and bathrooms, all decorated with family photos.[64] French doors opened from these rooms to a terrace, where Alexandra spent summer mornings reclining on a wicker chaise longue, shaded by the canvas awnings and the shadows cast by the fronds of the potted palms, taking her morning coffee, writing letters, and reading.

The children's rooms in the new wing were bright, their walls hung with floral cretonne, and their simple oak floors inlaid with walnut and covered with blue and green pile carpets. Mahogany was used for the wainscoting, either left stained a natural color or painted in crisp white enamel. Other decorative details, including moldings, cornices, chimneypieces, lintels, and window frames, were picked out in amaranth. The art nouveau taste for strong color was echoed in friezes of bright red poppies and blue cornflowers, and painted green furniture upholstered in velvet sewn with stylized yellow and blue cornflowers and strutting peacocks.[65] Their drawing room seemed, at first glance, a typical bourgeois interior, with floral patterned wallpaper and simple architectural details. In reality, however, it served as a showplace for some of the Lower Palace's most exquisite examples of art nouveau–style furniture. The Meltzers had provided most of these pieces: sensuously curved mahogany armchairs with ribbed sides and backs, walnut side chairs with exaggerated back rests in the manner of Charles Rennie Mackintosh, and a walnut cozy corner with a built-in sofa, tiers of shelves, and a mirror. The upholstery on the furniture, too, was a highly stylized combination of form and color: gray velvet with pink and blue flowers, red velvet with yellow floral designs, and gray with blue and red poppies.[66]

The room, like much of the Lower Palace itself, was undoubtedly unique, and the four girls filled it with favorite photographs, watercolors, and, in imitation of their mother, bits of art glass from Copenhagen and Darmstadt. But the drawing room, and the Lower Palace itself said more about the taste of the empress than of her family; Nicholas II himself is known to have particularly disliked many of the art nouveau interiors installed by his wife. Yet he and his children, figuratively and literally, were surrounded and engulfed by the more forceful personality of the empress.

The story of the last imperial family of Russia often seems inexorably bound to their more famous residence, the Alexander Palace at Tsarskoye Selo. The Lower Palace, however, actually served as the setting for some of the most important personal and political events in the reign of Nicholas II, including the births of the imperial couple's last three children, Marie in 1899, Anastasia in 1901, and Tsesarevich Alexei in 1904. These happy occasions, however, were soon tempered by more ominous events. It was at the Lower Palace, in October of 1905, that Nicholas gave way to pressure from his government and agreed to create the Duma and grant Russia a constitution. And barely two weeks later, it was from the Lower Palace that Nicholas and Alexandra set out for Znamenka, the neighboring estate of Grand Duke Nicholas Nikolaievich, to first meet Gregory Rasputin.

In July 1914, the imperial family was at the Lower Palace, following the growing diplomatic crisis over the assassination of Archduke Franz Ferdinand in Sarajevo. A steady stream of ministers filtered in and out of the Lower Palace, advising the emperor of the growing threat of war. "During the short intervals of the day when we saw the Emperor," recalled Anna Vyrubova, "he seemed half-dazed by the momentous decision he was called upon to make."[67] It was in his study, where framed photographs of the kaiser gazed down on him from the walnut shelves, that Nicholas II ordered Russian troops to be mobilized against imperial Germany and Austria-Hungary.

13

THE MOSCOW PALACES

IF ST. PETERSBURG WAS FILLED WITH imperial palaces, the same could not be said of Moscow, the former capital, which had suffered from centuries of neglect in favor of the city on the Neva. As the Romanovs rarely went to Moscow except on state occasions, they had no need of a dozen palaces. Instead, Moscow had only three main Crown properties: Neskuchnoye Palace, Petrovsky Palace, and the palaces inside the Kremlin.

Neskuchnoye Palace, ringed by a fringe of green trees and wide lawns, lay in a quiet southern suburb off the Garden Ring, some two miles from the Kremlin. Built in 1756 by the aristocratic Demidov family, it was purchased by Nicholas I, who commissioned the architect Evgraf Tiurin to wrap the structure in a refined, neoclassical facade.[1] The resulting palace, rooted in the work of Andrea Palladio, was a building of three storeys, dominated by projecting porticoes, Venetian windows, and a hipped roof crowned with a small belvedere. Within, an imperial staircase, wrapped in balustrades of polished brass and wrought iron embellished with gilded inserts, ascended to a suite of rooms decorated in the Empire style, their marble walls, pilasters, and grisaille ceilings speaking of cool restraint.

Neskuchnoye Palace.
See plate 28.

Few of the Romanovs were fond of the palace, although they appreciated its situation. The land had been the Pleasaunce Garden, a favorite spot for afternoon strolls and picnics until Nicholas I purchased the property and ringed it with a tall protective fence. Sprawled near the banks of the Moskva River, its

Petrovsky Palace.
See plate 29.

tree-lined allées and groves of fir and birch offered a hint of bucolic solitude in the midst of the hectic city, a benefit not lost on Nicholas and Alexandra, who preferred to reside here when in Moscow so that their children could enjoy its gardens.[2]

On the other side of the city stood the Petrovsky Palace, a late-eighteenth-century structure in a curious gothic, neo-medieval style. Matvei Kazakov was the architect responsible for this derivative pastiche, bristling with white arches, windows, battlements, and gingerbread trim spread across a red-brick facade crowned with a low dome. One English visitor termed it "a curious, fanciful edifice" in which "every principle of art appears to have been violated," though he noted that the effect "is quaint and impressive."[3] The interior, how-ever, was an exercise in sobriety, with exquisitely plastered rooms opening from a tall rotunda, decorated in the Empire and neoclassical styles. Nicholas and Alexandra occasionally used the palace during their visits to Moscow; in May of 1896, they spent several quiet days here in prayer, preparing for the coronation.[4]

Grand Kremlin
Palace. See plate 30.

The most important of all imperial residences in the former capital, though, was located in the Kremlin. Sprawled along a bend in the Moskva River, its cobbled squares, brightly painted palaces, and onion domes crowned the crest of Borovitsky Hill. In the fourteenth and fifteenth cen-turies, the grand princes of Moscow imported Italian architects to design its palaces and cathedrals, buildings that carried the technological and artistic advances of the Renaissance but remained Russian in character. "This curi-ous conglomeration of Palaces, towers, churches, monasteries, chapels, barracks, arsenals, and bastions," wrote one visitor, "this incoherent jumble of sacred and secular buildings; this complex functions as fortress, sanctuary, seraglio, harem, necropolis and prison; this blend of advanced civilization and archaic barbarism; this violent conflict of crudest materialism and most lofty spirituality; are they not the whole history of Russia, the whole epic of the Russian nation, the whole inward drama of the Russian soul?"[5]

Sixty-foot-high redbrick walls enclosed the Kremlin's citadels of spiritual and temporal authority, interrupted at intervals by twenty towers adorned with bat-tlements and topped with steeply pitched roofs and domes, their distinctive sil-houette dominating the city's skyline for miles.[6] Within these walls lay sixty-nine acres of gardens and paved squares, imposing cathedrals, and magnificent palaces that served as visible links with Russia's turbulent past.

At the center of the Kremlin lay Cathedral Square, an enormous cobbled space surrounded by the great churches of the Orthodox faith. The Annunciation

Cathedral, with its nine golden onion domes shining brightly above the white walls, served as the sovereign's private chapel. Like the other Kremlin churches, its interior was dim, lit only by narrow windows and the light that filtered down from the cupolas piercing the roof. The Cathedral of the Archangel Michael, built under Ivan III by the Italian Alovisio Novo, served as the burial church for the grand princes of Moscow, their metal tombs nestled beneath walls awash with medieval frescoes. It stood next to Ivan the Great's 265-foot-tall Bell Tower, its spire and onion visible from across the city.

The Cathedral of the Assumption, designed by the Italian Aristotle Fioravanti di Rodolfo in 1479 and modeled after the Cathedral of the Assumption in Vladimir, stood at the center of the square.[7] Five golden onion domes threw shafts of light across the greens, yellows, blues, and reds of the frescoed walls. Four central columns supported the painted roof, adding a spaciousness not usually found in Russian churches. At the front of the cathedral, a tall iconostasis rose toward the ceiling, its five tiers of icons enclosed in frames composed of five tons of gold.[8] Enormous solid silver chandeliers weighing more than eight hundred pounds, gilt altar stands, tent-roofed private pews decorated with murals and studded with precious and semiprecious stones, and impressive tombs and reliquaries all contributed to the splendid interior.[9]

A number of imperial residences stood within the Kremlin walls: the Nicholas Palace, the Palace of Facets, the Terem Palace, the Amusement Palace, and the Tsaritsa's Golden Chamber, linked by galleries and staircases that created a warren of corridors and endless enfilades of rooms.[10] The oldest of these buildings dated to the sixteenth century; the most recent, the Grand Kremlin Palace, had been built during the reign of Nicholas I. The Tsaritsa's Golden Chamber was a relic from the old palaces built by the grand princes of Moscow. A single room sitting on top of a high, arched ground floor, it was richly decorated with frescoes that covered every surface of the vaulted chamber's walls. Two churches were built onto this room, the Cathedral of Our Savior and the Church of the Crucifixion. The Golden or Holy Vestibule linked the Tsaritsa's Golden Chamber with the Palace of Facets, the Terem Palace, and the Grand Kremlin Palace. The low vaulted ceiling and walls were covered with murals, and the doorways were enormous, intricate works of art, carved and gilded with foliage, flowers, and heraldic beasts.[11]

To one side of the Holy Vestibule stood the Palace of Facets. Italian architects had raised its diamond-cut, white limestone walls at the end of the fifteenth century; on its northern exterior, the famous Red Staircase descended to Cathedral

Square. The structure contained but a single room, seventy-seven feet square and entirely decorated with brightly painted frescoes, its vaulted ceiling supported by a massive central pier.[12] On the other side of the Holy Vestibule, doors led to the Terem Palace, a five-storeyed building wrapped in a brightly painted exterior adorned with carved windowsills, cornices, and ornate little balconies. Small mica windows filtered light into the palace, suffusing its dim interior with soft, multicolored shadows. The Golden Stairway, hidden behind massive arches and painted in the lush medieval patterns and colors predominant throughout the palace, led to an intricate maze of lavishly decorated vaulted rooms, which were filled with carved and gilded furniture covered in tapestry and leather and were heated by elaborately tiled porcelain stoves.[13] The last sovereign to live in the rooms had been Peter II, the grandson of Peter the Great.

High above the Moskva River, its long, pale-yellow facade rising three storeys to a green hipped roof, stood the Grand Kremlin Palace. Though it evoked traditional Russian forms in its architecture, it had been built between 1839 and 1849 in place of a former palace that had been occupied and burned during Napoleon's tenure in the Kremlin.[14] Nicholas I commissioned the new structure from the architect Konstantin Ton, who fused the classical with a new neo-Russian style that drew its inspiration from medieval models.[15] Ton's Grand Kremlin Palace was a building of impressive size, stretching four hundred feet along the crest of Borovitsky Hill.[16] A raised ground floor pierced by arched windows provided a base for the piano nobile, whose two storeys were marked along the facade with tall rows of double windows in carved frames that echoed those of the adjoining Palace of Facets. At the center of the main facade, Ton raised a belvedere adorned with a series of arches copied from the traditional Russian peasant headdress, the *kokoshnik*.[17]

Visitors to the Grand Kremlin Palace entered a structure in which symbolism subsumed utility, an imposing evocation of Nicholas I's aspirations on the nineteenth-century world stage. The first room, the State Parade Antechamber, was a cool, classical space of white scagliola walls adorned with polished granite pilasters. Ton reinforced the Hellenic imagery by introducing four tall columns of polished blue-gray granite, with bases and Doric capitals in white Carrara marble, and continued the monochromatic theme with a floor of polished gray marble. From the antechamber, massive bronze candelabras framed the Parade Staircase, its five flights of gray marble rising in a straight line to the piano nobile.[18]

At the top landing, immense crystal vases with gilt bronze details flanked elaborately inlaid fifteen-foot-tall rosewood and mahogany doors opening to the State

Vestibule.[19] In contrast to the sober restraint of the antechamber and the staircase, the vestibule was awash with color, from its vibrant blue walls to its intricate wooden floor, inlaid with a dazzling array of ebony, mahogany, rosewood, palmetto, amaranth, yew, and maple in a swirl of colors. An immense canvas by Repin depicted peasants paying homage to Alexander III; above, crowning the two-storey hall, a leaded glass dome flooded the room with light.[20] The State Vestibule offered a tantalizing hint of the splendors of the palace, where immense halls, rich in decoration, opened in gilded succession to reveal the power and wealth of the Romanov Dynasty. These state halls took their names from the principal orders of the Russian empire—St. George, St. Vladimir, St. Alexander Nevsky, St. Andrei, and St. Catherine—and were decorated according to the colors in their cordons.

The Hall of St. Vladimir, designed to link the old palaces with Ton's structure, rose sixty feet, between walls of light pink scagliola, to an elaborately stuccoed ceiling adorned with gilded reliefs of the order's insignia. Below, a floor of oak and walnut was laid in an intricate pattern that echoed the reliefs of the ceiling panels. Pilasters and arches encircled the first floor, opening to niches filled with immense ormolu candelabra. A wide flight of marble steps, wrapped with intricate ormolu balustrades, swept in curves to arcaded galleries. Above, from the center of a glass skylight set within the vaulted ceiling, hung an eight-ton ormolu chandelier, its two hundred candles arrayed in three tiers embellished with heraldic shields and double-headed eagles.[21]

From the Hall of St. Vladimir, intricately inlaid wooden doors opened to the largest room, the Hall of St. George. Two hundred feet long, seventy feet wide, and sixty feet high, it stretched along Cathedral Square and faced onto the Moskva River at its southern end.[22] Eighteen massive piers, ringed by alabaster columns adorned with gilded spirals of oak garlands and Corinthian capitals, supported a carved frieze crowned by clusters of allegorical marble statuary.[23] The white of the walls and stucco-relief barrel-vaulted ceiling inset with ormolu emblems, coupled with the gilt bronze of the numerous decorations and the double rows of tall windows, lent the hall an unusual sense of light. Pale gray marble panels, inscribed with the names of those who held the order and crowned with ormolu laurels, offered a poignant tribute to the empire's fallen heroes. Six immense ormolu chandeliers, each weighing over one ton and together holding three thousand lights, hung from the vault of the stuccoed ceiling. They were electrified in 1895, in time for the coronation ball of Nicholas II, which took place in this room a year later. Below them, an intricate floor, composed of more

St. George's
Hall.
See plate 31.

than twenty different types of rare wood laid out in marquetry patterns, echoed the order insignia and emblems.[24]

Adjoining the Hall of St. George was the Hall of St. Alexander Nevsky, a hundred feet in length and nearly seventy feet wide. Boiseries and moldings in gold complemented the light pink and cream scagliola of the walls, framing panels whose canvases depicted events in the life of Alexander Nevsky. Massive hollow piers, adorned with twisted columns that were strewn with carved flowers picked out in gilt, supported the ceiling nearly seventy feet above, its vaults covered in an elaborate pattern of gilded foliage and insignia. Fourteen windows, matched by mirrors inset on the opposite wall, flooded the room with light that shimmered against the gold of the imperial plate displayed on consoles and tiers around the hall. The delicate colors of the room were echoed in light woods laid in intricate geometric patterns that danced across the floor. Above, scintillating with gilded double-headed eagles and escutcheons, hung ormolu chandeliers, their five thousand lights providing a blaze of fire by night.[25]

The parade rooms culminated in the Hall of St. Andrei, the most lavishly decorated of the palace's rooms. The hall was 160 feet long by 68 feet wide; its walls were hung with watered blue silk, encased in gilded boiseries. Ten hollow zinc columns, faced in artificial marble and covered entirely in elaborately carved gilded relief panels, supported the vaulted ceiling, embellished with gilt ornaments. Below, the floor was inlaid in an intricate design of scrolls and flowers, using twenty rare woods. A massive gilt sunburst, surrounded by the coats of arms of the Romanov Dynasty, stood guard against the vault of the western wall. Beneath it, from the edges of a gilded canopy festooned with ostrich plumes, cloth-of-gold—embroidered with double-headed eagles in black—hung in folds to embrace the gilded Chairs of State made for Nicholas II's coronation in 1896.[26]

Beyond the Parade Halls, the State Apartments occupied the entire west wing of the palace's first floor. Used for diplomatic receptions, they were deliberately anachronistic, echoing the eighteenth-century French idea of a formal enfilade culminating in a state bedroom. Like their French models, they conveyed grandeur but were never intended to be occupied. Instead, they offered a sumptuous backdrop against which the imperial court could impress distinguished visitors.

It was through this suite that the members of the imperial family made their formal entrance to the Parade Halls on ceremonial occasions, and the first apartment, the Chevalier Guards' Room, served as a physical representation of the distinct boundary between the multitude of guests and the few privileged participants who gathered beyond to await word from the grand marshal that all was ready. A simple room of white scagliola walls and a parquet floor, it offered a formal, restrained appearance in keeping with its military and ceremonial functions.

From the Chevalier Guards' Room, visitors passed between fifteen-foot-high doors of mahogany and rosewood to the Hall of St. Catherine, named after the Russian order founded by Peter the Great. Decorated in the neoclassical style, the room's white scagliola walls were hung with silver moiré panels encased in carved and gilded frames adorned with bas-reliefs of vibrant crimson. Pilasters and columns of rich green malachite ringed the walls and fringed two large piers, framing an alcove where a small dais held the empress's throne. From the ceiling embellished with ribbons and swags of foliage, all picked out in crimson, gold, and malachite, hung large ormolu and crystal chandeliers; below, arranged in careful groupings, stood Empire-style sofas and chairs upholstered in silver moiré.[27]

The formality of the Hall of St. Catherine gave way to the splendors of the State Drawing Room. A rich green and gold silk floral brocade hung upon its walls, its colors echoed in the thick green, gold, and black patterned carpet and in the panels of the vaulted ceiling, which were decorated with subtle floral designs framed by carved and gilded moldings. Two white marble niches, set with porcelain and bronze candelabra, flanked an apse pierced by a mirrored door that was encased in a lavishly gilded frame. Large standing torchères and an enormous crystal chandelier cast their glow across a suite of gilded Louis XV–revival furniture by Gambs, upholstered in the same patterned brocade that hung on the walls. The tables and consoles, executed in a style reminiscent of the Parisian craftsman Boulle and inlaid with mother-of-pearl, bronze, and tortoiseshell, completed the extravagant decor.[28]

Beyond lay the State Bedchamber. Four green-gray marble columns, said to be the largest of their kind in Russia, marked the eastern alcove, where a gilded bed rested on a dais. Similar pilasters framed walls that were hung with golden silk damask and crowned by an elaborate cornice of marble adorned with gilded carvings. Intricate traceries of gold covered the white ceiling, from which hung an ormolu chandelier; in contrast, the mantel of the fireplace was of carved jasper, embellished with gilded medallions. Gambs Brothers provided the immense bed, draped in gold brocade, to complete the illusion, but, like the parade bedchamber at Versailles, the Grand Kremlin Palace's State Bedchamber was destined to remain unoccupied.[29] Elaborate doors, inlaid with mother-of-pearl, bronze, gold, and tortoiseshell, opened to the final apartment, the Walnut Dressing Room, lined with panels of dark wood and lit by an alabaster chandelier.

Nicholas and Alexandra, when in residence, occupied apartments on the ground floor, to the left of the State Parade Hall. They were known as the Sobstvennaya Polovina, or Own Half, and their layout was determined by the curious floor plan into which they had been worked. To support the weight of the steel floor beams above, massive piers divided these rooms in half, creating intimate areas to the rear, closed off with groupings of furniture or screens. There were less than a dozen rooms; here, Empress Alexandra did not impose her own tastes for mauve silks and art nouveau furniture.[30] Decorated in a comfortable, eclectic fashion, the rooms contained a wealth of important objets d'art, furniture, tapestries, paintings, porcelains, and bronzes. Mirrors, gilt, and marble were used to great effect, forming perhaps the most luxurious suite in any of the imperial palaces.[31]

A massive central pier divided the Dining Room, the ceiling vaults resting on its corners. Four arched windows pierced the cream walls, inset with panels and pilasters of yellow scagliola to heighten the sense of airiness. The vaults of the ceiling were framed with raised stucco panels modeled on classical themes, the only architectural decoration in the otherwise deliberately restrained room.[32] The Empress's Reception Room that followed was a neo-rococo fantasy of cream and gilt. Cream moiré woven with delicate floral designs in silver thread hung in gilt-framed panels on the walls, offering a feminine contrast to the classical Dining Room. The central pier divided the ceiling into three vaults, crossed with gilt cornices and etched and painted in light blue and pink pastels; in the corners of the vaults, roundels in bas-relief depicted allegorical representations of *Morning, Day, Evening,* and *Night.* Two large crystal chandeliers hung from the shallow vaults at the front while, at the rear, a magnificent porcelain chandelier, embellished with pineapples and foliage, flooded the area with light. The rococo suite of rosewood furniture, gilded and encrusted with mother-of-pearl, bronze, and tortoiseshell, was also upholstered in silver moiré.[33]

The Empress's Drawing Room was carried out in the French rococo style, with crimson brocaded silk, patterned with gold, hung upon the walls; the same fabric was also used on the upholstery of the rosewood and walnut sofas and chairs, inlaid with mother-of-pearl and ebony. Two central piers, decorated with white pilasters enriched with gilded bases and capitals, rose to ceiling vaults embellished with gilded reliefs, from which hung sparkling, clover-shaped crystal chandeliers. Despite the room's private function, the Empress's Drawing Room contained the palace's most exquisite pieces of furniture: desks, consoles, a piano, and a tall clock in a rococo case, all in polished black rosewood inset with mother-of-pearl, ormolu, and tortoiseshell after the designs of Andre Boulle. In

The Empress's Drawing Room. See plate 32.

PLATE 13. The Jordan Staircase in the Winter Palace

PLATE 14.
St. George's Hall in the
Winter Palace

PLATE 15.
Nicholas II's Gothic Library
in the Winter Palace

PLATE 16. The Catherine Palace at Tsarskoye Selo

PLATE 17. The Cameron Gallery at Tsarskoye Selo

PLATE 19. The Feodorovsky Sobor in the
Alexander Park at Tsarskoye Selo

PLATE 18. View into the Great
Gallery of the Catherine Palace

PLATE 20.
View through the
Semi-Circular Hall
enfilade in the
Alexander Palace

PLATE 21. The Alexander Palace
at Tsarskoye Selo

PLATE 22. Nicholas II's
restored formal study in
the Alexander Palace

PLATE 23. The Grand Palace and Cascade at Peterhof

PLATE 24. The Ballroom in the
Grand Palace at Peterhof

PLATE 25. The Throne Room in the Grand
Palace at Peterhof

PLATE 26. The East Chinese Lobby in
the Grand Palace at Peterhof

PLATE 27. The Cottage Palace at Alexandria, Peterhof

PLATE 28. Neskuchnoye Palace, Moscow

PLATE 29. Petrovsky Palace, Moscow

PLATE 30. View of the Grand Kremlin Palace

PLATE 31. St. George's Hall in the Grand Kremlin Palace

PLATE 32. The Empress's Drawing Room in the private apartments of the Grand Kremlin Palace

contrast to this ebullience, a large band of black Carrara marble formed the lower wainscot of the walls, and the fireplace was of white marble in the rococo style.[34]

Two tall arched windows, heavily draped in richly patterned cream, pink, gray, and red silk, lit the Empress's Boudoir, its walls hung in the same fabric. The ceiling, a double vault resting on the central pier, was painted in delicate traceries of green, gray, silver, and pink to complement the fabrics and was surrounded by an elaborate, gilt relief cornice. Louis IV–revival furniture, in walnut and rosewood, stood across a deep red, gold, and black patterned carpet. Between the two windows stood a fireplace fashioned of pieces of malachite so carefully melded together that it appeared to have been carved from a single stone.[35]

Avoiding the gilded splendor of the formal rooms, the Imperial Bedroom was hung with a patterned blue moiré. The central pier divided the corridor section of the room from an angled alcove, where the emperor and the empress slept in twin brass beds concealed behind a gilded screen hung with blue silk. A white Carrara marble fireplace stood between the two arched windows, and the white ceiling was delicately outlined with gilt. The furniture—chaises, chairs, and sofas—was overstuffed, covered in blue moiré, and fringed with bullion in the Victorian manner.[36]

The Emperor's Study, where panels of green silk brocade and light ash concealed bookcases, occupied the corner of the suite. A narrow room, the study rose to a vaulted ceiling, painted en grisaille, from which hung an ormolu art nouveau chandelier. The furniture echoed Nicholas II's own tastes: Karelian birch sofas and chairs upholstered in dark green Moroccan leather and writing desks covered in green baize.[37] Beyond lay the Emperor's Reception Room, its pale blue walls devoid of decoration. The furnishings were exceptional, however: a suite of gilded chairs and sofas covered in bronze satin brocade, embroidered with green, gold, and brown floral motifs in cut velvet, and lacquered consoles inlaid with mosaics of semiprecious stones.[38]

The Grand Kremlin Palace stood as a visible symbol of Nicholas I's grandiose aspirations on the world stage. By the reign of Nicholas II, it was rarely used, for the emperor and the empress came only infrequently to Moscow. When they did arrive, however, they could indulge themselves in the most luxurious palace in the world, a masterpiece of Russian interior decoration and artistic craftsmanship. "When filled with light, its rooms perfumed by fresh flowers, filled with precious pieces of furniture, and scintillating like the diamonds of an elegant woman's *toilette*," recorded one turn-of-the-century visitor, "the Grand Kremlin Palace sumptuously displays the full glory of the Imperial Court."[39]

Part Three

POSSESSIONS

14

IMPERIAL RICHES

AT THE TURN OF THE CENTURY, Nicholas II was undoubtedly one of the wealthiest men in the world. He ruled one-sixth of the total land surface of the globe as sole autocrat, responsible to no one. As emperor, he presided over the most brilliant court in Europe and lived in enormous palaces filled with exquisite French furniture and historic works of art. He took his holidays on luxurious yachts and elaborate trains, showered his wife and his mother with priceless objets d'art by the great jeweler Fabergé, and could lay claim to millions of acres of untapped timber and mineral reserves spread across his empire.

Although raised in the opulent surroundings of the Russian court, Nicholas was unaware of his family's immense wealth. Nicholas and his brothers and sisters had no allowance or pocket money and, consequently, never understood the value of the ruble. At Christmas, jewelry, objets d'art, bottles of scent, clothing, games, and personal items were laid out in a drawing room for inspection and the children were admitted to select gifts to give their parents and siblings; the bills were sent to the Treasury. Once, when a box of jewelry was unpacked in the presence of the children, Nicholas's sister Xenia spotted a small scent bottle, its stopper studded with sapphires. She immediately seized it to present to her mother. The scent bottle had come from the Paris shop of Jacques Cartier and cost several hundred rubles.[1]

Even as an adult, Nicholas had little practical concept of money. He carried none, a fact that sometimes led to difficulties. Once, in the midst of a church service, Grand Duchess Tatiana leaned over to Baroness Buxhoeveden, whispering, "Can you lend Papa a ten ruble gold piece?" As the collection plate neared, she continued, "They will start with him," adding, "he did not know, so of course he hasn't any money." The baroness found the requested sum, handing it to the grand duchess who passed it to her father just in time.[2]

As emperor, Nicholas had two distinct sources of income: the State Budget and his private fortune. The first of these was derived from payments made to him by the Russian government in the form of a Civil List, while the second consisted of funds that belonged to the emperor himself. As an autocrat, Nicholas theoretically held immense capital. He had the largest private gold reserve in the world, some $1 billion in both bullion and coin. More than 150 million acres of land were attached to the Crown, including vast timber and mining reserves, as well as oil fields in Southern Russia. The Crown owned palaces, hunting lodges and preserves, yachts, trains, garages, and stables, as well as the crown jewels; furniture and china collections; and the art treasures in the Hermitage. The frozen asset value of the Romanov crown jewels alone was estimated at approximately $80 million in pre-1917 figures.[3] Most of these assets were considered entailed: they were Crown property, at the emperor's discretion to use and to enjoy but not to dispose of as he might wish, passing from one generation to the next. The emperor took possession of these palaces and treasures in his name, but the rights remained with the state. Nicholas could have sold off these assets as he saw fit; as autocrat, he was answerable to no one. But the outcry from both the government and the public would almost certainly have prevented any financial exploitation of his position as emperor.

There were important exceptions to this division, however. The emperor's collection of motorcars, though purchased with state funds, was regarded as his personal property, as were the estates in Poland and the Crimea. In 1905, at Nicholas's request, Count Vladimir de Freedericksz submitted an inquiry to Ivan Vsevolozsky, the director of the Imperial Hermitage, asking "whether we can consider the artistic works located in the Imperial Hermitage as the property of the Museum, or if in the collection there are works that form the property of His Imperial Majesty." After consulting with the Administration Board, Vsevolozsky replied that "the pictures and other treasures of the Hermitage have always, since the time of Catherine II, formed the property of the reigning Emperors, in the same way as objects decorating Imperial palaces, only allocated from among their artistic possessions to be shown in the said Museum. Everything kept in it must be considered the property of His Imperial Majesty."[4]

Nicholas's annual disposable income from the state was derived from two sources. The first formed the Civil List proper, paid by the Imperial Treasury from the State Budget to the Ministry of the Imperial Household. Each year, Nicholas received 250,000 rubles for his personal expenses ($2,500,000, in 2005 figures), Alexandra received 200,000 rubles ($2,000,000 in 2005 figures), and the tsesarevich, 100,000 rubles ($1,000,000 in 2005 figures). From their births until they reached the age of twenty, the emperor's daughters received 33,000 rubles each year for personal expenses ($330,000 in 2005 figures), with 45,525 rubles allocated for servants and staff ($455,250 in 2005 figures); at the age of twenty, the stipend was increased to 75,000 rubles for personal expenses ($750,000 in 2005 figures).[5] With no delineation between the public and the private wealth of the Russian state, this situation was tantamount to the emperor paying himself with funds that were already his.

The second source of income was the Ministry of the Imperial Household–controlled Appanages Department, a collection of interests in timber, mining, agricultural, fishery, and vineyard concerns. Created by Emperor Paul in 1797, the Appanages Department consisted of lands purchased by Catherine the Great to ensure the financial stability of the family. In 1826, Nicholas I solidified this as the Ministry of State Domains, through which all appanages monies were filtered.[6] The appanages lands encompassed 11 million acres owned by the emperor; another 9.5 million acres provided revenues shared between the ministry and the actual landowners, who sublet the land. In addition, the Appanages Department maintained a liquid reserve of 60 million gold rubles ($600,000,000 in 2005 figures). The value of the land alone, not counting proceeds from mining, timber, agriculture, and other revenues, was estimated at $50 million in 1914, just before the start of the First World War (approximately $611,520,00 in 2005 figures).[7]

In all, the emperor received an annual state income of some 24 million gold rubles ($240,000,000 in 2005 currency). From these resources, the emperor had to pay for the upkeep of his relatives. By 1886, annual stipends to various grand dukes and duchesses, as well as to princes and princesses of the imperial blood—all paid according to title—had risen to ruinous amounts. To curtail this immense financial drain on his annual state income, Alexander III issued an imperial ukase that restricted the use of the titles of "Grand Duke" and "Grand Duchess," confining the use of "Prince and Princess of the Imperial Blood" to great-grandchildren of emperors and their eldest sons. This restriction on the use of titles was accompanied by new guidelines that defined annual payments to members of the imperial family. Each grand duke received 250,000 gold rubles annually ($2,500,000 in 2005 currency), while each grand duchess received, as an imperial dowry, one flat payment of 1 million gold rubles ($10,000,000 in 2005 currency) when she married. Princes and princesses of the imperial blood were provided with a one-time payment of 1 million gold rubles at their births. At the turn of the century, Nicholas II had twenty-three grand dukes to whom annual payments were made, amounting to a total outlay of 5,750,000 gold rubles ($57,500,000 in 2005 currency). This figure fluctuated with the number of grand dukes, and, as none were born in the reign of the last emperor, save for his own son, the amount of the payments naturally decreased with each death. This money came from the state funds, not from the emperor's private purse.[8]

Funds allocated to the sovereign by the Ministry of the Imperial Household were used to pay for the upkeep of the palaces. All routine maintenance and operating expenses were paid from this settlement. The emperor himself was financially responsible for any additional expenses incurred—the food service; the costs of entertainments, balls, receptions, and state banquets; the costs of any redecoration—all of which were deducted from the Civil List funds. The emperor also paid, from his annual Civil List, the salaries of all the members of the Suite and the Household; although some sixteen thousand people made up the Russian court proper, not all of these received financial compensation or salaries, yet the number who did was over a thousand. All court uniforms were paid for from the Civil List, along with the food provided during working hours and gifts presented to every member of the suite and the household at Christmas and on their name days.

Nicholas and Alexandra also used their annual state grants to pay the salaries of members of their personal Households (valets, maids, and various servants), while the children's servants were paid from the funds they received. Salaries, even for those in the Upper Household, were minimal: Elizabeth Ersberg, Alexandra's third lady's maid, was paid 600 rubles each year ($6,000 in 2005 currency)[9]; and Andrei Derevenko, the tsesarevich's *dyadya*, was paid a salary of 120 rubles a year ($1,200 in 2005 currency). In comparison, Jim Hercules, who had served as a court Abyssinian Guard for several decades, received 720 rubles ($7,200 in 2005 currency).[10] Room and board were also included, and the figure did not reflect annual gifts and grants, including holiday pay and sick benefits. These salaries, while exceptionally low, were in keeping with those paid by any royal or noble family of the era: a lady's maid, working for a member of the

English aristocracy, could expect roughly £30 a year (£1,670, or $2,839, in 2005 currency).

The salaries of people employed in the imperial theaters—the Mariinsky, the Alexandrinsky, and the Maly Theaters in St. Petersburg, and the Bolshoi and the Maly in Moscow—including directors, dancers, teachers, and pupils, were also paid from the Civil List, as all were considered to be members of the Emperor's Household. At the end of every season, as Mathilde Kschessinska remembered, all of the pupils at the Imperial Ballet School and the dancers in the ballet itself received presents from the emperor. "In most cases," she wrote, "it consisted of a jewel in gold or silver, enriched sometimes with precious stones according to the class of gift and always bearing a crown or Imperial eagle. Male dancers usually received a gold watch. On the whole, these gifts were not particularly beautiful."[11] The annual cost of funding the imperial theaters alone amounted to some 2 million rubles a year.[12] Also included were the upkeep of the Imperial Academy of Fine Arts, the Alexander III Museum of Russian Arts, and the Hermitage in St. Petersburg.

Thus the emperor's outlay each year was certainly enormous. According to the Romanovs in exile, Nicholas was lucky to survive from financial year to financial year, so strained were his resources. His cousin and brother-in-law Grand Duke Alexander Mikhailovich wrote in 1933, "It had always been conceded by financial experts and awe-stricken laymen alike that the late Tsar was one of the ten richest men in the world. Even now . . . we are still occasionally being informed by the gentlemen of the American press that the Bank of England remains in possession of the 'vast fortune of the Romanovs.' Had he reigned longer, Nicholas II would have found himself a rather poor man at the close of the great European conflict."[13] And the emperor's sister Olga Alexandrovna later declared, "The fiscal year began on the first of January. Often enough Nicky would be broke by the autumn."[14] While it is true that there may not have been much money left over at the end of each year from the Civil List after expenses had been paid, it is almost certain that the emperor was never forced to dip into his private resources to pay for the day-to-day running of his court. All monies expended on court expenses and costs came solely from the emperor's Civil List and not from his private fortune.

The emperor's private fortune was entirely separate from the money received as part of the Civil List payments and was Nicholas's personal property to dispose of as he wished. He inherited the vast majority of his personal fortune from both his father and his grandfather after their deaths. In addition to the cash resources, the emperor held, in his own name, a number of financial interests. This included timber reserves in Siberia, mining districts in Nertchiask, and gold and precious metal reserves in the Altai Province.[15] Most of the emperor's private fortune had been invested with foreign financial institutions and companies. It is known with certainty that there were reserves held in at least two famous European banks, the Bank of England and the Mendelssohn Bank in Berlin. Alexander II had originally deposited £20 million in the Bank of England during his reign, a private fortune to which Alexander III and Nicholas II added regularly. By the beginning of the First World War, the Romanov fortune in the Bank of England was estimated at £40 million, or approximately $200 million in 1914 figures. Only the deposits to the Bank of England were actually made in the name of the Romanov family; the other foreign investments and deposits were made under holding companies and trustees.

In 1917, the Provisional Government of Russia undertook an investigation of the emperor's private foreign investments, in an attempt to determine whether he would be able to support himself and his family in exile without government assistance. The Provisional Government, working with the emperor on the question during his imprisonment at Tsarskoye Selo, found that Nicholas had, by his own account, at least 14 million gold rubles invested or in foreign deposits, or approximately $140 million.[16] And immediately following the Revolution, Alexandra told her friend Lili Dehn, "At least we shan't have to beg, for we have a fortune in the Bank of England." Lili Dehn did not recall the actual amount but later declared that the empress "spoke of millions, and in gold."[17]

Even if $140 million existed outside of Russia at the time of the Revolution, there is a large gulf between this figure and that of $200 million in the Bank of England prior to the First World War. Where did the rest of the money go? Both Alexander Mikhailovich and Olga Alexandrovna asserted that at the beginning of the First World War, the emperor immediately commanded all members of the imperial family to repatriate any foreign investments to help the war effort. The emperor, according to his relatives, naturally followed suit. In fact, the emperor seems to have left his English deposits intact at the beginning of the war and did not immediately transfer the funds back to Russia. Nicholas regularly withdrew funds from this capital in England, to aid in the war effort and support the Russian Red Cross. In 1915, Alexandra wrote to Nicholas at Military Headquarters, "I see Buchanan [the British Ambassador in St. Petersburg] tomorrow as he brings me again over 100,000 p. [pounds] from England."[18] This letter alone clearly proves that the emperor did not repatriate his English deposits at the beginning of the First World War. There are no accurate financial records of these withdrawals or of their frequency, so it is impossible to say how much money actually may have remained at the time of the Revolution.

In complete contrast to this, Sir Edward Peacock, the director of the Bank of England from 1920 to 1924, and again from 1929 to 1946, declared in a 1960 deposition, "I am pretty sure there was never any money of the Imperial Family of Russia in the Bank of England, nor any other bank in England. Of course it is difficult to say 'never,' but I am positive at least there was never any money after World War I, and during my long years as director of the Bank."[19] Clearly, however, Peacock was wrong. The Romanov family did have money in the Bank of England up to the start, and at least into the middle, of the First World War. Empress Alexandra's statement to her friend after the Revolution, along with the Provisional Government's own accounting in cooperation with the emperor himself, place several million pounds still in the institution in 1917. If money remained in the Bank of England after 1917, and Peacock was the director in 1920, the money was either still there during his tenure, or else someone had withdrawn it. But since it was on deposit in the name of Nicholas II, who could have done so? None of his heirs were in a position to lay claim to the money.

This complex situation was exacerbated by the confused financial position of the imperial children. The State Budget allocated a large annual grant to each of the children, but this money was invested, and none of them could touch these funds until they reached their eighteenth birthday. Instead, the four grand duchesses and the tsesarevich received from their parents an allowance of roughly nine dollars a month, a substantial sum at the turn of the century but certainly not an impressive amount for royalty. With this, they bought personal items: scent, toys, books, and writing paper. When they gave presents to each other or to their parents and friends, the gifts were purchased with this allowance rather than being paid for by the Treasury.[20] "In this way," Buxhoeveden explained, "their mother hoped to make them realize the value of money, a thing that Princes find hard to understand. But etiquette prevented their going into any shops but those of the little stationers at Tsarskoye Selo and Yalta and they never had any clear idea of the value and price of things."[21] Raised in isolation, they had little idea of the world beyond the confines of their father's estates. Only on foreign holidays did they venture into shops and as a result had little idea of the value of money.

By the time of the Revolution, their personal fortunes in Russia were immense: as calculated by Count Paul von Benckendorff, working with Alexandra's private secretary Count Rostovtsev and Feodor Golovin, the commandant in charge of the former imperial court for the Provisional Government, Olga had a balance of 3,185,500 rubles ($31,855,000 in 2005 currency); Tatiana, 2,118,500 ($21,285,000 in 2005 currency); Marie, 1,854,430 ($18,544,300 in 2005 currency); and Anastasia, 1,612,500 ($16,125,000 in 2005 currency).[22] Only Olga and Tatiana, having reached the age of eighteen before the Revolution, were able to enjoy use of these funds; even so, both spent large sums not on themselves but on funding private charities, on Red Cross trains, and on their war hospitals at Tsarskoye Selo.

In 1933, the Berlin Civil Court granted a certificate of inheritance to seven collateral heirs of the last emperor of Russia for funds held in the Mendelssohn Bank in Berlin. In December of 1905, in the aftermath of the First Russian Revolution, Nicholas II had made deposits for all of his children in the Mendelssohn Bank. The accounts were opened under the coded names "A., B., C., D., and E." and initially included some 2 million gold rubles. The following year, he opened another account at the same bank, with a personal check for 1.5 million gold rubles. These assets were frozen at the beginning of the First World War, and the chaos of runaway inflation in 1920s Germany meant that their value, at the beginning of the 1930s, was a mere million Reichmarks, or approximately £1,000.

Sir Peter Bark, an Anglicized Russian who served as Nicholas II's minister of finance until the Revolution, made the arrangements for the initial deposits, as well as further additions to the children's funds. Bark, of course, knew all the details of these private transactions, but, after the fall of the Romanovs, he maintained a discreet silence on the subject. Legend has long held that there were additional deposits for each of the children in an English bank, and that the accounts each contained approximately 1 to 2 million gold rubles. This money was, like the undisputed deposits in the Mendelssohn Bank in Berlin, to provide dowries for the daughters if they married outside of Russia.[23] These figures, if not the nations in which they were deposited, were supported by Count Paul von Benckendorff, who recalled that each of the children had "several million" rubles deposited abroad.[24] None of these funds were touched, according to these sources, during the First World War, because they were regarded as the children's property alone and not part of the emperor's private fortune.[25]

Exiled members of the Romanov family believed these stories to have some foundation in truth. The emperor's sister Grand Duchess Xenia spent some fifteen years searching for her late brother's Western finances, authorizing at least two lawyers, Sir Harold Brooks and Miss Fanny Holtzmann, to conduct inquiries and undertake a sweeping investigation of bank deposits and transactions.[26]

The Western funds, however—apart from any monies deposited in Berlin for the imperial children—seem largely to have been imperial state property: gold bullion and money dispatched to secure favorable rates of exchange for the ruble appear to have constituted these funds. As autocrats, it appears that neither Nicholas nor Alexandra made the important distinction between these state funds and their personal deposits. The emperor and the empress assumed that the monies deposited by the Russian government abroad were their own personal property, while in actual fact they technically belonged to the state. Alexandra's remark to Lili Dehn most likely referred to money that belonged to the Russian government and not to the imperial family, although neither the emperor nor the empress understood this.

It appears that neither Nicholas nor his family had any private money left outside Russia at the time of the Revolution. Aside from the money deposited for the children in Berlin, all of their private fortunes remained in Russia. Count von Benckendorff estimated that the emperor had a private fortune of 1 million gold rubles, Alexandra approximately 1.5 million rubles, and the five children between 2 and 3 million rubles each.[27] These figures closely match those estimated by Alexander Kerensky on behalf of the Provisional Government, who determined that the imperial family's private fortune in Russia stood at approximately 14 million gold rubles. Count Benckendorff estimated that their private fortune ranged from 12.5 to 17.5 million gold rubles.[28] This was certainly an enormous amount, but whatever the size of the funds, they were all confiscated when the Bolsheviks came to power in the fall of 1917, leaving the doomed Romanovs, once the wealthiest family in the world, destitute and living off soldiers' rations.

15

FASHION AT THE RUSSIAN COURT

THE BEGINNING OF THE TWENTIETH CENTURY was a particularly fruitful era all over the Western world where dress was concerned. It was a time of concentrated wealth, coupled with the ostentatious sensibilities and refined tastes of the aristocracy. Nouveau riche hostesses in America needed fashionable clothing, to compete with each other and to impress the European visitors they frequently tried to win as husbands for their eligible daughters. The introduction of photography, periodicals devoted exclusively to fashion, and the ease of world travel meant that for the first time, there was a widespread market for current fashion. Rich Americans and socially prominent aristocrats from across Europe were eager for direction, and a handful of brilliant designers were more than willing to flood the world with their creations.

Members of the Russian court proved to be no exception. During the reign of Nicholas II, clothing from various periods and styles could often be seen, with dowagers dressed in the fashions of their youth to the young debutantes in the latest Parisian gowns. The royal courts of Europe had always ensured a market for couture clothes, but in style, the court was so removed from everyday life that it failed to set trends. For society women, not to mention the grand duchesses and empresses, it was necessary to plan wardrobes far in advance of the forthcoming season. The financial strain on many families was enormous, as orders for bespoke clothing went out to fashionable dressmakers and couture houses several times a year. Even in a relatively modest aristocratic establishment, it was necessary to order dozens of dresses and outfits. A woman might purchase perhaps ten to twelve tea gowns for afternoon social functions and luncheons; two dozen day dresses; at least five or six ball gowns; and assorted cloaks, evening gowns, nightclothes, and lingerie, as well as accessories: hats, shoes, boots, gloves, handbags, and parasols.

In the fashion race, Europe still influenced Russia. The greatest purveyors of style were the Houses of Doucet, Cheruit, Doeuilley, Paquin, Poiret, and, most especially, Worth. Charles Worth had established his shop in Paris at the end of the 1850s and soon acquired a reputation without parallel. Not only Parisians, but also English, German, Austrian, and Spanish women flocked to his salon, to say nothing of American hostesses like Caroline Astor and Alva Vanderbilt. By the turn of the century, Worth's influence as the ultimate arbiter of taste had reached such heights that not only did he regularly dress such illustrious clients as Empress Alexandra, Dowager Empress Marie Feodorovna, Queen Alexandra of England, and Kaiserin Augusta Viktoria of Germany, but they gave him carte blanche as to style and material.

Worth certainly had his competitors in Russia, and aristocratic women patronized couturiers along the Nevsky Prospect. There were seven principal dressmakers in the capital, all catering to the elaborate needs of society. Anna Gindus had trained in Paris at the House of Paquin before opening her own shop, offering elaborate concoctions of silk, velvet, and tulle. At the corner of Nevsky Prospekt and Bolshaya Morskaya Ulitsa stood Chernyshevs, whose elegant gowns and fashionable ensembles were favored by older, more refined, and less adventurous women, including those of the imperial family. The store held royal warrants for Empress Alexandra, the dowager empress, Queen Olga of Greece, and Grand Duchess Vladimir. Down the Nevsky were the workshops of Madame Olga Bulbenkova, who specialized in Russian court dress. Nadezhda Lamanova, Anna Ivanova, and Izembard Chanceau also supplied gowns to the imperial court, while Bertrand offered both couture and ready-made dresses and gowns.[1]

The most fashionable of all the Russian designers, however, was undoubtedly Madame Auguste Brissac, whose elegant couture house at No. 42 Moika Embankment served all the women of the imperial family. Although her gowns were considered de rigueur for *haute société*, everyone complained loudly about her outrageous prices. To Alexandra, she once confessed, "I beg Your Imperial Majesty not to mention these things to anyone, but I always cut my prices for Your Imperial Majesty." Later, however, when discussing Madame Brissac with her sister-in-law Olga Alexandrovna, Alexandra heard what the dressmaker had told the grand duchess: "I beg Your Imperial Highness not to mention these things at Tsarskoye Selo, but I always cut my prices for you." It was a line undoubtedly used on many other unsuspecting clients, and Alexandra and Olga laughed over the shrewdness of the clever dressmaker.[2]

A typical day during the social season might involve up to six changes of clothing. Ordinary long-sleeved day dresses of serge or muslin were worn during the morning. If a woman joined guests for lunch, she changed into a more elaborate dress, usually of silk or serge overlaid with lace. Women changed into tea dresses for the afternoon; if calling on another member of society, they changed into more formal dresses, often of chiffon, lace, or silk. An evening gown, of brocade, satin, velvet, or silk, was worn for dinner, and this was often followed by a change into a ball gown if a reception or a ball was taking place. On evenings when more than one invitation had been accepted—either to several parties or to the ballet, the opera, or a symphony followed by supper or a ball—a change of clothing was sometimes made between each event.

Debutantes faced their own challenges. Helene Izvolsky, the daughter of the Russian ambassador in Paris, later recalled the intense preparations for her presentation at the imperial court: "We had to order a complete new wardrobe of formal and semiformal gowns, as well as the warm clothes indispensable in the northern city. Mother had to have her jewelry reset: the small diamond tiara, the fine pearl choker, and the sapphire brooch, the three main pieces in her jewelry box. The famous couturier Worth agreed to make our formal gowns at a reduced price since to cater to the Embassy was good publicity. The minor items were done by the *petites couturiers* of Paris, the little seamstresses expert in their art. I was provided with a sealskin coat, muff, and hat."[3]

Most of these dresses, even the most simple for a morning at home, were encumbered with flounces of lace, rows of buttons down the back, high necks, and long sleeves adorned with appliqué. By the turn of the century, stiff Victorian corsets had largely given way to newer, less painful versions, but a woman still required the assistance of a lady's maid to lace her up to achieve the desired effect. In

Grand Duchess Olga Nikolaievna in Russian court dress, 1913

the evenings, for balls, most ladies wore rather more stiff corsets ribbed with whalebones, to compress their waists and push their bosom up and out to create fashionable décolletage.

The complexities of aristocratic life were further modified to suit the court calendar. If the court was in official mourning or a family suffered a death, mourning clothes were pulled out. For the first six months of mourning, only black was worn, except on formal occasions when white was allowed. For the last six months, half-mourning was traditional, with dresses of gray, white, or mauve, although in public it was still considered in bad taste to wear anything but black for a full year.[4]

Olga
Nikolaievna's
gown.
See plate 33.

Morning and day dresses at the turn of the century crossed a number of styles. Loose dresses, with flowing skirts and sleeves, were in vogue; materials ranged from muslin to silk, satin to velvet brocades, embellished with embroidery, lace, and bows. Tea gowns, less formal than evening gowns, were often in soft pastels, covered with beading or lace to convey an ethereal appearance. Evening gowns ranged from the simplicity of the Empire style, with severely restrained decoration, to the elaborate creations of Worth and his competitors—both European and Russian—composed of velvets, satin, and brocades trimmed with pearls, expensive furs, jet beading, silver and gold thread, and fringe; these gowns often had encompassing folds of diaphanous tulle, trains, flowing sleeves, and a plunging décolletage. But the most detail and money were lavished on Russian court dress, a style that eventually began to influence European fashion to such an extent that Worth produced an entire line of gowns *à la Russe.*

Until the reign of Nicholas I, the court had no dress regulation for women, and ladies attending balls and receptions wore European gowns. Then, in 1834, Nicholas issued an edict that established regulations on court dress and spelled out the accepted colors, materials, decoration, and length of train both for members of the imperial family and, rank by rank, for those ladies who had entrance to the imperial court. With minor exceptions, these rules remained enshrined until 1917. Russian court dresses were modeled on the traditional *kapot,* a type of medieval peasant dress composed of a caftan split down the front to reveal a second gown beneath. Although Catherine the Great introduced a modified version of the kapot as a gown to be worn at formal court ceremonies, this early model still relied on eighteenth-century tastes, with long sleeves and a full, pannier skirt. Only after Nicholas I's 1834 edict were court gowns required to conform to specific standards.

A Russian court gown was composed of three separate parts: the underskirt, the bodice, and the jacket, which formed the train. The underskirt was of white silk or satin, worn over layers of stiff petticoats to give the desired bell shape and embroidered with gold or silver thread in a variety of foliate designs. Bodices of velvet, satin, or silver brocade were tightly fitted and boned, with short puffed sleeves and a boat-shaped décolletage cut low to reveal the neck and the shoulders. Over the bodice, a floor-length velvet jacket, decorated with jeweled buttons and panels richly embroidered with foliage designs, garlands, and scrolls sewn in gold and silver thread and adorned with sequins and seed pearls, was split from the waist down in an inverted V to reveal the underskirt. Each long, stiff sleeve of this jacket was split with oblique slits from under the shoulder and fell back to expose the arm, which was inevitably covered with above-the-elbow white gloves. The folds of the jacket formed a flowing train, embroidered in gold or silver thread with foliate and arabesque designs, and a separate train, attached to the waist, fell back in folds to the floor. The length of each train was dictated by rank: women of aristocratic birth had six-foot trains; those of the imperial family, nine-foot trains; and those of empresses were fifteen feet long.[5]

Ladies-in-waiting wore court gowns of white silk with jackets and trains of green velvet embroidered in gold thread. Maids of honor wore white satin skirts and bodices and crimson velvet jackets and trains embroidered in gold thread. For women who held no rank, a modified gown was designed, similar in style to those worn by members of the court but sewn in different fabrics and colors.[6] Not surprisingly, these gowns were terribly expensive. In 1913, Baroness Agnes de Stoeckl considered herself lucky to purchase a secondhand gown for her daughter, who had been appointed a *freilina* to Empress Alexandra; even so, it cost some 1,360 rubles ($13,600 in 2005 figures).[7]

The gowns worn by members of the imperial family followed this same pattern, but more elaborate materials were used. Empresses generally wore gowns of silver brocade, embroidered with silver and gold thread, while each grand duchess was assigned an exclusive color for her own court: the gowns worn by Grand Duchess Vladimir were executed in dark orange, sewn with silver and gold thread, while those worn by Grand Duchess Elizabeth Mavrikievna, the wife of Grand Duke Konstantin Konstantinovich, were of dull yellow.[8] Brocades were woven with silver thread, velvets embroidered in gold, and silks sewn with pearls. As a final flourish, the edges of the décolletage, hemline, train, and sleeves were often trimmed with silver fox, mink, sable, or ermine.

These gowns were usually worn with a kokoshnik, a crescent-shaped headdress based on those worn by Russian peasants and later adopted by the medieval *boyarin*. Protocol dictated red or white velvet or silk kokoshniki for women of noble birth, with blue reserved for the imperial family. The kokoshniki were often embellished with pearls, diamonds, and other jewels. From this headdress flowed a veil of tulle. Unmarried women wore a fillet, a low, modified kokoshnik adorned with a satin bow and a veil at the rear. These gowns were so heavy that pages often had to carry them. Not surprisingly, few women enjoyed wearing them, and, within the imperial family, dressing in a Russian court gown was known as putting on "the armor."[9]

For men, too, fashion was of paramount importance. St. Petersburg being the capital of a great empire, military uniforms were abundant. "There were only a few white ties and tails," noted a guest at one ball, "mostly foreign diplomats. Everybody in Russia seemed to be in uniform."[10] One aristocratic lady explained that "uniforms have always been preferred to dull black and white evening clothes, which do not differentiate a gentleman from his lackey."[11]

Americans posted to the imperial court in St. Petersburg, lacking suitable military uniforms, were subjected to constant difficulties. In 1904, Charlemagne Tower, the American minister in Russia, received an invitation to the christening ceremony of the new tsesarevich Alexei Nikolaievich. On arriving at Peterhof Palace, however, the guards "exchanged incredulous glances when he announced himself as the American Ambassador," recalled one lady. "He had been driven to the door in the very plainest equipage, and he wore no court dress, not even a solitary decoration. Coming as he did on the heels of a glittering procession of the representatives of every country in Europe in glorious array, it was hardly surprising that they regarded him with distrust."[12]

For those gentlemen not on active military duty, appearances at social occasions often brought a panorama of splendid official uniforms. Members of the Imperial Senate wore dress uniforms of white trousers sewn with gold galloon, with long dark-blue or scarlet broadcloth coats adorned with stylized oak and laurel leaves in gold thread and gilt buttons; atop their heads, they wore elaborate, two-cornered black felt hats with gold galloon and black ostrich feathers.[13] Ministers calling on the emperor wore, by etiquette, long black frock coats adorned with gold epaulets and galloon.[14] If a gentleman was unfortunate enough to lack the credentials allowing him to dress in uniform, he could always resort to the uniform of the nobility, worn on formal occasions such as weddings and balls. This outfit was composed of white broadcloth trousers and a midlength, Prussian-style black frock coat decorated with gold lapels, collars, and cuffs and ornamented with gold galloon.

Gentlemen of the imperial court wore a wide range of dress. Each court position included four specific uniforms: regular day dress or uniform, for ordinary occasions; semistate liveries or uniform, for lesser ceremonial occasions, including imperial balls; parade dress or uniform, for formal appearances; and state dress, reserved for the most important ceremonial occasions.[15] The higher the court rank, the more elaborately decorated with gold embroidery and braid were the uniforms. The cost of these various outfits was enormous and could run into thousands of rubles. Court chamberlains wore white broadcloth trousers trimmed with gold galloon and single-breasted, black broadcloth coats decorated with gilt buttons crested with double-headed eagles sewn with stylized laurel leaves and peacock feathers in gold thread. The standing collars and cuffs were of scarlet, sewn with stylized floral motifs in golden thread; beneath this, scarlet and gold waistcoats, sewn with double-headed eagles, covered white silk shirts.[16]

Footmen had three sets of dress: ordinary duties called for regulation cutaway black coats worn over white shirts, gold waistcoats sewn with double-headed eagles, and black trousers; semistate liveries consisted of red velvet knee breeches and white stockings, scarlet waistcoats embroidered in gold with double-headed eagles, and long scarlet coats; on ceremonial occasions, they wore blue velvet breeches, scarlet waistcoats, and longer jackets of dark green broadcloth, adorned with gold galloon on the collars and cuffs, and sewn with rows of double-headed eagles on the fronts and sides.[17] Even waiters at the imperial table wore elaborate liveries of dark-blue broadcloth trousers and matching tailcoats with gold galloon collars and double rows of gilt buttons over white silk shirts.[18]

In matters of everyday dress, men usually followed the conventions of the day. Shirts were, almost without exception, of white cotton, worn with stiffly starched wing collars embellished with bone studs; only rarely would a gentleman be seen wearing a turned-down collar. For formal dress, the front of the shirt was starched as well and decorated with jeweled studs. Colored shirts were considered bad taste, and striped shirts were only slightly less unacceptable. Cravats and knotted ties, held in place with jeweled stickpins, were set against low-cut waistcoats. Trousers, in wool or flannel in winter and cotton in summer, were generally creased at the sides, although the fashion for front creases eventually won its own set of admirers. For formal day events, a man without uniform wore the standard morning suit of striped gray trousers and black frock coat with tails. Those without uniform always wore cutaway jackets on formal occasions, with white tie and tails for the theater, balls, and receptions. Overcoats, trimmed with collars of Astrakhan fur or velvet, hung below the knees, revealing short patent leather boots. Hats were hard or soft, with bowlers, derbys, and homburgs favored.[19]

In the country, fashion was dictated by utility. For women, long white skirts, with matching blouses and bolero jackets, were de rigueur, while wide-brimmed hats, veils, and parasols protected their skin from the harsh rays of the sun. There were prescribed lawn tennis, croquet, and boating outfits, and wrap-over skirts with matching jackets and hats adorned with ribbons for riding. Men tended to dress in English-style wool tweed jackets, with plus fours and matching capes and hats for shooting or hunting. Tightly fitting leather or sealskin gloves were an indispensable part of the outfit.

Empress Alexandra dictated the wardrobes of her children. She clothed her daughters, as infants, in fussy satin and silk dresses adorned with lace and colored ribbons. "Among a people madly extravagant," reported the wife of one American diplomat, "she has Queen Victoria's weakness for petty economies, and has been known to order the St. Petersburg shops to send their newest designs in baby bonnets for her inspection, and then return them after copying off the most charming of the patterns."[20] As they grew older, Alexandra habitually dressed the grand duchesses in simple matching dresses of white cambric sewn with lace, each decorated at the waist with a colored sash, or in dresses of subtle pastels adorned with floral patterns. As the two eldest, Olga and Tatiana were often seen in identical dresses, while slightly different variations might be selected for Marie and Anastasia. Even when they reached their teenage years, the empress continued to clothe her daughters in matching ensembles, often skirts and blouses of muslin or serge, with short jackets and Edwardian picture hats; only the subtle variation in the lengths of the skirts differed. For formal ceremonies when they were younger, the grand duchesses all wore shorter versions of Russian court dress, without trains but complete with kokoshniki trimmed with a satin bow at the rear.[21]

By 1913, when the Romanov Dynasty celebrated its Tercentenary, Olga and Tatiana were allowed more say in selecting their own clothing, although they often continued to appear in matching skirts and jackets. Their Russian court gowns now extended to the floor, and their day dresses, tea dresses, and evening gowns, frequently ordered from the Moscow couture house of Lamanova, began to break away from the confines of Edwardian fashion. Olga, in particular, seems to have favored the current trend of shapeless dresses that foreshadowed the sleek lines that came into vogue just before the First World War erupted, a look she accentuated with her new stylish coiffure.

As an infant and a young boy, Tsesarevich Alexei wore skirts and dresses and velvet or linen playsuits and was occasionally dressed in a miniature regimental uniform for official photographs. These alternated with sailor suits, following the trend that was popular not only among Europe's royal families but also with the middle class. As he grew older, short pants gave way to trousers, but this was the only concession he made, for the tsesarevich rarely appeared in private in anything other than trousers and a shirt, often worn with a cap emblazoned with the name of his father's yacht *Standart*. For public appearances, he inevitably wore military uniforms, drawn from his own extensive collection of regimental kits.

Nicholas II, having been raised in a military environment, habitually favored uniforms. His wardrobes held the kits of all regiments in the empire, along with naval uniforms and those of the various foreign regiments to which he had been appointed honorary commander. Cabinets and shelves displayed rows of military caps and helmets, along with cuirasses and ceremonial dress swords. Like his father, Nicholas occasionally wore simple peasant blouses and baggy trousers, though he always preferred a uniform. He rarely wore suits, saving them for certain occasions, like private holidays, when he wished to avoid attention. Holidays on the imperial yacht found the emperor in naval uniform, while shoots in Poland called for tweed knickers, coats, capes, and hats. Although his wardrobe was immense, Nicholas—like his father—was frugal to the point of parsimony; coats and tunics were regularly sent out to have collars and cuffs replaced and worn spots patched. For ceremonial occasions with their regiments, his wife and his daughters also had military uniforms: tunics and long skirts manufactured by the House of Kitaev in St. Petersburg, which had long been a purveyor to the imperial court.

Empress Alexandra herself had little interest in fashion. People in St. Petersburg society who expected the empress to set the latest trends and dictate style were sadly disappointed. When she married Nicholas immediately after his father's funeral, she was plunged into the deep mourning of the Russian court, and her first year in her new country found her inevitably attired in black dresses. Although her marriage had been rushed, Alexandra had a formidable trousseau. One contemporary newspaper detailed this extensive wardrobe: "Little, dainty twilled morning jackets, having finely tucked Vandyke collars trimmed with lace" in "very pale colors." There were "silk and satin broche blouses . . . trimmed in various pretty ways with velvet or lace. One, having black Spanish lace over the yoke and on the sleeves to the elbow, is in particularly good style, as is a tea-gown in twilled silk, with insertion and trimming of ecru lace. The colors are chiefly those that the Princess likes best—soft pinks and delicate grays."[22]

Dowager Empress Marie Feodorovna quickly stepped in to advise her new daughter-in-law on her clothing. Alexandra duly purchased the gowns her mother-in-law recommended, but more often than not they were soon dispatched to wardrobes, never to be seen again. "My mother liked fussiness, trimming, and certain colors," recalled Grand Duchess Olga Alexandrovna. "She never allowed for Alicky's own taste. My mother would order dresses and Alicky did not wear them. She knew but too well that severity suited her best."[23]

Alexandra's fashion sense caused much unfavorable comment among the sophisticated ladies of St. Petersburg society. Inevitably, they found fault with her gowns: too fussy and too matronly, they might declare one day; too severe and not stylish enough, they would say on another occasion. No matter what she did, the empress's tastes seemed destined to offend. And Alexandra, too, offended. On more than one occasion, presiding over an imperial ball, the empress was known to have spotted ladies whose gowns she deemed too revealing, their décolletage cut too low. She once dispatched a *freilina* across a crowded hall to say, "Madame, Her Majesty wants me to tell you that in Hesse, we do not wear our dresses that way."

"Really?" came the unflinching reply. "Tell Her Majesty that in Russia, we do wear our dresses this way."[24]

On other occasions, Alexandra simply summoned carriages and dismissed those ladies whose gowns she considered too revealing.[25] Not surprisingly, St. Petersburg society fought back, not only whispering its condemnations but actively provoking incidents. After one reception, Alexandra complained that several of the ladies had purposely worn exceptionally long feathers in their aigrettes, sending her into a fit of sneezing as they slowly bent in curtseys that were deliberately delivered to sweep their feathers across her face.[26]

Alexandra dressed for her own comfort, and, although she patronized the most prestigious couturiers of the day, she had no enthusiasm for the latest trends. Each season, she ordered dozens of new dresses from establishments in St. Petersburg and in Paris. At the beginning of each year, a list of all official engagements, proposed state visits, and other ceremonial occasions was consulted to determine her annual requirements. When its basic outline was settled, various couturiers were summoned to the palace, bringing sample books, fabrics, and sketches for the empress's approval. Within several months of receiving an order, the dressmakers returned for fittings, an ordeal Alexandra hated. At the same time other designers, from milliners to shoemakers, were shown the couturiers' designs and samples and were asked to complete the ensembles. Alexandra constantly made additions to her wardrobe when she found a gown with a style she particularly liked, though she frequently wore her favorite dresses for several years.

At the beginning of each week, Alexandra read through her coming schedule; working from this, she would either select her own wardrobe for the week or ask her chief lady's maid to do so. Alexandra personally approved each selection, which was then noted in a leather-bound plan book. Every morning, the maid on duty laid out the empress's first wardrobe selection in her dressing room; when Alexandra finished bathing, she would find the clothes waiting for her. Throughout the day, other dresses and gowns appeared at designated intervals, all according to the initial selections made at the start of the week.

For morning and day, Alexandra favored flowing dresses in white, mauve, floral, or soft pastel cambric, batiste, muslin, crepe de chine, or silk. Collars, sleeves, and hemlines were often adorned with bands of embroidery or decorative lace to accentuate the design. Pleated blouses, fringed with velvet collars, matched long, wrap-over skirts whose panels flared at the hem to add depth. For official appearances in the day, the empress often wore elaborate silk dresses with frilled lace collars and pin-tucked bodices; long, cutaway coats opened to reveal flared skirts bedecked with flounces of lace and appliquéd silk flowers; large, wide-brimmed hats, trimmed with ostrich feathers or clusters of silk flowers, held fine veils that shielded her face from the sun. In the country, she often selected muslin or velvet skirts, with silk or cambric blouses and short bolero jackets trimmed with lace embroidery.[27]

Alexandra's evening gowns were inevitably elaborate concoctions of satin, silk, or velvet, embroidered with delicate acanthus and oak leaves in gold or silver thread, sewn with antique lace, and decorated with jet, beaded fringe, or seed pearls. Occasionally, she wore gowns of silver brocade or silver or gold tissue, covered with flounces of lace, chiffon, or tulle netting sprinkled with sequins or embroidered with miniature roses that decorated their tiered trains.[28] With these gowns, Alexandra wore low-heeled court shoes in suede or leather and decorated with lace or beaded embroidery, manufactured by the firms of Andreas Neider or H. Weiss in St. Petersburg.[29] She disliked the more elaborate satin slippers favored by the period. "I can't bear satin shoes," she once told her friend Lili Dehn. "They worry me."[30] In the day, she always carried a parasol; at night, she clutched a small velvet or lace-covered evening bag.

The empress found many of the famous fashions of the day, including the "hobble skirts," an impossible nuisance. "Do you really like this skirt?" she once asked Lili Dehn.

"Well, Madame, it's the fashion," replied Lili.

"It's no use whatever as a skirt," Alexandra shot back. "Now, Lili, prove to me that it is comfortable—run, Lili, run—and let me see how fast you can cover ground in it!"[31]

Alexandra's wardrobe rooms contained an immense collection of dresses and gowns, folded in tissue and packed in cupboards hung with sachets of violet. Drawers held row after row of everyday gloves in kid leather, linen, satin, buckskin, suede, or lace, and the formal *mousquetaires*, the long, skintight buttoned gloves that were demanded on formal occasions at court.[32] One chest contained a priceless collection of fans, of ostrich or peacock feathers or painted scenes and graced with ivory, tortoiseshell, mother-of-pearl, ormolu, or porcelain ribs and handles. One entire room was reserved for the empress's collection of furs: sable cloaks, ermine wraps and coats, mink stoles, and chinchilla muffs and hats. The care of this wardrobe required the constant attention of the empress's maids. Seamstresses were employed to mend small tears, attach loose ribbons and appliqués of lace, and alter dresses. Most of the empress's wardrobe required cleaning by hand, a long, meticulous process made somewhat easier by the assortment of modern steamers and irons that filled the workrooms of the Alexander Palace. Regular day dresses, blouses, skirts, and underclothing were all gathered in large wicker hampers each week and transported to Anichkov Palace in St. Petersburg, where the imperial laundries were located.

Fashion at court under Nicholas II did not change much, save for the usual influx of new styles and trends customary during any era. The emperor himself, although he favored military uniforms or loose peasant-style shirts and trousers, once toyed with the idea of reintroducing medieval dress, the long, embroidered, richly jeweled caftans of his early ancestors' reigns. Only after the expense of such costumes was pointed out did Nicholas reluctantly give up the idea.[33]

16

JEWELRY, REGALIA, AND OBJETS D'ART

I sincerely think that if monarchs appeared more often
in their crowns, there would be fewer republics!
—Grand Duchess George of Russia

"AMONG THE SEVERAL ARTICLES of sumptuousness which distinguish the Russian nobility," wrote one Western visitor, "there is none perhaps more calculated to strike a foreigner than the profusion of diamonds and other precious stones, which sparkle in every part of their dress."[1] There was nothing subtle about this love of jewelry or the manner in which it was worn. The size of the stones used in Russian jewels was rarely seen in the rest of Europe. Alexander Mossolov recalled the wife of the marshal of the nobility in St. Petersburg attired in a gown adorned with "nine or ten emeralds as buttons, each bigger than a pigeon's egg."[2] Not surprisingly, the Russian demand for such jewels was enormous, as women raced to display the largest, most valuable, and rarest pieces.

The most famous Russian jeweler was Peter Carl Fabergé; he competed with a number of other firms that also had been awarded the title of "Purveyor to the Imperial Court," including Koechli, Bolin, Bock, Khlebnikov, Denisov, and Ovchinnikov; the Finnish jeweler Alexander Tillander on Bolshaya Morskaya Ulitsa; and Kurt Hahn, whose shop at No. 26 Nevsky Prospekt was favored by Empress Alexandra. Women were just as likely to shop in Paris, where they patronized Cartier and his fellow Parisians Frederic Boucheron and Lucien Falize; the taste for art nouveau–inspired pieces led them to Vever and René Lalique.

Russian men also formed suitable collections. They wore jeweled belt buckles, cuff links, shirt studs, tie clasps, cravat pins and hoops, and cabochons and signet rings set in gold. Full military dress often called for jeweled sword hilts and epaulets. The decorations of the various Russian orders—St. George crosses, St. Vladimir cordons, St. Andrei diamond order stars, and St. Alexander Nevsky diamond collars—also embellished the military tunics of guards officers. One guest at a ball recalled that the men there were "almost covered with diamonds; their buttons, buckles, hilts of swords, and epaulets, were composed of this valuable material; their hats were frequently embroidered . . . with several rows of them; and a diamond star upon a coat was scarcely a distinction."[3] Even on ordinary afternoons, wrote a visiting American, gentlemen could be seen with "rubies and diamonds in their studs and cuff links, and they would likely offer cigarettes from a gold case strewn with the monograms of various friends traced in jewels."[4]

Nicholas II possessed hundreds of such jeweled pieces; he recorded those given to him and made simple watercolor sketches of the items in a small leather-bound book recording his collection.[5] Among these were five sets of cuff links, given to him by Alexandra on the births of each of their children. Shaped like

The crown jewels and other imperial jewels confiscated by the Bolsheviks. At the center of the table is the Imperial State Crown, flanked by the two diamond crowns of the empresses, the Diamond Chain of the Order of St. Andrei, and the Romanov Nuptial Crown. Empress Alexandra's pearl and diamond tiara, made by the jeweler Kurt Hahn, can be seen in the middle row, second from the left.

hearts and adorned with the empress's initials in diamonds, they were finished in different guilloche enamels: mauve for Olga, red for Tatiana, blue for Marie, yellow for Anastasia, and gray for Alexei.[6]

Nowhere was this love of jewelry displayed to more stunning effect than within the imperial family. The regalia included not only physical adornments but the imperial thrones as well, used for the last time during Nicholas II's coronation in 1896. Nicholas II sat upon the Diamond Throne of Tsar Alexei, made by the court jeweler to the shah of Persia, and presented in the seventeenth century by Armenian merchants in recognition of trade concessions.[7] The chair, though made of wood, was completely covered with gold and silverwork plates whose surfaces were encrusted with 870 diamonds.[8] Alexandra occupied the Throne of Ivan the Terrible, which had open arms, a high back, and a small footrest. Its entire surface was covered with richly carved ivory panels depicting biblical scenes; according to legend, it had been brought from Constantinople by Ivan III's wife, Zöé Paleologue, on their marriage.[9]

In the strong room of the Winter Palace, steel-lined vaults held the most important crown pieces. The centerpiece of the entire collection was the Imperial State Crown, created by Gerald Pozier for Catherine the Great for her coronation in 1762. Shaped like a low miter and split into identical hemispheres, the crown weighed nearly nine pounds, which made it terribly uncomfortable to wear. Between the hemispheres, a garland of oak leaves and acorns was executed in diamonds, with eleven larger diamonds inset at intervals and a 56-carat diamond, presented to Empress Elizabeth in 1754, set at the base.[10] The shell of the crown was covered with more than forty-nine hundred diamonds set in a silver lattice frame adorned with diamond laurel branches and fringed with a band of twenty-eight large diamonds and thirty-eight perfectly matched pearls.[11] At the apex of the crown, five large diamonds formed a cross, set with a magnificent uncut ruby of 415 carats, the largest in the world.[12] The imperial scepter, made for Catherine the Great, was a chased gold rod, ringed with double rows of diamonds and topped with a gilded, double-headed eagle holding the famous Orlov Diamond of 194 carats.[13] The smoothly polished golden sphere of the Imperial Orb was set with bands of diamonds and crowned by a diamond cross set with an oval Ceylon sapphire of 200 carats at its center.[14]

The Imperial Regalia also included the Diamond Chain of the Order of St. Andrei; the Sword of State; the Shield of State; and the Seal of State. The main piece of the empress's regalia was her crown, made by the French jeweler Duval in 1801 for Empress Elizabeth, the wife of Alexander I. Of silver, its surface was

The Imperial Rivière Necklace

completely covered with diamonds, and its two spheres topped with a diamond cross. These jewels of state were supplemented by the crown jewels, including the Imperial Diadem; the Diadem of Catherine the Great, consisting of a band of large diamonds at whose center was inset a large pink diamond; the Romanov Nuptial Crown, its six arches of some fifteen hundred diamonds sewn on red velvet and surmounted by a cross studded with an 80-carat diamond; the Diamond Festoon Earrings of Catherine the Great, so heavy that they had to be supported with wires around the ear lobes; and the Imperial Rivière Necklace, composed of twenty-one enormous diamonds of graduated size, the largest weighing 32 carats, with another fifteen pear-shaped diamond drops of between 15 to 25 carats each. The total weight of the diamonds in the Imperial Rivière Necklace was just over 470 carats, making it the single largest diamond necklace in the world. In 1909, its value alone was estimated at 498,000 rubles ($4,980,000 in current values).[15]

The private collections of the women of the imperial family were staggering. In 1874, when Grand Duchess Marie Alexandrovna, the daughter of Alexander II, married Queen Victoria's second son, Prince Alfred, the duke of Edinburgh, she brought to England a collection of jewels that far outshone those of the queen. Among them was a diamond and ruby suite consisting of a tiara, a necklace, earrings, a stomacher, and brooches; diamonds, pearls, emeralds, and sapphires adorned further diadems, necklaces, bracelets, earrings, brooches, hair clips, and stomachers, so rich that members of the British royal family felt poor by comparison. Once, the grand duchess, bedecked in her priceless gems, appeared before a plainly adorned Queen Victoria; the elderly queen shrugged her shoulders, "like a bird whose plumage has been ruffled," recalled one witness, "drawing down the corners of her mouth in an expression those around her had grown to dread."[16]

Even though Marie Alexandrovna possessed an extensive collection of jewelry, minor women in the imperial family also appeared covered in a blaze of diamonds, rubies, sapphires, pearls, and emeralds. Many of these jewels were received as wedding presents. On her marriage to Grand Duke George Mikhailovich in 1900, Marie Georgievna's father-in-law, Grand Duke Michael Nikolaievich, gave her a magnificent diamond and ruby tiara and four perfectly matched strings of pearls, set with a diamond clasp adorned with an enormous sapphire, that had belonged to his late wife. Her husband presented her with a diamond tiara and a matching parure of jewels that had also belonged to his mother, while Nicholas and Alexandra gave her three matched ropes of pearls, a sapphire and diamond clasp, and a sapphire and diamond brooch. "I was quite overwhelmed by all these riches," Marie Georgievna later wrote. "Certainly I had had few brooches of my own before, and one beautiful rope of pearls that had belonged to my grandmother Queen Louise, which my father gave me."[17]

She kept this collection in a series of glass-topped cabinets arranged round her dressing room. As Baroness Agnes de Stoeckl recalled, "In the first lay all her diamonds: tiaras of all sizes, necklaces, stomachers, earrings, bracelets, etc. Another held similar ornaments, but all in emeralds, some of stupendous size and value. Others held sets in sapphires, turquoise, rubies, and pearls. Here in this room lay jewels worth a king's ransom, varying from tiaras for state occasions to small ones for private parties."[18]

Of the Romanovs, however, the three greatest collections belonged to Grand Duchess Vladimir, the dowager empress, and Empress Alexandra. Many of Grand Duchess Vladimir's exquisite pieces came from the Paris shop of Jacques Cartier. In 1900, she commissioned a collar of six strings of pearls, with two double-headed eagles composed of diamonds.[19] On her marriage, she had received from Alexander II an emerald and diamond brooch that had belonged to Catherine the Great; the emerald, of 107 carats, was said to be the second largest in the world.[20] Shortly after the turn of the century, Cartier set the brooch within a necklace, suspended on a gold chain and surrounded with square-cut emeralds encased in diamond borders that supported emerald drops; between the emeralds hung platinum pendants set with diamonds, each containing separate oval-cut diamonds of 10 to 16 carats each.[21]

Other commissions followed, particularly after Cartier opened a branch in St. Petersburg. In 1908, the grand duchess ordered a briolette aigrette tiara, as well as a tiara that incorporated a ruby that had belonged to Empress Josephine.[22] The following year, she commissioned a sapphire and diamond kokoshnik, with a 137-carat sapphire at its center, and her famous diamond loop tiara, with interchangeable cabochon sapphire and diamond pendants.[23] In 1910, Cartier designed a stomacher for the grand duchess, with a 162-carat sapphire at its center.[24] Adorned with this priceless collection and presiding over gatherings in her splendid palace, the formidable grand duchess inevitably left a vivid, glittering impression. She enjoyed showing visitors the fantastic treasures, which she kept in glass-topped cabinets in her boudoir. The duchess of Marlborough, the former Consuelo Vanderbilt, later recalled, "There were endless *parures* of diamonds, emeralds, rubies and pearls, to say nothing of semi-precious stones such as turquoises, tourmalines, cat's eyes, and aquamarines."[25]

After the Revolution, Albert Stopford, who was attached to the British Embassy in St. Petersburg, rescued much of the grand duchess's jewelry from the hands of the Bolsheviks. Queen Mary of Great Britain purchased several of the most important pieces when they were sold at auction in Europe. Today, Queen Elizabeth II often wears the magnificent diamond loop tiara that had once graced the grand duchess during her glittering entertainments in St. Petersburg.

Dowager Empress Marie Feodorovna thrived on jewelry. On her marriage in 1866, the formerly impoverished Danish princess was stunned by the quantity of jewelry she received, saying that she would never be able to wear it all.[26] Within a few years, however, she had become enamored of the riches at her disposal, and her collection became the finest in the world. Marie Feodorovna owned more than twenty tiaras, consisting of rubies, emeralds, pearls, diamonds, and sapphires. Her favorite necklace, nine strands of perfectly matched pearls, had been a gift from Alexander III, but Marie Feodorovna also had an unusual assortment of decorative pieces: twenty large pink diamond stars, worn cascaded through her hair and across the bodice of her gown; a long diamond spear, to hold back the folds of a skirt; and fifteen diamond, sapphire, emerald, ruby, and topaz butterflies worn sprinkled across her bodice and set off by a large jeweled moth of pearls and diamonds in her hair.[27]

Marie Feodorovna used this wealth of jewels to powerful effect. "The Empress wore four rows of diamonds around her neck," the wife of the American minister to the court of Alexander III recalled of one imperial ball, "with pendants in front and at the back; a beautiful tiara, in which the splendid stones were set open with just enough silver to hold them together; brooches all around the neck of her dress, two of them, at least, consisting of single stones of incredible size; and diamond ornaments on her skirt." The impression, she wrote, was of "a blaze of splendor."[28]

Relations between Alexandra and Marie Feodorovna were strained by the incident over the imperial jewels. It was customary for a dowager to hand over certain pieces of imperial jewelry to a reigning empress. But the necklaces and tiaras meant too much to Marie Feodorovna, and, although by protocol they belonged to Alexandra, she gave her new daughter-in-law only a number of older tiaras and parures that had belonged to Catherine the Great and those that she herself found too uncomfortable to wear. Alexandra was insulted. Nicholas asked his mother to hand over the main jewels, but the dowager empress made a great fuss about it and, in the end, refused. When she heard of this, Alexandra was not only hurt but also angry. She knew just how to retaliate. Saying that she no longer cared about the jewels, Alexandra told Nicholas that even if the dowager empress gave them to her, she would now refuse to wear them. The emperor passed this message along to his mother and reminded her that Alexandra would, by tradition, be expected to appear in certain of the jewels on state occasions. If she failed to do so, and Marie Feodorovna was seen wearing them, a scandal would ensue.[29] To save her reputation, Marie Feodorovna duly sent the most important jewels to her daughter-in-law, keeping for herself seventy-seven pieces that, by right, should have gone to Alexandra. This included three diadems, five necklaces, more than forty brooches, and a number of pendants, earrings, and bracelets.[30]

Empress Alexandra herself came to the Russian throne with only a small personal collection of jewelry. At her father's court in Darmstadt, elaborate jewels had not been much in evidence. There was little demand for extravagant pieces; moreover, the Hessian royal family lacked the resources with which to purchase a greater number. Her personal collection of jewelry, including the gifts she had received as Princess Alix of Hesse, amounted to a mere 308 items, all neatly recorded in her own hand in a small book similar to the jewelry album kept by her husband.[31] On learning of the engagement, Empress Marie Feodorovna wrote to her son, Tsesarevich Nicholas: "Ask Alix which stones she likes most, sapphires or emeralds? I would like to know for the future." The letter came accompanied by an emerald bracelet and a jewel-encrusted Easter egg, Alix's first taste of the Russian passion for jewels.[32]

Her first substantial pieces came from her future husband and his parents when Nicholas arrived to spend the summer of 1894 with her and her grandmother Queen Victoria at Windsor Castle. Nicholas's formal engagement presents included a pink pearl ring and a beautiful necklace of perfectly matched pink pearls, a sapphire and diamond brooch, and a gold chain bracelet with a huge emerald pendant drop. With all of these dazzling jewels laid out before her, Queen Victoria eyed her granddaughter and warned, "Now, Alix, do not get too proud."[33] Upon her marriage, the empress added to her collection. Nicholas gave his bride a tiara of diamond *fleurons* set with pearl spikes, and she received a number of pieces from Marie Feodorovna on behalf of herself and her late husband. Before his death, Alexander III had ordered a diamond kokoshnik tiara for her from

Empress Alexandra's pearl and
diamond tiara, made by Kurt Hahn

Fabergé as his wedding gift, and his widow presented another commission, a magnificent diamond and Ceylon sapphire parure from the jeweler Friedrich Koechli, consisting of a necklace, a brooch, bracelets, and a tiara, its seven hundred diamonds—weighing 400 carats—arrayed in starbursts and set with sixteen large sapphires weighing 222 carats.[34]

Alexandra's tiaras encompassed a number of styles. She had several modeled on the kokoshnik, the simple, medieval form of peasant headdress that had become part of the Russian court dress. Her kokoshnik tiaras were executed in a diamond fringe pattern, inset with larger diamonds or other jewels. Other tiaras were based upon interlaced foliage: rose florets, oak leaf clusters, laurel wreaths, diamond garlands, and wheatears. There were festoon, meander, and trellis designs, intricately exhibiting gems in a lacy network of platinum and silver supports. A number of the empress's tiaras were drawn from exquisite parures, including a diadem of 529 diamonds weighing 120 carats set with 18 large pear-shaped pearls; a diamond circlet and bow-knot tiara embellished with large sapphires; a tall diadem of 5 floral diamond ovals adorned with Burmese rubies; and a diamond garland tiara, made by Bolin to match a suite of jewels by Fabergé and set with Colombian emeralds. Alexandra took an active interest in commissioning new jewels, sketching designs for them herself, often to accompany special gowns. The empress designed a *demi-parure*, consisting of a diadem and a large brooch, composed of aquamarines set within a foliate pattern of diamonds on platinum, which she wore on numerous public occasions.[35]

After the turn of the century, bandeaus—low scrollwork headbands containing contrasting jewels as centerpieces—became fashionable, and Alexandra's were interpreted in the art nouveau style. Perhaps her most distinctive piece was the Imperial Diadem, of 840 diamonds weighing 287 carats and set in a modified kokoshnik design. Its open scrolls and diamond fleurons were set with 13 large pearl spikes and pendants, and the edges ornamented with another 101 smaller pink pearls that had originally belonged to Catherine the Great.[36] The empress often wore the imposing diadem on important occasions, including the installation ceremony of the first State Duma at the Winter Palace in 1906.

Additional ornaments for the empress's hair included diamond stars and crescents, moons, feathers, arrows, clusters of leaves, and birds. Aigrettes and diamond sprays, holding groups of ostrich and eagle feathers, were also worn. On most occasions, these tiaras and hair ornaments were worn without any additional accessories, although, in the case of the jeweled kokoshniki required for court functions, veils of tulle or lace hung from the bow at the back of Alexandra's head. Often, these veils were themselves sewn with diamonds or sprinkled with tiny beading, to catch the light and give the impression of a jeweled cascade.

The empress had a number of parures, consisting of a tiara and a matching necklace, earrings, and brooches. Her most formal necklaces, in festoon, fringe, and collet designs, shimmered with diamonds, aquamarines, rubies, and emeralds. Queen Alexandra of England, Dowager Empress Marie Feodorovna's sister, was responsible for the fashion of diamond and pearl dog collars, as well as the famous collar *résille*, a lacy net of diamonds, or diamonds and pearls, suspended on silk threads, which completely covered the neck and draped down to the low neckline of the gown. Other necklaces reflected the art nouveau movement, including a lavaliere, a long chain of silk thread studded with diamonds and set with hanging pearls and rubies, and a negligee necklace, of two long strings of diamonds set in platinum, worn draped over her shoulders, with the two free ends ending in diamond tassels.

Above all other jewels, Alexandra favored pearls. The firms of Fabergé, Bolin, and Hahn had standing orders to allow her first choice of any pearls that were obtained. She had dozens of ropes of carefully matched freshwater pearls worn in multiple strings; a dog collar of pearls and diamonds; a pearl coronet, made by Fabergé and studded with diamonds; and a cap of dozens of pearls linked by silk threads. Her most famous necklace was undoubtedly a magnificent *sautoir*, a long string of pearls that fell in ropes below her waist and could be pinned to folds of her gowns to form an ornamental cascade. Created by Fabergé, it had been a wedding gift ordered by Alexander III and had cost a quarter of a million rubles ($2,500,000 in 2005 figures).[37]

Alexandra's earrings ranged from simple button-style clasps and drops to elaborate waterfalls of diamonds, sapphires, and emeralds. Diamond and pearl drop earrings were particular favorites, but the empress disliked the heavier chandelier-style pendants of the era. Her bracelets reflected the late Victorian and Edwardian eras, and most often came from a parure of jewels. She had a number of diamond collets, or pearl and diamond pendant bracelets, as well as platinum bands set with diamonds and combinations of emeralds, sapphires, or rubies. Elegant, animal-inspired designs—leopards, snakes, and panthers, with jeweled eyes or tongues of diamonds—echoed the taste for art nouveau–inspired pieces, and Alexandra had a number of charm bracelets, hung with small reminders of anniversaries, births, and other special occasions.

To adorn the bodices of her gowns, Alexandra had numerous brooches. Diamonds were used as drop pendants or in network with other jewels like sapphires and emeralds to form cascades. Bowknot brooches were particularly fashionable, as were pearl drop pendants set in platinum. Floral brooches in the form of sprays in multicolored gemstones were often worn during the day, and diamond wheatears, oak leaf clusters, stars, and crescents decorated bodices and were sometimes used to pin back sautoirs, or ropes of diamonds and pearls. On formal occasions the empress also wore stomachers, stretching from the neckline to the waist of her gown and consisting of pearls and diamonds, in cascades of varying length, inset with other gems and sweeping in ropes of diamond knots and jeweled pendants to cover the bodice. Influenced by her brother Grand Duke Ernst Ludwig's patronage of the art nouveau movement, the empress owned a number of stylized pieces: brooches and clasps, hair ornaments and necklaces, composed of diamonds, platinum, and gold; bits of lavender, rose, and amethyst-colored glass; and semiprecious stones, all used to create miniature animals, jeweled insects, and even lightning bolts.

Alexandra kept most of her pieces in safes in the Alexander Palace and in trays in her dressing room. "Only rubies today," she might say to a maid when dressing, or "Pearls and sapphires with this gown."[38] In the evening, when dressing for dinner, she followed a predictable pattern, as Baroness Buxhoeveden recalled, wearing pearls and amethysts with light-colored gowns, and sapphires and diamonds with those of darker colors.[39]

When Alexandra wore one of the crown pieces, an elaborate ritual ensued. After receiving a request for a piece, the empress's first lady's maid had to send a written note to the head treasurer in charge of the strong room at the Winter Palace, where the jewels were kept.[40] This gentleman called an escort of three soldiers of the guard, opened the vaults, pulled the requested item, and, accompanied by these three sentries, delivered the piece to the first maid. She, in turn, was required to write out a receipt for the jewelry before he would turn it over. As soon as Alexandra took the piece of jewelry off, the ritual was repeated, the notes exchanged, and the treasurer appeared to collect the item and, surrounded with his sentries, made his way back to St. Petersburg to deposit it safely in the strong room of the Winter Palace.[41]

Perhaps the most precious legacies of the last years of the Romanov Dynasty were the objets d'art produced by the great jeweler Peter Carl Fabergé. Fabergé was an artist rather than a craftsman; his genius lay in his interpretation of commonplace, everyday objects—clocks, paperweights, pots of flowers, cigarette cases, snuff boxes, picture frames, opera glasses, cuff links, and desk sets—which, in his hands, became masterpieces of soft pastel enamels, chased gold and silver, and filigree metal work, composed of lapis lazuli, agate, chalcedony, jasper, nephrite, sandstone, tiger's eye, and other precious and semiprecious gemstones. His use of colored enamels, semiprecious stones, and polished metals often resulted in delightful surprises: Karelian birch picture frames with chased ormolu mounts; clocks of silver gilt with guilloche enamels, surrounded by chased silver filigree swags and bows and pendants; miniature malachite and gold cabinets and tables; silver and enamel sedan chairs; cigarette cases of chased silver, gold, platinum, or guilloche enamels, embossed with Romanov crests or imperial monograms; turtles, doves, gulls, bears, seals, and fish carved from nephrite, rock crystal, agate, chalcedony, and jasper, set with ruby eyes and silver gilt whiskers; miniature figures of peasants and soldiers detailed with precious gems; and flowerpots of rock crystal, filled with gold, silver, and platinum-stemmed flowers of pearls, rose diamonds, nephrite, and jade.

Much of what Fabergé produced went necessarily to the imperial court. A special vault in the Winter Palace, next to the strong room holding the crown jewels, was reserved especially for Fabergé's latest pieces. When special occasions like family birthdays, anniversaries, or weddings called for gifts, the emperor or the empress had only to call for the key and enter this Aladdin's Cave of treasures to select what they required.[42] The members of the imperial family were prestigious and important customers, although Fabergé often complained that when it came to their commissions, he was expected to drop everything else and work exclusively on pieces for the Romanovs. They were, he said, terribly impatient and always insisted that their special orders take priority, even if it meant keeping a staff of craftsmen working round the clock.[43]

It is the imperial Easter eggs for which Fabergé is best remembered. The tradition began in 1885 when, at his brother's request, Grand Duke Vladimir commissioned an Easter gift for Marie Feodorovna.[44] Fabergé responded with a simple white enamel egg-shaped shell that, when broken apart, contained a golden yolk that opened to reveal a smaller chased gold hen with ruby eyes. Marie Feodorovna was so delighted that the emperor commissioned Fabergé to design a new egg each year, a tradition carried on by his son Nicholas II, who always ordered two, one for his mother and one for his wife. In all, Fabergé produced some sixty-four Easter eggs, most of which have survived to the present day.

The *Standart*
Egg.
See plate 34.

Fabergé's great success with his Easter eggs lay in his unique designs; no two imperial eggs ever featured the same style or concept. In addition, he always used the shell of the egg to form the basis for a surprise within: sometimes miniature portraits that rose from the top of the shell when a concealed button was pushed, clocks inset into the sides of the shells that chimed the hour, and replicas of palaces and statues of importance to the imperial family. Although Fabergé was not the first jeweler to create surprise Easter eggs, his use of enamels, silver and gold, platinum, precious and semiprecious gems, as well as the intricacy of the miniature surprises and exquisite craftsmanship of the product, set his eggs apart and raised them from being merely derivative to true works of art in their own right.

The eggs given to Alexandra were often more elaborate than those commissioned for the dowager empress. The Coronation Egg of 1897 contained a perfectly articulated golden replica of the coach that Alexandra had used the previous May during her husband's coronation festivities in Moscow, a model so detailed that it had taken some fifteen months to create.[45] The Colonnade Egg of 1910 was a masterpiece of pale green chalcedony and bowenite, decorated with silver cherubs and love birds and containing a rotary clock around the top of the egg with Roman numerals set in diamonds. Several of the eggs replicated favorite residences or yachts, like the Alexander Palace Egg of 1908 and the *Standart* Egg of the following year. In 1911, to celebrate their fifteenth wedding anniversary, Nicholas gave his wife an egg of gold and platinum decorated with translucent enamels and containing miniature portraits of the imperial family, as well as of important events during the emperor's reign. It was the most personal and poignant of all the eggs that the jeweler produced.

During the First World War, the tradition continued, but the eggs were scaled down, owing to wartime austerity. In 1915, Alexandra received a simple white enamel shell decorated with a Red Cross that broke apart to form a triptych with small icons; a year later, the Steel Military Egg of 1916 was actually composed of cartridge cases and contained a miniature painting of the emperor and his son reviewing the Russian troops at the front. Fabergé was at work on the eggs for 1917 when the emperor abdicated, preventing their final delivery to its imperial recipients who, by Easter, were prisoners of the Provisional Government. These last magnificent works disappeared in the chaos of revolution.

17

IMPERIAL TRANSPORTATION

IN 1868, OR SO THE STORY GOES, Grand Duchess Alexandra Iosifovna traveled to Montreux for a short holiday. In her suite were Admiral Baron Boye, the marshal of her court; two of her ladies-in-waiting; a physician; a pianist; a masseuse; a hairdresser; a jewelry maid; the keeper of her purse; two footmen; a wardrobe maid; and four ordinary lady's maids. In addition, along with the dozens of trunks and suitcases, the grand duchess had brought her own grand piano, for she disliked playing any other. All of this cost an enormous amount, which was duly paid for by the Imperial Treasury, so that the grand duchess could have her holiday in comfort.[1]

Such luxurious extravagance was common at the Russian imperial court. When the Romanovs left their palaces, they did not abandon the comforts surrounding their positions. Instead, travel became its own pleasure. Some measure of this luxury can be gauged from a private railway carriage ordered by Nicholas II's uncle and brother-in-law, Grand Duke Serge Alexandrovich, to convey him the eighteen miles from Moscow to his country estate at Ilinskoye. The carriage, a masterpiece of lavishly gilded furniture, consisted of a drawing room, a bedroom, a bathroom, and an anteroom; as governor-general of Moscow, the grand duke had authorized some £3,500 alone on the upholstery and decoration, expenses billed to the Moscow-Brest Railway Company. The resulting miniature palace, however, was so heavy that it remained in service for less than a decade.[2]

Transportation had always been an important element in the imperial show of power. On ceremonial occasions, fantastic carriages and state landaus rolled through the streets of St. Petersburg or Moscow, drawn by carefully trained horses led by grooms in exquisite liveries, forming an impressive display of wealth and prestige. The Office of the Imperial Stable employed grooms, coachmen, and veterinarians, as well as craftsmen to repair the coaches; stable boys to polish the silver harnesses, stirrups, and bridles; and artisans to sew the blankets with silver thread and golden double-headed eagles.

The Imperial Stables were under the direction of General Artur von Grunwald, who held the post of *ober-shtalmeister*, or master of the imperial horse. "He has continually been considered a substantial pillar of the barons of the Baltic provinces," noted one observer, "and in the event of any important occurrence, they always apply to him to have their requirements successfully attended to."[3] The administration of the Imperial Stables operated within the Russian court as a division of the imperial household, and Grunwald reported directly to the emperor. His deputy, Baron Gustav Mannerheim, held the position of *shtalmeister*, charged with the daily running of the Imperial Stables and acting as liaison with the imperial security division during public appearances. With Colonel Paleologue, the director of the Imperial Stud, he coordinated the selection of horses for these occasions.[4]

Colonel Paleologue had general care of the horses within the Imperial Stables and those belonging to the Imperial Stud. A man of astute eye and diligent in his approach to horseflesh, he personally appraised potential additions, often traveling to France, Germany, and England to inspect and purchase new stock.[5] Each of the imperial palaces had a set of stables within its grounds. At the Alexander Palace, there was a massive gothic structure, complete with turrets and battlements, while the stables at Peterhof had been designed after Hampton Court, Henry VIII's great palace on the Thames outside London; an Imperial Stud was also located at Gatchina.[6] In St. Petersburg, the Imperial Stables were housed in a long, elaborate building adorned with Doric columns stretching from the Moika to the Catherine Canal.[7] Being confined to the city, the horses at these stables were exercised daily, at either the Imperial Riding School on the Catherine Canal or on the Champs de Mars.

Paleologue maintained between five and six hundred horses in the St. Petersburg area; another hundred were kept at the Imperial Stables and Stud in Moscow. Of this number, only a few were selected as personal mounts for members of the imperial family, with the remainder designated for carriage and ceremonial duties. Nicholas II had six personal horses: two at Tsarskoye Selo and two at Peterhof for both private rides and public appearances; one in St. Petersburg, for use in military parades and reviews; and one at Gatchina, for hunting and shooting. These horses were carefully bred and trained to fulfill their ceremonial functions. Those selected to pull carriages were often paired at birth, matched in size and color, and subjected to difficult exercises before being entrusted to public duties: the noise of crowds on the great occasions of state could be deafening, and stable boys and grooms huddled round the yards shouting and waving flags as the horses were put through their paces. The famous black Orlov trotters were reserved exclusively for the carriages of the emperor and the empress.[8]

The imperial family's personal mounts were carefully looked after in exquisitely fitted stables with warmed floors and bundles of inspected hay. When the horses became too old to continue their functions, they were retired to a corner of the park at Tsarskoye Selo, looked after by a specially selected team of grooms. On their deaths, the horses were buried in a cemetery just beyond the stables, beneath stone monuments commemorating their names and dates of service.[9]

Catherine the Great's
state carriage.
See plate 35.

During the reign of Nicholas II, the dozens of ornate carriages were rarely used. For the coronation, the parade carriages collected by the Romanovs throughout the centuries conveyed the imperial family through the streets of Moscow. Most of these state carriages were elaborate affairs from the reigns of Empress Elizabeth and Catherine the Great, reflecting European style and tradition. Empress Elizabeth's great state carriage, heavily carved and covered in gilt, contained side panels painted in rococo style. The largest of all the state carriages was made in Berlin in 1746; a massive collection of cherubs, rococo garlands, swags, and foliage, together with carved double-headed eagles, crowns, laurel leaves, and sea shells—all heavily gilded—framed side panels depicting romantic scenes of court life.[10] For the coronation, Alexandra rode in a carriage made for Catherine the Great in 1793, its scarlet exterior decorated with golden trelliswork knotted with double-headed eagles.[11]

Although the interiors of these carriages were lined with velvets, silk brocades, and *point d'Espagne* lace, they were anything but comfortable. Most of the windows could not be opened for ventilation, and the boxes containing the seats were slung from braces supporting the wheels, without springs or cushions. As a result, a carriage ride was unenviable: every uneven spot in the roadway, every bump or hole, caused jolts to the passengers inside. On warm days, with the sun shining on the closed interiors, they became unbearably hot miniature infernos, especially when the men were in full military uniform and the women in heavy court gowns. Few of those cheering the processions realized how uncomfortable the Romanovs were inside their elaborate vehicles.

Foreign monarchs had presented many of the saddles, bridles, and harnesses adorning the horses. On state occasions, the horses were outfitted in a special set of red Moroccan leather saddles, harnesses, and bridles stitched in silver thread, with stirrups of chased and gilded bronze. The saddlecloths from this set were of gold lace, embroidered with double-headed eagles in gold thread. To complete the elaborate picture, the horses sported sprays of ostrich plumes on their heads, drawn together in gold bands embossed with crowns.

For most occasions, the imperial family used a series of red and gold semistate landaus, calèches, and victorias; in the winter, brightly painted troikas and sleighs appeared, complete with bells and ermine and sable lap blankets embroidered with double-headed eagles.[12] All bore imperial crests on their doors, a distinction that caused another conflict between Alexandra and her forceful mother-in-law. It was customary, at the beginning of each reign, for imperial carriages to be painted with the new emperor's initials and monogram; in 1894, these were joined by the initials of his consort. Dowager Empress Marie Feodorovna spotted the change and went directly to her son. "Since when," she asked Nicholas, "did I cease to be Empress?" It turned out that several of her personal carriages had unwittingly been fitted with the new crests—a mistake that the dowager empress quickly noticed and even more quickly corrected.[13]

On ordinary occasions, the footmen, grooms, postillion riders, and coachmen accompanying these vehicles wore semistate liveries, black with crimson and gold detailing; state occasions called for elaborate gold and crimson liveries, with tricorn hats and white silk stockings, or blue jackets with silver braid and blue velvet hats with ostrich plumes over their powdered wigs. Nicholas II kept three personal coachmen, but his favorite was M. Notto, an Italian who first came to Russia in the reign of Alexander II. In addition to his immense collection of ordinary and state liveries, Notto received 1,800 rubles a year, making him one of the highest paid members of the household.[14]

In time, carriages gave way to motorcars. In 1896, during a visit to Paris, Nicholas II was offered one of the first motorcars manufactured by Dion Bouton; he declined, saying he preferred to wait until the machine had been perfected.[15] After 1900, however, Nicholas—fascinated by the new motorcars—purchased a number of landaus, phaetons, and limousines from Mercedes-Benz, Daimler, and Renault; he supplemented these with French Delauney-Belleville open touring cars, which quickly became his favorites. The French firm responded to this important patronage by producing special models for the Russian imperial court, including a larger, longer touring motorcar, the "S. I. M." or "Son Impérial Majesté" model in 1909.[16] Imperial garages were built at Tsarskoye Selo and Peterhof to house this growing collection and, on the recommendation of Prince Vladimir Orlov, Adolphe Kegress came from France to supervise the burgeoning department, a task for which he received 1,885 rubles a year. Four men served as the imperial family's personal chauffeurs; they received 1,400 rubles a year and wore distinctive khaki overcoats sewn with double-headed eagles and peaked caps of dark blue Swedish moleskin, uniforms designed by Empress Alexandra in 1910.[17] The taste for motorcars soon caught on; by 1913, there were 2,585 automobiles in St. Petersburg alone.[18] The most privileged owners sought membership in the Imperial Automotive Club, presided over by Count de Freedericksz.[19]

Journeys across the Russian empire were conducted in the imperial train, its ten cars—painted deep blue and decorated with golden double-headed eagles—stretching over a thousand feet in length. It had been manufactured at the Alexandrovsky Mechanical Works between 1894 and 1896, working from the plans of the train that had been built for Alexander III in 1892. Individual carriages and components were manufactured at private railway companies not only in Russia, but also in Warsaw, Berlin, and Paris, with fittings ordered from firms in Finland and Austria.[20]

The carriages were luxuriously decorated, with fittings and furnishings of teak, oak, walnut, beech, maple, Karelian birch, red beech, and satinwood. Floors were covered with specially designed linoleum tile and with deep carpets, and the walls hung with floral English cretonne, silk, leather, and wooden panels inlaid with satinwood, beech, tortoiseshell, and mother-of-pearl. A power station in the final carriage supplied the train with electricity, ran its telephones, and regulated individual temperature controls in the compartments. For safety, the train was equipped with both Westinghouse compressed air brakes and Hardy air discharge brakes; there was also a third set of emergency brakes, in the unlikely event that the first two failed.[21]

The first car contained rooms for the escort, composed of ordinary members of the palace protection squad, and officers of the Railway Battalion. The second carriage held the kitchen, a pantry, a wine room, and compartments for the chef, kitchen boys, the butler, and the wine steward. A small anteroom in the third carriage opened to the dining room, decorated with silk brocade set between

The drawing room aboard the imperial train

mahogany panels; blue-gray velvet and satin curtains hung from the carved window pediments, a color repeated in the floral carpet. The ceiling, divided into
white panels, was set with small crystal fixtures and ormolu chandeliers with
frosted glass globes. Sixteen people could dine here, sitting at the oak table in
chairs covered with brown leather. Nicholas usually sat at the middle of the table,
with his daughters and son to either side; Alexandra almost always took her meals
alone, in her boudoir.

The walls of the drawing room, in the fourth carriage, were covered in olive-
colored damask set between mahogany moldings. Art nouveau–style ormolu
chandeliers, sconces, and lamps fitted with silk shades provided light for the
mahogany sofas and chairs, covered in striped green and cream silk. In one corner, atop a green carpet woven with a trellised floral pattern, stood an upright
piano. Compartments for the imperial couple filled the fifth carriage. Nicholas
had a study furnished with a built-in sofa upholstered in dark leather, nestled
between bookcases of Karelian birch. Between the two windows stood his desk,
its surface crowded with a lavish ormolu, crystal, and marble writing set in the
Renaissance style and silver ashtrays and paper knives by Fabergé.[22] The imperial
bedroom, hung in blue silk, held twin brass beds beneath a cluster of icons; the
adjoining bathroom held a sunken tub of copper lined with silver, set into a corner whose ledges prevented water from spilling when the train was in motion.
Alexandra's boudoir, with mauve silk on the walls and furniture of cedar and
Karelian birch, opened to a small dressing room and compartments for the

emperor's valet and the empress's maid.[23] Rooms for the children and members of the empress's suite and household occupied the sixth carriage, while the emperor's suite was housed in the car that followed. Beyond this, two cars were reserved for domestic staff and the imperial luggage; a few years after the train's construction, a church car was added to the end, its chapel richly decorated with an iconostasis and topped with a small belfry whose bell jingled as the train raced across the countryside.[24]

The imperial train required a permanent staff of twenty-six, including electricians, mechanics, four engineers, four valets, four cooks, and a staff manager.[25] In addition, a security detail traveled with the train at all times. "Railway journeys involved a mass of complications," recalled Alexander Mossolov. Before each trip, the inspector of the imperial train surveyed the carriages and personally checked the route to be taken; members of the palace protection squad guarded the imperial family on the train itself, with members of the Railway Battalion dispatched to various points along the route to do sentry duty and sentinels posted at every bridge and tunnel the train would pass.[26] The train always ran at twenty miles an hour, to prevent excess rocking or the possibility of derailment.[27] In addition, both the old and the new imperial trains were sent on every journey to confuse potential assassins. Not surprisingly, security for these trips was terribly expensive, costing some 100,000 rubles, or $1,000,000 in contemporary terms.[28]

Above all, Nicholas II and his family relished their time aboard the imperial yachts. Each June, as the northern sky over St. Petersburg was suffused with the brilliant pearls, blues, and magentas of the famous White Nights, Nicholas, Alexandra, and their five children cruised through the Finnish Skerries, enjoying the simple pleasures of life at sea. The imperial yachts provided the most luxurious means of travel. By the turn of the century, royal yachts were necessities. European sovereigns used them for state visits to fellow monarchs, where they functioned as miniature floating palaces, serving not only for entertainment but also for discreet diplomacy.

In the first year of his reign, Nicholas II had several yachts at his disposal, but he regularly used *Polar Star*. Completed in 1890 for Alexander III, the vessel had cost 3,557,100 rubles—the most expensive private yacht built to that date.[29] *Polar Star* was 337 feet in length, with a displacement of 4,100 tons; during her trials, she managed a cruising speed of just over 17 knots.[30] In design, she resembled a sleek clipper ship. An elongated bowsprit encrusted with gold leaf lengthened her profile, while three masts, flanking the two white funnels, added to the illusion of a sailing vessel. The architects Ippolit Monighetti and Nicholas Nabokov

Standart

had finished her rooms with a variety of rare woods: the drawing room, located aft and lit by large windows and leaded-glass skylights, was the most elaborate apartment, its walls covered in mahogany panels inlaid with ash, oak, walnut, and Karelian birch, while the dining saloon was faced in light Hungarian ash and bird's eye maple.[31] In addition to rooms for the imperial family, the vessel carried a crew of 349, including 19 officers.[32] This sleek yacht, filled with happy memories of life with her beloved husband and children, remained Marie Feodorovna's favorite vessel.

But above all other vessels, Nicholas II preferred *Standart*, commissioned from Copenhagen's Burmeister and Wain Shipyard in 1893. The public rooms were nearly twice as large as those on *Polar Star*, and no expense was spared in its construction. Alexander III died before the ship was finished, and it was not until September 1896 that Nicholas II took possession during a visit to Denmark.[33] By the time construction had finished, *Standart* had cost 4 million rubles; it was the largest, most expensive, and most luxurious private yacht in the world.[34]

Kaiser Wilhelm II, whose smaller white and gold yacht *Hohenzollern* had been converted from a military destroyer, once told Nicholas he would be proud to receive such a fine vessel as a gift. This rather unsubtle hint prompted the dowager empress to write to her son: "I am sure the beautiful lines of *Standart* would be an eyesore to Wilhelm. Still, his joke about how happy he would be if the yacht were given to him was in very doubtful taste. I hope he will not have the cheek to order himself a similar one here, this really would be the limit, though

The dining room aboard *Standart*

just like him.”[35] More diplomatically, the prince of Wales requested plans, and their study certainly influenced the design of the new British royal yacht *Victoria and Albert III*, launched in May of 1899.

Everything about *Standart* was on a massive scale. She was 420 feet in length, 50 feet in breadth, and weighed in at 5,300 tons. Twin screws propelled her through the water at a top speed of 22 knots, fueled by steam and coal.[36] Yet she was extremely graceful and elegant. In appearance, *Standart* resembled a clipper, with a sleek black hull and a jutting bowsprit encrusted with a gilded, double-headed eagle.[37] There were eight main lifeboats and four steam cutters; three tall masts rose from her gleaming teak decks; twin funnels, painted buff, were the only sign that she was indeed a modern ship.

Standart had three principal decks, with two lower decks devoted to service. Behind the flying bridge, the wheelhouse, and the funnel casings, the stern quarter of the upper deck was given over to four formal rooms. First came the Imperial Day Cabin, with windows on two sides. Designed to serve as a combination reception room and study for the emperor, its walls, faced in panels of ash and birch, were hung with family photographs and nautical paintings. A desk, situated beneath a window looking out over the starboard side, held an elaborate

Fabergé desk set, while low bookcases contained some of the emperor's books. It adjoined the Imperial Lobby, paneled in ash and provided with a leather-covered sofa and several chairs; from here, the forward staircase descended to the Forward Corridor on the main deck below.

The dining saloon was situated directly behind the Imperial Day Cabin and the Imperial Lobby, entered through two pairs of doors flanking a large console and a mirror that reflected its length. The mahogany table in the ash-paneled saloon could be extended to accommodate eighty people in simple chairs upholstered in leather. For dinners, places were set with the ship's own china adorned with the imperial standard and double-headed eagles and crystal etched with the Romanov coat of arms and *Standart* in Cyrillic.[38] The wainscot and cornice of the room were undertaken in a darker, contrasting mahogany, while ten large windows on each side filled the room with light. The center of the white ceiling above the dining saloon was raised and set with windows, further flooding the room with light; at intervals hung three crystal and ormolu chandeliers.

From the dining saloon, doors opened to the Aft Lobby, also paneled in ash. The room was kept deliberately simple, its plain carpet strewn with wicker tables and chairs and its walls flanked by a built-in, leather-covered sofa. Beyond the Aft Lobby, doors opened to a small, covered sitting area, with L-shaped wooden benches snuggled against the half walls and to the stern deck. During cruises, white canvas awnings here shaded wicker chairs, tables, and chaises, offering a pleasant, cool retreat from the summer sunshine.

From the Aft Lobby, a staircase, its balustrade of elaborately carved and twisted trelliswork, descended to the Aft Corridor and the imperial cabins on the main deck below. These apartments were all finished in a rich variety of ash, cherry, teak, and birch, with bright English chintzes on the walls, matching fabric for the furniture and curtains, and deep carpets sewn with gold flowers and a pattern of fleur-de-lis. The central Aft Corridor divided the vessel lengthwise, with apartments both port and starboard. Tsesarevich Alexei had a suite of rooms on the port side, with a bathroom, a bedroom, and a sitting room, all decorated in rich woods and chintz fabrics. Although the dowager empress retained use of *Polar Star*, she had her own suite of rooms aboard *Standart*. Situated on the port side of the vessel directly following the tsesarevich's suite, they included a combination wardrobe and bathroom, a bedroom with a brass bed, and a sitting room with a corner fireplace. The bedroom and the adjoining sitting room were hung in a bold floral chintz fabric, which was also used on the upholstered furniture.[39] Later, these rooms were redecorated for Grand Duchesses Olga and Tatiana.

The dowager empress's suite opened to the imperial drawing room, with two large windows piercing the port side of the yacht. Above the walnut wainscot, the walls were hung with floral damask set within walnut moldings. At one end, where the wall of the room curved inward to meet the corridor, nestled a built-in cozy corner topped with shelves, its seats and back upholstered in the same floral damask as the walls. Sofas, tables, and chairs were arranged in comfortable groups beneath the white segmented ceiling hung with ormolu chandeliers; there was even an upright piano, for music at sea. The walls were lined with portraits of foreign relatives, among them Kaiser Wilhelm II.[40]

Beyond the drawing room, members of the imperial family had their private dining room, its walls faced in birch panels between contrasting cherry moldings and lit by three large windows. Up to eighteen people could dine here, seated in walnut chairs with leather seats gathered around the rectangular table. Above, from the segmented white ceiling, hung a ten-light ormolu and crystal chandelier. A small doorway at the forward end opened to a curved staircase that descended to the imperial pantry below, while another doorway led to the Forward Corridor, with a staircase connecting to the Imperial Lobby above.

On the starboard side of the main deck were two apartments, each with a bedroom and an adjoining bathroom, which were used by the two eldest grand duchesses. Beyond them was the emperor's suite. First came his bathroom and his wardrobe room, followed by his bedroom and his study. The bedroom and the study were both adorned with ash and walnut wainscot and trim, framing walls that were hung in light olive glazed cloth. Built-in leather upholstered sofas, topped with open shelves, nestled into the corners of each room, with chairs covered in green leather scattered over the floral carpet. Alexandra's boudoir adjoined Nicholas's study; the walls were hung in mauve chintz, and the same fabric was also used on the built-in sofa and on upholstered chairs. In one corner, nestled against the door opening to the imperial drawing room, was a curved cozy corner topped with shelves. It was, recalled Baroness Buxhoeveden, "full of photographs and snapshots on every available ledge."[41] The empress's bedroom and a small adjoining bathroom completed her suite.

Beyond the Forward Corridor, situated in a paneled passage with large windows open to the engine room below, was a portable chapel. The semicircular iconostasis held six painted icons on either side of the Royal Door opening to the

Nicholas II and his daughters aboard *Standart*, 1912

altar. When members of the imperial family went to sea, Father Dobrovolsky of the Holy Synod joined them, assigned to conduct daily services.[42] When the weather was good, the portable iconostasis would be moved to the upper deck and services held in the open air for the imperial family and the yacht's crew.

Kitchens, pantries for food and wine, galleys, a dining room for the crew, and separate suites of rooms for officers, including their general sitting room and their mess, were scattered across the three decks.[43] In addition to the engine room, boiler rooms, and coal bunkers, the lower decks contained holds for ice and cargo, a distillation plant that could produce sixty tons of hot and cold fresh water daily, and a teak-lined stable for a cow to provide fresh milk.[44] Quarters also housed *Standart*'s 275-person crew, including officers and sailors from the Imperial Navy, cabin boys, stewards, bakers, cooks, kitchen boys, engineers, stokers, and deck hands, along with an entire platoon of the Garde Équipage or the Marine Guard, the men of the ship's brass band, and a special balalaika orchestra. The accommodations for these men, with the exception of the officers, were deep within the hull: cabins with low ceilings crossed with pipes and vents, making them less than ideal. The yacht also had its own wireless room and operator, who maintained constant contact with the government and the ships of the escort.[45]

As modern and impressive as *Standart* was, however, the yacht was forever plagued with an infestation of rats. No amount of cleaning could rid the vessel of the unwelcome creatures, and members of the imperial family simply accustomed themselves to the rats' presence. When Baroness Buxhoeveden first sailed aboard the yacht, she recalled Alexandra warning her to be on guard; if a rat crept into her cabin, the empress declared, the baroness should simply throw a shoe at it.[46]

Each June, the imperial family boarded a tender at Alexandria, Peterhof, and crossed the Gulf of Finland to Kronstadt, where *Standart* lay at anchor just off the naval base. In the weeks before a cruise, the yacht regularly underwent a flurry of activity. Decks were scrubbed and polished, cabins cleaned, furniture reupholstered, and provisions loaded into the hold. The arrival of the imperial family aboard the yacht was always a great occasion, and the Romanovs—especially the four grand duchesses, as Alexander Grabbe recalled—looked forward to their holiday with "joyful anticipation." According to Grabbe, the grand duchesses "loved the sea" and the "intimacy with their beloved father which was otherwise impossible. To be at sea with their father—that was what constituted their happiness."[47]

On those June days when members of the imperial family arrived on their yacht, the ship was dressed, colorful pennants and flags flying from the rigging and waving gently above the glistening teak decks. Below, the entire company of ship's officers and crew, clad in bright white uniforms, stood in rows along the railings. As the tender pulled alongside, the imperial family was piped aboard. At the precise moment the emperor set foot upon the deck, the band of the Garde Equipage struck up "God Save the Tsar," and the entire company saluted. The emperor was received by the captain and the senior officers, passing down the line to receive their salutes. When Tsesarevich Alexei was older, he usually accompanied the emperor, marching along the deck as the men stood rigidly at attention. They were followed by the empress, invariably clad in a long white gown and a picture hat or a parasol as protection against the sun. As she passed along the rows, she offered her hand to each man, who bent forward to kiss it, a practice they continued as the four grand duchesses walked behind her. As soon as the formal reception had ended, the captain gave the orders for steam. With a barely discernible roar, the twin screws began their motion, gradually easing the yacht astern and away from the safety of Kronstadt harbor. Once the graceful vessel had floated into the deeper waters of the gulf, she slid away from the naval base, churning a thin spit of white foam in her wake as she disappeared into the horizon.

The men in charge of *Standart* enjoyed especially close relationships with the imperial family. The yacht had a permanent assignment of seventeen officers, led first by Captain Neverovsky who, on his retirement in 1912, was replaced with Captain Chaguin.[48] Chaguin held the post for less than a year; that October, he committed suicide after his seduction of a young girl threatened to cause a scandal.[49] Captain Rostislav Zelenetsky replaced Chaguin. Born in 1865, Zelenetsky had joined the Garde Équipage in 1886 and was one of the first officers assigned to the new *Standart* on its maiden voyage in 1896. Appointed a senior officer on the imperial yacht in 1903, he remained attached to the vessel until his elevation to commander.[50] Zelenetsky was assisted by Nicholas Sablin and by another senior officer from the Garde Équipage, Knüpffer. Rear-Admirals Lomen and Nilov served as the emperor's flag-captains, responsible for the security arrangements aboard the yacht.[51] Konstantin Nilov, wrote one contemporary observer, "is devoted to the Emperor, and when in men's society he can be very amusing and has a remarkable fund of funny stories. Always known as a woman hater, his unexpected marriage some years ago caused no little amazement

Nicholas II and his children aboard *Standart*, 1912

in society."[52] In contrast, Lomen was regarded as something of a tyrant. Alexander Mossolov later recalled that "the entire Naval Administration stood in mortal fear" of him. "It is true that he asked a great deal, and if he was annoyed, he could be extremely rude." Lomen was fond of boasting that as soon as the emperor set foot on the yacht, Nicholas II himself "was under his orders," though once off duty, Lomen was, Mossolov remembered, "pleasant and sociable."[53]

Of this group, two men were particularly close to the imperial family. Lieutenant Paul Voronov, born in 1888, was the scion of a noble family from Kostroma; when he joined the crew of *Standart*, he soon became one of the children's favorite companions, joining the young grand duchesses in excursions and serving as a tennis partner during their games ashore. Olga Nikolaievna quickly fell in love with the tall, handsome Voronov, confiding her longings to her diary. Aware of the growing attraction and unwilling to see the situation continue, Nicholas and Alexandra urged Voronov to marry Countess Kleinmichel's niece, Olga, in 1914.[54] Born in 1880, Nicholas Sablin was a tall, thin man with a dashing little mustache and a charming manner. A graduate of the Imperial Naval Academy, he had served on a cruiser in the Russo-Japanese War before joining the Garde Équipage in 1906. Appointed a *fligel-adjutant* in 1912, he joined *Standart* as senior officer the same year. A great favorite of the empress, he accompanied members of the imperial family on their annual cruises and also acted as a trusted companion to the grand duchesses.[55]

When the children boarded the yacht, each was assigned a dyadya, a sailor charged with looking after them. At the end of each cruise, these sailors were presented by the emperor with a gold watch, in recognition for their services.[56] Grabbe noted that "the relationship of the Imperial Family to its entourage was very friendly and informal. It was especially cordial with the officers of *Standart*. These young men were exemplary—charming, modest, possessed of a great deal of dignity and tact, and incapable of any intrigue."[57]

Life aboard *Standart* stood in deliberate contrast to the rigid etiquette of the imperial court. "All possible formality was dispensed with," Baroness Buxhoeveden noted, "and the Court led a simple life, in which the officers of the yacht took part."[58] Nicholas invited officers to dine with his family and join them in games of dominoes. "On such occasions," Grabbe recalled, "the Empress usually sat nearby, sewing, the Tsesarevich ran about with his playmates, while the Grand Duchesses, surrounded by all the young men, scattered throughout the yacht." It was a privileged glimpse into the intimate life of their sovereigns. "We form a united family," the empress would happily remark while observing the scene.[59]

Twice weekly, wherever the ship might be, tenders scurried over the waters, carrying state papers for the emperor's attention; otherwise, Nicholas was left alone.[60]

An escort of destroyers dispatched by the Imperial Navy shadowed *Standart* wherever she went, to protect the emperor and his family, but even they could not avert disaster. On August 29, 1907, the yacht was cruising through the Ganko Archipelago near Horso off the Finnish coast, guided by a local pilot, Captain Libek, when she struck a submerged rock, buckling plates in her hull.[61] The empress's friend, Anna Vyrubova, recalled, "We were seated on deck at tea, the band playing, a perfectly calm sea running, when we felt a terrible shock which shook the yacht from stem to stern and sent the tea service crashing to the deck. In great alarm we sprang to our feet, only to feel the yacht listing sharply to starboard. In an instant the decks were alive with sailors obeying the harsh commands of the captain, and helping the suite to look to the safety of the women and children."[62]

With every passing minute, *Standart* took on more water, her list progressing and making it imperative that she be abandoned. "The Empress," recalled Baroness Buxhoeveden, "was always resourceful and full of energy and never lost her head in face of danger. She arranged that the children and the ladies' maids should be first lowered into the boats."[63] As soon as her children were safe, Alexandra grabbed Anna Vyrubova and ran below. Stripping sheets from the beds, the two women piled precious icons, scrapbooks, family photographs, and important souvenirs into makeshift bundles, tied them together, then carried them to the lifeboats to be saved.[64]

Throughout, the emperor stood at the rail. Every few seconds, he leaned over to look at the waterline and the numbers painted on the bow and then again turned to his pocket watch. To Princess Elizabeth Obolensky, he explained that he meant to remain on board until the very last minute and was trying to determine how long the ship had left. The situation seemed hopeless, and Nicholas announced grimly that he expected *Standart* would only stay afloat for another twenty minutes.[65] Alexandra was the last woman to leave the yacht. With Anna Vyrubova at her side, she stepped into the unsteady lifeboat, watching intently as the sailors on deck lowered away until it had reached the water.[66]

After some minutes, however, it became obvious that the watertight bulkheads would hold, and Nicholas II reluctantly left the wounded vessel. The Finnish pilot boat *Ellekeinen* witnessed the incident and collected passengers from the lifeboats, transferring them to the Russian cruiser *Asia* as soon as it arrived. "Happily," recalled Buxhoeveden, "no one suffered from anything but great discomfort and agitation. But had the seas been high, the matter would have been serious, for the yacht would undoubtedly have sunk and the boats were very full."[67] Conditions aboard *Asia* were cramped. Alexandra and Alexei shared the captain's cabin, while Nicholas took a small officer's cabin on deck. "The little Grand Duchesses were crowded in a cabin by themselves," recalled Vyrubova, "their nurses and attendants finding beds where they could. The ship was far from clean, and I remember the Emperor, rather disheveled, himself bringing basins of water to the Empress and me in which to wash our faces and hands. We had some kind of a dinner about midnight and none of us passed an especially restful night."[68] *Standart* was soon pulled off the rocks, towed to a shipyard, and repaired in time for the following summer's cruise.[69]

Life aboard the yacht followed its own pleasant routine. Nicholas generally awoke early, visiting the bridge, where he consulted with the captain on the day's route.[70] He frequently suggested changes of course in order to take in some particularly favorite isolated bay or remote fishing spot. He also regularly made the rounds of the crew, inspecting the yacht and greeting members of the company; occasionally, he would be presented with sailors' rations, tasting each dish before approving what the galleys produced below. Nicholas was everywhere on the vessel, walking the decks, smoking and chatting with the officers, or playing shuffleboard and games of dominoes with them.

The empress, Anastasia, Alexei, and Marie enjoy a picnic during a trip ashore to Finland while cruising aboard *Standart*, 1910

"Generally," wrote Baroness Buxhoeveden, "these cruises were limited to that part of the coast that lies between Kronstadt and Helsinki, for the Emperor had to be within easy reach of his government. A favorite place of anchorage was the lonely bay at Pitkopas, near Bjorke."[71] The spot, a secluded cove of deep blue water dotted with small islands and surrounded by rocky granite outcroppings and a shielding forest of pine and birch, was soon dubbed "the Bay of *Standart*" and became a regular stop on summer cruises.[72] There were, Buxhoeveden recalled, "no houses in sight. Dark forests stretched far into the mainland, and here were hidden a few lonely fishermen's huts. The transparent waters were still and quiet in the wonderful White Nights of May and June, when the light of one day lasted long till the dawn of the next."[73]

Many afternoons, with *Standart* at anchor in the secluded Finnish fjord, the imperial family, along with several officers and members of the crew, boarded tenders and smaller boats and left the yacht for their private sanctuary. At the edge of the sandy beach, *Standart*'s crew had built a long wooden pier, allowing the imperial party to come ashore safely. As soon as the emperor landed, the Imperial Standard was hoisted atop a tall pole that rose from the end of a wide, open meadow. Here, the yacht's crew had built a wooden court, along with several rustic pavilions shaded with striped awnings, where the imperial family could play tennis and picnic. The emperor and his children foraged through the forest for mushrooms and berries or swam in shallow coves while Alexandra lay on carpets spread across the beach, reading and watching her family at play. Occasionally, Nicholas, joined by members of his Suite and some of the yacht's officers, took to the woods to shoot or hunt for a few hours, or he raced his crew in rowboats and kayaks from the yacht.[74] Large wicker baskets containing sandwiches, bread and butter, pastries, tea, and wine were brought ashore from the ship, and the family took tea sitting along the sandy beaches or beneath the sheltering pines.[75]

Occasionally, there were visitors to this secluded sanctuary. On July 23, 1912, *Polar Star* slowly steamed into the Finnish waters, dropping anchor next to *Standart*. It was, in the Russian Orthodox Church, the name day for both Marie Feodorovna and her granddaughter Grand Duchess Marie. The dowager empress, accompanied by her youngest daughter, Olga Alexandrovna, had come to share the family holiday with her son. Attired in a long white skirt and a jacket and shaded from the summer sun by a large black picture hat adorned with ostrich feathers, the dowager empress was escorted to the meadow. There she joined her daughter-in-law Alexandra in watching the emperor, partnered with

Anna Vyrubova, take on officers from *Standart* in a game of tennis while Olga Alexandrovna romped with her four nieces along the beach. At the end of the afternoon, the party returned to *Standart* for an early dinner, followed by dancing under the shade of awnings stretched over the aft promenade deck. The four grand duchesses, clad in white summer dresses and hats, circled the deck, their smiles caught in the flickering images of an early home movie. Just before sunset, the dowager empress and Olga Alexandrovna returned to *Polar Star*, this rare family holiday at its end.[76]

Alexandra enjoyed these holidays. "She had loved the sea from childhood," wrote Baroness Buxhoeveden, "and the greatest pleasure she had was when the Imperial Family was on their yacht, cruising in Finnish Waters."[77] While Nicholas was occupied with his official duties and the children played or had lessons, Alexandra sat on deck knitting, reading, or writing, or she played the piano in the drawing room, often singing duets with Anna Vyrubova. "We spent hours playing four-hand pieces," Anna recalled, "all our early loved classics, Bach, Beethoven, Tchaikovsky and others. The Empress had a lovely contralto voice, which, had she been born in other circumstances, might easily have given her a professional standing."[78]

Returning to the yacht after long, lazy days ashore, the imperial family gathered on deck for evening prayers at sunset, sung by the choir of the Garde Équipage as the Imperial Standard was lowered.[79] "The Empress loved the long, still days," recalled Baroness Buxhoeveden, "the bright, moonlight nights on the water, the evening prayer of the sailors on deck before the lowering of the flag, when the last rays of the setting sun rested in the sea, on the woods, and on the escorting ships, while the deep voices of the men, singing the Lord's Prayer, echoed far away into the silence."[80] By eleven o'clock, the lights on deck had been extinguished, and members of the imperial family had retired to their staterooms below, watching from their portholes as the sky danced with the pinks, blues, and reds of the northern lights.[81]

After the Revolution, *Standart* was confiscated by the new regime, was renamed *Vosemnadtsat Marta*, and served as a training ship for the fledgling Soviet Navy. In 1932, she was again refitted as a minelayer in Leningrad and renamed *Marti*. This time, her superstructure was gutted, and her formerly elegant profile and clean lines disrupted with the introduction of gun turrets and mine stores. During the Second World War, *Marti* prowled the Gulf of Finland, laying mines and engaging in heavy artillery action against the Nazi forces. After the war, she was again refitted, this time as a training ship named *Oka*. For the next twenty years, thousands of young Soviet sailors thundered over her formerly elegant teak decks, where Nicholas and Alexandra had entertained Kaiser Wilhelm II and King Edward VII. In 1963, the Soviet Navy, deciding that she had outlived her usefulness, finally ordered the former *Standart* scrapped at a yard at Tallinn in Estonia.[82]

18

COUNTRY ESTATES

SINCE HIS EARLIEST DAYS, NICHOLAS II had nursed an intense passion for physical exercise and outdoor activity. As a young man, he spent every free hour walking, riding, or rowing in the imperial parks at Gatchina and Peterhof. In the winter, when he and his family returned to the capital, he led his brothers and sisters on ice-skating parties and sledding expeditions; he hated nothing so much as being confined indoors by ill health or inclement weather. Shortly after Nicholas became tsesarevich, his father presented him with his first gun and took his eldest son shooting for crows and small game in the forests surrounding St. Petersburg. Nicholas loved country life, and, as emperor, he had ample opportunity to indulge his passion. Like every other wealthy aristocrat, the emperor retired each year to one of his country estates to holiday, to shoot, fish, hunt, and stalk game.

In 1857, Alexander II had moved the Imperial Hunt from Peterhof to Gatchina, and thereafter the forests were carefully stocked with game for the emperor's amusement. Prince Dimitri Golitsyn, the master of the Imperial Hunt, supervised the estates and the employees attached to them, carefully tending stock and nurturing the wildlife. One English visitor recalled the "mass of buildings" at Gatchina: "the stables and kennels, and all the appurtenance belonging to the sport of kings. I was most kindly entertained and shown over it all, and thought myself fortunate to see what few have seen." Flying through the snowy forest, she noted "plenty of deer—red, fallow, and roe; a few pheasants; some hares that turn white in winter; and flights of woodcock that passed over every evening at sunset." Here, Golitsyn maintained a pack of sixty borzois for hunting wolves, along with a pen filled with wild brown bear cubs, savagely used for baiting the dogs and training them in their pursuit through the forests.[1]

As emperor, Nicholas II maintained three country estates in Poland, encompassing many thousands of acres, although these were visited only rarely. Visits took place only in the fall; in the spring, when the bucks were in velvet, the gamekeepers carefully fed and nurtured the herds, awaiting the rut and the arrival of the imperial party. According to custom, Nicholas normally spent only a few days at Skernevetski, a rather severe palace that had been purchased by Emperor Alexander I. Most of his time in Poland was divided between the other two lodges, Bielovezh and Spala.

Skernevetski stood in a large park on the outskirts of Warsaw. The former country estate of a Catholic archbishop, the house—originally built in 1463—had been altered over the centuries into an elaborate, neoclassical jewel, surrounded by a large English-style park with an artificial lake and carefully placed glades dominated by groups of classical statuary. In 1820, Alexander I purchased the estate for his brother Grand Duke Konstantin Pavlovich, who served as governor-general of Poland, and the architect Carlo Rossi made extensive renovations to the Bishop's Palace. Eleven years later, Nicholas I signed the estate over to the imperial Crown, and thereafter it was used as not only a hunting lodge but also as the emperor's official Polish residence. In the reign of Alexander III, Skernevetski played host to an important meeting of the emperors of Russia, Germany, and Austria-Hungary. By the beginning of Nicholas II's reign, the former country estate was surrounded by the urban sprawl of Warsaw, and the emperor confined his stays to short periods, preferring to spend his holidays in the countryside.[2]

The imperial estate of Bielovezh stood some 150 miles northeast of Warsaw, near Brest-Litovsk. Bielovezhskaya Pushcha, as the compound was called, had long been a favorite retreat for hunting. In the fifteenth century, Lithuanian dukes had built a lodge here, and in the following centuries, the kings of Poland occupied the property. Alexander I purchased the estate in 1803, but it was Alexander II who first came here in 1860, drawn by the ample game available in the surrounding forests. Bounded and cleaved by the Lesnaya, Belaya, Hwozna, and Narewka Rivers, Bielovezh consisted of a quarter-million acres of carefully maintained primeval forest, offering the finest shoot in Europe.[3]

At the time of Alexander II's visit, only a wooden manor house, built by the governor of Grodno Province, stood in the preserve. In 1889, Alexander III commissioned the architect Count Nicholas de Rochefort to design a new residence more suited to the demands of the imperial court. The architect selected a spot called Oak Hill, a small mound marked by four ancient trees; the site was leveled in 1890 and, five years later, the lodge stood completed, a massive, picturesque structure standing sentinel over an enveloping fringe of forest.[4]

The palace at Bielovezh

From the end of the small village, a sandy road ended abruptly at a redbrick gatehouse topped by a steep roof and flanked by guards standing erect in their striped sentry boxes. Beyond, a paved drive curved through dense stretches of pine, evergreen, and birch trees, between banks of fragrant summer roses to the depths of the estate. At the edge of the wood, the trees parted to reveal a glade, the road gently sweeping up Oak Hill to meet a piece of eclectic romanticism as the new lodge dominated the landscape. Nicholas de Rochefort had designed a striking, multi-storeyed building, the monotonous length of its redbrick facade relieved by horizontal bands of yellow bricks, gray stone window lintels, and alternating projections and inset bays. Resting on a stone terrace, the lodge was crowned with deeply overhanging carved wooden cornices resting on curved brackets that in turn supported tall, steeply pitched metal roofs dotted with gables and peaked dormer windows. Above, gilded wrought-iron railings followed the intricate roofline, further adding to the building's height. Loggias and overhanging wooden balconies angled out from wings and gables, and two tall, spidery towers thrust themselves upward from the eastern and the western ends of the building. The taller, circular one on the southwestern side of the lodge rose to an open wooden gallery on the fourth floor, from which the emperor and his guests could view the rolling preserve, beneath a tall, steep conical roof topped with a gilded double-headed eagle.[5]

The driveway on the northern side led to an immense porte cochere resting on stone piers that had sweeping carved wooden brackets. Double doors of oak, embellished with inlays of polished, blackened iron adorned with red copper, opened to the hall, which spanned the width of the lodge. A large staircase of maple and birch ascended to a columned gallery that circled above. Enormous plate glass windows and French doors overlooked the southern terrace, with its wide, semicircular sweep of steps descending to the park. Much of the wood used in the interior came from the surrounding forest, and the rooms were decorated with inlaid brass, beaten copper, and polished metal chandeliers and sconces. The new lodge contained 134 rooms spread over two floors, making it only slightly smaller than the Alexander Palace at Tsarskoye Selo. The drawing room, paneled in ash, was adorned with bearskin rugs and mounted animal heads. The walls of the immense dining room were decorated in contrasting wainscoting and carved panels of maple and birch, set between slender columns that supported inlaid arches and arcades. From the beams of the coffered wooden ceiling hung beaten copper and crystal chandeliers; below, the thirty-foot-long mahogany table could be extended to comfortably seat a hundred guests in the carved, leather-upholstered chairs. Throughout the new building, rooms were paneled in mahogany, yew, birch, ash, oak, and maple; hung with bright English chintzes; and furnished with overstuffed sofas and chairs lurking behind banks of potted palms.[6]

The emperor's reception room opened to a billiard room, its walls hung with hunting trophies and Russian landscapes and lit by a copper chandelier above the English billiards table. The second floor held a number of suites, incorporated into the building at the request of Alexander III: each set of apartments consisted of a sitting room, a bedroom, a dressing room, a wardrobe, and a bathroom, and each was finished in a different style. The walls of the emperor's suite, on the southern side of the lodge overlooking the lake, were hung in English chintz patterned with rushes and flowers.[7] Nicholas II, who first visited the lodge in 1894 when still tsesarevich, wrote in his diary: "Its position on top of a hill is absolutely beautiful." He found that the rooms had been decorated with "simplicity, taste and comfort. . . . I have four delightful rooms—almost too luxurious. . . . Sank with delight into the enormous heavenly bath, like a swimming pool, next to my bedroom."[8]

Surrounding the lodge were a number of smaller buildings, including houses for members of the Suite, the Entourage, and the Household; a lodge for the imperial huntsmen; two bathhouses; a wooden dacha that served as a tea pavilion; a small Russian Orthodox Church; an extensive stable for forty horses; kennels; and a power plant at the edge of the Narewka River, hidden from the lodge by a screen of trees. The landscape architect Valery Kronenberg laid out the garden, preserving the 400-year old maple and elm trees and damming the Hwozna River to create a large artificial lake that mirrored the new lodge in its surface. Graveled walks led through glens of pine, oak, spruce, and linden to sunken flower gardens and picturesque memorials. At the end of the Royal Allée stood an obelisk commemorating a spectacular shoot given by King Augustus III of Poland in 1752, during which fifty-seven animals had been brought down.[9]

Despite its magnificent situation and luxurious rooms, Bielovezh was rarely used. In the twenty-three years of Nicholas's reign, the imperial family stayed there only five times: in 1897, 1900, 1903, 1906, and 1912. Other members of the dynasty, including Grand Duke Vladimir and his family, occasionally used the lodge, but it was more often sadly ignored.[10] Even when members of the imperial family came to Poland, they were often forced to abandon these private holidays: at various points during his reign, Nicholas was joined by Kaiser Wilhelm II and the emperor of Austria, as well as by members of his own, and his wife's, family. The emperor would receive a delegation of local Polish nobles for a day of hunting, followed by a ceremonial dinner. During visits, a regiment of Grodno Hussars, with their colorful green, amaranth, and silver uniforms, or the Warsaw Lancers, in yellow and blue tunics, patrolled the park and served as extra hands on shoots.[11]

Bielovezh offered a number of sporting pleasures: there was fishing for salmon and trout in the rivers flowing through the estate; hunting for wolf, wild boar, and bear; shooting for pheasant, duck, hare, partridge, and woodcock; and stalking for red deer, elk, and moose. These expeditions were as carefully choreographed as an exquisite ballet. In the dim blue light of a late-summer morning, as the lodge slumbered against the long shadows and pale mist hung over the encircling meadows, dozens of men, their faces etched with disturbed sleep, filled the yard surrounding the stables and kennels. Hoofs crunched across gravel and wheels rattled over cobbles as Mitrophane Golenko, the proctor at Bielovezh, prepared for the day's excursion. By seven, when sunlight danced against the tall windows of the lodge, he had taken his place outside the main entrance, sounding his horn to summon the emperor and his guests to the day's hunt. As they filtered out of the villa, they boarded waiting carriages that sped them into the dark forest. By imperial decree,

only stags of ten or more points could be shot. The emperor disliked shooting at groups of game driven by beaters, once expressing his fear that in bringing his target down, he might also wound one of his men.

For shoots, the emperor and his guests, accompanied by a number of loaders, took up their positions at the edges of a forest glade. The proctor offered the men a black velvet bag, from which they all drew lots to pick the positions of their stands. Nicholas always had two loaders for his guns, while the other shots each had one loader.[12] As each drive progressed, the morning silence was shattered by the crack of repeated shots. From the rustling thickets and low-hanging foliage, one bird, then another, would speed toward the sky, only to be brought down against the incessant barking of the dogs that raced to retrieve the fallen prizes. Nicholas was an excellent shot; after one occasion, he recorded, "The hunting was very successful: in all, we bagged 879 things. My tally was 115: 21 partridges, 91 pheasants, a white hare, and two rabbits."[13] His single largest shoot was 1,400 pheasants.[14]

The highlight of the stay at Bielovezh was the hunt for aurochs, or European bison. By the turn of the century, these magnificent animals had almost become extinct; only eight hundred remained in Poland and in the Caucasus.[15] Alexander III instituted a program to guard the breed, and gamekeepers carefully nurtured and fed the wild herd at Bielovezh to provide the emperor and his guests with this rarest of all trophies. Only a few could be brought down each season; by the beginning of the First World War, the number of aurochs had reached some sixteen hundred.[16] One witness at a hunt for aurochs recalled, "A *battue* of between 1,500 and 2,000 peasants and guns is assembled, it covers an area of the forest . . . where advance reconnaissance has discovered the presence of adult Aurochs. If during this they come upon a herd of cows with young calves, the keepers remove them from the drive beforehand. To be as sure as possible of holding the Aurochs in, they light fires all around and keep them burning until the end of the hunt. The military Governor-General of the region nearly always participates in the hunt with a large number of units and lovers of the sport, for whom they make a particularly elevated booth hidden with firs and other tree branches. They decide on a given number of shots and mark them on the trees that the hunters have no right to leave. The other peasants and shooters should have guns with blank cartridges. When everything is ready, a shot is fired as a signal for the drive to start."[17]

At midday, a small convoy of carriages and sleds left the main lodge, carrying folding tables, chairs, carpets, and baskets of food and wine. Alexandra often

Spala.
See plate 36.

accompanied their guests' wives when they went to join their husbands for lunch in the forest. Footmen threw large Oriental carpets across the pine needles, constructing the collapsible table and camp chairs on them. An imperial picnic in the forest did not lack elegance: butlers spread white linen cloths over the tables, setting each place with china, crystal, and silver. The emperor's guests dined on roasted venison, pig, fowl, pickled tongue, onions, caviar, black bread, sauerkraut, toasted mushrooms, cakes, pastries, and wild berries, all washed down with vintage sherry, hock, red wine, and port from the imperial cellars as a brass band or a balalaika orchestra serenaded them.[18]

At the end of a few weeks, the emperor and his family traveled to Spala, the third of the imperial hunting estates in Poland. Here, in 1511, the Spalov family built a grinding mill along the banks of the Pilitsa River, near the village of Rava in the Petrokovsky District; a century later, the kings of Poland confiscated the land as a hunting estate. When Poland was forcibly incorporated into the Russian empire, the Spala estate, as it had come to be called, was largely abandoned, its forests left to encroach on the old wooden lodge that had stood in a clearing for nearly two hundred years. It was Nicholas I who purchased the estate for the imperial Crown. Although it was an older, more stable reserve than Bielovezh, Spala was much smaller, with less acreage and less variety of game, but its isolation greatly appealed to Alexander III. In 1874, when he was still tsesarevich, he first came to Spala to hunt while on a visit to Bielovezh. A year after he became emperor, Alexander commissioned the Krakow architect Leon Mikuckiego to design and build a new lodge to accommodate his family and their guests. Mikuckiego selected a grassy glade at the edge of the surrounding forest, ringed on three sides by the long, low waters of the Pilitsa River and a vista of flat meadows and marshes. He supervised the contingent of Polish craftsmen who built the new lodge using traditional methods of construction and decorative details drawn from local models. Work continued for two years, and, by the autumn of 1884, the lodge was ready to receive the imperial family.

A long road, fringed by thick groves of evergreen, spruce, fir, and pine trees, led through the forest and across a long wooden bridge over the Pilitsa River to the clearing where the lodge nestled against the green forest wall. Resembling a large Swiss chalet, Spala was a long, forty-room, two-storeyed building with projecting gabled bays, wrapped in polychrome brickwork and adorned with ornate, twisted wooden columns and carved windowsills that relieved the otherwise somber exterior. Most of the ground floor was given over to reception and drawing rooms, inevitably hung with mounted animal heads and adorned with stuffed birds and bearskin rugs. A small reception room, paneled in oak with inset panels of ash, was decorated with vases from the Imperial Porcelain Factory and contained two chairs made from stags' horns. It opened to the drawing room, with white wainscoting and simple overstuffed sofas and chairs covered in bright English chintz. The emperor's study was faced in knotty pine and furnished with sofas covered with oriental throws. The dining room, painted white and simply furnished with a long table and leather-upholstered chairs, occupied one wing; French doors opened to a covered porch, strewn with wicker chairs and tables. A narrow wooden staircase, its walls lined with elk, deer, and moose heads and antlers, ascended to the second floor, divided in half by a long, low corridor so dark that even in the middle of the day, the electric lights had to be left on. It was all oppressively planned, a collection of unfortunate rooms that offered little in the way of beauty or comfort. Alexandra tried to enliven these rooms, opening up windows that had long been shuttered and covering the walls with bright English chintzes, but the effect remained depressing. Anna Vyrubova called Spala "one of the dampest, gloomiest places" she had ever seen.[19]

Surrounding the lodge, Mikuckiego erected a number of service buildings for members of the Suite and the Household, along with a barracks for the troops of the Cossack Konvoi Regiment. Taking advantage of the Pilitsa River, he built a small dam, whose waterfall fed a power station tucked behind a grove of trees that provided the electricity so necessary to the dim rooms. Until 1899, the lodge was without running water; Nicholas II solved this dilemma by ordering a reservoir dug and linked by a series of viaducts to a tall brick tower housing new machinery to supply the estate with rudimentary plumbing.

It is not surprising that members of the imperial family chose to spend most of their time at Spala out of doors. From the sloping lawn, the Pilitsa River swept its fresh mountain waters into the dark forests, with half a dozen tiny streams leading off in different directions. An English-style park was laid out around the villa, with trees imported from the Caucasus. Small rustic bridges crossed the waterways, leading to sanded paths cut through the groves of fir and pine trees. Wild mushrooms grew in abundance at Spala; one woodland path was called the Road of Mushrooms, for it ended some distance from the lodge at a clearing with a bench surrounded by thousands of mushrooms.[20] "The woods are magnificent," Nicholas wrote to Queen Victoria, "and the trees grow up to a huge height. Some places in that forest remind me so much of the Indian jungles, except that we have no creeping plants. This place is very dry and though there are many woods about, still it is a more open country, rather sandy."[21]

Nicholas II improved the hunting facilities, founding a stud along with a farm, where deer were specially bred for eventual release into the forests. The stud and the farm fell under the direction of Count Vladislav Velepolsky, the director of the imperial estates in Poland. It was Velepolsky who arranged hunts for the emperor and his guests far in advance of the imperial family's arrival. While the emperor hunted, the empress rode or drove her four-in-hand through the forest. Although she had often joined in the fishing and stalking activities while staying with her grandmother Queen Victoria at Balmoral Castle in the Scottish Highlands, Alexandra disliked blood sports and preferred to devote herself to more peaceful pursuits. There was a clay tennis court at Spala, and the empress often watched games between her guests and her children. Some afternoons, the emperor abandoned his hunting and joined his wife for walks through the forest, following paths that wove through the groves of evergreen and pine to benches where they could enjoy the view over the dam.

Each evening, at the end of the day's shoot or hunt, the gamekeepers at Spala, after carefully weighing and logging the bag into the Moroccan-leather estate books with illuminated pages, laid out the catch on the front lawn of the lodge. The emperor, the empress, and their guests inspected the dead animals, the scene lit by flaming torches. Dinners were largely casual affairs. By imperial tradition, anyone in the shooting party who had bagged a stag on the first or the last day of the hunt was asked to drink a whole bottle of champagne from a large stag's horn. One night during each stay, members of the local Polish nobility were invited to dinner with the emperor, during which the game of the day was served and scenes from plays were acted on a makeshift stage by the young grand duchesses.[22]

It was at Spala, in the autumn of 1912, that Tsesarevich Alexei nearly died. A week earlier, when the imperial family had been at Bielovezh, Alexei had slipped "from an awkward movement he made while jumping into a boat," as his father noted.[23] Doctors found a swelling just below the groin, and for several days, the tsesarevich was in considerable pain. By the end of the week, however, he seemed to have recovered, and the family moved on to Spala. For the first few days at Spala, Alexei seemed lethargic. Thinking an excursion would do her son good, the empress ordered a carriage and, with the tsesarevich and Anna Vyrubova, set off down the uneven, sandy road into the forest. Within a few minutes, however, Alexei complained that he was unwell; the bumps had dislodged the clot, and he was hemorrhaging internally. "That return drive," wrote

Anna Vyrubova, "stands out in my mind as an experience in horror. Every move-ment of the carriage, every rough place in the road, caused the child the most exquisite torture, and by the time we reached home, the boy was almost uncon-scious with pain."[24]

Botkin found that the swelling had dislodged itself; the tsesarevich's upper left thigh had turned an ugly purple, as blood flowed into the joints near the groin. Professor Serge Fedorov cabled St. Petersburg, asking that specialists come at once to the remote lodge, but there was little they could do. Within a day, Alexei's temperature had risen dramatically; the blood flowed from torn vessels into the lower abdomen, forming a swelling the size of a small grapefruit. In pain, Alexei drew his left leg up, allowing the excess of fluid more space, but, eventually, there was no more room, and the pressure became unbearable.

Screams pierced the walls of the villa, mournful, agonizing wails of pain cou-pled with gasps for breath.[25] Servants and members of the Suite were forced to stuff their ears with cotton in order to continue their work. "During the entire time," recalled Anna Vyrubova, "the Empress never undressed, never went to bed, rarely even laid down for an hour's rest. Hour after hour, she sat beside the bed where the half conscious child lay huddled on one side, his left leg drawn up."[26] Alexandra sat beside her son's bed, holding his hand, kissing him, wiping the sweat from his forehead, and praying for the life of her son, as he screamed out, "Mama, help me!" But there was nothing she could do but listen as Alexei begged to be allowed to die, asking plaintively, "When I am dead it will not hurt anymore, will it Mama?"[27] During one lucid moment, the eight-year-old boy asked his parents to build him a monument in the forest after he was gone.[28] It was unbearable, impotent torture.

But life at Spala continued. With Alexei's hemophilia a carefully guarded secret, no one knew what was wrong with him, and the emperor and the empress entertained groups of Polish nobles at teas and dinners.[29] "The dinners in the company of their Suite," recalled Princess Elizabeth Naryshkin-Kuryakin, "con-tinued as before, the same meaningless conversations were held, and the Emperor went shooting as if nothing were happening. This manner of hiding every manifestation of emotion or excitement was also taught to the children."[30] One evening, Grand Duchesses Marie and Anastasia performed two scenes from Molière's *Bourgeois Gentilhomme* for a room of assembled guests. Watching from the wings of the makeshift stage, Pierre Gilliard noticed the empress sitting in the front row, laughing and smiling as she chatted with her guests. A few minutes later, he saw her rush past him, face set and eyes wide, down a corridor and into Alexei's room, following the sound of his low moans. When she reappeared in the drawing room, the empress was again genial, exchanging pleasantries with the assembled crowd.[31]

This terrible charade came to an abrupt end on October 6, when Professor Fedorov announced that Alexei's stomach was hemorrhaging; the tsesarevich, he warned, might well die. Only then did Nicholas and Alexandra consent to the publication of regular medical bulletins on their son's condition; for the first time, Russia learned that the heir to the throne was gravely ill, though the bulletins made no mention of his hemophilia. Across the empire, churches and cathedrals were thronged as special services were held to pray for Alexei's recovery. There was no church at Spała; instead, a green canvas tent, erected on the front lawn of the villa, witnessed the prayers of members of the Suite and the Household.[32]

On October 8, Alexei's condition was so grave that no one thought he would survive the night. Nicholas and Alexandra knelt at his bedside as a priest began the Last Rites of the Orthodox Church.[33] The medical bulletin, already prepared for release the following day, announced his death. In those terrible hours, the empress sent a cable to Rasputin, pleading with him to pray for the life of her son. The answer came early the next morning: "The Little One will not die."[34] Clutching the cable, Alexandra burst into a meeting between her husband and Count Velepolsky, her face lit with an exhausted smile. "The doctors," she told them, "notice no improvement yet, but I am not the least bit anxious myself now. During the night I received a telegram from Father Gregory, and he has reassured me completely."[35] And, indeed, within twenty-four hours, the hemorrhage stopped. Alexei lay pale and wasted, but alive.

In a letter to Bishop William Boyd-Carpenter, Alexandra described the ordeal: "It was a terrible time we went through, and to see his fearful suffering was heartrending—but he was of an *angelic* patience and never complained at being ill—he would only make the Sign of the Cross and beg God to help him, groaning and moaning from pain. In the Orthodox Church one gives children Holy Communion, so twice we let him have that joy, and the poor, thin little face with its big suffering eyes lit up with blessed happiness as the Priest approached him with the Sacrament. It was such comfort to us all and we too had the same joy—without trust and faith implicit in God Almighty's great wisdom and ineffable love, one could not bear the heavy crosses sent one."[36]

Alexei's recovery was slow, though after a few weeks he ventured out in a pony cart. An early autumn snow had cloaked the surrounding forest in a blanket of white by the time the imperial family left Poland. As a measure of safety, Alexandra ordered all of the roads hand-smoothed, and the imperial train back to St. Petersburg crawled along at a mere fifteen miles an hour to avoid any unexpected jolts.[37] The following year, the Romanovs did not return to Spala, preferring to spend the autumn in the warm climate of the Crimea; they would never again see their Polish estates.[38]

Part Four

———————————— ❖ ————————————

PAGEANTRY

19

IMPERIAL CEREMONIES

MONARCHIES, WHETHER AUTOCRATIC or constitutional, surround themselves with courtiers and ceremonies. The Russian court existed not only to serve the sovereign, but also to provide a visible demonstration of power and authority. The aura of majesty that accompanied ceremonial events, carefully contrived to enhance the image of the monarchy, remained the raison d'être of the Russian court until the Revolution.

Ceremonies during the reign of Nicholas II followed traditional models, presenting the emperor as the all-powerful head of an imposing imperial court. They fell into four distinct categories. First, there were state ceremonies, displays of pomp and power witnessed in every Romanov reign. Nicholas II's reign opened with the funeral of his father, quickly followed by his own marriage to Princess Alix of Hesse und Bei Rhein. Two years later, Nicholas was crowned in Moscow in an extraordinary display of imperial wealth and power not only to the court and the empire, but also to the world at large. In 1913, Nicholas presided over the Tercentenary of the Romanov Dynasty, a six-months' succession of religious services, parades, and tours of the country. A host of annual ceremonies comprised the second category, rituals that followed a regular pattern beginning on the first day of each New Year and continuing on throughout the months that followed. They included the annual reception for members of the Diplomatic Corps, the Epiphany celebrations, imperial balls, parades, and military reviews.

A third category encompassed dedications, memorials, important anniversaries, and special ceremonies, the most important being the invocation of the new State Duma in 1906. The final category consisted of personal occasions in the life of the imperial family, including majority ceremonies and christenings.

Nicholas II used the ceremonial of the imperial court to present an idealized image of himself and his family to his empire and to the world at large. In this, he followed the tradition of his predecessors, who looked to such occasions as opportunities to impress and impose support for the throne, at the same time evoking fear and awe at the majesty and might of the empire itself. He copied the example laid down by his father of evoking the Russian nature of what was, in all aspects but location, a European court, but Nicholas took this one step further. As his reign progressed, and he became disillusioned with the political realities of his rule, Nicholas used public ceremonies to solicit personal support. Promoting himself and his family as symbols of national authority, he attempted to present a modicum of independence, a shadow play in which he still remained autocrat.

The most impressive of all ceremonies were Their Majesties' Processions. These fell into two classes: a Maly Vykhod, or Lesser Procession, which took place with great regularity; and a Bolshoi Vykhod, or Great Procession, at which all members of the court were in attendance. These processions were held throughout the year, wherever the court was in residence, on religious as well as festive and diplomatic occasions. They formed a visible display of the power and unity of the throne and the court, a magnificent parade of authority and prestige designed to impress those fortunate enough to witness them.[1] The majority of Their Majesties' Processions took place in the Winter Palace, leading from the private apartments to the cathedral and back again, and the entire imperial court participated. The long line of Parade Halls was filled with officials, representatives from the military, and specially invited guests. "The crush at these receptions surpassed everything that could be imagined," commented one guest. "There was hardly elbow room, and to enjoy oneself was quite out of the question."[2]

A guard of honor, composed of members of the Chevalier Guards Regiment in their white parade uniforms with red tunics, stood stiffly before the doors leading from the Nicholas Hall to the Concert Hall. Courtiers belonged to only one of two categories: those who had the right, as members of the Entourage or the Suite of the emperor or the empress, to go beyond the Chevalier Guards into the Concert Hall and march with Their Majesties' Procession as it left the room, and those who did not. On no other occasion was the division within the court so apparent. Those who did not possess the right of passing the Chevalier Guards assembled in the Nicholas Hall; diplomats, military generals, and lower members of the court waited in the adjoining anteroom; civil officials and delegations of merchants took up positions in the Field Marshal's Hall, behind serried ranks of His Majesty's Cossack Konvoi Regiment; lesser members of the court, various officials, and invited guests were confined to the Peter the Great Throne Room, the Hall of Armorial Bearings, the 1812 Military Gallery, and the Picket Hall at the far end of the Great Enfilade.[3]

The whole of the imperial family waited in the Malachite Hall, chatting, sipping champagne, or smoking. Gradually, as the hour approached, they fell into place; everyone knew his or her exact position in the procession, and they moved toward the center of the room, the ladies smoothing their dresses, the gentlemen adjusting cordons and medals. Inevitably, there were problems: the wives of Grand Dukes Nicholas Nikolaievich and Peter Nikolaievich, the Montenegrin sisters Militsa and Anastasia, were particularly zealous about their precedence over lesser members of the family, and no one dared form the procession until they arrived. Once, Grand Duchess Marie Georgievna, observing the sisters jostling for position before her, loudly declared, "We can start now that Scylla and Charybdis have taken their places."[4]

Rows of chamberlains and footmen, attired in state livery, led the Great Processions. The grand masters of ceremonies came next, closely followed, in ascending rank, by the principal dignitaries of the court and members of the military suite. The grand marshal of the imperial court, walking backward and holding his gilded staff of office, preceded the imperial party. Nicholas came first, his mother, according to the protocol of the Russian court, on his arm, followed by Alexandra, on the arm of the most senior grand duke, and the remaining members of the imperial family. Behind them walked the minister of the imperial court, members of the Emperor's Military Entourage, and the women of the imperial court.[5] "We trooped in, two by two, just like a team of well-groomed, well-trained poodles," recalled Nicholas II's younger sister Olga.[6]

These processions were imposing spectacles. As one witness recalled, "Thousands of generals and officers of all ranks, down to that of captain, as well as the high functionaries of the civil service, were arranged in lines in the immense halls of the palace, to bow at the passage of the Emperor and his family, as they solemnly proceeded to the Church." He observed "the immense train" of the empress's gown, "attended by her two Pages, who had to support the train at the turnings and to spread it out again in all its beauty," the endless parade of grand dukes and duchesses, "in the order of their right of succession to the throne," and "a long procession of the ladies in attendance, old and young," all in Russian court dress, with kokoshniki and veils. "As the procession passed, I could see how each of the eldest military and civil functionaries, before making his bow, would try to catch the eye of the Emperor, and if he had his bow acknowledged by a smiling look of the Sovereign, or by a hardly perceptible nod of the head, or perchance by a word or two, he would look round upon his neighbors, full of pride, in the expectation of their congratulations." But he also noted the general apathy of the gathered crowd: "Apart from a few devotees and some young ladies, not one in ten present at these levees regarded them otherwise than as a tedious duty."[7]

On January 1 of each year, the emperor and the empress received the entire Diplomatic Corps at the Winter Palace. The imperial family began the day early, with a Great Procession to the cathedral for a divine liturgy. All members of the Romanov family in St. Petersburg, from the emperor on down, were expected to attend. A luncheon followed, one of the only occasions when the entire Romanov family was together, before its members retired to change for the diplomatic reception. Grand dukes were required to wear full military dress uniform, while the grand duchesses all dressed in Russian court gowns and parures of jewelry. Full ceremonial dress was required of the Diplomatic Corps; military uniform, morning dress, or white tie and tails for the men, with the women in evening gowns with regulation trains. Ambassadors and envoys, along with their wives, were presented to the emperor according to the length of their service. Thus, the ambassador of the French Republic, the Russian empire's closest European ally, might be forced to follow the representative of a diplomatically unimportant country like Siam or Sweden. Each accredited ambassador or envoy was presented down the receiving line, greeting the emperor, the empress, the dowager empress, and the grand dukes and duchesses before wandering to the side tables arrayed with zakuski. Throughout the afternoon, waiters moved in and out of the crowd, holding silver trays filled with iced vodka, champagne, and Hungarian and French wines, while the diplomats chatted about the latest political developments.

The beginning of the New Year also brought with it the *baisemain*, the empress's formal reception for the women of St. Petersburg society. A thread of dowagers, matrons, and their young daughters, each attired in Russian court dress, waited impatiently in the halls of the Winter Palace. Alexandra, presented with this opportunity to charm the ladies of society, instead looked upon it as an ordeal. "I am struck dumb when I see that row of ladies facing me," she once explained to Baroness Sophie Buxhoeveden.[8] On her orders, movement in the line was swift. The empress rarely uttered more than a word or two of greeting to the ladies, who curtsied before her and kissed her hand before moving on. Even without conversation, however, the ceremony normally took several hours, and sometimes a thousand women were presented in a single afternoon.

The ladies were led by the senior *dames à portrait*, followed by the women of the imperial court, arrayed in a procession strictly dictated by their positions, and those from the first four ranks of aristocratic society. Each woman held the train of the lady in front of her as they slowly shuffled through the Nicholas Hall of the Winter Palace to the Concert Hall, where the empress waited. The procedure called for three curtsies: one dropped at the doors of the Concert Hall, one at the center of the Hall to the emperor, who generally stood at his wife's side, and one to the empress. It was a difficult maneuver, remembered Baroness Buxhoeveden. Princess Serge Beloselsky-Belozersky, in charge of the baroness's train, was less than attentive, and her constant tugs to keep it straight left Buxhoeveden reeling as she entered the hall. As she dropped into her first curtsy, one last tug sent her sprawling to the gleaming wooden floor. Two chamberlains rushed forward to help her to her feet, but "in my haste to be gone," she recalled, "I almost ran past." She ignored the second required curtsy to the emperor and, after dropping a curtsy to the empress and kissing her hand, quickly fled the room.[9]

Alexandra, unwilling and unable to set aside her personal discomfort, "seemed to have difficulty in finding anything to say," as one lady recalled.[10] A critic noted, "She extended her hand for the traditional kiss, and seemed to impose it. She mostly granted her audiences standing, and in the stiffest manner possible, never making a distinction where she ought to have done so. This incensed people against her, and all the dowagers who had come out of their retirement to be presented to her upon her marriage bitterly resented the haughty, disdainful way in which she received them."[11] And Princess Elizabeth Naryshkin-Kuryakin recalled, "Her almost morbid shyness prevented her from acting as freely and naturally as she ordinarily would have. The consciousness of her exalted position seemed to fluster her and her nervousness during these receptions caused her face to break out in red blotches that came and went and made her nod her head convulsively as she spoke."[12] Inevitably, the ladies left the Winter Palace and spread their tales of the cold, haughty empress.

A few days after the diplomatic reception, on January 6, came the Epiphany Ceremony. Although a religious service, Epiphany, or the Blessing of the Waters, was one of the few ceremonies to be witnessed by ordinary Russians, conducted as it was along the banks of the Neva River in front of the Winter Palace. The halls in the Winter Palace were filled with chosen guests, as Meriel Buchanan, the daughter of the British ambassador in St. Petersburg, later recalled, "Inside the Winter Palace the warm, hushed stillness was full of a subdued murmur of voices, a rustle of silken skirts, soft footsteps and the jingling of spurs. Court servants in gorgeous liveries, wearing queer round hats covered with ostrich feathers, lined the staircase. A mass of colored uniforms thronged the vast rooms through which we passed." As Their Majesties' Great Procession passed, "a sudden hush stilled the chattering voices"; the only sound, she remembered, was "the murmur of the long trains of many colored velvet or brocade, the rustle of gorgeous robes opening over the embroidered underskirts of stiff white satin. The blaze of jewels that covered their kokoshniks, the long white veils, seemed to set them in a world apart, made all our dress look somehow insignificant, our hats either absurd or dowdy."[13]

Along the Neva River Embankment, the granite quay was covered with a strip of crimson carpet, leading from the Winter Palace to the Neva, where an elaborate open chapel, complete with gilded columns and crosses, fluttering religious banners, and glittering icons, rested over a hole cut in the frozen river.[14] Court officials and members of the Orthodox clergy filled the quay, awaiting the arrival of the emperor. "A row of soldiers placed at long intervals kept a space clear for a large circle around the chapel," wrote Théophile Gautier. "They stood bareheaded, their helmets placed near them, their feet in the snow, so absolutely motionless they might have been taken for sign posts."[15]

The metropolitan of St. Petersburg led the procession from the Winter Palace, followed by bishops, archimandrites, and priests attired in festive dalmatics, stoles, and copes studded with pearls and diamonds. As they walked, they swung smoking censers of incense that perfumed the chill air with the rich aromas of cloves and rose oil. The emperor and his court, heads bared to the freezing wind, followed the clergy down the Jordan Staircase and between lines of smart soldiers to the edge of the Neva, in "a spectacle both magnificent and imposing," recalled Théophile Gautier.[16] Clustered around the chapel, they listened as the sonorous, moving liturgy chanted by the priests swept across the frozen river. Finally, the metropolitan took a golden cross on a chain and dipped it three times into the hole cut in the ice, blessing the crowd. "At the supreme moment," wrote Gautier, "the cannon placed on the other side of the river thundered, one after the other. A cloud of blue smoke, a flash of light, floated between the snowy carpet of the river and the gray-white sky. Then the detonation shook the windows till they rattled."[17] At the same time, the bells of the city's churches rang out, the guns of the Fortress of St. Peter and St. Paul across the Neva thundered salutes, and the massed soldiers broke into cheers. After the participants had returned to the Winter Palace, the people who had gathered to watch the scene flocked to the hole cut in the ice, filling pitchers and even dipping infants into the Neva in the belief that the blessed waters held curative powers.[18]

The Epiphany Ceremony of 1905, in the midst of the Russo-Japanese War, proved most memorable. At the moment of benediction, recalled a witness, "suddenly there was the detonation of a cannon from the esplanade of the Fortress of St. Peter and St. Paul across the river. The smoke of the discharge rose in a spherical cloud. The regulation salvo was beginning. But to our amazement a similar detonation had resounded above the Imperial platform. The gun had been loaded with shrapnel and the shell had burst over the Imperial party and Suite."[19] Baroness Buxhoeveden, standing in the Nicholas Hall, recalled, "I heard a tremendous crash of glass after the first loud report. To the intense surprise of all, we saw pieces of glass all over the floor."[20] The shell that hit the Winter Palace splintered, crashing through the windows and exploding on the granite quay, wounding a policeman on duty.[21] Throughout, the emperor remained calm, standing on the quay as the procession quietly reassembled and made its way back inside the palace. According to one witness, as he walked along the crimson carpet, Nicholas stopped to retrieve a piece of shrapnel, commenting, "I'll keep this as a souvenir."[22]

In addition to imperial balls and receptions, presentation of debutantes at the Russian court had always taken place each January, in an event presided over by the emperor and the empress at the Winter Palace. For the first few years of her husband's reign, Empress Alexandra continued the tradition. In time, however, her ill health, coupled with her extreme dislike of such affairs, led Alexandra to abandon traditional presentations, thus losing the opportunity to win back the affections of an alienated society. Instead, she instituted small receptions for two or three young women, held several times a week in the privacy of one of the imperial palaces, with complete ignorance of the importance attached to this ceremony by the Russian court. Baroness Buxhoeveden, herself presented at one of these small gatherings, recalled that the empress "was very silent at first, nervously twisting her handkerchief after she had asked all the ladies to be seated. There was an awkward pause, which my mother broke, contrary to custom, but greatly to the relief of the Empress. Mama made some remark about the exceptionally shy contingent of girls whom the Empress was seeing that day. The moment it was brought home to her that four at least of those present were fellow sufferers probably even more nervous than herself the Empress's face lit up with a charming smile and she became quite talkative. She immediately set us girls at our ease by enquiring about our parties, whether we knew many people and if we were enjoying our dances."[23]

Helene Izvolsky, the daughter of the Russian ambassador to France, recalled a far different presentation to the empress at the Alexander Palace. The reception, she recalled, "was strained. Mother and I were invited to sit down on the hard art nouveau chairs and the Empress seemed to have difficulty in finding the words of greeting for which we were respectfully waiting. A forced smile was all that she could muster up for a few moments and when she spoke it was with downcast eyes and in a strange hollow voice. Alexandra's extreme coldness, usually attributed to shyness, was one of the causes of her unpopularity in Russian society. In spite of her great beauty she did not attract but rather repulsed her subjects harshly. I felt frozen to the bone and when at last she spoke I heard myself giving her the most absurd answers. Thus for instance when she mentioned her son the Tsesarevich Alexei I recalled that on the day that he was born we were happy because our professors canceled our lessons. The Empress gave me a severe look."[24]

Additional ceremonies included military reviews and parades on the Champs de Mars, commemoration services, and festive Te Deums, along with the less glamorous but more frequent duties of laying foundation stones, inspecting factories, commissioning new battleships, and opening hospitals. In private, charitable organizations regularly dispatched delegations of representatives to meet with either the emperor or the empress, to report on work, ask for financial assistance, and request attendance at fund-raising events or receptions. Other imperial duties carried out by the emperor, the empress, and members of their family included annual reviews and graduation luncheons of cadets at the various military institutions such as the Corps des Pages. Dowager Empress Marie Feodorovna, as patroness, usually attended the graduation ceremony at the Smolny Institute for Young Ladies of Noble Birth, personally handing out diplomas to the students, while the emperor, as patron of the Alexander Lyceum, performed a similar function each spring.

In 1834, Nicholas I introduced the majority ceremony to mark the sixteenth birthday of the future Alexander II; it soon became established ritual for the male members of the Imperial House.[25] By imperial ukase, most grand dukes were made adjutants to the emperor at their majority, which took place after their twentieth birthdays. The future Nicholas II marked his sixteenth birthday,

May 6, 1884, in a majority ceremony that followed the established pattern. Attired in the dark blue uniform of an ataman in the Imperial Cossack Guards Regiment, he joined his parents and several hundred officials in a Great Procession through the Winter Palace to its cathedral, where priests conducted a Te Deum. At the end of the service, Alexander III led his son to the altar, watched by members of the imperial family, the Imperial Entourage and Suite, members of the Imperial Council and the Imperial Senate, and the Diplomatic Corps.[26] Nicholas, right hand held aloft, swore "to serve truly and faithfully" his father, "without sparing my body, until the last drop of blood, to guard and defend all the rights and privileges pertaining to the autocracy."[27] At the end of the Te Deum, the congregation moved to the Hall of St. George, where hundreds of military officers waited to witness the tsesarevich as he recited the Oath of the Russian Army. Accompanied by the standard bearer of his chief military regiment, Nicholas ascended the dais, grasped the regimental standard in his left hand, and read the oath. After receiving congratulations from representatives of the various imperial regiments, Nicholas joined as the crowd sang the national anthem, its conclusion marked by the booming of cannons fired from the Fortress of St. Peter and St. Paul across the Neva.[28]

A luncheon for eight hundred guests was held in the Nicholas Hall. In addition to the imperial family, the Russian court, the Diplomatic Corps, government officials, and representatives from the Armed Forces and the Orthodox Church, the guests included a number of foreign royal relatives who had come to St. Petersburg especially to attend the service, including the future Kaiser Wilhelm II, who presented the tsesarevich with the Prussian Order of the Black Eagle on behalf of his grandfather, Wilhelm I.[29] Round tables, draped in white cloth, each held twelve guests, their place settings marked with elaborately illuminated menus decorated with imperial monograms and a pastoral view of an isolated Orthodox church perched at the side of a tranquil river.[30] "I am quite happy that it all went so well," Nicholas recorded in his diary, though several guests present noticed his distinct nervousness and the quake in his voice when he read the two oaths.[31] The tsesarevich, as he confided in an essay, would have been happy to have postponed the ceremony until his twentieth birthday.[32]

Romanov christenings also formed an important part of the ceremonial at the Russian court. The most elaborate christening during the reign of Nicholas II was undoubtedly that of his son, Tsesarevich Alexei Nikolaievich. Born at 1:15 P.M. on the afternoon of July 30, 1904, in the Lower Palace at Alexandria, Peterhof, Alexei Nikolaievich was an immense, lusty infant; at birth he weighed eleven pounds. Alexei had an illustrious group of godparents, including Nicholas's mother, Dowager Empress Marie Feodorovna; Grand Duke Alexei Alexandrovich; King Christian IX of Denmark; King Edward VII of Great Britain; and Kaiser Wilhelm II. "What a very kind thought that was of yours to ask me to be Godfather to your little boy!" the jubilant kaiser wrote on hearing the news. "You can well imagine what our joy was when we read your telegram announcing his birth. May he grow up to be a brave soldier and a wise and powerful statesman."[33] At his birth, the infant was awarded the Russian Orders of St. Andrei, St. Alexander Nevsky, and St. Anna, and the Polish Order of St. Stanislaus; enrolled as a member of the Imperial Guards Corps; designated an honorary member of the 89th White Sea Infantry Regiment; and appointed ataman of all Cossacks. As a final flourish and an astute piece of loyalty-inspiring propaganda, Nicholas announced that all members of the Imperial Army then fighting in the ill-fated war against Japan would be named honorary godfathers.[34]

Eleven days later, on "a fine August morning," as Baroness Buxhoeveden recalled, the tsesarevich was christened.[35] At half-past nine that Wednesday morning, a long line of red and gold carriages, drawn by six perfectly matched white horses, drew up in front of the Lower Palace to convey the imperial family

The state carriage conveying Tsesarevich Alexei to his christening at Peterhof, August 1904

to the nearby cathedral of the palace of Peterhof, where the ceremony would take place. Beneath the hot, late-summer sun, the carriages followed the gravel drive, lined by members of the emperor's Cossack and Hussar Life Guards Regiments, as it meandered through the lush park, the crunch of the wheels drowned out by massed bands playing "God Save the Tsar" amid the cheers of the soldiers.[36] "First came the trumpeters of the Cossack Escort," recalled one witness, "in red and on dashing bays. This was followed by a detachment of the Chevalier Guards in their white uniforms, with gilt cuirasses glittering in the sun. Then came an open state carriage containing high court officials, their uniforms a blaze of gold." Finally, as the cheering reached a crescendo, the coach bearing the infant came into view, "all glass and gilding, drawn by six white horses in gilded harness, with nodding plumes on their heads. Inside, we could see billows of lace, the christening robe of the heir to Russia's thorny crown. A coachman in gold-laced livery held the reins, and powdered footmen in gold-laced coats stood on the box. Courtiers in full uniform rode beside the coach."[37]

Nearly a thousand members of the Russian court had assembled in the glittering rooms of the Great Palace; through the open windows, the tall spray from the hundred fountains dotting the Grand Cascade splashed and sparkled in the brilliant light. By eleven, the enfilade of parade rooms, stretching the 800-foot length of the palace, were full. The men, clad in their regimental dress or in court uniforms covered with gold galloon and rows of shining medals, stood silently, while the ladies, adorned "with jewels, in gowns of gold and silver cloth with long trains," whispered in anticipation.[38]

At last, the carriages arrived at the Great Palace, greeted by a guard of honor, sabers drawn in salute. The sound of Tchaikovsky's "Fanfare," played by the State Trumpeters, shattered the silence of the immense palace, calling those gathered within its halls to attention. Shortly before eleven, the grand master of ceremonies appeared at the end of the enfilade, tapping his ebony and gilt-encrusted staff on the floor to signal the start of the procession. Behind him walked a hundred court officials: chamberlains and footmen, attired in state livery embellished with gold thread, followed by the dignitaries of the court and members of the Emperor's Suite. Finally, Princess Marie Golitsyn, the empress's *ober-gofmeisterina*, appeared, carrying the new tsesarevich on a cushion of cloth-of-silver. "The old Princess," Buxhoeveden remembered, "was terrified of dropping the baby. The cushion prevented her from seeing what was under her feet, so she had carefully pinned up the front of her dress to help her in getting up the stairs, and a generous display of white silk stockings appeared above her very large, flat heeled shoes with rubber soles to prevent her slipping—an additional safety measure."[39]

On either side of her walked chamberlains, holding the ends of the long, flowing cloth-of-gold mantle lined and edged with ermine that nearly covered the infant. Alexei was clad in a white cambric shirt; over this, he wore a christening gown of silver brocade, sewn in golden thread and covered with flounces of lace and tulle.[40] Behind them came the dowager empress, flanked by the tsesarevich's two eldest sisters, Grand Duchesses Olga and Tatiana, in miniature Russian court gowns of pink and silver. White kokoshniki, adorned with flowing silver bows, graced their heads, and they each wore the crimson cordon of the Order of St. Catherine across their bodices. The girls were just nine and seven years old. It was their first official appearance at a court function, and they had been warned not to misbehave. "Solemn as judges," Buxhoeveden recalled, they walked with their heads held high, eyes straight ahead; only when they passed a group of their young cousins did they break into wide smiles.[41]

Finally, the procession reached the cathedral, its white and gold walls glistening in the sunlight and its floor crowded with the imperial family, foreign princes, and members of the court. Only the parents, according to orthodox custom, were

The ceremonies on the battlefield at Poltava, 1909

absent from the service.[42] At the front of the church, before the glittering, gilded iconostasis stood Metropolitan Anthony of St. Petersburg and Father Ioann Yanishev, the personal confessor to the imperial family. Princess Golitsyn carefully handed the infant to the dowager empress, who carried him to the gilded font adorned with carved cherubs and roses. At her side, Grand Duchess Olga Nikolaievna proudly held a corner of the cushion as they approached Father Yanishev, who stripped the tsesarevich of his mantle and gown before dipping him bodily into the water three times.[43] In response, the new tsesarevich, recalled Baroness Buxhoeveden, "lustily bellowed."[44] After he was dressed in his christening gown and wrapped in the golden mantle, Alexei's godparents carried him around the dais three times, as priests anointed his face, eyes, ears, hands, and feet with holy oil. A shattering salute of 301 guns, fired simultaneously from the cannon of nearby Kronstadt and from the Fortress of St. Peter and St. Paul, signaled the end of the ceremony.

In June of 1909, Nicholas celebrated the Bicentennial of the Battle of Poltava, commemorating Peter the Great's victory over Charles XII of Sweden. He arrived at the site of the battle on June 25, attending a dinner with officers of the Preobrazhensky Guards Regiment. The following day, he presided over a military review; at his side stood Victor Kochubey, Alexander Sheremetiev, and Paul Skoropadsky, three direct descendants of men who had served with Peter the Great during the battle.[45] During the Procession of the Cross, Nicholas was surrounded by several thousand peasants, who cheered him and fell to their knees as he passed. It was, Grand Duke Konstantin Konstantinovich noted in his diary, "very touching and significant."[46]

In a speech to the gathered military officers and cadets, Nicholas reaffirmed his faith in the Russian people and their loyalty to the throne: "I have lived through the last two days, as probably all of you have done, with feelings of the deepest emotion, as you stood on these very fields of Poltava, where 200 years ago the fate of our country was decided. Here by the will of God and thanks to the genius of Peter and the stubborn endurance of the Russian people the victory was won that gave Russia her greatness. Our country has just passed through a period of misfortune. I believe that today it is entering on a period of development and prosperity and that it will be easier for future generations to live and to serve their country. To secure this it is necessary that all my subjects should help their Emperor. We must have faith in the strength of our country; we must have love for it and love for our past and our ancient customs." He ended with a plea for "close fellowship between the whole nation and the Emperor."[47]

"In the shouts of 'Hurrah!' drowning out the Emperor's words," wrote Grand Duke Konstantin Konstantinovich, "one could see the extraordinary spiritual forces beneath them, a feeling that none of us have experienced for some time."[48] Nicholas used the occasion, as Richard Wortman has noted, as a "partisan device, to compete with the Duma and to show himself as sole focus of national sentiment."[49] After Poltava, he told a French military attaché, "no one could say that the Russian people did not love their Emperor." He took the manifestations as evidence that "the landowners, the nobility, and the Army" remained loyal, commenting contemptuously that the revolutionaries were "all Jews, students, landless peasants, and workers."[50]

In August 1912, Nicholas presided over the Centennial of the Battle of Borodino outside Moscow. The emperor, joined by his wife and most of the grand dukes and duchesses, reviewed a large detachment of soldiers drawn up on the battlefield. Nicholas, in the uniform of the Imperial Horse Guards Regiment— a unit that had distinguished itself at the battle—watched as soldiers carried the miraculous icon of the Smolensk Mother of God across the dusty field; it was the same icon with which General Field Marshal Kutuzov had blessed his troops before hostilities commenced. "It was a very moving, solemn procession," recalled

Nicholas II and his family leaving a church service commemorating the Centennial of the Battle of Borodino, 1912

Vladimir Dzhunkovsky, the governor of Moscow. "Every face displayed excitement."[51] As a regimental band struck up the hymn "Kol' Slaven," Nicholas joined the procession, following it beneath the hot August sun to a chapel where golden-vested priests conducted a Te Deum. At the end of the service, the icon was paraded before the ten thousand massed troops, who dropped their rifles to their sides, heads lowered, an "extraordinarily moving" moment, according to Dzhunkovsky.[52]

On August 26, the emperor attended a Te Deum at the Spaso-Borodinsky Monastery before watching a reenactment of the battle. For several weeks, military engineers had reconstructed the old redoubts, and entire platoons of appropriately costumed soldiers occupied the positions of the French and the Russian Armies. As the morning sun shone upon the lines of trimly uniformed men, they raced across the field, their regimental standards and the double-headed eagle waving proudly against the blue sky. At the climax of the mock fight, the emperor rode across the field atop a white stallion, between the lines of cheering men.[53]

The festivities were marred only by a public eruption of the simmering feud between Empress Alexandra and Grand Duchess Vladimir. Although the centennial was a national celebration, in which all members of the Romanov family were expected to participate, Alexandra had pointedly excluded her husband's aunt, directing that she be excluded from the ceremonies. Word of this deliberate slight soon became public, and, as Prince Felix Yusupov recalled, Alexandra was roundly criticized for her pettiness. Felix, always eager to embarrass Alexandra, invited the grand duchess to accompany him to the ceremony, suggesting that they attend incognito. But with his usual theatrical flair, he ensured that they arrived on the field just as the review began. Officials, recognizing the grand duchess, insisted on seating her in the imperial box, but Marie Pavlovna refused, saying she would watch from the public stands. Officials duly escorted her, accompanied by the prince, to a tribune, where her presence caused a commotion. Catching sight of the pair, Felix later wrote, Alexandra "cast very cold glances in our direction."[54]

At the end of the reenactment, as Nicholas wrote to his mother, "they managed to find a few old men who remembered the arrival of the French, and, most incredibly, among them was one who actually participated in the battle, former Sergeant-Major Vintonyuk, 122 years old. Can you imagine—talking to a man who remembers everything, and can describe every detail of the fighting, and can show you the place where he was wounded and so on; I told them to stand near us in the tent during the service and I watched them. They were all able to kneel down with the aid of a stick, and to get up again without anyone's help!"[55] It was an impressive moment, though, as Dzhunkovsky recalled, the men had forgotten details of the battle and had been coached to create the touching scene for the emperor's benefit.[56]

On August 27, Nicholas and Alexandra attended a reception given by members of the Moscow nobility at the Hall of Nobles. Alexander Samarin, the marshal of the nobility of the Moscow Province, presented the emperor with, as Nicholas recalled, "a beautiful banner, of ancient design," as a symbol of continued loyalty to the throne.[57] In his address, Samarin vowed the eternal support of Russia's nobility to the throne; when he referred to "our August, Autocratic Sovereign," Nicholas was so moved at this echo of his own beliefs that his eyes filled with tears.[58] The emperor responded by singling out the aristocracy as a bastion of loyalty, speaking of "the enduring and permanent bond that exists between the Russian nobility, the highest class in Russia, and their Emperors. I am convinced that the nobility's spirit of loyalty and devotion to their rulers, and the boundless love that they and the whole nation bear toward our sacred motherland will never die."[59]

Tsesarevich Alexei being presented with a souvenir of the Centennial
of the Battle of Borodino, 1912

The next day, Nicholas conducted an immense military review on Khodynka Field, the site of the terrible tragedy that occurred during his coronation in 1896. Four Army corps, a total of 75,000 soldiers, participated in the ceremonial march past, watched over by the empress and the grand duchesses, all clad in long white summer dresses and picture hats. The celebrations culminated on August 30, with a Te Deum held in the Cathedral of the Assumption in the Kremlin. Nicholas and Alexandra led the entire imperial family in a procession down the Red Staircase of the Grand Kremlin Palace, preceded by some 200 priests, gonfalon, and icon bearers and more than 300 members of the imperial court in their resplendent uniforms.[60] Below them, Cathedral Square was filled with an immense crowd, "a sea of heads," as Nicholas recorded, "in perfect order and quiet," behind ranks of soldiers drawn from the Moscow Garrison.[61] After the Te Deum, sung by the choir of the Holy Synod and a choir composed of more than 3,000 Muscovites, the metropolitan of Moscow offered a prayer in memory of Alexander I; it ended with a shattering salute, fired from the guns of the Kremlin, and a cacophony of tolling church bells.[62]

Nicholas had crafted the ceremonies to make himself the center of attention, in an effort to link his own reign with the past glories of the empire. Although many officials were present at the Borodino ceremonies, on Nicholas's orders the members of the Imperial Council of Ministers and the State Duma were denied invitations. It was a deliberate insult, designed to reinforce the emperor's conception of himself as the only legitimate source of power and authority in Russia. On learning of this, Michael Rodzianko, the president of the Duma, lodged an official complaint with Baron Korff, the master of ceremonies. Korff was less than understanding, replying, "members of the Duma do not enjoy the right of access to the Court." Rodzianko, however, pointed out the inequity of the situation. "This is not a Court, but a national celebration," he declared. "Besides, Russia was saved not by Masters of Ceremony, but by her people." No amount of protest, however, could convince the emperor to relent.[63]

Less exciting but more common ceremonies included dedications of various monuments. In 1909, Nicholas unveiled a statue of his father, Alexander III, in St. Petersburg's Znamenskaya Square, just opposite the Nicholas Railway Station. Nicholas II selected Prince Paul Trubetskoy, a noted sculptor, to design the memorial. It took Trubetskoy nearly a decade to complete the sculpture, and the resulting work cost more than a million rubles (over $10,000,000 in 2005 figures), an unheard of sum for a memorial. The Ministry of Finance had to divert funds marked for the development of the Trans-Siberian Railway to ensure the statue's completion.[64]

The State Opening of the Duma in St. George's Hall at the Winter Palace, April 1906

The ceremony on May 23, 1909, was one of the first occasions on which the entire imperial family had appeared in public since the Revolution of 1905. A salute of cannon, fired from the Fortress of St. Peter and St. Paul, marked the beginning of the festivities. An immense crowd ringed Znamenskaya Square, where flags and banners floated in the late spring breeze. The emperor, followed by his wife and his mother, both in white gowns and wide-brimmed hats, descended from carriages and circled the center of the square, watched by the Diplomatic Corps, the Council of Ministers, members of the Duma, and representatives of the military. Together, Nicholas and his mother unveiled the monument. The statue stood upon a massive red granite pedestal inscribed "To Emperor Alexander III, Sovereign Founder of the Great Siberian Railway." Trubetskoy depicted Alexander III on a large horse, in the Russian style of a *bogatyr* or ancient warrior. The imperial family liked it, and Dowager Empress Marie Feodorovna even kept a small working model in bronze on the writing desk in her boudoir.[65] But its ponderous lines brought a swift, negative reaction.

Soon enough, cartoons depicting Trubetskoy's massive statue appeared in the press, mocking the artist and his vision. One editorial, in *Novoe Vremia*, termed the dedication of the statue "an event in our Russian life and, regretfully, another unhappy event, as it is a failure."[66] Trubetskoy was forced to defend his work to the press: "I of course understand that Petersburg is quite unused to new works in this field of art. . . . They heap criticism on my fat horse, yet I had to select a large horse for the monument, taking into account the *bogatyr*-like figure of the Emperor."[67] Privately, however, Trubetskoy explained, "I just depicted one animal on top of another."[68]

Perhaps the most peculiar of all the ceremonies during the reign of Nicholas II was the State Opening of the Duma, the Russian parliament. The ceremony, which took place on April 27, 1906, formally inaugurated the new parliament in suitably imperial fashion. Ironically, it was held in the sanctum sanctorum of the autocracy, St. George's Hall, the Imperial Throne Room, in the Winter Palace. All of the newly elected members of the Duma had been invited, and the cross-section of delegates included not only landed nobles and representatives from the middle classes but also peasants and socialists. The palace, recalled Grand Duchess Marie Pavlovna, "looked more like a fortress, so greatly did they fear an attack or hostile demonstrations."[69]

Nearly all members of the Romanov Dynasty were present. "We all wore our full dress uniforms," recalled Grand Duke Alexander Mikhailovich. "Deep mourning would have been more appropriate."[70] The women were adorned with exquisite jewels, "naively believing," wrote Vladimir Gurko, the assistant minister of the interior, "that the people's representatives, many of whom were peasants, would be awed by the splendor of the Imperial Court." Instead, as he noted, "the effect was altogether different. This oriental method of imposing upon spectators a reverence for the bearers of supreme power was quite unsuited to the occasion. What it did achieve was to set in juxtaposition the boundless Imperial luxury and the poverty of the people."[71]

Shortly before two that afternoon, a fanfare of trumpets announced the start of the processions: chamberlains, attired in their golden liveries; masters of ceremony, carrying their maces; members of the Emperor's Entourage and military suite; and twelve imposing soldiers from the Palace Golden Grenadier Regiment. The grand marshal of the imperial court, holding his ebony staff of office, slowly walked backward in front of the emperor, who wore the full dress uniform of the Preobrazhensky Guards Regiment. Behind him came the empress, in a Russian court dress richly embellished with intricate foliate designs in gold thread, the tall diamond and pearl kokoshnik made by the jeweler Kurt Hahn holding a long lace veil in place. According to one witness, she "appeared as cold and disdainful as usual; she seemed bored more than anything else, and scarcely noticed the low salutations with which the Imperial party were greeted when they came into the room."[72] At her side was the dowager empress, her Russian court dress of brown velvet and gold thread.[73] She "was extremely moved and agitated," remembered one observer. "Her eyes were red, and she kept putting up her handkerchief as if to wipe away tears. She remained slightly behind her son and daughter-in-law, but keenly observed the assembly, as if trying to read their countenances and to guess what lay behind them."[74]

As a regimental band, concealed in the upper gallery, filled the hall with the strains of "God Save the Tsar," Nicholas crossed the expanse of bare floor. On his left, across from the deputies, stood the members of the State Council and the imperial court, in uniforms dripping with gold braid and medals. At the end of the room, the crimson velvet throne had been draped—it was said by Alexandra herself—with the Imperial Mantle lined with ermine.[75] To the side, on plump cushions, rested the Imperial State Crown, the Imperial Orb, and the scepter, shimmering symbols of autocratic power. As she followed her brother into the hall, Grand Duchess Xenia Alexandrovna cast a quick glance at the deputies, "men with repulsive faces and insolent disdainful expressions! They neither crossed themselves nor bowed, but stood with their hands behind their backs or in their pockets, looking somberly at everyone and everything."[76] And Alexander Izvolsky noted that their faces "were lighted by triumph in some cases and in others distorted by hatred, making altogether a spectacle intensely dramatic and symbolic."[77]

Nicholas mounted the dais and slowly read from a prepared speech, announcing his conviction that the sovereign and the Duma must work together in an effort to reform the country. There was no mention of the turmoil that had forced him to make this concession; instead, Nicholas clung to the illusion that "the care for the welfare of the country entrusted to me by the Most High has caused me to summon representatives elected by the people to assist in the work of legislation." At several points, he emphasized that "order is the basis of law," a clear warning that he expected this hated compromise to work within the existing monarchical system and put an immediate halt to the chaos sweeping the empire. It was, he said, his "intense desire to see My People happy, and to bequeath to My Son an inheritance of a strong, well ordered, and enlightened state."[78] One onlooker recorded, "Nicholas II appeared nervous; he was paler than was his wont, and he kept twisting his white military gloves. But there was no kindness in his blue eyes."[79]

When he concluded, remembered Grand Duchess Xenia Alexandrovna, "a cheer broke out, which was taken up by everyone including in the other halls—it sounded magnificent." Looking up, she saw that both Alexandra and Marie Feodorovna were crying, and "poor Nicky was standing there in tears—his self control finally overcome, he could not hold back his tears!"[80] Baroness Buxhoeveden, catching sight of Empress Alexandra, thought that she "looked tragic. Her large, sad eyes seemed to foresee disaster, and her face became alternately red and pale. Her knuckles as she clutched her fan were quite white, she gripped it so tightly."[81] The minister of the imperial court, Freedericksz, declared that the representatives "gave one the impression of a gang of criminals who are only waiting for the signal to throw themselves upon the ministers and cut their throats! What wicked faces! I will never again set foot amongst those people!"[82]

At the conclusion of the ceremony, Nicholas and Alexandra returned to the Lower Palace at Alexandria, Peterhof. "I did a lot of work," the emperor wrote in his diary, "but with a light heart, after the satisfactory way in which today's ceremony had gone."[83] But Nicholas continued to live in a world of dreams. Although he had transformed Russia, he refused to accept the democratic changes; he still believed that he remained an autocrat, responsible, as before, only to God for his rule. Others were more prescient. After the ceremony, Princess Naryshkin-Kuryakin took tea with Princess Marie Golitsyn, Alexandra's *ober-gofmeisterina*. The elderly Princess Golitsyn, she recalled, "told me that at that moment she had the feeling that something great was crashing—as if all Russian tradition had been annihilated in a single blow."[84]

20

AN IMPERIAL FUNERAL

BY THE AUTUMN OF 1894, Emperor Alexander III had been diagnosed with nephritis.[1] "Your Majesty's malady," his doctor warned, "is incurable. With care and attention, your valuable life may be prolonged for many months, but it is useless to conceal the fact that no remedies will avail beyond a certain period."[2] Alexander accepted his fate with quiet resignation; although kept from the Russian public, word of his illness soon spread throughout the imperial family. His cousin Queen Olga of the Hellenes offered her villa, Mon Repos, on Corfu, and the doctors all agreed that the warmer climate might improve the emperor's condition.[3] Alexander reluctantly agreed, and Marie Feodorovna asked her brother, King George I of Greece, to make the arrangements, but on reaching the imperial estate of Livadia in the Crimea, he was too weak to continue the journey. Hearing this, scattered members of the imperial family made their ways south, fearing the worst.[4]

At Livadia, the days passed in uncertainty. At first, Alexander seemed to improve, spending long hours in the warm sunshine on balconies of the Maly Palace; within a few days, however, the devastating illness again took hold. "Every movement became an agony," remembered his youngest daughter, Olga, then a girl of twelve. "He could not even lie in bed. He felt slightly more comfortable when they wheeled his chair to an open window."[5]

By the first week of October, it was obvious the emperor was dying, and Empress Marie hastily dispatched a pitiful telegram to her sister Alexandra, the princess of Wales, begging her to come to Livadia. Alexandra and her husband left London for Russia that same evening.

Alexander III felt himself gradually slipping away. "Tell me the truth," he asked his doctor one afternoon, "how long do I have to live?" Uncomfortable, the physician replied, "That is in God's hands, but with this disease I have seen cases of marvelous cures." Not satisfied, the emperor demanded, "Can I still live for a fortnight?" On being told he could, Alexander sent for Tsesarevich Nicholas, asking that he summon his fiancée, Princess Alix, to Livadia.[6] Alix immediately left Darmstadt, traveling across the continent to Warsaw, where her sister Grand Duchess Elizabeth Feodorovna quickly ushered her into a regularly scheduled passenger train bound for the Crimea. Court officials were too involved in the unfolding drama at Livadia to concern themselves with her arrival, and Russia's future empress traversed her new country without ceremony, alone except for her sister and a few servants. Nicholas met her train at Simferopol, and by four o'clock on the afternoon of October 10, they had reached the little palace high above the Black Sea.

The Maly Palace at Livadia

Despite his illness, Alexander III insisted on receiving his future daughter-in-law in full dress uniform, ensuring that every medal and decoration was in its proper place. The tall, beautiful, golden-haired princess entered his second-floor corner bedroom, kneeling before the emperor, who could scarcely rise and kiss her.[7] The ordeal proved too much for the dying man; an official bulletin, released the next day, noted that the visit had "strongly excited the patient, in spite of the joy it caused him."[8] Within a few days, the emperor was vomiting uncontrollably, suffering from daily nosebleeds, and unable to sleep. In a futile attempt to ease his pain, the doctors turned to heavy injections of morphine.[9]

On the morning of Thursday, October 20, Marie Feodorovna entered her husband's bedroom to find his breathing labored; he had not slept all night. "I feel the end approaching," he said to her. "Be calm; I am quite calm." With the assistance of his valet, the emperor put on a light gray military tunic, and the doctors helped move him across the room to an overstuffed armchair. Alexander asked that the French doors to the small balcony be opened, so that he might hear the birds singing.[10] Slowly, members of the imperial family crowded the corners of the room. An eerie, hushed silence settled over them, mesmerized and terrified as they were at the rasping coughs and guttural moans of the dying man. Prince Nicholas of Greece likened it to watching "a magnificent building crumbling away."[11] Just after two that afternoon, as Marie Feodorovna cradled her husband in her arms, his head fell to his heaving chest, and Alexander III, the emperor of Russia, lay dead at the age of forty-nine.

"My God, my God, what a day!" the new emperor, Nicholas II, wrote in his diary. "The Lord has summoned our adored, dear, deeply beloved Papa to Him. My head is spinning, I don't want to believe it—the awful reality seems so unjust. We spent the whole morning upstairs with him! He had difficulty breathing and they kept having to give him oxygen to inhale. . . . It was the death of a saint!"[12]

At the moment of death, the machinery of the imperial court swung into action. An adjutant, his uniform covered in gold braid and shining medals, sent a courier down to the small harbor at Yalta; within a few minutes, the guns of the cruiser *Pamyat' Merkuriya* boomed across the dark blue waters, announcing Alexander III's passing. The guns were soon joined by tolling church bells, creating a cacophony of sounds that split the tranquility of the late afternoon along the Crimean coast.

The first act in Nicholas II's reign took place against the crimson of a fading autumn sunset. Father Ioann Yanishev, clad in the golden dalmatic of his ecclesiastical office, led the mourners to a hastily erected altar, where officials gathered to witness the new emperor's formal accession to the throne. In the midst of mourning, the women wore white, following the tradition of the imperial court and providing visible witness to the aphorism *"Le roi est mort, Vive le roi!"* As warships in the harbor fired their salutes, Yanishev consecrated the shaken young man, proclaiming him "His Imperial Majesty, the Emperor and Autocrat of all the Russias, the Rightful Sovereign Tsar, Nicholas II."

Beyond the sweep of green lawns, Alexander III's valets were busy within the Maly Palace. They carefully lifted his stiffening corpse from the chair where he had died and laid it on a nearby camp bed, covering the body from the chest to the feet with a white eiderdown. Between his folded hands, they placed an icon and a cross. Tall silver candlesticks circled the bed, their candles providing an eerie illumination to the dead sovereign's pale features. As dusk settled over the Crimea, Count Hilarion Vorontzov-Dashkov, the minister of the imperial court, began the onerous task of presiding over the Mourning Committee, which would oversee the elaborate funeral rituals. Pages were ordered into trunks to unearth endless yards of black bunting and crepe. Throughout the night, the palaces at Livadia were covered with the unmistakable symbols of death: windows and doorways hung with heavy swags; columns twisted with black festoons; facades draped with mourning ribbons; and chandeliers wreathed in black tulle. Even the ordinary crested writing paper and envelopes on the desks had disappeared by sunrise, replaced with heavy, black-edged vellum.

Livadia awoke wreathed in a veil of mist and incessant rain. Below the exquisite gardens and marble terraces, the Black Sea pounded against the rocky beach, spitting angry sprays of white foam into the gray air. The black crepe and bunting fluttered miserably in the sea breeze as courtiers, heads bent against the driving rain, made their ways from palace to palace. Livadia, steeped in mourning, had become a place of whispers.

Amid this desolate scene, a vivid splash of pageantry and color took place. That morning, after a requiem for the dead emperor, Princess Alix was officially confirmed into the Russian Orthodox Church. The Church of the Exaltation of the Cross at Livadia, a small, Byzantine-style structure of white limestone, stood sheltered against the balconies of the Great Palace. Within, arches supported an intricately frescoed roof, where the faces of saints looked on in beatific peace. Alix wore black, and her future mother-in-law wept openly. Yanishev held a conversion book as the princess read her responses in half-learned Russian. After she recited the Creed of the Orthodox Church, Yanishev led Alix through her new

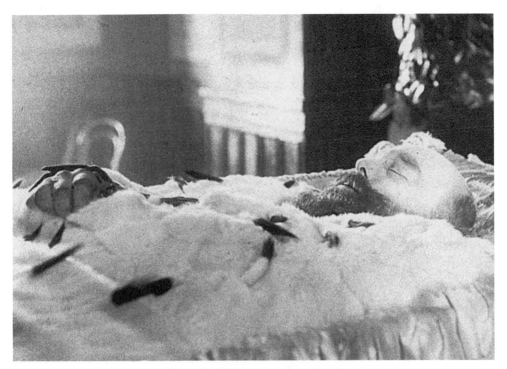

Alexander III lying in state at Livadia

Orthodox catechism; she was not, as a special dispensation, required to repudiate Lutheranism or renounce her former faith.[13]

Yanishev then anointed her forehead, eyes, neck, throat, and the palms and wrists of her hands with holy oil. "In the midst of our deep sorrow," Nicholas wrote in his diary, "the Lord has sent us a quiet and radiant joy: at 10 o'clock in the presence of the family my dear darling Alix was anointed with the holy oils and after the service we took communion together, with dear Mama and Ella. Alix repeated her responses and prayers wonderfully well and distinctly!"[14]

Alix had apparently wished to take the name of Catherine on entering the Orthodox Church; the new emperor, however, suggested Alexandra, echoing not only the closest Russian equivalent of Alix, but also evoking the reign of his great-grandfather Nicholas I and his wife, Empress Alexandra.[15] When the service ended, Vorontzov-Dashkov issued one of the new emperor's first imperial ukases or proclamations, announcing that the former Princess Alix of Hesse had been received into the Russian Church as "the Orthodox Grand Duchess Alexandra Feodorovna."[16]

That long Friday, the new emperor led his grieving family in the first of what were to become twice daily services for his father. "The expression on Dear Papa's face," he wrote, "is beautiful; he looks as if he were about to smile."[17] For thirty hours, Alexander III's body lay untouched on his bed. By the end of the second day it had begun to decompose, and Nicholas, along with his uncles, carried it down the narrow staircase of the Maly Palace to a corner drawing room, whose windows provided better ventilation and whose heavy mahogany doors could be closed against the increasing stench.[18]

Vorontzov-Dashkov had ordered an oak coffin, decorated with gilded mounts and golden tassels and lined with ivory satin, from an undertaker in Yalta. It arrived on October 23, and, three days after the emperor's death, physicians and morticians finally began their work, conducting a postmortem examination and removing Alexander III's heart and internal organs for separate burial. Although the morticians worked on the emperor all afternoon, the results were less than impressive; over the weeks that followed, Alexander's body would rapidly decay and rot while still on public display. When they had finished, the body was washed and attired in the dark-green dress uniform of the Preobrazhensky Guards. "I still cannot bring myself to go into the corner room where dear Papa's body is lying," Nicholas wrote in his diary. "He is so changed since being embalmed, I cannot bear to lose the wonderful impression of the first day!"[19]

The following evening, in the orange glow of a full moon, Nicholas II, along with his brother George and their four uncles, Vladimir, Alexei, Serge, and Paul, themselves carried the emperor's coffin from the drawing room to the front door of the Maly Palace. A group of Terek Cossacks, in long blue coats and bearskin hats, lifted the coffin onto their shoulders and bore it down the stairs, following the weaving brick walkway round the Maly Palace, the wrought-iron gas lamps casting eerie halos in the gray fog, and the escort's torches licking their flames into the misty night. The sad cortege crossed the Imperial Park, the white-robed bishops of Taurida and Simferopol leading a military escort along the roadway beneath the shaking palms and rapidly thundering skies, to the Church of the Exaltation of the Cross where the body would lie in state. Guns in the harbor at Yalta below thundered their salutes, while the dozen priests chanted the Liturgy for the Dead. Against the tolling bells and whistling wind, the Regimental Band of the Crimean Sharpshooters played "Kol' Slaven Nash Gospod' v Sione" (How Great and Glorious Is God in Zion). Behind the cortege walked the mourners: Nicholas, leading his mother, who was heavily veiled in black; Queen Olga of the Hellenes; the grand dukes and duchesses, including the new

Alexandra Feodorovna; and members of the Suite and the Household, surrounded on all sides by robed soldiers with crackling torches that glowed against their golden helmets.

Two days after Alexander's death, the prince and the princess of Wales arrived in the Crimea. While Princess Alexandra comforted her grieving sister, holding her, praying with her, and even sleeping at her side, her husband immediately thrust himself into the midst of the intricate funeral preparations. Vorontzov-Dashkov was too deferential to protest, and the prince of Wales spent endless hours questioning him about the route for the train to Moscow, church services in the former capital, and the state funeral in St. Petersburg itself. "I wonder," Alexander III's daughter Grand Duchess Olga Alexandrovna said many years later, "what his tiresome old mother would have said if she had seen everybody accept Uncle Bertie's authority! In Russia of all places!"[20]

Alexander III left Livadia for the last time six days after his death. The storm over the Crimea had passed, replaced with a cloudless cerulean sky. More than a thousand soldiers, stationed every twenty feet along the winding, steep hillside, lined the length of the three-mile roadway to Yalta, its surface watered and strewn with rose petals, cypress branches, and laurel leaves. The boom of guns in the harbor, accompanied by the sound of muffled drums and the constant tolling of church bells, announced the start of the procession. A group of white-robed clergy, including the bishops of Taurida and Simferopol, walked before the coffin, its polished oak lid draped in a purple pall. It rested on the shoulders of eight Terek Cossacks who wound their way down the slope of the mountain to Yalta. The emperor's favorite charger, led by a black-clad groom, bore Alexander III's boots, placed backward in the stirrups, its saddle empty. The new emperor and his brothers, uncles, and cousins all walked, heads bared, behind the coffin, with the empress and the women of the imperial family clad in black silk and thick veils and hidden in carriages. Dozens of court officials marched solemnly behind the procession, followed by two squadrons of mounted Cossack guards, two infantry battalions, and a field battery platoon; a contingent of merchants from Yalta; and a group of white-clad schoolchildren, holding lighted tapers.[21]

Beneath the shade of the cypress and palm trees lining the quay, the procession reached the dock at Yalta, decorated with swags of black bunting. Sixteen Cossacks carried the coffin aboard the *Pamyat' Merkuriya* as a nearby regimental band struck up the haunting strains of "Kol' Slaven." They placed the coffin beneath a black canopy on the ship's quarterdeck, forming a guard of honor round it; members of the imperial family followed up the gangway.[22] Six other warships of the Russian Black Sea Fleet lay at anchor in the harbor, flags at half-mast and decks lined with sailors, their heads bowed in silence. At last, the mighty roar of the *Pamyat' Merkuriya*'s engines shook the great vessel as she slowly steamed out of the harbor. Above, a flock of circling gulls escorted the ship until it disappeared into the horizon, her screws churning waves of white foam against the dark blue sea.

Pamyat' Merkuriya entered the placid harbor of Sevastopol at sunset, to the salute of artillery batteries on shore. An honor guard, formed from the oarsmen of the vessel, gently lifted the coffin from the catafalque and carried it down the gangplank, where an escort of officers from the Preobrazhensky and the imperial horse guards regiments lined the quay, standing rigid as the coffin was taken to the end of the Mole, which had been swagged in black crepe and hung with silver crepe rosettes. Here, two imperial trains waited to convey the dead emperor and his family on their journey across Russia. The dark-blue saloon cars, embellished with gilded, double-headed eagles, had been plumed with black ostrich feathers, their windows shuttered and roofs draped in heavy mourning swags. Once the coffin had been placed on board, the empress, her face hidden behind a thick veil, climbed the steps of the second train, followed by her sister and her family, and, with a shrill whistle and a burst of steam, the two locomotives set off for Moscow.

For three days, the trains made their thirteen-hundred-mile journey across Russia, leaving behind the sun-washed Crimea as they headed toward the cold, gloomy north. "Three times," remembered Prince Nicholas of Greece of the funeral train, "it halted while the priests chanted their intercessions for the dead; at every station, as it rumbled slowly through, crowds of peasants fell upon their knees in prayer. At night it would draw up at some wayside halt, and as it stood there, black and forbidding and surrounded by guards, people swarmed out of the countryside, and knelt for hours in the frosts."[23]

Finally, at half-past nine on the morning of October 30, the funeral train slowly steamed into Moscow, the city's medieval silhouette rising in shadow beyond the fogged windows of the passenger carriages, into which members of the imperial family had transferred. The locomotive came to a stop beneath the glass and cast-iron roof above the railway station, hung with black crepe and bunting held by gold swags; a long Oriental runner covered the platform, dotted with tall potted palms.[24] Eleven young cadets from the Corps des Pages in St. Petersburg, attired in white chamois breeches, black dress coats, silver helmets surmounted with double-headed eagles and white plumes, and polished black dress boots with silver spurs, waited along the platform.[25]

One by one, members of the imperial family, led by Nicholas II, crowded the platform, welcomed not, as on so many other occasions, by joyous shouts and colorful banners but with solemn, overwhelming silence. No brass bands played rousing marches, no group of smiling deputies waited to present congratulations, no cascading bouquets of fresh flowers scented the air. All that stood beyond the station doorway was an enormous hearse, the breath of the eight black horses harnessed to its carriage exploding in puffs of steam. As the coffin was carried from the train, the grieving family knelt, and a nearby choir sang "Eternal Memory."[26]

Thousands of Muscovites waited along the route that would take the funeral procession to the Kremlin. Arches, garlanded with crepe, spanned the roadways, above ranks of soldiers whose appearance signaled the approach of the hearse. From the windows, doorways, balconies, and rooftops, the cortege became an endless ribbon of mourning banners, dark uniforms, and court carriages festooned with black, snaking its way through the streets, the respectful silence broken only by the droning dirges of the orchestras and the incessant tolling of the church bells.

An officer's long greatcoat shrouded the figure of Nicholas II as he walked behind his father's coffin, his bare head bowed in grief. Slowly, he led his brothers, uncles, and cousins as they climbed the twisting cobbled streets, followed by foreign princes, dignitaries, and diplomats struggling to keep pace over the uneven roadways, until they reached the broad Tverskaya Avenue, which sliced through the ancient city to the Kremlin. Court carriages moved in unison, rolling through the streets in this lurid parade of death. Soldiers from the Moscow Garrison and cadets from the city's military academies lined the route, standing beneath street lamps whose gas lights flickered in the gray fog.[27] "It is difficult to do justice to the impressiveness of the scene," reported the correspondent for one British paper, "from the moment of the arrival of the train until the deposit of the coffin on its bier in the Cathedral. The absolute silence of the thousands who lined the roads and windows and crowded the roofs was broken only by the sound of the bells and the minute guns. The gray, still cold of the Russian winter gave a spectral aspect to the snow-covered houses which were draped with black and displayed fluttering black and white flags through which passed the stately mourners representing every class and every age of this colossal Empire from the Emperor to the village mayor, from tottering old age to the freshest youth. All combined to form a picture which will be ineffaceable from the memories of those who witnessed it."[28]

At ten different churches, the cortege stopped, as black-robed priests circled the coffin, chanting pensive prayers, before the procession reached the heights of Borovitsky Hill. From the gloom, the Kremlin appeared like some fantastic apparition, a sea of gilded and painted onion domes, burnished Orthodox crosses, and turrets rising above the swirling mist. Soldiers escorted the hearse through the narrow Iberian Gate, beyond lawns grown brown with autumn frosts, to the cobbled expanse of Cathedral Square. With deliberate pace and heads held high, the mourners followed the coffin. Each step took them past some poignant reminder, some visible link, to Alexander's life. Here, in the imposing Cathedral of the Assumption, the emperor had been crowned; on that warm May morning eleven years earlier, the bells in the Tower of Ivan the Great had joyously rung their salutes as Alexander and his wife crossed the square in triumph. Now, Marie Feodorovna watched as her husband's body was carried into the Cathedral of the Archangel Michael. Pale shafts of light spilled from the five domes piercing the frescoed ceiling, bathing the green and blue columns in delicate shades. The coffin was set upon an immense catafalque at the head of the cathedral, between enormous sweeps of cloth of gold embroidered with double-headed eagles in black, as a hidden choir chanted Orthodox prayers for the dead. "The scene was resplendent," wrote the correspondent for the *Daily Chronicle* of London. "The silver gilt icons vied with the silver and gold paneling of the walls in reflecting the light of countless tapers burning within the sanctuary by the altar screen and around the catafalque. Anything more solemn than the office it was impossible to imagine. Many of those present were unable to restrain their emotion. Tears were seen rolling down the cheeks of noble ladies. Sobs broke on the ear almost rhythmically with the cadences of the sacred music."[29]

For twenty hours, Muscovites filed past the old tombs of forgotten tsars to look upon the face of their late emperor. On Monday, October 31—"a dark, gloomy day," as M. A. Bera, one of the cadets from the Corps des Pages noted—the coffin was sealed, then removed from the cathedral, borne to the waiting hearse that took it to the railway station.[30] As a fresh storm erupted over the ancient capital, the train headed northwest, toward St. Petersburg.

From Moscow, the imperial train traveled through murky forests of pine and fir, past dank swamps turned to ice and distant villages of rough wooden cottages grouped around white-washed churches. Within the train's gently rolling saloon cars, relentless grief had descended upon the imperial family, but officials of the court had no respite as they prepared for the coming ceremonies. Thirteen years had passed since St. Petersburg draped itself in black to mourn Emperor

The funeral procession of Alexander III in St. Petersburg

Alexander II, who had been eviscerated by a terrorist's bomb, and detailed accounts of the ceremonial were studied for precedent. As the train continued its journey, workers in the capital were busy preparing a crypt in the Cathedral of St. Peter and St. Paul, the traditional resting place of Romanov sovereigns since Peter the Great.

At the edge of the Russian plain, the train slowed, as the first rays of morning light crept across the land. In the suburbs, where smokestacks belched their clouds of industrial waste, small crowds watched as the train disappeared into St. Petersburg's looming horizon, lost in a haze of rain and sleet. The Nicholas Station, where the imperial train was to end its journey, bustled with activity. Grand Duke Vladimir Alexandrovich waited impatiently beneath the arched roof, pacing back and forth, the heels of his shining black knee-high boots clicking angrily against the concourse floor. A black carpet stretched along the length of the platform, lined with motionless soldiers in crisp uniforms drawn from the Russian guards regiments.[31] Finally, at ten on the morning of November 1, the lights of the locomotive appeared through the fog, and, with a great burst of steam and deafening noise from the engine's brakes, the line of blue carriages came to a halt.

A group of Orthodox priests, dressed in richly decorated robes and tall miters studded with jewels, bowed low as Nicholas II descended from the compartment. "After greeting me," recalled his cousin Grand Duke Konstantin Konstantinovich, "he gave me a deep, expressive look with his lovely, thoughtful and now sad eyes, and kissed me."[32] Nicholas watched as his father's remains were gently handed down, and, with his uncles, he grasped the coffin and carried the heavy load to the end of the platform, where a hearse stood waiting.

A thunder of cannon rent the sky, announcing the start of the procession, and the cortege began its slow, methodical movement. At the same time, church bells across the imperial capital began to toll out, and the guns of the Fortress of St. Peter and St. Paul fired their salutes, one shot every minute until the late emperor's body reached the cathedral. St. Petersburg slumbered in the relentless wrath of approaching winter. The low winter sun, which normally shone on canals choked with ice, was shrouded in a sky cast with gray clouds, the city streets bound in slush. Nearly a hundred thousand soldiers, culled from the elite guards regiments and the St. Petersburg Garrison, stood rigidly at attention along the three-mile route down Nevsky Prospekt to the fortress. They were wrapped in heavy greatcoats against the knife-edge of the Baltic wind that blew down the hollow, cavernous shaft of the great avenue and carried occasional swirls of snow mingled with the sleet. The crowds along the route were small and, as the correspondent for the *Daily Chronicle* of London noted, filled "not with such external marks of devotion as impressed me in Moscow."[33]

The procession, so immense that it took two hours to pass any given point, was divided into 13 sections, with 156 divisions of officials and representatives.[34] A detachment of mounted imperial guards, holding halberds wrapped with black crepe, led the cortege, followed by State Drummers and State Trumpeters. Behind them came the gentlemen of the imperial court, clad in long black cloaks and wide-brimmed hats. Masters of ceremony, their brilliant uniforms covered in mourning ribbons, carried the standards of the Russian provinces: the display of heraldic shields and provincial emblems served as a visible reminder of the breadth of the Russian empire, with the escutcheons of Siberia, Poland, Kazan, Finland, Astrakhan, Novgorod, Vladimir, Kiev, and Moscow shining in the pale light. They were followed by hundreds of officials, representing provincial assemblies, educational institutions, city councils, and bureaucratic and workers' organizations and guilds. Marching slowly behind them were the members of the Imperial Senate and the State Council of Ministers.

Tall, dignified gentlemen, the gold aiguillettes and crested monograms of their epaulets distinguishing them as members of the late Emperor's Suite, were followed by general-adjutants, generals, and admirals of the Suite, their velvet cushions holding pieces of the Imperial Regalia and Alexander III's decorations and foreign orders. The shimmering, jewel-encrusted crowns, from those of Astrakhan, Poland, and Kazan, to the medieval Cap of Monomakh, symbolized the ancient Russian territories. Hussars and Lancers, Chevalier and Cuirassier Guards, all walked in step, their silver breastplates and polished sabers washed in the soft light of gas street lamps whose golden halos glowed in the mist. Two knights followed: one in shining silver and gold armor with richly colored ostrich plumes in his helmet, his shining sword drawn and held proudly upright, rode upon a white horse led by two grooms in golden liveries; the second wore black armor and walked at his side, head lowered and sword covered with black crepe. Together, they represented Joy and Sorrow, Life and Death, signaling the approach of the corpse.[35]

Swaying ranks of court priests, archbishops, bishops, and deacons followed in the cortege, holding icons and religious banners, as the Court Choir intoned a low dirge. Finally, the hearse appeared, drawn by eight horses covered in black palls embroidered with silver thread. An arched catafalque, topped with a gilded replica of the Imperial State Crown, rested on carved and gilded columns bound with thin strips of black; from each of the four corners, ostrich plumes waved in the powerful wind. Twelve general-adjutants—members of Alexander III's Suite—walked at the sides of the hearse, holding the poles supporting the canopy; another twelve generals à la Suite held the golden cords of the top of the catafalque. They were surrounded by a sea of sixty young cadets from the Corps des Pages, holding aloft flaming torches. The coffin lay hidden beneath a pall of gold brocade, lined with ermine and embroidered with the Romanov double-headed eagle in silver thread.[36] The "small dimensions of the vehicle," noted one spectator, "and the over-abundance of cheap gilding and of gold hangings under which it almost disappeared," reminded him of "one of the chariots in which the fairies are drawn in a Drury Lane pantomime."[37]

Nicholas II led the Romanov grand dukes and princes, foreign royals, members of the Diplomatic Corps, and officials, all walking in careful, calculated step behind the hearse. "He had a pale, impassive face," recalled Baroness Buxhoeveden.[38] "He was very pale," noted Princess Anatole Bariatinsky, "and appeared deeply moved by his sorrow and the gravity of the moment." When the cortege passed Anichkov Palace, where Alexander III and his family had lived when in the imperial capital, the new emperor was seen to wipe tears from his eyes.[39] The widowed empress and the grand duchesses followed in court carriages cloaked in black and purple mantles, each drawn by four horses shrouded in black cloth.[40] Faces strained to catch a glimpse of the future empress. As Alexandra's carriage rolled past, people lowered their heads, shaking them in sad resignation while muttering, "She has come to us behind a coffin. She brings misfortune with her."[41]

The clatter of hooves, the crunch of iron-rimmed wheels against the uneven stones, tolling church bells, wailing laments, and shattering cannon salutes echoed against faded yellow palaces as the cortege moved through the capital. Faces were set in unyielding masks, footsteps methodical, as the participants passed Alexander's subjects. There was no hint of grief, no emotion, as they walked in quiet, uniform step, actors in this monotonous, extravagant display of pomp and power. Genuine sympathy for the stricken family, paraded down the avenue before thousands of staring eyes, had been replaced by empty, macabre splendor.

Halfway down Nevsky Prospekt, the haze parted, revealing the curving colonnades and the tall dome of Kazan Cathedral. The cortege came to a halt as Metropolitan Palladi of St. Petersburg stepped from the portico, hand raised in blessing over the hearse. With a slow and weary step, Nicholas II ascended the staircase and, led by the metropolitan, disappeared through the bronze doors to pray for his father's soul.

For four long hours, the funeral procession made its grim, laborious way across the bleak boulevards of the imperial capital: down the Nevsky; along Admiralty Prospekt; through St. Isaac's Square, with its hulking granite cathedral; past the Senate and the Synod Buildings; following the length of the English Embankment to the Nikolaievsky Bridge over the Bolshaya Neva; along the edge of Vasilevskiy Island; around the Strelka and across the Malaya Neva, drawing ever closer to the tall spire of the cathedral rising from the grim Fortress of St. Peter and St. Paul. As soon as the cortege crossed the bridge to the fortress, the Russian tricolor atop the Naryshkin Bastion was lowered, and a black standard hoisted in its place. A ring of Preobrazhensky Guards, drawn up in ranks across the cobbled courtyard, dipped their colors in salute as Metropolitan Palladi met the coffin at the west door of the cathedral, sprinkling it with holy water as general-adjutants carried it through the nave to the catafalque, standing on a dais in front of the gilded iconostasis.

The interior of the cathedral, with its richly colored, smooth marble walls, had been hung with black crepe, ornamented with silver and gold tassels. The coffin rested on an inclined bier, its lid removed to display the dead emperor's remains, the lower half of his body draped with an Imperial Standard that fell away in folds. A baldachin, surmounted with a gilded replica of the Cap of Monomakh surrounded by escutcheons and ostrich plumes, hung from the cathedral dome. Long sheets of black and silver crepe, sewn with double-headed eagles and edged with ermine and heavy gold and silver bullion fringe, cascaded to the corners of the catafalque, attached to four piers with gilded crowns.[42]

On the steps of the dais lay velvet cushions, each holding a glittering piece of the Imperial Regalia or insignia that Alexander had been entitled to wear in life: at the center stood the Imperial State Crown, the Imperial Scepter, the Imperial Standard, and Imperial Orb, with the Crowns of Siberia, Astrakhan, Kazan, Poland, Finland, Novgorod, and Kiev arrayed on cushioned stools. The thousands of diamonds, rubies, emeralds, and sapphires sparkled in the soft light cast from wax tapers burning in the silver candelabra that circled the catafalque.[43]

Through the intermittent sleet and snow, thousands of Alexander's subjects stood patiently in queues that stretched around the cobbled square in front of the cathedral, waiting to pay their last respects, but, like every aspect of the proceedings, this followed an elaborate ritual. People in the military were admitted in the early morning, followed by students and cadets until noon. From two to four in the afternoon, those who held places in the six highest levels of Peter the Great's Table of Ranks and had been sent special engraved cards by the minister of the imperial court paid their respects. People without rank or position were admitted for several hours each evening and then again from nine at night until two in the morning. Inside, the cold marble walls and floor magnified the chill of the tomb. All was silent, except for the shuffling of feet and the occasional, barely audible sob. As they moved past the catafalque, men and women bowed, curtsied, dropped flowers, and knelt in prayer. Illuminated in the pale half-light from hundreds of candles, the faces of members of the guard of honor glowed eerily like ghosts in the night. Bishops in long black caftans circled the platform, swinging censers of fragrant incense whose smoke curled in phantom wisps to the painted dome. The whole of the interior was filled with funeral wreaths, including some five thousand from France alone. Queen Victoria's wreath of lilies and violets bore the inscription "To My Well-Beloved and Never-to-Be-Forgotten Brother."[44]

More than a dozen men stood duty in the guard of honor, each holding an upside-down sword in one hand and a helmet in the other. Next to a mass of palms, funeral wreaths, and massed flowers, members of the Corps des Pages stood at attention, their young faces frozen in sorrow. The strain of this post soon took its toll. The cadets changed positions every two hours, to avoid overexposure to the tear-stained faces and sobs of the public.[45] The pages on duty remained at the fortress throughout their term of service, sleeping on straw mats in two chilly adjoining rooms.[46]

In his first days as emperor, Nicholas II found himself caught in an inescapable, exhausting drama, as much a servant of the intense protocol and etiquette of the Russian court as were any of the young pages. Sixty-one European royals had journeyed to St. Petersburg to mourn Alexander III. Empress Marie Feodorovna's father, King Christian IX of Denmark, had come in person, as had her brother the king of Greece. The king of Serbia arrived with his entourage, and the prince and princess of Wales were joined by their eldest son, George, the duke of York, all representing Queen Victoria. The duchess of Edinburgh, Alexander's sister Marie, arrived from Coburg, while Princess Alix's brother Grand Duke Ernst Ludwig IV of Hesse came from Darmstadt. Representing the Habsburgs was Archduke Karl Ludwig; the king of Baden sent his eldest son and heir; and from Italy came the prince of Naples. The hereditary grand duke of Luxembourg; the hereditary prince of Oldenburg; Prince Ferdinand of Romania; Prince Eugene of Sweden; and Prince Friedrich Augustus of Saxony all represented their own states and countries. Kaiser Wilhelm II had sent his brother, Prince Heinrich of Prussia, the husband of Alexandra's sister Irene. Ambassadors, diplomats, consuls, and envoys filled the train stations and docks as they disembarked with their secretaries, pages, and valets. All of these foreign representatives had to be lodged, fed, acknowledged, and allowed to make their personal condolences to the new emperor. Day after day, the columned ballroom and the crimson salons of Anichkov Palace blazed with light as Nicholas stood with his courtiers to greet this solemn crowd, who offered their sympathy and exchanged honors and awards in a seemingly endless parade of grief.[47]

Twice a day, once at noon and again in the early evening, Nicholas led members of his family, along with the visiting royal representatives, to the Fortress of St. Peter and St. Paul, where services were held for the late emperor. On November 3, Grand Duke Konstantin Konstantinovich noted that Alexander's body had begun to turn black; the pall had been pulled from the lower torso upward to the neck, to cover the disfigured hands. His face, which had also begun to rot, could not be covered and remained exposed.[48] At nine o'clock on the evening of November 6, the night before Alexander III's funeral, the cathedral was closed to visitors. Once the doors were shut, workers prepared the burial vault, lining it with heavy slabs of Putilov stone. The minister of the imperial court presided over a ceremony in which the silver urn containing the emperor's heart was set within a small niche at the bottom of the vault.[49]

After a week filled with terrible ordeals, the divine liturgy for the repose of Alexander III finally took place. A burst of three cannon salutes, fired from the top of the Trubetskoy Bastion in the fortress over the broad Neva, shattered the quiet morning of November 7, announcing the start of the service. As space within the cathedral was so limited, aside from the imperial family, foreign royal guests, and the Diplomatic Corps, only members of the two highest court ranks were given passes to attend the ceremony. The crowd of mourners stood shoulder to shoulder, a vivid sea of uniforms and shining medals, frock coats and black silk gowns, their faces flushed and eyes cast toward the doorway to observe the entrance of the imperial family.

At half-past ten that morning, the emperor and his family arrived. The women wore plain black dresses, relieved only by the crimson and blue silk order sashes across their bodices; small caps held long veils of tulle and lace in place.[50] Nicholas and his family gathered round the steps of the dais as the choir burst into a mournful litany for the dead. Priests took up the chant, as tapers were handed to the congregation until the cathedral was a sea of flickering flames. The metropolitans of St. Petersburg, Moscow, and Kiev anointed the body with holy oil, placing a band of silk, richly embroidered with emblems of the church, across the gray forehead. Then, one by one, the mourners advanced, climbed the dais, and kissed the corpse.[51]

For two long weeks, Alexander's family had received condolences and messages of grief, listened to the rich tones of wailing laments and dirges, and viewed the glittering world of the imperial court through black veils and tear-stained eyes. They had watched as the face of their husband, father, brother, and emperor grew more sallow, his skin darker, his closed, sunken eyes circled with growing purple lines, his shrunken body bloated and filled with the stench of putrefaction. Day after day, they stared at his still features, watching them crumble into memory even while he remained before them. Marie Feodorovna stood near the iconostasis, leaning heavily on her sister the princess of Wales. She watched as her eldest son, his face a pale mask, stepped to the brim of the coffin and gently placed the folds of the Imperial Mantle around his father's body. Eight general adjutants fastened the lid in place, and Nicholas and the grand dukes lifted the coffin and carried it to the edge of the burial vault. The entire congregation knelt as an artillery salute from the guns of the fortress thundered in the cold November sky, rattling the large plate-glass windows of the cathedral as the coffin was lowered. Slowly, the mourners filed past the open grave, collecting handfuls of white sand from a silver salver and sprinkling them across the top of the coffin.

As choirs sang and priests chanted amid the haze of incense and overwhelming heat from the flickering votive candles, the weeks of pomp and pageantry, decay and desolate grief, finally enveloped the family. Alexander's widow, her ears filled with the ceaseless chants and her eyes stung with tears, collapsed into the arms of the princess of Wales, her heartbreaking screams of "Enough! Enough! Enough!" echoing through the vast gilded cathedral as the polished coffin holding her husband's remains disappeared from view through the stone floor.[52]

21

AN IMPERIAL WEDDING

ONE WEEK AFTER ALEXANDER III'S FUNERAL, the second great ceremony of Nicholas II's reign took place. This was his wedding to Princess Alix of Hesse und Bei Rhein, in the cathedral of the Winter Palace. The incredible irony of the situation was lost on no one: what should have been the happiest day in Nicholas's life was instead a depressing reminder of the tragedy that had just befallen the imperial family.

Weddings of grand dukes and duchesses and members of the imperial family generally followed a recognized procedure. The round of parties and receptions varied greatly according to the rank of the bride or the groom, and the venue also differed according to personal choice. But these marriages, the etiquette surrounding them, and all the details of their ceremonial were conducted according to precedent and tradition laid out by the minister of the imperial court and the grand master of ceremonies. Imperial weddings were never considered state occasions; that honor was reserved exclusively for the nuptials of the sovereign, or the heir to the throne.

Under normal circumstances, Nicholas II's wedding would have been a grand affair. The ceremony itself had been in the planning stage since the tsesarevich's engagement in April of 1894. The wedding would have formed the centerpiece of a week of public celebrations and parades. The death of Alexander III changed all of this. Just after his father's death, Nicholas II declared his intention of marrying Alix while they were still at Livadia, quietly and without ceremony. "There has been a good deal of argument about the question of where to arrange my marriage," Nicholas wrote in his diary. "Mama, many others, and I think it would be better to celebrate the marriage here quietly, while dear Papa is still under this roof, but all the uncles are against it, saying that I should marry in Petersburg after the funeral. To me, this seems quite unfitting."[1]

These four uncles, the Grand Dukes Vladimir, Alexei, Serge, and Paul Alexandrovich, all vetoed their nephew's idea of a quiet wedding. They argued that the marriage of the Emperor of All Russia was too important to be cast aside for the sake of personal emotions; at the very least, it should take place in St. Petersburg, in appropriate surroundings, and with a suitable guest list. Although this ran counter to Nicholas's own wishes, he let himself be persuaded that it was the only course to follow.

Nicholas II was the first Romanov since Empress Elizabeth to accede to the imperial throne without a consort at his side. Had he not been so determined to wed immediately, the actual ceremony itself might have proved a far more glamorous and memorable affair, taking place with the splendor accompanying the emperor's position. He could, of course, wait until the following spring, when the wedding had originally been planned, but because court mourning would still be in effect, the ceremony itself would, of necessity, have had to have been a small, private one. Nicholas II considered all of his options: he decided that he could not wait eighteen months to have a state wedding. Monday, November 14, was Empress Marie Feodorovna's birthday, and even though her husband had just died, court mourning would be relaxed somewhat. Using this as a convenient excuse, Nicholas decided that his wedding would take place on his mother's birthday.

This decision meant that although a certain amount of pomp would be allowed, the wedding would be dominated by mourning. At first, Nicholas declared that the wedding would be a private family occasion. Only after considerable pressure from his four uncles did he relent and allow members of the aristocracy, the imperial court, and the Diplomatic Corps to be invited, to view the procession to and from the cathedral; they would still be restricted from the actual ceremony itself. Although not a full-scale state ceremony, the wedding nonetheless retained elements of grandeur and was considered a state occasion, even though it was celebrated in private. Preparations had to be telescoped into the space of a few days. Even the bride's trousseau was not ready, and extra seamstresses were hastily called in to complete her wedding gown.

On Friday, November 11, the formal wedding contract was signed. A magnificent parchment, illuminated and embossed in gold, it stated that Nicholas II accepted his intended bride and her "magnificent dowry," a piece of official fiction that concealed the relative poverty of the Hessian royal family. Paragraph by paragraph, the contract stipulated precisely what personal items, jewels, and wealth the bride brought to the marriage, promising that these would remain under her complete personal control. Should Nicholas die, his widow—as well as any children the pair might have—was promised a substantial annual allowance for the duration of her life. Nicholas de Giers, the Russian minister of foreign affairs, and Count Vorontzov-Dashkov signed the document on behalf of the emperor; General von Werder, an official representing the bride's brother Grand Duke Ernst Ludwig IV of Hesse und Bei Rhein, signed on behalf of Princess Alix.[2]

The weekend leading up to the wedding passed quietly. The emperor and his family continued to attend daily services for Alexander III as snow blanketed the capital. On Sunday afternoon, Nicholas and his fiancée took tea with his family, then shared the evening together at her sister Ella's Sergeievsky Palace facing the Fontanka. "I cannot see her any more until the wedding," Nicholas wrote in his diary. "It seems to me the whole time that this must be somebody else's wedding and not mine. It seems so impossible that it should take place in such circumstances. We dined and spent a quiet evening sitting with Mama."[3]

In anticipation of the wedding, Nicholas issued an imperial ukase, in which he declared November 14 and 15 public holidays and forgave a number of debts owed to the government, including repayment of loans undertaken by peasants, tax debts, and various fines. Certain penal sentences were relieved or shortened, and those accused of treason but who had remained at large for fifteen years without prosecution were pardoned. Finally, some forty thousand workers from St. Petersburg's factories were to be fed at special dinners, the expense borne by the emperor himself.[4]

The day of the wedding dawned cold but clear in St. Petersburg. The previous night, thousands of spectators had poured into the capital, selecting spots lining the route from Anichkov Palace along Nevsky Prospekt to the Winter Palace. At seven o'clock, members of the imperial guards regiments, who had been detailed to stand at intervals along the route down Nevsky Prospekt, took up their posts.[5] An hour later, the quiet of the early winter morning was shattered by a twenty-one-gun salute, fired from the cannon of the Fortress of St. Peter and St. Paul and calling St. Petersburg to celebrate the coming festivities.

Two weeks earlier, in the midst of the lengthy funeral services for Alexander
III, some three thousand invitations to attend the new emperor's wedding had
gone out from the office of the minister of the imperial court. Surmounted by a
double-headed eagle and embossed in gilt, the engraved vellum cards summoned the guests to the Winter Palace on Monday, November 14, to witness the
ceremony. For the day, the deep mourning imposed by Alexander III's death was
set aside. Gentlemen were ordered to come in full regimental dress; bureaucrats
and civil servants were to don the uniform stipulated by their position in Peter
the Great's Table of Ranks, while those in the Diplomatic Corps were requested
to wear white tie and tails, with orders. Russian ladies were to wear full court
dress and foreign women, evening gowns, with full jewelry, including tiaras and
veils and awards. At nine that morning, the first guests began to arrive, their carriages depositing them at the entrances to the Winter Palace specified on their
invitations, according to their rank. They were met by pages and court chamberlains in uniforms dripping with gold braid, who escorted them up the Jordan
Staircase, lined with members of the Chevalier Life Guards Regiment in silver
cuirasses and helmets, sabers drawn in salute, and to the Parade Halls where they
were to view the procession to and from the palace cathedral. The gathered
crowd, noted one foreign correspondent, "was a splendid spectacle, with the
variety of brilliant uniforms, and the costly dresses and jewels worn by the
ladies."[6] There was much anticipation; for most of them, it would be their first
intimate glimpse of the woman who was to be their new empress.

At half-past eleven, the emperor, accompanied by his sixteen-year-old brother,
Grand Duke Michael Alexandrovich, left Anichkov Palace in an open, semistate
landau drawn by four white horses, with Cossack outriders galloping in front of
and behind the carriage. As soon as the gates of the palace swung open and the
groom appeared on Nevsky Prospekt, reported one witness, he was "greeted
with a vociferous burst of cheering, which was renewed again and again." An
escort, drawn from the Chevalier Guards, His Majesty's Imperial Hussar Guards,
and Her Majesty's Lancer Guards Regiments, joined the landau as it rolled down
the Prospekt, their brilliant uniforms and the silver liveries on their mounts shimmering in the pale morning light.[7]

The one-and-a-half-mile route leading from Anichkov Palace to the Winter
Palace was decorated with flags and bunting, and was thronged with cheering
crowds who waved miniature tricolor imperial flags. Detachments of soldiers from
the Preobrazhensky Life Guards Regiment stood rigidly at attention along the way,
holding back the masses of people, all trying to catch a glimpse of the imperial

procession. Military bands, stationed every half-mile along the avenue, each struck up "God Save the Tsar" as the procession appeared to it, the strains taken up by the crowd that joined in as Nicholas passed before them. After a short, fifteen-minute ride, the landau left Nevsky Prospekt and entered Morskaya Ulitsa, rolling beneath Rossi's great Triple Archway spanning the General Staff Building to cross Palace Square. "There was not an inch of space to spare," noted one observer.[8]

A few minutes after Nicholas and his brother left Anichkov Palace, Empress Marie Feodorovna climbed into a closed red and gold court carriage beneath the portico that, at a signal from the driver, circled the courtyard and rolled through the gates onto Nevsky Prospekt. The empress drove down the Nevsky and across the Fontanka to the Sergeievsky Palace to collect the bride. Alexandra descended the heart-shaped staircase and crossed the Entrance Hall, wrapped in heavy furs to protect her against the chill of the winter morning. She wore not her wedding gown, which awaited her arrival at the Winter Palace, but a simple traveling dress. Once the bride had joined her future mother-in-law in the carriage, the two women set off down the broad avenue to the Winter Palace, escorted by divisions of Lancer and Hussar Guards.[9]

As the bride's procession, with its line of closed carriages conveying the members of the imperial family, the foreign royal guests, and the highest dignitaries of the Empress's Suite, made its way down Nevsky Prospekt, recalled one observer, it received, "if possible, even a more hearty greeting than the Emperor himself. Handkerchiefs and hats were waved in the air and the most intense enthusiasm prevailed."[10]

At the Winter Palace, the bride's coach came to a halt to the wild cheers of the crowd that filled the immense Palace Square. Boris Gerois, one of the pages in attendance, recalled, "Alexandra Feodorovna was beautiful and majestic, too, and resembled her sister closely, but still she took second place. We met them at the doors of the carriage and helped them get out. The bride offered her hand for us to kiss, but with an awkward and embarrassed gesture. A sense of unease was thus the first thing you noticed on meeting the young Empress, and this impression she never managed to dispel. She was so obviously nervous of conversation, and at moments when she needed to show some social graces, her smile would become suffused with little red spots and she would look intensely serious. Her wonderful eyes promised kindness, but instead of a bright spark, they contained only the cold embers of a dampened fire. There was certainly purity and loftiness in this look, but loftiness is always dangerous: it is akin to pride and can quickly lead to alienation."[11]

While the emperor waited in the Blackamoor Hall, smoking and chatting with various guests, his bride, accompanied by his mother and her sister, walked to the Malachite Hall, where her wedding dress was prepared. Alexandra sat before a large gilded looking glass, used by all Russian grand duchesses on their wedding days, while maids fluttered about, completing her toilette. On the lace-covered dressing table stood Empress Anna's ornate, solid gold toilette service, the work of an eighteenth-century craftsman from Augsburg.[12] Alexandra nervously awaited the arrival of Monsieur Delcroix, the court hairdresser, who was to style her coiffure. Delcroix appeared as scheduled, but the sentry on duty failed to recognize him and believed that his pass was a forgery. As Alexandra waited, increasingly agitated, her hairdresser stood on the street. Finally, after much argument, Delcroix was admitted and taken to the anxious bride.[13]

By tradition, the maids of honor of every grand duchess participated in the ceremonial robing of the bride in her splendid gown. Alexandra's wedding outfit was the most intricate ensemble she would ever wear. Her stockings were of lace, her shoes embroidered and decorated with seed pearls and lace overlays. Over these, she wore layers of wide, starched petticoats, which added volume to her skirt. The gown was modeled on the traditional Russian court dress. The wide, full overskirt, of silver brocade, was open from the waist to the floor in an inverted V to reveal a second underskirt of silver tissue, edged along the hemline with ermine. The décolletage, also edged with white ermine, was cut low, to reveal her neck and shoulders. The long sleeves, split from just below the shoulders, were edged with white ermine and hung in stiff folds below the waist. The tightly fitted, boned bodice was embroidered with a foliate design in gold thread adorned with diamonds, which sparkled at every movement.[14] The overskirt fanned out from the waist into a fifteen-foot train, also edged with ermine.[15] Over this, Alexandra wore an Imperial Mantle. Ordinarily, grand duchesses wore a mantle of crimson velvet, but Alexandra's mantle, as a concession to her rank as bride of the emperor, was of cloth-of-gold, lined and edged with ermine.[16] These robes were so heavy that eight pages—four on each side—and the chamberlain, carrying the hem, had to help carry them; without their assistance, Alexandra could scarcely move.[17]

Alexandra wore her hair swept back and coiled into a bun at the back of her head; by tradition, Delcroix attached two ringlets, which hung down to her bare shoulders, from her own hair on either side of her face. Her long veil of Honiton lace had been designed by her grandfather Prince Albert and had previously been worn by her mother, Princess Alice, and by her sisters Victoria, Elizabeth, and Irene on their wedding days. It was held in place by a Russian fringe tiara of diamonds set in platinum, surmounted by a large pink diamond.[18] In addition, she wore the Romanov Nuptial Crown, of diamonds sewn on red velvet. This was placed on her head, according to tradition, by Empress Marie Feodorovna. Surrounding these traditional headpieces was a wreath of orange blossoms, brought from the imperial conservatory in Warsaw.[19]

Across the bodice of her gown stretched the blue sash of the Order of St. Andrei, held in place by a large diamond star. Along with a number of diamond-and-pearl bow brooches and a diamond stomacher, Alexandra wore, by tradition, the Imperial Rivière, a diamond necklace of 475 carats, with matching earrings, all of which had belonged to Catherine the Great. These earrings were so heavy that they had to be supported with wires looped around the top of the ears. As the day wore on, the wire cut into the flesh, causing Alexandra much pain.[20] She carried a small bouquet of white roses with sprigs of myrtle, tied together with long, white velvet ribbons embroidered with Peter the Great's monogram in gold thread.[21] On her right hand, she wore a ring sent from her grandmother Queen Victoria as one of her wedding gifts.[22] "The bride," wrote her future mother-in-law, "was thoroughly *enchanting*, so lovely and beautiful and [with] an Imperial calm and dignity."[23]

At ten minutes past twelve, the guns of the Fortress of St. Peter and St. Paul across the Neva River opened fire, beginning a fifty-one-gun salvo that announced the beginning of the processions. At the same time, the doors of the private apartments swung open and the wedding procession marched out. A hundred officials appeared in pairs: quartermasters of the court, in scarlet and gold livery; the gentlemen-at-arms, in white and gold; the masters of ceremony; the grand master of ceremonies; the gentlemen of the Household, in uniforms covered in gold braid; chamberlains; and, finally, the grand marshal of the imperial court, swinging his ebony wand of office topped with a gilded, double-headed eagle. His raised the staff slowly, then brought it down on the inlaid wooden floor with three loud thuds, announcing, "Her Imperial Majesty the Empress."[24] At that moment, Marie Feodorovna appeared, leading her future daughter-in-law at the head of the imperial procession.

In deference to the occasion, Marie Feodorovna wore a long, white velvet court gown, decorated with scallops of gold lace and panels of white crepe embossed with pearls.[25] A pearl-and-diamond tiara and a matching necklace sparkled as she walked. She held her head high, but her eyes were red and swollen from crying. "It was painful to watch the poor Empress," wrote Grand

Duke Konstantin Konstantinovich. "She seemed even paler and more frail than usual, like a victim being led to the slaughter; finding herself in front of thousands of eyes at such a difficult and grief stricken time was inexpressibly painful for her."[26]

Alexandra walked at her side. One witness later recalled the favorable impression made by the young bride: "'How beautiful she is!' That expression followed her all along her path, and it is true that her appearance was positively magnificent as she stood there in her bridal array of silver cloth. . . . Her unusual height helped her to bear the weight of her dress and set off its splendor in its best light. Her mouth quivered a little and this relieved her habitual hard expression that was the one defect of an otherwise perfectly beautiful face, the straight classical features of which reminded one of an antique Greek statue. The glow upon her cheeks only added to the loveliness of her countenance and her eyes, modestly lowered, gave to her whole figure a maidenly shyness that made it wonderfully attractive."[27] And Lord Carrington wrote to Queen Victoria, "She looked the perfection of what one would imagine an Empress of Russia on her way to the altar would be and moved along quite simply and with great dignity. She makes very marked bows with her head, when she greets anyone; and this is much noticed and appreciated."[28]

Nicholas walked behind his mother and his bride. He wore the ceremonial dress uniform of a colonel in the Life Guards Hussar Regiment. His scarlet broadcloth tunic was decorated with gold braid, golden epaulets with the diamond initials of his father, gold aiguillcttes denoting his rank as adjutant general to Alexander III, and several rows of medals that shone against the crimson backdrop. His Hussar breeches, of dark blue cloth, were trimmed with gold braid, and he wore low boots of black patent leather. Across his chest stretched the orange sash of the Order of Hesse und Bei Rhein; from his shoulders hung a dolman of white broadcloth, decorated in gold braid and edged with fur.[29] In his hand, he held a Hussar hat of beaver fur, with a long white ostrich plume.

Count Vorontzov-Dashkov followed the emperor, leading members of Nicholas II's Entourage and Suite. The foreign royal guests came next, a long procession headed by Marie Feodorovna's father, King Christian IX of Denmark; her brother King George I of the Hellenes and his wife, Queen Olga; Alexandra's brother Grand Duke Ernst Ludwig IV of Hesse; Prince Alfred, the duke of Edinburgh and of Saxe-Coburg-Gotha, in Russian naval uniform, with his wife, Grand Duchess Marie Alexandrovna, an aunt of Nicholas II; the prince and the princess of Wales, the former in the uniform of a colonel in chief of the Russian Dragoons, his wife in a long white court gown; Prince Ferdinand of Romania; Prince George, the duke of York, in a British naval uniform; and Alexandra's sister Irene with her husband, Prince Heinrich of Prussia. They were followed by members of the imperial family; all of the grand dukes wore the cordon of the Order of Hesse, and the princes, the cordon of the Order of St. Andrei.[30]

The empress's *ober-gofmeisterina* led the procession of the ladies of the imperial court, all richly attired in Russian court gowns embroidered in gold and silver thread, with velvet or satin kokoshniki and long veils of lace or tulle: the *starshaya dami*; the *dames à portrait*; the *kamer-freilini*; the *kavaler-dami*; and the *freilini*.[31] Behind them came the highest officials in the government, including members of the Imperial Senate, in their dark blue uniforms embellished with gold braid and tricorn hats, and nearly a hundred officials who held places in the first four ranks of Peter the Great's *Chin*.

The processions followed the ribbon of crimson carpet as it wound from room to room. At the doors of each hall, the grand marshal of the imperial court announced their entrance, and members of the guard of honor who were posted drew their sabers in salute as the assembled crowd bowed and sank into deep curtseys.[32] The three thousand guests invited to witness the processions to and from the cathedral had been strictly divided according to rank and precedence. The Concert Hall was filled with members of the imperial court and state officials, who watched from either side of the carpet before joining the end of the procession. Members of the Emperor's Military Secretariat, along with officers attached to the grand dukes, military officials on active duty, and the suites belonging to the foreign royal guests, filled the adjoining Nicholas Hall and the anteroom. In the Field Marshal's Hall and the Throne Room of Peter the Great, they passed before municipal representatives and mayors, civic officials, foreign industrialists, and members of the Russian and the international press. The Hall of Armorial Bearings was crowded with nearly a thousand guests, including aristocrats, former court officials, and hundreds of maids of honor, the latter all in Russian court gowns of white satin and velvet brocades. So immense was this procession that it took nearly half an hour for the wedding party to pass the guests who waited in the halls.

An extraordinary assemblage joined the procession when it reached the 1812 Gallery. At a signal from the grand master of ceremonies, members of the Diplomatic Corps, the Imperial Council, and the Council of Ministers all took up

The wedding of
Nicholas and
Alexandra, 1894.
See plate 37.

positions at the rear of the procession, following it down the immense gallery to the cathedral. Waiting at the cathedral doors was a host of clergymen: the metropolitan of St. Petersburg; Father Ioann Yanishev, the personal confessor to the imperial family; archbishops; bishops; archimandrites; and court priests. These elderly, white-haired men were attired in golden copes and stoles embroidered with silver and encrusted with diamonds and pearls. As the choir burst into an anthem, the clergymen led the procession down the aisle of the cathedral to the red-carpeted dais beneath the dome, which was flanked by huge bowers of roses, orchids, lilies, and lilacs. Nicholas ascended the dais first, then turned to face the congregation.[33] Slowly, Empress Marie Feodorovna took the hand of her future daughter-in-law and led her up the steps to the waiting emperor. The red velvet curtains at the enormous cathedral windows had been raised, and the sun shining against the snow-covered roofs and sills, along with the strong electric lights, lent a strange, luminescent sparkle to the festivities.

As Nicholas and Alexandra knelt, the choir began a litany, followed by two prayers intoned by the metropolitan. A priest handed the bride and groom each a lighted taper, tied with silk ribbons and sprigs of myrtle, while the metropolitan blessed them, swinging a smoking censer filled with fragrant incense. From the altar, a court priest brought a golden tray, on which rested the two wedding rings. He took the tray to the dais, where he held it before Father Yanishev. Yanishev blessed them, making the sign of the cross over the tray and announcing loudly, "The Servant of God, Nicholas, betroths himself to the Servant of God, Alexandra," and "The Servant of God, Alexandra, betroths herself to the Servant of God, Nicholas." He then took the rings from the tray and himself placed them on the right ring fingers of the bride and the groom, exchanging them three times, in recognition of the Trinity. Nicholas and Alexandra again knelt, while prayers were read, after which the choir burst into the 77th Psalm.

The emperor and his bride exchanged traditional wedding vows: she promised to love, honor, and obey; he, to cherish and worship. While Alexandra made her responses in a low but firm voice, Nicholas, clearly nervous and overwhelmed with emotion, had to be prompted several times by Father Yanishev.[34] A priest brought two golden nuptial crowns from the altar, which the metropolitan then blessed. The four best men, Grand Dukes Michael Alexandrovich, Kirill Vladimirovich, and Serge Mikhailovich, and Prince George of Greece, took turns holding the crowns over the heads of the bride and the groom, again exchanging them three times. "The Emperor is just a little shorter than his bride," noted Grand Duke

Konstantin Konstantinovich, "but not so much as to be noticeable. They both stood motionless under the crowns. I was able to see their faces as they circled round the lectern; their eyes were lowered, their expressions concentrated."[35]

Nicholas and Alexandra, their joined hands covered with the metropolitan's stole, were led around the altar three times as a deacon blessed them with incense. Returning to the steps of the dais, the bride and he groom knelt once more, the metropolitan intoned a final prayer, Nicholas and Alexandra kissed a golden cross, and, shortly after one o'clock in the afternoon, they were pronounced husband and wife.

At the end of the benediction, the Court Choir burst into the great Te Deum; at the same time, by a prearranged signal, the bells of the city's churches tolled, joined by the guns of the Fortress of St. Peter and St. Paul as their salutes echoed across the St. Petersburg sky.[36] Within the cathedral, however, the atmosphere was more subdued. Marie Feodorovna, now the dowager empress, had cried throughout the service.[37] And, according to Grand Duke Alexander Mikhailovich, "The whole thing looked grotesque. I doubt whether the greatest of theatrical producers could have staged a more appropriate prologue for the tragedy of the last Tsar of Russia."[38]

The ceremony ended, the procession left the cathedral, this time with Nicholas and Alexandra marching at its head. The emperor, noted one witness, "was very pale, and was visibly affected."[39] It was Alexandra, beautiful and attired in her rich gown, who made the most lasting impression. Princess Elizabeth Naryshkin-Kuryakin recalled that she "looked so impressive that the Emperor seemed almost insignificant beside her."[40]

There was no reception or wedding luncheon to celebrate the occasion. "When all the family and friends gathered around Nicholas with their congratulations," remembered Grand Duke Ernst Ludwig IV of Hesse und Bei Rhein, "I went unofficially to look for Alix. I found her by herself, standing alone in the middle of a room. I slipped in, and went to her to hug her, and she told me that the silver dress and gold mantle were so heavy that she could not move from her spot. I went quickly to find Nicky and told him. Quickly, two *kamer-herren* were sent to help her, and soon she could move again."[41]

After Alexandra changed out of her wedding gown into a traveling outfit, husband and wife climbed into a waiting, open, semistate landau drawn by four white horses and left the Winter Palace for Anichkov Palace, "amid the unbounded enthusiasm of the immense crowds gathered to greet them," recorded one witness. "The Emperor graciously saluted the crowds on the either side of the route."[42] Alexandra, wrote an observer, "kept bowing repeatedly, but she was so nervous that she appeared to move her head mechanically, and her eyes were filled with tears that she tried to restrain."[43] "The streets were so crowded," Nicholas recorded in his diary, "that we could hardly drive through them."[44] And the *Illustrated London News* reported, "Popular acclamation in the streets and public places through which the state carriage passed amply compensated, by its unbidden, hearty greetings and expressions of friendly congratulations, for this suppression of festive signs of the joyful occasion."[45]

Halfway down Nevsky Prospekt, the landau halted at Kazan Cathedral so that Nicholas and Alexandra could pray before its celebrated icon. "There was literally a sea of heads extending up the Nevsky Prospekt," recorded one witness, "and the multitudes were so densely packed that the troops had a great difficulty in preserving a passage for the wedding march." As the emperor and the empress entered the packed cathedral, the choir burst into a Te Deum that ended with a benediction by the metropolitan of St. Petersburg, asking for God's blessing as they embarked on a life of duty to the Russian empire.[46]

As the newly married couple emerged from the cathedral, reported one observer, "the enthusiasm of the people was beyond all description. The brilliancy of the spectacle at this moment was enhanced by a sudden burst of sunshine from the clouds that had hitherto darkened the city. The appearance of the golden rays was regarded as a good augury by the immense crowds present, which cheered themselves hoarse."[47] Overwhelmed, Nicholas ordered that the Cossack outriders who formed the escort, as well as the soldiers lining the route, be removed, so that the people could surge forward round the landau for a better view, a move that the correspondent of the French newspaper *Journal des Débats* called "a daring and beautiful gesture."[48]

The emperor and his new wife were met with a salute from members of the Life Guards Uhlan Regiment as their landau rolled into the courtyard of Anichkov Palace. Waiting beneath the porte cochere was the dowager empress. She met her son and new daughter-in-law with the traditional Russian welcome of bread and salt, signifying plenty and good luck. Together with Nicholas's youngest sister, twelve-year-old Grand Duchess Olga Alexandrovna, the emperor and the empress appeared at an upper window of the palace. "Here they stood for fifteen minutes," wrote one reporter, "bowing repeatedly in response to the acclamations of the multitude gathered outside the Palace. Grand Duchess Olga, with girlish enthusiasm, repeatedly kissed her hand to the crowd. The Empress leaned on the arm of her husband and smiled radiantly on the throng."[49]

There was no honeymoon, and Nicholas and Alexandra spent their first night together as husband and wife in the emperor's former childhood bedroom. "We all sat together during the evening," Nicholas recorded in his diary, "reading and replying to telegrams. We dined at eight o'clock, and went to bed early as Alix had a bad headache."[50] Sadly, to the new empress, her wedding "seemed to me a mere continuation of the masses for the dead, with this difference, that now I wore a white dress instead of a black one."[51]

22

THE CORONATION

In MAY OF 1896, RUSSIA CELEBRATED the coronation of Nicholas II. A coronation symbolized the supreme moment in a sovereign's life. It was not merely his crowning; a coronation was the physical and spiritual anointing, at the hands of Orthodox clergy, of God's Representative on earth, the Father of the Russian People. Each coronation not only relied on the rigid tradition and iron etiquette that ruled the imperial court, but also renewed these precedents as living witnesses to the power of autocracy and the primacy of the Orthodox Church. As such, a coronation was a celebration of the Orthodox faith, with all of its pomp, pageantry, and majesty vested in the person of the emperor. Coronations took place in Moscow, the citadel of Russian Orthodoxy. St. Petersburg, with its Western influences and imported ideas, was considered far too European to be entrusted with such a sacred and holy rite.

Preparations for Nicholas II's coronation began as soon as his father's funeral was over. Initially, Grand Duke Serge Alexandrovich, the emperor's uncle who held the post of governor-general of Moscow, had insisted that he alone should be responsible for all of the arrangements. According to Princess Elizabeth Naryshkin-Kuryakin, he was "keenly disappointed in this ambition when he discovered that the Court Ministry had reserved the chief functions for its own. Deeply hurt, he declared that in that case he would leave all responsibility on the shoulders of the Ministry." He threatened, in protest, to leave Moscow for the length of the ceremonies. Nicholas II, the princess recalled, "was greatly embarrassed by this conflict and tried to mediate between the two contestants. He succeeded in bringing about a compromise, whereby some of the arrangements fell to the Grand Duke and others to the Court Ministry."[1]

Eventually, a special Coronation Commission was formed to oversee the plans, headed by the grand duke and assisted by the minister of the imperial court, Count Hilarion Vorontzov-Dashkov; his deputy, Count Vladimir de Freedericksz; and the grand master of imperial ceremonies, Count Konstantin von der Pahlen. Court mourning for Alexander III ended on October 20, 1895. After several lengthy meetings with the Coronation Committee, the emperor issued a decree on March 8, 1895. A magnificently illuminated parchment, decorated with Byzantine-style drawings, announced that the coronation would take place on May 14 of the following year, following the emperor's wish that the festivities be held as close as possible to the anniversary of his father's own coronation in 1883.[2]

Nothing concerning the coronation was left to chance. Scale models were built of Moscow, detailing the processional routes, along with models of the Kremlin and the Cathedral of the Assumption, where the actual ceremony would take place, to allow the committee to study in detail the necessary requirements. The Coronation Commission dispersed hundreds of thousands of rubles to refurbish the Moscow palaces, theaters, streets, and churches where special events would take place. The total cost of the coronation came to a staggering 965,925 rubles ($9,659,250 in 2005 figures); even so, this was frugal compared with the 2,715,704 rubles ($27,157,040 in 2005 figures) that had been spent for Alexander III's coronation in 1883.[3]

In anticipation of the coronation, the Moscow of May 1896 presented a dazzling sight: freshly painted and whitewashed buildings, capped with multicolored tile roofs and hung with white, blue, and red Russian tricolor flags and bunting, strings of electric lights, and garlands of evergreen boughs and moss; Turks in black fezzes, Persians with white turbans and robes; Hussars in white and gold cloaks with plumed caps and Cossacks in long red coats with black astrakhan kolpaki hats and shining sabers; wide avenues lined with elegant colonnaded mansions, decorated with flags, bunting, and baskets of spring flowers pouring forth their aromas into the sky; and, emblazoned upon every doorway, over every window, and atop steeply pitched roofs, the initials *H* and *A* for Nicholas and Alexandra in Cyrillic.[4]

Thousands of visitors, from all parts of the empire, as well as foreign guests, royals, members of the Diplomatic Corps, and special envoys, crowded into the former capital. Wooden stands were built along the processional route and inside the Kremlin, and doorways, windows, balconies, and rooftops overlooking the route, reported Vladimir Nemirovich-Demchenko, a correspondent for the popular Russian periodical *Niva,* were rented for as much as 500 rubles ($5,000 in 2005 figures). Prices for horses and carriages were ten times higher than normal: when Nemirovich-Demchenko went to rent a vehicle at the regular price of 75 rubles ($750 in 2005 figures), he was informed that he would instead have to pay between 800 and 900 rubles ($8,000 to $9,000 in 2005 figures). Fine French clothing at Korday's in Moscow was much in demand: trains for ladies' gowns went for up to 400 rubles each ($4,000 in 2005 figures), while court gowns fetched up to 2,000 rubles ($20,000 in 2005 figures).[5]

Several thousand of these guests were specially invited on the emperor's orders. Representing the world's different faiths was a wide body of delegates. For the first time, the Vatican sent a deputation on behalf of the Pope, while the archbishop of Canterbury sent a group of Anglican bishops to represent the Church of England. The Patriarch in Constantinople sent a delegation, and there were representatives of the Patriarchs of Jerusalem, Antioch, and Alexandria as well.[6] The Danish, Italian, Bulgarian, Romanian, and Greek royal families sent their crown princes as representatives, while the duke and duchess of Connaught attended the coronation on behalf of the empress's grandmother, Queen Victoria. Kaiser Wilhelm II sent his brother, Prince Heinrich of Prussia, who was married to Alexandra's sister Irene. According to protocol, no crowned sovereign was allowed to witness the coronation service; in 1896, two exceptions were made, one for Dowager Empress Marie Feodorovna, the other for Nicholas II's great aunt, Queen Olga of the Hellenes.[7]

These visitors and dignitaries had to be housed and fed. Apartments rented for as much as 2,500 rubles ($25,000 in 2005 figures) for the month of May.[8] The imperial court had taken over all of the city's hotels. Members of the empire's nobility and military officers were housed at the Hotel Metropol; foreign princes, princesses, and other diplomats were lodged at their respective embassies. The government of France rented the Hunt Club, at a cost of 22,000 rubles ($220,000 in 2005 figures), with some 900,000 francs allocated for their entertainment. The Germans took over the Von Derviz Palace, where the empress's brother-in-law was lodged.[9]

At the beginning of 1896, the Cathedral of the Assumption, where the service would take place, was closed to the public and renovated. For several months, the ancient walls echoed with the sounds of carpenters' hammers, as the men built the wooden stands that would line the interior. The cathedral was given a new lead roof, the wall paintings and frescoes were cleaned, the iconostasis regilded, the wooden window frames replaced with iron ones, and new oak doors were fitted. At the end of April, the interior was hung with red velvet damask, and a dais and a canopy were installed at the front of the iconostasis. For the first time, the Kremlin was wired for electricity.[10]

Invitations to witness the coronation service in the Cathedral of the Assumption were precious commodities, and the selection process became a veritable nightmare of protocol and precedence for the minister of the imperial court, the grand marshal of the imperial court, and members of the Coronation Committee. "It was their duty," recorded one journalist, "to decide between an aide-de-camp from Bulgaria and a Russian ambassador at home on leave, a Japanese Prince and an English general, a German Duchess and the correspondent of the Paris *Figaro*. It was a matter of so many square inches chiefly, and one man or woman who got in kept a dozen applicants for the space out; and the pressure that was brought to bear in order to gain a footing—and a footing was actually all one obtained— threatened the peace of Europe, and caused tears of disappointment and wounds that will rankle in the breasts of noble Russian families for years to come."[11]

Nicholas and Alexandra arrived in Moscow on Monday, May 6, the emperor's twenty-eighth birthday. In the midst of a terrible storm, their train slowly steamed into a siding at Smolensk Station, where they were greeted by a guard of honor formed from Her Majesty's Lancer Regiment.[12] As governor-general, Grand Duke Serge Alexandrovich formally welcomed them, saying, "In lucid recognition of the grandeur of the historical moment in which we are living, Moscow lays down before you, Most Autocratic Monarch, its most loyal congratulations and its prayerful wishes that the coming year, in which an intensified blessing from the Holy Spirit will descend on your holy head, may be the entrance to a long range of tranquil and glorious years, to the gladness and happiness alike of your Imperial Family, and of the hundred million family of your loyal subjects."[13]

By tradition, they did not enter the city center but instead retired to the suburban Petrovsky Palace, to pray in preparation of the coming ceremony. Waiting in the palace courtyard was another guard of honor, formed from the Ekaterinslav Life Guards. After a brief Te Deum, held in the Palace Rotunda, Nicholas and Alexandra dined that evening with Prince Heinrich of Prussia, before retiring.[14]

Dowager Empress Marie Feodorovna arrived in Moscow on May 8. Following dinner, the imperial family gathered on the balcony of the Petrovsky Palace for a concert. Below, in the courtyard, stood a massed choir, composed of twelve hundred members drawn from churches and academies from across Moscow. Each person carried a small lantern, turning the courtyard into "a sea of flickering lights," as Grand Duke Konstantin Konstantinovich recalled.[15] As soon as the emperor and the empress took their seats, the choir, recalled one English visitor, serenaded them "with the very sweetest and wildest of music—grand old choruses and plaintive folksongs, wailing always in a minor key—the Russian landscape put into music."[16] After the first song, Nicholas turned to his relatives and said, "Let's applaud."[17] The concert concluded with the "Glory Chorus" from Glinka's *A Life for the Tsar* and the national anthem, "sung with loyal fervor" as the empress, dressed in white, came to the edge of the balcony and bowed to the assembled choir in appreciation.[18]

Nicholas II, on horseback, leading the state entrance procession through the Kremlin for his coronation

On Thursday, May 9, the imperial family made its state entrance into Moscow. "It was calm and warm, the sun was shining joyfully, as if wishing to join the Muscovites in greeting the Emperor," wrote Grand Duke Konstantin Konstantinovich.[19] Early that morning, a nine-gun salute, sounded by the guns of the Kremlin and accompanied by a constant tolling of church bells, summoned the participants from their slumber. From Petrovsky Palace, the procession would travel down the Petersburgskoye Chaussee through the Triumphal Arch and along Tverskaya to Red Square and the Kremlin. The entire length had been decked in festive finery, hung with flags, banners, bunting, and swags of evergreen boughs. Tall, gaily painted Venetian masts, adorned with twisted ribbons of white, blue, and red, marked squares and supported strings of fluttering pennants that crossed the roadways in a colorful grid.[20]

Members of His Majesty's Own Escort, the Imperial Horse Guards Regiment, the Dragoon Guards Regiment, the Hussar and Lancer Guards Regiments, the Grenadier Guards Regiment, and the Life Guards Uhlan Regiment were detailed to line the length down which the parade would pass.[21] They stood in two ranks; behind them were mounted Cossack guards; behind the Cossacks, members of the Moscow police; and behind the police, the public.[22] Soldiers from the imperial guards regiments marched in solemn procession, the sun glinting on the helmets and cuirasses of gold worn by the imperial guards cavalry and the long red coats and black Astrakhan kolpaki hats of the Cossack guards.

More than a million people turned out to witness the spectacle. Restless, filled with anticipation, they strained their necks to gaze up and down the boulevards, watching the comings and goings of the soldiers and members of the imperial court. At two-thirty that afternoon, a twenty-one-gun salute rent the sky; the bells of the city's churches soon took up the salute, ringing from one end of Moscow to the other. The guard of honor snapped rigidly to attention, the gates of Petrovsky Palace swung open, and, amid the thunderous cheers of the people lining the streets, the imperial procession slowly marched out, onto the broad avenue leading to the Kremlin.

The procession was led by the master of ceremonies, adorned in his elaborate gold-embroidered livery, and fourteen gendarme officers, each attired in a shining golden cuirass and helmet, and all mounted on sleek black horses.[23] They were followed by four Cossack squadrons of the Konvoi guard of His Majesty's Premier Personal Escort, dressed in long crimson tunics and black kolpaki hats. "At their appearance the crowd's admiration burst forth into hurrahs and shouts of pleasure," noted the correspondent for the *New York Times*.[24] After them came the Life Guards Cossack Regiment and the mounted horsemen of the Cossack guards, also greeted with tremendous cheers. A contingent of representatives from "the subjugated Asian tribes" followed, led by the emir of Bokhara and the khan of Khiva.[25] Members of Moscow's nobility, wearing gold-braided uniforms, followed in the procession. Behind them came the Court Orchestra, led by Major-General Baron von Stackelberg; the State Trumpeters of the Imperial Hunt; Prince Golitsyn, the grand master of the Imperial Hunt, leading his huntsmen in their green, red, and gold uniforms; four members of the Abyssinian Guards, attired in their colorful costumes and white turbans; and the imperial footmen in red velvet knee breeches, white silk stockings, powdered wigs, and tricorn hats.[26]

A string of carriages followed, carrying high-ranking members of the imperial court: two masters of ceremonies; the grand master of ceremonies, in a coach drawn by six white horses; twenty-four *kamer-junkers*, or gentlemen-of-the-bedchamber; and twelve chamberlains, "all in uniforms covered with gold, and in Tricorn hats with white feathers."[27] Immediately after this group came the grand marshal of the imperial court, in a state phaeton; a squadron of the Chevalier Guards, and a squadron of the Garde à Cheval.[28] "We watched the fairytale scene in a strange reverie," recalled one French visitor. "Never before had we seen such an amount of gold. Perhaps we had imagined it in Versailles or the Trianon, but had not expected to see such a sight in the present hour."[29]

A mounted contingent consisting of the minister of war, the duty adjutant, a general-adjutant, and representatives from the military services and the Emperor's Military Secretariat and Entourage came next, signaling the approach of the imperial family.[30] Finally, the emperor appeared, riding his favorite English horse, Norma, a light dapple gray mare that wore shoes of silver.[31] Nicholas wore the full dress uniform of a commander in the Preobrazhensky Guards, with the sash of the Order of St. Andrei across his chest, along with gold aiguillettes and two rows of shining medals. "At the moment that the Emperor appeared," recalled one witness, "simple and modest on his white horse, unbelievable cheers erupted. And how one heard the conviction, the love in the cheers!"[32] As he passed, people dropped to their knees, shouting fervently, "We would die for our Tsar!"[33] Nicholas, as several witnesses recalled, was "deathly pale" as he rode along the avenue.[34] Finally, however, the warmth of the crowd won him over, and he observed them, according to Crown Princess Marie of Romania, with "an almost wistful smile."[35] The Romanov grand dukes rode behind him, proudly erect in their various regimental uniforms, their hands frozen in salute.

Empress Alexandra riding in her carriage during the state entrance to Moscow

Alexandra's gown, worn at Nicholas's coronation. See plate 38.

The women of the imperial family followed in elaborate gilded coaches. Dowager Empress Marie Feodorovna rode alone in the Imperial State Coach, made for Catherine the Great and topped with a gilded replica of the Imperial State Crown; it was drawn by eight white horses.[36] She wore a Russian court gown of silver tissue embellished with embroidery in golden thread; atop her head, a diamond tiara flashed fire as she bowed from side to side to the gathered crowd. Grand Duke Konstantin Konstantinovich noted that she cried the entire afternoon.[37]

Empress Alexandra Feodorovna followed in a gilded state carriage, the side panels painted in the style of Watteau; the interior was lined with red velvet brocade and gold lace. The eight white horses, led by imperial equerries in crimson and gold livery and surrounded by a contingent of members of the emperor's Cossack Konvoi Regiment, sported white, black, and yellow ostrich plumes atop their bobbing heads and had been fitted with magnificent new liveries of red Moroccan leather engraved in gold and stitched in silver, made in Paris.[38] The saddle cloths were covered with gold lace, designed in the form of the Russian coat of arms, and the saddles, also of red Moroccan leather, were decorated with silver stitching and had stirrups of gilded bronze.[39] Alexandra wore a Russian court gown of silver brocade, with a diamond tiara and a superb diamond neck-lace.[40] She took no joy in the occasion. Her cousin Crown Princess Marie of Romania recalled her expression as one of "almost painful earnestness," as if "she were holding Fate off at arm's-length, as though darkly guessing that life might be a foe, she must set out to meet it sword in hand."[41]

According to tradition, each Romanov emperor, before entering the Kremlin, went first to the Chapel of the Iverskaya Mother of God, which stood at the head of Red Square and was home to a revered icon. Nicholas helped his wife out of her carriage and led her into the cool chapel, where they prayed before the icon and received the blessing of Metropolitan Serge of Moscow. Honor done, Nicholas, followed by his mother, wife, and family and surrounded by hundreds of officials, made his way across Red Square, the great space filled with a cheering mass of faces, to the Gate of the Redeemer and entered the fortress. As they did so, a massed band struck up the national anthem, and the bells of the Kremlin's cathedrals rang out in salute. Enormous arcades had been built all round the walls of the Kremlin, which held thousands of cheering spectators.[42] The procession stopped at the Cathedrals of the Assumption, the Annunciation, and the Archangel Michael, where Te Deums were sung for the imperial family.[43] At the end of the ceremonies, amid a salute of 101 guns fired from the Kremlin, Nicholas and Alexandra crossed Cathedral Square and, on reaching the top of the Red Staircase, bowed three times to the crowd gathered below.[44] "Everyone who witnessed the scene on this vast square," commented Nemirovich-Demchenko, "will remember the sight for the rest of their lives."[45] At the end of the day, the imperial family quietly slipped from the Kremlin and retired to apartments in the Neskuchnoye Palace.

On the morning following the imperial procession into Moscow, the emperor and the empress gave a breakfast for 180 of the most important guests at Petrovsky Palace. That afternoon, in the Kremlin, there was another reception, this one for the foreign representatives and ambassadors who had gathered in Moscow. More than five hundred diplomats, in full court dress with orders and decorations, paraded through the rooms of the Grand Palace, the long line slowly wending its way to the Hall of the Order of St. Catherine, where the emperor and the empress received them. Over the two days that followed, deputations of heralds were sent out from the Kremlin to formally proclaim the news, "to the good people of Our Former Capital," that the date for the coronation ceremony had been fixed for May 14, 1896.[46] The heralds wore silk trousers with yellow, black, and white stripes, the colors of the Imperial Standard; tunics of gold silk embroidered with yellow, black, and white stitching; golden silk brocade dalmatics embroidered with the imperial coat of arms; and wide-brimmed, dark red hats embellished with gold lace and yellow, black, and white ostrich plumes.[47]

Souvenir copies of these parchments were precious prizes, as the English writer Maude recalled, "So great was the crush and throng to obtain them that several accidents occurred; the gilt carriage was carried by storm and wrecked, its lining was torn to shreds, and even one of the eagles disappeared from its panels. Report says that the decorations were stolen from the breast of the Master of Ceremonies distributing the proclamations." In all, he reported, eighteen people were crushed to death as they scrambled for the parchments.[48]

On Sunday, May 12, Orthodox clergy consecrated the Imperial Banner. A symbolic representation of power and authority, the Imperial Banner had been woven in the Moscow workshops of the Sapozhnikov Factory of rich golden silk and satin brocade, embroidered with a double-headed eagle by nuns from the Novodievechi Convent outside Moscow.[49] At half-past three that afternoon, Nicholas led the entire imperial family, along with the foreign princes and princesses and members of the Imperial Suite and Entourage, through the Grand Kremlin Palace to the Hall of St. Andrei. Father Ioann Yanishev blessed the banner, ending the service with an appeal to the emperor: "Most Pious Sovereign! Divine Providence has entrusted You, by virtue of the law of succession to the Throne, Autocratic Leader of the Peoples of the Russian Empire, with this Holy Standard, symbol of the unity and of the power of the Nation. We pray to the Heavenly Father that this Standard will unite all peoples in boundless loyalty to the Throne and the Motherland, and in the devoted fulfillment of patriotic duty."[50]

The Cathedral of the Assumption. See plate 39.

On the following afternoon, Nicholas and Alexandra watched as the Imperial Regalia was carried on velvet cushions from the Armory in the Kremlin to the Hall of St. Andrei, where it rested overnight on a table draped in golden cloth edged with ermine, guarded by two rows of Chevalier Guards.[51] Every now and then, an unobtrusive elderly man would clamber on his hands and knees, up one row of soldiers, then down the other; the guards could not move, and it fell to this shuffling figure to gently sweep and polish their boots.[52] That night, without ceremony, Nicholas and Alexandra moved into the private apartments in the Grand Kremlin Palace, in preparation for the following day's service. "May the Merciful Lord help us, may He strengthen us tomorrow and bless us for a lifetime of peaceful works," the emperor wrote in his diary.[53]

The day of the coronation, Tuesday, May 14, 1896, was greeted by a brilliant sunrise over Moscow, promising a golden stage upon which to enact this most spectacular of imperial pageants. "The very weather, the blue sky, and the sun seemed to collaborate with the effort of man to excel even nature in a special and unique act of creation," wrote Grand Duke Kirill Vladimirovich.[54] The early morning was rent by a thunder of cannons, firing in salute from the walls of the Kremlin to announce the dawn; they were quickly joined by the bells of the citadel's cathedrals, ringing out in a joyous cacophony of sound that spread across the expectant city in waves.[55]

Invitations issued to people who would witness the processions across Cathedral Square or view the ceremony in the Cathedral of the Assumption itself had called for an early arrival. "We were in our places at 7:30," recorded the wife of an American diplomat, "which had meant breakfast at six o'clock, and maids and valets in attendance at four. And, as the fashionable Russian is seldom abed before 3 A.M., most of the party made sure of being up in time by not going to bed at all, beginning with an impromptu dance at midnight, and sitting at the card tables an hour or two later, changing then one festive garment for another."[56]

By dawn, recalled one American journalist, "the high banks of the Kremlin, the streets around it, the bridges and open squares, and the shores of the river that cuts Moscow in two, were black with the people who had spent the night in the open air."[57] Diplomats and dignitaries began arriving at the Kremlin, their carriages disappearing behind its tall redbrick walls draped with Imperial Standards and heraldic escutcheons of the empire's provinces. Once inside, they departed their carriages, following the ribbons of crimson carpet to the grandstands, erected to provide them with comfortable seats for the lengthy pageant, or to the Cathedral of the Assumption. "As the ticket holders appeared at the passage leading up to the tribunes," recalled one guest, "they were met by graceful young masters of ceremonies in white and gold costumes and cocked hats with waving plumes, who directed their progress by ebony wands tied with ribbons."[58]

Only Christians were allocated places within the cathedral; members of other faiths were given seats in the tribunes and arcades surrounding Cathedral Square. The emir of Bokhara took up his place early that morning, attired in a richly decorated caftan and a turban studded with jewels. Nearby sat Li-Hung-Chang, the Chinese minister, "conspicuous in yellow jacket and peacock feather accompanied by his suite," recalled one visitor.[59] Westerners wore military uniform; those not entitled to do so wore formal court attire: black velvet knee breeches, black silk stockings, black patent leather shoes, stiffly starched white shirts, black dress coats with silver buttons, and black silk top hats. The ladies wore silk and satin gowns with velvet trains; their heads were adorned with tiaras from which billowed lace and tulle veils, their hair studded with diamond crescents and stars.[60] "The air," remembered one man, "was charged with electricity."[61]

Entrance to the Cathedral of the Assumption to view the service was restricted to two thousand guests. All of the foreign royals and members of the Diplomatic Corps received invitations, as well as representatives of the nobility, merchant, and peasant classes.[62] The lower walls of the cathedral had been draped in panels of red velvet embroidered with double-headed eagles in gold thread, while the columns were wrapped in crimson and purple velvet, adorned with imperial monograms sewn in gold thread. Above them, the frescoes shimmered in the light of hundreds of candles and the shafts of brilliant sun cascading from the high windows and golden domes.[63] At the front of the cathedral, a red-carpeted dais spread before the iconostasis, shielded from the nave by a gilded balustrade. Above, suspended on golden chains, hung an ornately carved, gilded baldachin adorned with double-headed eagles and ostrich plumes and fringed with heavy gold bullion; from its edges, long curtains of red velvet, embroidered with double-headed eagles in gold thread, cascaded to the dais below.[64]

From the French doors of the Grand Kremlin Palace stretched a long ribbon of crimson carpet, strewn with palm fronds and sprinkled with holy water. Lining the carpet were ranks of members of the Chevalier Guards and the Horse Guards Regiments, as it flowed down the ceremonial Red Staircase and across the cobbled Cathedral Square to the doors of the Cathedral of the Assumption.[65] The steps of the Red Staircase were lined with pages and footmen from the imperial household, all in gold-braided uniform. At the top of the balcony that ran the length of the palace facade, generals, lieutenants, adjutants, and maids of honor took up their respective positions.

Nicholas and Alexandra had been up since dawn, preparing for the intricate ritual. He wore the dress uniform of a colonel of the Preobrazhensky Guards Regiment. His thigh-length tunic, of dark blue broadcloth, had a red broadcloth collar and cuffs, embroidered with oak leaves in gold thread. Gold epaulets were trimmed with heavy gold bullion and decorated with the diamond initials of his father, Alexander III. His trousers were white, worn with black knee-high boots lined with white leather. Across his chest stretched the light blue Sash of the Order of St. Andrei, worn with its matching Diamond Star, as well as the Diamond Star of the Order of St. Vladimir and several rows of medals.

Alexandra's coronation gown cost 4,920 rubles ($49,200 in 2005 figures).[66] In the style of a Russian court dress, it was of smooth silver brocade over silver tissue and had been woven and embroidered by the nuns of the Ivanovsky

Convent.[67] The full overskirt was split down the front in an inverted V-shape, revealing a smooth, white silk underskirt. The long, split sleeves, as well as the bodice and the outer skirt, were entirely covered with leaves and flowers embroidered in silver thread and studded with more than ten thousand pearls.[68] The boat-shaped neckline was trimmed with gauze and lace, and the outer skirt fell back in folds to form a fifteen-foot train, also decorated with embroidery of silver thread and pearls. The crimson Sash of the Order of St. Catherine stretched across her breast, held in place by its Diamond Star. Alexandra wore a single strand of pink pearls round her neck and matching pink pearl earrings, engagement gifts from her husband.[69] Her low-heeled court shoes were of unadorned white satin, and her stockings of pure white, semitransparent silk.[70]

During Alexander II's coronation, Empress Marie Alexandrovna's crown had not been fastened properly to her coiffure, and it slipped from her head.[71] To avoid a similar ill omen, Alexandra had rehearsed the moment with her husband. Princess Elizabeth Naryshkin-Kuryakin, summoned to assist, remembered, "The Emperor was there when we entered. He was evidently very nervous, smoking one cigarette after another. The Empress's hairdresser was there, too. On the table stood a large *etui*, and presently the Emperor opened it and took from it the Imperial crown, covered with diamonds. He placed it on his wife's head, and the hairdresser stepped up to her, took up a diamond-studded hairpin, and explaining the manipulation to me stuck it in the Empress's hair. She uttered a piercing scream, and jumped from the chair. It developed that she had a very sensitive nerve on that very spot, and that the slightest touch caused her the most exquisite pain."[72]

By eight forty-five, all of the imperial family, as well as those foreign royals attending the ceremony, had gathered in the Hall of St. George, awaiting the appearance of the dowager empress. She wore a gown of silver cloth, embroidered with silver thread; upon her head rested a small diamond crown, and she wore a purple mantle, lined and edged with ermine.[73] From her neck hung the famous Imperial Rivière, its five strands of large oval diamonds flashing fire in the brilliant sunshine. Above these, she wore a single strand of large, perfectly matched pearls. "Our hearts bled when we saw her," recalled Grand Duke Konstantin Konstantinovich, who noted that she appeared "like a victim prepared for the sacrifice. Her face expressed suffering."[74]

At nine, a thunder of cannon announced the start of the imperial processions. Within Cathedral Square, all eyes turned to the top of the Red Staircase. Amid the salutes and the ringing of church bells, the dowager empress appeared with her brother Crown Prince Frederick of Denmark, her brother-in-law Grand Duke Alexei Alexandrovich, and members of her Suite.[75] She was followed by twelve court pages holding the train of her magnificent gown, her maids of honor and ladies-in-waiting, and the *dames à portrait*. At the bottom of the Red Staircase, she stepped beneath a tall baldachin of cloth-of-gold, decorated with sprays of waving ostrich plumes at each of the four corners and held aloft by a contingent of major-generals. Then she followed the crimson carpet across Cathedral Square. "The Kremlin bells were ringing out with thunderous peals," recalled one witness, "the bands had struck up the National Anthem, and the people were shouting in a mighty volume that drowned every sound as she advanced, preceded by heralds, whose gigantic white plumes almost covered their cocked hats, and then by the uniformed gentlemen of her household; a little woman of lofty mien, whose face was full of the pride of ruling and the determination not to lay it down, her diamond crown, from which the hair fell unconfined, catching the sun in a thousand flames of dazzling radiance as she bowed right and left, her robes of golden tissue and ermine sweeping out behind her."[76] Once inside the cathedral, she ascended the dais, seating herself on a small throne.[77]

After the dowager empress had entered the cathedral, members of the Romanov family, along with the foreign royals attending the coronation, descended the Red Staircase and walked in procession into the church. They were followed by the treasurer of the emperor, clad in a black uniform covered with gold embroidery, who slowly walked the same length of red carpet from the Grand Kremlin Palace to the west door of the cathedral, sprinkling the path with holy water. As he did so, a great fanfare of trumpets echoed over the Kremlin ramparts.[78] The procession of the Imperial Regalia came next. Slowly, in pairs formed according to rank and title, these general-adjutants, generals à la Suite, and adjutants descended the Red Staircase and walked toward the cathedral. They held red velvet cushions upon which rested the Imperial Regalia: the Diamond Chains of the Order of St. Andrei for both the emperor and the empress, the Imperial Banner of State, the Sword of State, the Imperial Orb, the State Seal, the Imperial Mantles of cloth-of-gold, the state scepter, the empress's crown, and the Imperial State Crown.

Finally, at half-past ten, Nicholas and Alexandra appeared at the top of the balcony, to the strains of Tchaikovsky's "Fanfare" and a cacophony of thundering cannons and joyous church bells.[79] The assembled crowd erupted with cheers as they walked down the Red Staircase. "Hats were thrown into the air, handkerchiefs waved, and men and women cheered, and cheered again until they were hoarse," recalled one observer.[80] Their imperial majesties' procession was headed by a detachment of Chevalier guards, followed by fifty-seven categories of delegations and officials, including the pages-in-ordinary, the pages-of-the-bed-chamber, the masters of ceremonies, a large group of rural representatives from all across the empire, the mayors of St. Petersburg and Moscow, delegates from the Grand Duchy of Finland, delegates from the various *zemstva*, the president and members of the Moscow bourse, delegates of the merchant classes and arti-sans, delegates of the major banking houses within the empire, delegates from the principal factories in Moscow, delegates from various public institutions in the former capital, and representatives of native and ethnic groups within the empire.[81] Nicholas, according to one observer, looked "pale, as though the tremendous strain of function on function had begun to tell; but there was a quiet determination in his mien, a simplicity and modesty that augured well for the future of Russia."[82] Alexandra walked at her husband's side, surrounded by the emperor's uncles the Grand Dukes Vladimir, Serge, and Paul Alexandrovich and his brother Grand Duke Michael Alexandrovich.[83] As they descended the Red Staircase and crossed Cathedral Square, their coronation procession was captured, for the first (and last) time on hand-cranked motion picture cameras by several enterprising young men dispatched from the French company Lumière Cinématographe to record the historic scene.[84]

At the bottom of the staircase, the imperial couple stepped beneath a bal-dachin of cloth-of-gold ornamented with the imperial monograms and bunched plumes of yellow, black, and white ostrich feathers. Sixteen major-generals à la Suite held the ebony and mother-of-pearl poles of the baldachin, and sixteen general-adjutants held the golden cords as they carried it over the heads of the emperor and the empress, following the red carpet toward the church. Nicholas walked at the front of the baldachin, Alexandra behind him at the rear, between a guard of honor of the imperial cavalry, resplendent in red, white, and gold uni-forms with silver metal helmets topped with burnished double-headed eagles. They were followed by the minister of war; the commander of the imperial resi-dences; the general-adjutant of the day; two general-adjutants; the grand marshal of the imperial court, accompanied by two ordinary marshals; the minister of the imperial court; the orderly major-general à la Suite; the commander of the Horse Guards Regiment; four ladies-in-waiting; four maids of honor; twelve pages holding aloft the empress's train; and six Horse Guards with drawn swords.[85]

Three metropolitans waited for the emperor and the empress at the tall copper-sheathed doors of the cathedral. Metropolitan Serge of Moscow greeted

Nicholas and Alexandra, beneath the baldachin at the bottom of the Red Staircase,
walk in procession to the Cathedral of the Assumption for their coronation

them with a gold cross, said to contain a relic of the True Cross, which the
imperial couple kissed. "Most Pious Sovereign!" he exclaimed, "Your solemn
progress, amidst outstanding splendor, has an exceptionally great end. You
come into this ancient sanctuary to assume the Crown and be anointed with holy
oil. Your hereditary Crown belongs to you alone, Autocratic Emperor!"[86]
Metropolitan Palladi of St. Petersburg blessed the couple with incense, and
Metropolitan Ioannikii of Kiev anointed their foreheads with holy oil. After a

final bow, the emperor and the empress entered the cathedral as the choir within intoned the 101st Psalm.[87]

The walls of the 500-year-old Cathedral of the Assumption were covered entirely with frescoes; icons studded with diamonds and gems sparkled in the dim light from thousands of flickering votive candles. Shafts of sunlight from the windows in the five golden domes cut across the rich panoply of color inside: from the blue and silver robes of the choir members, who sang ancient Russian hymns from an out-of-the-way corner to the gold vestments of the bishops, sewn with silver thread and embroidered with precious stones; the reds, greens, and blues of the military uniforms, all covered with gold braid and shining medals; and the glowing rubies, diamonds, pearls, silver, and gold in the regalia on its red velvet cushions.

In a slow, solemn procession, Nicholas and Alexandra walked through the cathedral and ascended the dais, its crimson-carpeted steps lined with members of the Chevalier Guards, broadswords drawn in salute. The dais, enclosed by a gilded balustrade, stood in front of the iconostasis, whose icons glowed in the shimmering light. The entire length of the platform was filled with participants in the coronation: one general-adjutant held the Sword of State; another, the Imperial Banner. Ministers, members of the State Council, and representatives from the guards regiments stood on the left side of the dais, while members of the imperial family occupied the right side. Nicholas and Alexandra sat in two elaborate chairs of state, made at the Schmidt Factory in Moscow and adorned with silver inlays, crowns, and double-headed eagles and covered in gold silk sewn with imperial monograms.[88]

The coronation
ceremony.
See plate 40.

Beyond the dais stretched a sea of heads. The gowns worn by the women were particularly splendid: Alexandra's sister Grand Duchess Elizabeth Feodorovna stood to one side, wearing a Russian court gown of cream-colored velvet embroidered with fuchsias in gold thread. Nearby was the wife of their brother Grand Duke Ernst Ludwig of Hesse, Victoria Melita, and her sister, Crown Princess Marie of Romania, both attired in white satin and cloth-of-gold gowns embroidered with flowers of silver and gold thread.[89] Standing at the front of the group, Grand Duchess Alexandra Iosifovna left a vivid impression. "Exceedingly tall and still astonishingly upright for her age," recalled Marie of Romania, "her hair was snow white; clothed from head to foot in silver she wore a sparkling diadem like frosted sun rays. . . . Having a too great wealth of pearls to wear them all round her neck, she had fixed half a dozen ropes at her waist with an enormous diamond pin; they hung down along her gown in a milky cascade. She was so pale and shining white that seen against the golden walls of the cathedral she seemed to be covered with hoar-frost."[90] "The air," recalled Grand Duke Kirill Vladimirovich, "was heavy with incense, the Cathedral resplendent with the flash of golden vestments and the sparkling of precious stones."[91]

Metropolitan Palladi approached the emperor, bowed, and invited him to make his confession. Nicholas stood and confessed, after which he received absolution and recited the Nicene Creed. Assisted by his uncles Vladimir, Serge, and Paul Alexandrovich and his brother Michael Alexandrovich, Nicholas removed the small collar of the Order of St. Andrei from around his neck. The three metropolitans stepped forward, followed by general-adjutants holding cushions on which rested the Imperial Regalia. They placed the Imperial Mantle of cloth-of-gold, lined and edged with ermine and embroidered with double-headed eagles, around Nicholas's shoulders, fastening its diamond clasps over his collar and draping the Diamond Chain of the Order of St. Andrei round his neck. Nicholas then knelt before Metropolitan Palladi, who prayed for his health and for divine inspiration. His face, recalled Grand Duke Konstantin Konstantinovich, "had an expression of piety and supplication; his whole countenance emanated majesty."[92]

Nicholas sat upon the Throne of Tsar Alexei, which was encrusted with 870 diamonds; nearby stood the empty Ivory Throne of Ivan the Terrible, upon which Alexandra would take her place.[93] As two general-adjutants carried velvet cushions on which rested the Imperial Orb and the imperial scepter, Metropolitan Palladi turned to the emperor, handed the two pieces to him, and said, "Receive this Scepter and this Orb, which are the visible representation of the autocratic power that the Almighty gives You to rule over Your People and to bring them prosperity."[94]

By tradition, a Russian sovereign crowned himself, a sign that his power came neither from man nor from the Church, but from God Himself. Nicholas had wished to use the eight-hundred-year-old Cap of Monomakh, weighing two pounds, edged with fur, and surmounted with an uncut ruby. But this was impossible, according to the tradition of the ceremony. Instead, he wore Catherine the Great's Imperial State Crown, which weighed nine pounds.[95] As a concession, a new red velvet lining had been fitted inside the crown, with a special opening over the space where it would rest on the scar Nicholas II had received during an attack on his life in Japan.[96]

Metropolitan Palladi blessed the Imperial State Crown, then addressed the emperor: "Truly Pious Autocrat and Great Emperor of all Russia! This adornment for Your Head represents the invisible act of Christ, King of Glory, who consecrates you Head of the Russian Nation, and with His blessing confirms

Your unlimited power over Your People."[97] Nicholas took the crown from the velvet cushion held by the metropolitan and placed it on his own head. "It looked a simple enough gesture," explained his sister, Grand Duchess Olga Alexandrovna, "but from that very moment, Nicky's responsibility was to God alone."[98]

At a summons from her husband, Empress Alexandra approached. "Of all the women there," recalled one witness, "she was the most simply robed, and of all the women there she was by far the most beautiful." As she approached her husband, "the color in her cheeks was high, and her eyes were filled with that shyness or melancholy that her pictures have made familiar; and in contrast with the tiaras and plumes and necklaces of the ladies of the court surrounding her, she looked more like Iphigenia going to the sacrifice than the queen of the most powerful Empire in the world waiting to be crowned."[99]

Alexandra swept her husband a deep curtsy before kneeling on a small red cushion edged with gold lace. Princess Elizabeth Naryshkin-Kuryakin, attending the empress, stepped forward with three ladies-in-waiting to assist in her robing. Alexandra was first invested with an Imperial Mantle of cloth-of-gold, its fifteen-foot train lined and edged with ermine, and its outer surface embroidered with double-headed eagles.[100] Nicholas himself fastened its diamond clasp as Alexandra knelt in front of him. The empress was crowned by the emperor himself, attesting to the fact that her power came through his grace alone. Nicholas removed the crown from his head and briefly touched it to her brow. Replacing it back on his own head, Nicholas took the smaller empress's crown, of two thousand diamonds, and gently set it atop his wife's hair.[101] With the crown secured, Alexandra rose and kissed her husband, who took her hand and led her to her place on Ivan the Terrible's throne.[102]

A proto-deacon bowed to the couple and, turning to the congregation, proclaimed that the emperor had been duly crowned "the Orthodox and Pious and Christ-Loving, the Absolute Autocrat and Great Lord by the Grace of God, Nicholas Alexandrovich, Emperor and Autocrat of all Russia." At that moment, as the bells of the Kremlin's churches rang out and a salute of 101 guns rent the sky, the choir burst into "Misericordiam et Judicum Cantabo Tibi Domine."[103] Three times, the proto-deacon proclaimed "Many Years," using the new emperor's full title and repeating this for the empress. "The waves of harmony rose and fell, rolled and broke like the sea in tones which were scarcely of this world, vibrating throughout the length and breadth of the cathedral, filling it to its smallest recesses," recalled Grand Duke Kirill Vladimirovich. "From sudden thunder, it would dwindle to a still whisper. It implored, it triumphed, and it sorrowed, it conveyed an idea of the infinite and while it lasted brought heaven down to earth."[104]

As Nicholas and Alexandra sat upon their thrones, their family within and members of the imperial court solemnly approached the dais to pledge their loyalty. The dowager empress was the first to offer her homage; as she approached, noted one witness, she was weeping openly.[105] "I swept a deep curtsey," the emperor's sister Olga recalled, "raised my head, and saw Nicky's blue eyes looking at me with such affection that my heart glowed. I still remember how passionately I vowed to dedicate myself to my country and her sovereign."[106] During her homage, one correspondent noted, Queen Olga of the Hellenes "scowled at the young couple like Lady Macbeth."[107]

At the end of the obeisance, Nicholas rose from his throne and, kneeling before Metropolitan Palladi, read a prayer from a large illuminated book. When he had finished, he reverently crossed himself, bowed low, and kissed the hand of the priest. The emperor remained standing while the rest of the congregation dropped to their knees, as he prayed for the Russian empire and his subjects: "O Lord God of Our Fathers, Supreme Ruler of all Sovereigns, Who Has Created everything by Thy Word, and in Thy Wisdom has set up Man that he may govern the World in Righteousness and Holiness, Thou has chosen Me as Sovereign and Judge over Thy People. I confess Thy inscrutable Providence in selecting Me, and bow down before Thy Majesty. I beg You Lord to Aid and Instruct Me in the Work for which You have selected Me. Inspire and Enlighten My Path and direct My Actions in this Awe-inspiring Mission. May the wisdom that descends always from Your Throne abide with Me. May it descend to Me from On High that I may understand what is pleasing in Thy Holy Heavens and in Thy Eyes, and Govern Me according to Thy Commandments. May My Heart be always in Your Hand, that I may Order all I do for the advantage of the People Thou has entrusted unto My Care and to Thy Glory."[108]

As he finished, the choir burst into the hymn "Thee, O Lord, We Praise."[109] Crown Princess Marie of Romania recalled, "Through a fragrant haze of incense, mysterious rituals were taking place; it was more like a dream than reality. With slow movements grandly vested priests moved hither and thither, hands raised in gestures of prayer or benediction. Their robes were in tone with those of the saints who, with heavily haloed faces, looked down from their walls upon the great of this world. Wherever the eye rested, gold, nothing but gold, with here and there the flash of a precious stone, red, blue, or green. All faces were dim in this atmosphere of solemn expectation; they had taken on something of the

The imperial procession leaving the Cathedral of the Assumption after Nicholas II's coronation

immaterialness of the frescoed saints. Alone, the figures of the Emperor and Empress stood out with symbolic significance, two shining apparitions imbued for an hour with transient glory. And the thousand tapers reflected in the glittering iconostasis were like stars in God's Heaven."[110]

Adjutants divested the imperial couple of their crowns and mantles, and Nicholas and Alexandra followed a gold and crimson carpet across the dais to the Royal Door in the center of the iconostasis. Metropolitan Palladi dipped a golden rod into an ampulla of holy oil and used it to anoint the emperor's brow, eyes, nose, ears, breast, and palms and tops of both of his hands, saying, "The Seal of the Gift of the Holy Spirit." Alexandra was anointed only on the brow.[111]

For the only time in his life, Nicholas entered the sanctuary to celebrate the Eucharist as a priest of the Orthodox faith. As he walked up the steps to the door in the iconostasis, the Chain of the Order of St. Andrei slipped from his shoulders and crashed to the carpet with a thud. Only a few people witnessed the incident; to avoid superstitious talk, they were later sworn to secrecy.[112] Within the sanctuary, bishops covered the emperor with a dalmatic, woven of golden brocade, before he participated in the celebration of the Eucharist.[113] Nicholas

Nicholas II, newly crowned, walking through Cathedral Square in the Kremlin

returned from the sanctuary and was rerobed and invested with the Imperial Regalia before taking his place on the throne at the side of his wife. Alexandra could not conceal her feelings. "All through the many ceremonies," recalled her cousin Crown Princess Marie of Romania, "the young Empress never relaxed this severely aloof attitude which was, in part, no doubt, timidity. Nothing ever seemed to give her pleasure, she seldom smiled, and, when she did, it was grudgingly, as though making a concession."[114] Her face remained still as Metropolitan Palladi intoned the final prayers. At the end of the service, Nicholas and Alexandra rose from their thrones and bowed three times to each of the four sides of the church before leaving the dais to return to the Grand Kremlin Palace to the strains of "God Save the Tsar."

In the afternoon sunshine, Nicholas and Alexandra walked into the cobbled Cathedral Square, to the cheers of the thousands of guests and foreign dignitaries, the joyous ringing of the church bells, and a thundering salute of 101 guns fired from the walls of the Kremlin. During the lengthy service, these guests, who had been unable to witness the actual crowning in the cathedral, lunched on sandwiches, pastries, ice creams, tea, and champagne, served by footmen in powdered wigs.[115] As Nicholas and Alexandra left the cathedral, they again stepped beneath a golden baldachin. The jewels in the couple's crowns flashed like "veritable suns" as they moved across the square.[116] Nicholas, recorded one witness, "was deathly pale from his long fasting, and the jeweled burden that he carried upon his head and in his hands, and in the heavy robes of cloth of-gold and ermine falling from his shoulders, and once or twice he faltered and seemed about to faint. But a Grand Duke upon either side quickly leaned over and supported his arms."[117]

When they reached the top of the Red Staircase, Nicholas and Alexandra turned to the crowd and bowed three times. "To describe the moment," recalled Alexandra's brother Grand Duke Ernst Ludwig IV, "it seemed as though a million people stood below them, and the endless cheering reached them like waves breaking in a giant storm, soaring up to the two sun-bathed, glittering people. And with each of the three bows that they made to their people, the ones below sank to their knees. I could see it all clearly; although one was forbidden on the terrace with them, I crawled out beside them on my hands and knees, and could see clearly, shielded by their Coronation robes. It was one of the greatest moments of my life."[118]

At three that afternoon, the coronation banquet, for eighteen hundred guests, was held in the magnificent, newly electrified halls of the Grand Kremlin Palace.[119] One room was specially reserved for Russians whose ancestors had, at one time or another through the centuries, saved the life of a sovereign. A fanfare, played by State Trumpeters, and the opening polonaise from Glinka's *A Life for the Tsar* signaled the start of the imperial procession. Nicholas, Alexandra, and the dowager empress dined in the frescoed Throne Room of the Palace of Facets, beneath a baldachin draped with cloth-of-gold sewn with double-headed eagles and adorned with gathered ostrich plumes and fringed with gold bullion.[120] Then some two hundred guests joined them, including the male members of the imperial family and the most senior dignitaries of the Russian court.[121]

A second fanfare of trumpets announced the beginning of the banquet, during which members of the Diplomatic Corps were admitted to the room to drink toasts to the sovereigns.[122] Before each toast, the grand cup bearer passed a different golden goblet to the emperor, announcing in a loud voice, "His Majesty deigns to drink!"[123] At the same time, as soon as the emperor touched his lips to the rim of the goblet, a fanfare of trumpets sounded from the galleries above, summoning all other guests to join in the toast. Five official toasts were made: the first was to the emperor, accompanied by a salute of 61 guns fired from the walls of the Kremlin;

the second, to his mother, Dowager Empress Marie Feodorovna, accompanied by a 51-gun salute; the third, to Empress Alexandra Feodorovna, also accompanied by a 51-gun salute; the fourth, to the imperial family, was accompanied by a salute of 31 guns; and the last toast, to the clergy of the Orthodox Church and all faithful subjects of the emperor, was accompanied by a salute of 21 guns.[124]

Most of the guests dined in the adjoining Golden Hall or in the Hall of St. Vladimir. The round tables were set with a mixture of pieces drawn from three different services: the Coronation Service of Nicholas I, adorned with the imperial coat of arms within a cobalt-colored border; the Kremlin Banquet Service of 1837, with its colorful, medieval-style designs; and the Coronation Service of Alexander III, with black double-headed eagles upon a simple white background.[125] Silken cords bound parchment rolls, elaborately illuminated with a scene from the coronation of Michael, the first Romanov tsar, and decorated with medieval-style scrollwork and foliate ornaments by the artist Victor Vasnestov, which stood on the tables.[126] They contained the menu: borscht, pepper pot soup, meat piroshki, steamed sturgeon, spring lamb, pheasant in aspic, roasted capon in cream sauce, salad, asparagus, sweet fruits in wine, and ice cream.[127] Written across the top of each menu, in Old Church Slavonic, were the words, "Glory to God on Heaven's Glory! To Our Lord on this Earth Glory! To all the Russian People Glory! To His Faithful Servants Glory! To His Eminent Guests Glory! May Truth in Russia be better and brighter than the Sun! Glory! This Song to bread we sing, to bread we sing, bread we honor! Glory!"[128] Throughout the banquet, the diners were serenaded by a chorus from the Bolshoi and the Mariinsky Opera companies and the Moscow Symphony Orchestra, performing Alexander Glazunov's special "Coronation Cantata."[129]

At four o'clock, the banquet ended, and the emperor and the empress walked in procession through the Grand Kremlin Palace, giving the thousands of guests within its immense halls a close view of both them and of their magnificent coronation robes and regalia. "The Empress's crown," recorded one American guest, "was a mass of great diamonds, perfectly matched; and I saw hundreds of jeweled *kokoshniks*, fashioned entirely of big stones of exquisite water—it seemed impossible even to hope to see the like again." Although the pressure of the ceremony had ended, neither Nicholas nor Alexandra evinced any hint of joy or even relief. The empress's face, she recalled, "was charged with profound emotion—it has haunted me ever since. It was like the face of a martyr walking with measured steps to her funeral pyre." Nicholas made a less distinct impression: "His narrow forehead and receding chin, visible even behind the beard, spoke little of intelligence and nothing of power; while the insignificance of his small form was emphasized beside the tall men of his family."[130]

That evening, in the midst of the festivities, Nicholas and Alexandra stepped onto the balcony of the Grand Kremlin Palace; below, thousands of people had gathered along the banks of the Moskva River. "It was a hot summer night," recalled one English visitor, "with the throb of a great national excitement in the air."[131] Immense projectors lined with mirrors shot streaks of brilliant white light into the night sky above the city and caught the imperial couple in their glare as they appeared on the balcony. An immense cheer rose from the crowd, which spontaneously broke into "God Save the Tsar" at their appearance. The mayor of Moscow presented Alexandra with a bouquet of flowers resting on a silver tray. The tray contained a signal to the Moscow Power Station, which simultaneously switched on nearly 200,000 tiny electric lights all across the city: they surrounded windows and doorways, lined rooftops, crept over the onion domes of churches, and sparkled in the spring foliage of the trees.[132] "It was a dream of beauty!" recalled one visitor. "The mass of golden domes, huge palaces, the encircling crenellated wall with its fantastic towers and turrets, the bridges spanning the river below, all scintillated in myriads of fairy lights—ruby, sapphire, emerald, amethyst!"[133] Against this sparkling backdrop, the night sky exploded with fireworks, their reflections turning the dark waters of the Moskva River into a twisting ribbon of color.

Although the actual coronation service was over, the ceremonies in Moscow continued. The following morning, the emperor and the empress received the traditional gifts of bread and salt from representatives who had come to Moscow from all parts of the empire. From their thrones, they greeted representatives from the Holy Synod and members of the Orthodox clergy; the Protestant clergy within Russia; the ministers of the government; the Council of the Empire; the members of the State Senate; the nobility; the secretaries of state; the Grand Duchy of Finland; and various city and provincial delegations. Each gift was presented on a gold or silver salver, engraved with scenes or arms depicting the organization, the group, or the province.[134] The cost of providing these salvers— over two hundred on that day alone—was immense, depleting the fragile resources of the smallest villages. Even Grand Duke Konstantin Konstantinovich derided this tradition as "a useless expense! How much good could that amount of money have been put to!"[135]

Nicholas and Alexandra leading the Coronation Ball

On the evening of May 16, Nicholas and Alexandra presided over seven thousand guests at the Coronation Ball. At ten, the grand master of ceremonies appeared, armed with an ebony staff topped with a double-headed eagle in silver. Three loud bangs on the floor silenced the crowd, as he cried out, "Their Imperial Majesties!" Nicholas and Alexandra appeared, followed by members of their families; the queen of the Hellenes; the crown prince and crown princess of Romania; the duke and the duchess of Connaught; and other royal representatives. Nicholas wore the uniform of the Chevalier Guards Regiment, while Alexandra was attired in a Russian court gown of silver tissue, magnificently embroidered with flowers sewn in diamonds and pale tulle roses.[136]

Nicholas and Alexandra led the first polonaise through the Halls of the Orders of St. George, St. Alexander Nevsky, and St. Andrei, before switching partners, the emperor taking the hand of his aunt Queen Olga of the Hellenes, while Alexandra danced with the Turkish ambassador.[137] Seven times they circled these halls, changing partners on each round, to include the most important royal and diplomatic guests present. One American guest was dazzled by the fabulous display of jewelry that evening: "When one has been to such balls as Russia gives, jewels elsewhere are nothing. On all sides, women were wearing necklaces, pins, tiaras, etc., that almost covered their heads and necks. Some of the jewels were as large as robin's eggs. Strings and strings of enormous pearls hung from the neck to the waist of many of the women. [Grand Duchess] Xenia wore emeralds, as did the Grand Duchess Elizabeth, and some of them were an inch long. Such a blaze makes one's eyes fatigued."[138]

On Friday, May 17, Empress Alexandra received the women of the imperial family, the wives of the Diplomatic Corps, and hundreds of aristocratic ladies.[139] That evening, the entire imperial family attended a gala performance at the Bolshoi Theater. For the event, the imperial loge had been enlarged to seat sixty-three guests, and the interior refurbished at a cost of 50,000 rubles ($500,000 in 2005 figures).[140] At eight o'clock Nicholas entered the imperial loge to the strains of "God Save the Tsar;" Empress Alexandra, in a gown of silver brocade, walked at his side.[141] The audience, reported Nemirovich-Demchenko, "positively blazed with the Orders of St. Andrei and St. Anna, the full dress uniforms of generals, and the crimson uniforms of the Senators."[142] The gala opened with the first and the last act of Glinka's *A Life for the Tsar*, ending with the famous "Glory Chorus." During the interval, the guests mingled in the foyer, enjoying a buffet and sipping champagne.[143]

The centerpiece of the gala was a new ballet, *La Perle*, choreographed by Marius Petipa and performed by members of the Mariinsky Company. Ivan Vsevolozsky, the director of the imperial theaters, gave the principal role to a visiting Italian dancer rather than to Mathilde Kschessinska, the famous prima ballerina who had been Nicholas II's mistress before his marriage. Indeed, the dowager empress, reviewing the programs several months previously, had spotted Kschessinska's name and had drawn a line through it.[144] When Kschessinska learned of this, she was beside herself with anger and asked Grand Dukes Vladimir and Serge Mikhailovich to intercede with Nicholas II. In the end, Nicholas—as usual—gave in and ordered the director of the imperial theaters to include his former mistress. Vsevolozsky was forced to completely redo the planned gala, with new music and choreography by Petipa, added just for Kschessinska. Undoubtedly, this appealed to her vanity, making her the centerpiece of the festivities, but it caused much resentment among members of the Mariinsky Corps.[145] As the emperor, the empress, and their relatives enjoyed the magnificent spectacle, a few miles away, on the outskirts of the city, hundreds of thousands of people were gathering in Khodynka Field for the great public coronation feast, which was due to take place the following day.

Khodynka Field lay to the northeast of the city center and had been used for Alexander III's open-air celebrations. Normally, it was a military training ground and, in consequence, was scored with a number of pits, trenches, and wells.[146] These obstacles had caused some deaths at Nicholas's father's festivities, but no one, including Grand Duke Serge Alexandrovich, who had been placed in charge of security arrangements, changed the venue.

"Every visitor to the field stalls," flyers plastered across Moscow announced, "will receive a kerchief containing sweets, gingerbread, sausage, an enamel mug, and a program of the festivities. They will also be given a bread roll, a pound in weight. Special stalls will be set up around the edge of the field for dispensing beer and mead."[147] Stalls were built to hold the buffets and casks of beer that were to be given away to the thousands of peasants and workers. In total, some four hundred thousand packages were prepared. Each contained a half-pound of sausage, small loaves of bread, nuts, gingerbread, and sweets, and a blue and white enamel mug decorated with the imperial monogram. These gifts from the imperial couple were wrapped in colored handkerchiefs that showed the Kremlin and portraits of the emperor and the empress and had been woven at the Prokhorov and the Danilov factories.[148] Circus performers, musicians, singers, and dancers were to entertain at a temporary theater, while priests of the Orthodox Church were to conduct an open-air liturgy for the throng. Finally, at two in the afternoon, the emperor and the empress were to make an appearance.

Only sixty police officers had been detailed to patrol Khodynka Field; throughout the warm summer night before the planned feast, these men watched in amazement as the crowd continued to grow and grow—thousands of people pouring in from every direction beneath a clear black sky twinkling with stars. People pushed and jammed against each other and stumbled and fell into the trenches crossing the meadow. Those arriving late, fearing that they would not receive their gifts, pressed ahead, unaware of what was taking place across the field. Hundreds of men, women, and children were forced down, from their knees to their stomachs and faces, while the people behind them, unable to resist the force against their own backs, struggled forward, stepping on the fallen bodies. As the terrible stampede continued through the night, screams rose above the dusty field, sending the horrified policemen into a panic. Fearing that the crowd had simply grown too large, they decided to begin distributing the gifts early that morning. This caused an even greater push toward the front, resulting in a crush in which hundreds were trampled. Those at the front and the middle of the field, pushed by the swell of the crowd at the rear, were forced to walk over the bodies as they fell before them, grinding hands, fingers, and faces into the dirt. As the police at the front realized what was happening, they sent for reinforcements, but it was too late.[149]

In the pale Moscow dawn, Khodynka looked like a battlefield. Bodies lay everywhere. Vladimir Nemirovich-Demchenko saw hundreds of faces, "dark purple, blue-black, and crimson," with "dried blood filling nostrils and the corners of their mouths."[150] Arms were twisted into strange positions, broken bones protruded through ripped flesh, eyes dangled from gouged sockets, ribcages had been crushed, the heads of children and babies smashed beyond recognition. For the rest of the morning, police and brigades arrived with large carts to haul away the dead or the injured. One visitor remembered "a large wagon lumbering along, heaped high with a quivering load of the dead—poor crushed peasants, still in their gaudy festal clothes, being driven through the city to the cemetery, followed by weeping friends."[151] When it proved impossible to remove all of the dead before the start of the ceremonies, the bodies were simply pushed under the Imperial Pavilion.

Nicholas II learned of the disaster at ten that morning. "Until now, all has gone smoothly," he recorded in his diary, "but today, a great sin occurred."[152] Although thousands had been killed, officials put the death toll at just under fifteen hundred, in an attempt to minimize the tragedy. In his capacity as governor-general, Grand Duke Serge Alexandrovich decided that news of the disaster should be concealed. Francis Doublier, one of the men sent by Lumière Ciné-matographe, had been at Khodynka with his camera early that morning when he heard "shrieks behind me, and panic spread through the people." Realizing what was happening, he began "to film the horrible scene" of "the shrieking, milling, dying mass." The police spotted him and arrested him before he could leave the field. "All our equipment was confiscated and we never saw our precious camera again."[153] A British correspondent, attempting to file a report by telegram that afternoon, found that officials refused to forward it. When Count Vorontzov-Dashkov learned of this, he went straight to the emperor and obtained Nicholas II's permission to authorize publication of details of the tragedy.[154]

Everyone expected that the imperial couple would cancel their appearance at Khodynka Field and the rest of the coronation schedule. Distressed by the catastrophe, Nicholas was uncertain of what to do. Serge Witte raised the issue with Grand Duke Serge Alexandrovich, asking, "Will there not be an order from the

Emperor, in light of the disaster, to turn the joyous celebration into an expression of grief, and to hold a solemn religious service instead of performances and concerts?" But Nicholas, the grand duke said, had declared that "although what had happened was a tragedy, it must not be permitted to cast a shadow over the joyous occasion of the Coronation."[155]

A few minutes past two that afternoon, Nicholas and Alexandra duly appeared in the Imperial Pavilion at Khodynka. People still on the meadow bowed reverently and crossed themselves, watching as battalions of infantry and cavalry rode by in review. Nicholas, recalled one witness, "was quiet, but very pale."[156] But after the crowd had sung "God Save the Tsar," the imperial couple entered an open landau and returned to the Petrovsky Palace, having spent just twenty minutes among their people.[157] Witte termed it "a festival on top of the corpses."[158] The emperor's sister Olga Alexandrovna recalled dozens of carts, with untold numbers of arms protruding over the sides. "At first, I thought that people were waving to us. Then my blood froze. I felt sick. Those carts carried the dead—mangled out of all recognition."[159]

At the Petrovsky Palace, the emperor received delegations from across his empire. Nicholas and Alexandra stood on a platform in the courtyard of the palace, as representatives of fourteen delegations paraded by, ending with the men who had baked the little loaves of bread put in the gift bundles distributed at Khodynka Field.[160] A luncheon followed. Two orchestras played military tunes as the guests dined on Poltava borscht, piroshki, cold whitefish, veal with fresh greens, roast spring chicken and fowl, fresh and pickled cucumbers, raspberry sweets, fresh fruits, and wines. According to Witte, "the Emperor's face showed grief; in fact, he looked sick."[161] Yet at the conclusion of the meal, Nicholas declared to his guests, "The Empress and I heartily thank you for your expressions of love and dedication. We do not doubt that these feelings are shared by your fellow villagers." He ended with words that, under the circumstances, were pregnant with irony: "Care for your welfare is as close to my heart as it is to that of our Father and Beloved Savior."[162] Even as he spoke, beyond the gates of the palace, carts were busy hauling away countless corpses of his subjects from Khodynka Field.

That night, Nicholas and Alexandra appeared at half-past ten, as scheduled, at a magnificent ball given in their honor by the French ambassador, Count Louis Gustave de Montebello. The French government had spent thousands of francs shipping gold plate and tapestries from Versailles to decorate the former Sheremetiev Palace. The immense foyer had been transformed into a tropical garden, with illuminated fountains and over a hundred thousand fresh roses, imported from the south of France.[163] Nicholas and Alexandra opened the ball, the emperor, dressed in the uniform of the Life Guards Uhlan Regiment, leading the countess while the empress danced with the count. Several guests noticed that the empress's eyes were red and swollen from crying. "It nearly broke my heart to hear of all their suffering," one later said, "and then to have to go on with all the celebrations."[164] According to Grand Duchess Xenia Alexandrovna, "Nicky and Alix wanted to leave after half an hour." But Grand Dukes Vladimir and Serge Alexandrovich pulled them aside, protesting that such thoughts were "useless sentimentality."[165] Seeing what was taking place, Grand Duke Nicholas Mikhailovich interrupted the conclave, saying, "You cannot revive the dead, but you must show your sympathy with their families. Do not let the enemies of the regime say that the young Emperor danced while his murdered subjects were taken to the Potter's Field." When, after further discussions, the imperial couple again took to the dance floor and remained for over three hours, Grand Dukes Nicholas, George, Alexander, and Serge Mikhailovich left the ball, creating a scandal and a burst of whispers across the room. Turning to his brother Serge Alexandrovich, Grand Duke Alexei exclaimed in disgust, "There go the four Imperial followers of Robespierre."[166]

The following day, Nicholas and Alexandra visited the wounded in St. Catherine's Hospital; in addition, the emperor publicly pledged that he would give 1,000 rubles ($10,000 in 2005 figures) to each of the families of the nearly fifteen hundred official victims, although he later failed to do so.[167] Many of the victims were buried in a communal grave at Vagonovsky Cemetery on the outskirts of Moscow, beneath a tall monument with the simple inscription "18 May 1896." But the damage had been done. The insult was made worse by the knowledge that two previously scheduled events in the coronation program, a military review on Khodynka Field—to have taken place on May 7—and a ball at the Austrian Embassy, on May 21, were canceled, on the emperor's orders, in deference to the death of Archduke Karl of Austria.[168] "To be able to make head or tail of the Coronation proceedings," wrote Aylmer Maude in disgust, "one has to grasp the idea that human beings are not brothers, sons of one Father as Jesus taught, but that they are made of various qualities of earth, and therefore an Austrian Grand Duke may well, in the sympathies of the Court of Russia, outweigh thousands of peasants."[169]

Amid the continuing controversy, the round of dinners, receptions, and balls continued. On the evening after the carnage at Khodynka, the emperor and the empress appeared at a great state dinner in the Hall of the Order of St. Alexander

Nevsky in the Grand Kremlin Palace, as though no catastrophe had taken place. The next night, May 20, Grand Duke Serge Alexandrovich presided over the glittering Governor-General's Ball, culminating in a magnificent midnight dinner for fifteen hundred, during which the orchestra of the Preobrazhensky Guards Regiment serenaded the guests.[170]

After nearly three weeks of festivities, the celebrations culminated in a great military review. This, the last event in the coronation schedule, took place, ironically enough, on Khodynka Field, where just a week earlier, the terrible deaths of thousands cast the first of the grim shadows that were to completely shroud the reign of Russia's last emperor. "The brown plain of baked mud lay sweltering under a brazen sky," wrote one witness, "and the stifling air was heavy with thick red dust that, like a fog, greatly interfered with the grand military spectacle before us. Sixty thousand men, Cavalry, Artillery, and Infantry, were drawn up for inspection. The Empress in a carriage with four white horses, and the Emperor—a gallant figure riding at the head of a brilliant group of princes and generals—passed between the lines of troops till all had been duly seen and approved. Soon after, Their Majesties came and took up their position once more in the Pavilion and stood in the burning sun, showing themselves to their soldiers as they had done, that day last week, to their peasants, or to such as had survived."[171]

It was fitting that the ceremonies ended on the dusty Khodynka Field, for its terrible tragedy became the overriding image of the festivities. The official account of the coronation claimed, "The people understood the suffering and emotion of their Sovereign, and sympathized with his great sorrow," portraying Khodynka as the emperor's personal disaster, rather than a tragedy endured by its victims.[172] The glorious image of the grand coronation, celebrating the traditional link between emperor and Orthodox Church, between sovereign and subject, was forever shattered, replaced with tales of a heartless Nicholas and his consort who danced and drank as their subjects suffered and died in the thousands. It stood in stark contrast to Nicholas's declaration on the very day of the tragedy, as a sovereign whose care and compassion for his subjects "is as close to my heart as it is to that of our Father and Beloved Savior."

23

THE TERCENTENARY

On a cold, early-spring day in 1913, the Romanov Dynasty celebrated its Tercentenary. Three hundred years earlier, a delegation of boyars from the Zemsky Sobor in Moscow had called upon sixteen-year-old Michael Romanov at the Ipatiev Monastery in Kostroma and offered him the crown. The Tercentenary of this momentous event turned out to be the last great state occasion in imperial Russia. After years of isolation, Nicholas and Alexandra commemorated the anniversary with a series of receptions and tours, designed to restore some of the public support that had eroded during the previous difficult decades.

The festivities were marked with a host of souvenirs. Engraved silver medals and ruble coins, struck at the Imperial Mint in St. Petersburg, were distributed through the office of the minister of the imperial court. Intended for guests and officials participating in the actual ceremonies, one side depicted the features of Nicholas II alongside those of Tsar Michael.[1] Along with the usual assortment of postcards and souvenir books, the Tercentenary Commission, chaired by former minister of the interior Alexander Bulygin, approved a number of cups, plates, candy dishes, boxes, trays, and calendars, all adorned with representations of Nicholas II and his family. This led to an official protest from the ministry of the imperial court, which declared, "The placing of the portraits of Imperial personages on objects having a utilitarian character is usually not permitted."[2] For the first time, stamps were issued bearing the emperor's features, a move that caused a scandal: the Holy Synod declared it improper to stamp the sovereign's face with a postmark. "Has the kike come and conquered Tsardom?" the Holy Synod asked in an editorial, leaving postal workers afraid to cancel the stamps.[3]

In the days leading up to the Tercentenary, workmen erected special stands to hold members of the public; decorated building facades with heraldic emblems, banners, and busts of Michael and of Nicholas II; and adorned lampposts along Nevsky Prospekt with twisted ribbons of yellow and black, the colors of the Romanov House standard.[4] At night, recalled Princess Michael Cantacuzené, "the Imperial Crowns and Monograms, with emblems of State designed in colored lamps, made vast decorations that lighted up the streets."[5] Yet, as one critic noted, "The festivities themselves provoked no enthusiasm from the crowds. They were damped externally by the rain, which fell in torrents during the whole time they lasted."[6]

The popular periodical *Niva*, in an editorial the week before the celebrations began, portrayed the founding of the dynasty not in the historically accurate terms of Michael's reluctant election to the throne, but as his personal sacrifice, in keeping with God's predestined plan for Russia. The empire had developed, it declared, "solely as a result of the sovereign's understanding of the demands and obligations of Russia itself."[7] This accorded with Nicholas II's beliefs, presenting, as Richard Wortman notes, "the Assembly's election of Michael not as the birth of a political nation, but as a divine designation of Michael Romanov and his descendants."[8]

Nicholas II's Tercentenary Manifesto kept to this theme. The Imperial Council and the State Duma unanimously called for an extensive amnesty for those involved in the 1905 Revolution.[9] One observer recorded the public hope "that mercies should be shown, miseries relieved, tears dried, an impulse given both to public and to private charities; something attempted to raise the moral standard of the people by the creation of new schools and educational establishments."[10] The manifesto, however, fell short of expectation. Written by Alexander Krivoshein, the minister of agriculture, it trumpeted the past glories of the imperial regime, at the same time referring to the emperor and his family as the sole source of Russian authority. Nicholas edited the document to remove references to the State Duma—an unwelcome reminder of the loss of the autocratic power and a public rival to attention and legitimacy.[11] As for the sweeping reforms and political amnesty many had anticipated, the manifesto made only the smallest concessions. The disappointment was palpable. "All the thieves and common malefactors who were crowding the prisons of St. Petersburg and

State processions leaving the Winter Palace to celebrate the Romanov Tercentenary, February 21, 1913

the other towns of the Empire were set free," recorded one critic, "but the political exiles, men of culture and the highest civic and private virtue, were left to their sad fate."[12]

At eight o'clock on the morning of February 21, a twenty-one-gun salute, fired from the guns of the Fortress of St. Peter and St. Paul, shattered the silence of the gray St. Petersburg dawn, announcing the start of the festivities. A Te Deum was scheduled to take place at noon, at Kazan Cathedral. The winter snow still lay deep on the ground, the temperature was frigid, and the sky heavy with threatening clouds. Count Vladimir Kokovtsov, the prime minister, recalled, "There was nothing in the feeling of the crowd but shallow curiosity."[13] Even the empress's loyal friend, Anna Vyrubova, later wrote of the "excited, but on the whole undemonstrative, masses of people," calling them "a typical Petersburg crowd."[14] Nicholas II, however, saw none of this. "The mood was joyous," he wrote in his diary, "reminding me of the Coronation."[15]

At noon, a salvo from the fortress signaled the beginning of the imperial processions. Palace Square was ringed with a guard of honor composed of members drawn from the imperial guards regiments, rigidly at attention as the massed band struck up "God Save the Tsar." At the same time, the elaborate wrought-iron gates of the Winter Palace's triple archway swung open, and a long line of carriages rolled out across the cobbled square, led by a squadron of the Cossack Konvoi Regiment in their scarlet coats and black kolpaki. Nicholas left the palace in an open, semistate landau with his son, nine-year-old Tsesarevich Alexei, at his side, both wearing the uniform of His Majesty's Rifle Regiment.[16] The emperor, recalled one witness, "looked grave and pale," his hand periodically raised in salute as he passed the gathered ranks of troops.[17] A correspondent for the *Times* of London noted that the tsesarevich "looked as well as any boy his age."[18] Behind them, surrounded by members of the Cossack Konvoi Escort, came the two empresses in a gilded state coach drawn by four white horses, followed by the four grand duchesses in an open barouche and a string of landaus and carriages filled with nearly all the members of the imperial house.[19] A sense of unease hung over the assembled crowds, kept at bay by triple rows of soldiers and members of the St. Petersburg police. According to one official, worries over bombs and a potential assassination attempt had turned the capital into "an armed camp."[20]

Nearly five thousand guests filled Kazan Cathedral. Michael Rodzianko, the president of the Duma, had come early that morning, to inspect the places reserved for the deputies and officials of the Russian parliament. He found that most of the seats were at the back of the cathedral. He objected strenuously and succeeded in having them moved toward the front. Soon, though, he was warned that "an unknown man, in peasant dress and wearing a pectoral cross, had placed himself in front of the space reserved for the Imperial Duma and refused to move." Rodzianko hurried to the spot, where he found Rasputin. "He was dressed in a magnificent Russian tunic of crimson silk, patent leather top boots, black cloth full trousers and peasant's overcoat. Over his dress he wore a pectoral cross on a finely wrought gold chain." Rodzianko immediately ordered the peasant out of the cathedral, but Rasputin refused, replying, "I was invited here at the wish of persons more highly placed than you," at the same time pulling out an invitation. But Rodzianko would have none of it. As Rasputin fell on his knees and began to pray, Rodzianko kicked him, saying, "Enough of this tomfoolery! If you don't clear out at once, I'll order my Sergeants-at-Arms to carry you out!" Rasputin shot the Duma president an angry look, slowly rose to his feet, and left the cathedral.[21]

Nicholas and Alexandra in procession in the Kremlin during
the Tercentenary Celebrations, 1913; Tsesarevich Alexei,
unable to walk, is carried by a court cossack

   A few minutes after this drama took place, the imperial processions arrived. As
the emperor's carriage came to a stop in front of the cathedral, recalled one witness, "the shy wintry sun came out and sharpened the splendor. The deafening
hurrahs drowned all other sounds."[22] Greeted by the metropolitan, the members
of the imperial family entered the massive cathedral and took their places in front
of the iconostasis, listening intently as the Te Deum began. Alexei was still unable
to walk without a limp, the lingering effects of his near-fatal hemorrhage at Spala
the previous autumn, and a member of the emperor's Cossack Konvoi Regiment
carried him in his arms. "The sight was inexpressibly sad," commented one witness, because it proved the truth of what had been whispered ever since the

autumn, that the heir to the throne was still suffering from disease. The white, pinched, small face of the boy, gazing anxiously around at the sea of human beings before him, engrossed with the beauty of the unaccustomed pageant, painfully impressed the spectators in the cathedral."[23] Standing in the congregation, the Comte de Chabrun noted the tsesarevich: "His ravishing face a little wooden, his eyes bright and questioning, his cheeks with the exquisite roundness of childhood all atop a graceful, slender neck. I observed it, thus, and he dominated the crowd."[24]

Members of the imperial family took up their places at the front of the cathedral, beneath a crimson velvet canopy shielding a dais. Alexandra, in a white gown with the blue cordon of the Order of St. Andrei across her breast, stood "immobile as a statue," noted one observer, "sadness upon her classically beautiful features."[25] Throughout the service, recalled the daughter of the British ambassador, Nicholas remained impassive, and his "almost stern gravity gave to the celebration no sense of national rejoicing."[26] A few observers saw Nicholas repeatedly gaze up into the great dome; he later told Anna Vyrubova that he had been watching some doves that had flown through the cathedral doors and up into the dome. To the impressionable emperor, it was a symbol of blessing on the continued rule of the House of Romanov.[27]

The Te Deum was followed by a state reception at the Winter Palace. For the first time in nearly a decade, the magnificent halls, with their marble, malachite, and granite columns and glowing crystal and ormolu chandeliers, were filled with the excited voices and rustling dresses of St. Petersburg society. It was the first state occasion at the palace since the opening of the Duma in 1906, and the entire imperial family was present to receive the guests and members of the Diplomatic Corps; only with great reluctance did Nicholas II consent to the inclusion of members of the State Duma.[28] Nicholas, in the uniform of the Preobrazhensky Guards, walked in with his wife, who wore a blue velvet Russian court gown and a pearl and diamond kokoshnik, from which floated a long tulle veil sewn with tiny diamonds and seed pearls. Their four daughters, making their first appearances at a Winter Palace reception, looked young and innocent in white Russian court gowns, worn with the red Sash of the Order of St. Catherine and white kokoshniki ornamented with pearls and satin bows tied at the back of their heads. Throughout the afternoon, as Alexander Spiridovich noted, Nicholas seemed unable to bring himself to greet the assembled crowd; instead, he stood smoking with members of his Entourage.[29] Another official recorded, "Two steps from the Emperor stood Dowager Empress Marie Feodorovna, openly and graciously smiling, having a young look despite her sixty-four years, thanks to heavy makeup. Then somewhat apart, about ten to fifteen feet from the Dowager Empress, the young Empress sat on an armchair, in a pose of exhaustion, all red, like a peony, with eyes that were almost mad. Next to her, also sitting on a chair, was the unmistakably weary Heir, in the uniform of the Rifles of the Imperial Family. The group had a most tragic look."[30] Nicholas and Alexandra's inability to hide their contempt for the ceremonies left a bitter impression.

The following evening, there was a gala performance of Glinka's opera *A Life for the Tsar* at the Mariinsky Theater. In addition to the emperor, the empress, and their daughter Olga Nikolaievna, the emir of Bokhara and the khan of Khiva, along with the Romanov grand dukes and duchesses, crowded the blue, white, and gold auditorium. The renowned prima ballerinas Mathilde Kschessinska and Anna Pavlova performed in the dances. "The three tiers of boxes blazed with jewels and tiaras and the huge parterre of stalls was filled solely with Court officials in scarlet uniforms," recalled Meriel Buchanan.[31] Baroness Agnes de Stoeckl later declared that the empress "looked listless, as though she were in pain," when she and the emperor entered the imperial box.[32]

Meriel Buchanan watched the scene from the ambassador's box on the second level, to the side of the imperial loge. When the emperor and the empress entered the theater, her attention was also immediately drawn to Alexandra, who appeared ill at ease. She later wrote, "She was very pale when she came in, the pale blue ribbon of the St. Andrei that crossed her breast matching the turquoises in her magnificent diamond tiara and parure, the soft folds of her white velvet dress setting off her stately figure. But her lovely tragic face was expressionless, almost austere as she stood by her husband's side during the playing of the National Anthem, her eyes, enigmatical in their dark gravity, seeming fixed on some secret inward thought that was certainly far removed from the crowded theatre and the people who acclaimed her. Not once did a smile break the immobile somberness of her expression when, the Anthem over, she bent her head in acknowledgement of the cheers that greeted its conclusion and sank down in the gold backed armchair that had been provided for her. The Diplomatic Body had been given places all along the first tier and our box happened to be the next to the Imperial one, and, sitting so close, we could see that the fan of white eagles' feathers the Empress was holding was trembling convulsively, we could see how a dull, unbecoming flush was stealing over her pallor, could almost hear the labored breathing which made the diamonds which covered the bodice of her gown rise and fall, flashing and trembling with a thousand uneasy sparks of light.

Presently it seemed that this emotion or distress mastered her completely, and, with a few whispered words to the Emperor, she rose and withdrew to the back of the box, to be seen no more that evening. A little wave of resentment rippled over the Theater."[33]

At the end, Feodor Chaliapin walked to the front of the stage, followed by the entire cast. As they stood bathed in the footlights, the orchestra struck up "God Save the Tsar"; instinctively, Chaliapin fell to his knees, reached his arms toward the imperial loge, and sang. The others quickly followed his lead, and all eyes turned upward, where the emperor stood in silence, head bowed slightly, tears in his eyes.[34]

Although the festivities had been conceived as a showcase for the imperial family, to the exclusion of all official institutions, neither Nicholas nor Alexandra made any effort to disguise their disinterest. The resentful manner in which they participated in the celebrations undertaken on their behalf demonstrated a tragic ineptitude in recognizing the opportunity at their disposal to win back an alienated public. The empress refused to preside over any entertainments at the Winter Palace; St. Petersburg's aristocracy gave the only ball, on February 23 at the Assembly Hall of the Nobility, facing Mikhailovsky Square. Even Alexandra could not avoid the ceremony. "The vast columns of cream marble," wrote Princess Michael Cantacuzené, "wound with garlands, the rich red velvet of draperies, the golden woodwork, the bronze and crystal of chandeliers or high candelabra, made a picture difficult to rival and one felt the proud nobles of the Empire had done their best and might well be proud of their success."[35] The emperor and the empress led the opening polonaise in the grand Hall of Columns, to the lyrical music of Chopin. Nicholas II, recalled Princess Cantacuzené, "looked uncomfortable and intimidated. He walked as rapidly as possible, in military fashion, as if anxious to get the ceremony over and hating to be stared at."[36] The empress, in a white gown worn with Catherine the Great's diamonds, circled the hall, taking the arm of a different partner at each end, but from the flush on her cheeks to the constant darting of her eyes, her discomfort was obvious.[37] "Her eyes were stern and sad," Princess Cantacuzené remembered, "her mouth made a straight, hard line, drawn in physical distress and mental rebellion at the necessity of carrying through a ceremony she disliked, amid a court and nobility she did not care for. Not once did she smile."[38]

At the end of the polonaise, the imperial couple retreated to a dais, set between a pair of Corinthian columns and crowned with a red velvet canopy embroidered with a double-headed eagle in gold thread. As Nicholas and

Alexandra watched, their eldest daughter, Grand Duchess Olga Nikolaievna, walked onto the dance floor, attired in a light pink satin gown decorated with garlands of artificial roses, her hair bound with a silver ribbon and a single string of pearls adorning her neck. It was her first formal appearance in St. Petersburg society, and she blushed with pleasure as all eyes turned on her and her partner, Prince Saltykov, as he led her through a waltz. Meriel Buchanan recalled her "wide, laughing mouth" and "sparkling blue eyes" as she swept across the floor.[39] As the evening wore on, Empress Alexandra grew increasingly restless. Nicholas happened to be chatting with a member of his suite when he noticed a frantic look from his wife. He managed to excuse himself and quickly escorted her from the hall. Nicholas was just in time; when the doors were closed behind them, the empress fainted into her husband's arms, completely exhausted.[40] Her physical frailty and nervous emotional state had, by 1913, nearly incapacitated her.

To celebrate the Tercentenary, the imperial family embarked on a pilgrimage across Russia. On May 15, the imperial train left St. Petersburg to retrace the route along the Volga River taken by young Michael on his way from Kostroma to Moscow to assume the throne. On May 16, the imperial train reached the ancient city of Vladimir. Nicholas and his family drove through the crowded streets to the town of Suzdal, visiting several monasteries and churches. "With great delight and interest," Nicholas wrote in his diary, "I inspected the wonderful treasures in the sanctuaries, and the ancient Russian churches. On our way there, and on our return, many people came from their villages with icons. I did not tire at all—the impressions were so strong and beautiful."[41]

The following day, the imperial train took the emperor and his family to the town of Nizhny-Novgorod. Nicholas, Alexandra, the tsesarevich, and the four grand duchesses climbed into waiting open carriages and set off through the crowded streets. Buildings had been hung with bunting, flags, and portraits of Tsar Michael and Nicholas II. The crowd, remembered Vladimir Dzhunkovsky, was "continually shouting 'Hurrah!' "[42] A Te Deum, held in the town cathedral, was followed by the dedication of a memorial to Kuzma Minin and Prince Pozharsky, who had helped thwart Polish troops on their way to capture young Michael Romanov.[43]

In the evening, the imperial party boarded a series of four steamboats that waited at dock on the Volga River. For the next week, Nicholas, Alexandra, and their children lived aboard the steamer *Mezhen*, which had been outfitted with carpets, furniture, paintings, and personal effects from the Alexander Palace for the duration of the voyage. The largest of the vessels, *Tsar Mikhail*

Feodorovich, had also been equipped with fittings from the imperial palaces, including china, crystal, and silver services for a hundred guests. Members of the Cossack Konvoi Regiment, along with detectives and regular infantry guards, traveled on a third ship, *Alexander the Blessed*, while the Entourage, the Suite, and government officials were lodged aboard *Strezhen*.[44]

That night, Nicholas and Alexandra gave a dinner for local officials aboard *Tsar Mikhail Feodorovich*. Local peasants and the town's inhabitants filled the docks and the river's edge, gazing on the vessels decorated with flags, their decks crowded with revelers and illuminated with strings of electric lights that shone brightly against the crimson sunset. At eleven that night, *Mezhen* cast off her lines, weighed anchor, and, followed by the three other ships, steamed from the docks, churning ribbons of white foam across the placid waters of the dark Volga. As the ships slowly pulled away, the town's church bells rang out and the crowd along the shore, a sea of heads holding flaming torches, broke into "God Save the Tsar," followed by the old Russian folk song "Down the Mother Volga."[45] "I will never forget the excitement and sense of patriotism," recalled Vladimir Dzhunkovsky. "In the meadows along the Volga, barrels of tar burned as bonfires."[46] Such scenes repeated themselves down the length of the Volga. The emperor's sister Olga Alexandrovna later recalled, "When our steamer went down the Volga, we saw crowds of peasants wading high in the water to catch a glimpse of Nicky. In some of the towns, I would see artisans and workmen falling down to kiss his shadow as we passed. Cheers were deafening."[47]

On May 19, 1913, *Mezhen* rounded a bend in the Volga and the town of Kostroma came into view, the tall white spires of its cathedrals and churches rising above the rambling houses and dusty streets. "From dawn," noted Vladimir Dzhunkovsky, "Kostroma was the scene of unusual activity: huge crowds of people headed to the banks of the Volga, and by 8 o'clock the whole riverside was a sea of heads. All the tributaries and even the Kostroma and Murayevka Rivers were full of rafts covered with people."[48]

As *Mezhen* steamed across the Volga toward the cheering throngs, cannons along the walls of the town's Kremlin thundered out in salute, and the bells of the city's churches joined in the cacophony of sound.[49] Kostroma was a town of modest size, but its imperial connections meant that its wide, dusty streets were graced with triumphal obelisks, neoclassical museums, and immense statuary of previous Romanovs, all of which shone beneath new layers of whitewash or glowed from endless cleanings.

It was, as Nicholas noted in his diary, "a heavenly morning."[50] At a quarter to ten, a burst of cannon fire greeted *Mezhen* as it reversed engines and came to a halt at the edge of a newly constructed dock. Waiting to welcome the imperial family was a group of provincial, town, and church officials, headed by Archbishop Tikhon and Governor-General Peter Stremukhov, who presented the emperor (who wore the uniform of the Erivansky Guards Regiment) with the traditional welcome of bread and salt. As members of the imperial family left *Mezhen*, they walked between serried ranks of a guard of honor drawn from the Erivansky Regiment.[51] The empress, leaning heavily on her tightly rolled parasol and clutching her husband's arm, as well as her four daughters, all wore long white summer dresses, their heads crowned by large picture hats adorned with ostrich feathers; behind the emperor and the empress, a member of the Cossack Konvoi carried Tsesarevich Alexei in his arms.

At the end of the dock, members of the imperial family climbed into a string of waiting landaus that conveyed them through the center of the town. Thousands of people crowded the streets. A public holiday had been declared, and merchants, peasants, and schoolchildren—turned out in crisp white uniforms— all jostled as the procession passed, waving flags and handkerchiefs and shouting greetings as the imperial family appeared. "The Emperor and his family," recalled Prime Minister Vladimir Kokovtsov, "were surrounded by a massive crowd of people. Unrestrained expressions of joy rang out, and as if from their own warmth their hearts melted."[52]

On the first day of the visit to Kostroma, the imperial family visited the Church of the Resurrection, the Officers' Assembly, and the Red Cross Headquarters and Nursing Facility. That afternoon, they drove to the Ipatiev Monastery, where young Michael Romanov had lived and been offered the Russian throne. Despite its historic ties to the dynasty, the monastery was one of the poorest in Russia; of the Romanov sovereigns, only Nicholas I had taken an interest in its welfare, providing funds for the restoration of its church and supporting its monks. After his death, however, the monastery had fallen on hard times, and none of Nicholas I's imperial successors intervened as it slipped first into poverty, then outright scandal. By 1913, the monastery had grown infamous, its monks discarding their clerical robes in favor of modern dress as they strolled through the town with their girlfriends and retreated to cells that rang with the sound of gramophone music. Nicholas II himself was saved the embarrassment of its financial and spiritual poverty only by the careful intervention of the hated State Duma, which appropriated adequate funds to clothe the priests in new vestments and quickly curtail their excesses.[53]

In the afternoon, following a visit to the town's new Romanov Museum, the imperial family attended a reception given by the Provincial Assembly of Nobles. In his address, the marshal of the provincial nobility welcomed the emperor, speaking of the empire's growth under his reign and citing the establishment of the State Duma as a sign of clear progress, a remark that stung the autocratically minded Nicholas, who interrupted the speech by loudly and angrily asking, "Are you finished?" The marshal quickly concluded his remarks, but both the emperor and the empress were incensed by the unwelcome mention of the hated Duma. During the reception that followed, Nicholas, as he had done in St. Petersburg, largely ignored the gathered representatives, choosing instead to chat with members of his Entourage, while Alexandra flatly refused to speak to anyone other than Madame Stremukhov, the wife of the governor-general. The imperial couple thus offended those who were present by this petulant behavior.[54]

That night, Nicholas and Alexandra gave a banquet on board *Tsar Mikhail Feodorovich* for a number of provincial and town officials, dining on a seven-course meal that included soup made from young greens, piroshki, steamed sturgeon, saddle of wild goat, roast chicken, salad, asparagus with sauce, and ice cream. The town was illuminated with strings of electric lights that twinkled against the dark sky; at eleven, the imperial family gathered on the deck of *Mezhen* to watch a magnificent fireworks display over the Volga River. "The steamships on the Volga were superbly lit," recalled Vladimir Dzhunkovsky, "their lights shimmering on the waters."[55]

The highlight of the visit came on May 20, when the entire imperial family attended the groundbreaking ceremony for the new Romanov Dynasty Memorial. Designed by the architect A. I. Adamson, the memorial would include depictions of sixteen of the eighteen Romanov sovereigns, including a statue of Nicholas II—the first such representation of a living monarch ever to be raised in Russia.[56] The emperor, the empress, and members of the imperial family attended a Te Deum in the Assumption Cathedral that beautiful early-summer day, the blue sky stretching for miles into the distance of the great Russian plain. "Their Majesties," recalled Dzhunkovsky, "were accompanied to the Cathedral by constant shouts of 'Hurrah!' that drowned the choir."[57] A large white canvas tent, decorated with double-headed eagles, had been erected next to the memorial site. Nicholas, Alexandra, Tsesarevich Alexei, the four grand duchesses, and Dowager Empress Marie Feodorovna each laid a foundation stone engraved with his or her name.[58] At the end of the ceremony, the assembled clergy, in their silver and gold robes and stoles, led a Te Deum, washed with the warm Volga breezes that filled the Russian tricolor proudly flying above the pavilion.

After two days, the members of the imperial family left Kostroma, and, at the end of May, they reached Moscow, their final destination. On May 24, the imperial train slowly steamed into Alexander Station. The platform had been decorated with flags and bunting, the siding lined with a regiment of horse guards; a military band played a rousing march. There was a lengthy procession through the streets of the city to the Kremlin, with thousands of church bells ringing out joyously into the Moscow sky. One side of the route was lined with cheering crowds, the other with troops drawn from the imperial guards regiments. A long string of landaus, court carriages, and barouches carried members of the imperial family down the Tverskaya to the Kremlin. Nicholas rode at the head of the procession atop a chestnut mare, surrounded by a mounted escort of the Cossack Konvoi Regiment. Bruce Lockhart recalled, "The mass emotion this visit engendered was overwhelming."[59]

The next day, the imperial family attended a Te Deum in the Kremlin's Cathedral of the Assumption. Kokovtsov remembered that the procession down the Red Staircase "was distinguished by a remarkable orderliness, given the far greater-than-usual crowds filling every inch of the Square. There was only one sad note—the sight of the Heir being carried the whole time in the arms of a Cossack. We were all used to this, but I well remember that as the procession slowed down momentarily, I heard loud exclamations of grief at the sight of the poor child."[60]

The celebrations convinced Nicholas of the loyal support of the Russian people. On their tour along the Volga, he was amazed at the emotion of the crowds, the endless sea of heads and waving flags, the loud cheers and spontaneous singing of the national anthem. "Now you can see for yourself what cowards those State Ministers are," Alexandra declared to Princess Elizabeth Naryshkin-Kuryakin. "They are constantly frightening the Emperor with threats and forebodings of a revolution and here—you see it yourself—we only need show ourselves and at once their hearts are ours."[61] But crowds in St. Petersburg and Moscow had greeted them with disinterest, a reflection of their alienation from public affection. At Kostroma, the imperial family had visited the Ipatiev Monastery, where the dynasty had been born; five years later, in a Siberian house owned by a merchant named Ipatiev, the Romanov Dynasty came to its brutal end when the emperor and his family were shot to death in the cellar.

Part Five

※

PLEASURES

24

IMPERIAL BALLS

IMPERIAL BALLS AT THE WINTER PALACE were the highlight of the St. Petersburg season, carefully choreographed and planned to present the imperial court in the most spectacular light, surrounded by unbelievable majesty, grandeur, and authority. These balls were designed "not just as entertainments, but spectacles," notes one historian. "The decoration of the halls, the selection of the rooms and their architecture, the lighting, and even the table settings, were all sublimated to the ideal of the Imperial presentation."[1]

During the season, only a dozen imperial balls were given, and the guest list changed with each occasion, allowing most of St. Petersburg society to attend at least one. Although, in theory, the guest lists were the sole domain of the empress, the man who held the real power was the minister of the imperial court, Count Vladimir de Freedericksz, and St. Petersburg society stood in awe of him, fearful of alienating the source of imperial favor. By the time of Grand Duchess Vladimir's Charity Bazaar a fortnight before Christmas, arrangements for the imperial balls were being finalized. Those aspiring to attend eagerly awaited the arrival of the stiff vellum cards, embossed in gold with double-headed eagles, that commanded the recipient, by order of the emperor, to appear at the Winter Palace on the appointed day and hour. These invitations were hand-delivered by officials known as *skorokhodi*, or court runners, attired in short dark-green jackets, ornamented with red collars and cuffs, and wearing golden caps decorated with black ostrich plumes. Once an invitation for an imperial ball was received, it could not be refused except for the most serious illness, or a death in the family.

The Nicholas Ball was the first event of the season, usually held on January 10 or 11. Only people in the first four levels of the Table of Ranks possessed the right of attendance. The guest list, drawn up by Count de Freedericksz, included members of the court, government ministers, senators, members of the State Council, commanders of the guards regiments, the heads of the St. Petersburg City Council, and representatives of the provincial nobility, who could be accompanied by their wives and unmarried daughters only if the women had already been presented to the empress. Members of the entire Diplomatic Corps and their families also received invitations. Foreign visitors of distinguished birth could sometimes secure an invitation by applying in person to the grand marshal of the imperial court. Typically, between five and eight thousand guests would attend.[2]

Representatives from the various guards regiments also received invitations. The grand marshal requested a number of officers from each regiment, who were selected by lottery. Before the ball, their commander instructed, "It is not an amusement. You must not think about having a good time. You are detached on duty, and you will be busily occupied with your duties. You have got to dance with the ladies and do your best to keep them amused. You are strictly forbidden to keep in a compact group . . . scatter, scatter!"[3] Officers sent to imperial balls were forbidden to drink, to avoid any hint of alcohol on their breath.[4]

A flurry of activity swept through the Winter Palace on the day of the ball. The grand marshal and the palace steward pored over massive leather-bound albums containing inventories and descriptions of china, silver, and crystal before selecting the appropriate service from the thousands of pieces held in storerooms below. The china used on these occasions had been commissioned from the Imperial Porcelain Factory in St. Petersburg, the Popov Factory, and the Gardner Porcelain Factory, with additional settings from Sèvres and Meissen. Most of the Romanov crystal in use at the turn of the century dated from the reign of Nicholas I: thousands of engraved goblets from Bohemia and Ireland, etched with heraldic emblems, imperial monograms, or double-headed eagles, and rimmed in gold; for the imperial family, there were goblets of similar design, executed in solid silver and gold. The thousands of plates, pieces of silver, and crystal were taken from their cupboards, drawers, and chests; placed on carts;

and rolled through the corridors to the state apartments above. Servants transformed the bare Parade Halls as the afternoon wore on, filling them with hundreds of delicate gilded chairs, potted palms, and tubs filled with orange trees, brought from the imperial conservatories at Tsarskoye Selo or Warsaw. Florists arranged cascades of roses, lilacs, hydrangeas, orchids, geraniums, lilies, and ivy, shipped from the Crimea across the snow-covered empire by a special train, behind elaborate treillages set in the corners of the halls. By seven o'clock, all was ready. As snow swirled across the frozen capital, covering the ornate pastel palaces in soft blankets of white, footmen laid fires, lit tapers, and switched on electric lights, until the tall windows of the palace blazed against the night sky. Before the guests arrived, servants carried censers through the palace, the clouds of sweet incense perfuming the halls.[5]

In distant corners of the palace, chamberlains, butlers, footmen, and pages collected freshly pressed uniforms from the palace laundries. The grand master of ceremonies normally summoned up to a thousand of these men into service for such an evening. He also determined which liveries should be worn and who would be called upon to "powder," the official designation for the wearing of white powder in one's hair to simulate a wig. This was an unwelcome ordeal. Towels were draped around shoulders and a special white paste was applied to the wet hair. When it dried, the result simulated a white wig.

Also summoned to the Winter Palace were *kamer-pages*, senior students from the Corps des Pages. "Formal dress," recalled Page Feodor Rerberg, "was very beautiful and fancy; it consisted of a helmet with a large puffy white sultan made of horsehair and decorated with gold braid. Coats were made so tight at the waist that in order to button them one servant would hold the material while another fastened the buttons. A wide belt of golden thread with a golden clasp encircled our waists, attached to them, long sabers. Breeches were of white chamois leather and lacquered boots were of the Cavalier design, with spurs." Court carriages collected the pages, who rode to the Winter Palace covered in white cloths, "so as not to soil our elegant outfits."[6]

In the palaces and houses lining the Neva River and winding canals, excited guests readied for the evening. Society ladies accustomed to leisurely afternoons promenading and taking tea with friends devoted themselves to the impending ball. Hairdressers, summoned from their shops, fussed and fretted over coiffures as lady's maids flitted about, dressing their mistresses in velvet, brocade, or satin gowns made in one of St. Petersburg's couturier houses or ordered from Paris. The men, too, were busy. Valets and, for those in the military, batmen cleaned medals and polished boots to a gleam as bright as patent leather. Officers' dress uniforms were brushed and laid out, beards trimmed, and mustaches waxed as darkness fell across the capital.

By evening, icy winds whistled off the Gulf of Finland, wrapping the city in their chill fingers as carriages and troikas raced guests muffled in sable, silver fox, ermine, or mink wraps through the haze of snow. Undulating drifts of snow cushioned the crunch of the horses' hooves as they sped down the broad avenues and along the frozen Neva, bound in thick blue ice. In the immense Palace Square, they swept past enormous braziers aglow with orange bonfires whose flames licked the dark sky, placed so that the hundreds of coachmen could warm themselves throughout the night. Occasionally, a driver, having imbibed too much vodka in the interim, would be found dead, sitting frozen atop his seat.[7]

The Winter Palace, recalled Théophile Gautier, "shone at every window, like a mountain pierced with holes and brilliant with interior fire. Perfect silence reigned in the Square; the severity of the weather kept away the curious who with us never fail to be attracted by the spectacle of such a fete."[8] The light from within the palace cast an eerie glow across the snow-covered ground as carriages deposited their passengers: grand dukes at the Saltykov Entrance, courtiers at Their Majesties' Entrance, officers at the Commanders' Entrance, and ordinary officials and guests at the Jordan Doorway. Inside Rastrelli's vaulted corridor, footmen in white silk stockings, velvet knee breeches, and shirts with lace jabots peeking through blue coats sewn with gold braid, collected military cloaks and officers' greatcoats, Astrakhan coats, fur wraps, hats, and gloves, as guests made their ways through the warm labyrinth, pausing to make last-minute adjustments of gowns and uniforms in pier glasses framed by potted palms, before reaching the magnificent Jordan Staircase. The wide marble steps, covered in crimson runners, were lined with footmen in scarlet coats whose golden double-headed eagles shimmered in the glow from the alabaster shades of the candelabra as guests ascended to the first floor.

The sweet smell of incense hung heavily in the rooms, along with the aromas of the beeswax candles and resin from evergreen boughs framing doorways. The halls, recalled Gautier, were a "furnace of light and heat." He noted, "Rows of lights along the cornices; in the embrasures of the windows great candelabra with a thousand arms blazed like burning bushes; hundreds of chandeliers hung from the ceiling in constellations of fire. And all these lights uniting their rays formed the most dazzling illumination that could be imagined to adorn a fete."[9] These rooms, desolate and cold by day, took on new life during a ball: the marble, malachite, jasper, and porphyry columns; the gilded ceilings and doorways; the polished inlaid wooden floors gleaming like mirrors—all created a setting of unparalleled magnificence. With faces flushed, guests moved from room to room, between banks of exotic flowers, fragrant orange and lemon trees, and lofty palms arranged in lush displays.[10] "The heat," noted one guest, "was excessive."[11]

Scattered across the halls, princes and princesses, dukes, barons, counts, and members of the Diplomatic Corps mingled with government ministers and elderly grandes dames. Bishops and priests, clad in black or purple robes and long white veils, chatted amiably in corners with the *dames à portrait*, their Russian court gowns adorned with diamond-framed miniatures of the empress. Officers from the various regiments clustered in small groups: Cossacks, in scarlet coats and black kolpaki; Hussars, in white tunics and red dolmans covered with gold aiguillettes; Lancers in blue, their silver helmets topped with cascades of eagles' feathers; Chevaliers Gardes and the Gardes à Cheval, with white tunics, silver breastplates, and helmets topped with double-headed eagles; and Golden Palace Grenadiers, in black tunics decorated with gold braid and heads adorned with tall bearskin hats.[12]

Through the blue haze of the cigarette smoke, jewels flashed their brilliant fires. "There was a general blaze of magnificence," recalled one guest.[13] Alexander Mossolov left a vivid portrait of one lady at an imperial ball: "She was already in her forties, but still slim, and her spangled dress displayed her figure wonderfully. Her light, almost chestnut hair was decorated with a diadem set with two rows of diamonds. A *ferronière* with a single diamond of two square centimeters crossed her forehead. A diamond necklace, the neck of her dress bordered with diamonds, with a flower at the back entirely of diamonds, set flat; two diamond chains leading, like enormous threads of fire, first to the front of the bodice, and then to the buckle at the waist."[14]

Music filled the palace. Gypsies in Hungarian uniforms played rousing melodies in one hall; in another, a symphony orchestra flooded the room with the music of Tchaikovsky, Rimsky-Korsakov, Borodin, Cui, and Glinka; while, in a third, the mournful sounds of a balalaika orchestra washed hauntingly over the guests. Footmen in sumptuous liveries handed round wines and spirits in crystal glasses balanced on silver trays. By nine, expectation had grown to a fever pitch. Crowds swelled near the entrance to the Nicholas Hall, awaiting the imperial family. In the adjacent Concert Hall, brilliantly attired Chevalier Guards stood in anticipation as processions began to form: court servants in their liveries, chamberlains in dark-blue frock coats with gold braid, senators, and members of the State Council.

The emperor and the empress, with members of the imperial family, gathered in the Malachite Hall; etiquette demanded that they appear en grande toilette, adorned with jewelry and cordons, orders and awards, covering their gowns and uniforms in a scintillating veneer of flashing colors.[15] A few minutes before nine, the *kamer-pages* took up their positions, and the emperor, with a short nod to the grand marshal, signaled that all was ready.[16] The moment of their appearance was pure theater: noiselessly, the fourteen-foot-high mahogany doors to the private apartments were opened by gaily costumed court Abyssinians. "There was a murmur of expectation," recalled one guest, "and every one seemed to know that the Emperor and Empress were coming."[17] Ranks of chamberlains and footmen slowly filtered out of the doors and into the Concert Hall, followed by the grand marshal of the imperial court, who carried a ten-foot ebony staff, topped with an ormolu double-headed eagle and tied with the blue silk ribbon of the Order of St. Andrei. Deliberately, he brought it down upon the polished floor with three loud bangs, crying out, "Their Imperial Majesties!"

At these words, the emperor and the empress appeared, followed by a string of grand dukes and duchesses and members of the imperial court. Nicholas inevitably wore the uniform of the Preobrazhensky or the Hussar Guards, his wife clad in a Russian court gown of silver brocade; she always wore the crown jewels to the Nicholas Ball, as required by court etiquette.[18] Women sank into deep curtsies, the men into low bows. As the emperor and the empress entered, an orchestra struck up "God Save the Tsar." "The beauty and splendor of the picture was overwhelming," recalled one *kamer-page*.[19]

The imperial procession from the Malachite Hall through the Concert Hall and to the Nicholas Hall was a delicate act, as more than a hundred people—the imperial family, court officials, and members of the Imperial Household—marched slowly through the rooms. Pages were careful to steer the ladies' velvet and brocade trains out of harm's way, but inevitably there were accidents. Once, Grand Duke Michael Nikolaievich caught the train of Grand Duchess Vladimir's gown with his spur, which she unknowingly dragged behind her. Her page ran forward, attempting to grab the yards of lace and velvet, but succeeded only in shredding even more of the fabric as the grand duchess struggled on.[20]

According to tradition, imperial balls opened with the polonaise, a stately promenade through the elegant rooms, led by the emperor and his wife. After the first round, he switched partners, selecting someone he wished to honor—usually, the doyenne of the Diplomatic Corps—while Alexandra Feodorovna took the arm of the doyen. To the rhythmic music of Glinka's *A Life for the Tsar*, they began the slow parade. "Our procession," remembered Grand Duke Alexander Mikhailovich, "had to pass through all the halls with six chamberlains in front of us announcing our approach. We circled the Palace three times, after which the dancing began in every hall."[21]

Returning to the Nicholas Hall, the emperor and his partner moved to the center of the room as the dancing began. Two orchestras sat in the galleries of the Nicholas Hall, the Court Musicians and the players of the Household Regiment of the Preobrazhensky Guards, including students of the Imperial Conservatory who thus fulfilled their military obligations.[22] After a few soft dances, the revelers began quadrilles. Usually, the emperor and the empress joined in the first quadrille but by tradition did not participate in the second; at that point, Nicholas moved through the crowds greeting guests, and the empress received selected ladies.[23] Inevitably, Alexandra's dislike of such occasions shone through; rather than using the occasion to draw people toward her, she left only bitter memories. "She danced badly, not caring for dancing; and she certainly was not a brilliant conversationalist. . . . She had red arms, red shoulders, and a red face which always gave the impression that she was about to burst into tears. . . . Everything about her was hieratic to the very way she was dressed in the heavy brocade of which she was so fond, and with diamonds scattered all over her, in defiance of good taste and common sense."[24]

After the third or fourth quadrille, the dancing changed to the mazurka, a difficult operation given the push of the crowds and the lack of space in the halls, as the couples swirled and men dipped to one knee, officers noting their spurs as they came dangerously close to the flying trains and rich gowns. "Amid the blaze of light, the brilliant costumes, the flashing of diamonds, and the mirrors with their endless reflections," wrote Théophile Gautier, "it is difficult to distinguish anything. A glowing scintillation prevents you from seizing any object."[25] They flew across the shining floors, beneath chandeliers whose prisms "sparkled like diamonds," until the room was a shifting panoply of color and motion.[26] "The whirling waltz puffs out dresses," Gautier recalled, "like the skirts of the spinning dervishes and amid the rapid revolution, knots of diamonds, and blades of gold and silver flash like lightning; little gloved hands placed on shoulders look like white camellias in massive gold vases."[27]

Grand duchesses dispatched adjutants to summon chosen partners who, flushed with honor, hurried through the crowd to lead them to the floor; grand dukes, attired in regimental uniform, were free to select their own partners. Weapons were removed before the grand dukes took to the floor, but this precaution did not prevent accidents. Once, Grand Duke Michael Alexandrovich was waltzing with Nadine Wonlar-Larsky when he caught his spur in the hem of her gown. He tried to disentangle his foot, but as he did so, he ripped the bottom of the dress away, dragging rows of lace and satin with him. His startled partner tried to balance herself against this tug-of-war, but both ended up in a heap on the floor, watched by thousands of mirthful eyes.[28]

At the stroke of midnight, a buffet supper was served. Long tables, covered with elaborate ice sculptures, flickering candles, and fresh flowers, filled the sides of the anteroom, the rotunda, and adjoining corridors. Guests began with the traditional zakuski, or hors d'oeuvres: chafing dishes of hot stuffed mushrooms; bowls of red, black, and gray caviar snuggled into beds of ice; platters spread with cold smoked salmon and sturgeon; salted cucumbers; sausages; slices of ham; and stuffed eggs. Between them, bowls of sour cream surrounded piles of little round blini. Although the zakuski amounted to a meal in itself, the main supper quickly followed, when guests dined on morsels of roasted pheasant, lamb, suckling pig, venison, veal, grilled sturgeon, and smoked salmon in cream sauce. Tureens held steaming borscht, grilled and steamed potatoes, and vegetables in hollandaise sauce. There were bowls of fresh fruits—pineapples, watermelons, grapes, fresh strawberries, and cherries—shipped north from the Crimea and arranged in artful pyramids; salvers covered with breads and rolls, pastries, cakes, and delicate tortes; and frosted bowls mounded with chocolate, vanilla, and fruit-flavored ice creams and sorbets. Waiters carried bottles of champagne, French and Crimean wines, and decanters of whiskey, cognac, sherry, and cassis. Vodka, flavored with either lemon peel, peppercorns, cranberries, or buffalo grass, chilled in beds carved from blocks of ice, was placed next to silver jugs of seltzer water, lemonade, and milk flavored with almonds; at the end of the tables, tea boiled atop samovars and coffee steamed in engraved silver and crystal pots.[29] Summing up the effect of this luxurious feast, one foreign visitor declared, "My dear, there was fresh asparagus for *everyone*."[30]

Orchestras, concealed in galleries, serenaded the diners throughout the meal. The empress dined in the Nicholas Hall with ladies of the imperial family, at a long table erected on a dais, surrounded by a bower of "hyacinths, mixed with tulips."[31] Below, the four hundred most important guests sat at round tables of twelve, while the others ate in adjoining halls.[32] Nicholas moved throughout the meal, an empty seat reserved for him at each table. This, recalled one guest, "created excitement and general unrest, for as soon as he approached a table, every one had to stand and enter into conversation as if he intimated his desire to talk; the guests had to keep their eyes open to watch for his approach and the servants never knowing exactly where he was were in constant terror of knocking into him."[33]

At the end of the supper, the emperor returned to the empress and, taking her hand, led her to the center of the Nicholas Hall to resume dancing. After the first waltz, however, Nicholas and Alexandra inevitably retired to their private apartments, bowing to the crowd before retreating to the seclusion of the Malachite Hall. Although the dancing continued for several hours, led by a ranking grand duke or duchess, for most guests, the departure of the imperial couple meant the end of the festivities. Descending the Jordan Staircase, they collected their greatcoats or fur wraps and waited as footmen summoned their carriages and troikas from the snow-covered square. Climbing inside, they hugged hot water bottles filled by their coachmen and, wrapped in fur rugs, sped across the frozen city to the warmth and comfort of their own houses.

Over the next six weeks, the brilliant rooms of the Winter Palace were regularly filled with thousands of guests. "Invitations to the other Court balls followed immediately after," noted one diplomat's wife, "decreasing in size and increasing in importance, and one's position could be easily ascertained by knowing which of these balls they attended."[34] Three Concert Balls followed the Nicholas Ball, to which up to eight hundred guests received invitations.[35] These were always held in the Concert Hall, followed by an elaborate sit-down dinner in the adjoining Nicholas Hall, during which the guests were serenaded with selections performed by the St. Petersburg Symphony Orchestra. At least one ball each season had a pastoral theme, and real turf was laid down on sheets of wood spread across the exquisitely inlaid floor. To heighten the effect, tubs holding small trees were placed at intervals round the room, their branches wired with tiny electric lights that sparkled as the guests dined.[36]

During any season, five or six Hermitage Balls might be given as January slipped into February. Limited to a thousand guests each, these exclusive balls took place in elaborate rooms hung with Catherine the Great's priceless collection of paintings and decorated with Siberian marble. "Everything was gold," recalled one guest, "even to the tall vases holding the flowers and a tiny fountain in the center of the Empress's supper table upon the dais, throwing an exotic fragrance into the air."[37] The evening's entertainment began with a single act from an opera, performance in the Hermitage Theater by members of the Bolshoi or the Mariinsky Company, followed by a short theatrical, and finally a ballet. Alexandra rigidly controlled the theatricals: she found many of the popular dramas and comedies of the day—particularly the racier French imports—unsuitable for imperial consumption, and Russian fairy tales, English dramas, Shakespeare, and French classics were frequently given. A ball, held in one of the Hermitage Galleries, was followed by a midnight supper in an adjoining hall. Dancing continued until two in the morning when, by tradition, a final polonaise signaled the end of the evening.[38]

The most exclusive of all imperial entertainments was the Palm Ball, given at the end of the season. Only five hundred guests received invitations, and competition among St. Petersburg's aristocracy ran high for this sign of imperial favor. After the usual polonaise and round of waltzes, guests at the Palm Ball moved into the Nicholas Hall for supper. Tubs held tall palm trees, brought from the imperial conservatories, and were ringed by circular tables for twelve covered with white damask embroidered with double-headed eagles and the emperor's monogram. Place settings were laid out and measured with a ruler to ensure that all were spaced correctly; a single setting might consist of thirty pieces, according to the menu and the variety of wines to be served. Once the places were set, florists began their work, arranging Jacqueminot roses, scarlet carnations, exotic orchids, and trails of ivy in solid gold and silver epergnes. Surrounding the flowers were silver and ormolu candelabra with tall snow-white tapers, salt cellars, and gold ashtrays. Even the French Sobrannes, Java cloves, and American Benson and Hedges cigarettes, as well as Havana cigars—placed at each setting in individual enamel or gold cases or crystal holders—were stamped and embossed with the double-headed eagle and banded in gold. Menus for the Palm Ball were not as elaborate as those for the Nicholas Ball, and usually only five courses were served. The meal began with consommé, served with pale sherry. This was followed by the fish course, which might be grilled sturgeon or salmon, accompanied by an imported white wine. The main course varied from meat or game that often came from the emperor's own reserves or farms. Following this, guests might have oysters and salad, finishing with ices, pastries, and puddings.[39]

These splendid scenes reached their zenith in 1903, when Nicholas and Alexandra gave perhaps the most famous imperial entertainment of the last century of Romanov rule: the Medieval Costume Ball at the Winter Palace. With the approach of the social season, Alexandra decided to give a fancy dress ball that evoked the glories of the Muscovite court under the first Romanovs. It was a theme in keeping with the popular Russian revival in both art and architecture that the Slavophile Nicholas II had warmly embraced.[40] "For at least one night," said Grand Duke Alexander Mikhailovich, "Nicky wanted to be back in the glorious past of our family."[41]

Guests were asked to come in costumes from the reign of Peter the Great's father, Tsar Alexei Mikhailovich. The invitations sent a wave of panic over St. Petersburg: aristocratic ladies might own dozens of expensive gowns from Worth or Paquin in Paris or Madame Olga's in St. Petersburg, but brightly colored caftans had not formed part of a society wardrobe for two hundred years. Designers, workshops, and theatrical costume houses were suddenly flooded with requests as society began to plan for what promised to be a memorable evening.

Alexandra helped to design costumes for herself and her husband, copied from clothing that had belonged to Tsar Alexei and his first wife, Marie Miloslavskaya. The emperor wore a long, open-fronted caftan with a turned-down collar, in raspberry velvet embroidered in white and gold, over a second caftan with a stand-up collar and cuffs decorated with jeweled buttons, pearls, and sable. He carried Alexei's iron staff and wore his sable-trimmed cap and pearl bracelets, items brought especially from the Kremlin Armory for the event.[42] The costume was impressive, but Grand Duke Alexander Mikhailovich thought, "Nicky was obviously not sufficiently tall to do justice to his magnificent garb."[43]

Nicholas II, dressed for the 1903 Medieval Ball

Alexandra's costume was said to have cost nearly 1 million rubles ($10,000,000 in 2005 figures).[44] Her dress, of gold brocade, was sewn with floral designs in silver thread, delicately embroidered with diamonds, sequins, and pearls; over this, she wore a *sarafan* of gold, its wide, long sleeves falling to the floor. A large kokoshnik, studded with diamonds, emeralds, and pearls, framed her face.[45] Around her neck she wore a cabochon sapphire of 400 carats, "larger than an ordinary matchbox," recalled Grand Duchess Marie Georgievna, and her pearl earrings were so heavy that she could not nod her head.[46] The ornate medieval outfit suited the imperious empress: "Alicky was just stunning," declared her sister-in-law Olga Alexandrovna.[47]

Nicholas II's 1903 Medieval Ball costume. See plate 41.

All of the guests jealously guarded their costumes, "so as to add the element of surprise to the event," recalled Marie Georgievna.[48] Grand Duke Alexander Mikhailovich wore the uniform of a seventeenth-century court falconer: a long white coat with a double-headed eagle embroidered in gold thread, a pink silk shirt, blue silk trousers, and boots of tooled yellow leather.[49] His wife, Nicholas

Alexandra, dressed for the 1903
Medieval Ball

Grand Duchess Xenia
Alexandrovna, dressed for the
1903 Medieval Ball

II's sister Xenia, came costumed as a seventeenth-century *boyarina*, in a gown sewn with floral designs in gold and silver thread. Strands of pearls cascaded from either side of her halo-shaped kokoshnik, its broad width decorated with arabesques picked out in diamonds and emeralds.[50]

Grand Duke George Mikhailovich selected the uniform of the Royal Postel'nitchi Guard, boyars attached as sentries to the Terem Palace in the Kremlin. A long velvet cloak, embroidered in gold thread and ornamented with a fur collar, covered his gold silk caftan, its sable edging sweeping the tops of white and yellow leather boots. His wife, Grand Duchess Marie Georgievna, appeared in an apple-green satin sarafan, embroidered in silver thread; over this, she wore a blouse of gold crepe sewn with colored silk flowers ornamented with seed pearls and a white velvet jacket embroidered in golden thread. Her kokoshnik, edged with gold and diamond chains, rested atop a pearl net cap and was studded with seven large diamonds encased in pearl-embroidered stars; four strands of perfectly matched pearls fell from either side of the headdress, framing her face.[51]

Grand Duke Serge Alexandrovich came as a Muscovite prince, in a tunic of gold brocade embroidered on the chest and shoulders with double-headed eagles in gold thread. Ermine edged his pearl-encrusted collar, matching a pearl sash around his waist. His billowing gold silk trousers were tucked into the tops of yellow Moroccan leather boots ornamented with crimson leather inlays, and in his hand he carried a jeweled dagger. His wife, Elizabeth, wore a costume designed after the court dress of a seventeenth-century Muscovite princess, a long sarafan of silver tissue and dark green brocaded velvet panels, sewn with pearls and edged with sable, over a *platno* of fine gold silk. Her kokoshnik, of lace laid over netting in a starburst design, was adorned with pearls and sapphires.[52]

Other members of the imperial family were attired in equally magnificent costumes. Grand Duke Alexei Alexandrovich came in a long caftan of gold and crimson brocade, heavily embroidered with floral designs in gold and silver thread and adorned with a collar ornamented with seed pearls and edged with sable. His tasseled waistband, of crimson silk sewn with arabesque designs in gold thread, held a small ceremonial dagger in place. Grand Duchess Vladimir appeared in a gold velvet sarafan, embroidered with jewels and sewn with floral designs in silver thread. Over this, she wore a crimson silk tunic, its floor-length sleeves encrusted with pearls. Her tall kokoshnik, studded with precious stones, complemented a *barma* collar of gold set with enormous emeralds, rubies, and diamonds.[53]

Prince Felix Yusupov wore the costume of a seventeenth-century boyar from Kazan, draped in a caftan of patterned silk brocade decorated with gold braid and embroidered with broad stripes sewn with pearls and pieces of colored glass. Beneath this, his cream silk shirt was wrapped at the waist with a velvet band and worn with knee-length, green velvet trousers tucked into the tops of yellow and red Moroccan leather boots.[54] His beautiful wife, Zenaide, wore a gown of silver brocade, with a short crimson velvet jacket embroidered with silver thread and trimmed with sable. Her tall, pointed kokoshnik, studded with rubies and diamonds, incorporated the Yusupov family's forty-one-carat Polar Star Diamond at its center.[55]

The Winter Palace glowed with light on the evening of February 11, as the 390 guests entered what palace commandant Vladimir Voyekov later described as "a living dream."[56] "Some mysterious magic," recalled Grand Duchess Marie Georgievna, "seemed to have changed all these familiar figures into splendid visions out of Russia's oriental past."[57] A fanfare from the State Trumpeters, attired in seventeenth-century costumes, announced the arrival of the emperor and the empress, who opened the ball with a polonaise from *A Life for the Tsar*. A medieval masque in the Hermitage Theater followed: Feodor Chaliapin sang several scenes from Mussorgsky's *Boris Godunov*, while Anna Pavlova danced in selections from Tchaikovsky's *Swan Lake*. As the evening wore on, guests danced ancient quadrilles in the glittering Pavilion Hall, followed by a lavish medieval feast laid out in the Spanish, Flemish, and Italian Galleries of the Hermitage.[58] Grand Duke Konstantin Konstantinovich deemed the evening "astonishingly beautiful," while the emperor himself

Grand Duke Alexei Alexandrovich, dressed for the 1903 Medieval Ball

Grand Duchess Vladimir, dressed for the 1903 Medieval Ball

noted laconically in his diary, "the Court looked rather pretty, full of people in ancient Russian costume."[59]

Two days later, the ball was repeated in the Winter Palace's Concert Hall for Dowager Empress Marie Feodorovna and her son Michael, as well as for members of the Diplomatic Corps. Although the dowager empress came in regular court dress, the grand duke wore the uniform of a seventeenth-century Streltsy Guard commander: a long caftan of gold brocade sewn with foliate designs in golden thread, with a soft cap of gold brocade trimmed with sable. To adorn the cap, he borrowed a large diamond aigrette, once owned by Emperor Paul, from the crown jewels. During the evening, the grand duke lost the priceless ornament, and, despite a frantic search, it was never found.[60]

Despite its oriental splendor, the 1903 Costume Ball proved to be a swan song. It was, Grand Duke Alexander Mikhailovich sadly noted, "the last spectacular ball in the history of the Empire."[61] Within a year, Russia was at war with Japan; revolution followed, and the glittering halls of the Winter Palace were abandoned.

PLATE 33. The gown worn by Olga
Nikolaievna on page 243.

PLATE 34. The *Standart* Egg, created by
Fabergé in 1909 for Empress Alexandra

PLATE 35. State carriage made for Catherine the Great and used by Empress Alexandra for the state entrance to Moscow during Nicholas II's coronation in 1896

PLATE 36. Spala

PLATE 37. The wedding of Nicholas and Alexandra, November 14, 1894,
painted by Laurenz Tuxen

PLATE 38. The gown worn by Alexandra at
her husband's coronation

PLATE 41. Nicholas II's 1903
Medieval Ball costume

PLATE 39. The Cathedral of the Assumption

PLATE 40. The coronation ceremony: Nicholas II is anointed as his brother Grand
Duke Michael Alexandrovich, fourth from the left, looks on. Alexandra stands on the
steps behind her husband; on her right is Grand Duke Serge Alexandrovich,
and immediately behind her is Grand Duke Paul Alexandrovich.

PLATE 42.
The Church of the
Exaltation of the
Cross at Livadia

PLATE 43. View of the White Palace at Livadia

PLATE 44. The White Hall in the White Palace at Livadia

25

STATE VISITS

AT THE TURN OF THE CENTURY, the etiquette of kings demanded the ceremonial exchange of visits and presents, honorary titles and decorations, elaborate ritual and stiff protocol. A few days before his father's funeral, Nicholas was made an honorary colonel in chief in the Scots Grays Regiment by the prince of Wales; in return, Nicholas made his Uncle Bertie an honorary colonel in chief in the 27th Kiev Dragoon Regiment.[1] European monarchs covered themselves with foreign awards and orders: the British Order of the Knights of the Garter, the French Légion d'Honneur, the Black Eagle of Germany, the Knights of Dannebrog of Denmark, the Golden Fleece of Spain, and the Knights of the Redeemer of Greece, all exchanged during the festivities that marked a state visit.

Foreign visits undertaken by the emperor and the empress required months of planning. Officials from the Russian court traveled to the intended destination, meeting their foreign counterparts to discuss details. Nothing was left to chance: parade routes were organized and walked, accommodations inspected, and potential guest lists carefully arranged. From the moment the sovereigns set foot on foreign soil, their visit was timed to the minute, following a laboriously detailed schedule. When the emperor and the empress traveled, they were accompanied not only by up to a hundred suitcases and steamer trunks, but also by a retinue of some hundred officials and members of their respective suites.

Shortly after coming to the throne, Nicholas and Alexandra embarked on a series of visits to their fellow sovereigns. In the fall of 1896, they visited Emperor Franz Joseph of Austria-Hungary and his wife, the beautiful Empress Elisabeth, in Vienna; made a brief call on their mutual cousin Kaiser Wilhelm II; and had family holidays with Alexandra's brother Grand Duke Ernst Ludwig IV of Hesse in Darmstadt and with Nicholas's royal cousins in Denmark. At the end of the Danish visit, Nicholas and Alexandra took possession of their new yacht, *Standart*, and sailed to Scotland for a holiday with the empress's grandmother Queen Victoria at Balmoral Castle before journeying to France.

A contingent of French warships joined *Standart* in the English Channel and escorted it across the rough waters to Cherbourg.[2] The storm was so intense that the French officials waiting to greet them had abandoned the quay for the shelter of a nearby pavilion. When Nicholas and Alexandra disembarked from the yacht, the landing was empty, and only the hurried appearance of President Félix Faure managed to save an embarrassing situation. As the ships of the escort fired a 101-gun salute, the imperial couple came ashore, Nicholas in naval uniform with the cordon of the Légion d'honneur across his chest, and Alexandra wearing a white dress and cloak adorned with lace, and a velvet toque with osprey feathers.[3]

For the official welcome, a special pavilion, built on pontoons at the edge of the harbor, had been erected, its white columns and arches draped with purple and adorned with armorial shields and double-headed eagles above a forest of potted palms. As the couple came ashore, members of the Marine Guard along the quay presented arms, and a band struck up "God Save the Tsar" and "The Marseillaise" as nearby artillery thundered its 101-gun salute across the gray waters.[4]

Despite the inclement weather, Nicholas continued on with the previously arranged naval review, returning to the imperial yacht to inspect the ships of the French fleet. "The Empress, although greatly fatigued by the difficult sea voyage," the press reported, "won the hearts of the French in her first hour in our country, when, despite her delicacy, she insisted on accompanying the Emperor in his inspection."[5] As the imperial yacht steamed up and down the serried lines of cruisers and battleships, it was met by the wild cheers of the French sailors gathered along their decks and the shattering boom of cannon salutes.[6]

At the end of the review, President Faure presided over an official dinner in Cherbourg, held in an immense exhibition hall near the quay that had been decorated with floral garlands, intertwined Russian and French flags, and a forest of palm trees.[7] As the incessant rain pelted against the arched glass roof, Faure

The imperial cortege at the Arc de Triomphe, 1896

offered a glowing speech of welcome: "As President of the Republic, I am bound to reflect the sentiments of the French nation, which unanimously extends its most respectful wishes to the Imperial Family for the glory of Your Majesty's reign and the continued happiness of Russia. Tomorrow, Your Majesty, in Paris, you will feel the beat of the heart of the French people, who will prove to the Emperor and Empress of Russia their sincere friendship." In reply, Nicholas declared, "Upon touching the ground of this friendly nation, I have come to share the feelings you express."[8]

The Paris visit, in October of 1896, was undoubtedly the most important state visit of Nicholas II's reign. France was Russia's only formal European ally; the ties that bound the two unlikely partners were firm and, in the end, catastrophic. The French government, under President Faure, went to enormous expense to charm the couple. To create just the right impression, thousands of artificial chestnut blossoms were wired to the branches of trees lining the processional routes. "Right up to the moment the cortege was due," recalled Baroness Agnes de Stoeckl, "men were climbing amongst the trees like monkeys, fastening small pink rubber buds all over the boughs."[9] Strings of electric bulbs linked the cast

The imperial couple departing from Ranelagh Station during their state visit to Paris, 1896

iron lampposts, providing a ribbon of light that illuminated the city's great avenues, and flags, bunting, and garlands of flowers draped every facade, providing "the most sumptuous decoration imaginable," according to the French press.[10] Nearly a million visitors poured into Paris to cheer the emperor, all at the encouragement of the government, which had given them a holiday and offered cheap railway passages as an incentive.[11]

When the emperor and the empress arrived at Ranelagh Station, their train was welcomed by the strains of "God Save the Tsar" and "The Marseillaise," as a 101-gun salute thundered in the Parisian sky. The empress, attired in "an exquisite white satin dress," stepped out of the train first, followed by Nicholas, who wore the uniform of a colonel in the Preobrazhensky Life Guards Regiment; as he set foot on the platform, according to one witness, he looked "somber and serious."[12] They entered a Louis XV–style pavilion hung with blue satin and draped with garlands of flowers, which had been erected alongside the platform, for the official welcoming ceremony. The entire length of the siding and the broad avenue beyond was ringed by a guard of honor; opposite the pavilion, a tribune held specially invited guests.[13]

At the end of the reception, the emperor and the empress climbed into an open landau, with President Faure seated directly opposite them. Two Cossack guards were seated behind them, and they rode into Paris between rows of soldiers, some mounted, all in full dress uniform, stationed at intervals along the roadway, to control the jubilant crowds. "The weather was divine, just like summer," Nicholas wrote to his mother.[14] The route took them through the Bois de Boulogne and into the city, through the Place de la Concorde and down the Champs-Elysées. One witness wrote, "The populace had all donned their Sunday clothes, and were gaily singing and shouting, the children waving small Russian flags. The roadways were covered with yellow sand. Guns in the distance announced the arrival of the august guests. . . . The sun shone forth from behind a cloud, as the head of the cortege came into view under the Arc de Triumphe."[15] A mounted division of Cuirassiers, "with their plumes waving from side to side," opened the procession, followed by a squadron of French Arabs, "a fantastic sight," noted one correspondent, "with their colorful, flowing caftans and broad, jeweled turbans."[16]

Finally, the imperial visitors appeared, to "frenzied acclamations."[17] The crowd, recalled one witness, "went mad, crying, *'Vive l'Empereur! Vive l'Imperatrice!'* The police, and even the troops lining the route, could scarcely hold them back. The little pink buds fluttered gaily on the bare branches, music from regimental bands greeted the procession as it passed, the glorious Russian Anthem was played again and again, the people taking it up and singing at the top of their voices."[18]

Nicholas was overwhelmed, calling the reception "tremendous" and noting that "the people behaved admirably, and not a single man stepped off the pavement! Such good order could be called exemplary anywhere, but for the emotional French it must have been a real tour de force."[19] The emperor, reported the French press, merely smiled at the ovations, but surprisingly, given her shy character, it was Alexandra who won the Parisians' hearts. The press noted how she responded with "gracious gestures" to the welcoming cheers.[20] And *L'Illustration* rhapsodized, "The young Empress was the very essence of the joyous occasion. With her brilliant responses, she seduced us, and she provided a gracious symbol of the friendship between France and Russia."[21]

Nicholas and Alexandra stayed at the sumptuous Russian Embassy in the Rue de Grenelle, where a suite of rooms overlooking the garden had been prepared. At the state dinner at the Élysée Palace, President Faure addressed the emperor with a jubilant toast: "The acclaim that has greeted Your Majesty's entrance to Paris proves the sincere feelings you have witnessed since setting foot in the

Republic. Your Majesty's presence among us seals, along with the acclamations of the public, the bonds that link our two countries in harmonious work and provides for the confidence of our mutual destinies. The union of a powerful Empire and a steady Republic will only exert a beneficial influence on the peace of the world." In his reply, Nicholas spoke of "the warm welcome, which has deeply touched Her Majesty and myself, as we arrived in Paris, a city of so much genius, cultivated taste, and of such influence." He ended by repeating the president's hopes "that this friendship can only have the happiest influence on the world."[22]

Nicholas and Alexandra spent their days visiting historic sites: the ornate Opera House, the Tuileries, the Palais de Justice, the Louvre, the Russian cathedral, and Notre Dame, where the organist greeted their arrival by playing "God Save the Tsar."[23] Nicholas was also shown a motorcar in Paris at a Dion Bouton exhibition; offered his choice of vehicle, he thanked the officials but declined, declaring that he wished to wait until the manufacturers had perfected the machine.[24]

There were also historical reminders. At the Pantheon, Nicholas and Alexandra placed a bouquet of orchids and lilacs on the grave of President Marie François Sadi Carnot who, with Alexander III, had cemented the Franco-Russian alliance, and at Les Invalides, they gazed down on Napoleon's enormous porphyry tomb.[25] At an official lunch at the Russian Embassy for members of the French nobility, Nicholas was startled to receive a low and courtly bow from an elderly gentleman attired in velvet knee breeches, a brocaded coat, a waistcoat trimmed with ruffles, and a tricorn hat atop a powdered wig. Seeing the emperor's puzzled expression, the man explained, "I should never have dared accept Your Majesty's invitation in the dress of the present day, and as our social life in France is at an end, it is only fitting I should appear before Your Majesty in Court dress."[26]

Throughout the visit, Nicholas and Alexandra were greeted with rapturous ovations. "Wherever we went," the emperor wrote, "huge crowds lined the streets with policemen about twenty yards apart in front, and the people stood absolutely still, everybody keeping his place in the most orderly manner while cheering as loud as they could, and frantically waving hats and handkerchiefs!"[27]

One day, Nicholas called on the president of the French Senate but did so incognito. He rode through the streets of Paris in an open landau, without an escort and accompanied only by a member of his Entourage. At the Luxembourg Palace, Nicholas remained in the landau as his aide disappeared inside to ask if the emperor might come in. As Nicholas sat in the landau, a passing man spotted him and, drawn to what he assumed to be his uncanny resemblance to the

The emperor lays the foundation stone for the Pont Alexandre III, 1896

emperor, strode over, gave a low bow, and yelled, "How's the Empress?" Nicholas thanked him for his greeting and replied, "The Empress is very well, and is delighted with her journey." As the aide came to the carriage, the man suddenly realized that it was, in fact, the emperor to whom he had spoken, doffed his cap, gave another bow, and backed away with wide eyes.[28]

On the afternoon of their second day Tuesday October 6, Nicholas laid the cornerstone of the new Pont Alexandre III over the Seine, constructed in honor of his father, as Alexandra, clad in a long white dress and matching hat, looked on. "This was a remarkably touching ceremony," Nicholas reported to his mother, "and Dear Papa's name was mentioned many times with such feeling of love, remembrance, and respect that nobody could help tears coming into their eyes."[29] That night, President Faure gave a dinner for the emperor and the empress in the Grande Salle of the City Hall, followed by a display of fireworks over the Seine culminating in an enormous illuminated figure of St. George that emerged from the second tier of the Eiffel Tower to spear a dragon.[30]

When the fireworks ended, the president and his wife escorted the emperor and the empress to a gala performance at the opera, where the presidential box had been decorated with wreaths of yellow chrysanthemums woven between the French and Russian tricolors and the word *Paix*. Nicholas appeared in Cossack uniform, while Alexandra wore a dress of sky-blue silk trimmed with lace and a magnificent parure of diamonds. "From the central box," reported *L'Illustration*, "where the most magnificent uniforms and sparkling, elegant toilettes were gathered, a ripple of light radiated across the auditorium, producing a stunning effect."[31] The orchestra played "God Save the Tsar," followed by "The Marseillaise," both fervently sung by the guests; at the end of the French anthem, Nicholas stepped to the edge of the box, placed his hand on his heart, and bowed to the audience.[32]

On Wednesday, October 7, they attended a reception at City Hall that began with a Russian hymn, sung by the choir of the Orthodox cathedral, and continued with a long list of entertainments in a room bedecked with palms and roses. On the third morning, the imperial couple left Paris, "I must confess not without regret," Nicholas wrote, "in spite of our days being rather tiring on the whole." Accompanied by the president, they drove to Versailles. "The road was lined with crowds just as in the streets of Paris," Nicholas wrote; "my hand got quite numb from so much saluting."[33] At Sèvres, they stopped to inspect the famous factory and were presented with several beautiful pieces of porcelain. They arrived at Versailles just as twilight settled over the great park. As they drove down the long allées, their path was lined with flaming torches, and the fountains had been turned on and illuminated especially for the imperial couple. After touring the vast palace, Nicholas and Alexandra were the guests of honor at a magnificent, nine-course banquet in the Galerie des Batailles, followed by a theatrical performance in the Hercules Salon given by members of the Comédie-Française and a poetry reading by Sarah Bernhardt.[34]

The following morning, the emperor and the empress traveled to Chalons-sur-Marne, where Nicholas II was guest of honor at a military review of eighty thousand French soldiers.[35] That afternoon, Nicholas and Alexandra reluctantly bade farewell to President Faure and began their return trip to Russia. They both left utterly won over, convinced that the Franco-Russian alliance was a glorious partnership destined to preserve the peace of Europe.

Often, these state and formal visits were family affairs, reuniting aunts, uncles, and cousins. There were frequent visits to Kaiser Wilhelm II: attending German army maneuvers at Breslau, shooting in Prussia, and yachting at Kiel. Cousin Willy also visited his Russian relatives, joining the emperor for stalking at Bielovezh and Spala or sailing on his yacht *Hohenzollern* to the remote Finnish Skerries to holiday with Nicholas and Alexandra on *Standart*. Alexandra never liked her flamboyant cousin. "He's nothing but a clown!" she once declared.[36]

Even the polite Nicholas found the kaiser's domineering attitude and condescending streams of advice a trial.

Until the beginning of the First World War, Wilhelm II remained a strong—if unlikely—presence in his cousins' lives. The kaiser could be arrogant, loud, boisterous, and suspicious. At times he was like an ill-tempered child, albeit one with an extraordinary wardrobe: the kaiser liked nothing more than donning one of his splendid uniforms, which he wore habitually and to great effect. They lent to him a presence and, together with his spiked, almost tyrannical mustache, distracted attention from his withered arm and disagreeable manner. His foreign relatives were almost universal in their contempt, and Wilhelm responded with overt attempts at ingratiating himself, usually to no effect. He became moody and paranoid, and not without reason, worried that his own family both feared and dismissed him. The kaiser's quest for admiration, cloaked in his bombastic manner, was met with quiet disdain, alienating him and wounding a fragile personality that sought only acceptance.

On July 14, 1897, Wilhelm, his wife, Kaiserin Augusta Victoria, along with his brother Prince Heinrich and his brother's wife, Princess Irene, Alexandra's sister, arrived at Peterhof aboard *Hohenzollern* for a six-day visit with their Russian cousins. "The Kaiser," recorded Alexander Mossolov, "was highly excitable—he gave me the impression of a sufferer from hysteria—and he had a special gift of upsetting everybody who came near him." When the kaiser was in a good mood, Mossolov complained, he ran about, "a broad smile on his face, whacking the Russians on their backsides."[37]

On the second night of the visit, Nicholas and Alexandra gave a state dinner for the kaiser and the kaiserin in the Great Palace at Peterhof. The tall windows of the State Apartments were thrown open, providing magnificent vistas over the Grand Cascade, where the gilded fountains glittered with mist, and on to the Gulf of Finland, shimmering in the early evening sunshine. "The weather was marvelous all through," Nicholas wrote, "and therefore no one could help being in good spirits."[38] Nicholas and Alexandra stood at the head of a receiving line in the Throne Room, its pale cream walls touched with light blues and pinks that mirrored the ever-changing sky outside. Princess Anatole Bariatinsky, presented to Wilhelm and his wife, later recalled, "He was in great spirits, talking and gesticulating a lot, and seemed very self-satisfied and confident. . . . The Kaiserin appeared a kind-hearted and gentle woman, but her ideas on etiquette were very pronounced."[39]

The visit took place in the midst of St. Petersburg's famous White Nights, when the sun hung low on the horizon until midnight before barely slipping away into a milky haze that continued to wash the sky with blues, crimsons, and pearls. At nine that evening, the emperor led the kaiserin, with Alexandra sitting at the side of her Cousin Willy, in a carriage procession through the allées of the Upper Park to Olgino, a serene sheet of water surrounded by undulating lawns that led to the reed-choked shoreline. A small flotilla of boats conveyed them to Olga Island, where an open-air amphitheater rose at the edge of the lake. In the middle of the water, classical columns framed a small theater stage set on piles driven into the lakebed, its sides and back open to reveal the gently rolling Babigon Hills beyond. An orchestra, hidden in an immense iron tub sunk below the surface of the lake, serenaded the party with the softly floating music of Delibes. At the same time, a spotlight picked out the lone figure of the ballerina Mathilde Kschessinska: she stood on a small mirror, which was pulled across the lake by underwater cables, giving the impression that she was gliding across the surface. When she reached the stage, Kschessinska lightly stepped from her mirror and began a selection of ballets arranged by the great Marius Petipa. A low, orange moon rose slowly over the stage as the performance reached its finale, when the Babigon Hills were suddenly bathed in a series of crimson and purple spotlights, creating a magical effect that delighted the unpredictable kaiser.[40]

The following morning, the kaiser reviewed the two regiments of the Russian Army of which he was colonel in chief at Krasnoye Selo, followed by an Offenbach operetta, performed at the camp theater. "Strict orders had been given to leave out all improper passages," Nicholas II wrote to his mother, but even this was not enough for the prim kaiserin.[41] "The actors spoke broken Russian, with a German accent, as was usual in this piece," noted Princess Anatole Bariatinsky. "It was not an intentional slight; but the piece was hardly appropriate to the occasion. Worse still, Mlle. Muguet, a French dancer, gave an impromptu turn, a *pas de deux*, in very short skirts. The Kaiserin rose from her seat, made a sign to her lady-in-waiting, and left the theater."[42] Such displays did little to endear the visiting Germans to Nicholas. "Thank God the German visit is over," the emperor wrote to his mother, "and one may definitely say without boasting that it went off successfully. On the whole Wilhelm was very cheerful, calm, and courteous, while *she* tried to be charming, and looked very ugly in rich clothes chosen without taste; the hats she wore in the evenings and at the performance at Olgino were particularly impossible."[43]

The visit had culminated in a review of the Russian Fleet, anchored off the Kronstadt naval base in the Gulf of Finland. Nicholas dreaded the occasion; as he explained to his mother, "I'm sorry to tell you we shall have to give Wilhelm the rank of Admiral in our Navy. Uncle Alexei reminded me of it; and I think, no matter how disagreeable it may be, we are obliged to let him wear our naval uniform; particularly since he made me, last year, a Captain in his own Navy and, what's much worse, I'll have to greet him as such at Kronstadt. It makes me want to vomit!"[44] At the lunch, Nicholas duly announced the honor, and Wilhelm, the emperor later wrote, "highly elated by his appointment in our Fleet, began to shower honors right and left."[45] In the following years, when the two imperial families would occasionally meet on their yachts, Wilhelm would stand on the bridge of *Hohenzollern*, signaling to Nicholas on *Standart*, "The Grand Admiral of the Atlantic salutes the Grand Admiral of the Pacific!" Observing this, Nicholas shook his head and declared, "He's raving mad!"[46]

In 1908, King Edward VII made the first state visit of a reigning British monarch to the Russian empire. It was a visit tinged on all fronts with uncertainty and suspicion. Although Nicholas II personally liked his Uncle Bertie, he also harbored doubts about British policies that had led English manufacturers to develop the fleet that ultimately wrought disaster on their own navy. This was followed, at the end of the war, by Great Britain's diplomatic overtures to the Japanese empire. Nicholas himself described his uncle as "the greatest mischief-maker and the most deceitful and dangerous intriguer in the world." The king, too, had his own concerns. His Jewish friends, particularly Lord Rothschild, had been pressing Edward VII to raise the issue of the ongoing pogroms with Russia. Then, too, Edward's friend, the banker Sir Ernest Cassel, wanted the king to discuss the idea of a Russian loan when he met his nephew.[47]

The idea of a Russian visit was sealed when, in late summer 1907, the Anglo-Russian Convention was signed, uniting Great Britain and Russia with France in a series of defensive agreements. On learning of this agreement, the kaiser was beside himself with anger, declaring, "It is aimed at us."[48] The defense pact, coupled with talk of a Russian visit, resulted in an immense outcry among Liberal politicians. George Bernard Shaw, Ramsay MacDonald, and John Galsworthy wrote a joint letter to the *Times* in which they protested "an arrangement which, for a very dubious and temporary advantage," allied Great Britain with Russia.[49] "The English people," added Henry Nevinson, "are being trapped by a Liberal Foreign Office into some sort of alliance with the forces of Russian tyranny."[50] MacDonald, in particular, was vocal in his criticism. In an article called "An Insult to Our Country," he labeled the Russian emperor a "common murderer" and protested at the very idea of a British king "hobnobbing with a bloodstained creature." Edward VII was so displeased that he refused to issue the customary invitations to a Buckingham Palace Garden Party to those who had spoken out against the proposed Russian visit.[51]

On the lovely, warm morning of May 28, two cruisers and a squadron of four British warships escorted the royal yacht *Victoria and Albert III* through the Baltic Sea to the Estonian harbor town of Reval. The emperor and his family waited aboard *Standart*, anchored off Reval; imperial security officers had deemed it too unsafe to hold the meetings on shore, where anarchists could easily attack the two sovereigns. Nicholas had insisted, as a matter of courtesy, on calling upon his Uncle Bertie and Aunt Alix first. As the tender pulled alongside *Victoria and Albert III*, His Majesty's Marine Band aboard struck up "God Save the King" and "God Save the Tsar." Nicholas II wore the uniform of a colonel in chief of the Scots Grays Regiment; Edward waited on deck to greet him, attired in the uniform of a colonel in chief of the Kiev Dragoon Regiment. Their two consorts, aunt and niece, each attired in billowing white satin and lace gowns with wide picture hats, exchanged kisses, and Queen Alexandra warmly greeted her sister Marie Feodorovna, whose own yacht, *Polar Star*, also lay at anchor.

A tender carried the Russian and the British sovereigns and their families to *Polar Star*, where a guard of honor formed from the Kiev Dragoons had been drawn up to greet the king. As Edward VII strode up to the soldiers standing rigidly at attention on the gleaming teak deck for inspection, he greeted them with a bellowed, "Good morning, my children!" in Russian, which won him a deafening cheer.[52] In the dining saloon below, the dowager empress presided over an informal lunch, where waiters handed around caviar sandwiches and goblets filled with kirsch.[53]

That evening, Nicholas and Alexandra gave a banquet for their aunt and uncle on *Standart*. The dinner concluded shortly before ten, when the emperor led his guests up to the main deck. The night was warm, scented with the salt air of the sea, while the sky was washed with a pale palette of blues and pearls from the late northern twilight. A local choir had come to serenade the party, but, due to the strict security, all men and women had to submit themselves to a strip search to ensure they carried no bombs or guns. Even then, they were only allowed onto the deck of an adjacent ship, singing their melodies across the water as the emperor and the king stood against *Standart*'s railings.[54] Midway through the festivities, Sir Charles Hardinge, a member of the king's household, went aft to smoke, where he found Empress Alexandra, her face buried in a handkerchief and weeping, apparently overwhelmed at having to force herself through even the social obligations of a family visit. Worried, Hardinge asked if there was anything he might do. But the empress only shook her head sadly, saying that there was nothing to be done, and broke into tears again.[55]

The following evening, it was King Edward and Queen Alexandra's turn to hold a state dinner on *Victoria and Albert III*. Both harbored vague fears that if forced by protocol to take second place behind her mother-in-law, Alexandra might find some excuse not to attend. To solve this potentially acrimonious situation, King Edward VII hit upon a brilliant idea. When the dinner was announced, he strode up to the spot where both women stood, held out an arm to each, and declared, "Tonight I am going to enjoy the unique honor of taking two Empresses in to dinner. It is I who shall have the privilege of taking your arms. We must keep step together."[56]

Following dinner, the party gathered on the deck. Jackie Fisher, who had accompanied the king, asked the gathered orchestra to strike up "The Merry Widow" and boldly bowed to Grand Duchess Olga Alexandrovna, presenting his arm and asking her to waltz. Delighted, Olga joined him, but the pair, conscious of all eyes on them, enacted a peculiar version of the dance, with both of them keeping their hands folded behind their heads. Seeing the looks they were receiving, Fisher whispered to Olga, "How about Siberia for me after this?" Olga collapsed in a fit of laughter, and even Alexandra, standing by the railing, broke into a wide smile.[57]

On the last day of the visit, diplomatic gifts were exchanged. According to custom, King Edward presented the most important members of the Emperor's Suite with gifts, and the Russians were to reciprocate that afternoon. With the assistance of a member of King Edward's suite, Alexander Mossolov had selected those items to be presented by the emperor. Before the audience, Mossolov delivered the gifts to Nicholas to distribute. Alexandra, who happened to be present, insisted that she be allowed to view the gifts herself; on looking at them, she declared that she would change the recipients of several items. "All my arrangements were in danger of being thrown into confusion," wrote Mossolov. When he tried to protest, the empress silenced him. "Besides," she declared, "these presents are all much too expensive. Another time, please let me see them beforehand." In reply, Mossolov pulled from his jacket a gold cigarette case with the royal monogram in diamonds, which King Edward had just presented to him, explaining that this single gift was more expensive than any of those he had chosen for the emperor to give to his uncle's suite. Seeing this, Alexandra relented.[58]

A year later, Edward VII was host to his Russian relatives. On a stormy day in August of 1909, *Standart* steamed slowly through the English Channel and into the Solent. A line of twenty-four battleships, sixteen armed cruisers, and forty-eight destroyers lay at anchor in the waters off Cowes on the Isle of Wight, firing their guns in salute as the yacht passed by. Nicholas stood on deck, attired in the uniform of an admiral in the British Royal Navy; at his side, Alexandra, in a flowing white Edwardian gown and a large picture hat, gazed out over the familiar waters. A motor launch from *Victoria and Albert III* carried King Edward VII and Queen Alexandra to *Standart* to greet their niece and nephew. As the king and the queen climbed the gangplank, a brass band struck up "God Save the King," followed by "God Save the Tsar," both anthems accompanied by booming salutes and cheers from the sailors of the Royal Navy.[59] That evening, sleek launches sped over the dark water, transporting guests in brilliant uniforms and extravagant gowns to *Victoria and Albert III*, where the king presided over a state dinner.[60]

By the following morning, the storm had passed. "The weather," recalled Alexander Spiridovich, "was exquisite, clear and warm." The visit took place during the annual Cowes Yachting Regatta, and the Solent was jammed with boats, their tall masts bobbing rhythmically with the flow of the tide. Nicholas and Alexandra joined their aunt and uncle aboard *Britannia*, the king's racing yacht, and sailed over the shimmering water to watch the races. The previous day, Nicholas had been named an honorary member of the Cowes Royal Yacht Club, and he took a keen interest in following the boats as they sped along the Solent. Before returning to *Standart*, the emperor and the empress visited Empress Eugenie, the widow of France's Napoleon III, who herself was watching from a nearby yacht. While their parents enjoyed the races, the four grand duchesses had gone ashore on the Isle of Wight, visiting Osborne House and playing on the beach. In the afternoon, Olga and Tatiana, accompanied by a few members of the Suite, drove down the hill to Cowes, exploring the shops. Spiridovich later recalled, "They seemed quite at ease, entering into the shops to buy postcards and various souvenirs." Soon enough, however, a few residents recognized them, collecting around the girls and following them along the streets. Terrified, their escorts suggested that they return to the yacht, but the grand duchesses refused; instead, they hired a carriage and continued sightseeing for several hours, clearly enjoying the experience.[61]

That evening, Nicholas and Alexandra gave a state banquet aboard *Standart*. Against the growing twilight, the yacht glistened with light that reflected over the rippling water while strains of music reached the shore as the privileged guests waltzed across gleaming teak decks and sipped champagne in tall glasses plucked from silver trays. In the distance, the ships of the English squadron had been strung with thousands of tiny electric lights. "Under the blanket of the dark night," Spiridovich recalled, "the giant vessels were transformed, their shapes bordered in silver."[62] Late that night, both families stood against the yacht's railings, necks strained as they watched fireworks exploding in fantastic patterns against the sky.[63]

In May 1913, Nicholas traveled to Berlin to attend the wedding of the kaiser's only daughter, twenty-one-year-old Princess Viktoria Luise, to Ernst Augustus, the duke of Brunswick. Although this was a family occasion, it had all the pomp and trappings of a full state visit. Viktoria Luise had always been her father's favorite child, and as she was the only daughter of the German emperor, there had been much talk that she would make a dynastic alliance. She surprised everyone by falling in love with the handsome but diplomatically unimportant Prince Ernst Augustus, the duke of Brunswick, the youngest son of the duke and duchess of Cumberland. His grandfather, George V, had been the last king of Hanover, which in 1866 had been forcibly annexed by Prussia at the end of the Seven Weeks' War. Incorporation meant exile for the Hanovers, and Ernst Augustus, whose mother, Thyra, was a sister of both Dowager Empress Marie Feodorovna and Queen Alexandra of England, had grown up impoverished.

A sense of unease hung over Europe in 1913, and the wedding was charged with political and diplomatic innuendo. One German newspaper declared, "Their Majesties the Emperor and Empress will upon the occasion of the marriage of their only daughter be surrounded by a brilliant circle of exalted guests. Together with the august parents of the bridegroom we welcome with special pleasure the King and Queen of England and the Emperor of Russia. Though their presence is due to a family festival, yet the cordiality between the three Monarchs which is thus signified constitutes valuable imponderables for the security of the undisturbed progress of the great nations of Europe." While the public pondered the political implications of a gathering of the three powerful sovereigns, a different kind of security was first and foremost in the minds of Berlin authorities. "The police," reported the *New York Times*, "are having their own troubles in guaranteeing the safety of so many exalted foreign crowned heads. In the case of the Tsar, they are on the lookout for bomb-throwing anarchists. In the case of King George and Queen Mary, the Kaiser's sleuths are watching for bomb-throwing suffragettes."[64]

Alexandra was unwell, and Nicholas II arrived alone on May 22, his ten-car, armor-plated train rolling slowly to a stop at Anhalter Station. As he alighted, a brass band played the Russian national anthem. According to the *Daily Mail*, the station "looked like a constabulary camp, police and detectives were every-where. On a platform fifty feet from that at which the Emperor's train was to come in was a line of infantrymen stretching far beyond the end of the station. They had rifles loaded with ball cartridge."[65] To honor his cousin, Nicholas stepped from the train wearing the uniform of the German Alexander Grenadier Guards Regiment, with a tall silver Friedrich the Great–style helmet and the Prussian Order of the Black Eagle.[66] With him, he brought a wedding present from him and Alexandra: a magnificent diamond and aquamarine necklace.[67]

That evening, Nicholas joined nearly a hundred other royal personages for a state dinner at the Berlin Palace. At eight o'clock, a brass band struck up "The Brunswick Military March" as the guests slowly paraded into the hall. Wilhelm II came first, leading Queen Mary. He wore the full-dress uniform of the British Royal Dragoons, with the sash and star of the Russian Order of St. Andrei. Both Nicholas II and George V donned Prussian military dress, the emperor in the uni-form of the Prussian Dragoons with the Order of the Black Eagle on his chest, while the king also wore a Dragoon tunic, breeches, and jacket. The guests sat at a long quadrangular table decorated with bouquets of roses and gleaming Prussian silver plate.[68] The following night, the emperor attended a gala performance of *Lohengrin* at the Royal Opera House, which had been decorated with thou-sands of pink carnations.[69] The emperor's box was crammed with nearly two dozen sovereigns, princes, dukes, and duchesses, the gold of the men's medals and the jewels in the women's parures casting flashes of light about the gilded interior.

The wedding took place on May 24 in the chapel of Berlin Palace. Brilliantly attired pages led the procession through the halls of the palace. Two heralds fol-lowed, carrying the Prussian and the Brandenburg coats of arms. The chief mar-shal of the kaiser's court, holding a large ivory staff, walked before the bride. Viktoria Luise wore a gown of cloth-of-silver decorated with old lace. Four bridesmaids in pale blue gowns carried the silver tissue train of her gown, which was edged in ermine.[70] Ernst Augustus wore the full-dress uniform of the Pruss-ian Zieten Hussar Guards Regiment.[71] Behind them came the kaiser, wearing the uniform of the 1st Guards Regiment, escorting the bridegroom's mother, the duchess of Cumberland, in a lilac-colored gown. The duke of Cumberland, who wore an Austrian uniform, escorted Kaiserin Augusta Victoria, in green satin and velvet. Nicholas, in a Hussar uniform, walked with Queen Mary of England, whose magnificent gold dress had been woven in India and sewn with sparkling diamante, while King George V escorted the crown princess of Prussia, who wore silver brocade and pink velvet.[72]

The Lutheran service in the palace chapel was short; at its conclusion, a thirty-six-gun salute was fired from a battery of the 1st Guards Field Artillery Regiment, and the chapel bells pealed joyously.[73] The reception took place in the White Hall, where the bride and her husband stood beneath the baldachin above the thrones to greet their guests. According to custom, the Torch Dance was performed in the White Hall, as the bride and the bridegroom led their guests across the polished floor in a polonaise, preceded by pages carrying silver candelabra. When their dance ended, Nicholas turned to Viktoria Luise, whispering, "My wish is that you will be as happy as I am," as the guests celebrated what was to be the last gathering of European monarchs before the beginning of the Great War.[74]

26

THE CRIMEA

THE UKRAINIAN STEPPE, with its golden fields of wheat and thick groves of trees, wide rivers flowing lazily through the flat countryside, and peasant villages grouped around brightly painted churches, ended at the Haila mountain range that separated the Russian mainland from the Crimean Peninsula. Beyond these mountains lay a tropical paradise: a sun-drenched land of palm trees, beaches, and rolling vineyards cooled by Black Sea breezes. In late spring, snow still glinted on Ai-Petri, the peninsula's highest peak. Clear, cold rivers rushed down mountain slopes covered with fir and pine, fell over cliffs, tumbled through deep gorges, and wound through lush orchards before emptying into the sea. Here, at their idyllic estate of Livadia, the Romanovs retreated to relax in the Crimean sunshine and escape from the rigid formality of the imperial court in St. Petersburg.

"I am only sorry for you who have to remain in this bog," Nicholas II once said to a group of ministers as he prepared to flee St. Petersburg for Livadia.[1] With the passing years, he looked to the Crimea as a refuge, a place, as Anna Vyrubova recalled, where the imperial family was "loved and revered."[2] Alexandra, too, adored the warm climate and relished the lack of the etiquette in which the St. Petersburg court was wrapped. Only in the Crimea could she move freely about, shopping in Yalta and visiting villages and hospitals. "In St. Petersburg we work," Grand Duchess Olga Nikolaievna once wrote, "but at Livadia, we live."[3]

Spring transformed the Crimea into an enchanted garden: apple, cherry, and peach trees burst into clouds of pink or white, their fallen blossoms carpeting the countryside in soft blankets of color. Lilies, lilacs, violets, and orchids flowered, their sweet perfumes scenting the air. Bougainvillea, wisteria, and roses grew in abundance, climbing in jubilant profusion over white walls and red-tile roofs, filling the eye and nose, as Prince Serge Obolensky recalled, with "a marvelous expanse of fragrance and color."[4] Palms, sequoias, cypress, ancient redwoods, and flowering magnolia spread their shadows over gardens, against a backdrop of mountains cut through by steep roadways.

The Church of the Exaltation of the Cross. See plate 42.

For centuries, the Crimea had been home to the Tartars, and until the Revolution, their communities flourished. Although incorporated into Russia, they remained fiercely independent, herding their sheep and farming their rich lands just as their ancestors had done. When the imperial family visited the Crimea, groups of Tartars waited patiently along the dusty roads to pay homage to the man they considered the rightful successor to their khan: men stood clad in baggy white trousers tucked into the tops of brightly colored leather boots, scarlet jackets, and small round fur caps atop their heads. Behind them, women were adorned in colorful robes of crimson, blue, green, or purple, embroidered with beads and silver thread and worn over colorful, tight-legged trousers or swirling skirts. Only married women still wore traditional veils from their small velvet caps, although invariably they sported hair dyed bright red and jingled with dozens of silver and gold necklaces.[5] In return, Nicholas granted them special privileges to preserve their culture and Moslem religion against the nationalism that dominated the rest of the empire.[6]

No Crimean estate was more fabled than the emperor's Livadia, some five miles west of Yalta high above the Black Sea. Alexander II purchased the 800-acre estate, named after the Greek word meaning "meadow," from a Polish aristocrat in 1860 and commissioned the architect Ippolit Monighetti to build a suitable residence.[7] The Great Palace, built between 1862 and 1866, was a relatively small, two-storeyed building of dark wood and stone; the lower floor was ringed with covered arcades overgrown with wild roses, ivy, and honeysuckle that enveloped the loggias and covered windows with their hanging tendrils.[8]

This profusion of shrubbery left the interior of the Great Palace unusually gloomy. Walls were paneled in dark mahogany and oak, windows filled with stained glass, and low ceilings crossed with imitation wooden beams; the effect, even on the sunniest of days, was somber.[9] To the southwest, Monighetti built the Church of the Exaltation of the Cross, a Byzantine-style structure whose shining white limestone walls and single dome stood in stark contrast to the dark palace facade.[10] A short distance from the Great Palace, nestled against a hillside thick with pines, was Monighetti's Maly Palace, an elaborate little villa of pink brick ornamented with contrasting bands of dark red and white stone, built for Alexander II's heir.[11] The rooms were decorated in English chintzes and light pastel glazes and furnished with overstuffed sofas and chairs. Alone of all the buildings at Livadia, it was a bright, sunny house, with unobstructed views to the sparkling Black Sea.[12]

In 1896, Nicholas II ordered that the Great and the Maly Palaces be electrified; the project allowed the empress to make much-needed repairs and to renovate rooms in the Great Palace, which had not been touched since it was built. While workers wired the palace and fitted it with telephone lines, and plumbers laid new piping to carry water to the upper floor for the first time, decorators gutted many of the old, dark rooms. Balconies were fitted with extra supports, laid with new wooden floors to hold the assortment of wicker chairs and chaise longues the empress dispatched from St. Petersburg, and draped in new white canvas awnings edged with red scallops.[13] Out of respect for the memory of Alexander III, Alexandra did not touch the Maly Palace. In the late emperor's bedroom, nothing had been changed; the armchair in which he had died still stood near the corner windows overlooking the Black Sea.[14]

Alexandra's renovations temporarily lent the old building new life. During the family's 1909 stay at Livadia, however, Tsesarevich Alexei fell ill, and Alexandra feared that he had contracted typhoid from the damp, musty wooden palace. Over the years, the moist sea air and humid summers played havoc with the building, rotting floors and feeding a dangerous mold. Alexandra was adamant that the entire building be pulled down and replaced with a new residence. Nicholas, ever reluctant to endorse change,

The White Palace.
See plate 43.

needed some convincing, but his more powerful wife eventually won, and the old palace was razed. Nicholas imposed one condition: all work on the new building was to be finished by September 1911, in time for his family's usual holiday.[15]

The imperial couple selected Nicholas Krasnov to design the new palace. Born in 1864, Krasnov had studied at the Moscow College of Art and, on his graduation in 1887, been named city architect to Yalta. His work in the Crimea followed local traditions: he restored the old Tartar khan palace of Bakhchisarai, and Romanov commissions soon followed, including the Crimean estates of Harax for Grand Duke George Mikhailovich, Tchair for Grand Duke Nicholas Nikolaievich Jr., and Koreiz and Kokoz for the Yusupov family. It was, however, his Dulber Palace, built for Grand Duke Peter Nikolaievich, that won Krasnov the commission for Livadia. Dulber, a fantastic Moorish-style palace, gleaming white against a dark forest and crowned with several turrets and domes, was the most elegant of all Crimean estates. Krasnov demonstrated an adept hand at the interplay between reception rooms and the informality of the courtyards, loggias, and balconies demanded by the Crimean climate, the same features Alexandra wanted in her new house.

Krasnov's White Palace, as the new building was called, was the only imperial residence commissioned by Nicholas and Alexandra. "It was designed and fulfilled," Krasnov later wrote, "in the style of the Italian Renaissance," the form dictated by the empress, who asked that he copy the Venetian palazzos and Tuscan villas, with their sun-washed courtyards and dramatically shadowed colonnades, that she had admired on a youthful visit to Italy.[16] After poring over prints and photographs with the empress, Krasnov selected the garden facade of the Villa Medici in Rome as a model for the exterior; he copied the Villa Medici's stark white exterior, open loggias, dentilated cornices, stucco bas-reliefs, and even its tower and rooftop belvedere.[17] Alexandra also asked that a courtyard, modeled on the cloisters of San Marco in Florence, be included; Krasnov complied, though his eventual design copied the colonnade of San Michele in Isola at Florence.[18]

In the end, the White Palace was a telling insight into Alexandra's troubled life in Russia. It was largely influenced by Osborne House, Queen Victoria's residence on the Isle of Wight, where the empress had spent many summers. By the time of its construction, Alexandra, suffering from illness and worry over her son's health, was alienated from most of the imperial family and St. Petersburg society. At Livadia, she attempted, albeit unconsciously, to recapture some of the happiness and security of her youth.

Visitors approached the new building along a drive shaded with pine, palm, and cypress and banked with fragrant roses and oleander that parted to reveal Krasnov's structure, glistening against a broad carpet of turf. Framed between tall cedars, the white limestone palace was a building of poetic beauty, its projecting bays and Ionic colonnades dominated by a four-storey tower. It was small by imperial standards—116 rooms occupied its two principal floors—yet they were finished and fitted with the latest technology: hot and cold freshwater and saltwater, a telegraph room, telephone lines, electric elevators, and a modern kitchen with separate refrigeration and smoke rooms.[19]

To carry out the interior decoration, Krasnov commissioned two St. Petersburg experts: the Friedrich Meltzer Company, which had done the imperial couple's private apartments in both the Winter Palace and the Alexander Palace at Tsarskoye Selo, as well as in the Lower Palace at Alexandria, Peterhof; and Silvio Danini, who had also done extensive work at the Alexander Palace. Together, they created a comfortable yet stylish marriage of the neoclassical, in keeping with the design of the palace, with the art nouveau interiors so beloved by the empress. Here, there was none of the cluttered, oppressive atmosphere found in the Winter Palace or the Alexander Palace; no deep saturation of colors and no unrestrained excess. The touches were light, relying on occasional exotic woodwork and a few decorative reliefs to convey the desired effect. While the rooms at the Alexander Palace and the Lower Palace had seemed dated soon after their completion, the interiors at Livadia evoked a timeless quality, framed by Krasnov's architectural shell with its neoclassical forms.[20]

The emperor's public rooms, at the northeastern corner of the ground floor, offered the palace's most flamboyant decoration. The walls of his audience room, paneled in African mahogany accented with ormolu inlays, were glazed a deep ocher color, while his billiard room copied Elizabethan models, with finely carved linen-fold paneling, a granite fireplace, and a ceiling crossed by plaster beams carved and painted to resemble oak. There were only three principal reception rooms in the palace. The Italian Hall, designed in the neoclassical style at Alexandra's request, featured a marble floor and scagliola walls lined with Corinthian pilasters. With its suite of Karelian birch furniture spread over an Oriental carpet held in place by Chinese porcelain tubs sprouting potted palms, it was the most formal room in the palace. The nearby Turkish Salon reflected the Crimea's Eastern heritage, with a colorful mosaic floor and walls adorned with inset mirrors and polylobate pilasters.[21]

The White Palace's White Hall. See plate 44.

The largest room in the palace was the White Hall. Six tall arched windows overlooked the northern garden, echoed by six French doors opening to the Italian Courtyard. Corinthian pilasters supported an entablature and cornice heavily decorated with bas-reliefs. Krasnov took advantage of modern technology and extended the cornice to provide hidden lights that played against the intricate stucco-relief ceiling. A hooded marble fireplace dominated one end of the room, balanced on the opposite wall by a screen of Corinthian columns flanking a marble statue of Penelope.[22] A room of restrained neoclassicism, the White Hall was deliberately formal, used for ceremonial meals and occasional balls.

At the heart of the White Palace lay the Italian Courtyard, open to the sky and

Alexandra's library in the White Palace at Livadia

circled with vaulted Tuscan colonnades paved in gray granite. This was a natural gathering spot, bright with sunshine; Nicholas came here to smoke after lunch and on ceremonial occasions used it as an extended reception room. At the center of a lawn planted with roses and palm trees stood a seventeenth-century Italian well, set between a pair of ancient Greek Corinthian columns.[23] Exquisite wrought-iron gates, made in Verona in 1750, opened to a colonnade that led to the Church of the Exaltation of the Cross.[24] Beyond the west door, topped by a mosaic depicting Christ robed in scarlet, the church shimmered with frescoes of the Annunciation and a broad marble and alabaster iconostasis adorned with gold.[25]

Tsesarevich Alexei had a suite of rooms along the southeastern side of the main floor, facing the Black Sea; beyond them, looking onto an enclosed cortile decorated with Moorish tiles and lit by a glass roof, a staircase ascended to the private apartments. The emperor's study, at the top of the landing, was hung with light, striped moiré above a stained maple wainscot and was flooded with light from a bay overlooking the Black Sea. In contrast to the oppressive opulence of their room in the Alexander Palace, Nicholas and Alexandra's bedroom featured cream-and-white-striped silk above a white-enameled wainscot; against one corner stood twin brass beds, covered in silk eiderdowns. The emperor's bathroom

Side view of the White Palace, showing the bay containing
Nicholas II's study

was paneled in mahogany, while that of Alexandra held a tub of engraved silver, a gift from the shah of Persia.[26]

Nicholas's library, lined with mahogany bookcases and paneling, was executed in the art nouveau style, with a curved desk and a built-in sofa surrounded by open shelves backed by mirrors. It adjoined Alexandra's boudoir, with a tall Palladian window and French doors opening to a balcony high above the sea and to a loggia at the palace's southeastern corner. Hung in mauve floral cretonne, the room was dominated by a curved, built-in sofa encased in an oak frame, its top ledges filled with family photographs, bits of porcelain, and vases of fresh flowers. Alexandra's library beyond was a more formal space. Lit by a Palladian window, its lower walls, as well as the glass-fronted bookcases, were paneled in honey-colored oak, the same wood used in the thin Corinthian pilasters that framed panels of gray and mauve silk.[27]

A small dining room, paneled in yew and hung with cream-and-gray-striped moiré, opened to the rooms of the four grand duchesses. As at Tsarskoye Selo, Olga and Tatiana had one bedroom and Marie and Anastasia a second, both simply decorated with mahogany paneling and bright floral fabrics hung upon the walls. Their sitting room, divided in half by a screen of paired Corinthian columns and furnished with comfortable chairs and sofas upholstered in English chintzes, led to classrooms whose French doors opened to balconies overlooking the gardens and distant mountains.[28]

Surrounding the White Palace was an exquisite tropical garden, as contrived as anything created for Peter the Great and his successors at Peterhof or Tsarskoye Selo. Sweeping lawns dotted with ancient Greek and Roman statuary and antique Italian fountains were lined with thick borders of roses and wisteria. Graveled walks led to formal parterres, edged with golden box, and to long avenues of pleached lime, clipped yews, or tall beech trees. Fragrant magnolias spread over glades reached by narrow, twisting paths banked with laurel and azalea. From the top of the cliff, wide marble stairs, their balustrades overgrown with ivy and wildflowers, led down to the protected beach of small pebbles, with a little bathing pavilion in the Turkish style nestled against the shore of the Black Sea. As a final exotic touch, Alexandra had peacocks introduced into the park.[29]

Both Nicholas and Alexandra were delighted with Krasnov's White Palace. Nicholas wrote to his mother, "We can't find words to express our joy and pleasure of having such a house, built exactly as we wished. The architect Krasnov is a remarkable stalwart—just think that during 16 months he has built the large Palace, the Suite's House, and new kitchen. What is more, he has wonderfully laid-out and decorated the garden all around the new buildings, together with out excellent gardener, so that this part of Livadia has gained much. The sights from every point are so nice, especially of Yalta and the sea. The rooms have lots of light, and you remember how dark it was in the old house."[30]

Life at Livadia was very different from the one led by the imperial family in St. Petersburg: it was free from the rigid etiquette their positions demanded when surrounded by the intense protocol of the Russian court. Even while on holiday, the business of government continued. The emperor devoted his mornings to meetings with the occasional minister, who came from the capital. Leather dispatch boxes arrived at the White Palace every other day with state papers for Nicholas to read and initial. Many of these ministers grumbled about the inconvenience of having to travel five days to spend two hours delivering a report. When one had the temerity to raise the issue during his audience, complaining of "how difficult it was for the government to be situated for so long away from the center of administration," Nicholas uncharacteristically cut him short by saying, "Where I am is the center of administration!"[31]

Generally, the emperor took a short walk before settling into his work, while Alexandra spent her mornings on the chaise longue in her boudoir or sat on the balcony above the Black Sea, writing letters to friends.[32] Lunch was served at one. When Alexandra felt well, she joined her husband, along with her daughters; Alexei rarely appeared. "Everyone living in the Palace was asked to luncheon," Baroness Sophie Buxhoeveden recalled, "even the children's teachers and the priest, as well as four or five of the officers of the *Standart*, which was anchored at Yalta during the Imperial sojourn in the Crimea. In addition to these, three or four people, local residents or visitors, were invited every day as well as the Ministers who came from St. Petersburg to report to the Emperor."[33] Even if the empress took lunch in her rooms, she always greeted the guests and members of the Suite when they gathered in the Italian Courtyard to smoke and talk.[34]

In the afternoon, Nicholas and Alexandra might visit one of the neighboring estates that adjoined Livadia. In 1889, Alexander III had purchased the old Vorontzov estate of Massandra, along with the adjoining vineyard at Ai-Danil, both of which lay across Yalta harbor from Livadia, and for which the usually parsimonious Alexander III willingly laid out some 250,000 rubles ($2,500,000 in 2005 figures).[35] At the center of Massandra stood a French Renaissance–style palace, finished by the St. Petersburg architect Maximilian Messemacher on Alexander III's orders. Massandra was designed to replicate the chateaus of the Loire Valley, but here the elements—tall pyramid roofs, Third Empire–style exterior detailing, steeply pitched slate roofs decorated with iron fretwork, chimneys, loggias, balconies, and elaborate carved stonework—were all at stark contrast with the tropical surroundings.[36] When Nicholas and Alexandra visited, Count de Freedericksz telephoned the lodge at Massandra, and the park would be closed to tourists. By the time the imperial couple arrived, the estate would be quiet and empty. They might take lunch in the palace, then walk in the gardens or ride up into the hills to the Uchan-Su waterfall, a torrent of icy water that tumbled from the cliffs to a tranquil pond surrounded by groves of pine and evergreen trees. Here, they would picnic, go off into the surrounding forest in search of mushrooms or berries, and relax under the shade of the trees on the long, hot afternoons.[37]

A few miles west of Livadia, perched on the edge of a cliff high above the Black Sea, stood the imperial estate of Orienda, which had been devastated by a fire in 1881. In September of 1894, Grand Duke Dimitri Konstantinovich, who owned the estate, sold the ruins to Alexander III, asking only that his own family be allowed to continue living in their little wooden dacha.[38] During the reign of Nicholas II, the once magnificent palace lay abandoned, its white walls charred and overgrown with honeysuckle and ivy, the silence broken only by the mournful wail of the wind as it flitted in and out of the long corridors and fallen colonnades cast in shadow by the tall fir and pine trees that grew without restraint amid the crumbling marble. It was a favorite place for picnics, especially by the young grand duchesses, who found the ruins a source of perpetual curiosity.[39]

Other afternoons, the emperor took long rides across the mountains. Invariably, he announced his intention, adding, "Anyone who would like to go, too, might have his horse got ready." The hillsides above Livadia were treacherous, and, usually, most guests begged off the ride. On one occasion, Nicholas was riding near Massandra when his horse slipped, tossing the emperor roughly onto the rocky ground. He hurt his side and was scarcely able to climb back into the saddle and return to Livadia before he collapsed. "The Empress," Mossolov recalled, "was so terrified that she begged her husband never to ride again."[40] Thereafter, the emperor usually took a long walk or a drive. On walks, the emperor proved indefatigable, and few could keep up with his pace as he strode over the mountains.

Occasionally, Alexandra ventured into Yalta to shop, something she could never do in St. Petersburg. One afternoon, she was out with Anna Vyrubova when a sudden storm erupted, and the two women fled to the safety of the nearest store. The empress entered, still carrying her rain-soaked umbrella, and the shopkeeper spotted her. He did not recognize her but strode across the shop, pointed to a stand, and said sternly, "Madame, this is for umbrellas!" Meekly, the empress folded up her umbrella and placed it in the stand as directed before continuing her shopping.[41]

The emperor loved to play tennis and had a clay court, hidden by a thick screen of pine and cedar trees, built at Livadia. All the family, except Alexei, whose hemophilia prevented vigorous activities, joined in the games. The men appeared in white linen trousers and shirts sewn with double-headed eagles in gold, escorting the women in their white skirts and blouses, large picture hats adorned with feathers perched atop their hair. "I was often the Emperor's partner," Anna Vyrubova wrote, "and a very serious affair I had to make of each game. No conversation was allowed and we played with all the gravity and intensity of professionals."[42] Nicholas played well, and he enjoyed a challenge; when he heard that Count Nicholas Sumarakov-Elston, the nephew of Prince Felix

Yusupov and his wife, Zenaide, and a Russian tennis champion, was staying with them at their Crimean estate, Koreiz, he asked the young man to join him for a game at Livadia. The young count easily won every game against the emperor in their first match, and Nicholas was determined to avenge his loss in a second battle that same afternoon. A few strokes into the match, however, the count hit a shot that pounded into the emperor's ankle. Nicholas collapsed and had to remain in bed for the next few days, unable to walk with his swollen ankle. The count was in despair, and when he returned to Koreiz, the Yusupovs, according to Mossolov, "hauled him over the coals." As soon as he had recovered, Nicholas asked the young man back to Livadia for another match, but this time the count was cautious and played without any real force.[43]

Many afternoons, the emperor, accompanied by his children and a group of young officers, went for a swim. Nicholas had a passion for swimming and taught his children to enjoy the water. The rocky beach at Livadia caused all sorts of hazards to scurrying feet, and runner carpets were laid down to the edge of the water. Usually, the Black Sea was tranquil, but on one occasion disaster was narrowly averted. Nicholas and his children were swimming in the surf, watched from the beach by Grand Duchess Olga Alexandrovna, when an unexpected wave swept over the group. In a few seconds, the emperor and his three eldest daughters came to the surface, but there was no sign of Anastasia. Nicholas, realizing that his daughter must have been sucked in by the wave, dove back beneath the water, retrieving Anastasia and pulling her ashore by her hair.[44] After this, Nicholas had a canvas swimming pool, filled with warmed saltwater, built so that his children could swim in safety.

No matter how far afield they might be, every day, at four in the afternoon, the imperial family gathered for tea. At Livadia, this was taken in the empress's boudoir, on the balcony above the Black Sea, or, more often, at the English cottage, a little half-timbered house hidden amid a grove of evergreen and cedar trees at the end of an overgrown meadow.[45] After tea, the emperor usually went to his study to read through state papers, while the empress read or lay resting on her chaise longue and the children worked on their lessons for the following day.[46] Dinner was served at eight.[47] "Dishes were sent up from the kitchens and pantries," Mossolov noted, "to be kept warm by boiling water dishes, so that sauces were often ruined. At Livadia, Freedericksz asked for engineers to arrange some kind of railway and lift from kitchens to pantries, but the cooks protested that such an arrangement would deprive the kitchen boys of their job and the motion would disturb the sauces."[48] Two or three times a week, the imperial family dined with all the members of the Household and the Suite at Livadia. On other evenings, relatives and friends would join them and, after the meal had ended, sit in the Italian Courtyard while the Balalaika Orchestra from *Standart* played or officers from the Cossack Konvoi Escort sang.[49]

One of the most eagerly anticipated visitors during the imperial family's annual holiday at Livadia was Sayed Abd al-Ahad Bakhadur-Khan, the emir of Bokhara. An enormous man, with a round face, dark, vibrant eyes, and small, neatly trimmed mustache and beard, he invariably appeared in richly colored brocaded robes adorned with the blue silk moiré cordon of the Imperial Order of St. Andrei and wore a turban festooned with jewels. The emir was undoubtedly one of the wealthiest men in the Russian empire, and his appearance at Livadia never failed to delight and impress the Romanovs. The children particularly looked forward to his visits, as he showered them with toys and other expensive gifts. Anna Vyrubova remembered the emir as "a big, handsome Oriental, in a long black coat, and a white turban glittering with diamonds and rubies. He seemed intensely interested in the comparative simplicity of Russian Imperial customs."[50]

Abd al-Ahad was always accompanied by an entourage of aides, doctors, secretaries, and Bokharan representatives, "dressed in long, Oriental robes of bright colors, with white turbans," as Baron Wrangell-Rokoassowsky later wrote.[51] When he left Livadia, the emir distributed extravagant gifts to the imperial family and members of their suite. Anna Vyrubova recalled "costly diamonds and rubies" presented to Nicholas and Alexandra, and his personal orders decorated with jewels to members of the emperor's suite.[52] On one occasion, Grand Duchess Olga Alexandrovna, the emperor's sister, who was staying at Livadia, was surprised when the emir lavished upon her "an enormous gold necklace from which, like tongues of flame, hung tassels of rubies."[53]

With its warm climate and fresh air, the Crimea was a popular health resort. Sanatoriums for tuberculosis patients, rest homes, and hospitals were built on the green hillsides above Yalta. By the turn of the century, there were more tuberculosis sanatoriums in the little Black Sea town than in all of the rest of Russia. The entire coast was dotted with pensions, villas, hospitals, and nursing homes that specialized in the care of patients; of this number, almost half were devoted to children. Empress Alexandra herself founded several of these institutions, funding them with her own private fortune. In 1901, she opened the Alexander III Sanatorium in Yalta, a large institution with 460 beds for tubercular patients, out of her own money. The empress hired a team of American tubercular experts to come and work in the facility, training Russians in the latest medical treatments.[54] Unwilling

Grand Duchesses Olga, Marie, and Anastasia with their wreaths
for the Day of White Flowers at Yalta, photographed in the
loggia of the Italian Courtyard of the White Palace, 1912

to carry out her imperial duties in St. Petersburg on the pretext of ill health, Alexandra magically transformed in the Crimea. The empress, as Sophie Buxhoeveden wrote, "herself went to see the worst cases, visiting private houses where illness was there. She would be helpful, full of practical suggestions, helping arrange the pillows, and sending the things that the people could not afford to buy."[55]

Alexandra often took her young daughters with her on these visits or sent them out on their own to visit patients. On one occasion, Elizabeth Naryshkin-Kuryakin asked the empress, "Is it safe, Madame, for the young Grand Duchesses to have people in the last stage of consumption kiss their hands?" Alexandra quickly replied, "I don't think it will hurt the children, but I am sure it would hurt the sick if they thought that my daughters were afraid of infection."[56] To the empress, this noblesse oblige was a necessary part of her children's education. "They should realize the sadness underneath all this beauty," she once said.[57]

To help raise awareness of the institutions and the necessary funds, the empress organized two regular yearly events at Livadia. The first of these was called the Day of White Flowers. Crown Princess Margarethe, the empress's cousin, had founded the Day of White Flowers in Sweden, and Alexandra transplanted the idea to Russia, selecting St. George's Day for the annual fund-raising. The idea was quickly transplanted to cities all over the empire, adding much-needed donations to help support the Crimean sanatoriums. The Day of White Flowers always began with a parade through the streets of Yalta, which were decorated with garlands and wreaths of white marguerites, in recognition of the Crown Princess of Sweden. Volunteers were stationed throughout the town, accepting collections; in addition, young schoolgirls attended booths in the shops, cafes, cinemas, and theaters.[58]

The imperial children also participated in the fund-raising. The four grand duchesses, dressed in white, and Tsesarevich Alexei, in a sailor suit, each carried a long staff, with clusters of white marguerites tied to it, topped with a portrait of St. George surrounded by flowers. Over their shoulders or hanging round their waists were wallets in which to collect money.[59] Arriving in Yalta, they drove up and down the streets, walking along the avenues and entering shops to solicit donations in exchange for a flower. All of them, according to Anna Vyrubova, approached the endeavor "as enthusiastically as though their fortunes depended on selling them all."[60] In 1912, the children raised between 100 and 140 rubles ($1,000 to 1,400 each in 2005 figures) to help fund the Crimean sanatoriums.[61]

The other great event organized by the empress was her annual Charity Bazaar, which was first held in 1911 and took place until the First World War broke out in 1914. The bazaar quickly became a fashionable event for the St. Petersburg women who spent holidays in their villas along the coast. Together with the empress and her daughters, they helped to produce watercolors, painted bookmarks, made articles in needlepoint, and knitted blankets, all of which were sold to the curious public. On the day of the bazaar, *Standart*, anchored at the Mole in Yalta, served as a lounge and a stockroom for the small booths set up along the whole length of the pier. Canvas tents and white awnings shaded the booths and white tables, draped in garlands of flowers and evergreen boughs, which were crowded with blankets, linens, vases, postcards of the imperial family, cookies and pastries, small pieces of furniture, and various household items.

The bazaars were always a great success, and everyone, even the emperor, manned a stall to raise funds for the charities. "The Empress and her ladies," recalled Anna Vyrubova, "worked very hard, and from the opening day, the Empress, however precarious the condition of her health, always presided at her own table, disposing of fine needlework, embroidery and art objects with energy and enthusiasm."[62]

The White Palace was formally inaugurated a month after the imperial family first arrived, with a ball given by the emperor and the empress to celebrate the sixteenth birthday of their eldest daughter, Grand Duchess Olga Nikolaievna. Olga, according to Anna Vyrubova, "was as excited over her debut as any other young girl." She spent the afternoon preparing for the ball; for the first time, one of her maids arranged her long golden hair in a new, becoming upswept coil. Before the ball, Olga received her parents' birthday presents: a diamond ring and a necklace composed of sixteen diamonds and sixteen pearls. These were her first jewels, collected by the emperor and the empress piece by piece, one diamond and one pearl for each year of their daughter's life, and she wore them for the first time that evening.[63]

For the evening, the rooms were transformed into a scented garden of roses, lilacs, and orchids. The French doors of the state apartments were thrown open, and guests wandered through the courtyard and along the terraces, listening to the music provided by a regimental orchestra in the Italian Courtyard. Officers from *Standart* and from the Alexander Cavalry Regiment, of which Olga was honorary colonel in chief, along with relatives and members of the Suite, comprised the 150 guests.[64] "The ladies were in rich colored gowns," recalled Baroness Agnes de Stoeckl, "the young girls mostly in white tulle, and the gorgeous uniforms seemed to belong to a feast from the Eastern hemisphere."[65] And Anna Vyrubova remembered, "It was a perfect night, clear and warm, and the gowns and jewels of the women, and the brilliant uniforms of the men, made a striking spectacle under the blaze of the electric lights."[66]

At ten o'clock, Olga, on the arm of her proud father, entered the White Hall, her pink tulle gown complementing her golden hair, and "a flush of excitement on her cheeks," as Olga Voronoff recalled.[67] Family, friends, members of the emperor's suite, and the young officers watched as Olga took to the floor with her father for her first waltz.[68] A candlelit supper, "elaborate and excellent," according to Agnes de Stoeckl, was served on small round tables decorated with pink roses, following the ball. Only Alexandra was absent; confronted with the prospect of a social evening, she pled illness and watched the scene from the balcony above the Italian Courtyard. At the end of the supper, though, she reluctantly appeared to greet the guests. "I shall ever remember how beautiful she looked," wrote Agnes de Stoeckl, "like a Greek icon, in a gown of cloth of gold; she had a priceless gold and diamond band in her fair hair, a glorious necklace of many rows of different stones coming down to her waist; she seemed to be a Byzantine picture. The Tsesarevich was next to her, his lovely little face flushed with the excitement of the evening."[69]

Guests strolled through the Italian Courtyard and along the gardens, "with the high and rocky mountains outlining their rugged silhouettes against the deep, southern sky glittering with myriads of stars," remembered Olga Voronoff.[70] The night, "clear and warm," as Anna Vyrubova recalled, was awash with the scent of thousands of flowers and the distant strains of the orchestra still playing for the young revelers, who continued to celebrate until the sun chased the moon from the sky and the new day broke over the Black Sea.[71]

27

THE LAST SEASON

BY THE BEGINNING OF 1914, the Russian court stood unknowingly poised on, the edge of an abyss. As the old year faded into memory, aristocrats greeted the new social season with a frenzied energy, whose very vibrancy seemed an ominous portent of things to come. Society remained isolated, proud, and oblivious to change. A mantle of false security lay across the pastel palaces and French gardens, enshrined in its brooding, magisterial buildings lined with columns. These outward signs of authority masked a world of subtle nuance balanced precariously on ritual and form, where aristocratic sanction also encompassed arbitrary exclusion. Never had this fragile reality seemed more apparent than in the last months before the outbreak of the First World War, and St. Petersburg, seductively wrapped in its brilliant milieu of glamour and privilege, slipped ever closer to an unseen conflagration, a smoldering volcano about to engulf its life in the fires of war and revolution.

It was a world peopled with polished old gentlemen and formidable dowagers, debutantes in the new shapeless dresses and bobbed hairstyles, and young men in crisp uniforms or white ties and tails, raised to respect convention even as they watched the world around them change at a startling pace. Their mothers might be respectable matrons and their sisters virginal creatures without blemish, but they knew their fathers regularly disappeared to Monte Carlo and Biarritz to gamble away their family fortunes or to one of the red velvet private dining rooms at Maxim's in the Rue Royale in Paris, to lavish diamonds on demanding mistresses to the salutes of Veuve Clicquot. All across Russia and Europe, from the salon cars of the Nord Express to the fashionable promenades at Marienbad and Biarritz, a new, not entirely welcome character had appeared: the nouveau riche gentleman, through whose hands money flowed like water, and his inevitable demimondaine lady, clad in the latest gowns and draped with enormous jewels in an attempt to impress fashionable society. Gamblers and stockbrokers encroached on the privileged drawing rooms in their ill-fitting tails, lounging on exquisite Empire sofas and waving expensive cigars with an air of defiance as they discussed their wealth in voices raised against the strains of ragtime. The once-exclusive bastions of the aristocracy had fallen victim to progress.

In its blanket of thick snow and frozen crystal, St. Petersburg sparkled that winter as never before. For the aristocratic and wealthy, that last season in St. Petersburg revealed its full glory as an immensely rich playground of artistic, culinary, and sensual delights. From December to the middle of February, dawn came late to the capital, a blanket of darkness that reflected the sluggish and deliberate existence within the houses of privilege. The lives of the aristocracy were carefully scheduled to allow for the maximum pleasure with the minimum of effort. Women usually rose late; in winter, when balls carried on into the early morning, it was often not until noon; "they appear," noted one British visitor, "to wish to exclude the light of day as far as possible."[1] Concerns were few: the housekeeper might be summoned to the boudoir to review menus or discuss proposed receptions. Otherwise, late mornings and early afternoons were passed in reading books and magazines in different languages, writing letters, and, most especially, telephoning friends to exchange the latest gossip.

Between the hours of two and four in the afternoon, the fashionable elements drove across the frozen city, giving them a chance to casually greet their friends and to show off their latest Parisian fashions. By late afternoon, carriages and troikas raced dowagers, their faces hidden behind veils that flowed from their toques, to the showrooms of Fabergé and Cartier; sped them to couture houses for fittings; waited in the slush as hairdressers completed coiffures; and flew across the frozen city to deposit them for afternoon teas. The rigid rules governing their lives were complex; in the latter half of the nineteenth century, handbooks described proper etiquette for Western visitors, explaining protocol and the necessity of the social call. "Strangers," one guide noted, "are expected to make the first call, which is returned either in person or by card. In leaving cards on persons who are not at home, one of the edges of the card should be turned up. It is necessary to leave a card next day on any person to whom the stranger may have been introduced at a party. Those who are introduced to the stranger will observe the same politeness. Great punctuality is exacted at St. Petersburg in the matter of leaving cards and entertainments and introductions. Visiting on New Year's Day may be avoided by giving a small contribution to the charitable institutions of the city, which will be duly acknowledged in the newspapers."[2]

"Every afternoon," recalled Baroness Sophie Buxhoeveden, "Mama and I got into a closed carriage and drove from house to house, leaving cards or attending At Homes. We generally managed from fifteen to twenty calls between two o'clock and seven. It meant hastily divesting oneself of one's fur coat and felt overshoes and staying for some fifteen or twenty minutes at the most."[3] These visits often proved startling for those who anticipated the rigid etiquette of St. Petersburg society. "Democracy is as striking a characteristic of the Russian aristocracy as is their extravagance," recalled one woman. "The foreigner must make the first call but it would be difficult to find a Russian great lady outside the circle of the Imperial Family who would sit at home and arrogate to herself the privilege of receiving but not returning calls. Russian women are ready at a moment's notice to discuss in the friendliest way with any stranger the geography, literature, and art of any country in the world and in its native language."[4]

Ladies often received complete strangers for tea or those who had called and left a card. Entering the house, recalled one woman, "the footman becomes a clever lady's maid. He begins by taking off your big fur boots, then he unties the Orenburg shawl, which envelopes your head under your fur cap and is tied behind, and then he frees you from your heavy *shuba* or long cape with high fur collar. The shawl and the shuba are de rigueur and it is a dangerous experiment to try to wear a hat in the winter. You ascend the broad staircase, your toilette achieved, and pass through one, two, or three salons. In the last you find the family, mother, children, aunts, cousins, all gathered around the tea table and the samovar. . . . You sit for an hour or two talking with comparative strangers, taking your tea. The Russians are capable of drinking from ten to fifteen cups, the first with cream, perhaps, the next with jam or lemon, then with cognac—an endless variety. All the family matters are discussed and settled in your presence. You are treated as one of them."[5]

While aristocratic women were thus occupied, their husbands, brothers, sons, and lovers pursued their own passions. By noon, most business concerns had been addressed, and men retreated to the stock exchange at the tip of Vasilevskiy

Island, where aristocrats mingled with the nouveau riche as they searched for an inside hint to parlay into a great fortune. On the long, stormy winter afternoons, many men sought refuge in their private clubs. The clubs in St. Petersburg, unlike those of London, Paris, or Berlin, were not strictly male territory. Women were nearly always welcome, as were accompanied children; because of this, the dining rooms were often the scenes of boisterous lunches *en famille*, lending a gaiety rarely seen in Pall Mall or the Wilhelmstrasse. Most of these private clubs were the exclusive domain of the aristocracy; membership rested not only on nominations and votes, but also on birth and family connections. Thus, it was not uncommon for a man to put down his son's name at birth, not only at the most fashionable schools and institutions, but also at the most exclusive private establishments found in the capital. Private clubs provided certain elements many men found indispensable. In the smoke-filled drawing rooms and libraries, countless business deals were concluded with a handshake and a glass of port, while other, more personal transactions were consummated in the private bedrooms kept exclusively for use by members seeking a discreet rendezvous.

The English Club, founded in the reign of Catherine the Great, was particularly in vogue in the reign of Nicholas II, favored by the older aristocracy for its aura of subdued power. The New Club, founded by Grand Duke Vladimir, attracted the more modern elements of society and was considered the domain of the "fast" set. But the most elegant of all the private clubs—and thus the most desirable—was the Imperial Yacht Club on the Morskaya. "His Majesty the Emperor," recalled Countess Kleinmichel, "had two kinds of subjects: those who were members of the Yacht Club, and those who were not." She continued, "How many people passing through the *Morskaya* used to raise their longing eyes to that Holy of Holies, the goal of their most ardent desires. I recollect the members of that select club gluing their noses against the window panes, pressing close against one another, persuaded of their superiority over all other beings, proud of their importance and spending hours looking down the *Morskaya*. A young man who, the day before his admission to membership, was inoffensive, kindly and modest, eight days later would be self-important and abusive, and would disparage everything and everybody, except his club."[6]

To round out the afternoon, men might pay a visit to the steam baths. Although most of the private clubs had their own steam baths, the most popular one in the capital was Yegorov's. In a heavy gothic setting, with dark mahogany walls, stained glass windows, and Oriental carpets, men could forget their business and social pressures and relax in an atmosphere of luxury. Pages in white tunics and black breeches ran noiselessly up and down the vaulted hallways, carrying towels, cigars, and glasses of brandy to the intimate dressing rooms where men stripped off their clothes and wrapped themselves in robes. At the press of a button, a masseuse, a tailor, or a laundry clerk hurried to the dressing room, or a waiter would arrive, from whom lunch could be ordered. Russian men found no shame in nudity, and they lounged in various states of undress in the Turkish Sitting Room, reading, smoking, or chatting happily with their friends. For the truly shy, there were small private sauna rooms, where the occupant could strip in complete isolation from the rest of the crowd.

The ritual of the steam bath was learned from an early age. After stripping, customers plunged into the swimming pool, set in a large paneled room filled with potted palms and statuary; an iron bridge spanned the center of the pool, covered with dripping foliage. A sweat in the sauna followed a swim. Sauna rooms centered around large stoves, with attendants dousing the hot surface with frequent showers of water to produce an endless cloud of steam. There were granite tables and benches for lying upon, as well as private cubicles for less sociable visitors. If no attendant was available, fellow bathers happily beat each other with birch twigs to stimulate the circulation, before plunging into the baths and then running back to the saunas to repeat the entire process.[7] Invigorated and refreshed, cleansed of the cares of the day, a man would order his carriage or motorcar and join his wife for the evening's entertainments.

During the season, couples dined early if at all, allowing time to change before the evening's festivities began, and the capital's numerous restaurants did a brisk business. Aside from the Russian fare served at such fashionable establishments as the Bear and at Cubat's on the Morskaya, a number of restaurants specialized in international cuisine: A'lours, Donon's, and Contant were French; Privato, Italian; and Ernest featured German dishes. Most of these restaurants included small private rooms for romantic dining; after the turn of the century, most of these private rooms were divested of their locks, thus preventing some of the more intimate pursuits for which they had been designed and which had led to a number of unenviable situations and ruined careers.[8] The Russian passion for food—with meals frequently lasting for three or four hours—was matched by a love of alcohol. Before the Revolution, fully half of all French wine was shipped to the Russian empire, to supplement domestic supplies from the Crimea.[9]

On winter evenings, society went to the theater, the opera, and the symphony, but the glory of all Russian arts was the ballet, which reached its zenith under Nicholas II. The Imperial Ballet School, in Rossi's neoclassical complex lining the famous Theater Street, was so exclusive that ninety percent of all applicants were refused admission. Pupils, recalled Mathilde Kschessinska, lived in enormous communal dormitories, divided by both sex and age; the boys wore white or blue trousers with matching jackets, while the girls were in long dresses with white hoods, "their hair strictly smoothed down and plaited." Despite the best efforts of the instructors, romances blossomed; as Kschessinska recalled, "Since all communication between boys and girls was strictly forbidden, many were the dodges which had to be used for an innocent exchange of looks, smiles, or words. Naturally the teachers did not let us out of their sight during rehearsals and dancing classes; however, despite our sentinels we always managed to snatch a few seconds' flirtation, for these gatherings provided us with our only opportunities. These secret intrigues were part of the School's tradition and each girl had her own particular boyfriend. But these meetings, these short idylls, were most naive and innocent."[10]

Under the influence of Marius Petipa, *chef maître de ballet*, the Imperial Ballet had no rival. Petipa was old-fashioned, a man devoted to classicism while all around him others were breaking free of traditions and soaring to new heights. Against this backdrop, the works of Serge Diaghilev were startlingly revolutionary. Although his famous Ballets Russes conquered the European continent before gaining renown in his native Russia, Diaghilev—through the combined talents of the composers Stravinsky, Rachmaninov, and Strauss; artists such as Bakst, Benois, and Fokine; and dancers Nijinsky, Karsavina, and Pavlova—was able to dominate the world of ballet.

Although Diaghilev cemented his fame in the West, in Russia he took second place to the most famous and revered figure in ballet, the great prima ballerina Mathilde Kschessinska. In St. Petersburg, Kschessinska was celebrated as the absolute mistress of her art, and she reveled in the admiration, living in splendor in a magnificent art nouveau mansion near the Fortress of St. Peter and St. Paul, where she entertained on a lavish scale. Kschessinska was rumored to still have a great influence over Nicholas II, her former lover, and her simultaneous affairs with his cousins Serge Mikhailovich and Andrei Vladimirovich, complete with illegitimate child, were the talk of the city.

The ballet was such an intrinsic part of life in society that entire weeks during the season were planned around its performances at the blue and gold Mariinsky Theater, where the stalls and boxes were permanently booked and handed down from father to son through subscription. Meriel Buchanan, the daughter of the British ambassador, later wrote, "For the opera one could sit in any part of the house one liked, but for the ballet no lady, belonging to so-called Society, could be seen anywhere but in a box, and it was also considered highly incorrect to remain seated during the interval; one was supposed to retire to the little room at the back of one's box, where one could smoke and talk, and receive visits from friends amongst the audience. Then, as soon as the first strains of the orchestra were heard, everybody would flock back to their seats and for a few minutes before the lights went out one could look round at the beautifully dressed women with their amazing jewels, catch a glimpse of a young Grand Duke in the Imperial box, look down at the stalls crowded with young officers, diplomats, and critics, see in one of the upper tiers a group of girls belonging to the Imperial School, their old fashioned white aprons and fichus making them look rather like little Puritan girls of a bygone age. I can still feel the individual atmosphere of that huge theater, the scent of amber and chypre, of Russian cigarettes and Russian leather, the smell of boiling hot water pipes, of age old dust and the resin the dancers used on their shoes to prevent them slipping. I can visualize the white and gold of the decorations, the blue velvet curtains and chairs, the Imperial eagles that surmounted all the boxes, the attendants in their court uniforms, braided with gold. I can remember one gala performance, when the blaze of jewels almost dazzled one, when the whole parterre of the stalls was filled with court officials in scarlet uniforms, looking rather like a gigantic field of poppies swayed by a gust of wind, when, with one single movement they rose to greet the arrival of the Emperor."[11]

Against this backdrop of hedonistic indulgence, St. Petersburg celebrated its last social season. "Even the dowagers," wrote one contemporary, "do not remember such a brilliant season as that of 1914. Balls and receptions followed one another, each more resplendent than the last. Magnificent festivities were organized, dinner parties were sandwiched in between an at home and a rout. Smart people got such numbers of invitations to parties that they could not accept all. It was a continual rush, as if there were an undefined presentiment current that this particular season was the last for many a gallant officer joyfully taking his part in the vortex of worldly gaiety."[12]

The season could be exhausting. One winter, seventeen-year-old Anna Vyrubova attended twenty-two balls, in addition to countless teas, receptions, and dinners.[13] "Upon these brief months of gaiety," reported one lady, "is spent everything that can be raked and scraped"; once launched upon, "entertaining went on with a verve typical of the Russian passion for pleasure. There were *fêtes* indoors and out, and fashionable people scarcely saw the daylight for weeks at a time during the six hours of the winter's sunshine."[14]

These aristocratic balls were restricted by the conventions of protocol. At *Bals blancs*, reserved for debutantes, young ladies appeared in white gowns and were accompanied by ever-watchful chaperones. Dancing was confined to quadrilles and waltzes; anything else was considered "slightly unrefined," and there was a standing order from the emperor that no officer in uniform was allowed to dance the one-step.[15] "The dances," recalled Helene Izvolsky, "were directed by the Master of Ceremonies, a colonel with a magnificent blond beard and a stentorian voice shouting commands in French, '*Grand Rond, s'il vous plait!*' or '*Balancez vos Dames!*' We would all join hands or change partners and this would be the occasion for a quick nod, the pressure of a white-gloved hand, the only chaste signs of love we could exchange."[16]

Debutantes collected in ballroom corners, gazing across wide expanses of parquet to lines of uncertain partners who stood in their own groups. "No enlisted man could be invited to these formal affairs," remembered Helene Izvolsky, "neither were students or any pupils of the elite schools admitted. The only exception was made for the senior class of the Corps des Pages who were commissioned before graduation." There was no orchestra at a Bal blanc: music was provided by an elderly *tappeur*, who played suitable selections on a piano. During the cotillion, carts of lavish flowers were wheeled into the room. "Roses, carnations, and Parma violets," recalled Helene Izvolsky, "shipped to Petersburg from the Riviera in refrigerated cars."[17] At midnight, couples rushed to round tables draped in crisp white linen to dine on salmon and sturgeon, caviar, "fruit from every corner of the world," as one lady remembered, and even "apples, peaches, and pears embossed with the silhouette of the Emperor."[18]

In contrast, a *Bal rose* was somewhat more relaxed. By 1914, the shifting tide of morality—never more flexible than in St. Petersburg—happily ignored many of those whose behavior would formerly have condemned them to social oblivion. "The traditional young ballroom set had its fringe of rebellion," Helene Izvolsky recalled. "These were a few young married women who were branded as fast. They danced with the civilians and sent in requests for the one step and the tango, strictly prohibited in our milieu. They wore bold evening gowns and high turbans and feathers and smoked perfumed cigarettes in long jade holders."[19] The music, as well as the dancing of polkas and mazurkas, was lively, and the atmosphere more sophisticated. There were also the latest dances imported from Paris: "the *pas de patineur*, a gliding motion resembling ice skating, and the *Tonkinoise*, danced to a lively tune."[20] The cotillion was followed by an early supper, allowing the young couples to attend other parties.[21]

Couples might venture on to the popular nightspots of the capital: the Aquarium, a cabaret where the walls were glass tanks filled with fish, or the Villa Rode, where gypsies played and sang all through the night. The more determined and energetic of revelers made their ways to the Island District, to visit the gypsy encampments spread along the Neva and the shore of the Gulf of Finland. They raced across the frozen imperial capital snuggled in fur wraps and nestled into brightly painted troikas that flew over compacted snow, beneath the black sky and the shimmering orange moon whose glow cast long shadows against granite palaces. "The Islands were covered with deep snow," recalled Nadine Wonlar-Larsky. "The branches of the trees sparkled like diamonds under the bright light of the moon. The extreme cold, the thrill of the rapid motion, the clear, crisp, frost-laden air, so bracing and so clean, was like the breath of one's nostrils to a child of St. Petersburg."[22]

The gypsies ran their own establishments, offering champagne and music until the early hours. The troikas halted, their passengers rushing through the cold night to the warmth of a small café where, as Théophile Gautier noted, "lights flash, the samovar steams, champagne of *Veuve Clicquot* is chilled, plates of caviar and ham, strings of herring and cold fowl, and little cakes are spread on the table. Then follows laughter and chatting and eating and drinking and smoking."[23] The gypsies were justly famous for their haunting songs and lively entertainment. The most famous of all gypsy entertainers was Varya Panina, a woman of Wagnerian proportions and a soulful voice so celebrated that Fabergé created a hardstone figurine of her. Her death was a true St. Petersburg legend: one evening, during a performance, she spotted a former lover in the audience. Fetching a bottle of poison, Panina sang a mournful ballad to her lost lover; with the final words, she drank the poison and died in front of the horrified audience.[24]

The balls of the 1914 season were among the most magnificent St. Petersburg had ever witnessed, as the gilded salons of the imperial capital glittered with light and echoed with the sound of laughter and music. In January, Countess Betsy Shuvalov gave her celebrated Black and White Ball for six hundred guests. Following the countess's wishes, the men all wore white ties and black tails, while the women came in gowns of silk, satin, tulle, or velvet, all in white. The Shuvalov Palace was filled with white roses, orchids, carnations, and lilies, scenting the warm air with an almost overpowering fragrance. Only Grand Duchess Vladimir, the countess's mortal enemy, had not received an invitation, and none of the grand duchess's friends, fearing retribution, attended.[25]

A week later, the countess played host to the king and the queen of Bulgaria.

"Nearly a thousand guests assembled in her magnificent ballroom," recalled Countess Nostitz, "with its wonderful stained glass windows, its walls covered with sculpted *bas-reliefs*. When supper came and the folding doors of another neighboring suite of brilliantly lighted salons were opened we saw rows and rows of flower decked supper tables laid with beautiful old linen, cut glass, and antique silver. Baron Peter Wrangel, very tall and erect, who later became the famous chief of the White Army, asked me to lead the cotillion with him. Together we opened the ball with great *éclat* when suddenly his spur caught in the tarlatan dress of Princess Nathalia Naryshkin. We tripped and fell, I on my back, he on top, just in front of the King of Bulgaria. It was a most embarrassing moment, but the King gallantly helped me to my feet and we continued dancing."[26]

The dowager empress gave the most important ball that season for her two granddaughters, Grand Duchesses Olga and Tatiana Nikolaievna, at Anichkov Palace on February 14. As Helene Izvolsky looked on, Nicholas II appeared, a "short, timid man," as she recalled, "wearing as usual his uniform of a colonel in the Infantry and stroking his beard with a mechanical gesture." Behind him came not the empress, who had remained at Tsarskoye Selo, but the two grand duchesses: "They were tall, slim, lovely creatures and they looked at us with a sort of amused curiosity. They wore very simple classic white gowns for it would have been considered bad taste to dress them up." Nicholas opened the ball with Olga at his side as he circled the hall in a stately polonaise. "As soon as the orchestra struck up the first quadrille," Izvolsky remembered, "there was embarrassment. Not a single young man made a move to ask the two Grand Duchesses to dance. Were they all too shy to make the plunge? Or was it the sudden realization that the two girls were strangers?" Finally, however, the master of ceremonies prompted a few officers from Tsarskoye Selo, men "completely unknown," remembered Izvolsky, "rather uncouth, and common looking." As the two grand duchesses took to the ballroom floor, "silence fell upon the guests" as they looked on in disbelief at "their obscure partners," who "seemed to enjoy themselves immensely. This was too much—jealousy was awakened in the hearts of the reluctant cavaliers. When the next dance was announced the most brilliant young officers stepped forward and asked Olga and Tatiana for this and all the other dances."[27]

At the midnight supper, Nicholas wandered from table to table, chatting with the guests. Catching sight of Helene Izvolsky's mother, he leaned close and whispered sadly, "I know no one here." It was, the young girl recalled, a stunning admission from "the Emperor of all Russia, in his mother's house, among the flower of his own most loyal subjects, the aristocracy. By now he was completely isolated." Once supper had ended, the two grand duchesses again took to the ballroom floor, delighted by the unaccustomed gaiety. Finally, at five in the morning, they bade their reluctant farewells and returned to their isolated existence at Tsarskoye Selo.[28]

A week later, the halls of Anichkov Palace once again glowed, as the imperial family celebrated the most important event of that season, the wedding of Princess Irina Alexandrovna, the only daughter of Grand Duke Alexander Mikhailovich and the emperor's sister Xenia Alexandrovna, to Prince Felix Yusupov. As the most handsome, most eligible, and wealthiest prince in all of Russia, Felix was bound to make a brilliant match, but he surprised nearly everyone by winning the hand of Princess Irina, the emperor's only Russian niece. As tall and beautiful as her husband, Irina was regarded, after Nicholas II's own daughters, as the finest catch in all of Russia. "I married my wife out of snobbery," Felix later declared. "My wife married me for money."[29]

Prince Felix Yusupov and his fiancée, Princess Irina Alexandrovna

Before their wedding, Nicholas II asked Felix if he would like an official position at court as a gift; instead, and in typical dilettantish fashion, Felix requested unlimited use of the imperial box at the Mariinsky Theater. The emperor granted the request but added to it by giving the newlyweds a collection of uncut diamonds, from three to seven carats each.[30]

Felix and Irina were married on February 9, 1914, in the private chapel of Anichkov Palace. Irina arrived in a state coach drawn by eight white horses led by footmen in silk stockings, knee breeches, and powdered wigs. Her stylish gown, of white satin, was embroidered with silver thread; the diamond, pearl, and rock crystal tiara, by Cartier, held Marie Antoinette's lace wedding veil in place atop her head.[31] Because Felix had no official or military rank, he wore the uniform of the nobility: a dark blue frock coat with gold lapels and epaulettes and white broadcloth trousers.[32] "There was a glitter of jewels and decorations," recalled Meriel Buchanan, "of brilliant uniforms, and women's gaily colored dresses."[33] Helene Izvolsky was enchanted by the princess's "severe, almost icon-like beauty. Both bride and bridegroom seemed to step out of some ancient legend as they knelt before the gold vested priest, who joined their hands in matrimony."[34] In the receiving line, as Meriel Buchanan recalled, one figure stood out: Princess Zenaide Yusupov, the groom's mother, who watched as her only remaining son joined the Romanov family. Buchanan remembered "her dark hair, already flecked with silver, under the hat of pale colored violets"; her gown, "in pearl gray satin, with a few beautiful diamonds gleaming among the tulles and laces," as she stood, "smiling faintly as the long line of guests filed before the bride and bridegroom. Her thoughts seemed very far away."[35]

It was a glorious celebration, a marriage between perhaps the two most beautiful people in St. Petersburg, between one of the noblest families in Russia and its own ruling house, between untold wealth and unlimited power. And yet, as Meriel Buchanan recalled, "there was at the same time a strange feeling of doom and impending tragedy, as if the menace of the coming years was already casting a shadow on all the people assembled in the brightly lighted room, while outside the windows the snow covered streets, the frozen river, the teeming millions of peasants and workers, waited breathlessly for all this splendor to pass away."[36]

Countess Kleinmichel's masquerade ball, 1914

Society was still in a festive mood when, five days later, Countess Marie Kleinmichel gave a Persian Ball in honor of her three young nieces. Only three hundred guests were invited: the countess felt obliged to seat each one for a midnight supper, and her kitchen could handle no higher number. Hundreds of others, left uninvited, all begged to be allowed to simply watch from the ballroom gallery, but the countess was adamant—"it would have spoilt the beauty of the evening," she declared. Léon Bakst, who created the celebrated outfits for Serge Diaghilev's Ballets Russes, designed many of the costumes worn that evening. The ball opened with an Oriental quadrille, led by the three Kleinmichel debutantes, Princess Serge Cantacuzené, Grand Duchess Kirill, and Grand Duke Boris Vladimirovich. This was followed with an Egyptian dance, a Cossack dance, a traditional folk dance, and a Hungarian folk dance. As exotic as the dances were the costumes worn by the guests: Grand Duchess Kirill wore a crimson silk gown in Oriental design, embroidered with gold lace; Prince Vladimir Paley was attired in loose blue silk trousers, a medieval-style white caftan embroidered with gold thread, red boots, and a white cap trimmed with sable; Princess Serge Cantacuzené wore loose pantaloons, a blue and silver silk jacket, and an aigrette of white feathers in her silver lamé turban; and Prince Nicholas de Basily had copied a costume from a painting in his family's portrait gallery showing a Venetian prince in Renaissance clothing of crimson silk woven with gold thread. Countess Kleinmichel's celebrated evening was the last great ball in imperial Russia before the start of the First World War.[37]

At the end of the social season, the imperial family retreated to Livadia. Alexandra gave a number of dances for Olga and Tatiana at the White Palace, and Grand Duchess Marie Georgievna held parties for them at Harax. The house had just been wired for electric light, and the loggias and balconies were hung with strings of tiny flickering lights, which had also been woven into the foliage of the cypress and magnolia trees and interlaced through the ivy, wisteria, and roses covering the trelliswork. The entire house and gardens shimmered with the light, lending a magical quality to the evening. "We dined late," Agnes de Stoeckl recalled, "all the windows open, the moonlight so bright and the landscape from every window a vision of fairyland." The emperor soon grew bored with the meal and began to grab small bits of black bread, rolling them between his fingers and flinging them across the table at unsuspecting diners. Several of the pellets hit Agnes's daughter Zoia, and she quickly grabbed a menu, scrawled a message on the back, and asked the grand duchess to hand it to the emperor. Marie Georgievna duly circled the room and handed the menu to her cousin, who turned it over and read Zoia's message: "Please ask His Majesty kindly to wash his hands before he throws any more bread, the bullets are black." Nicholas, eyeing his infuriated target, collapsed into laughter "till the tears ran down his cheeks."[38]

The next evening, Nicholas returned to dine at Harax, this night bringing Alexandra and their two eldest daughters. "Owing to the intense heat," remembered Agnes de Stoeckl, "we all dined on the terrace overlooking the sea. The table was adorned with flowers; the urns on the terrace wall and the gardens below were ablaze with blossom."[39] Sitting on the terrace after dinner, Nicholas nervously flicked the ashes from his cigarette into a bronze ashtray. Agnes de Stoeckl, at his side, later recalled how tired he appeared. "When I go back to Livadia tonight," he said with resignation, "I shall have to read and sign papers for hours."[40]

One of the guests that evening, Grand Duchess Marie Georgievna's brother Prince Christopher of Greece, "was suddenly overcome with a passionate desire" to propose to the emperor's eldest daughter, as Agnes de Stoeckl recalled. "He told me," wrote the Baroness, "that he greatly admired Grand Duchess Olga . . . and asked me if I thought he had any chance." After discussing the situation, the prince, his courage bolstered by a stiff whiskey and soda, drove to the White Palace the following afternoon. A few hours later, he returned to Harax, looking "pale but dignified." Pressed for what had taken place, Christopher related that he had asked the emperor for Olga's hand. Nicholas, he said, "had been most kind," but ultimately dismissed him, saying firmly, "Olga is too young to think of such a thing as marriage yet."[41]

In fact, unknown to the prince, plans were already under way to secure a suitable husband for Olga Nikolaievna. On May 31, 1914, the imperial family sailed on *Standart* from Yalta to the Romanian port of Constanza on the Black Sea, ostensibly on a courtesy visit, but in reality hoping to explore a potential match between Olga and Prince Carol of Romania. The previous winter, Nicholas and Alexandra had asked the prince's mother, Crown Princess Marie, to bring her husband, Ferdinand, and her son to Tsarskoye Selo so that their eldest children might meet. Marie had little enthusiasm for the idea, aware of the possibility that Olga might be a hemophilia carrier, but "considered it ungracious to refuse."[42] Once brought together, however, neither Olga nor Carol showed any real interest in such an alliance.[43] During the Romanian visit of 1913, recalled Princess Elizabeth Naryshkin-Kuryakin, "Grand Duchess Olga had maintained a state of cold reserve in the face of this courtship, and it seemed to me that she was far from delighted at the thought of marriage to a Romanian Prince."[44]

As *Standart* steamed into the harbor at Constanza, the entire Romanian royal family stood waiting to greet them, King Carol at the side of his eccentric wife, Queen Elizabeth. The Romanians were Hohenzollerns by blood and thus directly related to both the emperor and the empress: Crown Princess Marie was both Nicholas's and Alexandra's first cousin, as well as a sister to the empress's former sister-in-law Victoria Melita, who had married Grand Duke Kirill Vladimirovich after her divorce from Grand Duke Ernst Ludwig of Hesse. A string of carriages conveyed the two families to a service at the town cathedral, celebrated in both Russian and Romanian, followed by a luncheon and a diplomatic reception. That evening, the king and the queen gave a magnificent banquet, in a pavilion decorated with palms and hung with strings of flickering electric lights.[45] Alexandra appeared in a gown of silver brocade, a wide bandeau of diamonds across her forehead, tired but, as Crown Princess Marie recalled, "making brave efforts to be as gracious as possible," though "her face was very flushed" and she appeared ill at ease.[46] After a fireworks display over the harbor, the imperial family boarded *Standart*, amid a thirty-one-gun salute, concluding the long day by sailing out of the harbor as a brass band played the Russian national anthem.[47] In the end, the visit had failed to evoke the slightest interest on the part of Grand Duchess Olga. "I don't want to leave Russia," she explained to Pierre Gilliard. "I am a Russian, and I mean to remain a Russian."[48]

On their return to Russia, the imperial family headed to St. Petersburg where, on June 6, the emperor welcomed the king of Saxony on a state visit, timed to coincide with the centenary of the Battle of the Nations at Leipzig. Nicholas and the king presided over a march past of His Majesty's Hussar Guards Regiment in the forecourt of the Catherine Palace before attending a luncheon in the Great Gallery. The king, recalled one witness, was "dull, pompous, and sleepy after meals. He made a very ungracious impression, and what struck most Russian courtiers, used to the courtesy and urbanity of our Imperial Family, was the fact that he did not offer to shake hands with any of the Emperor's Suite who were presented to him, not even making an exception for the Minister of the Imperial Court, Count de Freedericksz, who had to content himself with a slight inclination of the royal head."[49]

At the height of that long, golden summer, word reached St. Petersburg that Archduke Franz Ferdinand of Austria-Hungary had been assassinated, along with his morganatic wife, Countess Sophie Chotek, by a Serb nationalist during a visit to Sarajevo. A first, there was little hint that the murder would cause any disruption, and Alexandra was more concerned by a second cable that arrived that same fateful day, announcing that Rasputin had been attacked by a former prostitute in his village of Pokrovskoye. For two weeks, his life hung in the balance; Rasputin would spend the next month confined to a hospital in Siberia as the momentous events of July 1914 played themselves out.

A week later, on Monday, July 7, the emperor and the empress welcomed Raymond Poincaré, the president of France, to St. Petersburg, watching from the deck of the imperial yacht *Alexandria* as the great battleship *France* churned slowly up the Gulf of Finland, the scene washed by the fading light and lengthening shadows of sunset. As the battleship came to a stop, brass bands on the assembled fleet of Russian naval vessels thundered into "The Marseillaise" and "God Save the Tsar," accompanied by shattering echoes from the gun salutes.[50] That night, the imperial couple gave a state banquet for the president at Peterhof. The magnificent Grand Palace blazed with thousands of shimmering candles that, as the Comte de Chabrun recalled, "made scintillating rivers of all the tiaras."[51] Through the open windows, spray from the gilded fountains of the Grand Cascade hung in the air, like diamonds twinkling in the gray half-light of evening. Maurice Paleologue, the French ambassador, was overwhelmed by the show of pomp and splendor, so alien to life in democratic Paris. "Thanks to the brilliance of the uniforms, superb *toilettes*, elaborate liveries, magnificent furnishings and fittings, in short the whole panoply of pomp and power, the spectacle was such as no court in the world can rival. I shall long remember the dazzling display of jewels on the women's shoulders. It was simply a fantastic shower of diamonds, pearls, rubies, sapphires, emeralds, topaz, beryls—a blaze of fire and flame."[52]

During the banquet, Paleologue sat opposite Empress Alexandra. In his diary he wrote, "Although long ceremonies are a very great trial to her she was anxious to be present this evening to do honor to the President of the Allied Republic. She was a beautiful sight with her low brocade gown and a diamond tiara on her head. Her forty-two years have left her face and figure still pleasant to look upon. After the first course she entered into conversation with Poincaré, who was on her right. Before long, however, her smile became set and the veins in her cheeks stood out. She bit her lips every minute. Her labored breathing made the network of diamonds sparkle on her bosom."[53] Paleologue's compatriot, the Comte de Chabrun, was less impressed. "Her fair beauty imposes more than it attracts," he recorded. "Her words are friendly, but an instinctive shyness grips her lips; just when she wants to like you, fear suddenly glazes her eyes, and she looks away."[54]

Several days later, there was a military review of some sixty thousand massed troops at Krasnoye Selo. The president rode in an open calèche with Empress

Alexandra; at their side, on a magnificent charger, Nicholas galloped at the head of a procession of grand dukes and army officers. At Krasnoye Selo, the imperial family climbed the steps up the side of the Emperor's Mound, where they were to watch the soldiers march past. All around, women in elegant white dresses, their faces shielded from the blazing sun by twirling parasols, whispered and waited, curtseying deeply as the Romanovs passed. Paleologue recalled, "The sun was dropping towards the horizon in a sky of purple and gold. On a sign from the Emperor, an artillery salvo signaled the evening prayer. The bands played a hymn. Everyone uncovered. A non-commissioned officer recited the Lord's Prayer in a loud voice. All those men, thousands upon thousands, prayed for the Emperor and Holy Russia. The silence and composure of that multitude in that great plain, the magic poetry of the hour . . . gave the ceremony a touching majesty."[55]

On the last night of the visit, Poincaré held a banquet on the deck of the battleship *France*. "It had, indeed, a kind of terrifying grandeur with the four gigantic 304 cm. guns raising their huge muzzles above the heads of the guests," recalled Paleologue.[56] Within a few hours, Poincaré had said his farewells and, aboard the battleship, steamed slowly into the Gulf of Finland. "It was a splendid night," Paleologue recalled. "The Milky Way stretched, a pure band of silver, into unending space. Not a breath of wind. The *France* and her escorting division sped rapidly away to the west, leaving behind her long ribbons of foam, which glistened in the moonlight like silvery streams." Watching the ships grow smaller and smaller on the horizon, the emperor and Paleologue stood on the deck of *Standart*, smoking in the dim light and discussing the possibility of a European conflict. "Notwithstanding appearances," Nicholas declared to the ambassador, "Emperor Wilhelm is too cautious to launch his country on some wild adventure and Emperor Franz Josef's only wish is to die in peace."[57] In less than ten days, Europe was at war.

EPILOGUE

July 20, 1914:
The Beginning of the End

THE SPLENDOR, POMP, AND PAGEANTRY of the Russian imperial court came to an abrupt end on Sunday, July 20, 1914. On this day, Nicholas II left Peterhof, boarded a motor launch that took him out to the imperial yacht *Alexandria* and, with his wife, sailed up the Gulf of Finland to St. Petersburg to formally declare war on Germany.

As she entered the mouth of the Neva, *Alexandria*'s paddlewheel churned the sapphire waters of the river into a ribbon of glistening foam. Small boats and rafts swayed in her wake, blowing their horns; their salute was soon taken up by the thunder of cannons fired from the Fortress of St. Peter and St. Paul, announcing the yacht's approach. Thousands of people had gathered along the granite embankments of the Neva, "one solid mass of humanity," wrote one English visitor, who noted the "frenzied waving of national flags and the display of cheaply-printed portraits of the beloved Little Father."[1] As *Alexandria* sailed past the baroque palaces and ornate cathedrals whose domes shimmered in the afternoon sunshine, people cheered, waved, and applauded. "Wherever I looked I saw nothing but joyous resolve expressed in the faces around me," recalled the chief of the St. Petersburg Police.[2]

All eyes were on Nicholas II, a lone figure "standing on the yacht's bridge dressed in naval uniform," a witness recalled. When the crowd caught sight of

Nicholas II, Empress Alexandra, and their four daughters arriving at the Winter Palace
on the day World War I was declared, July 20, 1914

him, the ovations rose "into a very tempest of sound, as the tidings of his advent
spread from the water's edge to the remoter parts of the city." The yacht stopped
at the English Quay, where the emperor boarded a small launch to carry him the
final mile up the Neva River.[3] The tender halted at the edge of the Palace Quay,
and Nicholas stepped out first; he wore the uniform of the Hussar Guards Regiment, the medals across his breast shining brightly in the sun. Alexandra followed, in a flowing white dress and a large picture hat whose veil she had turned
back to reveal her face. Like their mother, the four daughters were also clad in
white gowns and hats; only Alexei was absent, having twisted his ankle the previous week. Hand in hand, Nicholas and Alexandra followed a ribbon of crimson carpet to the Winter Palace, whose dull red facade seemed to stretch into the
blue horizon, and they disappeared within, to the Malachite Hall. Here, every
member of the Romanov family in the capital had gathered, the men in full dress
uniform, the grand duchesses, like their empress, clad in the white of summer. A
few minutes before three, General Vladimir Voyekov announced that everything
was in readiness. Footmen in scarlet and black livery opened the tall gilded doors,
and the emperor and the empress, preceded by the grand marshal of the imperial
court, began a slow, solemn procession through the immense building.

Their destination was the Nicholas Hall. Its tall windows had been thrown open and, along with a welcome, cooling breeze, the songs and cheers of the masses on the quay below carried to the five thousand guests crowded into the hall: ladies of the court, generals and army officers, representatives of all branches of the service, regimental commanders, governmental ministers, and the hierarchy of the Orthodox Church.[4]

"Faces were strained and grave," recalled Grand Duchess Marie Pavlovna. "Hands in long white gloves nervously crumpled handkerchiefs, and under the large hats . . . many eyes were red with crying. The men frowned thoughtfully, shifting from foot to foot, readjusting their swords, or running their fingers over the brilliant decorations pinned on their chests."[5] Grand Duchess Vladimir stood at the edge of the hall, her eyes awash with tears.[6]

When Nicholas and Alexandra appeared, the crowd erupted in an enormous cheer. The emperor, noted Princess Cantacuzené, "was paler than usual, and seemed somewhat startled, but not displeased. He advanced with the Empress still upon his arm, and continuing its mighty cheers, the crowd parted in front of them, forming an aisle from the altar to the immense double doors opposite."[7]

In the middle of the room, on a dais, stood an altar draped in a golden cloth; at its center stood the Miraculous Kazan Icon of the Mother of God, its seven-hundred-year-old paint looking fresh and strong. Ivan the Terrible's armies had taken it from Kazan in the fifteenth century when they captured the town, and it had become a powerful symbol of Russian unity. During the Time of Troubles, when the country was without a legitimate ruler and suffered at the hands of Polish invaders, it had been hidden by the faithful. When the Poles were defeated, it was brought back to Moscow in triumph. Peter the Great had taken it to his new capital of St. Petersburg to commemorate his victory over Charles XII of Sweden at the Battle of Narva, and Field Marshal Kutuzov, the great hero of the War of 1812, had knelt in its shadow before waging his attack against Napoleon.

As the metropolitan of St. Petersburg intoned the Te Deum, the congregation knelt on the parquet floor, with heads bowed as bishops in silver copes and stoles circled the altar, swinging their censers. The strong bass voices of the priests filled the hall with "the noble and pathetic chants of the Orthodox Liturgy," as Maurice Paleologue recorded. Nicholas, he observed, "prayed with a holy fervor that gave his pale face a movingly mystical expression." During the liturgy, Paleologue saw Alexandra "gazing fixedly, her chest thrust forward, held high, lips, crimson, eyes glassy. Every now and then she closed her eyes and then her livid face reminded one of a death mask."[8]

A deacon read the emperor's declaration of war; when he had finished, the crowd spontaneously erupted into the hymn "Lord, Save Thy People." As its thunderous strain rolled through the hall, Nicholas, overcome with emotion, bowed his head, tears streaming down his face. With eyes still moist, he ascended the dais, placing his hand upon a Bible. According to Paleologue, he seemed "even more grave and composed, as if he were about to receive the sacrament."[9] In a low voice, he declared, "I welcome you in these solemn and anxious days, through which all Russia is passing. Germany, followed by Austria, has declared War on Russia. The great wave of patriotism and loyalty to the Throne that has swept our native land is to me, and presumably also to you, a token that our great Mother Russia will carry on that War, sent us as a visitation by God, to its desired consummation. This unanimous impulse of love on the part of my people and their readiness to sacrifice everything, even life itself, gives me the necessary strength, calmly and steadfastly to anticipate the future. I am certain that each of you, at your respective posts, will help me to bear the trials which are sent to us, and that we all, beginning with myself, will do our duty to the end. Through you, the representatives of my dear Guards and St. Petersburg Garrison assembled here, I greet my entire Army, united as it is, in body and spirit, standing firm as a wall of granite, and I give it my blessing. I solemnly swear that I will never make peace so long as the enemy is on the soil of our Holy Motherland. Great is the God of the Russian Land."[10]

Nicholas II on the balcony of the Winter Palace, July 20, 1914

For ten minutes, the crowd applauded and cheered.[11] Grand Duchess Marie Pavlovna recalled the "almost sublime patriotism, the reality of which none could doubt. The feeling of national consecration, of national unity, was sincere."[12] The empress, unable to hide her tears, bowed her head as her husband received the thunderous ovation.

At the conclusion of the service, Nicholas and Alexandra began to make their way through the Winter Palace. "General Voyekov, the Commandant of the Palace, always quick to be officious, rushed forward to reinforce the Grand Master of Ceremonies and his aides," recorded one witness, "and he roughly pushed back men and women in their places, saying, 'Space must be left clear.' It was the Empress who gently stopped him; and it was she who seemed best to understand the movement towards her husband, and to welcome it. Voyekov returned to his position in the procession with the Imperial Household, and the Sovereigns continued down the room, the crowd gone wild with love for them. Old men and young, red in the face and hoarse from the effort, kept up the noise. They, and the women too, bowed low, or threw themselves upon their knees, as their Rulers passed. His Majesty, in absolute silence, showed no recognition of any special kind. Our beautiful Empress, looking like a Madonna of Sorrows, with tears on her cheeks, stretched her hand in passing to this or that person, now and then bending gracefully to embrace some woman who was kissing her hand. Her Majesty that day seemed to symbolize all the tragedy and suffering that had come upon us; and feeling it deeply, to give thanks to this group for the devotion their attitude implied. Her expression was of extraordinary sweetness and distress, and possessed beauty of a quality I had never seen before in the proud, classic face. Everyone was moved by Her Majesty's manner in a moment when she must be tortured by thoughts of her old home."[13]

The emperor and the empress moved slowly, to the southern side of the palace and to the balcony overlooking Palace Square. The French doors opened and they stepped onto the red-draped balcony, hung with the imperial coat of arms; below, beneath the sweltering afternoon sun, thousands of people had jammed the square. "A great silence seemed to hold us all in a tense suffocation," recalled Olga Voronoff. Nicholas, she remembered, "was terribly pale. At the sight of him, a tremendous cheer shook the air."[14] As Nicholas surveyed the scene, the crowd knelt, a rolling wave stretching the cobbled length from the palace to the curving arms of the General Staff Building amid "a tremendous acclamation."[15] Nicholas tried to speak, but the cheers and shouts from the crowd drowned him out. Overcome, Nicholas slowly made the sign of the cross over them and, hand in hand with Alexandra, bowed his head.[16]

Someone in the crowd below began to sing the national anthem; soon, the sea of humanity had joined in, their massed voices rising to the lone couple on the balcony:

God Save the Tsar!
Mighty and Powerful!
May He Reign for Our Glory,
Reign that Our Foes may quake!
O Orthodox Tsar!
God Save the Tsar!

Such unity of thought and purpose was unknown in imperial Russia. To Pale-ologue, watching the scene from a window in the palace, it seemed as if "the Emperor really was the autocrat appointed by God, the military, political, and religious leader of his people, the absolute sovereign of their bodies and souls."[17]

It was a moment of sublime, bittersweet triumph for Nicholas II, who had struggled against so much public and private agony, innumerable misfortunes, and crushing defeats. Yet it also signaled the beginning of the end for the Romanovs; in less than three years, the glittering, isolated Russian court crumbled in the fires of revolution, leaving only ghosts of its former brilliance to haunt the baroque palaces along the embankments of the sweeping Neva.

ACKNOWLEDGMENTS

When I began this book in 1990, I had little idea of the work involved in exploring so complex a subject, or of the permutations the text would take over the next fifteen years. Throughout, I have been sustained and encouraged by a number of friends and colleagues, who have offered suggestions, research, and valuable insight.

In these years, it has been my privilege to meet Romanov descendants and aristocratic émigrés, a few born in Russia before the Revolution. They have read this book and allowed me access to their memories and to certain unpublished letters and diaries that I have used to fill in this story. I have respected their wishes that these contributions remain largely unacknowledged, but all have my profound gratitude.

Those who have contributed to this book, answered questions, and provided important information over the years include David Adams, Dominic Albanese, Bob Atchison, Lisa Aubry, Zoia Belyakova, Christine Benagh, Lucia Bequaert, Dr. Thomas Berry, Daniel Briere, Katherine Caron-Greig, William Clarke, Lisa Davidson, Frances Dimond, Tamara Dubko, George Fedoroff, Professor Joseph Fuhrmann, Candace Gahring, Julia Gelardi, the late George Gibbes, Paul Gilbert, Coryne and Colin Hall, Robert Hall, Nils Hanson, Christine Harper, Gretchen and David Haskin, Kathy Hoefler, DeeAnn Hoff, Brien Horan, Pauline Holdrup, Douglas Huntzinger, the late Ingrid Kane, Pavel Kann, John Kendrick, Marlene Eilers Koenig, Peter Kurth, Steven Lavallee, Ian Lilburn, the late W. Bruce Lincoln, Prince and Princess M. Lobanov-Rostovsky, Dimitry Macedonsky, Thomas Mansfield, Christophe Martyn, Grant Menzies, Ilana Miller, Paul Minet, Rob Moshein, Annette Nason-Waters, Nicholas Nicholson, Pepsi Nunes, Steve O'Donnell, Robin Piguet, Raymond Piper, Linda Predovsky, Philip Proctor, Edvard Radzinsky, George Rome, Ivan Schubichev, Valerian Sokolov, the late Lady Sarah Spencer-Churchill, Marilyn Pfeifer Swezey, Monika Szabalowska-Koczuk, the late G. Nicholas Tantzos, Dr. Idris Traylor, Elena Tsvetkova, David Vernall-Downes, Katrina Warne, Janet Whitcomb, Allen Wilson, Barbara Wilson, Tom Wilson, Sue Woolmans, Marion Wynne, and Charlotte Zeepvat. There are many others—friendly curators, drivers, translators, and researchers in Russia—who worked miracles on my behalf, often at their own peril. To them all, both named and anonymous, I express my thanks for helping to craft this book.

Through most of the life of this book, I have had the good fortune to work for an outstanding company, Half Price Books, which has never been anything less than supportive of my endeavors. I owe my coworkers past and present an enormous debt for understanding the demands of my writing and my somewhat erratic schedule that frequently forced them to do my work: Jennifer Absher, Tim Brown, Dennis Demercer, Betsy Gaines, Nicole Germain, Joseph Gramer, Molly Harvey, Nikki Kent, Kristal Kimmich, Beth Kuffel, Jay Larson, Kris Layman, Cindy Masuda, Cynthia Melin, Kat Melin, Ashley Navone, Joey Owens, Judy Prince, Guy Tennis, Crystal Perrigoue, Virginia Smith, Amy Squire, Michelle and Corey Urbach, and Craig Windham. Special thanks go to Alyssa Gourley, Ken Hetland, and Dan Raley for their extra efforts on my behalf; to Justin Harder, for the inconvenience of having to live in the chaos of my library; to Mathew Kirshner, for his generosity when my old computer abandoned life; and to Anne Von Feldt and Trinh Kossey, for providing stability and encouragement at a time when things fell apart just as I was completing this book.

My friends have put up with my lack of communication and disappearance from their lives as I struggled to craft this book into its present form. Sharlene Aadland, Erna Bringe, Laura Enstone, Jacob Gariepy, Chuck and Eileen Knaus, Angela Manning, Ceceilia Manning, Mark Manning, Russ and Deb Minugh, Robin Olson, Anne Shawyer, and Debra Tate have my appreciation for never complaining. And a special thank you to Gavin Creel and Christopher Gorham, and to Scott Stine, whose collection of odd and obscure videos and DVDs of highly questionable taste kept me entertained throughout the long nights of work.

My agent in London, Dorie Simmonds, signed this work more than five years ago; throughout the long process of shaping it into a form suitable for publication, she has remained steadfast in her conviction and managed small miracles on my behalf. And Stephen S. Power, my editor at John Wiley & Sons, has shepherded the manuscript through numerous meetings, always believing in the project and providing astute direction through these last, crucial months.

As always, my parents, Roger and Helena King, have been understanding and nothing less than supportive of my work, through circumstances both good and bad.

A final word for some exceptional friends whose comments, criticism, and research have added immeasurably to this finished work. Margarita Nelipa read the manuscript at a furious speed, correcting numerous mistakes, and through her research helped provide the monumental list of members of the imperial court in the appendices. Antonio Perez Caballero offered copious advice, sharing his own expertise and his vast collection of unique materials. Janet Ashton gave freely of her time, sharing such a wide variety of obscure sources, as well as her thoughtful analyses, that this book could never have reached its final form without her incredible generosity. Penny Wilson, my friend and coauthor on *The Fate of the Romanovs*, was at work on this manuscript nearly a decade ago, translating materials, running down obscure information for my benefit, and assembling the illustrations contained within. And, finally, Susanne Meslans endured numerous clumsy drafts of the manuscript for fifteen years, always driving me onward with her forthright opinions and critical insight to create something memorable. It is a tribute to her efforts that it has finally come to fruition.

Appendix A

FAMILY TREE OF
NICHOLAS I

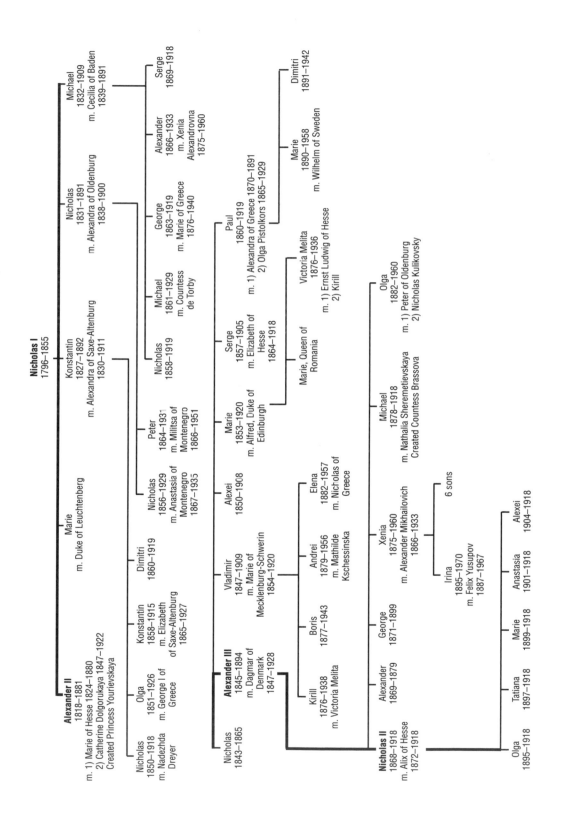

Nicholas I
1796–1855

Alexander II
1818–1881
m. 1) Marie of Hesse 1824–1880
2) Catherine Dolgorukaya 1847–1922
Created Princess Yourievskaya

Konstantin
1827–1892
m. Alexandra of Saxe-Altenburg
1830–1911

Nicholas
1831–1891
m. Alexandra of Oldenburg
1838–1900

Michael
1832–1909
m. Cecilia of Baden
1839–1891

Marie
m. Duke of Leuchtenberg

Serge
1869–1918

Nicholas
1850–1918
m. Nadezhda
Dreyer

Olga
1851–1926
m. George I of
Greece

Konstantin
1858–1915
m. Elizabeth
of Saxe-Altenburg
1865–1927

Dimitri
1860–1919

Nicholas
1856–1929
m. Anastasia of
Montenegro
1867–1935

Peter
1864–1931
m. Militsa of
Montenegro
1866–1951

Nicholas
1858–1919

Michael
1861–1929
m. Countess
de Torby

Alexander
1866–1933
m. Xenia
Alexandrovna
1875–1960

George
1863–1919
m. Marie of Greece
1876–1940

Paul
1860–1919

Dimitri
1891–1942

Marie
1890–1958
m. Wilhelm of Sweden

Nicholas
1843–1865

Alexander III
1845–1894
m. Dagmar of
Denmark
1847–1928

Vladimir
1847–1909
m. Marie of
Mecklenburg-Schwerin
1854–1920

Alexei
1850–1908

Marie
1853–1920
m. Alfred, Duke of
Edinburgh

Serge
1857–1905
m. Elizabeth of
Hesse
1864–1918

Paul
1860–1919
m. 1) Alexandra of Greece 1870–1891
2) Olga Pistolkors 1865–1929

Victoria Melita
1876–1936
m. 1) Ernst Ludwig of Hesse
2) Kirill

Marie, Queen of
Romania

Kirill
1876–1938
m. Victoria Melita

Boris
1877–1943

Andrei
1879–1956
m. Mathilde
Kschessinska

Elena
1882–1957
m. Nicholas of
Greece

Olga
1882–1960
m. 1) Peter of Oldenburg
2) Nicholas Kulikovsky

Nicholas II
1868–1918
m. Alix of Hesse
1872–1918

Alexander
1869–1879

George
1871–1899

Xenia
1875–1960
m. Alexander Mikhailovich
1866–1933

Michael
1878–1918
m. Nathalia Sheremetievskaya
Created Countess Brassova

Irina
1895–1970
m. Felix Yusupov
1887–1967

6 sons

Olga
1895–1918

Tatiana
1897–1918

Marie
1899–1918

Anastasia
1901–1918

Alexei
1904–1918

Appendix B

ORGANIZATION CHART OF THE RUSSIAN IMPERIAL COURT

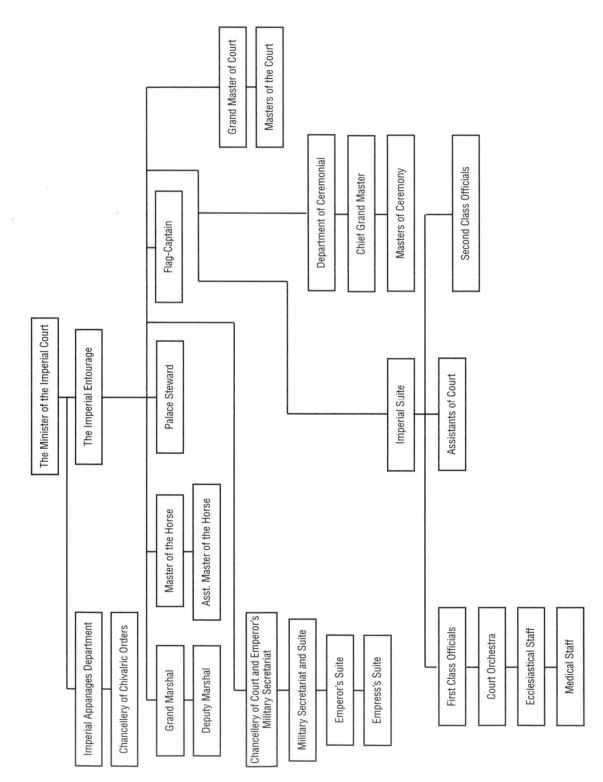

The Minister of the Imperial Court

The Imperial Entourage

Imperial Appanages Department

Chancellery of Chivalric Orders

Palace Steward

Flag-Captain

Grand Master of Court

Masters of the Court

Department of Ceremonial

Chief Grand Master

Masters of Ceremony

Second Class Officials

Master of the Horse

Asst. Master of the Horse

Grand Marshal

Deputy Marshal

Chancellery of Court and Emperor's Military Secretariat

Military Secretariat and Suite

Emperor's Suite

Empress's Suite

Imperial Suite

Assistants of Court

First Class Officials

Court Orchestra

Ecclesiastical Staff

Medical Staff

Appendix C

THE IMPERIAL COURT IN 1914

The following is the official list of members of the Russian imperial court. Although those who held office fluctuated throughout Nicholas II's reign, this list consists of the principals attached to the Imperial Suite, the Imperial Entourage, and the Emperor's Military Secretariat at the beginning of the First World War. Margarita Nelipa has my sincere gratitude for sharing her extensive research on the subject.

THE MINISTRY OF THE IMPERIAL COURT
(*Ministerstvo Imperatorskogo Dvora*)

Ministr Imperatorskogo Dvora (Minister of the Imperial Court): General-Adjutant Count Vladimir de Freedericksz

The Imperial Appanages Department
(*Imperatorskogo Glavnoe Upravlenie Udelov*)

Ministr Imperatorskogo Glavnoe Upravlenie Udelov (Minister of the Imperial Appanages Department): Count Vladimir de Freedericksz

Zaveduyushii Glavnogo Upravlenie Udelov (Head of the Imperial Appanages Department): General-Adjutant Prince Victor Kochubey

Sovereign and Regal Orders Chancellery
(*Kantselyariya Imperatorskih i Tsarskih Ordenov*)

Kantsler Ordenov (Chancellor): Count Vladimir de Freedericksz

Ober-tseremoniimeister Ordenov (Master of Ceremonies): C. M. Zlobin

THE IMPERIAL ENTOURAGE
(*Okrujenie Imperatora*)

Dvortsovii Komendant (Palace Commandant): Major-General Vladimir Voyekov

Komendant Alexandrovskogo Dvortsa (Commander of the Alexander Palace) and *Vremeno-zamestitel' Komendanta Voyekova* (Occasional Relief to Voyekov): Paul Groten

Zaveduyushii Gofmarshalskoe Otdeleniya (Chief of the Marshal's Department and Grand Marshal of the Imperial Court): General-Adjutant Count Paul von Benckendorff

Ober-Truchsess (Palace Steward): Alexander Bobrinsky

President of the Red Cross Society: Alexei Ilin

Grand Masters of the Court
(*Ober-gofmeistera Visochaishego Dvora*)

Ober-Gofmeister (Grand Master of the Court): Prince Nicholas Repnin

Pochetnii Sovetnik (Honorary Adviser): George Alexeyev

Pomoshnik Visochaishego Dvora (Assistant of the Court): Major-General Prince Dimitri Golitsyn

Gof-Meistera (Masters of the Court): Count Alexei Bobrinsky, Alexander Tanyeev, Baron Roman Rozen, Prince M. S. Volkonsky, Count A. S. de Broel-Plater, Peter Kaufmann-Tyrkestanskii

The Imperial Hunt
(*Imperatorskoi Ohoti*)

Ober-Egermeister (Master of the Imperial Hunt): Major-General Prince Dimitri Golitsyn

Egermeistera Visochaishego Dvora (Masters of the Imperial Hunt): Prince Efim Demidov, Prince Vladimir Volkonsky, Nicholas Dobrovolsky

Department of the Imperial Horse
(*Zaveduishii privdvornoi Konyushennoi Chast'yu*)

Ober-Shtalmeister (Chief Master of the Imperial Horse): General Artur von Grunwald

Shtalmeistera Visochaishego Dvora (Masters of the Horse): Lieutenant-General Prince Dimitri Golitsyn, Baron Feodor Meyendorff, Prince Konstantin Gorchakov, Count Paul Ignatiev, Arkadii Kelepovskii

Sovetnikii (Advisers): Alexander Rimsky-Korsakov, George Urusov

Shtalmeister i Verhoynii Zaveduyushii Sanitarnoi i Evakuatsonni Chasti (Stable Master and Supreme Head of the Sanitary and Evacuation Procedures Department): Count Vassili Gudovich

Pomoshnik Verhovnogo Nachal'nika Sanitarnoi i Evakuatsonni Chasti
(Assistant to the Supreme Head of Sanitary and Evacuation Procedures
Department): General-Adjutant Feodor Trepov

Predsedatel' Tsarskoselskoe Evakuatsonnoi Chasti (President of the
Evacuation Department): Major-General Serge Vilchkovskii

Chancellery of the Imperial Court
(*Kantselariya Imperatorskogo Dvora*)

Zaveduyushii Kantselyarii Ministerstva Imperatorskogo Dvora (Head of the
Court Chancellery): General-Lieutenant Alexander Mossolov

Zaveduyushii Ego Velichestva Kantselyarii-Pros'bi (Head of the Emperor's
Secretariat for Petitions): General-Lieutenant Alexander Mossolov

Glavno-upravlyushii Sobstvenoi Ego Velichestvo Kantselyarii (Chief Steward
to His Majesty's Chancellery): Alexander Tanyeev

Kantselyariya Tainogo Sovetnika po Delam Pridvornih Vedenii (Chancellery of
the Confidential Adviser for Matters under the Court's Authority): Prince
Alexander Golitsyn

*Kantselyariya Nachal'nika Glavnogo Shtaba pri Ego Imperatorskogo
Velichestvo* (Chancellery of the Chief of the Main Headquarters Attached
to His Imperial Majesty): Prince P. Volkonsky

The Ceremonial Department
(*Tseremonial'noye Otdelenie*)

Ober-tseremoniimeister (Grand Master of Ceremonies): Count Alexei
Ignatiev

Zaveduyushii Tseremonial'nogo Otdeleniya pri Dvore (Head of the
Ceremonial Department): Nicholas Evreinov

Ober-tseremoniimeister Visochaishego Dvora (Chief Grand Master of
Ceremonies): Baron Paul von Korff

Zamestitel Tseremoniimeister Visochaishego Dvora (Deputy Master of
Ceremonies): Serge Tanyeev

Tseremoniimeistera (Masters of Ceremonies): Prince Peter Kochubey,
Alexander Polovtsov, Nicholas Rudmann, and Edvard Volkov

Tsarskoye Selo Palace Department
(*Tsarskosel'skogo Dvortsovogo Upravlenie*)

Pomoshnik Nachal'nika Tsarskosel'skogo Dvortsovogo Upravleniya (Assistant
Chief): Serge Vilchkovskii

St. Petersburg Palace Department

Pomoshnik (Assistant): Major-General Edvard Zeime

Attached to His Imperial Majesty the Emperor
(*Pri Ego Imperatorskoe Velichestvo Imperator*)

Flag-Kapitan (Flag Captain): Admiral Konstantin Nilov

Attached to Her Imperial Majesty Dowager Empress Marie Feodorovna
(*Pri Ee Vdovstvuushei Imperatritse Marii Feodorovna*)

Ober-Gofmeister pri Dvora Vdovstvuushei Imperatritse (Grand Master of the Court): Prince Vladimir Bariatinsky

Gofmeistera pri Dvora Vdovstvuushei Imperatritse: Prince George Schervaschidze

Starshaya Dama Ober-Gofmeisterina pri Dvora Vdovstvuushei Imperatritse (Mistress of the Robes): Countess Elena Kochubey

Kamer-Freilini pri Dvora Vdovstvuushei Imperatritse (Ladies-in-Waiting): Countess Algaida Golenistchev-Koutouzova, Countess Marie Golenistchev-Koutouzova, and Countess Catherine Ozerova

Freilini pri Dvora Vdovstvuushei Imperatritse (Maids of Honor): Countess Marie von Benckendorff, Countess Olga Heyden, and Countess Zenaide Mengden

Major-General à la Suite: Prince Serge Dolgorukov

Attached to Her Imperial Majesty Empress Alexandra Feodorovna
(*Pri Ee Imperatorskogo Veluchestvo Aleksandra Feodorovna*)

Zaveduyushii Kanselyariei Tsaritse (Chief of Her Majesty's Chancellery): Count Ivan Rostovtsov

Pomoshnik zaveduyushego Kantselyariei (Assistant to the Head of Her Majesty's Chancellery): Boris Ordin

Ee Lichnii Sekretar' Tsaritse (Private Secretary to Her Majesty): Count Ivan Rostovtsov

Ober-Gofmeister (Grand Master of the Court): Count Peter Apraxin

General-Adjutant to Her Majesty: Baron Feodor Meyendorff

Dovorennoe Litzo Tsaritse (Spiritual Confidant to Her Majesty): Colonel Dimitri Loman

Sekretar' Upravleniya Bladotvositel'nimi Komitetami i Voennimi Gospitalyami (Secretary of the Department of Her Majesty's Charity and Military Hospitals): Count Peter Apraxin

Starshaya Dama Ober-Gofmeisterina Visochaishego Dvora (Mistress of the Robes and Chief Lady-in-Waiting): Princess Elizabeth Naryshkin-Kuryakin

Starshiye Dami pri Visochaishego Dvora (Ladies-in-Waiting of the Highest Rank): Princess Alexandra Kozena and Countess Emma de Freedericksz

Kamer-Freilini pri Visochaishego Dvora (Personal Ladies-in-Waiting): Baroness Sophie Buxhoeveden, Princess Sonia Orbeliani, and Countess Anastasia Hendrikova

Starshiye Freilini pri Visochaishego Dvora (Ladies-in-Waiting): Princess Marie Bariatinsky, Princess Olga Butzova, Princess Elizabeth Cantacuzené, Princess Elizabeth Kochubey, Princess Elizabeth Obolenskaya, Princess Olga Orlov, Princess Marie Vasilchikova, Countess Marie Karlova, Countess Zenaide Tolstoy, Countess Heyden, Countess Catherine Adlerberg, Countess Marie Lambsdorff, and Countess D. A. Bobrinskaya

Freilini (Maids of Honor): Princess Olga Bariatinsky, Mlle. A. Olenina, Mlle. Margarita Hitrovo, Countess Elizabeth Kelepovskaya, and Madame Anna Vyrubova

Gof-lektrisa Imperatritse (Court Lectrice to the Empress): Mlle. Catherine Schneider

Attached to the August Daughters of Their Imperial Majesties

(*Pri Avgusteishie Docheri Ego Imperatorskogo Velichestvo I Ee Imperatorskoe Velichestvo*)

Upravlyaushii Delami Tsarskih Detei (Steward in the Affairs of the Imperial Children): Count Ivan Rostovtsov

Freilina (Maid of Honor): Margarita Hitrovo

THE IMPERIAL SUITE ATTACHED TO THE MINISTRY OF THE COURT

(*Sviti Imperatora Nikolaya II pri Ministersve Dvora*)

First Class

Upravlyaushii Kabineta Nikolaya II (Head of Nicholas II's Cabinet): Prince Nicholas Obolensky

Upravlyaushii Pridvornogo Proizvodstvo i Imperatorskogo Ruchatel'stvo (Chief of Court Manufacturers and Imperial Warrants): N. N. Novosselsky

Zamestitel' Pridvornogo Proizvodstvo i Imperatorskogo Ruchatel'stvo (Deputy of Court Manufacturers and Imperial Warrants): Alexander Polovtsov

Ober-Kamerger (Grand Chamberlain): Count Konstantin Pahlen

Upravlyaushii Imperatorskoi Ohoti (Master of the Imperial Hunt): Prince Dimitri Golitsyn

Komandushuyii Imperatorskoi Glavnoi Kvartiroi (Commander of the Main Imperial Apartment): Nicholas Evreinov

Pomoshnik Komandushuyeshego Imperatorskoi Glavnoi Kvartiroi (Assistant to the Commander of the Main Imperial Apartment): Konstantin Maximovich

Upravlyaushii Imperatorskim Farforovim i Steklyannim Zavodom (Chief of the Imperial Porcelain and Glass Factory): Nicholas Strukov

Institutions Attached to the Court Administration for Culture
(*Uchrejdenie Pridvornogo Upravleniya Kulturi*)

Upravlyaushii Sobstvenoi Ego Imperatorskogo Bibliotekoi (Head of His Majesty's Personal Libraries): Vassili Scheglov

Upravlyaushii Imperatorskogo Akademiya Khudozhestv (Head of the Imperial Academy of Fine Arts): Grand Duchess Marie Pavlovna

Upravlyaushii Arkeologichicheskogo Otdelenniya (President of the Archaeological Commission): Count Alexei Bobrinsky

Upravlyaushii Imperatorskogo Emitajha (Head of the Imperial Hermitage Museum): Count Dimitri Golitsyn

Upravlyaushii Imperatorskogo Teatra (Head of the Imperial Theaters): Vladimir Teliakovsky

Upravlyaushii Russkogo Muzeya Imperatora Aleksandra III (Head of the Alexander III Museum of Russian Art): Grand Duke George Mikhailovich

Orchestra and Choir Attached to the Imperial Court
(*Pridvornii Orkestr i Pevcheskaya Kapella*)

Zaveduyushii Pridvornogo Orkestra i Kapella, Direjer Orkestra i Kompositor (Chief of the Court Orchestra and Choir, Conductor and Composer): Major-General Alexander Sheremetiev

Adjutant: N. Sokolov

Tseremoniimeister Pridvornogo Orkestra (Director of the Court Orchestra): Baron Nicholas Stackelberg

The Ecclesiastical Staff Attached to the Imperial Court
(*Pridvornaya Duhovenstvo*)

Sovetnik Imperatorskogo Dvortsa (Adviser to the Imperial Court): Proto-Presbyter Father Ioann Yanishev

Duhovnik Tsarskoi Semyi (Personal Confessor to the Imperial Family): Proto-Presbyter Father Petrovich

Lichnii Duhovnik Ego Imperatorskogo Velichestvo (Personal Confessor to His Imperial Majesty): Proto-Presbyter Father Alexander Vassiliev

Staff: Proto-Presbyter Afanasy Belyaev

Starosta Fedorovskogo Sobora (Warden of the Feodorovsky Cathedral at Tsarskoye Selo): Colonel Dimitri Loman

Medical Service Attached to the Imperial Court
(*Pridvornaya Meditsinskaya Chast'*)

Ober-Leib-Medik (Head Physician-in-Ordinary to His Majesty the Emperor): Professor Eugene Botkin

Physicians to the Imperial Court and the Military Household

Pochetnii leib-hirurg (Honorary Surgeon-in-Ordinary): Vladimir Derevenko

Leib-hirurgi (Surgeons-in-Ordinary): Professor Serge Federov, Professor Nicholas Veliaminov, Professor Eugene Pavlov, and Professor George Rein

Pochetnii leib-medik (Honorary Physician-in-Ordinary): Serge Ostrogorskii

Leib-akushera (Obstetricians-in-Ordinary): Professor Dimitri Ott and N. Fenomenov

Leib-Mediki (Physicians-in-Ordinary): Nicholas Simonovskii and L. Bellyarminov

Leib-pediatri (Pediatricians-in-Ordinary): N. Bistrov and Karl Rachfus

Assistants of the Imperial Court
(*Pomoshniki Imperatorskogo Dvora*)

Pochetnii Sovetnik (Honorary Adviser): Paul Golenistschev-Koutuzov-Tolstoy

Glavnii Pomoshnik (Chief Assistant of the Court): Lieutenant-General Prince Dimitri Golitsyn

Pomoshnik (Assistant): Nicholas Balashev, Count Serge Sheremetiev, and Ivan Balashev

Chief of the Separate Corps of Gendarmes Attached to Court Security
(*Nachal'nik Otdel'nogo Korpusa Jandarmov Dvortsovoi Ohrani*)

Major-General Alexander Spiridovich

The Military Secretariat and Suite Attached to His Imperial Majesty

(Voyennaya Kantselyariya i Sviti pri Ego Imperatorskogo Velichestvo)

Upravlyaushii Voenno-pohodnoi Kantselyariyei (Chief of the Emperor's Military Chancellery): Count Vladimir de Freedericksz

Upravlyaushii Voenno-pohodnoi Kantselyariyei (Chief of the Military Field Chancellery): General Prince Vladimir Orlov

Shtab-ofitser prikomandirovannii k Imperatorskoi glavnoi kvartire (Headquarter Officer and Major-General Attached to Special Military Household Missions): *Fligel-Adjutant* Captain Alexander Drenteln

Dezhurnyi General (General on Constant Duty): Major-General Alexei Ressin

Komandir Dvora i Zaveduyushii Politsii Dvora (Commander of the Palace and Head of the Court Police): Major-General Vladimir Voyekov

General-Adjutant to His Majesty the Emperor of Germany, King of Prussia: Count Ilya Tatischev

Major-Generals à la Suite Attached to His Imperial Majesty

Grand Duke Andrei Vladimirovich

Grand Duke Boris Vladimirovich

Grand Duke Nicholas Mikhailovich

Prince Anatole Bariatinsky

Prince Alexander Bagration-Mukhransky

Prince Vassili Dolgoruky

Prince Dimitri Golitsyn

Prince Victor Kochubey

Prince Nicholas Obolensky

Prince Ivan Obolensky

Prince Alexei Orlov

Prince George Romanovsky, Duke of Leuchtenberg

Prince Yuri Trubetskoy

Count Alexander Adrianov

Count Nicholas Fersen

Count Alexander von Grabbe

Count Michael von Grabbe

Count George Mengden

Count Alexander Sheremetiev

Count Dimitri Miliutin

Baron Nicholas Budberg

Baron Lev Girard-de-Soucanton

Vladimir Dzhunkovsky

Nicholas Dobrovolsky

Eugene Arseniev

Vladimir Bakulin

Afrikan Bogoaevskii

Eugene Bernov

Dimitri Dashkov

Vladimir Dragomirov

Daniel Dratchevsky

Alexander Drenteln

Arsene Goulevich

Nicholas Kisselevsky

Dimitri Knyajevich

Nicholas Komstadius

Ilya Kulnev

Michael Maslov

Serge Mezentzov

Alexander Nikolayev

Alexei Resin

Peter Orlov

Alexei Rodionov

Vadim Schebeko

Paul Skoropadsky

George Shevitz

Boris Petrovo-Solovovo

Nicholas Schipov

Eugene Volkov

Khan Housseine-Nahitchevansky

General-Adjutants Attached to His Imperial Majesty

Generals of the Artillery

Grand Duke Serge Mikhailovich

Michael Belyaev

Nicholas Ivanov

Paul Mistchenko

Generals of the Cavalry

Grand Duke Nicholas Nikolaievich

Grand Duke Dimitri Konstantinovich

Grand Duke Paul Alexandrovich

Prince Felix Yusupov, Count Sumarakov-Elston

Prince Michael Golitsyn

Prince Serge Vasiltchikov

Count Vladimir de Freedericksz

Count Hilarion Vorontzov-Dashkov

Baron Feodor Meyendorff

His Highness Prince Said-Abdul-Akhad-Khan, Emir of Bokhara

Konstantin Maximovich

Konstantin Arapov

Peter Baranov

George Skalon

Alexander Kozlov

Alexander Strukov

Captains of the Cavalry

Prince Gabriel Konstantinovich

Prince Alexander Romanovsky von Leuchtenberg

Prince George Eristov

Count Alexander Vorontzov-Dashkov

Count Feodor Nieroth

Peter Daragan

Paul Lavrinovsky

Alexander Linevich

Alexander Mandrika

Boris Micheyev

Nicholas Petrovsky

Michael Skalon

Lev Stefanovich

Vladimir Svetchin

Konstantin Zelenoy

Generals of the Infantry

Grand Duke Konstantin Konstantinovich

Prince Vladimir Bariatinsky

Prince Nicholas Dolgorukov

Prince Paul Engalytchev

Prince Alexander Oldenburg

Count Ilya Tatischev

Count Ivan Tatischev

Baron Lev de Freedericksz

Alexei Kuropatkin

Peter Durnovo

Alexander Panteleyev

Michael Alexeiev

Ivan Fonlon

Oscar-Ferdinand Grippenberg

Feodor Trepov

Nicholas Zarubayev

Naval Suite Attached to His Imperial Majesty

Nachal'nik Morskih Sil i Nachal'nik Baltiiskogo Flota (Chief of the Naval Power and Chief of the Baltic Fleet): Admiral Nicholas von Essen

Nachal'nik Nikolaevskogo Morskogo Akademii i Morskogo Uchilisha (Chief of the Nikolaievsky Naval Academy and College): Admiral Dimitri Arseniev

Glavnii Morskogo Shtaba (Chief of Staff): Vice-Admiral Count Alexander Heyden

Admirals

Moskoi Ministr (Naval Minister): Ivan Grigororovich

Grand Duke Kirill Vladimirovich

Grand Duke Alexander Mikhailovich

Baron Nicholas von Schilling

Eugene Alexeiev

Ivan Dikov

Feodor Dubassov

Konstantin Nilov

Nicholas Tchihatchov

Feodor Avelan

Rear-Admirals

Michael Veselskin

Komandir Yahti "Polyarnaya Zvezda" (Commander of the Imperial Yacht
   Polar Star): Prince Nicholas Viasemsky

Komandir Yahti "Standart" (Commander of the Imperial Yacht *Standart*):
   Rostislav Zelenetsky

Starshii Ofitser Imperatorskoi Yahti "Standart" (Senior Officer on the
   Imperial Yacht *Standart*): Nicholas Sablin

Nicholas Volkov

Semyon Fabritzky

Rear-Admiral Vladimir Litvinov

Rear-Admiral Count Nicholas Tolstoy

Lieutenant-Generals Attached to His Imperial Majesty

Grand Duke Michael Alexandrovich

Grand Duke Peter Nikolaievich

Grand Duke George Mikhailovich

Prince Serge Beloselsky-Belozersky

Prince Vladimir Orlov

Prince Peter Sviatopolk-Mirsky

Count Paul von Benckendorff

Count Feodor Keller

Vladimir Danilov

Vladimir Dedulin

Artur von Grunwald

Nicholas Kleigels

Vladimir Komarov

Konstantin Nilov

Alexander Pavlov

Alexander Poretzky
Nicholas Prescott
Paul Schipov
Ilya Tatischev
Dimitri Tatischev

Fligel-Adjutants Attached to His Imperial Majesty

Prince Vladimir Obolensky
Prince Peter Oldenburg
Prince Kirill Naryshkin
Prince Ivan Saltykov
Count Dimitri Sheremetiev
Count Andrei Shuvalov
Turia-Djane Said-Mir-Alim, Heir to the Emir of Bokhara
Peter Arapov
Alexander Drozd-Boniatchevsky
Vassili Gavrilov
Konstantin Holthoer
Vladimir Jitkevich
Eugene Kazakevich
George Ketkhudayev
Anatoli Mordvinov
Andrei Polovtsov
Paul Schipov
Peter Sivitzky
Vladimir Souhich
Maximilian Tzwetzinsky
Vadim Schebeko
Camille Boysmann

Staff Rotmeister Attached to His Imperial Majesty

Prince Ioann Konstantinovich

Lieutenants Attached to His Imperial Majesty

George Andeyev
Nicholas Demidov
Vladimir Verevkin[1]

Appendix D

PALACE FLOOR PLANS

The Winter Palace, first floor plan

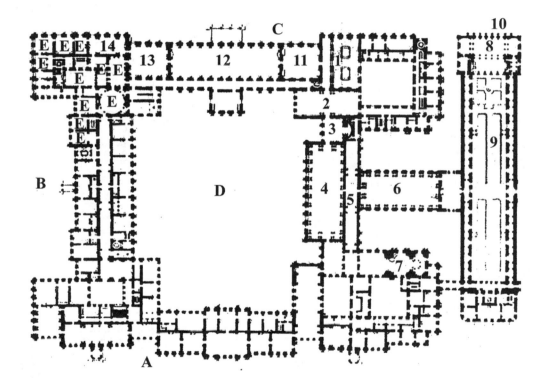

A. Palace Square
B. Private garden
C. Neva Embankment
D. Quadrangle
E. Nicholas and Alexandra's private apartments
1. Jordan Staircase
2. Field Marshal's Hall
3. Small Throne Room
4. Hall of Armorial Bearings

5. 1812 Gallery
6. St. George's Hall
7. Cathedral
8. Pavilion Hall
9. Hanging Garden
10. To the Hermitage
11. Anteroom
12. Nicholas Hall
13. Concert Hall
14. Malachite Hall

Plan of the private apartments in the Winter Palace

1. Nicholas Hall
2. Concert Hall
3. Malachite Hall
4. Blackamoor Hall
5. White Dining Room
6. Empire Drawing Room
7. Silver Drawing Room
8. Alexandra's private drawing room
9. Nicholas and Alexandra's bedroom
10. Alexandra's boudoir
11. Nicholas II's study
12. Alexandra's dressing room and bathroom
13. Nicholas II's dressing room and bathroom
14. Inner courtyard
15. Rotunda
16. Private chapel
17. Nicholas II's Gothic Library
18. Billiard room
19. Nicholas II's reception room
20. Saltykov Staircase
21. Dark Corridor

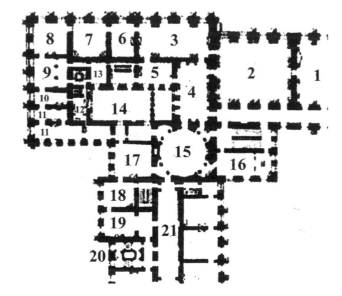

Plan of the Alexander Palace

A. East wing
   (private apartments)
B. Corinthian colonnade
C. West wing
D. Entrance to Alexander Park
1. Private apartments
2. Courtyard
3. Great Library
4. Imperial Anteroom
5. Portrait Hall
6. Semi-Circular Hall
7. Marble Hall
8. Chapel

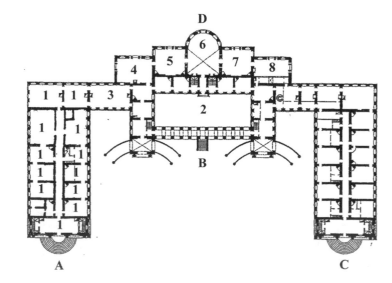

Plan of Nicholas and Alexandra's private apartments in the Alexander Palace

1. Imperial entrance
2. Vestibule
3. Waiting room
4. Nicholas II's study
5. Nicholas II's bathroom
6. Bathtub
7. Nicholas II's dressing room
8. Room for adjutant
9. Formal Study
10. Small Library
11. Corner Salon
12. Empress Alexandra's balcony
13. Maple Drawing Room
14. Rosewood Drawing Room
15. Mauve Boudoir
16. Nicholas and Alexandra's bedroom
17. Alexandra's dressing room
18. Alexandra's bathroom
19. Room for maid
20. Passage
21. Corridor
22. Elevator

Grand Kremlin Palace, first floor plan

1. Parade Staircase
2. State Vestibule
3. Hall of St. Vladimir
4. Holy Vestibule
5. Palace of Facets
6. Red Staircase
7. Hall of St. George
8. Hall of St. Alexander Nevsky
9. Hall of St. Andrei
10. Chevalier Guards' Room
11. Hall of St. Catherine
12. State Drawing Room
13. State Bedchamber
14. Walnut Dressing Room

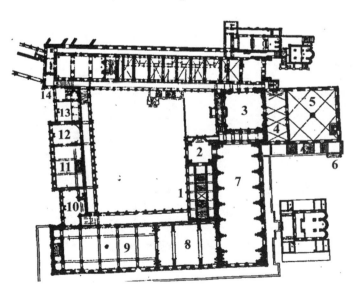

Appendix E

MAPS OF THE IMPERIAL ESTATES

Plan of the Imperial Park at Tsarskoye Selo

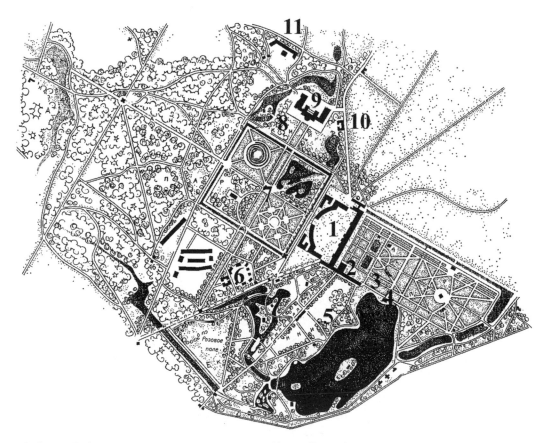

1. Catherine Palace
2. Agate Pavilion
3. Cameron Gallery
4. Lower Bathhouse
5. Great Lake
6. Chinese Village
7. Alexander Park
8. Children's Lake
9. Alexander Palace
10. Alexander Palace Kitchen
11. Feodorovsky Sobor and Gorodok

Plan of the Imperial Park at Peterhof

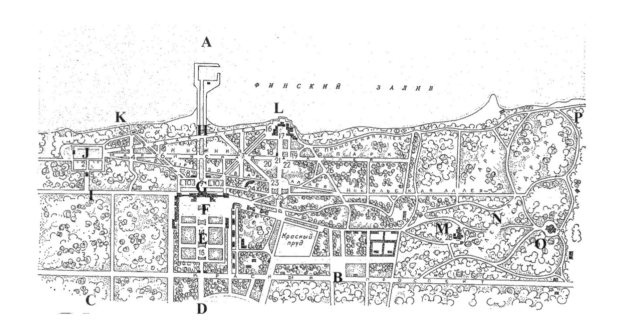

A. Gulf of Finland
B. Volkonsky High Road
C. To the English Park and Palace
D. To the Meadow and Colonists' Parks
E. Upper Park
F. Grand Palace
G. Grand Cascade
H. Canal

I. Golden Hill
J. Marly Gardens and Palace
K. Hermitage
L. Mon Plaisir Palace and Garden
M. Farmhouse Palace
N. Gothic chapel
O. Cottage Palace
P. Site of the Lower Palace

Appendix F

MAP OF ST. PETERSBURG

St. Petersburg, nineteenth century

(overleaf)

1. Winter Palace
2. Palace Square
3. Admiralty
4. Senate Square
5. St. Isaac's Cathedral
6. The Imperial Senate and the Holy Synod
7. Former Nikolaievich Palace
8. The English Embankment
9. Yusupov Palace
10. Palace of Xenia Alexandrovna and Alexander Mikhailovich
11. Mariinsky Theater
13. New Mikhailovsky Palace
14. Palace of Grand Duke Vladimir
15. Marble Palace
16. Champs de Mars
17. Mikhailovsky Castle
18. Summer Garden
19. Tauride Palace, home of the Duma
20. Smolny Institute
21. Fortress of St. Peter and St. Paul
22. The Exchange and the Strelka
23. Palace of Olga Alexandrovna and Prince Peter of Oldenburg
24. Mikhailovsky Palace (the Alexander III Museum of Russian Art)
25. Kazan Cathedral
26. Imperial Mews
27. Theater Street
28. Anichkov Palace
29. Sergeievsky Palace
30. Rasputin's apartment
31. Church on the Spilt Blood
32. Michael Alexandrovich's Palace
33. Paul Alexandrovich's Palace
34. Kschessinska's House
35. Fabergé
36. Gostiny Dvor
37. Alexander Nevsky Monastery

NOTES

Material utilized in this book is drawn from both published and unpublished archival sources. Archival abbreviations used within the Source Notes are listed here.

GARF — Gosudarstvennyi Arkhiv Rossiiskii Federatsii (State Archives of the Russian Federation), Moscow

RGB — Rossiiskii Gosudarstvennyi Biblioteka (Russian State Library), St. Petersburg

RGIA — Rossiiskii Gosudarstvennyi Istoricheskii Arkhiv (Russian State Historical Archives), St. Petersburg

BL — British Library, Department of Manuscripts

Complete citation details can be found within the individual source notes.

INTRODUCTION
1. Prince Christopher of Greece, 50.
2. Paleologue, 1:106.
3. Ibid., 1:65.
4. Wortman, 1:25.
5. See ibid., 1:334, for details.
6. Ibid., 2:118.
7. Buxhoeveden, *Before*, 317.
8. Kleinmichel, 111.
9. Poliakoff, *Mother Dear*, 141.
10. Lowe, 183.

PROLOGUE: ST. PETERSBURG
1. George and George, 30.
2. Gautier, 143.
3. Almedingen, *Tomorrow*, 10.
4. Alexander Mikhailovich, *Once*, 244.
5. Hickley, 4.
6. MacCallum Scott, 235–36.
7. Buchanan, *Dissolution*, 5.
8. *Intimacies*, 124–26.
9. Gautier, 105.
10. Gogol, 3.
11. MacCallum Scott, 229.
12. Gogol, 4.
13. Ibid., 4–5.
14. Gautier, 118.
15. Ibid., 124–25.
16. Ibid., 128.
17. Lincoln, *Between Heaven and Hell*, 110.
18. Vasilevskaya, 89; Humphreys and Richardson, 58; Syknovalov, 142; Zinovieff and Hughes, 195.
19. Vasilevskaya, 80.
20. Shvidkovsky, *St. Petersburg*, 156; Ovsyannikov, 542–44.
21. Vasilevskaya, 66–67; Ovsyannikov, 462–67; Ivanova, 4–6.
22. Brumfield, 298; Prince Michael of Greece, *Imperial Palaces*, 127–28; Kennett and Kennett, 90–92; see also Ivanova, 6–7, for further details.
23. Vasilevskaya, 63.
24. Steveni, 102–4.
25. Gautier, 114–15.
26. Steveni, 164.
27. Steveni, 164; MacCallum Scott, 254.
28. Vasilevskaya, 73.
29. Steveni, 164.
30. Vasilevskaya, 20.
31. Shvidkovsky, *St. Petersburg*, 18, 34; Ovsyannikov, 24–26.
32. Ovsyannikov, 105–8.
33. Shvidkovsky, *St. Petersburg*, 36; Gendrikov and Senko, 13.
34. Vasilevskaya, 286: Gendrikov and Senko, 27.
35. Vasilevskaya, 16–17; Mawdsley, 237; Ovsyannikov, 504–5.
36. Vasilevskaya, 17; Ovsyannikov, 493–97.
37. Zinovieff and Hughes, 111; Ovsyannikov, 501–2.
38. Vasilevskaya, 246.
39. Humphreys and Richardson, 117.
40. Vasilevskaya, 256.
41. Ibid., 32.
42. Ibid., 28.

43. Belyakova, *Romanov Legacy*, 140–56; Vasilevskaya, 131–32; Kann, *Ploshad Tryda*, 51–58.
44. Mawdsley, 285.
45. Belkovskaia, 2–4.
46. Prince Michael of Greece, *Imperial Palaces*, 113; Brumfield, 288–89.
47. Kennett, 87–88; Brumfield, 287–89; see also Kalnutskaia, *Mikhailovskii Zamok*, and Kalnutskaia and Frantsizov, *Mikhailovskii Zamok*.
48. Vasilevskaya, 115; Shvidkovsky, *St. Petersburg*, 39; Floryan, 18–23; Ovsyannikov, 72–75.
49. Ignatiev, 95.
50. de Robien, 120.
51. Talbot Rice, 25.
52. Izwolsky, *No Time*, 30.
53. Gautier, 156.
54. Marie Pavlovna, 38.
55. Kohl, 13.
56. de Basily, 32.
57. Buchanan, *Dissolution*, 28.
58. Izwolsky, *No Time*, 53.
59. Buchanan, *Dissolution*, 39.
60. Ovsyannikov, 278–86.
61. Ridge, 57.

CHAPTER 1: THE LAST TSAR
1. Alexander Mikhailovich, *Once*, 168–69.
2. Mossolov, 6.
3. Surguchev, 26.
4. Information to author from Pepsi Nunes.
5. Witte, 359.
6. Flourens, 77–78.
7. Lobanov-Rostovsky, 163.
8. Nicholas II, Diary, May 2, 1890, in GARF, F. 601, Op. 1, D. 224.
9. Buxhoeveden, *Before*, 156.
10. Lathrop, 67.
11. Private information to author.
12. Witte, 125.
13. Private information to author.
14. Tsesarevich Nicholas, Diary, December 21, 1891, in GARF, F. 601, Op. 1, D. 227.
15. Davis, *Ambassadorial*, 56.
16. Princess Alix of Hesse und Bei Rhein to Grand Duchess Xenia Alexandrovna, November 8, 1893, in Maylunas and Mironenko, 32.
17. Naryshkin-Kuryakin, 140.
18. Prince Christopher of Greece, 55.
19. Buxhoeveden, *Before*, 156.
20. Kussner Coudert, 846–47.
21. Souiny, 106–7.
22. Queen Marie of Romania, 1:573.
23. Vyrubova, 4.
24. Bariatinsky, 66.
25. Quoted in Cockfield, 173.
26. Botkin, 27.
27. Gilliard, 73.
28. Buxhoeveden, *Life*, 153.

29. Vyrubova, 78.
30. Dehn, 76.
31. Vyrubova, 79.
32. Gilliard, 75.
33. Vyrubova, 79; Voronoff, 53.
34. Gilliard, 76.
35. Voronoff, 52.
36. Dehn, 78; Gilliard, 75; Vyrubova, 78.
37. Mossolov, 64.
38. Eager, 40; Gilliard, 75.
39. Voronoff, 52.
40. Chavchavadze, *Crowns*, 57.
41. Botkine, *Au Temps*, 81.
42. Grabbe and Grabbe, 69.
43. Vorres, 112.
44. Vyrubova, 79.
45. Private information to author.
46. Mossolov, 247.
47. Gilliard, 40.
48. A. A. Mordvinov, in Barkovets and Tenikhina, *Nicholas II*, 106.
49. Gibbes, deposition given to Nicholas Sokolov, July 1, 1919, in Nicholas Sokolov, Unpublished Dossiers, vol. 5, doc. 31.
50. Grand Duke Konstantin Konstantinovich, Diary, March 30, 1912, in GARF, F. 660, Op. 2, D. 53.
51. Grabbe and Grabbe, 49.
52. Lambsdorff, *1894–1896*, 74.
53. Grand Duke Konstantin Konstantinovich, Diary, December 7, 1894, in GARF, F. 660, Op. 1, D. 41.
54. Benckendorff, 113–14.
55. Grabbe and Grabbe, 21.
56. Witte, 329.
57. de Grunwald, 46–49.
58. Mossolov, 10–11.
59. Alexander Mikhailovich, *Once*, 178–79.
60. Odom, 20–21.
61. Wortman, 2:341.
62. Hoare, 347.
63. Paleologue, 1:176.
64. Oldenburg, 2:306; *Krasni Arkhiv*, 1925, vol. XII, 440.
65. Lincoln, *Romanovs*, 662.
66. Elchaninov, 129; Elbogen, 398–99.
67. Florinsky, 17–18.
68. See Wortman, vol. 2, chap. 15, for further discussion.
69. Grabbe and Grabbe, 34.
70. Mossolov, 119.
71. See Wortman, 2:13 and 2:333, for further discussion.
72. See Wortman, 2:326, for further discussion.
73. Elchaninov, 3.
74. Ibid., 17.
75. Ibid., 51.

CHAPTER 2: THE IMPERIAL FAMILY
1. Chavchavadze, *Grand Dukes*, 93.
2. Bolitho, 29.
3. Hall, 21.
4. Vorres, 21.

5. Aronson, 26.
6. *Marie Feodorovna*, 82–86.
7. Hall, 46.
8. Polovtsov, 139.
9. Vorres, 26.
10. *Intimacies*, 155.
11. Polovtsov, 210.
12. Vassili, 214.
13. Vorres, 40.
14. George, *Romanov Diary*, 81.
15. Buchanan, *Victorian Gallery*, 160.
16. Prince Christopher of Greece, 37.
17. Buchanan, *Victorian Gallery*, 170; *Intimacies*, 155.
18. Gurko, 127.
19. Prince Christopher of Greece, 56.
20. Fabergé, Proler, and Skurlov, 41.
21. Vorres, 82.
22. Prince Christopher of Greece, 56.
23. Vassili, 232.
24. Buxhoeveden, *Before*, 265.
25. Ernst Ludwig, 68–69.
26. Private information to author.
27. Souiny, 93.
28. Shelking, 211.
29. Paleologue, 2:65.
30. Baylen, 37.
31. Bing, 158.
32. Kennett, 72–73; see also Demicheva and Akselrod; and Bylankova for further details.
33. de Robien, 188.
34. Hall, 218.
35. Ibid., 174.
36. Ular, 244, 257–58; Cantacuzené, *Revolutionary Days*, 132; Gibbon, 609–12.
37. Quoted in Kudrina, 156.
38. Yusupov, 158.
39. *Russian Court Memoirs*, 177.
40. *Russian Court Memoirs*, 113; Chavchavadze, *Grand Dukes*, 190.
41. Vorres, 59.
42. Tsesarevich Nicholas to Grand Duke George Alexandrovich, May 9, 1895, in Maylunas and Mironenko, 73.
43. Grand Duke George Alexandrovich to Tsesarevich Nicholas, June 9, 1894, in Maylunas and Mironenko, 73.
44. Lehr, 222.
45. Bogdanovich, 465.
46. Private information to author.
47. Polovtsov, Diary, July 29, 1901, in GARF, F. 583, Op. 1, D. 54.
48. Marie Pavlovna, 52.
49. *Russian Court Memoirs*, 81.
50. Polovtsov, Diary, July 29, 1901, in GARF, F. 583, Op. 1, D. 54.
51. Vorres, 86.
52. Bing, 148.
53. Ibid., 148.
54. Vorres, 86–87.
55. Ibid., 87.

56. Ibid., 94.
57. Ibid., 87.
58. Ridge, 100–1.
59. Phenix, 45.
60. Paoli, 118–19.
61. Ibid., 119.
62. Hall, 176; *The New York Times*, August 12, 1899; Vassili, 309; and private information to the author.
63. Grand Duke George Alexandrovich to Nicholas II, June 15, 1899, in Maylunas and Mironenko, 185.
64. Grand Duchess Xenia Alexandrovna, Diary, July 14, 1899, in Maylunas and Mironenko, 188–89.
65. Majolier, 89.
66. Mossolov, 95.
67. Nikitine, 220.
68. Abrikossow, 232–33.
69. Lyons, N-80.
70. Bruce Lockhart, 160.
71. Nicholas II to Dowager Empress Marie Feodorovna, July 25, 1907, in Bing, 213–14.
72. Dowager Empress Marie Feodorovna to Nicholas II, October 23, 1907, in Bing, 230–31.
73. Abrikossow, 231, 236.
74. Grebalskii, 172–73.
75. Dowager Empress Marie Feodorovna to Nicholas II, November 4, 1912, in Maylunas and Mironenko, 283.
76. Nicholas II to Dowager Empress Marie Feodorovna, November 21, 1912, in Maylunas and Mironenko, 363.
77. Abrikossow, 234–35.
78. Ibid., 235.
79. Paleologue, 2:172.
80. Private information to author.

Chapter 3: A Rival Court

1. Buchanan, *Victorian Gallery*, 55.
2. Ponsonby, 92.
3. Balsan, 123.
4. Romanovsky-Krassinsky, 33.
5. Alexander Mikhailovich, *Once*, 137.
6. Vassili, 122.
7. Brayley-Hodgetts, 2:149.
8. Souiny, 148.
9. Bogdanovich, 81; Ignatiev, 78; Brayley-Hodgetts, 2:227.
10. Lambsdorff, *1886–1890*, 203–4; Brayley-Hodgetts, 2:230–31; Chavchavadze, *Grand Dukes*, 180; Souiny, 148–49.
11. Vorres, 59.
12. Private information to author.
13. Waddington, 62.
14. Queen Marie of Romania, 1:98.
15. George, *Romanov Diary*, 43.
16. Buchanan, *Mission*, 1:175–76.
17. Lehr, 223.
18. Paleologue, 2:138.
19. Polovtsov, 1:170.
20. Vassili, 164–65.
21. Vorres, 95.
22. Bogdanovich, 81.

23. Letter of Queen Marie of Romania, 1909, in private collection.
24. Dowager Empress Marie Feodorovna to Nicholas II, August 8, 1895, in Bing, 96–97.
25. Nicholas II to Grand Duke Vladimir Alexandrovich, January 29, 1897, in GARF, F. 652, Op. I, D. 619.
26. "Czar's Rage Is Astir and It Falls upon the Royal Head of an Erring Aunt," in *The San Francisco Chronicle*, September 4, 1900.
27. Nicholas II to Grand Duke Vladimir Alexandrovich, November 26, 1896, in GARF, F. 652, Op. I, D. 619.
28. Vassili, 386.
29. Letter of Grand Duke Nicholas Mikhailovich, in RGB, Department of Manuscripts, F. 585, Op. 1, D. 582.
30. Buchanan, *Dissolution*, 47.
31. Vasilevskaya, 104; Velichenko and Miroliubova, 44–47.
32. Belyakova, *Romanov Legacy*, 172–73.
33. *Intimacies*, 160.
34. Ular, 84.
35. Ibid., 84–88.
36. Kleinmichel, 201.
37. Mossolov, 79.
38. Yusupov, 83.
39. Buxhoeveden, *Before*, 217.
40. Vickers, 69.
41. Grand Duke Konstantin Konstantinovich, Diary, May 24, 1900, in GARF, F. 660, Op. 1, D. 47.
42. Ibid., June 19, 1902, in GARF, F. 660, Op. 1, D. 49.
43. Queen Marie of Romania, 1:338.
44. Athlone, 139; private information.
45. Cited in Perry and Pleshakov, 126.
46. Ibid., 70.
47. Bogdanovich, 446.
48. Lastochkin and Rybejanskii, 123–26.
49. Abrikossow, 235.
50. Prince Christopher of Greece, 71–72.
51. Vyrubova, 86.
52. Steinberg and Krustalev, 380; Lyons, N-37.
53. Bobrov and Kirikov, 34–37.
54. Nijinska, 46–47.
55. Chavchavadze, *Grand Dukes*, 216.
56. Teliakovsky, 242.
57. Kirill Vladimirovich, 168–69.
58. Elsberry, 62; private information to author.
59. Chavchavadze, *Grand Dukes*, 226.
60. In Maylunas and Mironenko, 228.
61. Kirill Vladimirovich, 99.
62. Ibid., 163–84.
63. Van der Kiste, 90.
64. Kirill Vladimirovich, 184; Brayley-Hodgetts, 2:226.
65. Kirill Vladimirovich, 183.
66. Nicholas II to Dowager Empress Marie Feodorovna, October 5, 1905, in Bing, 142.

CHAPTER 4: THE ROMANOVS

1. Fitzlyon and Browning, 17.
2. George, *Romanov Diary*, 75.
3. Abrikossow, 234.
4. Gabriel Konstantinovich, 129.
5. Polovtsov, 370.
6. Ular, 71.
7. Infanta Eulalia of Spain, 171.
8. Queen Marie of Romania, 1:79.
9. Alexander Mikhailovich, *Once*, 173.
10. Ibid., 41.
11. Vassili, 126; Witte, 153.
12. Brayley-Hodgetts, 2:148–49.
13. Tarsaïdzé, *Katia*, 148.
14. Tarsaïdzé, *Czars and Presidents*, 274–80.
15. Kleinmichel, 51.
16. Brayley-Hodgetts, 2:229–30.
17. Polovtsov, 2:192.
18. Prince Nicholas of Greece, 42.
19. Kirill Vladimirovich, 52–53.
20. Ular, 96.
21. Ular, 96–97; Cantacuzené, *Life*, 276.
22. Ular, 97.
23. Maud, 136; Witte, 488; Bogdanovich, 446; Gibbon, 613.
24. Maud, 137.
25. Alexander Mikhailovich, *Once*, 41.
26. Queen Marie of Romania, 1:85–86.
27. Queen Marie of Romania, 1:7.
28. Paleologue, 1:152.
29. Marie Pavlovna, 17.
30. Queen Marie of Romania, 1:87; Alexander Mikhailovich, *Once*, 140.
31. Ular, 78.
32. Zainchkovsky, 76, 97; Greenberg, 2:41–42; Dubnow, 2:399–404.
33. Byrnes, 207.
34. Elbogen, 219.
35. Marie Pavlovna, 19.
36. Brayley-Hodgetts, 2:231–32; Ular, 78.
37. Mossolov, 80.
38. Witte, 240.
39. Nostitz, 118.
40. Private information to author.
41. Röhl and de Bellaigue, 123.
42. Vyrubova, 13.
43. Röhl and de Bellaigue, 649–50.
44. Marie Pavlovna, 17.
45. Hoare, 326.
46. Buchanan, *Victorian Gallery*, 148.
47. Fuhrmann, 81–82; see also Cunningham, 197; Curtiss, 370–71; and Oldenburg, 3:109.
48. Paleologue, 1:161; in *Royalty Digest*, issue no. 38, vol. IV, no. 2, August 1994, 59.
49. Private information to author.
50. Lyons, N-46.
51. *Russian Court Memoirs*, 178.
52. Mossolov, 81.
53. Nicholas II to Dowager Empress Marie Feodorovna, October 20, 1902, in Bing, 169–70.
54. Sokolovoi and Kondratiev, 68–69.
55. *Almanach de St. Petersbourg*.
56. Mossolov, 82.

57. "Grand Duke Exposes Secrets of Russian Revolution," in *The San Francisco Chronicle*, September 2, 1917.
58. George, *Romanov Diary*, 133; Souiny, 164.
59. *Russian Court Memoirs*, 85.
60. Marie Pavlovna, 91.
61. Ibid., 93.
62. Ibid., 107.
63. Private information to the author.
64. Ferrand, *Grand-Duc Paul Alexandrovitch*, 66.
65. Buchanan, *Victorian Gallery*, 149.
66. Ibid., 149.
67. Stopford, 43.
68. Buchanan, *Victorian Gallery*, 150–52.
69. Chavchavadze, *Grand Dukes*, 58.
70. Ibid., 59.
71. Buxhoeveden, *Before*, 219–20.
72. Chavchavadze, *Grand Dukes*, 62.
73. Chavchavadze, *Grand Dukes*, 60; Zemlyanichenko, 142; Miliutin, 4:85–87.
74. Kleinmichel, 65–66; information from Zoia Belyakova to author, August 1996.
75. Witte, 224–25; Poliakoff, *Mother Dear*, 87.
76. Tarsaïdzé, *Czars and Presidents*, 315–18; Kleinmichel, 65–66.
77. Brayley-Hodgetts, 2:143; information from Zoia Belyakova to author, August 1996; Ferrand, *Il est Toujours*, 250–53.
78. Buxhoeveden, *Before*, 218.
79. *Almanach de St. Petersbourg.*
80. Grand Duke Konstantin Konstantinovich, Diary, April 10, 1884, quoted in Barkovets, Federov, and Krylov, 120.
81. Grand Duke Konstantin Konstantinovich, Diary, September 12, 1904, in GARF, F. 660, Op. 1, D. 54.
82. Ibid., December 15, 1903, in GARF, F. 660, Op. 1, D. 51.
83. Grand Duke Andrei Vladimirovich, Diary, October 10, 1915, in GARF, F. 650, Op. 1, D. 2.
84. Sokolovoi and Kondratiev, 141.
85. Buxhoeveden, *Before*, 218.
86. Alexander Mikhailovich, *Always*, 88.
87. Alexander Mikhailovich, *Once*, 143.
88. Gabriel Konstantinovich, 95–96.
89. Mossolov, 83–85.
90. Ibid., 85.
91. Alexander Mikhailovich, *Always*, 88.
92. Alexander Mikhailovich, *Once*, 143.
93. Alexander Mikhailovich, *Always*, 88.
94. Alexander Mikhailovich, *Once*, 143.
95. Prince Christopher of Greece, 32.
96. Chavchavadze, *Grand Dukes*, 69.
97. Belyakova, *Romanov Legacy*, 153; and Zoia Belyakova to author, August 1996.
98. George, *Romanov Diary*, 84.
99. Ignatiev, 81.
100. Lobanov-Rostovsky, 14.
101. Davis, *Ambassadorial*, 184; Ignatiev, 97.
102. Bikov, 99; Chavchavadze, *Grand Dukes*, 167; Sokolovoi and Kondratiev, 142; Alexander Mikhailovich, *Once*, 145.
103. Nostitz, 144.
104. Yusupov, 52.
105. Naryshkin-Kuryakin, 163.
106. Bikov, 99.
107. Witte, 404; Tarsaïdzé, *Katia*, 52; Empress Alexandra Feodorovna to Nicholas II, November 4, 1916, in GARF, F. 601, Op. 1, D. 1157.
108. Witte, 619.
109. de Stoeckl, *Not All Vanity*, 86.
110. Alexander Mikhailovich, *Once*, 146.
111. de Stoeckl, *Not All Vanity*, 56.
112. Cockfield, 105–6; private information to author.
113. Izwolsky, *No Time*, 97; Mossolov, 92.
114. Chavchavadze, *Grand Dukes*, 171.
115. Buchanan, *Mission*, 1:177.
116. L. V. Anisimova, in Nikolaiev, 3–4; Grebalskii, 188.
117. Kleinmichel, 161.
118. Grand Duke Nicholas Mikhailovich, undated letter, in RGB, Department of Manuscripts, F. 585, Op. 1, D. 582.
119. Quoted in Cockfield, 103.
120. See Cockfield, 64; and Naryshkin-Kuryakin, 129.
121. Lambsdorff, *1891–1892*, 80.
122. Naryshkin-Kuryakin, 129.
123. Alexander Mikhailovich, *Once*, 18–19.
124. Chavchavadze, *Grand Dukes*, 183.
125. Chavchavadze, *Crowns*, 55.
126. George, *Romanov Diary*, v–vi.
127. Chavchavadze, *Grand Dukes*, 183.
128. Lyons, N-58.
129. George, *Romanov Diary*, 83.
130. Grand Duke Serge Mikhailovich to Grand Duke Nicholas Mikhailovich, March 9, 1917, in GARF, F. 670, Op. 1, D. 185.
131. Vorres, 114–15.
132. Paleologue, 1:260.

CHAPTER 5: THE RUSSIAN COURT

1. Lathrop, 66.
2. Grabbe and Grabbe, 19.
3. *Almanach de St. Petersbourg.*
4. Mossolov, 182.
5. Iroshnikov, Protsai, and Shelayev, *Sunset*, 277.
6. Lyons, N-57.
7. Witte, 156.
8. Radziwill, *Nicholas II*, 78–79.
9. Hanbury-Williams, 165.
10. Lyons, N-44.
11. Nostitz, 170.
12. *Almanach de St. Petersbourg.*
13. Mossolov, 107–8.
14. Vyrubova, 193.
15. *Almanach de St. Petersbourg.*
16. *Russian Court Memoirs*, 45–46.
17. Botkin, 41.
18. Lyons, N-44.
19. *Almanach de St. Petersbourg.*

20. Izwolsky, *No Time*, 44.
21. *Almanach de St. Petersbourg.*
22. Benckendorff, v–vi.
23. Botkin, 46–47.
24. Buxhoeveden, *Left Behind*, 51.
25. *Almanach de St. Petersbourg.*
26. Wortman, 2:277.
27. George, *Romanov Diary*, 78.
28. *Almanach de St. Petersbourg.*
29. Mossolov, 184.
30. *Almanach de St. Petersbourg.*
31. *Almanach de St. Petersbourg*; Iroshnikov, Protsai, and Shelayev, 128; Mossolov, 179–82; Morris, 487.
32. *Almanach de St. Petersbourg*; Lyons, N-36.
33. Iroshnikov, Protsai, and Shelayev, *Sunset*, 128; Mossolov, 179–82; Morris, 487; Grabbe and Grabbe, 19; Almanach de St. Petersbourg.
34. *Almanach de St. Petersbourg*; Iroshnikov, Protsai, and Shelayev, 128; Mossolov, 179–82; Morris, 487.
35. Mossolov, 179–82.
36. Botkin, 80–81.
37. Iroshnikov, Protsai, and Shelayev, *Sunset*, 128; Mossolov, 179–82; Morris, 487.
38. *Almanach de St. Petersbourg.*
39. Prince Christopher of Greece, 67.
40. Grey, 32.
41. Botkine, *Les Morts*, 18–19.
42. Botkin, 15.
43. Morris, 487.
44. Botkine, *Au Temps*, 52.
45. *Almanach de St. Petersbourg*; RGIA, F. 525, Op. 2, D. 2. (Chancellery of Empress Alexandra Feodorovna).
46. Vassili, 262–64.
47. Vorres, 73.
48. Naryshkin-Kuryakin, 193.
49. Vassili, 266.
50. Buxhoeveden, *Before*, 321.
51. *Almanach de St. Petersbourg*; Mossolov, 181–82; Iroshnikov, Protsai, and Shelayev, *Sunset*, 128; Vyrubova, 74–76; RGIA, F. 525, Op. 2, D. 2 (Chancellery of Empress Alexandra Feodorovna).
52. Buxhoeveden, *Life*, 54.
53. Naryshkin-Kuryakin, 95.
54. Buxhoeveden, *Before*, 323.
55. Ibid., 320.
56. Buxhoeveden, *Before*, 321; Voronoff, 88.
57. *Almanach de St. Petersbourg*; RGIA, F. 525, Op. 2, D. 2 (Chancellery of Empress Alexandra Feodorovna).
58. Vyrubova, 1–2.
59. Naryshkin-Kuryakin, 187.
60. Ibid., 188.
61. Gilliard, 83.
62. Vorres, 137.
63. Nostitz, 87.
64. Grabbe and Grabbe, 43.
65. Souiny, 157.
66. Vyrubova, 73.
67. Botkin, 79.
68. Voronoff, 58.
69. Grabbe and Grabbe, 19.
70. Mossolov, 192.
71. Iroshnikov, Protsai, and Shelayev, *Sunset*, 123.
72. Swezey, 87.
73. Vyrubova, 158–59.
74. Grabbe and Grabbe, 76.
75. Ignatiev, 73.
76. Lyons, N-45.
77. Ignatiev, 73.
78. Spiridovich, 1:29; Lyons, N-44; *Almanach de St. Petersbourg.*
79. Vernova, *Treasures of Russia*, 91; Grabbe and Grabbe, 40.
80. Spiridovich, 1:29; Lyons, N-130.
81. Grabbe and Grabbe, xi.
82. Spiridovich, 1:30.
83. Paleologue, 1:244; Lyons, AA-5; Spiridovich, 1:30; *Almanach de St. Petersbourg.*
84. Paleologue, 1:244; *Almanach de St. Petersbourg.*
85. Paleologue, 1:243–45.
86. Lyons, N-41.
87. Botkin, 42–44.
88. Mossolov, 122, 163.
89. Izwolsky, *No Time*, 79.
90. *Russian Court Memoirs*, 52–53.
91. Grand Duke Andrei Vladimirovich, Diary, March 9, 1917, in GARF, F. 650, Op. 1, D. 2.
92. Wortman, 1:324.
93. *Moscow: Treasures and Traditions*, 132–41.
94. Botkin, 61.

CHAPTER 6: BELOW STAIRS AT THE PALACE

1. Alexander Mikhailovich, *Once*, 158; Pelham-Clinton, 493.
2. Swezey, 2.
3. RGIA, F. 471, Op. 1, D. 2077 (Ministry of Imperial Court, Department of the Marshal of the Court, Service Lists, 1890–1917).
4. Cockfield, 101.
5. Vorres, 86.
6. Volkov, 64.
7. Vyrubova, 75; RGIA, F. 471, Op. 1, D. 2077 (Ministry of Imperial Court, Department of the Marshal of the Court, Service Lists, 1890–1917).
8. Alexander Palace Association; RGIA, F. 471, Op. 1, D. 839 (Hofmarschall Department of the Ministry of Imperial Court).
9. Alexander Palace Association; RGIA, F. 471, Op. 1, D. 2077 (Ministry of Imperial Court, Department of the Marshal of the Court, Service Lists, 1890–1917); RGIA, F. 471, Op. 1, D. 839 (Hofmarschall Department of the Ministry of Imperial Court).
10. Mossolov, 11–12.
11. Vyrubova, 75.
12. RGIA, F. 525, Op. 2, D. 2 (Chancellery of Empress Alexandra Feodorovna).
13. Vyrubova, 75.
14. Ibid., 75.

15. Empress Alexandra to Nicholas II, December 21, 1915, in GARF, F. 601, Op. 1, D. 1150.

16. Radzinsky, 116; RGIA, F. 525, Op. 2, D. 2 (Chancellery of Empress Alexandra Feodorovna).

17. Volkov, 64.

18. Vyrubova, 74.

19. Vyrubova, 74–76; Buxhoeveden, *Before*, 316; RGIA, F. 525, Op. 2, D. 2 (Chancellery of Empress Alexandra Feodorovna).

20. Details drawn from Volkov's memoirs.

21. RGIA, F. 471, Op. 1, D. 2077 (Ministry of Imperial Court, Department of the Marshal of the Court, Service Lists, 1890–1917).

22. Vyrubova, 75.

23. Radzinsky, 116; RGIA, F. 525, Op. 2, D. 2 (Chancellery of Empress Alexandra Feodorovna).

24. Benagh, 224.

25. Bykov, 34.

26. RGIA, F. 471, Op. 1, D. 2077 (Ministry of Imperial Court, Department of the Marshal of the Court, Service Lists, 1890–1917).

27. Buxhoeveden, *Before*, 232.

28. RGIA, F. 471, Op. 1, D. 839 (Hofmarschall Department of the Ministry of Imperial Court); private information to the author.

29. Queen Marie of Romania, 1:79.

30. Vyrubova, 11.

31. Pitcher, 51–52.

32. Ridge, 18.

33. Vorres, 100.

34. RGIA, F. 471, Op. 1, D. 2077 (Ministry of Imperial Court, Department of the Marshal of the Court, Service Lists, 1890–1917).

35. RGIA, F. 471, Op. 1, D. 2077 (Ministry of Imperial Court, Department of the Marshal of the Court, Service Lists, 1890–1917).

36. Ibid.

37. Gilliard, 17.

38. Botkin, 79.

39. George Gibbes to author, May 1989.

40. Trewin, 13–14; Benagh, 11–18; on Gibbes's homosexuality, see Welch.

41. Leudet, 134; RGIA, F. 471, Op. 1, D. 2077 (Ministry of Imperial Court, Department of the Marshal of the Court, Service Lists, 1890–1917).

42. RGIA, F. 471, Op. 1, D. 839 (Hofmarschall Department of the Ministry of Imperial Court).

43. RGIA, F. 471, Op. 1, D. 2077 (Ministry of Imperial Court, Department of the Marshal of the Court, Service Lists, 1890–1917); Leudet, 135.

44. RGIA, F. 471, Op. 1, D. 839 (Hofmarschall Department of the Ministry of Imperial Court).

45. Lastochkin and Rybejanskii, 73–74; Petrov, *Suburbs*, 110.

46. Alexander Palace Association.

47. Brayley-Hodgetts, 2:230–31.

48. RGIA, F. 471, Op. 1, D. 2077 (Ministry of Imperial Court, Department of the Marshal of the Court, Service Lists, 1890–1917); Morris, 487.

49. RGIA, F. 471, Op. 1, D. 2077 (Ministry of Imperial Court, Department of the Marshal of the Court, Service Lists, 1890–1917); Leudet, 135.

50. RGIA, F. 471, Op. 1, D. 2077 (Ministry of Imperial Court, Department of the Marshal of the Court, Service Lists, 1890–1917).

51. Mossolov, 225–29; Almedingen, *Empress Alexandra*, 120–21; Vyrubova, 76.

52. Mossolov, 221; RGIA, F. 471, Op. 1, D. 839 (Hofmarschall Department of the Ministry of Imperial Court).

53. Kropotkin, 204.

54. Mossolov, 224.

55. Ibid., 227.

56. Vyrubova, 57–58.

57. Vyrubova, 39; Volkov, 65–66; Eager, 39; Dehn, 46.

58. Timms, 146; Piper, 12.

59. Odom, 48; Piper, 13; Znamenov, 50.

60. Piper, 13; Znamenov, 50; Swezey, 116; Odom, 49.

61. Timms, 146.

62. Vernova, *Treasures of Russia*, 233.

63. Norman, *Hermitage*, 67.

64. *Intimacies*, 291.

65. Swezey, 5.

66. Vernova, *Treasures of Russia*, 207; RGIA, F. 471, Op. 1, D. 839 (Hofmarschall Department of the Ministry of Imperial Court).

67. Vyrubova, 9.

68. RGIA, F. 471, Op. 1, D. 2077 (Ministry of Imperial Court, Department of the Marshal of the Court, Service Lists, 1890–1917).

69. de Stoeckl, *My Dear Marquis*, 140.

70. Vorres, 26; RGIA, F. 471, Op. 1, D. 2077 (Ministry of Imperial Court, Department of the Marshal of the Court, Service Lists, 1890–1917), and F. 468, Op. 14, D. 839 (Hofmarschall Department of the Ministry of Imperial Court), Petition of January 21, 1902, "Concerning permission to provide allowance for six months to James Hercules in advance of his holiday abroad"; and information from Penny Wilson to author.

71. Korshunova, *Russian Style*, 127; Vyrubova, 9.

72. Prince Christopher of Greece, 50–51.

73. *Intimacies*, 134.

74. Leudet, 140.

75. Steveni, 162.

76. Volkov, 67; Mossolov, 227.

77. Vernova, *Treasures of Russia*, 216; RGIA, F. 471, Op. 1, D. 839 (Hofmarschall Department of the Ministry of Imperial Court).

78. Volkov, 67; Mossolov, 227; Leudet, 142; Steveni, 162; RGIA, F. 471, Op. 1, D. 839 (Hofmarschall Department of the Ministry of Imperial Court).

79. Prince Christopher of Greece, 52.

80. Voyekov, 216.

81. Paleologue, 2:137.

82. Mossolov, 62.

83. Voyekov, 216.

84. Mossolov, 62.

85. Voyekov, 216.
86. Buxhoeveden, *Before*, 254.
87. Volkov, 67.

CHAPTER 7: THE MILITARY

1. Ometev, 118.
2. Ibid., 196.
3. Kropotkin, 171.
4. Shoumatoff, 64–65; Ometev, 196.
5. George, *Romanov Diary*, 95.
6. Ignatiev, 58.
7. Lobanov-Rostovsky, 4.
8. Lyons, AA 3–4.
9. Lobanov-Rostovsky, 5–8.
10. Mossolov, 191.
11. Vernova, *Treasures of Russia*, 91.
12. Vorres, 15.
13. Ibid., 33.
14. Ibid., 84.
15. Wortman, 2:415.
16. Radziwill, *Nicholas II*, 24.
17. Ignatiev, 80.
18. Romanovsky-Krassinsky, 32.
19. Vorres, 48–49; George, *Romanov Diary*, 25–26; Ignatiev, 80–88.
20. Iroshnikov, Protsai, and Shelayev, *St. Petersburg*, 10.
21. *Niva*, No. 118, May 8, 1901.
22. Cited in de Jonge, 72.
23. Ignatiev, 76.
24. *Niva*, No. 18, May 8, 1901.
25. Nicholas II, Diary, May 1, 1901, in GARF, F. 601, Op. 1, D. 242.
26. Ignatiev, 128.
27. Botkine, *Au Temps*, 50; Mossolov, 22.
28. Botkine, *Au Temps*, 50.
29. Mossolov, 22.
30. Mossolov, 22; Vorres, 173.
31. Botkine, *Au Temps*, 50.

CHAPTER 8: THE ARISTOCRACY

1. Lieven, 47.
2. Kochan, 35.
3. Naryshkin-Kuryakin, 110.
4. Shoumatoff, 47.
5. Voronoff, 21.
6. Gautier, 201–3.
7. Vorres, 91.
8. *Russian Court Memoirs*, 253–54.
9. Buchanan, *Dissolution*, 50.
10. Vasilevskaya, 90–91.
11. *Russian Court Memoirs*, 259–60.
12. Ibid., 259–60.
13. *Intimacies*, 129.
14. Lyons, N-23.
15. *Intimacies*, 128.
16. *Russian Court Memoirs*, 293; Tsedidat, 99–101.
17. *Russian Court Memoirs*, 294.
18. Buchanan, *Victorian Gallery*, 178.
19. Stephan, 5.

20. Obolensky, 48.
21. Vorres, 98.
22. Yusupov, 29–34.
23. Shvidkovsky, *St. Petersburg*, 62; Vasilevskaya, 138.
24. Yusupov, 61–62.
25. Dorr, 104.
26. Yusupov, 64–66.
27. Sheremetevskii, 14–15.
28. *Intimacies*, 166.
29. Roosevelt, 3.
30. Ibid., 148.
31. Izwolsky, *No Time*, 64–65.
32. Ibid., 60–61.
33. Marie Pavlovna, 246.
34. Roosevelt, 104.
35. Buxhoeveden, *Before*, 37–38.
36. Buxhoeveden, *Before*, 96.
37. Kropotkin, 99.

CHAPTER 9: THE RUSSIAN ORTHODOX CHURCH

The epigraph to this chapter is drawn from Dostoevsky, 234.
1. George and George, *St. Petersburg*, xxxiii.
2. Wortman, 1:176.
3. Trufanov, 88.
4. Naryshkin-Kuryakin, 142.
5. *The Times*, November 14, 1894.
6. Longford, *Darling Loosey*, 284.
7. Witte, 375.
8. Essed-Bey, 128.
9. Nicholas II, Diary, July 13, 1901, in GARF, F. 601, Op. 1, D. 242.
10. Ibid., July 19, 1901, in GARF, F. 601, Op. 1, D. 242.
11. Nostitz, 117.
12. Shulgin, 259.
13. Witte, 242.
14. Vorres, 122; Dillon, 155–56; Oldenburg, 2:49.
15. Naryshkin-Kuryakin, 175.
16. Vorres, 124.
17. Robert L. Nicholas, "The Friends of God: Nicholas II and Alexandra at the Canonization of Seraphim of Sarov, July 1903," in Timberlake, 209.
18. Nicholas II, Diary, July 18, 1903, in GARF, F. 601, Op. 1, D. 246.
19. Nichols, in Timberlake, 210.
20. Mossolov, 134–35.
21. Oldenburg, 2:50–51.
22. Vasilevskaya, 52.
23. Ibid., 53.
24. Brumfield, 351.
25. Lobanova, 56.
26. Lincoln, *Romanovs*, 458–59.
27. Gautier, 160.
28. Lincoln, *Romanovs*, 464.
29. Butikov, *Isaakievskii Sobor*, 109–10; Butikov, *St. Isaac's Cathedral*, 16–22.
30. Gautier, 111.
31. Butikov, *Isaakievskii Sobor*, 117–27; Vasilevskaya, 29–30.
32. Mawdsley, 239.
33. Izwolsky, *No Time*, 58.

34. Almedingen, *Tomorrow*, 14.
35. Talbot Rice, 23–24.
36. Ometev, 17.
37. Talbot Rice, 23.
38. Massie, *Firebird*, 366–70.
39. Hamilton, 105–7.

CHAPTER 10: THE WINTER PALACE

1. Londonderry, 48.
2. Vorres, 100.
3. Sitwell, 194–196; Ovsyannikov, 156–57.
4. Ovsyannikov, 222–25.
5. Vasilevskaya, 7; Piotrovsky, *Ermitage*, 34–36; Norman, *Hermitage*, 17.
6. Ovsyannikov, 553–55.
7. Norman, *Hermitage*, 31.
8. Vasilevskaya, 11.
9. Ibid., 11–12.
10. Hamilton, 101.
11. Kennett, 36–41; Shapiro, 8–10; Piotrovsky, Hermitage, 28; Ovsyannikov, 352–53.
12. Piotrovsky, *Hermitage*, 22.
13. Piotrovsky, *Ermitage*, 39; Norman, *Hermitage*, 16; Kennett, 42; Shapiro, 13; Piotrovsky, *Hermitage*, 22.
14. Piotrovsky, *Ermitage*, 168, 220–21; Shapiro, 10–12; Piotrovsky, *Hermitage*, 22.
15. Kennett, 42; Shapiro, 13–14; Piotrovsky, *Hermitage*, 23; Ovsyannikov, 484–85.
16. Shapiro, 14–17; Piotrovsky, *Ermitage*, 140, 226–27; Piotrovsky, *Hermitage*, 23.
17. Komelova, 30; Piotrovsky, *Hermitage*, 24; Nesin, 101–2; Ovsyannikov, 354; Tallerchik, 6–7, 21–25.
18. Sokolova, 7; Norman, *Hermitage*, 5, 37.
19. Norman, *Hermitage*, 5.
20. Norman, *Hermitage*, 38; Voronikhina, Korshunova, and Pavelkina, 87; Korshunova, 114.
21. Vasilevskaya, 14.
22. Ibid.
23. Kennett, 42–43; Kann, *St. Petersburg*, 25; Brumfield, 407; Piotrovsky, *Hermitage*, 29; Petrova, *Stackenschneider*, 176.
24. Piotrovsky, *Hermitage*, 15.
25. Vasilevskaya, 15; Norman, *Hermitage*, 75.
26. Norman, *Hermitage*, 21; Baedeker, 144–45.
27. Piotrovsky, *Hermitage*, 109–12.
28. Norman, *Hermitage*, 36; Piotrovsky, *Hermitage*, 114.
29. Norman, *Hermitage*, 88.
30. Piotrovsky, *Hermitage*, 130; Norman, *Hermitage*, 97, 108–9.
31. Vasilevskaya, 15; Piotrovsky, *Hermitage*, 40–41; Kann, St. Petersburg, 40; Vasilevskaya, 15; Voronikhina, Korshunova, and Pavelkina, 175–76; Korshunova, 198–201.
32. Piotrovsky, *Hermitage*, 30; Voronikhina, Korshunova, and Pavelkina, 184–87; Korshunova, 214–16.
33. Nesin, 79–81; Mawdsley, 257; Voronikhina, Korshunova, and Pavelkina, 193–95; Korshunova, 221–23.
34. Piotrovsky, *Ermitage*, 131–33; Nesin, 67–69; Voronikhina, Korshunova, and Pavelkina, 206–8.

35. Kennett, 41; Shapiro, 19; Piotrovsky, *Hermitage*, 24–26, 37.
36. Norman, *All the Russias*, 16–17.
37. Nesin, 13; T. A. Petrova and T. A. Malinina, "The Private Rooms of the Imperial Family in the Winter Palace," in Timms, 22.
38. Nesin, 21; Borisova and Sternin, 176–77; Kirikov, 57.
39. Nesin, 127–32.
40. Petrova and Malinina, in Timms, 22; Nesin, 133.
41. Hepworth, 23.
42. Nesin, 13.
43. Nicholas II, Diary, December 31, 1895, in GARF, F. 601, Op. 1, D. 235.
44. Petrova and Malinina, in Timms, 26.
45. Petrova and Malinina, in Timms, 23; Nesin, 140–42.
46. Timms, 178.
47. Petrova and Malinina, in Timms, 23; Nesin, 144.
48. Timms, 172; Nesin, 146.
49. Petrova and Malinina, in Timms, 24.
50. Timms, 168; Nesin, 143.
51. Eager, 5–10; Conway, 112–13; Petrova and Malinina, in Timms, 24; Nesin, 147–49.
52. Piotrovsky, *Nikolaii i Aleksandra*, 11–17; Nesin, 153.
53. Kussner Coudert, 853–54.
54. Petrova and Malinina, in Timms, 25.
55. Conway, 112; Herriot, 27–32; Petrova and Malinina, in Timms, 25; Nesin, 132.
56. Conway, 112; Herriot, 27–32.
57. Studemeister, 125–28.
58. Piotrovsky, *Nikolaii i Aleksandra*, 17.
59. Petrova and Malinina, in Timms, 26; Nesin, 138–39.
60. Tarsaïdzé, *Katia*, 265.

CHAPTER 11: TSARSKOYE SELO

1. Botkin, 18.
2. Petrov, *Suburbs*, 14–15; Lastochkin and Rybejanskii, 7–8, 42–46.
3. Brumfield, 238; Ducamp, 7; Petrov, *Suburbs*, 22–24; Ovsyannikov, 304–6.
4. Lastochkin and Rybejanskii, 172; Koloskov et al., 117.
5. Benagh, 81.
6. Belyakova, *Romanov Legacy*, 18; Petrov, *Suburbs*, 24; Lastochkin and Rybejanskii, 53.
7. Petrov, *Suburbs*, 66.
8. Quoted in Heard Hamilton, 334.
9. Jellicoe, 565; Floryan, 36–37.
10. Botkin, 18–19.
11. Hobhouse and Taylor, 340–44.
12. Kann, *Environs*, 91; Lastochkin and Rybejanskii, 62–63, 186–87; Petrov, *Suburbs*, 64, 90–91; Floryan, 112–15.
13. Massie, *Firebird*, 125–26; Petrov, *Suburbs*, 80–88; Prince Michael of Greece, *Imperial Palaces*, 80–82.
14. Belyakova, *Romanov Legacy*, 34–36; Lastochkin and Rybejanskii, 56–58.
15. Kennett, 137; Belyakova, *Romanov Legacy*, 34–37; Shvidkovsky, *The Empress*, 45–62; Brumfield, 279; Petrov, *Suburbs*, 52–54.
16. Kennett, 137; Brumfield, 280; Petrov, *Suburbs*, 58; Lastochkin and Rybejanskii, 54–56.

17. Prince Christopher of Greece, 50–51.
18. Petrov, *Suburbs*, 20; Lastochkin and Rybejanskii, 51.
19. Belyakova, *Romanov Legacy*, 18.
20. Viltchkovsky, 79.
21. Norwich, 102.
22. Rindina, 4; Raymer, 69; Viltchkovsky, 119.
23. Kennett, 122; Belyakova, *Romanov Legacy*, 20–21; Rindina, 5; Cerwinske, 36–37; Massie, *Firebird*, 125; Viltchkovsky, 121.
24. Lemius, 33; Kennett, 123.
25. Belyakova, *Romanov Legacy*, 21; Lemius, 44–45.
26. Kennett, 123–24; Belyakova, *Romanov Legacy*, 22; Ducamp, 34; Beck, 78–79.
27. Koloskov et al., 66.
28. Belyakova, *Romanov Legacy*, 21; Lemius, 15; Viltchkovsky, 111.
29. Belyakova, *Romanov Legacy*, 28.
30. Kennett, 128; Ducamp, 32; Viltchkovsky, 88.
31. Kennett, 127–28; Brumfield, 278; Lemius, 58–66; Sitwell, 192; Belyakova, *Romanov Legacy*, 28; Ducamp, 42.
32. Ducamp, 46; Petrov, *Suburbs*, 47; Viltchkovsky, 124.
33. Brumfield, 278; Shvidkovsky, *The Empress*, 85; Rae, 46–49.
34. Kennett, 128; Belyakova, *Romanov Legacy*, 34–35; Ducamp, 60; Petrov, *Suburbs*, 46; Viltchkovsky, 125; Beck, 115.
35. Ducamp, 54.
36. Shvidkovsky, *The Empress*, 88; Viltchkovsky, 127–29.
37. Shvidkovsky, *The Empress*, 89–90; Viltchkovsky, 129–30.
38. Viltchkovsky, 133–35.
39. Ducamp, 48–50; Belyakova, *Romanov Legacy*, 32; Shvidkovsky, *The Empress*, 90–95; Rae, 46–49; Viltchkovsky, 136–39.
40. Petrov, *Suburbs*, 120.
41. Ibid., 110.
42. Petrov, *Suburbs*, 112–17; Lastochkin and Rybejanskii, 79–80; Floryan, 106–11.
43. Lastochkin and Rybejanskii, 83–84.
44. Shvidkovsky, *St. Petersburg*, 218; Lastochkin and Rybejanskii, 80–81; Petrov, *Suburbs*, 82.
45. Petrov, *Suburbs*, 126.
46. Lastochkin and Rybejanskii, 158–64; Petrov, *Suburbs*, 126–29.
47. Petrov, *Suburbs*, 128.
48. Petrov, *Suburbs*, 128; Lastochkin and Rybejanskii, 162–63; Kirichenko, *Tsarskoye Selo*, 43–66.
49. Petrov, *Suburbs*, 126.
50. Nicholas II, Diary, August 20, 1912, in GARF, F. 601, Op. 1, D. 258.
51. Lastochkin and Rybejanskii, 159–62.
52. Petrov, *Suburbs*, 106; Lastochkin and Rybejanskii, 70–71; Korshunova, *Dzhiakomo Kvarengi*, 216.
53. Viltchkovsky, 212; Korshunova, *Dzhiakomo Kvarengi*, 217; Voronikhina, Korshunova, and Pavelkina, 231–32.
54. Bott, 8; Lastochkin and Rybejanskii, 71; Petrov, *Suburbs*, 108; Korshunova, *Dzhiakomo Kvarengi*, 218; Voronikhina, Korshunova, and Pavelkina, 247–49.
55. Alexander Palace Association; *Alexander Palace*, World Monuments Fund, 39; Korshunova, *Dzhiakomo Kvarengi*, 220.
56. Alexander Palace Association; *Alexander Palace*, World Monuments Fund, 36; Ducamp, 98; Swezey, 25; Voronikhina, Korshunova, and Pavelkina, 253.
57. Petrov, *Suburbs*, 108; Borisova and Sternin, 67; Demidenko, *Inter'er v Rossii Traditsii*, 295; Kirikov, 197.
58. Petrov, *Suburbs*, 108.
59. Bott, 11; Demidenko, *Inter'er v Rossii*, 294.
60. *Alexander Palace*, World Monuments Fund, 15.
61. Bott, 10; Eager, 21; Alexander Palace Association.
62. Fulop-Miller, 82.
63. Marie Pavlovna, 34.
64. Alexander Palace Association.
65. Dehn, 78–79; Eager, 21.
66. Bott, 9; Eager, 21; Swezey, 16, 35; Alexander Palace Association.
67. *Alexander Palace*, World Monuments Fund, 36.
68. Gabriel Konstantinovich, 82–83.
69. *Alexander Palace*, World Monuments Fund, 36.
70. Ibid., 35.
71. Spiridovich, 1:37; Swezey, 15–16.
72. Vyrubova, 55.
73. Mossolov, 31.
74. Empress Alexandra Feodorovna to Nicholas II, July 6, 1900, in GARF, F. 640, Op. 2, D. 473.
75. *Alexander Palace*, World Monuments Fund, 35.
76. Swezey, 16–17, 34.
77. *Alexander Palace*, World Monuments Fund, 35.
78. Vorres, 128.
79. *Alexander Palace*, World Monuments Fund, 35.
80. Ibid., 39.
81. Alexander Palace Association.
82. *Alexander Palace*, World Monuments Fund, 33; Swezey, 12, 34–35.
83. Vyrubova, 56.
84. *Alexander Palace*, World Monuments Fund, 33.
85. Gabriel Konstantinovich, 61; Swezey, 12.
86. Bott, 12.
87. *Alexander Palace*, World Monuments Fund, 27.
88. Dehn, 71–72.
89. *Alexander Palace*, World Monuments Fund, 27.
90. Ibid.
91. Alexander Palace Association.
92. *Alexander Palace*, World Monuments Fund, 27; Swezey, 31.
93. Dehn, 71–72; Massie, *Pavlovsk*, 179.
94. *Alexander Palace*, World Monuments Fund, 29.
95. *Alexander Palace*, World Monuments Fund, 29; Swezey, 6; Demidenko, *Inter'er v Rossii*, 295–97; Kirikov, 263–64.
96. Marie Pavlovna, 35.
97. *Alexander Palace*, World Monuments Fund, 29; Demidenko, *Inter'er v Rossii*, 297–98.
98. Dehn, 70.
99. *Alexander Palace*, World Monuments Fund, 30; Demidenko, *Inter'er v Rossii*, 298.

100. Alexander Palace Association.
101. Swezey, 11.
102. *Alexander Palace*, World Monuments Fund, 30; Demidenko, *Inter'er v Rossii*, 298.
103. Spiridovich, 1:41.
104. Izwolsky, *No Time*, 87.
105. Bott, 8.
106. *Alexander Palace*, World Monuments Fund, 32.
107. Bott, 8.

CHAPTER 12: PETERHOF

1. de Robien, 70.
2. Prince Michael of Greece, *Imperial Palaces*, 23.
3. Ibid.
4. Petrov, *Suburbs*, 322–23.
5. Plumptre, 99.
6. Petrov, *Suburbs*, 334.
7. Ibid., 344.
8. Grabar, 134; *Petrodvorets: The Grand Palace*, 4–5.
9. Vernova and Znamenov, 34; Vernova, *Treasures of Russia*, 165; Petrov, *Suburbs*, 370–71; Ovsyannikov, 290–91.
10. Petrov, *Suburbs*, 369; Baltsykevich, 36.
11. Raskin and Znamenov, 130; Kann, *Environs*, 28; *Petrodvorets: The Grand Palace*, 7.
12. Vernova, *Treasures of Russia*, 24.
13. Raskin and Znamenov, 124; Kennett, 207; Petrov, *Suburbs*, 362.
14. Vernova and Znamenov, 42–43.
15. Raskin and Znamenov, 116.
16. Raskin and Znamenov, 86; Petrov, *Suburbs*, 352–57; *Petrodvorets: The Grand Palace*, 8.
17. Raskin and Znamenov, 76; Petrov, *Suburbs*, 362.
18. Vernova and Znamenov, 51; Kennett, 207.
19. Kennett, 207; Petrov, *Suburbs*, 348–49.
20. Vernova and Znamenov, 64.
21. Raskin and Znamenov, 108; Vernova and Znamenov, 68; Petrov, *Suburbs*, 348.
22. Raskin and Znamenov, 163; Kann, *Environs*, 8; Petrov, *Suburbs*, 372–80; Floryan, 194–97; Vernova, *The Great Cascade*, 12–18.
23. Raskin and Znamenov, 154; Petrov, *Suburbs*, 386.
24. Gaynor, 74; Petrov, *Suburbs*, 426–27.
25. Vernova and Znamenov, 148–49.
26. Raskin and Znamenov, 228; Petrov, *Suburbs*, 428–32.
27. Raskin and Znamenov, 230; Vernova and Znamenov, 170–71; Petrov, *Suburbs*, 432–33; *Petrodvorets: Fountains*, 7–8.
28. Raskin and Znamenov, 236; Vernova and Znamenov, 172.
29. Raskin and Znamenov, 238; Vernova and Znamenov, 172; Floryan, 24–26.
30. Petrov, *Suburbs*, 428–29; Vernova and Znamenov, 152.
31. Petrov, *Suburbs*, 412.
32. Raskin and Znamenov, 260; Petrov, *Suburbs*, 418.
33. Vernova and Znamenov, 140–42; Petrov, *Suburbs*, 409–11.
34. Raskin and Znamenov, 287; Petrov, *Suburbs*, 392–93.
35. Brumfield, 219; Norwich, 97; Kennett, 204; Vernova and Znamenov, 105–6; Gaynor, 62–67; Petrov, *Suburbs*, 393–99.

36. Petrov, *Suburbs*, 440–42.
37. Petrov, *Suburbs*, 456–57; Shvidkovsky, *St. Petersburg*, 325.
38. Petrov, *Suburbs*, 456–63; *Russkie Imperatorskii Dvortsi*, 6; Shurgin, 56–57.
39. Petrov, *Suburbs*, 464–67.
40. Shvidkovsky, *St. Petersburg*, 326; Petrov, *Suburbs*, 452–55.
41. Petrov, *Suburbs*, 461; Brumfield, 291.
42. Brumfield, 291–92; Petrov, *Suburbs*, 468–69; Shurgin, 59.
43. Hallmann, 45; Vernova and Znamenov, 173.
44. Vernova and Znamenov, 173; Petrov, *Suburbs*, 327.
45. Granin et al., 44; Hallmann, 44; Petrov, *Suburbs*, 444–45; Shurgin, 51.
46. Vernova and Znamenov, 175; Petrov, *Suburbs*, 450.
47. Petrov, *Suburbs*, 452; Syknovalov, 231.
48. Petrov, *Suburbs*, 448–49; Gaynor, 82.
49. See *Cottage Palace* for further details.
50. Hallmann, 44.
51. In GARF, F. 490, Op. 4, D. 1199.
52. Spiridovich, 1:63; Znamenov, 38; Petrov, *Suburbs*, 446.
53. Tsesarevich Nicholas, Diary, May 31, 1884, in GARF F. 601, Op. 1, D. 219.
54. Nicholas II, Diary, June 9, 1895, in GARF, F. 601, Op. 1, D 236.
55. Znamenov, 39; Petrov, *Suburbs*, 445–46; Baltsykevich, 51–52.
56. Letter from Nicholas II to Queen Victoria, May 24, 1899, in GARF, F. 601, Op. 2, D. 472.
57. Spiridovich, 1:63; Znamenov, 38; Shurgin, 52–53.
58. Znamenov, 43–44.
59. Ibid., 44–48.
60. Dehn, 39.
61. Baylen, 49–50.
62. Vernova, *Petergof, Novye Postynlenya*, 157; Paleologue, 1:59–60; Spiridovich, 1:61–65; Petrov, *Suburbs*, 445–46; and Znamenov, 39–43.
63. Znamenov, 48–49.
64. Ibid., 49.
65. Ibid., 62.
66. Ibid., 54–62.
67. Vyrubova, 103.

CHAPTER 13: THE MOSCOW PALACES

1. Brumfield, 319.
2. Freeman and Burton, 203–5; Floryan, 214; Mawdsley, 182; Kiselev, 202–10.
3. Grenfell, 25.
4. Brumfield, 328; Kirichenko, 19; Shvidkovsky, *The Empress*, 207–9; Freeman and Burton, 113–15; Kiselev, 172–78.
5. Paleologue, 1:93.
6. Voyce, 4–5.
7. Ibid., 33–38.
8. Lincoln, *Between Heaven and Hell*, 9.
9. Beable, 83; Leger, 32–33.
10. Leger, 33; Kiselev, 49.
11. Voyce, 53; Leger, 47.

12. Voyce, 53–54.
13. Ibid., 45–50.
14. Ibid., 66.
15. Markova, 13; Voyce, 65–66; Kiselev, 12–14.
16. Voyce, 66.
17. Timofeyev, 141.
18. Rodimzeva, Rakhmanov, and Raimann, 196; Voyce, 68.
19. Rodimzeva, Rakhmanov, and Raimann, 196.
20. Voyce, 68.
21. Rodimzeva, Rakhmanov, and Raimann, 198; Voyce, 111; Leger, 46–47; Kiselev, 50.
22. Raiguel and Huff, 289; Voyce, 68.
23. Timofeyev, 144.
24. Rodimzeva, Rakhmanov, and Raimann, 200; Voyce, 112; Leger, 43–44.
25. Raiguel and Huff, 288–89; Stoddard, 331; Voyce, 68; Logan, 170; Kiselev, 48.
26. Raiguel and Huff, 290; Voyce, 68; Leger, 46.
27. Rodimzeva, Rakhmanov, and Raimann, 202; Leger, 46.
28. Rodimzeva, Rakhmanov, and Raimann, 205.
29. Ibid., 205.
30. Lauritzen, 94.
31. Kiselev, 22.
32. Rodimzeva, Rakhmanov, and Raimann, 211.
33. Rodimzeva, Rakhmanov, and Raimann, 215; Lauritzen, 96; Kiselev, 22.
34. Rodimzeva, Rakhmanov, and Raimann, 217; Kiselev, 23.
35. Rodimzeva, Rakhmanov, and Raimann, 218; Lauritzen, 98.
36. Rodimzeva, Rakhmanov, and Raimann, 221; Lauritzen, 97; Kiselev, 23.
37. Rodimzeva, Rakhmanov, and Raimann, 221; Lauritzen, 97.
38. Rodimzeva, Rakhmanov, and Raimann, 222.
39. Leger, 46.

CHAPTER 14: IMPERIAL RICHES

1. Vorres, 28.
2. Buxhoeveden, *Before*, 311.
3. Alexander Mikhailovich, *Once*, 157; Mossolov, 178–79; Vorres, 87.
4. Norman, *Hermitage*, 86–87.
5. Clarke, 265.
6. Pipes, 70.
7. Alexander Mikhailovich, *Once*, 156.
8. Ibid., 158.
9. In RGIA, F. 525, Op. 2, D. 2 (Chancellery of Empress Alexandra Feodorovna).
10. In RGIA, F. 468, Op. 14, D. 839 (Hofmarschall Department of the Ministry of Imperial Court), Petition of January 21, 1902.
11. Romanovsky-Krassinsky, 76.
12. Timms, 331.
13. Alexander Mikhailovich, *Once*, 155–56.
14. Vorres, 87.
15. Mossolov, 177.
16. Alexander Kerensky, in Sokolov, 34–35.
17. Testimony of Lili Dehn, given in 1955 during the case of *Anna Anderson v. Barbara, Duchess of*

Mecklenburg, Hamburg, Germany, quoted in Kurth, 238.
18. Empress Alexandra to Nicholas II, August 26, 1915, in GARF, F. 601, Op. 1, D. 1149.
19. Vorres, 245.
20. Dehn, 78.
21. Buxhoeveden, *Life*, 157.
22. Benckendorff, 89; Clarke, 101.
23. Botkin, 125.
24. Benckendorff, 125.
25. Kurth, 236–39.
26. Berkman, 149.
27. Benckendorff, 89.
28. Clarke, 101.

CHAPTER 15: FASHION AT THE RUSSIAN COURT

1. Korshunova, *Russian Style*, 38, 155.
2. Vorres, 93.
3. Izwolsky, *No Time*, 73.
4. Buchanan, *Dissolution*, 19.
5. Korshunova, *Russian Style*, 93, 124.
6. Timms, 202; Korshunova, *Russian Style*, 34.
7. de Stoeckl, *Not All Vanity*, 126.
8. Ignatiev, 97.
9. Vorres, 74; Mossolov, 189.
10. Izwolsky, *No Time*, 79.
11. Souiny, 28.
12. Lehr, 200.
13. Vernova, *Treasures of Russia*, 217.
14. Izwolsky, *No Time*, 39.
15. Mossolov, 183.
16. Timms, 206; Vernova, *Treasures of Russia*, 218.
17. Timms, 208; Vernova, *Treasures of Russia*, 222.
18. Vernova, *Treasures of Russia*, 222.
19. Cowles, 36; Windsor, 94–98.
20. *Intimacies*, 150.
21. Timms, 184.
22. "Trousseau of an Empress," in *The Call*, San Francisco, November 27, 1894.
23. Vorres, 73.
24. Botkin, 26.
25. *Intimacies*, 149.
26. Botkin, 31.
27. Vernova, *Petergof, Novye Postynlenya*, 136.
28. Ibid.
29. Ibid., 141–42.
30. Dehn, 68.
31. Ibid.
32. "Trousseau of an Empress," in *The Call*, San Francisco, November 27, 1894.
33. Mossolov, 21.

CHAPTER 16: JEWELRY, REGALIA, AND OBJETS D'ART

The epigraph to this chapter is drawn from George, *Romanov Diary*, 103.
1. Quoted in Kelly, 70.
2. Mossolov, 189.
3. Quoted in Kelly, 70–71.

4. *Intimacies*, 141.
5. von Solodkoff, 55.
6. Ibid., 76.
7. Polynina and Rakhmanov, 101.
8. Goncharenko and Narozhnaya, 128.
9. Goncharenko and Narozhnaya, 126; Polynina and Rakhmanov, 98.
10. Prince Michael of Greece, *Crown Jewels*, 38.
11. Polynina and Rakhmanov, 144–48; Alexander Mikhailovich, *Once*, 157.
12. Hammer, 227.
13. Hammer, 227; Twining, 534.
14. Polynina and Rakhmanov, 148; Twining, 534.
15. Alexander Mikhailovich, *Once*, 157; Nadelhoffer, 187; Twining 535; Meylan, 10.
16. Buchanan, *Queen Victoria's Relations*, 115.
17. George, *Romanov Diary*, 77–78.
18. de Stoeckl, *My Dear Marquis*, 104–5.
19. Nadelhoffer, 129.
20. Snowman, 190.
21. Snowman, 190–91; Meylan, 22.
22. Nadelhoffer, 118.
23. Ibid., 71, 118.
24. Ibid., 118.
25. Balsan, 127.
26. Poliakoff, *Mother Dear*, 57.
27. Chavchavadze, *Grand Dukes*, 95.
28. Lathrop, 157.
29. Almedingen, *Empress Alexandra*, 43.
30. See *Marie Feodorovna*, 360–84, for a complete listing.
31. Clarke, 261–62.
32. Dowager Empress Marie Feodorovna to Nicholas II, in Bing, 66.
33. Buxhoeveden, *Life*, 38.
34. Twining, 540.
35. *Intimacies*, 141.
36. Twining, 535; Alexander Mikhailovich, *Once*, 157; Nadelhoffer, 187; Meylan, 10.
37. Bainbridge, 56.
38. Vyrubova, 74.
39. Buxhoeveden, *Before*, 287.
40. Nesin, 26.
41. Hammer, 223–24.
42. Habsburg and Lopato, 24.
43. Ibid., 33–34.
44. Fabergé, Proler, and Skurlov, 15–17.
45. Habsburg and Lopato, 107; Fabergé, Proler, and Skurlov, 47.

CHAPTER 17: IMPERIAL TRANSPORTATION

1. Kleinmichel, 34.
2. de Monte Alto, 24.
3. *Russian Court Memoirs*, 57.
4. Leudet, 215.
5. Ibid.
6. Petrov, *Suburbs*, 476.
7. Vasilevskaya, 110–11; Shvidkovsky, *St. Petersburg*, 172; Mawdsley, 332.

8. Leudet, 216–19.
9. *Le Monde*, January 25, 2001, Wilson, 81–82.
10. Rodimzeva, Rakhmanov, and Raimann, 213.
11. Timms, 172.
12. Prince Christopher of Greece, 50.
13. Leudet, 218–19.
14. Ibid., 218.
15. Bariatinsky, 62.
16. Swezey, 82–84.
17. Ibid., 84–85.
18. Ometev, 213.
19. Lyons, N-80.
20. Vernova, *Treasures of Russia*, 198; Baltsykevich, 54–57.
21. *L'illustration*, October 3, 1896; Iroshnikov, Protsai, and Shelayev, *Sunset*, 136.
22. Vernova, *Treasures of Russia*, 199–202.
23. Ibid., 198.
24. Mossolov, 241–42; Vyrubova, 97; Vernova, *Treasures of Russia*, 198.
25. *L'illustration*, October 3, 1896.
26. Mossolov, 240.
27. Prince Christopher of Greece, 21.
28. de Jonge, 198.
29. Alexander M. Golubev and Andrei L. Larionov, "Two Ships," in *Marie Feodorovna*, 230–36, 440.
30. Znamenov, Larionov, and Nosovich, 250.
31. Ibid., 187.
32. Golubev and Larionov, 440.
33. Ibid., 230–36.
34. Ibid., 452.
35. Dowager Empress Marie Feodorovna to Nicholas II, August 8, 1897, in GARF, F. 601, Op. 1, D. 1163.
36. Golubev and Larionov, 452.
37. Znamenov, Larionov, and Nosovich, 198.
38. Znamenov, Larionov, and Nosovich, 210; Piper, 13.
39. Golubev and Larionov, 230–36.
40. Spiridovich, 1:193.
41. Buxhoeveden, *Before*, 285.
42. Elchaninov, 41.
43. Znamenov, Larionov, and Nosovich, 202.
44. Golubev and Larionov, 454.
45. Golubev and Larionov, 230–36; Mossolov 246; Spiridovich, 1:187–93.
46. Buxhoeveden, *Before*, 289.
47. Grabbe and Grabbe, 57.
48. Elchaninov, 41; Grabbe and Grabbe, 106.
49. Spiridovich, 2:38.
50. Lyons, N-61; Grabbe and Grabbe, 95.
51. Mossolov, 246.
52. *Russian Court Memoirs*, 61.
53. Mossolov, 245.
54. Voronoff, 49.
55. Lyons, N-52.
56. Vyrubova, 29.
57. Grabbe and Grabbe, 90–91.
58. Buxhoeveden, *Life*, 119.
59. Grabbe and Grabbe, 90–91.
60. Vyrubova, 29.

61. Hoff, 92.
62. Vyrubova, 33.
63. Buxhoeveden, *Life*, 114.
64. Buxhoeveden, *Life*, 114; Vyrubova, 33.
65. Buxhoeveden, *Life*, 114.
66. Buxhoeveden, *Life*, 114; Vyrubova, 33.
67. Buxhoeveden, *Life*, 114.
68. Vyrubova, 32–33.
69. Spiridovich, 1:194–95; Mossolov, 247.
70. Grabbe and Grabbe, 95.
71. Buxhoeveden, *Life*, 119–20.
72. Grabbe and Grabbe, 104.
73. Buxhoeveden, *Life*, 120.
74. Grabbe and Grabbe, 104–6.
75. Vyrubova, 18.
76. Grabbe and Grabbe, 109–13.
77. Buxhoeveden, *Life*, 199.
78. Vyrubova, 28.
79. Elchaninov, 41.
80. Buxhoeveden, 120.
81. Vyrubova, 29.
82. See Golubev and Larionov, 230–36; and Zuev for further details.

CHAPTER 18: COUNTRY ESTATES

1. Hickley, 54–55.
2. In 1919, Skernevetski was confiscated by the Polish government and used as an official residence. During World War II, the German Army occupied the palace, and its neoclassical rooms served a more ominous purpose, as Warsaw Headquarters for the dreaded Gestapo. After a period of restoration, the Bishop's Palace housed several official institutions; in 1998, it was converted into a museum.
3. Falinski, 11–17; Keczynscy and Keczynscy; information from Monika Szabalowska-Koczuk to author.
4. Keczynscy and Keczynscy; information from Janet Ashton, and from Monika Szabalowska-Koczuk, to author.
5. Keczynscy and Keczynscy; information from Janet Ashton, and from Monika Szabalowska-Koczuk, to author.
6. Spiridovich, 2:274–76; information from Janet Ashton to author.
7. Keczynscy and Keczynscy; information from Janet Ashton, and from Monika Szabalowska-Koczuk, to author.
8. Tsesarevich Nicholas, Diary, August 19, 1894, in GARF, F. 601, Op. 1, D. 233.
9. Keczynscy and Keczynscy; information from Janet Ashton to author.
10. Information from Janet Ashton to author.
11. Kleinmichel, 20.
12. Mossolov, 253.
13. Nicholas II, Diary, January 11, 1904, in GARF, F. 601, Op. 1, D. 247.
14. Buchanan, *Mission*, 1:168.
15. Perry and Pleshakov, 46.
16. Mossolov, 251–54; Mamontov, 109–10; Spiridovich, 2:261–62.
17. Iroshnikov, Protsai, and Shelayev, *Sunset*, 84.
18. In 1918, Bielovezh was seized by the newly independent Polish government, which installed a number of organizations within its rooms, including the Bialowieza Provincial Offices and the Polish Forestry School. In 1930, the lodge became the country retreat of the president of Poland, though the interior was not substantially altered. During the Second World War, the palace was seized by occupying German troops and used as their local headquarters. Hermann Göring came here to hunt in 1935 and again during the war. When, on the night of July 17, 1944, the Germans retreated, they set fire to the building; at the end of three days, only the exterior brick walls were left. The Polish authorities considered the building a danger, and in 1947 it was blown up. For fourteen years, the ruins lay neglected; then, in 1960, the last vestiges of de Rochefort's lodge were carted away, replaced with a tourist hotel (Keczynscy and Keczynscy; information from Monika Szabalowska-Koczuk to author). Officially established as a National Park in 1932, the Bialowieza Puscha was added to the list of World Heritage Sites in 1979. In 1999, a permanent exhibition, "The Tsar's Palace at Bialowieza," was established in the old gatehouse. (Information from Monika Szabalowska-Koczuk and from Janet Ashton, to author.)
19. Vyrubova, 91.
20. Ibid.
21. Nicholas II to Queen Victoria, September 11, 1894, in Maylunas and Mironenko, 94–95.
22. Mamontov, 109–10; Spiridovich, 2:261–62.
23. Nicholas II to Dowager Empress Marie Feodorovna, October 20, 1912, in Bing, 275.
24. Vyrubova, 92.
25. Gilliard, 29.
26. Vyrubova, 93.
27. Buxhoeveden, *Life*, 132.
28. Vyrubova, 93.
29. Gilliard, 29–31.
30. Naryshkin-Kuryakin, 196.
31. Gilliard, 29.
32. Ibid., 31.
33. Vyrubova, 93.
34. Ibid., 94.
35. Paleologue, 1:148.
36. Empress Alexandra to Boyd-Carpenter, January 24/February 7, 1913, in BL, Additional Manuscripts, 47621, F. 240–43.
37. Vyrubova, 96.
38. In 1920, the Polish Republic nationalized Spala, and for a time it served as a country retreat for the president. In the late 1920s, the lodge was substantially altered by the Warsaw architect Ignaty Molcicki, who provided modern amenities for the president's use. In the 1930s, the lodge played host to a number of visiting Nazi officials, including Reichsmarshal Hermann Göring and Joachim von Ribbentrop, Hitler's minister of foreign affairs. During the Second World War, the Germans occupied the estate, and the lodge served as German Military Headquarters

in Poland for a time. In 1943, Adolf Hitler himself stayed here, sleeping in Nicholas and Alexandra's former bedroom. On January 17, 1945, as they retreated, the Nazi troops set fire to the villa; in less than six hours, flames reduced the wooden lodge to a smoldering pile of ashes. Today, the estate functions as the Polish Olympic Training Center.

CHAPTER 19: IMPERIAL CEREMONIES

1. Wortman, 1:324–25.
2. Vassili, 156.
3. Zinovieff and Hughes, 139, 141; Hancock, 213.
4. Vorres, 100.
5. Mossolov, 190; Wortman, 1:324–25.
6. Vorres, 100.
7. Kropotkin, 201–2.
8. Buxhoeveden, *Before*, 202.
9. Ibid., 205–7.
10. Buchanan, *Victorian Gallery*, 160.
11. Vassili, 230.
12. Naryshkin-Kuryakin, 145–46.
13. Buchanan, *Queen Victoria's Relations*, 196–98.
14. Nesin, 48–49.
15. Gautier, 173.
16. Ibid., 172.
17. Ibid., 174.
18. Massie, *Firebird*, 363; George, *Romanov Diary*, 117.
19. Weber-Bauler, 121.
20. Buxhoeveden, *Before*, 208.
21. Nicholas II, Diary, January 6, 1905, in GARF, F. 601, Op. 1, D. 248.
22. Weber-Bauler, 122.
23. Buxhoeveden, *Before*, 202–3.
24. Izwolsky, *No Time*, 86–88.
25. Wortman, 2:19.
26. Alexander Mikhailovich, *Once*, 87; Wortman, 1:359–61.
27. Brayley-Hodgetts, 2:21.
28. Alexander Mikhailovich, *Once*, 87; Wortman, 1:359–61.
29. Naryshkin-Kuryakin, 100.
30. Vernova, *Treasures of Russia*, 212; Timms, 420.
31. Tsesarevich Nicholas, Diary, May 6, 1884, in GARF F. 601, Op. 1, D. 219.
32. Wortman, 2:309.
33. Wilhelm II to Nicholas II, August 29, 1904, in GARF, F. 601, Op. 1, D. 1199; Nicholas II to Dowager Empress Marie Feodorovna, in Bing, 270–71.
34. Marie Pavlovna, 65.
35. Buxhoeveden, *Before*, 238.
36. Nicholas II, Diary, August 11, 1904, in GARF, Op. 1, D. 247.
37. Buxhoeveden, *Before*, 239.
38. Marie Pavlovna, 66.
39. Buxhoeveden, *Before*, 239–40.
40. Buxhoeveden, *Before*, 240; Swezey, 88.
41. Buxhoeveden, *Before*, 240.
42. Marie Pavlovna, 66.
43. Grand Duke Konstantin Konstantinovich, Diary, August 11, 1904, in GARF, F. 660, Op. 1, D. 53.
44. Buxhoeveden, *Before*, 240–41.
45. Spiridovich, 1:328–29; Grand Duke Konstantin Konstantinovich, Diary, June 25, 1909, in GARF, F. 660, Op. 1, D. 61.
46. Grand Duke Konstantin Konstantinovich, Diary, June 26, 1909, in GARF, F. 660, Op. 1, D. 61.
47. Elchaninov, 111–12.
48. Grand Duke Konstantin Konstantinovich, Diary, June 27, 1909, in GARF, F. 660, Op. 1, D. 61.
49. Wortman, 2:422.
50. Cited in Lieven, 167.
51. Dzhunkovsky, 2:19.
52. Ibid., 2:27–28.
53. Dzhunkovsky, 2:35–36; Spiridovich, 1:324–31.
54. Yusupov, 142.
55. Nicholas II to Dowager Empress Marie Feodorovna, September 10, 1912, in GARF, F. 642, Op. 1, D. 2332.
56. Dzhunkovsky, 2:19–20.
57. Nicholas II to Dowager Empress Marie Feodorovna, September 10, 1912, in GARF, F. 642, Op. 1, D. 2332; Spiridovich, 2:226.
58. Spiridovich, 2:266.
59. Elchaninov, 71.
60. Ibid., 78.
61. Nicholas II to Dowager Empress Marie Feodorovna, September 10, 1912, in GARF, F. 642, Op. 1, D. 2332.
62. Dzhunkovsky, 2:59–61; Bruce Lockhart, 73.
63. Rodzianko, 65–66.
64. Schanoshnikova, 2–4; Kedrinskii et al., 189; Petrov, *Pamyatniki arkitekturi Leningrada*, 214.
65. Ometev, 43.
66. *Novoe Vremia*, May 28, 1909.
67. Schanoshnikova, 2–3.
68. Cited in George and George, *St. Petersburg*, 349.
69. Marie Pavlovna, 84.
70. Alexander Mikhailovich, *Once*, 226–27.
71. Gurko, 470.
72. Vassili, 345.
73. Nesin, 178–79.
74. Vassili, 345.
75. Wortman, 2:403.
76. Grand Duchess Xenia Alexandrovna, Diary, April 27, 1906, in Maylunas and Mironenko, 282–83.
77. Izvolsky, *Recollections*, 74–76.
78. *Novoe Vremia*, April 28, 1906.
79. Vassili, 345.
80. Grand Duchess Xenia Alexandrovna, Diary, April 27, 1906, in Maylunas and Mironenko, 289.
81. Buxhoeveden, *Before*, 276.
82. Kokovtsov, 129–31.
83. Nicholas II, Diary, April 27, 1906, in GARF, F. 601, Op. 1, D. 251.
84. Naryshkin-Kuryakin, 189.

CHAPTER 20: AN IMPERIAL FUNERAL

1. Cited in Lowe, 277.
2. Ibid., 281.
3. Lowe, 285.

4. George, *Romanov Diary*, 48.
5. Vorres, 51.
6. Lowe, 285.
7. Vorres, 63.
8. Lowe, 286.
9. Ibid., 283.
10. Ibid., 288–89.
11. Prince Nicholas of Greece, 116.
12. Nicholas II, Diary, October 20, 1894, in GARF, F. 601, Op. 1, D. 233.
13. Tsesarevich Nicholas to Princess Alix of Hesse und Bei Rhein, April 23, 1894, in Maylunas and Mironenko, 60; *The Times*, October 17, 1894.
14. Nicholas II, Diary, October 21, 1894, in GARF, F. 601, Op. 1, D. 233.
15. *The Times*, November 14, 1894.
16. Lowe, 367.
17. Nicholas II, Diary, October 21, 1894, in GARF, F. 601, Op. 1, D. 233.
18. Ibid., October 22, 1894, in GARF, F. 601, Op. 1, D. 233.
19. Ibid., October 24, 1894, in GARF, F. 601, Op. 1, D. 233.
20. Vorres, 56.
21. Lowe, 292–93.
22. George, *Romanov Diary*, 50.
23. Prince Nicholas of Greece, 118.
24. "The Death and Burial of Emperor Alexander III," by M. A. Bera, in Barry, 92.
25. Ibid., 91.
26. Ibid., 93.
27. Ibid.
28. Lowe, 294–95.
29. Ibid., 295.
30. M. A. Bera, in Barry, 93.
31. Ibid., 93–94.
32. Grand Duke Konstantin Konstantinovich, Diary, November 1, 1894, in GARF, F. 660, Op. 1, D. 41.
33. Lowe, 297.
34. Ibid., 296.
35. Bariatinsky, 34; Lowe, 296–97.
36. Bariatinsky, 34.
37. Lowe, 297.
38. Buxhoeveden, *Before*, 147.
39. Bariatinsky, 34–35.
40. Buxhoeveden, *Before*, 148.
41. Gilliard, 48.
42. Gendrikov and Senko, 132.
43. Lowe, 298–99.
44. Ibid., 300.
45. Ignatiev, 57.
46. M. A. Bera, in Barry, 95.
47. Lowe, 300–1.
48. Quoted in Maylunas and Mironenko, 104.
49. Gendrikov and Senko, 131.
50. Hamilton, 166; Queen Marie of Romania, 1:197.
51. Lowe, 301–3; *The Illustrated London News*, November 24, 1894.
52. Witte, 208.

CHAPTER 21: AN IMPERIAL WEDDING

1. Nicholas II, Diary, October 22, 1894, in GARF, F. 601, Op. 1, D. 233.
2. Poliakoff, *Tragic Bride*, 69–70.
3. Nicholas II, Diary, November 13, 1894, in GARF, F. 601, Op. 1, D. 233.
4. "Nicholas and Alix: Joined at Last in Holy Matrimony," in *The Call*, San Francisco, November 27, 1894.
5. Ibid.
6. *The Illustrated London News*, December 8, 1894.
7. "Nicholas and Alix: Joined at Last in Holy Matrimony," in *The Call*, San Francisco, November 27, 1894.
8. Ibid.
9. *The Times*, November 27, 1894.
10. "Nicholas and Alix: Joined at Last in Holy Matrimony," in *The Call*, San Francisco, November 27, 1894.
11. Gerois, 1:36–37.
12. Norman, *Hermitage*, 16.
13. Vassili, 209.
14. Buxhoeveden, *Life*, 43; Ernst Ludwig, 68.
15. Poliakoff, *Mother Dear*, 234–35.
16. Vassili, 207.
17. Buxhoeveden, *Life*, 43; "Nicholas and Alix: Joined at Last in Holy Matrimony," in *The Call*, San Francisco, November 27, 1894.
18. Mager, 162.
19. Poliakoff, *Tragic Bride*, 76.
20. Hough, *Louis and Victoria*, 126.
21. Grand Duke Konstantin Konstantinovich, Diary, November 15, 1894, in GARF, F. 660, Op. 1, D. 41.
22. Empress Alexandra to Queen Victoria, November 16, 1894, in Maylunas and Mironenko, 112.
23. Dowager Empress Marie Feodorovna to Queen Louise of Denmark, November 17, 1894, cited in *Marie Feodorovna*, 166.
24. Poliakoff, *Tragic Bride*, 76; "Nicholas and Alix: Joined at Last in Holy Matrimony," in *The Call*, San Francisco, November 27, 1894.
25. Poliakoff, *Tragic Bride*, 76.
26. Grand Duke Konstantin Konstantinovich, Diary, November 15, 1894, in GARF, F. 660, Op. 1, D. 41.
27. Vassili, 206.
28. Quoted in Maylunas and Mironenko, 110.
29. Timms, 186; Poliakoff, *Tragic Bride*, 76; "Nicholas and Alix: Joined at Last in Holy Matrimony," in *The Call*, San Francisco, November 27, 1894; Beck, 122.
30. "Nicholas and Alix: Joined at Last in Holy Matrimony," in *The Call*, San Francisco, November 27, 1894; Poliakoff, *Tragic Bride*, 76.
31. Poliakoff, *Tragic Bride*, 76.
32. Ibid.
33. "Nicholas and Alix: Joined at Last in Holy Matrimony," in *The Call*, San Francisco, November 27, 1894.
34. Vassili, 209.
35. Grand Duke Konstantin Konstantinovich, Diary, November 15, 1894, in GARF, F. 660, Op. 1, D. 41.
36. "Nicholas and Alix: Joined at Last in Holy Matrimony," in *The Call*, San Francisco, November 27, 1894.

37. Grand Duke Konstantin Konstantinovich, Diary, November 15, 1894, in GARF, F. 660, Op. 1, D. 41.
38. Alexander Mikhailovich, *Once*, 169.
39. "Nicholas and Alix: Joined at Last in Holy Matrimony," in *The Call*, San Francisco, November 27, 1894.
40. Naryshkin-Kuryakin, 145.
41. Ernst Ludwig, 68.
42. "Nicholas and Alix: Joined at Last in Holy Matrimony," in *The Call*, San Francisco, November 27, 1894.
43. Vassili, 210.
44. Nicholas II, Diary, November 14, 1894, in GARF, F. 601, Op. 1, D. 233.
45. *The Illustrated London News*, December 8, 1894.
46. "Nicholas and Alix: Joined at Last in Holy Matrimony," in *The Call*, San Francisco, November 27, 1894.
47. Ibid.
48. Quoted in Oldenburg, 1:46.
49. "Nicholas and Alix: Joined at Last in Holy Matrimony," in *The Call*, San Francisco, November 27, 1894.
50. Nicholas II, Diary, November 14, 1894, in GARF, F. 601, Op. 1, D. 233.
51. Fulop-Miller, 80.

CHAPTER 22: THE CORONATION

1. Naryshkin-Kuryakin, 146.
2. Iroshnikov, Protsai, and Shelayev, *Sunset*, 20; Demidenko, *Reveling St. Petersburg*, 18; Chakirov, 259.
3. Bokhanov, 94–96.
4. Bovey, 10, 32; Hickley, 11.
5. Vladimir Nemirovich-Danchenko, in *Niva*, No. 19, May 1896, 448–51.
6. Iroshnikov, Protsai, and Shelayev, *Sunset*, 22.
7. Vladimir Nemirovich-Danchenko, in *Niva*, No. 19, May 1896, 448.
8. Vladimir Nemirovich-Danchenko, in *Niva*, No. 19, May 1896, 450.
9. Salisbury, 52.
10. Polynina and Rakhmanov, 184.
11. Davis, *A Year*, 39.
12. de Vianzone, 6–7.
13. de Monte Alto, 33.
14. Nicholas II, Diary, May 6, 1896, in GARF, F. 601, Op. 1, D. 236.
15. Grand Duke Konstantin Konstantinovich, Diary, May 8, 1896, in GARF, F. 660, Op. 1, D. 41.
16. Hickley, 10.
17. Grand Duke Konstantin Konstantinovich, Diary, May 8, 1896, in GARF, F. 660, Op. 1, D. 41.
18. Hickley, 10; de Monte Alto, 34.
19. Grand Duke Konstantin Konstantinovich, Diary, May 9, 1896, in GARF, F. 660, Op. 1, D. 41.
20. Davis, *A Year*, 21; Logan, 83; *The Times*, Weekly Edition, May 29, 1896.
21. Bokhanov, 96.
22. Logan, 102–3.
23. Bovey, 15.
24. *New York Times*, May 22, 1896.
25. LaPauze, 77.
26. Hickley, 12; LaPauze, 77; de Monte Alto, 38; Grenfell, 27.
27. de Monte Alto, 38.
28. Logan, 99–100; Bovey, 15–17; Bokhanov, 98.
29. LaPauze, 78.
30. Logan, 103.
31. Nicholas II, Diary, May 9, 1896, in GARF, F. 601, Op. 1, D. 236; Bokhanov, 98; *Les Solennites*, 206.
32. de Vianzone, 9.
33. Bovey, 16.
34. LaPauze, 79; Hickley, 13.
35. Queen Marie of Romania, 1:330.
36. Buxhoeveden, *Before*, 150.
37. Grand Duke Konstantin Konstantinovich, Diary, May 9, 1896, in GARF, F. 660, Op. 1, D. 41.
38. Davis, *A Year*, 32–34.
39. Pelham-Clinton, 489.
40. Ignatiev, 61.
41. Queen Marie of Romania, 1:331.
42. Logan, 104.
43. de Monte Alto, 41.
44. *Les Solennites*, 214.
45. Vladimir Nemirovich-Danchenko, in *Niva*, No. 20, May 1896, 505–6.
46. Buxhoeveden, *Life*, 64.
47. Polynina and Rakhmanov, 200; Hancock, 171, 174; Logan, 106–8.
48. de Monte Alto, 44.
49. Polynina and Rakhmanov, 133, 184.
50. *Les Solennites*, 220.
51. Ibid., 230.
52. Logan, 118.
53. Nicholas II, Diary, May 13, 1896, in GARF, F. 601, Op. 1, D. 236.
54. Kirill Vladimirovich, 63.
55. *Les Solennites*, 233.
56. *Intimacies*, 114.
57. Davis, *A Year*, 36.
58. *Intimacies*, 114.
59. Hickley, 16.
60. Bovey, 20–22.
61. Logan, 114.
62. Polynina and Rakhmanov, 203.
63. Davis, *A Year*, 45.
64. LaPauze, 103; *Les Solennites*, 233.
65. LaPauze, 103.
66. Bokhanov, 94.
67. Wortman, 2:353.
68. Goncharenko and Narozhnaya, 140.
69. Polynina and Rakhmanov, 195; Buxhoeveden, *Life*, 64.
70. Bothmer, 61.
71. Tiutcheva, 2:121–22.
72. Naryshkin-Kuryakin, 148.
73. Bovey, 23.
74. Grand Duke Konstantin Konstantinovich, Diary, May 14, 1896, in GARF, F. 660, Op. 1, D. 41.
75. *Les Solennites*, 236.
76. *Intimacies*, 117.

77. Logan, 122.
78. Ibid.
79. *Les Solennites*, 238.
80. Logan, 121.
81. Logan, 123–24; *Les Solennites*, 238.
82. Logan, 124–25.
83. *Les Solennites*, 241.
84. Leyda, 19.
85. Polynina and Rakhmanov, 203–4; Bokhanov, 104.
86. *Les Solennites*, 241.
87. *Les Solennites*, 241; de Monte Alto, 53.
88. Vernova, *Treasures of Russia*, 89; Beck, 59.
89. Buxhoeveden, *Life*, 66–67; Queen Marie of Romania, 1:336.
90. Queen Marie of Romania, 2:79.
91. Kirill Vladimirovich, 64.
92. Grand Duke Konstantin Konstantinovich, Diary, May 14, 1896, in GARF, F. 660, Op. 1, D. 41.
93. *Les Solennites*, 233; Polynina and Rakhmanov, 204; Buxhoeveden, *Life*, 63.
94. *Les Solennites*, 245–47.
95. Buxhoeveden, Life, 64.
96. Polynina and Rakhmanov, 184.
97. *Les Solennites*, 246.
98. Vorres, 75.
99. Davis, *A Year*, 55.
100. Polynina and Rakhmanov, 192.
101. Polynina and Rakhmanov, 184; Essed-Bey, 63.
102. Polynina and Rakhmanov, 204; Bokhanov, 104.
103. Logan, 125; Polynina and Rakhmanov, 204; Bokhanov, 104.
104. Kirill Vladimirovich, 64.
105. Grenfell, 35.
106. Vorres, 76.
107. Davis, *A Year*, 61.
108. *Les Solennites*, 1:248.
109. Oldenburg, 1:59–60.
110. Queen Marie of Romania, 1:333.
111. Polynina and Rakhmanov, 210.
112. Buxhoeveden, Life, 65.
113. Polynina and Rakhmanov, 156; *Les Solennites*, 254.
114. Queen Marie of Romania, 1:331.
115. Logan, 136.
116. Bovey, 25.
117. *Intimacies*, 120.
118. Ernst Ludwig, 73.
119. Logan, 138.
120. *Les Solennites*, 267–69.
121. Buxhoeveden, *Before*, 151.
122. *Les Solennites*, 267–69.
123. Mossolov, 183.
124. *Les Solennites*, 267–69.
125. Piper, 9, 12.
126. Demidenko, *Reveling St. Petersburg*, 24.
127. Bovey, 26.
128. Bokhanov, 104.
129. *Les Solennites*, 267–69.
130. *Intimacies*, 122–23.
131. Hickley, 25.
132. Souiny, 102; Romanovsky-Krassinsky, 59.
133. Hickley, 25.
134. Logan, 167–68; *Les Solennites*, 280.
135. Grand Duke Konstantin Konstantinovich, Diary, May 15, 1896, in GARF, F. 660, Op. 1, D. 41.
136. *Les Solennites*, 288.
137. Ibid., 288–89.
138. Bovey, 40.
139. *Les Solennites*, 289–90.
140. Salisbury, 52.
141. Grand Duke Konstantin Konstantinovich, Diary, May 17, 1896, in GARF, F. 660, Op. 1, D. 41.
142. Vladimir Nemirovich-Danchenko, in Niva, No. 22, May 1896, 564.
143. *Les Solennites*, 308–10.
144. Bobrov and Kirikov, 22.
145. Romanovsky-Krassinsky, 57–58; Bobrov and Kirikov, 22–23.
146. Harcave, 293.
147. Decree on public festivities at Khodynka Field, May 18, 1896, in GARF, F. 601, Op. 1, D. 140.
148. Polynina and Rakhmanov, 221; Iroshnikov, Protsai, and Shelayev, 30.
149. Salisbury, 56–57; Harcave, 293–94; Alexander Mikhailovich, *Once*, 171–72.
150. Vladimir Nemirovich-Danchenko, in *Niva*, No. 22, May 1896.
151. Hickley, 29.
152. Nicholas II, Diary, May 18, 1896, in GARF, F. 601, Op. 1, D. 236.
153. Leyda, 19.
154. de Monte Alto, 89.
155. Witte, 241.
156. Grenfell, 47.
157. *Les Solennites*, 311.
158. Witte, 242.
159. Vorres, 78.
160. Salisbury, 56.
161. Witte, 240.
162. *Les Solennites*, 312.
163. *Les Solennites*, 317; Vorres, 79; Barkovets, *Sredi Shtynogo Bala*, 39.
164. Buxhoeveden, *Before*, 154.
165. Grand Duchess Xenia Alexandrovna, Diary, May 18, 1896, in Maylunas and Mironenko, 146.
166. Alexander Mikhailovich, *Once*, 172.
167. In a public letter, Nicholas pledged that the families of each victim would receive a thousand rubles; this money came not from the emperor's own funds, but from the State Budget. The official account of the inquiry, *Otchet osoboi Kommissii, Obrazovannoi dlia vyiasneniia lichnosti pogibshikh na Khodynskom Pole 18-go Maia 1896 goda*, listed 1,386 victims, but only 374,580 rubles were granted for payments, which would, if divided equally, have meant 270 rubles per victim. The commission allocated grants based on the economic positions of the dead. Only 277 families

received a thousand rubles; 125 received five hundred rubles; smaller amounts were given to some 500 families, while nearly 400—mainly those who had lost children or older members—were denied any grants. Many in the latter group petitioned the emperor for relief, but Nicholas refused to honor his public promise. For more information, see Baker, 106–144.

168. *Les Solennites*, 332.
169. de Monte Alto, 34.
170. *Les Solennites*, 327; Vernova, *Treasures of Russia*, 213.
171. Hickley, 33.
172. *Les Solennites*, 309.

CHAPTER 23: THE TERCENTENARY

1. Hancock, 24.
2. Cited in Wortman, 2:484.
3. Ibid., 2:483.
4. Nesin, 40.
5. Cantacuzené, *Life*, 315.
6. Vassili, 403.
7. *Niva*, February 16, 1913.
8. Wortman, 2:443.
9. Ibid., 2:457.
10. Vassili, 399–400.
11. Cited in Wortman, 2:462.
12. Vassili, 399–400.
13. Kokovtsov, 361.
14. Vyrubova, 98.
15. Nicholas II, Diary, February 21, 1913, in GARF, F. 601, Op. 1, D. 259.
16. Ibid.
17. Vassili, 403.
18. *The Times*, March 7, 1913.
19. Spiridovich, 1:315–16.
20. Dzhunkovsky, 2:148.
21. Rodzianko, 75–77.
22. Almedingen, *I Remember St. Petersburg*, 162.
23. Vassili, 404.
24. Chabrun, 236.
25. Vassili, 405.
26. Buchanan, *Dissolution*, 35.
27. Vyrubova, 98.
28. Rodzianko, 78.
29. Spiridovich, 1:317.
30. Cited in Wortman, 2:464.
31. Buchanan, *Dissolution*, 35.
32. de Stoeckl, *My Dear Marquis*, 143.
33. Buchanan, *Dissolution*, 36.
34. de Stoeckl, *My Dear Marquis*, 143–44.
35. Cantacuzené, *Life*, 317.
36. Ibid., 315–16.
37. Buchanan, *Dissolution*, 37.
38. Cantacuzené, *Life*, 316.
39. Buchanan, *Queen Victoria's Relations*, 211.
40. Buxhoeveden, *Life*, 175.
41. Nicholas II, Diary, May 16, 1913, in GARF, F. 601, Op. 1, D. 259.
42. Dzhunkovsky, 2:192–94.

43. Spiridovich, 2:333–34.
44. Dzhunkovsky, 2:191 95; Spiridovich, 2:334–35.
45. *Novoe Vremia*, May 21, 1913.
46. Dzhunkovsky, 2:195–96.
47. Vorres, 130.
48. Dzhunkovsky, 2:197–98.
49. Ibid., 2:198.
50. Nicholas II, Diary, May 20, 1913, in GARF, F. 601, Op. 1, D. 259.
51. Dzhunkovsky, 1:198.
52. Kokovtsov, 169.
53. Cited in Wortman, 2:472.
54. Spiridovich, 2:340; Wortman, 2:475.
55. Dzhunkovsky, 1:199.
56. See Wortman, 2:452–55, for more details.
57. Dzhunkovsky, 2:199.
58. Nicholas II, Diary, May 20, 1913, in GARF, F. 601, Op. 1, D. 259.
59. Bruce Lockhart, in Bing, 10.
60. Kokovtsov, 224.
61. Naryshkin-Kuryakin, 206.

CHAPTER 24: IMPERIAL BALLS

1. Dukov, 179.
2. Hancock, 214; Vassili, 155–56; Mossolov, 192.
3. Mossolov, 197.
4. Ignatiev, 154.
5. Salisbury, 240–42; Cerwinske, 166–67; Alexander, 161–62; Prince Michael of Greece, *Imperial Palaces*, 150–51; Massie, *Firebird*, 274–79.
6. "Remembrances of Major General Feodor Petrovich Rerberg," in Barry, 77.
7. Sir Horace Rumbold, "Recollections," quoted in Brayley-Hodgetts, 2:71.
8. Gautier, 208.
9. Ibid., 209.
10. Lathrop, 65; *Intimacies*, 131.
11. Londonderry, 102.
12. Mossolov, 193–94.
13. Lathrop, 69.
14. Mossolov, 196.
15. Naryshkin-Kuryakin, 94.
16. "My Last Ball," by P. P. Gudim-Levokovich, in Barry, 73.
17. Lathrop, 66.
18. Vassili, 155–56.
19. Rerberg, in Barry, 162.
20. Rerberg, in Barry, 80.
21. Alexander Mikhailovich, *Once*, 56.
22. Gudim-Levokovich, in Barry, 73.
23. Rerberg, in Barry, 163.
24. Radziwill, *Intimate Life*, 75–76.
25. Gautier, 210.
26. Lathrop, 66.
27. Gautier, 215.
28. Wonlar-Larsky, 79.
29. Ignatiev, 154.
30. Vassili, 156.
31. Ibid., 157.

32. Mossolov, 198–202; Gautier, 217.
33. *Intimacies*, 135.
34. Ibid., 132.
35. Vassili, 157.
36. Wonlar-Larsky, 79.
37. *Intimacies*, 133.
38. Wonlar-Larsky, 80.
39. Private information to author.
40. Odom, 21.
41. Alexander Mikhailovich, *Once*, 211.
42. Polynina and Rakhmanov, 196.
43. Alexander Mikhailovich, *Once*, 211.
44. Eager, 175.
45. Timms, 214.
46. Prince Michael of Greece, *Crown Jewels*, 150–51; George, *Romanov Diary*, 102; Vorres, 102; Hancock, 224–25.
47. Vorres, 102.
48. George, *Romanov Diary*, 102.
49. Alexander Mikhailovich, *Once*, 211.
50. Buchanan, *Victorian Gallery*, 183.
51. George, *Romanov Diary*, 102; Timms, 214; Buxhoeveden, *Life*, 98–99.
52. Buchanan, *Victorian Gallery*, 183.
53. Ibid.
54. Timms, 216.
55. Buchanan, *Victorian Gallery*, 183.
56. Voyekov, 38; Timms, 214.
57. George, *Romanov Diary*, 103.
58. See *Al'bom kostiumirovovannogo bala* and *Album du Bal Costume* for further details.
59. Grand Duke Konstantin Konstantinovich, Diary, February 11, 1903, in GARF, F. 660, Op. 1, D. 51; Nicholas II, Diary, February 11, 1903, in GARF, F. 601, Op. 1, D. 245.
60. Vorres, 102.
61. Alexander Mikhailovich, *Once*, 210.

CHAPTER 25: STATE VISITS

1. Cited in Magnus, 247.
2. Poliakoff, *Tragic Bride*, 122.
3. *L'Illustration*, October 10, 1896; Bariatinsky, 59.
4. Baschet, 7.
5. Ibid., 8.
6. Ibid., 9.
7. Ibid., 10.
8. Ibid., 4.
9. de Stoeckl, *My Dear Marquis*, 52.
10. Baschet, 16.
11. Oldenburg, 1:69–73.
12. *Monde Illustre*, October 1896, 230; Baschet, 10, 12.
13. Baschet, 11–13.
14. Nicholas II to Dowager Empress Marie Feodorovna, October 2, 1896, in Bing, 119–20.
15. de Stoeckl, *My Dear Marquis*, 53.
16. de Stoeckl, *My Dear Marquis*, 53; Baschet, 14–16.
17. Baschet, 14.
18. de Stoeckl, *My Dear Marquis*, 53.
19. Nicholas II to Dowager Empress Marie Feodorovna, October 2, 1896, in Bing, 120.
20. *Monde Illustre*, October, 1896, 230.
21. *L'Illustration*, October 10, 1896.
22. Baschet, 4.
23. Buxhoeveden, *Life*, 75.
24. Bariatinsky, 60.
25. *L'Illustration*, October 10, 1896.
26. Bariatinsky, 62.
27. Nicholas II to Dowager Empress Marie Feodorovna, October 2, 1896, in Bing, 121–22.
28. Paoli, 129–31.
29. Nicholas II to Dowager Empress Marie Feodorovna, October 2, 1896, in Bing, 122.
30. *L'Illustration*, October 10, 1896.
31. Ibid.
32. *Petit Parisien*, October 7, 1896.
33. Nicholas II to Dowager Empress Marie Feodorovna, October 2, 1896, in Bing, 122–23.
34. Buxhoeveden, *Life*, 75.
35. Baschet, 49.
36. Yusupov, 168.
37. Mossolov, 236.
38. Nicholas II to Dowager Empress Marie Feodorovna, August 1, 1897, in Bing, 128.
39. Bariatinsky, 82–83.
40. Romanovsky-Krassinsky, 63–64.
41. Nicholas II to Dowager Empress Marie Feodorovna, August 1, 1897, in Bing, 129.
42. Bariatinsky, 82–83.
43. Nicholas II to Dowager Empress Marie Feodorovna, August 1, 1897, in Bing, 129.
44. Nicholas II to Dowager Empress Marie Feodorovna, July 23, 1897, in Bing, 128.
45. Nicholas II to Dowager Empress Marie Feodorovna, August 1, 1897, in Bing, 130–31.
46. Mossolov, 203.
47. Hibbert, 315.
48. St. Aubyn, 359.
49. *The Times*, June 11, 1907.
50. St. Aubyn, 358.
51. Lee, 2:587.
52. Maurois, 199; Brook-Shepherd, 325.
53. St. Aubyn, 361.
54. Maurois, 199–200; Brook-Shepherd, 325; Longford, *Louisa*, 157, 168–71.
55. St. Aubyn, 361.
56. Tisdall, 211; Duff, 243.
57. Hough, *Edward and Alexandra*, 290.
58. Mossolov, 42.
59. Donaldson, 45.
60. Spiridovich, I:172.
61. Ibid., I:173.
62. Ibid.
63. Heckstall-Smith, 77.
64. *New York Times*, May 23, 1913.
65. *Daily Mail*, London, May 23, 1913.
66. Viktoria Luise, 68; *Journal de St. Petersbourg*, May 12, 1913.
67. Viktoria Luise, 69.
68. Koenig, 34.

69. Viktoria Luise, 69.
70. Ibid., 68–69.
71. Koenig, 36.
72. Viktoria Luise, 70; Koenig, 36.
73. Viktoria Luise, 71.
74. Ibid., 71–73.

CHAPTER 26: THE CRIMEA

1. Kokovtsov, 304.
2. Vyrubova, 37.
3. Fromenko, 8.
4. Obolensky, 172.
5. Vyrubova, 36–38; Yusupov, 92; de Stoeckl, *Not All Vanity*, 128; Eager, 127; Botkine, *Au Temps*, 85.
6. Vyrubova, 36–38.
7. Lashenko, 10.
8. Fromenko, 9–12; Zemlyanichenko, 36–38; Lashenko, 11; Fromenko, 10.
9. Fromenko, 12.
10. Lashenko, 11; Fromenko, 11–13; Zemlyanichenko, 38–39.
11. Fromenko, 13.
12. Vyrubova, 41–42; Lowe, 282.
13. Fromenko, 11–12.
14. Paley, 16.
15. Fromenko, 16–17.
16. Lashenko, 12.
17. Cresti and Rendina, 158; Fromenko, 18.
18. Buxhoeveden, *Life*, 177; Kaminski, 490–92.
19. Fromenko, 19.
20. Ibid., 19–20.
21. Ibid., 20–21.
22. Ibid.
23. Grabbe and Grabbe, 78.
24. Fromenko, 22; Lashenko, 11.
25. Lashenko, 11.
26. Ibid., 14.
27. Ibid.
28. Ibid. In addition to published sources, this description of the interior of the White Palace draws upon information provided by Coryne and Colin Hall, DeeAnn Hoff, Marion Wynne, Katrina Warne, Sue Woolmans, and Charlotte Zeepvat.
29. Fromenko, 14–15.
30. Lashenko, 12–13.
31. Lambsdorff, *Dnevnik (1894–1896)*, 36.
32. Volkov, 64.
33. Buxhoeveden, *Life*, 179.
34. Naryshkin-Kuryakin, 207.
35. *Marie Feodorovna*, 106.
36. Nashokina, 301–2.
37. Fromenko, 12.
38. Zemlyanichenko, 20–21.
39. Eager, 126.
40. Mossolov, 237.
41. Botkine, *Au Temps*, 9.
42. Vyrubova, 39.
43. Mossolov, 238–39.
44. Vorres, 110.

45. Vyrubova, 39; Volkov, 65–66; Eager, 39.
46. Volkov, 67.
47. Volkov, 67; Mossolov, 227.
48. Mossolov, 228.
49. Buxhoeveden, *Life*, 179.
50. Vyrubova, 39.
51. Wrangell-Rokoassowsky, 192–93.
52. Vyrubova, 39.
53. Vorres, 92.
54. Fromenko, 14.
55. Buxhoeveden, *Before*, 297.
56. Ibid., 296.
57. Buxhoeveden, *Life*, 180.
58. Fromenko, 15.
59. Ibid., 16.
60. Vyrubova, 48.
61. Fromenko, 16.
62. Vyrubova, 46.
63. Ibid., 43–44.
64. Naryshkin-Kuryakin, 201.
65. de Stoeckl, *Not All Vanity*, 119.
66. Vyrubova, 44.
67. Voronoff, 51.
68. Vyrubova, 44.
69. de Stoeckl, *Not All Vanity*, 119–20.
70. Voronoff, 51.
71. Vyrubova, 44.

CHAPTER 27: THE LAST SEASON

1. Lord Augustus Loftus, "Reminiscences," quoted in Brayley-Hodgetts, 2:75.
2. Kelly, 285.
3. Buxhoeveden, *Before*, 204.
4. *Intimacies*, 144.
5. Ibid., 145, 169.
6. Kleinmichel, 132–33.
7. Ometev, 38.
8. MacCallum Scott, 264.
9. Massie, *Firebird*, 254.
10. Romanovsky-Krassinsky, 23–25.
11. Buchanan, *Victorian Gallery*, 73–74.
12. *Russian Court Memoirs*, 64.
13. Vyrubova, 5.
14. *Intimacies*, 165, 138.
15. Buchanan, *Dissolution*, 14–15.
16. Izwolsky, *No Time*, 80.
17. Ibid., 79–80.
18. *Intimacies*, 139.
19. Izwolsky, *No Time*, 80.
20. Ibid., 55.
21. Buchanan, *Dissolution*, 17.
22. Wonlar-Larsky, 95–96.
23. Gautier, 165.
24. Ometev, 79.
25. *Russian Court Memoirs*, 262.
26. Nostitz, 134.
27. Izwolsky, *No Time*, 84–85.
28. Ibid., 85.
29. Erté, 56.

30. Yusupov, 182.
31. Ibid., 183.
32. Izwolsky, *No Time*, 86.
33. Buchanan, *Victorian Gallery*, 184–85.
34. Izwolsky, *No Time*, 86.
35. Buchanan, *Victorian Gallery*, 184.
36. Ibid., 185.
37. Ometev, 129; Kochan, 44; Kleinmichel, 176–78; de Basily, 26–27; Cantacuzené, *Life*, 319; and private information to author.
38. de Stoeckl, *My Dear Marquis*, 154–55.
39. Ibid., 152.
40. Ibid., 126.
41. Ibid., 127.
42. Queen Marie of Romania, 1:569.
43. Ibid., 1:575.
44. Naryshkin-Kuryakin, 209.
45. Gilliard, 95.
46. Queen Marie of Romania, 1:582.
47. Buxhoeveden, *Life*, 181–83.
48. Gilliard, 94.
49. *Russian Court Memoirs*, 69–70.
50. Paleologue, 1:13.
51. Chabrun, 3.
52. Paleologue, 1:14.
53. Ibid., 1:14.
54. Chabrun, 4.
55. Paleologue, 1:22.
56. Ibid., 1:24–25.
57. Ibid., 1:27–28.

EPILOGUE: JULY 10, 1914

1. Merry, 83–84.
2. Ometev, 237.
3. Merry, 84–85.

4. Nesin, 189–93.
5. Marie Pavlovna, 162.
6. Cantacuzené, *Revolutionary Days*, 16.
7. Ibid., 14–15.
8. Paleologue, 1:45–46.
9. Paleologue, 1:46.
10. Rodzianko, 109–10; Paleologue, 1:50.
11. Paleologue, 1:51.
12. Marie Pavlovna, 163.
13. Cantacuzené, *Revolutionary Days*, 15–16.
14. Voronoff, 73.
15. Voyekov, 59.
16. Voronoff, 73.
17. Paleologue, 1:46.

APPENDIX C: THE IMPERIAL COURT IN 1914

1. Information on the imperial court in 1914 is drawn from *Almanach de St. Petersbourg*; Bariatinsky, 65, 348; Barkovets and Krylov, *Tsesarevich*, 49–50, 61, 66–67, 95, 110–11, 129; Buxhoeveden, *Life*, 48, 54, 152, 227; Cantacuzené, *Revolutionary Days*, 64; Dmitrieva, 130; Marie Feodorovna, *Dnevniki*, 629, 632–34, 642–43, 645, 647, 649–50, 653, 656, 658, 664, 667–68, 671–73, 678, 683, 687, 690–92; Maylunas and Mironenko, 666; Mossolov, 113, 185; Platonov; Shepelov, "Imperatorskii Dvor," 47–51; Shepelov, "Pridvornie Tityli"; Vorres, 249; Zaharova, 28, 34, 310–11; http://www.allpravo.ru; http://www.george-orden.nm.ru; http://www.vgd.ru; http://www.his.1september.ru; http://www.mogilevhistory.narod.ru; http://www.korabel.ru; http://www.rgis.narod.ru; http://www.rulex.ru; http://www.orthorus.ru; http://www.kdpmc.ru; http://www.sedmeitza.ru; http://www.vipmed.ru; and http://www.geocities.com/henrivanoene/genleuchtenberg.

BIBLIOGRAPHY

Books

Abrikossow, Dimitri. *Revelations of a Russian Diplomat: The Memoirs of Dimitri Abrikossow.* Edited by George Alexander Lensen. Seattle: University of Washington, 1964.

Al'bom kostiumirovovannogo bala v Zimnem Dvortse v fevrale 1903g. St. Petersburg: Gosudarstvenni, 1904.

Album du Bal Costume au Palais d'hiver, fevrier 1903. Moscow: Troika, 1998.

Alexander Mikhailovich, Grand Duke of Russia. *Always a Grand Duke.* New York: Farrar & Rinehart, 1933.

———. *Once a Grand Duke.* New York: Farrar & Rinehart, 1932.

Almanach de St. Petersbourg, Cour, Monde et Ville. Issued by the Ministry of the Imperial Court. St. Petersburg: Societe M. O. Wolff, 1912.

Almedingen, M. E. *The Empress Alexandra.* London: Hutchinson, 1961.

———. *I Remember St. Petersburg.* London: Longmans, 1969.

———. *Tomorrow Will Come.* Suffolk, UK: Boydell Press, 1983.

Aronson, Theo. *A Family of Kings: The Descendants of Christian IX of Denmark.* London: Cassell, 1976.

Athlone, Princess Alice, Countess of. *For My Grandchildren.* London: Evans, 1966.

Baedecker, Karl. *Russia, with Teheran, Port Arthur, and Peking.* New York: Baedecker, 1914.

Bainbridge, Henry Charles. *Peter Carl Fabergé: His Life and Work.* London: Hamlyn, 1966.

Balsan, Consuelo Vanderbilt. *The Glitter and the Gold.* London: Heinemann, 1953.

Baltsykevich, I. *Petergof: Dvoretsi i Parki.* Leningrad: Lensoveta, 1935.

Bariatinsky, Princess Anatole. *My Russian Life.* London: Hutchinson, 1923.

Barkovets, Alia, and Valentina Tenikhina. *Nicholas II: The Imperial Family.* St. Petersburg: Arbis, 1998.

———. *Sredi Shtynogo Bala: Bal i imperatorskaya sem'ii (Vtorya Polovina XIX–Nachalo XX Veka).* Moscow: Iskusstvo, 2001.

Barkovets, Alia, and Alexander Krylov. *Tsesarevich.* Moscow: Vagrius, 1998.

Barkovets, Alia, Feodor Federov, and Alexander Krylov. *Peterhof ist ein Traum: Deutsche Prinzessinnen in Russland.* Berlin: Verlangs-GmbH, 2001.

Barry, Thomas E., ed. *Memoirs of the Pages to the Tsars.* Mississauga, Ontario: Gilbert's Royal Books, 2001.

Baschet, Ludovic. *Le Panorama Les Cinq Journées Russes, 5–9 Octobre, 1896.* Paris: Librairie d'Art, 1897.

de Basily, Prince Nicolas. *The Abdication of Emperor Nicholas II of Russia.* Princeton, N.J.: Princeton University Press, 1984.

Baylen, Joseph. *The Tsar's Lecturer-General: W. T. Stead and the Russian Revolution of 1905.* Atlanta: School of Arts and Sciences, Georgia State College, 1969.

Beable, William. *Russian Gazetter and Guide.* London: Russian Outlook, 1919.

Beck, J. Spencer, ed. *Palaces of St. Petersburg: Russian Imperial Style.* Exhibition Catalogue. Charlottesville, Va.: Thomasson-Grant, 1996.

Belkovskaia, Valentina. *The Marble Palace.* St. Petersburg: Palace Editions, 1996.

Belyakova, Zoia. *The Romanov Legacy: The Palaces of St. Petersburg.* London: Hazar, 1994.

Benagh, Christine. *An Englishman in the Court of the Tsar.* Ben Lomond, Calif.: Conciliar Press, 2000.

Benckendorff, Count Paul von. *Last Days at Tsarskoe Selo.* London: William Heinemann, 1927.

Berkman, Ted. *The Lady and the Law: The Remarkable Life of Fanny Holtzmann.* Boston: Little, Brown, 1976.

Bikov, Aleksandr. *Pyuti Na Golgofii: Mronika Gibeli Velikii Knizei Romanovik.* Vologda, Russia: Izdatelbstvo Musei Diplomaticheskogo Korpiusa, 2000.

Bing, Edward J., ed. *The Letters of Tsar Nicholas and Empress Marie: Being the Confidential Correspondence between Nicholas II, Last of the Tsars, and His Mother, Dowager Empress Maria Feodorovna.* London: Ivor Nicholson and Watson, 1937.

Bobrov, V. D., and B. M. Kirikov. *Osobnyak Kschessinskoi.* St. Petersburg: Beloe i Chernoe, 1996.

Bogdanovich, A. V. *Tri poslednikh samoderzhtsa. Dnevnik A. V. Bogdanovich.* Moscow/Leningrad: Frenkel, 1924.

Bokhanov, Alexander, ed. *The Romanovs: Love, Power, and Tragedy.* London: Leppi, 1993.

Bolitho, Hector. *Victoria, the Widow and Her Son.* New York: Appleton-Century, 1934.

Borisova, Elena, and Grigory Sternin. *Russian Art Nouveau.* New York: Rizzoli, 1988.

Bothmer, Countess A. von. *The Sovereign Ladies of Europe.* London: Hutchinson, 1899.

Botkin, Gleb. *The Real Romanovs.* New York: Fleming H. Revell, 1932.

Botkine, Peter. *Les Morts Sans Tombes.* Paris: Louis Conard, 1921.

Botkine, Tatiana. *Au Temps des Tsars.* Paris: Grasset, 1980.

Bott, I. *The Alexander Palace.* St. Petersburg: State Museum Preserve Tsarskoye Selo, 1997.

Bovey, Kate Koon. *Russian Coronation, 1896.* Minneapolis: Privately Printed, 1942.

Brayley-Hodgetts, E. A. *The Court of Russia in the Nineteenth Century.* 2 vols. London: Methuen, 1908.

Brook-Shepherd, Gordon. *Uncle of Europe: The Social and Diplomatic Life of Edward VII.* London: William Collins & Sons, 1974.

Bruce Lockhart, Sir Robert. *Memoirs of a British Agent.* London: Putnam, 1932.

Brumfield, William Craft. *A History of Russian Architecture.* Cambridge: Cambridge University Press, 1993.

Buchanan, Sir George. *My Mission to Russia.* 2 vols. Boston: Little, Brown, 1923.

Buchanan, Meriel. *The Dissolution of an Empire.* London: John Murray, 1932.

———. *Queen Victoria's Relations.* London: Cassell, 1954.

———. *Victorian Gallery.* London: Cassell, 1956.

Butikov, Grigorii. *Isaakievskii Sobor.* Leningrad: Lenizdat, 1979.

———. *St. Isaac's Cathedral.* Leningrad: Smart, 1990.

Buxhoeveden, Baroness Sophie. *Before the Storm.* London: Macmillan, 1938.

———. *Left Behind.* London: Longmans, Green, 1929.

———. *The Life and Tragedy of Alexandra Feodorovna, Empress of Russia.* London: Longmans, Green, 1929.

Bykov, Paul. *The Last Days of Tsar Nicholas.* New York: International, 1934.

Bylankova, L. P. *Stranitsii Zhiznii Anichkova Dvoretsa.* St. Petersburg: St. Petersburgskii Gorodskoii Dvorets Tvorchestva Iunikh, 1992.

Byrnes, Robert F. *Pobedonostsev: His Life and Thought.* Bloomington: Indiana University Press, 1968.

Cantacuzené, Princess Michael, Countess Spéransky. *My Life Here and There.* New York: Charles Scribner's Sons, 1922.

———. *Revolutionary Days.* Boston: Small, Maynard, 1919.

Cerwinske, Laura. *Russian Imperial Style.* New York: Prentice Hall, 1990.

Chabrun, Louis Charles Pineton, Comte de. *Lettres a Marie: Petersburg-Petrograd, 1914–1917.* Paris: Librairie Plon, 1941.

Chakirov, N., ed. *75th Jubilee Coronation Celebration of Nikolai II.* New York: Holy Trinity Monastery, 1971.

Chavchavadze, Prince David. *Crowns and Trenchcoats: A Russian Prince in the CIA.* New York: Atlantic International, 1990.

———. *The Grand Dukes.* New York: Atlantic International, 1990.

Clarke, William. *The Lost Fortune of the Tsars.* New York: St. Martin's, 1994.

Cockfield, Jamie H. *White Crow: The Life and Times of Grand Duke Nicholas Mikhailovich Romanov, 1859–1919.* Westport, Conn.: Praeger, 2002.

Conway, Sir Martin. *Art Treasures in Soviet Russia.* London: Edward Arnold, 1925.

The Cottage Palace. St. Petersburg: Petrodvorets State Museum Reserve, 1990.

Cowles, Virginia. *1913: The Defiant Swansong.* London: Weidenfeld & Nicolson, 1967.

Cresti, Carlo, and Claudio Rendina. *Palazzi of Rome.* Cologne: Konemann, 1998.

Cunningham, James W. *A Vanished Hope.* Crestwood, N.Y.: St. Vladimir Seminary Press, 1981.

Curtiss, John. *Church and State in Russia: The Last Years of Empire.* New York: Columbia University Press, 1940.

Davis, John W. *The Ambassadorial Diary of John W. Davis.* Edited by Julia Davis and Dolores Fleming. Morgantown: West Virginia University Press, 1993.

Davis, Richard Harding. *A Year from a Reporter's Note Book.* New York: Harper & Brothers, 1903.

Dehn, Lili. *The Real Tsaritsa.* London: Thornton Butterworth, 1922.

Demicheva, N. N., and V. I. Akselrod. *Zodchie i Stroitelii Anichkova Dvoretsa.* St. Petersburg: St. Petersburgskii Gorodskoii Dvorets Tvorchestva Iunikh, 1994.

Demidenko, Julia. *Inter'er v Rossii: Traditsii, Moda, Stil.* St. Petersburg: Aurora, 2000.

———. *Reveling St. Petersburg: An Artistic Chronicle of High Society Life.* St. Petersburg: Palace Editions, 1994.

Dillon, E. J. *The Eclipse of Russia.* London: J. M. Dent & Sons, 1918.

Dmitrieva, E. K. *300-Letiyu Sankt Peterburga.* St. Petersburg: Korona, 2003.

Donaldson, Frances. *Edward VIII.* New York: Random House, 1974.

Dorr, Rheta Childe. *Inside the Russian Revolution.* New York: Macmillan, 1918.

Dostoevsky, Feodor. *The Possessed.* New York: New American Library, 1962.

Dubnow, S. M. *History of the Jews in Russia and Poland.* New York: Jewish Publishing Society, 1916.

Ducamp, Emmanuel, ed. *Imperial Palaces in the Vicinity of St. Petersburg.* Paris: Alain de Gourcuff Editions, 1992.

Duff, David. *Alexandra, Princess and Queen.* London: Collins, 1980.

Dukov, V. *The Culture of Entertainment in 18th–19th Century Russia.* St. Petersburg: Arbis, 2001.

Dzhunkovsky, Vladimir. *Vospominaniia.* 2 vols. Moscow: Progress, 1997.

Eager, Margarette. *Six Years at the Russian Court.* London: Hurst and Blackett, 1906.

Elbogen, Ismar. *A Century of Jewish Life.* Philadelphia: Jewish Publication Society, 1953.

Elchaninov, Major-General Andrei. *The Tsar and His People.* London: Hodder and Stoughton, 1914.

Elsberry, Terrence. *Marie of Roumania.* New York: St. Martin's, 1972.

Ernst Ludwig, Grand Duke of Hesse und Bei Rhein. *Erinnertes: Aufzeichnungen des letzten Grossherzogs Ernst Ludwig von Hessen und bei Rhein.* Darmstadt: Eduard Rocther Verlag, 1983.

Erté. *Things I Remember: An Autobiography.* London: Peter Owens, 1975.

Essed-Bey, Mohammed. *Nicholas II: Prisoner of the Purple.* London: Hutchinson, 1936.

Fabergé, Tatiana, Lynette G. Proler, and Valentin V. Skurlov. *The Fabergé Imperial Easter Eggs.* London: Christie, Manson and Woods, 1997.

Falinski, Janusz. *National Park in Bialowieza Forest.* Warsaw: Kluwer Akademic, 1968.

Ferrand, Jacques. *Le Grand-Duc Paul Alexandrovitch de Russie, Sa famille, sa descendance.* Paris: Jacques Ferrand, 1993.

———. *Il Est Toujours des Romanovs.* Paris: Jacques Ferrand, 1995.

Fitzlyon, Kyrill, and Tatiana Browning. *Before the Revolution.* New York: Viking, 1982.

Florinsky, Michael T. *The End of the Russian Empire.* New York: Collier Books, 1961.

Floryan, Margrethe. *Gardens of the Tsars: A Study of the Aesthetics, Semantics and Uses of Late 18th Century Russian Gardens.* Portland, Ore.: Sagapress, 1996.

Flourens, E. *Alexandre III, sa vie; son oeuvre.* Paris: E. Dentu, 1894.

Freeman, John, and Kathleen Burton. *Moscow Revealed.* New York: Abbeville, 1991.

Fromenko, Irina. "Krymskii Al'bom Nikolaya II." In *Krymskii Al'bom: Istoriko-kraevedcheskii i literaturno-khudozh.* Sevastopol: Taurida, 1998.

Fulop-Miller, Rene. *Rasputin, the Holy Devil.* New York: Garden City Publishing, 1928.

Fuhrman, Joseph T. *Rasputin: A Life.* New York: Praeger, 1990.

Gautier, Théophile. *Russia.* Translated from the French by Florence MacIntyre Tyson. Philadelphia: John C. Winston, 1905.

Gabriel Konstantinovich, Grand Duke of Russia. *V mramornom dvortse: iz khroniki nashei semyi.* New York: Izdatelstvo imeni Chekova, 1955.

Gaynor, Elizabeth. *Russian Houses.* New York: Stewart, Tabori & Chang, 1991.

Gendrikov, Vladimir, and Sergei Senko. *The Cathedral of St. Peter and St. Paul.* St. Petersburg: Liki Rossi, 1998.

George, Arthur L., and Elena George. *St. Petersburg: Russia's Window to the Future: The First Three Centuries.* Oxford: Taylor Trade, 2003.

George, Grand Duchess of Russia (Marie Georgievna). *A Romanov Diary.* New York: Atlantic International, 1988.

Gerois, B. V. *Souvenirs de Ma Vie.* Paris: Academie, 1969.

Gilliard, Pierre. *Thirteen Years at the Russian Court.* New York: George H. Doran, 1923.

Gogol, Nikolai. "Nevsky Prospect." In *Plays and Petersburg Tales.* Translated and edited by Christopher English. Oxford: Oxford University Press, 1995.

Goncharenko, Valentina, and Valentina Narozhnaya. *The Armory Chamber.* Moscow: Progress, 1979.

Grabbe, Paul, and Beatrice Grabbe. *The Private World of the Last Tsar: In the Photographs and Notes of General Count Alexander Grabbe.* Boston: Little, Brown, 1984.

Grabar, I. *Petersburgska arkhitektura v XVIII i XIX vekakh.* St. Petersburg: Iskusstvo, 1994.

Granin, Daniel, Ilya Gurevich, Galina Khodasevich, and Valeria Belanina. *Risen from the Ashes: Petrodvorets, Pushkin, and Pavlovsk.* Leningrad: Aurora Art, 1992.

Grebalskii, Petr. *Tsarstvennyie Yezniki Rossii.* Los Angeles: Kovcheg, 2001.

Greece, Prince Christopher of. *Memoirs.* London: Right Book Club, 1934.

Greece, Prince Michael of. *Crown Jewels of Europe.* New York: Crescent Books, 1986.

———. *Imperial Palaces of Russia.* London: Tauris Parke Books, 1992.

Greece, Prince Nicholas of. *My Fifty Years.* London: Hutchinson, 1926.

Greenberg, Louis. *The Jews in Russia.* New Haven, Conn.: Yale University Press, 1944.

Grenfell, Francis W. *Three Weeks in Moscow.* London: Harrison & Sons, 1896.

Grey, Marina. *Enquete sur le massacre des Romanov.* Paris: Librairie Academique, 1987.

de Grunwald, Konstantin. *Le Tsar Nicolas II.* Paris: Payot, 1955.

Gurko, Vladimir. *Features and Figures of the Russian Past.* Stanford: Stanford University Press, 1939.

Habsburg, Geza von, and Marina Lopato. *Fabergé: Imperial Jeweler.* New York: Harry N. Abrams, 1993.

Hall, Coryne. *Little Mother of Russia: A Biography of Empress Marie Feodorovna.* London: Shepheard Walwyn, 1999.

Hallmann, Gerhard. *Sommer-Residenzen Russischer Zaren.* Leipzig: VEB E. A. Seemann Verlag, 1986.

Hamilton, Lord Frederick. *The Vanished Pomps of Yesterday.* New York: Doubleday, 1934.

Hammer, Armand. *The Quest of the Romanoff Treasure.* New York: William Farquhar Payson, 1932.

Hanbury-Williams, Major General Sir John. *The Emperor Nicholas II as I Knew Him.* London: Arthur L. Humphreys, 1922.

Hancock, Ralph, ed. *Treasures of the Czars: From the State Museum of the Moscow Kremlin.* London: Booth-Clibborn Editions, 1995.

Harcave, Sidney. *Years of the Golden Cockerel: The Last Romanov Tsars, 1814–1917.* New York, Macmillan, 1968.

Heard Hamilton, George. *Art and Architecture in Russia.* London: Harmondsworth, 1987.

Heckstall-Smith, Anthony. *Sacred Cowes.* London: Anthony Bland, 1965.

Hepworth, Philip. *Royal Sandringham.* Norwich, UK: Wensum Books, 1978.

Herriot, Eduard. *Eastward from Paris.* London: Gollancz, 1934.

Hibbert, Christopher. *The Royal Victorians.* Philadelphia: J. B. Lippincott, 1976.

Hickley, Mary. *Gold, Glitter, and Gloom.* Devon: Brenda Marsault, 1997.

Hoare, Sir Samuel. *The Fourth Seal: The End of a Russian Chapter.* London: William Heinemann, 1930.

Hobhouse, Penelope, and Patrick Taylor, eds. *The Gardens of Europe.* New York: Random House, 1990.

Hough, Richard. *Edward and Alexandra.* New York: St. Martin's, 1993.

———. *Louis and Victoria: The First Mountbattens.* London: Hutchinson, 1974.

Humphreys, Rob, and Dan Richardson. *St. Petersburg: The Rough Guide.* London: Rough Guides, 1995.

Ignatiev, Lieutenant General A. A. *A Subaltern in Old Russia.* Translated by Ivor Montagu. London: Hutchinson, 1944.

Intimacies of Court and Society: An Unconventional Narrative of Unofficial Days, by the Widow of an American Diplomat. New York: Dodd, Mead, 1912.

Iroshnikov, Mikhail, Lyudmila Protsai, and Yuri Shelayev. *Before the Revolution: St. Petersburg in Photographs: 1890–1914.* New York: Harry N. Abrams, 1991.

———. *The Sunset of the Romanov Dynasty.* Moscow: Terra, 1992.

Ivanova, Elena. *Mikhailovskii Dvorets.* St. Petersburg: Palace Editions, 1996.

Izvolsky, Alexander. *Recollections of a Foreign Minister.* New York: Doubleday, 1921.

Izwolsky, Helen. *No Time to Grieve.* Philadelphia: Winchell, 1985.

Jellicoe, Sir Geofffrey, ed. *The Oxford Companion to Gardens.* Oxford: Oxford University Press, 1986.

de Jonge, Alex. *The Life and Times of Grigorii Rasputin.* New York: Dorset, 1982.

Kalnutskaia, Elena. *Mikhailovskii Zamok, Dvorets Russkogo Museya.* St. Petersburg: Palace Editions, 1996.

Kalnutskaia, Elena, and Vladimir Frantsizov. *Mikhailovskii Zamok.* St. Petersburg: Palace Editions, 1996.

Kaminski, Marion. *Venice: Art and Architecture.* Cologne: Konemann, 1999.

Kann, Pavel. *The Environs of St. Petersburg: Petrodvorets, Lomonosov, Pushkin, and Pavlovsk.* Moscow: Welcome Books, 1995.

———. *Ploshad Tryda.* Leningrad: Lenizdat, 1981.

———. *St. Petersburg.* Moscow: Welcome Books, 1994.

Keczynscy, Andrzej, and Ewa Keczynscy. *The Tsar's Palace at Bialowieza.* Bialowieza, Poland: Bialowieza State Preserve, 2003.

Kedrinskii, A. A., M. G. Kolotov, B. N. Ometov, and A. G. Raskin. *Vosstanovlenie Pamiatnikov Architekturii Leningrada.* Leningrad: Stroizdat-Leningradskoye Otdelenie, 1987.

Kelly, Laurence. *St. Petersburg: A Travellers' Companion.* London: Constable, 1983.

Kennett, Audrey, and Victor Kennett. *The Palaces of Leningrad.* London: Thames and Hudson, 1973.

Kirichenko, Eugenia. *Russian Design and the Fine Arts, 1750–1917.* New York: Harry N. Abrams, 1991.

Kirikov, B. M. *Petersburgski Moderni Stil'.* Moscow: Iskusstvo, 1987.

Kirill Vladimirovich, Grand Duke of Russia. *My Life in Russia's Service, Then and Now.* London: Selwyn & Blount, 1939.

Kiselev, A. S. *Tsarskie i Imperatorskie Dvoretsi: Staraya Mockba.* Moscow: Mosgorarkiv, 1997.

Kleinmichel, Countess Marie. *Memories of a Shipwrecked World.* London: Brentano's, 1923.

Kochan, Miriam. *The Last Days of Imperial Russia.* New York: Macmillan, 1976.

Kohl, J. G. *Russia: St. Petersburg, Moscow, Kharkoff, Riga, Odessa, the German Provinces on the Baltic, the Steppes, the Crimea, and the Interior of the Empire.* London: Chapman and Hall, 1842.

Kokovtsov, Count Vladimir. *Out of My Past: The Memoirs of Count Kokovtsov.* Palo Alto, Calif.: Stanford University Press, 1935.

Koloskov, P., I. Gurevich, G. Khodasevich, V. Belanina, L. Ivanova, and E. Levenfish. *Places of Interest in the Environs of Leningrad: Historical and Architectural Monuments.* Leningrad: Aurora Art, 1975.

Komelova, G. N. *Treasures of Imperial Russia: Catherine the Great: From the State Hermitage Museum, Leningrad.* London: Booth-Clibborn, 1990.

Korshunova, M. F. *Dzhiakomo Kvarengi.* Leningrad: Stroizdat, 1977.

Korshunova, Tamara. *Russian Style, 1700–1920: Court and Country Dress from the Hermitage.* London: Barbican, 1987.

Kropotkin, Peter. *Memoirs of a Revolutionist.* New York: Houghton Mifflin, 1899.

Kudrina, Iulia. *Imperatritsa Mariya Fedorovna.* Moscow: Mokba Olma-Press, 2001.

Kurth, Peter. *Anastasia: The Riddle of Anna Anderson.* Boston: Little, Brown, 1983.

Lambsdorff, V. N. *Dnevnik (1886–1890).* Moscow: Gosudarstvennoye Izdatelstvo, 1926.

———. *Dnevnik (1891–1892).* Moscow: Gosudarstvennoye Izdatelstvo, 1934.

———. *Dnevnik (1894–1896).* Moscow: Mezhdunarodnye Otnosheniya, 1991.

LaPauze, Henri. *De Paris au Volga.* Paris: Lemerre, 1896.

Lashenko, T. A. *Livadiiskii-Dvorets-Museii Livadia.* Simferopol: Taurida, 1997.

Lastochkin, S., and Yu. F. Rybejanskii. *Tsarskoye Selo: Rezidentsia Rossiiskij Monarkov.* St. Petersburg: Byukmoryma, 1998.

Lathrop, Mrs. George van Ness. *The Court of Alexander III: Letters of Mrs. Lathrop, Wife of the Honorable George van Ness Lathrop, Minister of the United States.* Edited by William Prall. Philadelphia: John C. Winston, 1910.

Lee, Sidney. *King Edward VII: A Biography.* 2 vols. London: Macmillan, 1925.

Leger, Louis. *Moscou.* Paris: Librairie Renouard, 1904.

Lehr, Elizabeth Drexel. *King Lehr and the Gilded Age*. London: Constable, 1935.

Lemius, Vera. *The Palaces and Park Complex at Pushkin*. Leningrad: Aurora, 1985.

Les Solennites du Saint Couronnement: ouvrage publie avec l'autorisation de Sa Majeste l'Empereur par le Ministere de la Maison Imperiale, sous la direction de M. V. S. Krivenko. St. Petersburg: Ministerstvo Imperatorskoago Dvora i Udielov, 1899.

Leudet, Maurice. *Nicolas II: intime*. Paris: E. Dentu, 1902.

Leyda, Jay. *Kino: A History of the Russian and Soviet Film*. Princeton, N.J.: Princeton University Press, 1983.

Lieven, Dominic. *Nicholas II: Twilight of the Empire*. New York: St. Martin's, 1993.

Lincoln, W. Bruce. *The Romanovs*. New York: Dial, 1981.

———. *Between Heaven and Hell: The Story of a Thousand Years of Artistic Life in Russia*. New York: Viking, 1998.

Lobanova, T. *St. Petersburg: History, Architecture, Museums*. St. Petersburg: Slavia, 2002.

Lobanov-Rostovsky, Prince Andrei. *The Grinding Mill: Reminiscences of War and Revolution in Russia, 1913–1920*. New York: Macmillan, 1935.

Logan, John A. Jr. *In Joyful Russia*. New York: Appleton, 1897.

Londonderry, Lady. *The Russian Journal of Lady Londonderry, 1836–1837*. Edited by W. A. L. Seaman and J. R. Sewell. London: John Murray, 1973.

Longford, Elizabeth. *Louisa, Lady-in-Waiting*. London: Jonathan Cape, 1979.

———. *Darling Loosey: Letters to Princess Louise, 1856–1939*. London: Weidenfeld & Nicolson, 1991.

Lowe, Charles. *Alexander III*. New York: Macmillan, 1895.

Lyons, Marvin, ed. *Diary of Vladimir Bezobrazov, Commander of the Russian Imperial Guard, 1914–1917*. Boynton Beach, Fla.: Dramco, 1994.

MacCallum Scott, Alexander. *Through Finland to St. Petersburg*. London: Grant Richards, 1908.

Mager, Hugo. *Elizabeth, Grand Duchess of Russia*. New York: Carroll & Graf, 1998.

Magnus, Philip. *King Edward the Seventh*. New York: E. P. Dutton, 1964.

Majolier, Nathalie. *Step-Daughter of Imperial Russia*. London: Stanley Paul, 1940.

Mamontov, Serge. *Carnots De Route D'un Artilleur à Cheval*. Paris: Harmatten, 2000.

Marie Feodorovna, Empress of Russia: An Exhibition about the Danish Princess Who Became Empress of Russia. Exhibition Catalogue. Copenhagen: Christiansborg Palace-Der Kongelige Udstillingsfond, 1997.

Marie Feodorovna, Empress of Russia. *Dnevniki Imperatritsi Marii Feodorovni, 1914–1920, 1923 godi*. Moscow: Vagrius, 2005.

Marie Pavlovna, Grand Duchess of Russia. *Education of a Princess*. New York: Viking Press, 1930.

Markova, G. *The Great Palace of the Moscow Kremlin*. Leningrad: Aurora Art, 1981.

Massie, Suzanne. *Land of the Firebird*. New York: Random House, 1982.

———. *Pavlovsk: The Life of a Russian Palace*. Boston: Little, Brown, 1990.

Maud, Rene Elton. *One Year at the Russian Court: 1904–1905*. London: John Lane, 1918.

de Monte Alto [Aylmer Maude]. *The Tsar's Coronation*. London: Brotherhood, 1896.

Maurois, Andre. *King Edward and His Times*. London: Cassell, 1933.

Mawdsley, Evan. *Moscow and Leningrad: The Blue Guide*. London: A & C Black, 1991.

Maylunas, Andrei, and Sergei Mironenko. *A Lifelong Passion: Nicholas and Alexandra, Their Own Story*. London: Weidenfeld & Nicolson, 1996.

Merry, W. Mansell. *Two Months in Russia: July–September, 1914*. Oxford: Holywell Press, 1916.

Meylan, Vincent. *Queens' Jewels*. New York: Assouline, 2002.

Miliutin, Dimitri. *Dnevnik D. A. Miliutina*. Moscow: Gosudarstvenaya Ordena Lenina Biblioteka, 1947.

Moscow: Treasures and Traditions. Seattle: University of Washington Press, 1990.

Mossolov, Alexander. *At the Court of the Last Tsar*. London: Methuen, 1935.

Nadelhoffer, Hans. *Cartier: Jewelers Extraordinary*. New York: Harry N. Abrams, 1984.

Naryshkin-Kuryakin, Princess Elizabeth. *Under 3 Tsars*. New York: Dutton, 1931.

Nashokina, M. V. *Dvoryanskie gnezda Rossii: Istoriia, Kultura, Arkitektura*. Moscow: Miraf, 2000.

Nesin, Vadim. *Zimnii Dvorets V Tsarstvovanye Imperatora Nikolaya II (1894–1917)*. St. Petersburg: Letny Sad, 1999.

Nijinska, Bronislava. *Early Memoirs*. New York: Holt, Rinehart, and Winston, 1981.

Nikitine, Colonel B. V. *The Fatal Years*. London: William Hodge, 1938.

Nikolaiev, A. B., ed. *Imperatorskaya familia v istorii rossii*. St. Petersburg: Kollektiv Avtorov, 1999.

Norman, Geraldine. *The Hermitage: The Biography of a Great Museum*. London: Jonathan Cape, 1997.

Norman, Henry. *All the Russias*. New York: Charles Scribner's Sons, 1903.

Norwich, John Julius, Viscount, ed. *Living in a Dream: Great Residences of the World*. New York: Simon and Schuster, 1993.

Nostitz, Countess (Lilie Bouton de Fernandez-Azabal). *Romance and Revolutions*. London: Heinemann, 1937.

Obolensky, Prince Serge. *One Man in His Time*. New York: McDowell, Obolensky, 1958.

Odom, Anne. *What Became of Peter's Dream: Court Culture in the Reign of Nicholas II*. Seattle: University of Washington Press, 2003.

Oldenburg, S. S. *Last Tsar: Nicholas II, His Reign, His Russia*. Gulf Breeze, Fla: Academic International Press, 1977.

Ometev, Boris. *St. Petersburg: Portrait of an Imperial City*. New York: Vendome, 1995.

Ovsyannikov, Yuri. *Velikye Zodchie Sankt-Petersburga*. St. Petersburg: Iskusstvo, 2000.

Paleologue, Maurice. *An Ambassador's Memoirs*. New York: Doran, 1925.

Paley, Princess Olga. *Memories of Russia, 1916–1919*. London: Herbert Jenkins, 1924.

Paoli, Xavier. *My Royal Clients*. London: Hodder and Stoughton, 1910.

Perry, John Curtis, and Constantine Pleshakov. *The Flight of the Romanovs*. New York: Basic Books, 1999.

Petrodvorets: Fountains. Leningrad: State Museum Reserve at Petrodvorets, 1990.

Petrodvorets: The Grand Palace. Leningrad: State Museum Reserve at Petrodvorets, 1989.

Petrov, Anatoli. *Pamyatniki arkitekturi Leningrada*. Leningrad: Stroyizdat, 1976.

———. *Architectural Monuments of the Leningrad Suburbs*. Leningrad: Stroyizdat, 1985.

Petrova, T. A. *Andrei Stackenschneider*. Leningrad: Stroyizdat, 1978.

Phenix, Patricia. *Olga Romanov: Russia's Last Grand Duchess*. Toronto: Viking, 1999.

Piotrovsky, Boris. *The Hermitage: Its History and Collections*. New York: Harcourt, Brace, Jovanovich, 1982.

———. *Ermitage: Istoryia, Stroyteltsvo, I arkitektura*. Leningrad: Lenizdat, 1991.

———. *Nikolaii i Aleksandra*. St. Petersburg: Aurora, 1994.

Piper, Raymond. *Imperial Russian Porcelain from the Raymond F. Piper Collection*. Privately printed, 1995.

Pipes, Richard. *Russia under the Old Regime*. New York: Macmillan, 1987.

Pitcher, Harvey. *When Miss Emmie Was in Russia: English Governesses Before, During, and After the October Revolution*. London: John Murray, 1977.

Plumptre, George. *The Water Garden*. London: Thames and Hudson, 1993.

Poliakoff, Vladimir. *Mother Dear: The Empress Marie of Russia and Her Times*. New York: D. Appleton, 1926.

———. *The Tragic Bride: The Story of the Empress Alexandra of Russia*. New York: Appleton, 1927.

Polovtsov, A. A. *Dnevnik gosudarstvennogo sekretaria A. A. Polovtsova*. Moscow: Izdatel'stvo Nauka, 1966.

Polynina, Irina, and Nikolai Rakhmanov. *The Regalia of the Russian Empire*. Moscow: Red Square, 1994.

Ponsonby, Sir Frederick. *Side Lights on Queen Victoria*. New York: Sears, 1930.

Radzinsky, Edvard. *The Last Tsar: The Life and Death of Nicholas II*. New York: Doubleday, 1992.

Radziwill, Princess Catherine. *The Intimate Life of the Last Tsarina*. London: Cassell, 1929.

———. *Nicholas II: The Last of the Tsars*. London: Cassell, 1931.

Rae, Isobel. *Charles Cameron, Architect to the Court of Russia*. London: Elek Books, 1971.

Raiguel, George Earle, and William Kistler Huff. *This Is Russia*. Philadelphia: Penn, 1932.

Raskin, Abram, and Vadim Znamenov. *Petrodvorets: Palaces, Gardens, Fountains, Sculptures*. Leningrad: Aurora Art, 1978.

Raymer, Steve. *St. Petersburg*. Atlanta: Turner, 1994.

Ridge, Antonia. *Grandma Went to Russia*. London: Faber and Faber, 1959.

Rindina, Margareta. *Pushkin: The Palace and Park Ensemble*. Leningrad: Sostavitel and Avtor Teksta, 1991.

de Robien, Louis. *The Diary of A Diplomat in Russia 1917–1918*. Translated from the French by Camilla Sykes. New York: Praeger, 1970.

Rodimzeva, Irina, Nikolai Rakhmanov, and Alfons Raimann. *The Kremlin and Its Treasures*. New York: Rizzoli, 1987.

Rodzianko, Michael. *The Reign of Rasputin, An Empire's Collapse*. Gulf Breeze, Fla.: Academic Press International, 1973.

Röhl, John C. G., and Sheila de Bellaigue. *Wilhelm II: The Kaiser's Personal Monarchy, 1888–1900*. Cambridge: Cambridge University Press, 2004.

Romania, Queen Marie of. *The Story of My Life*. 2 vols. New York: Charles Scribner's Sons, 1934.

Romanovsky-Krassinsky, Princess [Mathilde Kschessinska]. *Dancing in Petersburg: The Memoirs of HSH the Princess Romanovsky-Krassinsky*. London: Gollancz, 1960.

Roosevelt, Priscilla. *Life on the Russian Country Estate*. New Haven, Conn.: Yale University Press, 1997.

Russian Court Memoirs, 1914–1916. New York: E. P. Dutton, 1916.

Russkie Imperatorskii Dvoretsi. St. Petersburg: LenArt, 1989.

Salisbury, Harrison. *Black Night, White Snow: Russia's Revolutions 1905–1917*. New York: Doubleday, 1977.

Schanoshnikova, Luduia. *Pamiatnik Aleksandr III Skulptov Pavel Trubetskoi*. St. Petersburg: Palace Editions, 1996.

Shapiro, Yuri. *The Hermitage: An Illustrated Guide*. Leningrad: Aurora Art, 1983.

Shelking, Evgenii. *Recollections of a Russian Diplomat: The Suicide of Monarchies*. New York: Macmillan, 1918.

Shoumatoff, Alex. *Russian Blood*. New York: Vintage Books, 1990.

Shulgin, Vassili. *The Years*. New York: Hippocrene Books, 1984.

Shurgin, Yakov. *Petergof Letopis' vostanoveleniya*. St. Petersburg: Arbis, 2000.

Shvidkovsky, Dmitri. *St. Petersburg: Architecture of the Tsars*. New York: Abbeville, 1995.

———. *The Empress and the Architect*. New Haven, Conn.: Yale University Press, 1996.

Sitwell, Sacheverell, ed. *Great Palaces*. London: Weidenfeld, 1964.

Snowman, A. Kenneth. *The Master Jewelers*. New York: Harry N. Abrams, 1990.

Sokolov, Nicholas. *Enquete judiciare sur l'Assassinat de la Famille Imperiale Russe*. Paris: Payot, 1924.

Sokolova, Tatiana. *The Hermitage: Buildings and Interiors*. St. Petersburg: Alfa-Colour, 1995.

Sokolovoi, Valerii, and I. V. Kondratiev. *Dom Romanovykh*. St. Petersburg: Lio Redaktor, 1992.

von Solodkoff, Alexander. *The Jewel Album of Tsar Nicholas II*. London: Ermitage, 1997.

Souiny, Baroness. *Russia of Yesterday and Tomorrow*. New York: Century, 1917.

Spain, Infanta Eulalia of. *Court Life from Within*. New York: Dodd, Mead, 1916.

Spiridovich, Alexander. *Les dernieres annees de la cour de Tsarskoie Selo*. Paris: Payot, 1928.

St. Aubyn, Giles. *Queen Victoria: A Portrait*. New York: Atheneum, 1992.

Steinberg, Mark, and Vladimir Krustalev. *The Fall of the Romanovs: Political Dreams and Personal Struggles in a Time of Revolution*. New Haven, Conn.: Yale University Press, 1995.

Stephan, John. *The Russian Fascists*. London: Hamish Hamilton, 1978.

Steveni, James William Barnes. *Petrograd, Past and Present*. London: Grant Richards, 1915.

Stoddard, John L. *John L. Stoddard's Lectures: Berlin, Vienna, St. Petersburg, and Moscow*. Chicago: George L. Shuman, 1911.

de Stoeckl, Baroness Agnes. *Not All Vanity*. London: John Murray, 1950.

———. *My Dear Marquis*. London: John Murray, 1952.

Stopford, The Honorable Albert [Published Anonymously]. *The Russian Diary of an Englishman, Petrograd 1915–1917*. London: William Heinemann, 1919.

Surguchev, I. *Detstvo Imperatora Nikolaya vtorogo*. Paris: Payot, 1952.

Swezey, Marilyn Pfeifer, ed. *Nicholas and Alexandra: At Home with the Last Tsar and His Family*. Washington, D.C.: The American-Russian Cultural Cooperation Foundation, 2004.

Syknovalov, A. E. *Leningrad*. Leningrad: Lenizdat, 1969.

Talbot Rice, Tamara. *Tamara: Memoirs of St. Petersburg, Paris, Oxford, and Byzantium*. London: John Murray, 1996.

Tallerchik, T. *Sobor Spasa Nerykotvornogo Obraza V Zimneii Dvorets*. St. Petersburg: Hermitage, 1998.

Tarsaïdzé, Alexandre. *Czars and Presidents: The Story of a Forgotten Friendship*. New York: McDowell/Obolensky, 1958.

———. *Katia, Wife before God*. New York: Macmillan, 1970.

Teliakovsky, V. A. *Vospominaniia, 1898–1917*. Petrograd: Vremia, 1924.

Timberlake, Charles E., ed. *Religious and Secular Forces in Late Tsarist Russia*. Seattle: University of Washington, 1992.

Timms, Robert, ed. *Nicholas and Alexandra: The Last Imperial Family of Tsarist Russia*. New York: Harry N. Abrams, 1998.

Timofeyev, R. V. *Gosudarstvennyie Museii Moskovskogo Kremlya*. Moscow: Iskusstvo, 1983.

Tisdall, Evelyn E. *The Dowager Empress*. London: Stanley Paul, 1957.

Tiutcheva, Anna. *Pri dvore dvukh imperatorov*. Moscow: Mysl, 1990.

Trewin, J. C. *The House of Special Purpose*. New York: Stein and Day, 1975.

Trufanov, Sergei [Iliodor]. *The Mad Monk of Russia: Life, Memoirs, and Confessions of Sergei Mikhailovich Trufanov (Iliodor)*. New York: Century, 1918.

Tsedidat, Marina. *Dvorets Beloselskii-Belozerski*. St. Petersburg: Beloye i Chernoe, 1996.

Twining, Baron Edward Francis. *A History of the Crown Jewels of Europe*. London: Batsford, 1960.

Ular, Alexander. *Russia from Within*. London: Heinemann, 1905.

Van der Kiste, John. *Grand Duchess Victoria Melita*. Stroud, England: Sutton, 1990.

Vasilevskaya, Nina. *St. Petersburg: A Guide to the Architecture*. St. Petersburg: Bibliopolis, 1994.

Vassili, Count Paul (pseudonym of Princess Catherine Radziwill). *Behind the Veil at the Russian Court*. London: Cassell, 1913.

Velichenko, M. N., and G. A. Miroliubova. *Dvorets velikogo kniazia Vladimira Aleksandrovicha*. St. Petersburg: Beloe i Chernoe, 1997.

Vernova, Nina. *Petergof, Novye Postynlenya 1997–1999*. St. Petersburg: Arbis, 1999.

———. *Peterhof: The Great Cascade*. St. Petersburg: Ego, 1996.

———. *Treasures of Russia: From the Peterhof Palaces of the Tsars*. New York: Forbes Custom, 1999.

Vernova, Nina, and Vadim Znamenov. *Peterhof*. St. Petersburg: Ego, 1994.

de Vianzone, Therese. *Lettres sur Couronnement de l'Empereur Nicolas II et de l'imperatrice Alexandra, et de leur sejour en France*. Paris: Privately Published, 1896.

Vickers, Hugo. *Alice, Princess Andrew of Greece*. London: Hamish Hamilton, 2000.

Viktoria Luise, Princess of Prussia. *The Kaiser's Daughter*. London: W. H. Allen, 1977.

Viltchkovsky, S. *Tsarskoe Selo*. Berlin: Meisenbach Riffarth, 1912.

Volkov, Alexis. *Souvenirs d'Alexis Volkov: Valet de Chambre de la Tsarine Alexandra Feodorovna, 1910–1918*. Paris: Payot, 1928.

Voronikhina, A. N., M. F. Korshunova, and A. M. Pavelkina. *Arkhitekturnye proekty i risunki Dzhakomo Kvarengi iz muzeev i khranilishch SSSR*. Leningrad: Lenizdat, 1967.

Voronoff, Olga. *Upheaval*. New York: Putnam, 1932.

Vorres, Ian. *The Last Grand Duchess*. London: Hutchinson, 1964.

Voyce, Arthur. *The Moscow Kremlin: Its History, Architecture, and Art Treasures*. Berkeley, Calif.: University of California Press, 1954.

Voyekov, Vladimir. *S tsarem i bez tsarya*. Moscow: Rodnik, 1994.

Vyrubova, Anna. *Memories of the Russian Court*. New York: Macmillan, 1923.

Waddington, Mary King. *Letters of a Diplomat's Wife, 1883–1900*. New York: Charles Scribner's Sons, 1903.

Weber-Bauler, Leon. *From Orient to Occident*. Oxford: Oxford University Press, 1941.

Welch, Frances. *The Romanovs and Mr. Gibbes*. London: Short Books, 2002.

Windsor, HRH The Duke of. *A King's Story*. New York: Putnams, 1947.

Witte, Count Serge. *Memoirs of Count Sergius Witte.* Translated and edited by Sidney Harcave. Armonk, New York: M. E. Sharpe, 1990.

Wonlar-Larsky, Nadine. *The Russia That I Loved.* London: Elsie MacSwinney, 1937.

Wortman, Richard S. *Scenarios of Power: Myth and Ceremony in Russian Monarchy, Volume One: From Peter the Great to the Death of Nicholas I.* Princeton, N.J.: Princeton University Press, 1995.

———. *Scenarios of Power: Myth and Ceremony in Russian Monarchy: Volume Two, From Alexander II to the Abdication of Nicholas II.* Princeton, N.J.: Princeton University Press, 2000.

Wrangell-Rokoassowsky, Baron G. *Before the Storm.* Ventimiglia, Italy: Tipo-Litografia Ligure, 1971.

Yusupov, Prince Felix. *Lost Splendor.* New York: G. P. Putnam's Sons, 1954.

Zainchkovsky, P. A. *Krizis samoderzhavia na ribezhe 1870–1880 godov.* Moscow: Moscow University Press, 1964.

Zemlyanichenko, Marina. *The Romanovs and the Crimea.* Moscow: Rurik, 1993.

Zinovieff, Kyril, and Jenny Hughes. *Companion Guide to St. Petersburg.* Rochester, New York: Companion Guides, 2003.

Znamenov, Vadim. *Nicholas II: The Imperial Family.* St. Petersburg: Arbis, 1998.

Znamenov, V. V., A. L. Larionov, and T. N. Nosovich. *Russkie Imperatorskie Yahti konetz XVII–nachalo XX Veka.* St. Petersburg: Ego, 1997.

ARTICLES

Abrosova, Ekaterina. "Arkitektor Vysochaishego Dvora Vladimir Alcksandrovich Pokrovskii." *Tsar'ino: Pravoslavnyi istoriko-kraevedcheskii almanakh* no. 4 (1998): 43–67.

Gibbon, Percival. "What Ails Russia?" *McClure's Magazine* no. 24 (1905): 601–37.

Hoff, DeeAnn. "Trans-Atlantic Times." *Atlantis Magazine: In the Courts of Memory* 1, no. 2: 91–92.

Kirichenko, Evgeniia. "Tsarskoye Selo in the Early Twentieth Century: An Expression of Nicholas II's Idea of Popular Monarchy." *Experiment* 7, no. 3 (2001): 43–66.

Koenig, Marlene Eilers. "An Affair of the First Magnitude: The Wedding of Princess Viktoria Luise to Prince Ernst August of Hanover." *Atlantis Magazine: In the Courts of Memory* 1, no. 1: 32–39.

Kussner Coudert, Amalia. "The Human Side of the Tsar." *Century Magazine* 72 (1906): 850–59.

Lauritzen, Peter. "The Czar's Private Apartments in the Kremlin." *Architectural Digest* 49, no. 5 (1992): 91–97.

Morris, Fritz. "The Czar's Simple Life." *Cosmopolitan Magazine* 23, no. 5 (September 1902): 482–90.

Pelham-Clinton, Charles. "The Russian Coronation." *Strand* 11 (1897): 482–96.

Shepelov, L. "Imperatorskii Dvor." *Rodina Spetsal'nii Vipusk Sankt-Peterbug 300 Let* 1 (2003): 47–51.

Sheremetevskii, V. "Neobkhodimoe dopolnenie." *Gender Dok* no. 2 (1996): 9–22.

Studemeister, Marguerite. "Czar Nicholas II: His Majesty's Own Libraries." *Libraries and Culture* 32, no. 1 (1997): 121–27.

Wilson, Penny. "The Pensioners' Graveyard: The Favorites of the Emperors." *Atlantis Magazine: In the Courts of Memory* 5 (2): 80–82.

Zuev, G. I. "Marti." *Gangut* 26, no. 1 (2001): 10–16.

NEWSPAPERS AND PERIODICALS

Dates referenced within individual source notes.
The Call, San Francisco
The Daily Mail, London
Illustrated London News, London
L'illustration, Paris
Journal de St. Petersbourg, St. Petersburg
Krasnii Arkhiv, Moscow
Le Monde, Paris
Monde Illustre, Paris
The New York Times, New York
Niva, St. Petersburg
Novoe Vremia, St. Petersburg
Petit Parisien, Paris
Royalty Digest, Ticehurst, UK
The San Francisco Chronicle, San Francisco
The Times, London

OTHER MEDIA

The Alexander Palace, Tsarskoye Selo, St. Petersburg, Russia: Preliminary Assessment Report for Restoration and Adaptive Re-Use. Prepared by the World Monuments Fund, in association with Page Ayres Cowley Architects, LLP, Henry Joyce, and the Alexander Palace Association. New York, 1998.

Alexander Palace Association, at http://www.alexanderpalace.org.

Baker, Samantha. "Nicholas II and the Khodynka Catastrophe, May 1896: A Study of Contemporary Responses." Unpublished Ph.D. dissertation. University of Leeds, 2002.

Platonov, Oleg. "Nikolai II v Sekretnoi perepiske. Slovar' Tsarskoe okrujenie," at http://www.russky.org.

Shepelov, L. E. "Pridvornie Tituli i Mundiri," at http://www.militera.lib.ru.

Sokolov, Nicholas, Dossiers of the White Army investigation into the murder of the Russian imperial family, made available to author from private collection.

www.allpravo.ru
www.geocities.com/henrivanoene/genleuchtenberg
www.george-orden.nm.ru
www.his.1september.ru
www.kdpmc.ru
www.korabel.ru
www.mogilevhistory.narod.ru
www.ortho-ru.ru
www.rgia.narod.ru
www.rulex.ru
www.sedmitza.ru
www.vgd.ru
www.vipmed.ru

INDEX

Page numbers in *italics* represent illustrations and photos.